TRUTH, ETC.

Truth, etc.

Six Lectures on Ancient Logic

JONATHAN BARNES

CLARENDON PRESS · OXFORD

OXFORD
UNIVERSITY PRESS

Great Clarendon Street, Oxford OX2 6DP

Oxford University Press is a department of the University of Oxford.
It furthers the University's objective of excellence in research, scholarship,
and education by publishing worldwide in

Oxford New York

Auckland Cape Town Dar es Salaam Hong Kong Karachi
Kuala Lumpur Madrid Melbourne Mexico City Nairobi
New Delhi Shanghai Taipei Toronto

With offices in

Argentina Austria Brazil Chile Czech Republic France Greece
Guatemala Hungary Italy Japan Poland Portugal Singapore
South Korea Switzerland Thailand Turkey Ukraine Vietnam

Oxford is a registered trade mark of Oxford University Press
in the UK and in certain other countries

Published in the United States
by Oxford University Press Inc., New York

Database right Oxford University Press (maker)

First published 2007

H

British Library Cataloguing in Publication Data
Data available

Library of Congress Cataloging in Publication Data
Data available

Typeset by Laserwords Private Limited, Chennai, India
Printed in Great Britain
on acid-free paper by
Biddles Ltd, King's Lynn, Norfolk

ISBN 978–0–19–928281–4

1 3 5 7 9 10 8 6 4 2

D.M.M.M

Preface

The six chapters of this book are revised and enlarged versions of the six John Locke Lectures which I gave in Oxford in the summer of 2004.

The Philosophy Faculty of the University of Oxford honoured me by their invitation to give the Lectures. Oxford University Press generously supported the invitation. I am profoundly grateful to those two resplendent institutions.

The Warden and Fellows of All Souls College elected me to a Visiting Fellowship for Trinity term. Their unobtrusive hospitality made my stay in Oxford more pleasurable and more intellectually profitable than I had dared to imagine. I am profoundly grateful to that nonpareil institution which ignorant or envious tongues traduce and whose service to the republic of letters is beyond praise.

The book owes much to many. I gained greatly from the questioning which followed the Lectures and from the numerous discussions which surrounded them. I benefited from the enthusiastic criticisms of the group of friends who invited me to Geneva for a dress rehearsal of the Lectures. I had the advantage of a sheaf of corrections from the hand of Suzanne Bobzien, who read the typescript for the Press.

Over the years I have appropriated more than I can remember from colleagues and acquaintances in various parts of the world. I had thought to dedicate the book to my friends pillaged within. Instead, it is dedicated to the memory of one of them from whom I learned most.

The book retains the informal style of the Lectures. In particular, it sports no scholarly references and boasts no bibliography. I have read much—perhaps most—of the modern literature on the subject; and its influence, in one direction or the other, might be observed on many of the following pages. But I have not taken explicit issue with it. On some of the questions which the book addresses I have already expressed myself. Some paragraphs may smell of reheated cabbage; but not, I think, of cannibalism.

The chapters are in English, save for those places in which I talk about the meaning and use of certain Greek (or Latin) words. All quotations from ancient authors are given in translation, the original text always being displayed in a footnote. Abbreviations of ancient titles are either standard or self-explanatory; and I have endeavoured to adopt for each ancient work whatever is the most convenient style of reference. The Greek and Latin texts in the footnotes occasionally differ from those of the standard editions; but I have called attention to such differences only when my argument turns upon them. Note also the Index of Passages.

Just as in principle the book does not demand Greek and Latin from its readers, so in principle it does not presuppose any prior acquaintance with logic, whether ancient or modern. I do not say that it could be read through in a hammock on a spring afternoon; for there are some parts of logic—and some parts of ancient logic—which demand a modest cerebral effort. But the book does its best to ease the spring: as a rule it avoids logical symbolism, save for a few elementary Ps and Qs; and it has been swept clean of professional jargon. The few lines of symbols may be cut without loss by those readers whom they offend. As for jargon, the word 'clean' must be taken generously; for however assiduously you wield your broom, the dust has a tendency to settle back again.

My story has a large cast of ancient characters, some of them less familiar than others. They are not formally introduced to the reader; and their quirks and foibles have no bearing on the plot. But the Onomasticon supplies dates, and occasionally a word or two of description.

The book is about ancient logic. Antiquity is the antiquity of Greece and Rome—which here starts in the fourth century BC and continues, discontinuously, to the sixth century AD. As for logic, the table of Contents indicates what sort of thing is on or under the carpet.

Ancient logic lacks sex appeal.

Most contemporary logicians have little interest in the history—or at least in the ancient history—of their subject. No doubt they suppose that their long-dead colleagues have little or nothing to teach them, and perhaps they prefer the present and the future to the past. If that is so, then it must be confessed that their supposition is quite true: no logician has anything to learn from a study of Aristotle; and the pages of this book make no contribution to logic or to philosophy. As for preferences, I myself rate the past way above the future. But *de gustibus*.

Most students of the ancient world have little interest in logic. Some indeed despise it, or affect to despise it; and some fear it, or affect to fear it. Such attitudes—which were sometimes assumed in antiquity—are lamentable, and they are vexing. But there is nothing much I or anyone else can do about them.

Nonetheless, on my own pink official form there is written: 'I like my work.' And I hope that a few discerning readers will find parts of the book engaging—and even entertaining.

Ceaulmont
December 2005

Contents

1. Truth

A PRINCIPLE OF BIVALENCE

According to Cicero, 'Chrysippus strains every sinew in order to persuade us that every assertible is either true or false' (*fat* x 21).[1] How did Chrysippus strain his sinews? Why did he strain them? And what exactly was he trying to persuade us of? Those are the questions which this chapter addresses. It will dawdle along the way and indulge in a number of perfectly unnecessary circumvagations.

Chrysippus says that certain items are either true or false, that they have one of two truth-values: his thesis is, in the modern argot, a principle of bivalence. Philosophers sometimes speak of the Principle of Bivalence, in the singular and ennobled with capital letters; and they sometimes express the Principle by the sentence

Every proposition is either true or false,

or by the semi-sentence

For any P, either it is true that P or it is false that P.

The thesis which Chrysippus defended is ill expressed by those formulas—for at least three reasons.

First, the 'either/or' in the Principle is inclusive, whereas Chrysippean disjunctions are exclusive—and strongly exclusive at that. The Principle, in claiming that every proposition is either true or false, leaves open the possibility that some, or even all, propositions are both true and false (that possibility being closed off by a separate principle). Chrysippus' thesis claims that every assertible must have one and only one of the two truth-values.

Inclusive disjunction was known to ancient logic and to ancient grammar. But the exclusive variety was the normal case, and it was defined as follows:

---

[1] *contendit omnes nervos Chrysippus ut persuadeat omne ἀξίωμα aut verum esse aut falsum.*

A sound disjunction announces that one of the items in it is sound and the other or the others false—together with conflict.

(Sextus, PH II 191)[2]

That is to say, a disjunction is true if and only if at least one of its disjuncts must be true and at most one of them can be true. Thus—to take a couple of ancient examples—

Either Apollonius will be here or Trypho will

is not true: after all, both may be here. And again

Wealth is either good or bad

is not true; for it may be neither good nor bad but indifferent. The grammarian Apollonius Dyscolus maintained, implicitly, that the disjunction in the Chrysippean thesis must be exclusive and cannot be inclusive; for he claimed that

the connexion made in <inclusive disjunctions> can never hold between conflicting sayings but only between others.

(conj 219.12–14)[3]

Since 'It is true' and 'It is false' are conflicting sayings, in

Either it is true or it is false

the disjunction must be exclusive. Apollonius' claim is, of course, false; but it has proved seductive. And in any event, a disjunction in a Stoic text may be assumed exclusive unless proved inclusive. Chrysippus' thesis surely uses an exclusive disjunction.

Secondly, where the Principle of Bivalence—as I have expressed it—invokes propositions (whatever exactly they are taken to be), Chrysippus' thesis invokes assertibles. What is an assertible? The Greek word is '*ἀξίωμα*'. It has several senses, of which 'axiom' is the most familiar. But it does not mean 'axiom' in the Chrysippean thesis—nor, more generally, in Stoic logical contexts. Cicero once refers to

that definition, according to which an assertible is that which is either true or false.

(Luc xxx 95)[4]

---

[2] τὸ γὰρ ὑγιὲς διεζευγμένον ἐπαγγέλλεται ἓν τῶν ἐν αὐτῷ ὑγιὲς εἶναι, τὸ δὲ λοιπὸν ἢ τὰ λοιπὰ ψεῦδος ἢ ψευδῆ μετὰ μάχης.

[3] καὶ ἡ γινομένη ἐν αὐτοῖς [sc. τοῖς παραδιαζευκτικοῖς] σύνδεσις οὐκ ἂν δύναιτό ποτε ἀπὸ τῶν μαχομένων παραληφθῆναι, ἀπὸ δὲ τῶν ἑτέρων λόγων.—Here, and generally, I translate the Greek 'λόγος' by 'saying' rather than by 'sentence' or 'statement' or 'account' or 'formula' ... In most contexts, 'saying' is a pretty rotten translation. But any translation is, in most contexts, pretty rotten; and if you want—as I do—to stick so far as possible to a single translation, then you must put up with the rot.

[4] ... *illa definitio effatum esse id quod verum aut falsum sit.*

The definition was known to Simplicius, six centuries later—he speaks of

the interpretations of the definition of assertibles which defines an assertible as what is true or false.

(in Cat 406.22–23)[5]

And what Cicero and Simplicius report is rather more circumspectly expressed by Aulus Gellius—who ascribes it to 'the logicians':

Whatever is said in a full and complete verbal sentence in such a way that it is necessarily either true or false, that the logicians call an assertible.

(NA xvi viii 8)[6]

The definition finds an echo in the Peripatetic tradition. Ammonius, for example, remarks that

we already have the definition of assertion in what Aristotle said earlier—it is a saying in which being true or being false hold.

(in Int 80.24–26)[7]

He refers to the passage in which Aristotle says that

not every saying is assertoric—only those in which being true or being false holds.

(Int 17a2–3)[8]

But you might doubt that Aristotle intends thereby to define the notion of assertion; and in any event it is not evident that the 'definition' means—or indeed was taken by Ammonius to mean—that every assertion is either true or false.

However that may be, if the term 'assertible' is defined as Gellius' logicians defined it, then Chrysippus' thesis is true. Indeed, it is trivially true. Perhaps Chrysippus took it to be trivial? Cicero, speaking in a Stoic context, affirms that

it is a foundation of logic that whatever is asserted ... is either true or false.

(Luc xxix 95)[9]

The metaphor suggests that the thesis is a first principle, an axiom, something to be taken for granted or grasped as self-evident.

---

[5] ... ἐν ταῖς ἐξηγήσεσιν τοῦ ὅρου τοῦ ἀξιώματος τοῦ ἀφοριζομένου τὸ ἀξίωμα ὅ ἐστιν ἀληθὲς ἢ ψεῦδος.

[6] *quidquid ita dicitur plena atque perfecta verborum sententia ut id necesse sit aut verum aut falsum esse, id a dialecticis* ἀξίωμα *appellatum est.*

[7] τὸν μὲν γὰρ ὁρισμὸν τῆς ἀποφάνσεως ἔχομεν ἤδη διὰ τῶν ἔμπροσθεν παραδεδομένων, ὅτι ἐστὶ λόγος ἐν ᾧ τὸ ἀληθεύειν ἢ ψεύδεσθαι ὑπάρχει.

[8] ἀποφαντικὸς δὲ οὐ πᾶς, ἀλλ' ἐν ᾧ τὸ ἀληθεύειν ἢ ψεύδεσθαι ὑπάρχει.

[9] *fundamentum dialecticae est quidquid enuntietur ... aut verum esse aut falsum.*

But that cannot be right. After all, if the thesis is a trifle, or a self-evidence, then why should—and how could—Chrysippus have strained a sinew in its defence? In any event, Chrysippus did not define assertibles in terms of truth and falsity; rather,

an assertible is ... a self-complete object which is assertoric so far as depends on itself, as Chrysippus says in his *Dialectical Definitions*: An assertible is what is assertoric so far as depends on itself—for example: It is day, Dio is walking about.

(Diogenes Laertius, VII 65)[10]

An 'object' in that definition is a sayable or λεκτόν; a sayable is something which you may say; and a sayable is complete, or 'self-complete', if in saying it you say something complete.

The Stoics recognized several sorts of complete sayable, distinguishing among them by reference to what we might call the type of speech-act to which they correspond. So, for example,

an assertible is an object saying which we assert something (which is either true or false), whereas a question, while being a self-complete object like an assertible, requests an answer—for example, Is it day? (that is neither true nor false). Hence 'It is day' is an assertible, 'Is it day?' a question.

(Diogenes Laertius, VII 66)[11]

So we might say that a sentence expresses an assertible if and only if by uttering it you may thereby assert something. Thus the sentence

France is a hexagon

expresses an assertible; for you may utter it and thereby assert something—namely, that France is hexagonal. And the sentence

Is France a hexagon?

expresses a question inasmuch as by uttering it you may thereby ask whether so-and-so—namely, whether France is hexagonal.

Thus Chrysippus hoped to show that if it can be asserted that such-and-such, then either it is true that such-and-such or else it is false that

---

[10] ἀξίωμα δέ ἐστιν ... πρᾶγμα αὐτοτελὲς ἀποφαντὸν ὅσον ἐφ᾽ ἑαυτῷ, ὡς ὁ Χρύσιππός φησιν ἐν τοῖς Διαλεκτικοῖς ὅροις· ἀξίωμά ἐστι τὸ ἀποφαντὸν ὅσον ἐφ᾽ ἑαυτῷ, οἷον ἡμέρα ἐστί, Δίων περιπατεῖ.

[11] ἀξίωμα μὲν γάρ ἐστιν ὃ λέγοντες ἀποφαινόμεθα, ὅπερ ἢ ἀληθές ἐστιν ἢ ψεῦδος· ἐρώτημα δέ ἐστι πρᾶγμα αὐτοτελὲς μέν, ὡς καὶ τὸ ἀξίωμα, αἰτητικὸν δὲ ἀποκρίσεως, οἷον ἆρά γ᾽ ἡμέρα ἐστί; τοῦτο δ᾽ οὔτε ἀληθές ἐστιν οὔτε ψεῦδος. ὥστε τὸ μὲν ἡμέρα ἐστίν ἀξίωμά ἐστι, τὸ δὲ ἆρά γ᾽ ἡμέρα ἐστίν; ἐρώτημα.

such-and-such. The modern Principle of Bivalence says nothing about assertion. How significant a difference that is depends in part on how the term 'proposition' is to be understood. For example, if a proposition is anything which may be proposed or put forward for consideration, and if something can be proposed if and only if it can be asserted, then something will be a proposition if and only if it is an assertible, and the Principle and the Chrysippean thesis will be, *pro tanto*, equivalent. But there are other ways of interpreting the word 'proposition'.

There is a third point of difference between Chrysippus' thesis and the modern Principle of Bivalence. It may be introduced like this. Some properties, we tend to think, belong to their owners timelessly, whereas others are timed. Individual numbers, say, own their properties—or at any rate, their arithmetical properties—timelessly: if you hear that the number 27 is a cube, you do not ask when or for how long. It is not a cube at a time, nor for a time, nor even for ever and ever. Individual bodies, on the other hand, have many of their properties—for example, their colours—at a time or for a time: if an individual item is coloured thus-and-so, it is coloured thus-and-so at a certain time, and for a certain time; you may ask 'For how long was his nose red?', 'When will the lawns be green again?', and in principle there will be an answer. (Not, perhaps, in all cases? 'The French flag is red, white and blue'—there is no 'when' to the matter. But then the French flag is not an individual item.) The colour-values of individual items are timed.

Are the truth-values of individual items timeless, like arithmetical properties, or timed, like colour-values? The Principle of Bivalence works—or is generally taken to work—with timeless notions of truth and falsity. In the Chrysippean thesis—and in ancient logic quite generally—truth-values are timed: you may ask when, or for how long, an item is true or false; and in principle you will get an answer. The point emerges casually from a number of ancient texts. For example, Sextus remarks of 'the logicians' that

they say that the determinate assertible, 'This man is sitting' or 'This man is walking' is then true when the predicate—i.e. to sit or to walk—holds of the item which falls under the demonstrative.

(*M* viii 100)[12]

---

[12] καὶ δὴ τὸ ὡρισμένον τοῦτο ἀξίωμα, τὸ οὗτος κάθηται ἢ οὗτος περιπατεῖ, τότε φασὶν ἀληθὲς ὑπάρχειν ὅταν τῷ ὑπὸ τὴν δεῖξιν πίπτοντι συμβεβήκῃ τὸ κατηγόρημα, οἷον τὸ καθῆσθαι ἢ τὸ περιπατεῖν.

Or again,

> they say that the assertible 'It is day' is at the present moment true, whereas 'It is night' is false.

(*M* viii 103)[13]

And on a more elevated plane, Cicero will explain that fate or destiny

> is sempiternal truth flowing from all eternity.

(*div* i lv 125)[14]

Truths may be 'sempiternal'; an assertible may be 'then true', or 'at the present moment true': the temporal phrases are not so many *façons de parler*.

The difference between timeless and timed truth-values seems, at first glance at least, to separate the Principle of Bivalence and the Chrysippean thesis in a far more significant fashion than do the other two differences which I have mentioned.

TIMES AND TENSES

There is nothing quaint or shocking in the idea that truth-values are timed. If standard contemporary logic—I mean, the logic which derives from Gottlob Frege and was discovered in 1879—treats truth-values as timeless, nevertheless timed truth and timed falsity have their champions among contemporary philosophers (even if their champions do not all fight in the same cause). Moreover, outside the philosophical study we all time truth-values often enough and without embarrassment. You may wonder if it is always true that there'll be an England, and fear that it will soon be true that anyone smoking in public will be hanged, drawn and quartered. You may doubt if it was really true in your grandfather's day that you could buy a house for a shilling and still have some change left over. You may be delighted if at the present moment it is true that Phyllis is thine. Those last few sentences are reasonably normal pieces of English; and they find reasonably normal counterparts in Greek and in Latin.

Many—perhaps most—of our ordinary ways of ascribing truth or falsity to an item seem to encourage the thesis that truth-values are timed; and

---

[13] ... ὅταν λέγωσι τὸ μὲν ἡμέρα ἔστιν ἀξίωμα ἐπὶ τοῦ παρόντος εἶναι ἀληθές, τὸ δὲ νὺξ ἔστι ψεῦδος ...

[14] *ea est enim ex omni aeternitate fluens veritas sempiterna.*

the encouragement may be articulated by way of a simple argument. Thus: 'When we ascribe truth or falsity to something, we generally do so by means of some verb or verbal phrase. Verbs are tensed. Tenses generally indicate times. So ascriptions of truth and falsity are generally timed.' I have not found that argument in any ancient text; and it may appear to be too strong for its own good—for it can be generalized without difficulty so as to conclude that all ascriptions of any property to anything are timed. Nonetheless, the notions which the argument organizes must have been part of the background of the ancient commonplace that truth-values are timed.

The first premiss of the argument is uncontroversial. After all, most ascriptions of truth and falsity will make use of the adjectives 'true' and 'false' (or of their local equivalents). The adjectives will typically be used to construct various verbal phrases—in particular, predicates ('... is true' and '... is false') and sentential prefixes ('It is true that ...' and 'It is false that ...').

Tell me that everything I say is true.

It is quite false that truth is easier to hit than a barn-door.

The predicate and the prefix contain finite verbs, and the finite verbs have tenses.

In Latin and in Greek, there are the same phenomena—but they are sometimes lightly disguised. For in Latin and in Greek it is far easier than it is in English to drop the verb 'is' or leave it to be understood, crying 'Oh true, true' for 'Oh 'tis true, 'tis true'. Another Greek phenomenon may also be mentioned: there is a pair of verbs which mean 'true-say' and 'false-say': 'ἀληθεύειν' and 'ψεύδεσθαι'. The two verbs may take a personal or an impersonal subject: 'Cretans always false-say', 'The saying that he's a man true-says'. One of them, 'ψεύδεσθαι', has a Latin counterpart (namely, '*mentiri*'). The other does not.

Dio true-says that it's day

is true if and only if Dio says that it's day and it's true that it's day.

That assertible false-says that it's night

is true if and only if that assertible says that it's night and it's false that it's night.

False-saying, so understood, is not the same as lying. But the Latin '*mentiri*' is often translated by 'to lie'; and the translation is often correct. And as for the Greek 'ψεύδεσθαι', Sextus, having presented a number of cases in which it is morally permissible or even obligatory to say something false, states that plainly there is a world of difference between saying something false and false-saying inasmuch as the former comes from a decent judgement whereas false-telling comes from a wicked judgement.

(M vii 45)[15]

The distinction between saying something false and false-saying is a matter of intention; and Sextus implies that false-saying is the same—or more or less the same—as lying. What Sextus implies is wrong. Or rather, the Greek 'ψεύδεσθαι', like the Latin '*mentiri*', sometimes means 'to lie'; but it does not always do so. And very frequently, especially in logical contexts and especially when it is twinned with 'ἀληθεύειν', you false-say that so-and-so if and only if you say that so-and-so and it is false that so-and-so. In any event, ascriptions of truth and falsity are often made in Greek with the aid of those two verbs.

The second premiss of the simple argument alleges that verbs have tenses. That is not a trivial truth—or rather, it is not at all evident that the notion of a verb should be so defined as to ensure that all verbs are tensed. The language of contemporary predicate logic has no tenses, nor does the symbolic language of arithmetic. (But perhaps those languages do not contain any verbs?) And there are allegedly natural languages which do not deck their verbs out with tenses. Nonetheless, English verbs are tensed (though the system of tenses is weak), and French verbs are tensed (and the system is relatively robust). The same is true of Latin and of Greek. Just as any finite part of any verb has a number and a person and a mood, so it has a tense. That is not a necessary truth, and it is not a universal truth. But it is true of many languages—and that is enough for the present argument.

The final premiss of the argument states that tenses indicate times. That sounds less well in English than in other languages. In English 'time' and 'tense', though etymologically identical, are different words: Greek makes do with a single term, 'χρόνος', and Latin makes do with '*tempus*' (and French with 'temps'). So the claim that verbs indicate times is indistinguishable, in Latin and in Greek, from the claim that verbs have tenses.

Now Plato, who—so far as we know—was the first person to distinguish verbs from names, did not mention time as a defining feature of the verb; rather, he suggested that

it is the indicator which is attached to actions, I suppose, that we call a verb.

(*Soph* 262A)[16]

---

[15] προφανὲς τοίνυν ἐστίν ὅτι καὶ τὸ ψεῦδος λέγειν τοῦ ψεύδεσθαι κατὰ πολὺ διενήνοχεν ᾗ τὸ μὲν ἀπὸ ἀστείας γίνεται γνώμης, τὸ δὲ ψεύδεσθαι ἀπὸ πονηρᾶς.

[16] τὸ μὲν ἐπὶ ταῖς πράξεσιν ὂν δήλωμα ῥῆμά που λέγομεν.

The Stoics, too, defined the verb without reference to time:

A verb is a part of a saying which signifies a non-compound predicate, as Diogenes
says; or, as some say, an element of sayings which has no case and which signifies
something about some item or items. For example: I write, I say.

(Diogenes Laertius, VII 58)[17]

Of course, the Stoics did not deny that verbs are tensed—on the contrary,
they developed rather a sophisticated theory of tenses. Nor did they deny that
tenses signify times.

But it was Aristotle who tied verbs definitionally to times:

A verb is that which additionally signifies a time … For example, illness is a name
but 'ails' is a verb; for it additionally signifies that it now holds.

(*Int* 16b6–9)[18]

He does not, of course, mean that verbs indicate what o'clock it is or signify
hours or days or years. He means that they indicate the past or the present or
the future. More precisely, verbs in the strict sense indicate the present time,
whereas what Aristotle calls cases of verbs indicate the past or the future:

'ailed' and 'will ail' are not verbs but cases of verbs. They differ from verbs inasmuch
as verbs additionally signify the present time whereas they signify the peripheral
times.

(*Int* 16b15–18)[19]

But whereas Aristotle's distinction between verbs and cases of verbs had no
future, his annexation of time to the verb became a commonplace of ancient
grammar.

The definition of the verb in the *Art of Grammar* which goes under the
name of Dionysius Thrax runs like this:

A verb is an expression which has no case, which accepts times and persons and
numbers, and which presents an activity or a passivity.

(13 [46.4–5])[20]

---

[17] ῥῆμα δέ ἐστι μέρος λόγου σημαῖνον ἀσύνθετον κατηγόρημα, ὡς ὁ Διογένης, ἤ, ὥς τινες,
στοιχεῖον λόγου ἄπτωτον σημαῖνόν τι συντακτὸν περί τινος ἢ τινῶν, οἷον γράφω, λέγω.

[18] ῥῆμα δέ ἐστι τὸ προσσημαῖνον χρόνον … οἷον ὑγίεια μὲν ὄνομα, τὸ δ᾽ ὑγιαίνει ῥῆμα·
προσσημαίνει γὰρ τὸ νῦν ὑπάρχειν.

[19] ὁμοίως δὲ καὶ τὸ ὑγίανεν ἢ τὸ ὑγιανεῖ οὐ ῥῆμα, ἀλλὰ πτῶσις ῥήματος· διαφέρει δὲ τοῦ
ῥήματος ὅτι τὸ μὲν τὸν παρόντα προσσημαίνει χρόνον, τὰ δὲ τὸν πέριξ.

[20] ῥῆμά ἐστι λέξις ἄπτωτος, ἐπιδεκτικὴ χρόνων τε καὶ προσώπων καὶ ἀριθμῶν, ἐνέργειαν
ἢ πάθος παριστᾶσα.

Here the reference to activities and passivities takes over and enlarges Plato; the reference to times and persons and numbers does the same for Aristotle; and the caselessness is Stoic.

Later grammarians found fault with the Dionysian definition in several respects; but their improved versions all retain the condition that verbs are receptive of times. An ancient scholar reports the definition which Apollonius Dyscolus set down in his lost essay *On Verbs*:

A verb is a part of a saying which has no case, which receives different times, has its own transformations, together with activity or passivity or neither, and which presents persons and numbers, when it also shows the dispositions of the soul.

(scholiast to Dionysius Thrax, 71.23–27)[21]

The dispositions of the soul are the verbal moods, and so in Latin Priscian has this:

A verb is a part of a saying with times and moods, without cases, signifying an activity or a passivity—in that definition all verbs, both finite and non-finite, are included.

(*inst* VIII i 1 [II 2–4])[22]

Verbs indicate times. Moreover, they do so essentially. For

it is necessary for a verb to have times. For if a verb is an object, and an object announces an activity or a passivity, it is necessary that what comes about by way of an activity or a passivity also has a time.

(scholiast to Dionysius Thrax, 248.13–16)[23]

No doubt that argument—like so many arguments in the late grammatical texts—is miserably confused. But it shows how seriously verbs were linked to times.

Aristotle refers to the past, the present, and the future. If verbs signify times and there are three real times, then you might expect there to be three verbal times or three tenses. But, in Greek and in Latin, there are more than three. The Dionysian *Art of Grammar* explains the apparent mismatch in this way:

---

[21] ῥῆμά ἐστι μέρος λόγου ἄπτωτον ἐν ἰδίοις μετασχηματισμοῖς διαφόρων χρόνων ἐπιδεκτικὸν μετ᾽ ἐνεργείας ἢ πάθους ἢ οὐδετέρου, προσώπων τε καὶ ἀριθμῶν παραστατικόν, ὅτε καὶ τὰς τῆς ψυχῆς διαθέσεις δηλοῖ.

[22] *verbum est pars orationis cum temporibus et modis, sine casu, agendi vel patiendi significativum—hac enim definitione omnia tam finita quam infinita verba comprehenduntur.*

[23] ἀνάγκη ἐστὶ τὸ ῥῆμα χρόνους ἔχειν· εἰ γὰρ τὸ ῥῆμα πρᾶγμά ἐστι, τὸ δὲ πρᾶγμα ἐνέργειαν ἢ πάθος ἐπαγγέλλεται, ἀνάγκη τὸ γινόμενον ἢ κατὰ πάθος ἢ κατ᾽ ἐνέργειαν καὶ χρόνους ἔχειν.

There are three times: present, past, future. Of these the past has four species: extensive, adjacent, supercompletive, indefinite. There are three correlations: present to extensive, adjacent to supercompletive, indefinite to future.

(13 [53.1–4])[24]

This distinction of six verbal times is found in all the later grammatical texts, both Greek and Latin (e.g. Priscian, *inst* VIII viii 38 [II 405.8–19]). Some learned men noticed that the Attics had a seventh time, the future adjacent (e.g. scholiast to Dionysius Thrax, 249.13–26); but no one attempted to argue that the Dionysian list was too generous, and that in fact there were only three verbal times.

Perhaps it should be noted that the four Greek terms for the species of the past are usually translated in a different way: what I have called the extensive is usually known as the imperfect, the adjacent is the perfect, the supercompletive is the pluperfect, and the indefinite is the aorist. With the traditional translations, several passages in the ancient discussions of time and tense are difficult to comprehend.

The apparent disparity of numbers—three real times and six (or even seven) verbal times—might have moved the grammarians to distinguish between times and tenses. It might have done, but it didn't. Rather, the grammarians ruminated on the nature of time. There is only one present time, since the present is indivisible. But the past is extended and divisible, so that different forms of a verb may refer to different parts of it—the adjacent or perfect, for example, refers to the recent past, and the supercompletive or pluperfect refers to the distant past. As for the future,

the future, having itself too an extension, ought to accept a division—for future items are going to come about either shortly or after a longer time. But since the future is unknowable and what is unknowable, insofar as it is unknown, cannot accept a division, for that reason the future does not accept a division. Nonetheless, the Athenians actually divided the future into the future and the near future.

(Choeroboscus, *proleg* 12.28–36)[25]

---

[24] χρόνοι τρεῖς· ἐνεστώς, παρεληλυθώς, μέλλων. τούτων ὁ παρεληλυθὼς ἔχει διαφορὰς τέσσαρας, παρατατικόν, παρακείμενον, ὑπερσυντέλικον, ἀόριστον· ὧν συγγένειαι τρεῖς, ἐνεστῶτος πρὸς παρατατικόν, παρακειμένου πρὸς ὑπερσυντέλικον, ἀορίστου πρὸς μέλλοντα.

[25] ὁ δὲ μέλλων καὶ αὐτὸς ἔχων τὸ πλάτος ὀφείλει ἐπιδέξασθαι διαίρεσιν· τὰ γὰρ μέλλοντα ἢ μετ᾽ ὀλίγον μέλλουσι γενέσθαι ἢ μετὰ πολύ. ἀλλ᾽ ἐπειδὴ τὰ μέλλοντα ἄγνωστά εἰσι, τὰ δὲ ἄγνωστα οὐ δύνανται ἅτε δὴ ἀγνοούμενα διαίρεσιν ἐπιδέξασθαι, διὰ τοῦτο οὐκ ἐπιδέχεται διαίρεσιν ὁ μέλλων· ὅμως δὲ οἱ Ἀθηναῖοι καὶ αὐτὸν διεῖλον εἰς μέλλοντα καὶ μετ᾽ ὀλίγον μέλλοντα.

Most of that is contestable, and some of it is plainly false. For example, the Greek adjacent and supercompletive do not signify the recent past and the remote past. Nor were all ancient theorists in agreement on the matter of verbal times. Here is one example (which will come back in a later context). It concerns the adjacent or perfect. Not everyone thought that the adjacent signified the past:

> The Stoics define the present as a present extensive, because it extends both into the past and into the future—for someone who says 'I am doing it' indicates both that he has done something and that he will do. The extensive they define as a past extensive—for someone who says 'I was doing it' shows that he has done the major part but has not yet completed it—he will do so, and in a short time (for if what is past is the major part, then what remains is little). And when that has been done, it will make a complete past, 'I have written', which is called adjacent because the completion of the activity is nearby. ... The adjacent is called the completive present.
>
> (scholiast to Dionysius Thrax, 250.26–251.4)[26]

The scholiast ascribes these views to the Stoics; and if his words are trusted—and they usually are, although they receive no confirmation from any other source—then the Stoics counted the adjacent or perfect as one of two presents, and they took it to indicate not a past time but a present time.

The same view was held by at least one of the grammarians. For according to Apollonius,

> we are persuaded that the adjacent signifies not a past but a present completion; hence it does not admit anything which will be capable of coming to be and for that reason does not need the connector 'ἄν'. We shall show this at greater length in the compilation on connectors.
>
> (*synt* III 21 [287.5–288.4])[27]

In the surviving part of Apollonius' *Connectors* the matter is not discussed; and for once the ancient commentators on the Dionysian *Art* pay no heed to Apollonius' voice.

---

[26] τὸν ἐνεστῶτα οἱ Στωϊκοὶ ἐνεστῶτα παρατατικὸν ὁρίζονται, ὅτι παρατείνεται καὶ εἰς παρεληλυθότα καὶ εἰς μέλλοντα· ὁ γὰρ λέγων ποιῶ καὶ ὅτι ἐποίησέ τι ἐμφαίνει καὶ ὅτι ποιήσει· τὸν δὲ παρατατικὸν παρῳχημένον παρατατικόν· ὁ γὰρ λέγων ἐποίουν ὅτι τὸ πλέον ἐποίησεν ἐμφαίνει, οὔπω δὲ πεπλήρωκεν, ἀλλὰ ποιήσει μέν, ἐν ὀλίγῳ δὲ χρόνῳ· εἰ γὰρ τὸ παρῳχημένον πλέον, τὸ λεῖπον ὀλίγον· ὃ καὶ προσληφθὲν ποιήσει τέλειον παρῳχηκότα, τὸν γέγραφα, ὃ καλεῖται παρακείμενος διὰ τὸ πλησίον ἔχειν τὴν συντέλειαν τῆς ἐνεργείας· ... ὁ δὲ παρακείμενος καλεῖται ἐνεστὼς συντελικός.

[27] καὶ ἐντεῦθεν δὲ πειθόμεθα ὅτι οὐ παρῳχημένου συντέλειαν σημαίνει ὁ παρακείμενος, τήν γε μὴν ἐνεστῶσαν· ὅθεν οὐδὲν δυνησόμενον γενέσθαι παρεδέξατο, καὶ διὰ τοῦτο ἀπροσδεὴς τοῦ ἂν συνδέσμου ἐγεγόνει. ἐν τῇ συνδεσμικῇ συντάξει ἐντελέστερον τὰ τοιαῦτα δεδείξεται.

If Apollonius and some Stoics had an unorthodox view about the adjacent or perfect tense, they did not think of denying that it signified time: the question was not whether it indicated time but rather what time it indicated. And so their view is no exception to the general contention that verbs indicate times.

Take that contention straightforwardly and it is straightforwardly false. For whatever the value of tenses may be, and whatever the link between tense and time, it is clear that the past, present and future tenses do not always signify the past, the present and the future times. There is no need to appeal to idioms such as the historic present, or the gnomic aorist; and I shall not mention them. There is no need to refer to the phenomenon which the grammarians call sequence of tenses; but I shall note that in

Everything Oscar said was witty

the tense of 'was' is determined by the tense of 'said'—the sentence does not suggest that his remarks have lost their salt. And in the same way the past tense of 'was' in

Whatever Aristotle said was true

does not put his truths in the past.

Uncomplicated and seemingly uncontroversial counterexamples to the contention are commonly taken from the sciences—

Two parts of hydrogen to one of oxygen make water.

The positive square root of 9 is 3.

The Principle of Bivalence is unrestrictedly valid.

Such sentences do not appear to say that something now holds, nor are they synonymous with the (rather odd) sentences

Two parts of hydrogen to one of oxygen now make water,

and so on. What holds for science holds equally for everyday generalizations:

The world is too much with us.

The expense of spirit in a waste of shame is lust in action.

On Wednesdays I go shopping.

Those sentences have each a verb in the present tense. None of them refers to the present time.

Those are trifling facts about English usage. They are mirrored, without much distortion, in Latin and in Greek. (I remark in passing that the present tenses in one of the stock illustrative sentences of Stoic logic—

If it's day, it's light.

—do not signal the present time, a fact which may be thought to have consequences for the interpretation of Stoic logic.) The relationship between tense and time is complicated, and it is a relationship which differs, to some degree at least, from one language to another. But one thing is plain: tenses do not always signal time.

So the third premiss of the argument for timed truth is false: to be sure, ascriptions of truth and falsity are generally tensed; but it may not be inferred that truth and falsity are timed. Nonetheless, whatever may be said of the present tense, which tends to be a maid-of-all-work, the past tense and the future tense do regularly—though not, to be sure, always—signify the past and the future times. The fact that such tenses are used freely in ascriptions of truth and falsity creates a presumption in favour of timed truth-values. And the presumption is corroborated by several associated facts—for example, by the fact that temporal adverbs are readily attached to 'be true' and 'be false'.

TIMELESS TRUTHS

Timed ascriptions of truth and falsity are normal in English and in Greek and in Latin. So too—or so it seems—are timeless ascriptions. There is nothing singular about that: on the contrary, for a vast range of predicates, both timed and timeless ascriptions are equally normal.

The tomatoes are red—it's time to pick them.

Tomatoes are red—they look pretty in salads.

If the ancient grammarians implicitly reject timeless ascriptions of truth—and indeed of anything else—then what can they say about the second of those two sentences? What can they say about arithmetical equations or about scientific generalizations? What can they say about the vast number of apparently timeless verbs?

Perhaps where we incline to find timelessness, they found omnitemporality? In that case, the present tense of the verb in

Two and two make four

is not a timeless tense: it signifies time—all and every time. One way of interpreting that idea is to take the sentence to be synonymous with

Two and two have made, make, and will make four.

But if that ensures that the present tense always indicates time, it does not ensure that it always indicates present time.

A different interpretation appeals to a certain conception of time. On that conception, the present is a stretch of time and not an instant or a durationless moment. But it is not a stretch between the past and the future; for there is no gap between past and future. Rather, it a composite stretch, a stretch consisting of a piece of the past and a contiguous piece of the future. According to a late grammarian,

there are three times—but according to the true account there are two: the past and the future. For what is being done either has been done or is going to be—it is never present.

(scholiast to Dionysius Thrax, 248.16–18)[28]

I am now writing—that is to say, I have been writing for a bit and I shall go on writing for a bit. The present tense indicates the present time; but the present time is part past and part future.

How much of the past and how much of the future? As much and as little as you like: it all depends on the context; and in the limiting case, the present will encompass the whole of time past and the whole of time future. So the verb in

Two and two make four

is present in tense and indicates the present time—but here the present time is forever.

The view that in truth there are only two times was accepted by the grammarians—if we believe Choeroboscus:

You must know that according to the grammarians, the present is extended. For it indicates a sort of extension compared to what the philosophers call an instantaneous time, as when we say 'The present year is such-and-such'. But according to the philosophers the present is instantaneous, i.e. its being is simultaneous with its being said, as in 'I strike', 'I write'; for both of those have their being at the same time as their being said.

(*proleg* 12.1–7)[29]

But the ancient testimonies are not coherent. Some authorities agree with Choeroboscus (see scholiast to Dionysius Thrax, 295.26–27; 403.28–31). Others give an opposite report. Thus one commentator, whom I have already cited, states that

---

[28] εἰσὶ δὲ τρεῖς, κατὰ δὲ τὸν ἀληθῆ λόγον δύο, ὅ τε παρεληλυθὼς καὶ ὁ μέλλων· τὸ γὰρ πραττόμενον ἢ πέπρακται ἢ μέλλει, οὐδέποτε δὲ ἐνίσταται.

[29] ἰστέον δὲ ὅτι παρὰ μὲν τοῖς γραμματικοῖς πλατικός ἐστιν ὁ ἐνεστώς—οἱονεὶ γὰρ πλάτος ὑπεμφαίνει ὡς πρὸς τὸν παρὰ τοῖς φιλοσόφοις ἀκαριαῖον λεγόμενον χρόνον, ὡς ὅταν εἴπωμεν ὁ ἐνεστὼς ἐνιαυτὸς τοιόσδε ἐστί—παρὰ δὲ τοῖς φιλοσόφοις ἀκαριαῖός ἐστι, τουτέστιν ἅμα τῷ λέγεσθαι ἔχει καὶ τὸ εἶναι, ὡς ἐπὶ τοῦ τύπτω γράφω· ταῦτα γὰρ ἅμα τῷ λέγεσθαι ἔχουσι καὶ τὸ εἶναι.

the Stoics define the present as a present extensive, because it extends both into the past and into the future.

(scholiast to Dionysius Thrax 250.26–27)

And another commentator affirms more generally that

the philosophers define two times ... But the most accurate judgement deriving from grammar defines a certain instantaneous time and calls it present in order that the verbal inflections may be coherently presented with the appropriate accuracy.

(scholiast to Dionysius Thrax, 248.18–23)[30]

The present tense signifies the present time; and the present time is not a stretch of time, part past and part future—it is a fleeting moment in between.

As an account of present time, that view is perverse; and as an account of the present tense, it is hopeless. Was it a philosophical view scorned by the grammarians or a grammatical view scorned by the philosophers? Or both?

However that may be, it is one thing to accept the two-timing thesis and to construct the present out of the past and the future, another thing to admit the possibility of a present time which includes all the past and all the future. Is the conception of such an everlasting present found in any ancient grammatical text? A passage in Apollonius might be cited. In a discussion of temporal adverbs, he distinguishes between those which are particular, or fix on a certain part of time (as 'yesterday' fixes on the past and 'tomorrow' on the future), and those which are universal. The adverb 'now', he says, is universal; for it

embraces time in general, not cutting off a divided part of time but pervading the whole—like a generic noun.

(*synt* IV 68 [489.9–12])[31]

The word 'now' pervades the whole of time: does that not mean that any time at all may be now, and the whole of time may be present?

I do not think that it does; for elsewhere Apollonius remarks that temporal adverbs

---

[30] καὶ γὰρ οἱ φιλόσοφοι δύο ὁρίζονται ... ἡ δὲ ἐκ τῆς γραμματικῆς ἀκριβεστάτη κρίσις ὁρίζεταί τινα ἀκαριαῖον χρόνον καὶ ὀνομάζει ἐνεστῶτα ἵνα τὰς κλίσεις τὰς ῥηματικὰς ἀκολούθως δυνηθῇ μετὰ τῆς ἐχούσης ἀκριβείας παραδιδόναι.

[31] ὁ αὐτὸς λόγος καὶ ἐπὶ τοῦ νῦν· πάλιν γὰρ χρόνου ἐστὶ τοῦ γενικωτάτου ἐμπεριεκτικόν, οὐ τέμνον τὸ ἐπιμεριζόμενον τοῦ χρόνου, διῆκον μέντοι δι' ὅλου, ὡσπερεὶ γενικὸν ὄνομα.

which do not divide time but show the common extent of all time are taken along
with any time—as 'I thought now', 'I think now', 'I will think now'.

(adv 123.21–23)³²

That is to say, 'now' is a universal adverb inasmuch as it may be taken with a
verb in any tense. We say 'I'll go now', and refer to the future. We say 'I was
there just now', and refer to the past. That is what Apollonius means: it does
not even suggest a two-time theory, let alone the notion of an everlasting
present.

So the grammarians do not claim that the present time may run on for
ever. Neither do they say that the present tense of the verb—the present
verbal time—sometimes indicates not the present real time but rather all
eternity. Then how did they deal with that use of tenses which we take to
be timeless? Well, it has been claimed that, despite the official remarks about
tense and time, ancient thinkers did in fact acknowledge a timeless use of
the verbal tenses—or at least of the verbal present. If the claim means that,
in numerous ancient texts, tensed verbs are in point of fact timeless, then it
is—in the present context—uninteresting; for it says nothing about ancient
views on times and tenses. But perhaps there are passages in which a timeless
tense is explicitly acknowledged?

I have found no such passage in the grammarians; but ancient philosophy
throws up a candidate or two, one of the least unpromising of which is the
following text from the *Prior Analytics*:

> You must take 'holds of every' not determining it as to time (e.g. now, or at such-and-
> such a time) but unqualifiedly. For we construct the syllogisms with such propositions
> inasmuch as if the proposition is taken with regard to now there will not be a syllogism.
> For presumably nothing prevents it from being the case that man holds at a given
> time of every moving item—i.e. if nothing else were moving. But moving item
> possibly holds of every horse—yet it is not possible for man to hold of every horse.

(APr 34b7–14)³³

In that dense paragraph, Aristotle is considering syllogisms of the following
form:

---

³² τὰ μέντοι οὐ διορίζοντα τὸν χρόνον, κοινὴν δὲ παράτασιν δηλοῦντα τοῦ παντὸς χρόνου,
συμπαραλαμβάνεται κατὰ πάντα χρόνον, ὡς ἔχει τὸ νῦν ἐφρόνησα, νῦν φρονῶ, νῦν φρονήσω.

³³ δεῖ δὲ λαμβάνειν τὸ παντὶ ὑπάρχον μὴ κατὰ χρόνον ὁρίσαντας, οἷον νῦν ἢ ἐν τῷδε τῷ
χρόνῳ, ἀλλ' ἁπλῶς· διὰ τοιούτων γὰρ προτάσεων καὶ τοὺς συλλογισμοὺς ποιοῦμεν, ἐπεὶ
κατά γε τὸ νῦν λαμβανομένης τῆς προτάσεως οὐκ ἔσται συλλογισμός· οὐδὲν γὰρ ἴσως κωλύει
ποτὲ καὶ παντὶ κινουμένῳ ἄνθρωπον ὑπάρχειν, οἷον εἰ μηδὲν ἄλλο κινοῖτο· τὸ δὲ κινούμενον
ἐνδέχεται παντὶ ἵππῳ· ἀλλ' ἄνθρωπον οὐδενὶ ἵππῳ ἐνδέχεται.

A holds of every B.
Possibly B holds of every C.
Therefore possibly A holds of every C.

He claims that the form is valid. But he notes that the following concrete argument is invalid:

All moving items are men.
Possibly all horses are moving items.
Therefore possibly all horses are men.

After all, it is perfectly possible for the two premises of that argument to be true and the conclusion false. So there is a counterexample, and the proposed syllogistic form is invalid. Or at least, that seems to be the inference to draw. But Aristotle does not draw it. Rather, he insists that in the first premiss of the syllogistic form, 'A holds of every B', the verb must be taken unqualifiedly and not restricted to a given time.

The question of the validity of the syllogistic form does not concern me here: I have cited the passage only because Aristotle's remark has been taken to show that, in syllogisms in general, 'holds of' must not be understood to indicate the present time; and that he therefore recognizes a timeless use of the present tense. Now that is certainly not quite right: Aristotle is discussing a particular syllogistic form, and he means that, in the syllogism under consideration, we must take 'holds of' unqualifiedly. There is no reason to generalize the remark to all syllogistic propositions—and excellent reason not to do so. Nonetheless, does the passage not recognize that tenses are sometimes timeless insofar as it insists that in some syllogistic contexts they must be taken timelessly?

Well, the adverb 'unqualifiedly' does not in itself imply timelessness. When Aristotle says that you must take 'holds of' unqualifiedly, what he means is that you must write 'All men are moving'—without any adverbial qualification—and not 'All men are now moving' or 'All men are moving on Friday' or the like. And Aristotle plainly implies that, in the present context, 'All men are moving' is true if and only if all men are always moving; for he contrasts the unqualified 'All men are moving' with statements to the effect that at some time or other all men are in motion. In that case, he is not acknowledging a timeless use of the verbal present 'are'. Rather, he tacitly admits that the verb 'are', despite its present tense, here signifies omnitemporality. How can it do so? There is no hint in the text; but presumably either 'are' indicates not the present but all time or else 'are' signifies an everlasting present.

I readily grant that that interpretation of the Aristotelian text is less than perfectly satisfying; and perhaps it is prudent to allow that, here and there, an ancient text half-acknowledges a timeless tense. Nonetheless, it remains true that whenever they reflected on tenses, the ancient logicians and grammarians took them to indicate times.

BIVALENCE DISPUTED

Ancient truth-values were timed. What then—to return to the fold—was Chrysippus' thesis? What principle of bivalence did he maintain? 'Every assertible is either true or false' means

> If it can be asserted that so-and-so, then either it is true that so-and-so or it is false that so-and-so.

But we must add temporal indicators to 'is true' and 'is false'—and also, no doubt, to 'can be asserted'. So the thesis will be something of this form

> If it can be asserted ... that so-and-so, then either it is true ... that so-and-so or it is false ... that so-and-so

—where the dots are to be replaced by the temporal indicators.

There are several possibilities. A modest version of the thesis holds that every assertible is at some time true or at some time false:

> If it can ever be asserted that so-and-so, then either at some time or other it is true that so-and-so or else at some time or other it is false that so-and-so.

The most aggressive version holds that every assertible is either at all times true or else at all times false:

> If it can ever be asserted that so-and-so, then either it is true at every time that so-and-so or else it is false at every time that so-and-so.

The modest version is certainly too weak for Chrysippus. The aggressive version is certainly too strong. There are several intermediate versions. I assume—though I cannot prove—that Chrysippus' thesis proposed that every assertible is either true or false throughout its existence; that is to say:

> Whenever it can be asserted that so-and-so, either it is true at that time that so-and-so or else it is false at that time that so-and-so.

The modest version of the thesis allows that assertibles may pass some part of their careers without a truth-value. The aggressive version requires that they pass the whole of time either in the company of one truth-value or in the company of the other. The version which I propose as Chrysippean is betwixt and between.

If Chrysippus strained every sinew to persuade us of the truth of his thesis, then the thesis must have been disputed—or at the least, it must have seemed disputable. And indeed, at first blush it looks pretty dubious.

Aphorisms are neither true nor false.

I have heard myself asserting that Strauss (R.) was a far greater operatic composer than Wagner (R.); one of my colleagues recently asserted that all students ought to be awarded the same marks in their examinations; my brother asserted that England would not have collapsed had Trescothick not been judged l.b.w.; and so on. There are assertions there, or else I do not know what an assertion is. Hence there are assertibles—for what is asserted can be asserted. But is each of the assertibles either true or false? The answer is far from evident; and ordinary speakers will ordinarily incline to find the terms 'true' and 'false' if not inapposite then at any rate less apt than other words of appraisal.

Philosophically, too, Chrysippus' thesis was—and remains—controversial. True, no ancient philosopher blenched at ascribing truth-values to moral or to aesthetic assertibles. (Some of them claimed that what they called admiratives—items such as 'How beautiful are the feet ...'—and what they called reprehensives—items such as 'False perjured Clarence ...'—are not assertibles at all. But that is another kettle.) Yet on other scores there were doubts. On the score of vague assertibles, for example. (I can assert that France is a hexagon. But is it true or false? Quite apart from any homespun reluctance so to assess it, there is the serpent of the sorites, whose bite Chrysippus knew, and one familiar antidote to which is the denial of truth-value to at least some vague assertibles.) Again, there are paradoxical assertibles. (Surely I can assert that this assertible is false. But then the Paradox of the Liar threatens me—and one way of placating it is to refuse the paradoxical assertibles a truth-value.) Or again, there are what they call 'future contingents'.

The director announces—perhaps more in hope than from conviction—that there will be a festival at Aix-en-Provence next year. Is what he asserts either true or false? Is it now either true or false? Well, the future of the festival is quite uncertain: perhaps it will take place and perhaps it won't. And if the festival hangs in the air, then surely so too does the truth-value of any assertible which announces it. Were the truth-value of the assertible now fixed, then the future of the festival would be now fixed. But it isn't.

The certainty or fixedness here is not a matter of our attitude to the future. The director may in fact be quite certain that the festival will come off—and the rest of us may think it cruelly unlikely. But that isn't to the point: the point is that—whatever we may think about it—the future of the festival hasn't yet been decided. The sun will rise over Aix: that is perfectly determined. Will it rise over a city in festival attire? That is not yet fixed. So there is, as yet, no fact of the matter about the festival of Aix-en-Provence. And where there is no fact of the matter, there there is no truth and no falsity.

Not, of course, that the whole of the future is in that way contingent or up in the air. On the contrary, innumerable future items are already fixed, and many have been fixed from all eternity. The future of the natural world is rough-hewn, and its general development is fixed. Much of the future of any man is fixed; and of those items which are unfixed for me now, most—or perhaps all—will get fixed some time before they happen. If it is not now fixed that there will be a festival in Aix, it will be fixed—one way or the other—before next July, and before the festival opens (if it does). Contingency is anything but universal. Nonetheless, there are future contingencies—and any assertible which deals with such a contingency is neither true nor false.

That, at any rate, is a view which has often been upheld; and sometimes for the reasons which I have rehearsed.

If an assertible is neither true nor false, then what is it? Some philosophers have suggested that it has a third truth-value: it is indeterminate, or neutral, or possible, or the like. No such notion is found in any ancient text, where there are precisely two truth-values, truth and falsity. An item which is neither true nor false does not have a filmy third value—it has no truth-value at all. Questions and commands and prayers and hypotheses are all—according to the Stoics—sayings and complete sayables. None of them is either true or false. None of them has a third truth-value. So too—according to some philosophers—with certain future assertibles.

So the thesis of bivalence was menaced, in antiquity, by paradoxical assertions, none of which—according to some philosophers—is ever either true or false; and by vague assertions, some of which—according to some philosophers—are never either true or false; and by future assertions, some of which—according to some philosophers—are sometimes neither true nor false.

In *On Fate*, Cicero places Chrysippus' thesis in the context of an argument over fatalism and the future. In particular, he sets Chrysippus against Epicurus:

Chrysippus strains every sinew to persuade us that every assertible is either true or false. For just as Epicurus feared lest, should he concede this, he would have to concede that whatever happens happens by fate (for if one or the other is true from eternity, then it is already fixed; and if it is fixed, then it is necessary—so that he thinks that both fate and necessity are confirmed in this way); in the same way Chrysippus was afraid that were he not granted that whatever is asserted is either true or false, he would not be able to maintain that everything happens by fate and on the basis of eternal causes of future things.

(*fat* x 21)[34]

So Chrysippus defended his thesis against Epicurus; and Epicurus had denied the thesis in connection with future contingencies, in order to avoid fatalism.

As for Epicurus, Cicero links his view to some arguments which had been advanced by Diodorus Cronus. At any rate, he says about certain contentions of Diodorus that

it is not because these things are so that Epicurus need fear fate and call on the help of his atoms …;

(*fat* ix 18)[35]

and that suggests that Epicurus' rejection of the thesis of bivalence was, in part at least, a reaction to Diodorus. But if Epicurus disagreed with Diodorus and Chrysippus disagreed with Epicurus, it should not be thought that Diodorus and Chrysippus were allies. On the contrary, they too were at loggerheads:

Be careful, Chrysippus, or you will abandon the cause in which you are wrestling mightily with Diodorus, the robust logician.

(*fat* vi 12)[36]

Now some of the arguments which Diodorus proposed are reminiscent of the ninth Chapter of the *de Interpretatione* in which Aristotle discusses the relation between certain propositions about the future on the one hand and truth and falsity on the other. According to Boethius,

some people, the Stoics among them, have thought that Aristotle says that future contingents are neither true nor false.

(*in Int²* 208.1–3)[37]

---

[34] *itaque contendit omnes nervos Chrysippus ut persuadeat omne ἀξίωμα aut verum esse aut falsum. ut enim Epicurus veretur ne si hoc concesserit concedendum sit fato fieri quaecumque fiant (si enim alterutrum ex aeternitate verum est, esse id iam certum, et si certum etiam necessarium—ita et necessitatem et fatum confirmari putat), sic Chrysippus metuit ne si non obtinuerit omne quod enuntietur aut verum esse aut falsum, non teneat omnia fato fieri et ex causis aeternis rerum futurarum.*

[35] *nec cum haec ita sint est causa cur Epicurus fatum extimescat et ab atomis petat praesidium …*

[36] *vigila, Chrysippe, ne tuam causam, in qua tibi cum Diodoro, valente dialectico, magna luctatio est, deseras.*

[37] *putaverunt autem quidam, quorum Stoici quoque sunt, Aristotelem dicere in futuro contingentes nec veras esse nec falsas.*

Aristotle has indeed generally been understood in such a way; and there is no reason to doubt that some Stoics so understood him.

So shall we imagine that Chrysippus strained his sinews while wrestling with Aristotle and with Diodorus and with Epicurus over future contingents? He indubitably wrestled with Diodorus. But Diodorus did not deny the Chrysippean thesis, and Chrysippus could not therefore have defended it against Diodorus. As for Aristotle, Boethius refers to the Stoics in general, not to Chrysippus in particular; and his report probably bears not upon Chrysippus but upon the imperial Stoics. For the imperial Stoics are known to have tried their hand at interpreting Aristotle, whereas how much Chrysippus knew about Aristotle's logic is a matter of dispute, and there is no evidence for (or against) the hypothesis that he had read and digested the *de Interpretatione*. In any event, Epicurus is presented by Cicero as the arch-adversary. Chrysippus is explicitly said to have rejected various Epicurean notions: there is no reason for scepticism, and we may believe that Chrysippus defended his thesis against Epicurus.

TRUTH AND CAUSATION

The dossier on the Epicurean attitude to bivalence contains four more Ciceronian snippets in addition to the passage which I have just cited. The Epicurean broth can be thickened: it will be served up at a later stage in my argument; but enough has already been said to suggest that it has an odd flavour.

Cicero's story runs like this. Diodorus had urged that whatever is true is necessary and whatever is false is impossible. Since everything is either true or false, everything is either necessary or impossible: there is no contingency in the world, not even in the future world; and we all roll forward inexorably along the iron rails of fate. In order to avoid that tremendous conclusion, Epicurus maintained that some propositions were neither true nor false, and in particular that some propositions about the future were neither true nor false. And he founded that thesis about truth and falsity on his doctrine of atomic swerves.

The first part of the Epicurean position is easy to understand. Epicurus agreed with Diodorus that if, say, it is true now that I shall be in Paris next week, then it is necessary now that I shall be in Paris next week; and if it is false now, then it is impossible now. But in fact it is, now, neither true nor false that I shall be in Paris next week, so that the

Diodoran theses do not establish that my whereabouts next week are already necessary.

It is less easy to understand the second part of the Epicurean position. The doctrine of the swerve is this: When an atom changes direction, it usually does so because it crashes into another moving atom; but every so often, an atom will alter its trajectory, by a minimal amount, without being involved in a crash. Such atomic swerves are causeless—or at any rate, they have no antecedent causes. Now my whereabouts next week depend, *inter alia*, upon various future atomic swerves. If atom A swerves at lunch-time, then I shall find myself in Athens; if atom B swerves at tea, then I shall be in Bologna; and so on. So far so good—or so bad. But what is the link between causeless atomic swerves and lack of truth-value?

The link is this: if atom A will swerve, causelessly, at some time in the future, then it is not now true (nor, of course, false) that A will swerve. And if my being in Athens next week depends on that particular swerve, then it is not now true (nor, of course, false) that I shall be in Athens next week. That is to say, Epicurus presupposes a link between the current truth-value of a proposition and the current causal situation with regard to the state of affairs which the proposition describes: if it is now true that such-and-such will be the case, then there is now some cause which ensures that such-and-such will be the case.

Perhaps that is unremarkable—after all, is there not something similar in Aristotle?

If there is a man, then the saying by which we say that there is a man is true; and the converse too: if the saying by which we say that there is a man is true, then there is a man. But the true saying is not in any way cause of the being of the object: rather, the object seems to be in a way cause of its being true—for the saying is said to be true or false by virtue of the object's being or not being.

(*Cat* 14b15–22)[38]

Or again, and more pithily:

It is not because we truly think that you are pale that you are pale: rather, because you are pale, we who say so say the truth.

(*Met* 1051b6–9)[39]

---

[38] εἰ γὰρ ἔστιν ἄνθρωπος, ἀληθὴς ὁ λόγος ᾧ λέγομεν ὅτι ἔστιν ἄνθρωπος. καὶ ἀντιστρέφει γε· εἰ γὰρ ἀληθὴς ὁ λόγος ᾧ λέγομεν ὅτι ἔστιν ἄνθρωπος, ἔστιν ἄνθρωπος. ἔστι δὲ ὁ μὲν ἀληθὴς λόγος οὐδαμῶς αἴτιος τοῦ εἶναι τὸ πρᾶγμα, τὸ μέντοι πρᾶγμα φαίνεταί πως αἴτιον τοῦ εἶναι ἀληθῆ τὸν λόγον· τῷ γὰρ εἶναι τὸ πρᾶγμα ἢ μὴ ἀληθὴς ὁ λόγος ἢ ψευδὴς λέγεται.
[39] οὐ γὰρ διὰ τὸ ἡμᾶς οἴεσθαι ἀληθῶς σὲ λευκὸν εἶναι εἶ σὺ λευκός, ἀλλὰ διὰ τὸ σὲ εἶναι λευκὸν ἡμεῖς οἱ φάντες τοῦτο ἀληθεύομεν.

It is the way things are which causes the truth (and the falsity) of sayings.

It may be objected that those Aristotelian passages are anodyne—or at least, that they hardly commit Aristotle to anything as specific as the thesis which I have just ascribed to Epicurus. But suppose that it is now true that

I shall die tomorrow, but you will die today:

what, according to Aristotle, is the cause of that present truth? Hardly the double death, or the fact of the double death; for how could future deaths be a cause of present truth? Surely the best understanding of Aristotle's view—or perhaps, the best extension of Aristotle's view—must be the Epicurean position, or something very close to it.

However that may be, the thesis which I have ascribed to Epicurus was certainly held by Chrysippus.

Chrysippus argues thus: If there are movements without causes, then not every assertible ... will be either true or false. For what will not have efficient causes will be neither true nor false. But every assertible is either true or false. Therefore there are no movements without causes.

(Cicero, *fat* x 20)[40]

'What will not have causes will be neither true nor false'. More particularly:

Future items cannot be true—Chrysippus says—if they do not possess causes why they are future, so that it is necessary that those which are true have causes.

(*fat* xi 26)[41]

The formulation leaves something to be desired; but the general sense is plain: it cannot now be true that it will be the case that so-and-so unless there is now some cause which ensures that it will be the case that so-and-so.

Those texts deal with truths about the future: present truth about the future requires present causes. For truths about the past, parity of reasoning will suggest that present truth requires present effects. And for truths about the present? Well, they are there in front of us, too late to have causes and too soon to have effects. So a first shot at a general thesis about present truth might look like this:

It is true now that so-and-so if and only if either it is now the case that so-and-so or there are now present elements in some causal chain which

---

[40] *concludit enim Chrysippus hoc modo: si est motus sine causa, non omnis enuntiatio ... aut vera aut falsa erit. causas enim efficientes quod non habebit id nec verum nec falsum erit. omnis autem enuntiatio aut vera aut falsa est. motus ergo sine causa nullus est.*

[41] *... quia futura vera, inquit [sc Chrysippus], non possunt esse ea quae causas cur futura sint non habeant. habeant igitur causas necesse est ea quae vera sunt.*

will bring it about that so-and-so or there are now present causal traces left by the fact that so-and-so.

The generalization of that to all times will be:

> It is true at a given time that so-and-so if and only if either it is the case at that time that so-and-so or there is at that time a cause why so-and-so or there is at that time an effect because so-and-so.

That will require some scrubbing before it is clean enough to be inspected. But for my present purposes it will do as it is.

For there are several immediate objections to such a causal thesis—objections which will be thrown against the cleanest version you may come up with. What, for example, are we to do with truths which are inherently causeless and effectless? I mean such things as mathematical or logical truths—or, come to that, causal propositions themselves. Plainly, the causal thesis will have to be afforced by the addition of a further clause, or of further clauses. To start with, you might think of appending something like: '... or it is necessarily the case that so-and-so'. But that addition will soon prove in need of modification; and perhaps it should simply be conceded that the causal thesis applies only to truths which enter into the causal affairs of the world.

But what are we to do with truths which no longer have any effects and with truths which do not yet have any causes?

Are there not innumerably many future events which nothing now in the world causally heralds? On 1 March 2014 the monarch of Great Britain will or will not have eggs and bacon for breakfast—is there anything in the present state of the world which will bring that event about, or prevent it from happening? Again, are there not innumerably many past events which have left no trace at all on the world? On the fatal Ides of March, either Julius Caesar had his morning rashers or he didn't—is there still a trace or smear of that breakfast to be found somewhere in the universe? Have there always been heralds of all our future lunches, and will there always be traces of all our past dinners? Are there, now, causes and effects of every one of those tedious little events which mark our petty pacing through life?

Those questions invite the answer No. Chrysippus returned the answer Yes. And his physics ensured the affirmative answer: the career of the Chrysippean universe is fixed by a vast number of infinite and interconnecting causal chains, such that everything which happens both has antecedent causes which had antecedent causes which had antecedent causes *ad infinitum* and also has subsequent effects which have subsequent effects which have subsequent effects *ad infinitum*. At any moment in the history of the world there will be found causes of every future happening and effects of every past happening. If it is true that Caesar ate a hearty breakfast, then the effects of that breakfast are still about us; and if it is true that he had an unhearty breakfast—or no breakfast at all—then, again, the effects are still with us.

That is Stoic fatalism. Or rather, it is a crude and inaccurate version of Stoic fatalism; and it is inaccurate in part because, Stoic causes being bodies and Stoic effects being incorporeal, nothing can be both a Stoic cause and a Stoic effect, so that no cause can have a cause and no effect an effect. We talk of causal chains, and so did the Stoics; but a Stoic chain is not constructed from links which are at once the effects of their predecessors and the causes of their successors. It is in fact quite a ticklish matter to give an account of a Stoic chain. But one thing is clear, and it is the only thing which matters here: Chrysippus' fatalism commits him to the view about Caesar's breakfast which I have ascribed to him.[42]

It will be said that Chrysippus' doctrine of fatalism is a piece of physics—or perhaps of metaphysics—and that it cannot be invoked to support a logical principle. Perhaps it ought not to be invoked. But I bet that Chrysippus did invoke it: the Stoics notoriously claimed that their philosophy formed a strongly unified system; and although the claim is largely eyewash, there are some drops of truth in it. One drop connects fatalism to bivalence.

However that may be, an appeal to fatalism—it will next be objected—can scarcely serve Chrysippus' needs. After all, his fundamental reason for associating truth and causation must have something to do with the conditions under which an item is rationally assertible: for example, I can reasonably assert, now, that I saw *Les Troyens* last October inasmuch as I can look, now, at the programme which I then bought and which is a causal trace of the event. And I can assert, now, that I shall split the logs this afternoon inasmuch as I have, now, a firm intention and a sharpened axe, which are causal heralds of the act.

That sort of notion, familiar enough to modern philosophers, can be found in a few ancient texts:

Carneades said that not even Apollo could predict future events unless nature contained causes in such a way that it was necessary for them to come about. For what could the god himself have looked at in order to predict that Marcellus—the Marcellus who was three times consul—would die at sea? That was indeed true from all eternity, but it had no active causes. In the same way, Carneades deemed that not

---

[42] This paragraph was added on the advice of Suzanne Bobzien.

even past events were known to Apollo if no signs of them exist as it were as their traces.

(Cicero, fat xiv 32–33)[43]

Apollo cannot predict the future unless there are current causes to which he can turn, and he cannot recount the past unless there are present traces. For in order to assert anything, he must have something to 'look at'. Surely Chrysippus' appeal to his fatalistic doctrine was meant to guarantee that Apollo would always have something pertinent to look at.

But does it do so? Chrysippean fatalism assures us that the world contains, now, traces of my last duchess and harbingers of those future bean-rows on Innisfree. Yet it does not assure us that those traces and harbingers are at our present disposition; and it would be a preposterous assurance to offer. Perhaps Chrysippus thought that all traces and harbingers were at our disposition, 'in principle', or that they were at Apollo's disposition? But we have no particular reason to suppose that he did so. What is more, we have no particular reason to suppose that his appeal to fatalism was meant to supply us—or anyone—with things to look at. The pertinent texts do not suggest that Chrysippus appealed to causes and effects in order to underwrite our present assertions about the past and the future: they suggest that he appealed to causes and effects in order to underwrite the present truth of what has been and of what is to come.

So there is a difference between Chrysippus' view and the view which Carneades outlined. Carneades' first remark about Apollo concerns prediction—that is to say, it concerns foreknowledge. Carneades' second remark about Apollo turns to retrodiction and to knowledge of the past. His thesis might reasonably be generalized as follows:

> It is knowable at a given time that so-and-so if and only if either it is the case at that time that so-and-so or there is at that time a cause why so-and-so or there is at that time an effect because so-and-so.

That generalization is calqued on the thesis about truth which I attributed to Chrysippus:

> It is true at a given time that so-and-so if and only if either it is the the case at that time that so-and-so or there is at that time a cause why so-and-so or there is at that time an effect because so-and-so.

<hr />

[43] *itaque dicebat Carneades ne Apollinem quidem futura posse dicere nisi ea quorum causas natura ita contineret ut ea fieri necesse esset. quid enim spectans deus ipse diceret Marcellum eum qui ter consul fuit in mari esse periturum? erat hoc quidem verum ex aeternitate, sed causas id efficientes non habebat. ita ne praeterita quidem ea quorum nulla signa tamquam vestigia extarent Apolloni nota esse censebat.*

But the two theses are quite different. Moreover, Carneades rejects the Chrysippean thesis; for he holds that it was always true that Marcellus would die at sea even though his death at sea did not always have causal harbingers.

Why did Chrysippus maintain his causal thesis about truth? Perhaps he was moved by some such thought as the following. It was true some fifty years ago that Roger Bannister ran a four-minute mile, it is true now that he did so, and it will still be true fifty years hence. Those three truths constitute three facts about the world. The facts are intimately connected to one another; but they are distinct—if only because they refer to different times in the history of the world. So there must have been something about that period fifty years ago which ensured that it was true then that Bannister ran a four-minute mile, and there must also be something similar about now, and there will have to be something similar fifty years hence.

You might say that what ensured the truth fifty years ago was the epoch-making event at Iffley Road, and that the very same event ensures the present truth and will ensure the future truth. No doubt that is correct; but it is not enough. What killed the nettles last year, what is killing them this year, and what will kill them next year? Why, a good dose of Praixone, each and every time. That is true. But there were three quite different dosings of the stuff; and the nettles died last year not because they were dosed but because they were dosed last year. In the same way, the event at Iffley Road secures all three truths about Bannister; but there are, as it were, three different dosings of the event—for otherwise the differences among the three truths would be elided. And if you look for different dosings, where could you better seek than in the web of causes and effects which is spun by the event?

That argument makes a mumbling impression. But perhaps it can be given a bite.

CHANGING TRUTH-VALUES

Chrysippean bivalence, I suggested, may be expressed by the following thesis:

> Whenever it can be asserted that so-and-so, either it is true at that time that so-and-so or else it is false at that time that so-and-so.

That may be distinguished from a neighbouring thesis, namely:

> Either whenever it can be asserted that so-and-so it is then true that so-and-so or whenever it can be asserted that so-and-so it is then false that so-and-so.

The neighbouring thesis excludes the possibility that an assertible might have now one truth-value and now the other, that an assertible might change its truth-value, the true turning false or the false true. The thesis I have ascribed to Chrysippus leaves open—or at least, does not directly exclude—the possibility of such changes.

If truth and falsity are timeless, then items cannot change their truth-values; for if truth-bearers don't have truth-values at times, then they can't have different values at different times. So if truth-values are to change, it is necessary that truth and falsity be timed. But it is not sufficient. If truth and falsity are timed, it does not follow that some items change their truth-value. Indeed, it does not follow that any item can change its truth-value; for there may be other impediments to change.

Nonetheless, ordinary conversation ordinarily supposes, or perhaps pre-supposes, that truth-values change; and timed ascriptions of truth and falsity are frequently used precisely to call attention to such changes. If I say that it's now true that you can get from Paris to London in 3 hours, I insinuate that it was not true in the past. If I lament that it's no longer true that Swiss railways are the most reliable in Europe, I imply that it was true in the past. In the one case, I indicate a change from false to true, and in the other a change from true to false. In that way, we all hold—or at least, we all speak as though we hold—that at least some truth-bearers may, and sometimes do, change their truth-value.

The Greeks spoke in the same sort of way, and so did the Romans; and ancient philosophers supposed—as a matter of course—that an item might be now true and then false, now false and then true. When—to recall a passage I quoted earlier—the logicians

say that the assertible 'It is day' is at the present moment true, whereas 'It is night' is false,

(Sextus, *M* VIII 103)

they plainly imply that, whereas now it is true that it is day, a little later it will be false that it is day, so that one and the same assertible, the assertible that it is day, is now true and later false.

That it is day is a simple assertible, and one which refers to the present time. But there is no reason in principle why other sorts of assertible—complex assertibles, say, or assertibles which look to the past or to the future—may not change in the same fashion. And the Stoics, at least, acknowledged such changes.

Of the ancient texts which mention changing assertibles—they are not very numerous—the most instructive is a passage in Simplicius' commentary on Aristotle's *Physics*:

According to Alexander, it is possible to show that those Stoic assertibles which some call indeterminately changing are not in fact so. I mean items such as:
If Dio is alive, Dio will be alive.
For if that is now true, inasmuch as it begins with something true ('Dio is alive') and ends with something true ('Dio will be alive'), nonetheless there will be a time when, the co-assumption 'But Dio is alive' being true, the conditional will change to being false inasmuch as there will be a time when, 'Dio is alive' still being true, 'He will be alive' will not be true—and when that is not true, the whole conditional changes and becomes false. For it is not always the case that when 'He is alive' is true, so too is 'He will be alive'—were that so, Dio would be immortal. Nonetheless, it is not possible to determine the matter and say when, him being alive, 'He will be alive' will not be true. That is why they say that the change in such assertibles takes place at an indeterminate and undefined time. Well, that is what they mean by an assertible which changes indeterminately.

(*in Phys* 1299.36–1300.11)[44]

The constipated style of the passage suggests that Simplicius is quoting Alexander more or less *verbatim*—no doubt from his lost commentary on the *Physics*.

The text demonstrates that the Stoics discussed changing assertibles in some detail. Thus they distinguished between different types of change in truth-value, inasmuch as some items change determinately, or at a definite time, and others indeterminately. Again, they considered changes in complex assertibles: the changing assertible which is the hero of the passage, namely
If Dio is alive, Dio will be alive,
is a conditional. Not only that: the verb in the antecedent is in the present tense and the verb in the consequent is in the future—and that particular fact is directly pertinent to the changing status of the assertible. Again, the Stoics

---

[44] ἐκ δὴ τούτων τῶν λόγων, φησὶν ὁ Ἀλέξανδρος, δυνατὸν ὁρμώμενον δεικνύναι τὰ παρὰ τοῖς Στωϊκοῖς ἀξιώματα ἃ μεταπίπτοντά τινες λέγουσιν ἀπεριγράφως μὴ ὄντα τοιαῦτα. ἔστι δὲ ταῦτα τοιαῦτα· εἰ ζῇ Δίων, ζήσεται Δίων. τοῦτο γὰρ εἰ καὶ ἀληθές ἐστι νῦν ἀρχόμενον ἀπὸ ἀληθοῦς τοῦ ζῇ Δίων καὶ λῆγον εἰς ἀληθὲς τὸ ζήσεται, ἀλλ' ἔσται ποτὲ ὅτε τῆς προσλήψεως ἀληθοῦς οὔσης τῆς ἀλλὰ μὴν ζῇ Δίων μεταπεσεῖται τὸ συνημμένον εἰς ψεῦδος τῷ ἔσεσθαί ποτε ὅτε ἀληθοῦς ὄντος ἔτι τοῦ ζῇ Δίων, οὐκ ἔσται ἀληθὲς τὸ καὶ ζήσεται, οὗ μὴ ὄντος ἀληθοῦς τὸ ὅλον συνημμένον γίνοιτο ἂν ψεῦδος μεταπίπτον· οὐ γὰρ ἀεὶ ὅτε τὸ ζῇ ἀληθές, καὶ τὸ ζήσεται, ἐπεὶ οὕτως ἀθάνατος ἂν εἴη ὁ Δίων. οὐ μὴν ἔσται ὁρίσαντας εἰπεῖν πότε οὐκ ἀληθὲς ἔσται ζῶντος αὐτοῦ τὸ ζήσεται. διὸ καὶ ἐν ἀπεριγράφῳ καὶ ἀορίστῳ χρόνῳ λέγουσι γίνεσθαι τὴν τῶν τοιούτων ἀξιωμάτων μετάπτωσιν. τοιοῦτον μὲν οὖν ἐστι τὸ ἀπεριγράφως μεταπίπτειν λεγόμενον ἀξίωμα.

considered such assertibles as potential premises of arguments: that is revealed by Alexander's casual reference to a co-assumption or πρόσληψις, where he employs the standard Stoic term for the second or supplementary premiss of a two-premissed argument. Finally, Alexander uses the verb 'μεταπίπτειν', and its associated noun, to describe change in truth-value; and although the word is a common enough term which means no more than 'change' or 'alter', it is plain, from this and other texts, that it came to be used as a piece of logical jargon to designate change in truth-value.

Alexander names no Stoic names, and it would be rash to suppose that the whole of his report goes back to Chrysippus. True, the catalogue of Chrysippus' writings includes two essays on changing arguments—that is to say, on arguments one or more of the components of which changes its truth-value in the course of the argument's being propounded; but the author of the catalogue took the two essays to be spurious (Diogenes Laertius, VII 195–196).⁴⁵ Changing arguments were certainly discussed by the imperial Stoics—as is shown by some of the conversations of Epictetus (see esp. *diss* I vii), and also by Sextus Empiricus, who preserves an example of a changing argument (*PH* II 134). But if changing arguments perhaps did not engage Chrysippus' attention, changing assertibles certainly did. Dionysius of Halicarnassus happens to tell us that they were discussed in Chrysippus' work *On the Construction of the Parts of Speech* (see *comp verb* iv 32); and there is further evidence in Cicero's *On Fate*.

If Stoic assertibles may change their truth-values, so too may Aristotelian sayings. Aristotle never discusses the phenomenon in any detail, but he alludes to it half a dozen times—for example, in the short essay on truth which ends Book Theta of the *Metaphysics*. There, having recalled the distinction between items which cannot be otherwise than they are and items which can, he remarks that

concerning those which can be otherwise, the same opinion is true and false, and so too the same saying, i.e. it is possible for them to be now true and now false; but concerning those which cannot be otherwise, an item is not now true and now false but the same things are always true and false.

(*Met* 1051b13–17)⁴⁶

---

⁴⁵ Περὶ τῶν μεταπιπτόντων λόγων πρὸς Ἀθηνάδην αʹ (ψευδεπίγραφον), Λόγοι μετα-
πίπτοντες πρὸς τὴν μεσότητα γʹ (ψευδεπίγραφα).

⁴⁶ περὶ μὲν οὖν τὰ ἐνδεχόμενα ἡ αὐτὴ γίγνεται ψευδὴς καὶ ἀληθὴς δόξα καὶ ὁ λόγος ὁ
αὐτός, καὶ ἐνδέχεται ὁτὲ μὲν ἀληθεύειν ὁτὲ δὲ ψεύδεσθαι· περὶ δὲ τὰ ἀδύνατα ἄλλως ἔχειν οὐ
γίγνεται ὁτὲ μὲν ἀληθὲς ὁτὲ δὲ ψεῦδος, ἀλλ' ἀεὶ ταὐτὰ ἀληθῆ καὶ ψευδῆ.

Aristotle's formulation might have been more careful; but what he means is clear. It is clear, too, where the weight of his remark falls: he wants to insist not that some opinions and sayings change their truth-value (that is an evidence) but that some opinions and sayings do not.

Some things can be otherwise than they are, and some things do in fact become otherwise than they are or were in fact otherwise than they have become. In a word, some things change. The melons were hard yesterday; they are ripe today; they will be rotten tomorrow—unless we take the precaution of eating them first. As the melons change their character, so—it seems easy to think—sayings about the melons change their truth-values. Yesterday the melons were not ripe, and the saying which says that they were ripe was false. Today the melons are ripe, and the saying is true. If states of affairs are not fixed and determined, then—or so some philosophers have held—the sayings which correspond to them have no truth-values. In a similar way, when states of affairs change, then—or so some philosophers have held—the sayings which correspond to them change their truth-values.

Sayings which concern items which cannot be otherwise do not—and presumably cannot—change truth-value. If it is the case that so-and-so and it cannot be otherwise—if, that is to say, it is necessarily the case that so-and-so—then it is true that so-and-so and it will never be false that so-and-so. That may seem sound enough: after all, if it were to turn false that so-and-so, then it would have to be possible for it to turn false that so-and-so—and hence it would have to be possible that not-so-and-so and not necessary that so-and-so.

But that argument is far too swift. After all, may not possibilities and necessities themselves change? What today cannot be otherwise may be possible tomorrow: technology and the law are forever creating new possibilities—and foreclosing old ones. If that is so, then what is necessary may cease to be necessary; and if it can cease to be necessary, then perhaps it can cease to be true. What Aristotle should have said—perhaps what he intended to say—is rather this: a saying or opinion concerning what cannot be otherwise cannot change its truth-value so long as the items it concerns cannot be otherwise.

Some things not only cannot be otherwise: they cannot come to be capable of being otherwise. In Aristotle's view, the past is like that: whatever is now true about the past will and must always remain true. That sounds immensely plausible; and it was a popular ancient view. Nevertheless, it was not universally upheld. Cicero informs us that all truths in the past are necessary, as Chrysippus held (disagreeing with his master Cleanthes), because they are immutable and past items cannot turn from truth into falsity.

(*fat* vii 14)[47]

Cleanthes, then, held that past truths were not necessary, that what is past can for all that be otherwise, and that a past truth may become a past falsity. In disagreeing with Cleanthes about the past, Chrysippus was agreeing with Diodorus, his adversary in what Cicero describes as 'a great wrestling match' (*fat* vi 12). They wrestled inasmuch as Chrysippus held that some truths about the future are mutable and Diodorus urged that past and future are alike immutable.

The matter is intrinsically difficult, and Cicero's presentation of it is in parts elusive. One question is this: the passage I have just quoted speaks of past and future truths: what of present truths? Cicero does not mention them (he has no particular reason to do so). No doubt Cleanthes allowed them sometimes to change, and perhaps Diodorus took them to be immutable. As for Chrysippus, most scholars doubtless suppose that on this point he followed his master and differed from Diodorus.

Again, when the passage talks of mutability, it is change from truth to falsity which Cicero has in mind. Thus Diodorus is credited with the thesis that

No past truths ever become false.

What of a change in the opposite direction? If past truths cannot become false, may past falsities become true? Cicero's text leaves open the possibility of such an asymmetry between past truth and past falsity; and the asymmetry is not without its charms. After all, it is now false that I have seen a performance of Handel's *Hercules*; but that past falsity will be a past truth by the time you read this sentence. Nonetheless the asymmetry is not easy to defend, for the following reason.

In general, it is true (at a given time) that so-and-so if and only if it is false (at that time) that not so-and-so; and an assertible is about the past (or the present, or the future) if and only if its contradictory is about the past (or the present, or the future). It follows that every past falsity is the contradictory of a past truth. Hence were a past falsity to become true, a past truth—namely,

---

[47] *omnia ... vera in praeteritis necessaria sunt, ut Chrysippo placet dissentienti a magistro Cleanthe, quia sunt immutabilia nec in falsum e vero praeterita possunt convertere.*

its contradictory—would become false. In other words, if past truths are immutable, then so are past falsities.

If that is so, then the general contours of the ancient discord may be delineated as follows. There were three double theses. Diodorus held that

No past assertibles ever change their truth-value.

No future assertibles ever change their truth-value.

Cleanthes held that

Some past assertibles sometimes change their truth-value.

Some future assertibles sometimes change their truth-value.

Chrysippus held that

No past assertibles ever change their truth-value.

Some future assertibles sometimes change their truth-value.

At first blush, the Chrysippean pair seems the most attractive: after all, Diodorus appears to make the world too solid and Cleanthes to make it too fluid.

Inasmuch as the past is closed, must not past assertibles also be closed or immutable? And insofar as the future is—at least to some extent—open, must not some future assertibles similarly be open or mutable? On the one hand, the Queen has reigned for more than fifty years, and nothing can change that fact. Hence the assertible

Elizabeth II has reigned for more than fifty years

is true now, and will always remain true. On the other hand, she will—let me patriotically pretend—reign for a further decade, so that

Elizabeth II will reign for another ten years

is true now. But that truth, unlike its past partner, will cease to be true and come to be false in a year or two's time. There is a striking difference between past and future—and therefore between past assertibles and future assertibles. The difference is reflected in the Chrysippean pair of theses.

Or so it appears. First, however, it must be noted that the distinction between immutable and mutable truth-values has nothing at all to do with the distinction between the alleged closedness of the past and the alleged openness of the future. The openness of the future resides in the fact that things may turn out one way or they may turn out another. Will there be a festival at Aix this year? Well, that is still an open question. But it has nothing to do with changing truth-values. An Epicurean or a Peripatetic will not suggest that, say, it is now false that there will be a festival—but that it may, with a bit of luck, later become true. Rather, he will suggest that it is now neither true nor false that there will be a festival—and that it will at some time become true or false. Conversely, when you are counting down before the start of a boat-race—

30 seconds, 20 seconds, 10, 9, ... ,

—the assertible which you express when you shout '20 seconds', namely

There are 20 seconds to the gun,

is perhaps false then true then false. But that doesn't imply that it's an open question whether the gun will fire or not.

In any event, the Chrysippean theses seem to be falsified—in so far as the past is concerned—by innumerable counterexamples. Consider, say:

I've taught in Paris for three years.
I've only read *La Débâcle* once.
I've never seen *Les Paladins*.
I was on Eurostar this morning.

Each of those items concerns itself, in a perfectly innocuous sense, with the past. Each of the items is now true. Each will in all probability turn false. It is easy to add to the list; and it is child's play to make a parallel list of past falsities which will become true.

It may be replied that, despite appearances, such items are not really about the past—or at least, they are not the sort of past assertibles to which Chrysippus' thesis addresses itself. After all, three of the examples use the perfect tense; and according to the Stoics (if we believe the grammatical scholiast at 250.26–251.4 whom I quoted earlier), the perfect tense does not concern the past—it is a 'completed present'. Something similar goes for

I was on Eurostar this morning,

inasmuch as the adverbial phrase 'this morning' refers to the present time.

More generally, the question of whether or not a given item is about the past is not always straightforward. Consider a compound assertible such as:

If I lectured yesterday, then I shall lecture tomorrow.

Is that about the past or about the future? If you incline to judge it by its main clause and say that it is about the future, then remember that it is equivalent to

If I shan't lecture tomorrow, then I didn't lecture yesterday

—where the main clause apparently is about the past. The right answer to the question whether those compound items are about the past or the future is: Yes.

So let us say that the Chrysippean thesis about past assertibles applies to items which are exclusively past, that it applies to 'pure' pasts (however purity is to be defined and detected). Just as pure pasts must be distinguished from impure pasts, so pure futures may be distinguished from impure futures. So, for example,

I shall die tomorrow

is not a pure future; for 'tomorrow', which means 'the day after today', and so 'the day after the present day', implicitly refers to the present. But although Chrysippus has a pressing reason to distinguish pure from impure pasts—for otherwise there will be counterexamples to his thesis—he has no pressing reason to do so for the future.

All that suggests that we might revise the first part of Chrysippus' double thesis so as to read:

No pure past assertibles ever change their truth-value.

What of the second part? According to Chrysippus,

some future assertibles sometimes change their truth-value.

Diodorus affirmed that that was not so; and Cicero agreed with him: after all,

those who say that what is future is immutable and that a future truth cannot turn into a falsity are not affirming the necessity of fate—they are explaining the meaning of terms.

(*fat* ix 20)[48]

It is not clear which terms are having their meaning explained, and Cicero tells us nothing more about the grounds of Diodorus' position. Moreover, that position is initially unattractive.

For there are innumerable apparent counterexamples. I have already spoken of the Queen's future demise. Here are a few more examples. Determined to see Naples before I die, I assert, in the summer of 2004:

I shall see Naples before I die.

In 2005 I visit Naples; and I do not repeat the experiment. What I asserted in the summer of 2004 was true then—if not before—and it remained true for about a year. Then, from 2005 onwards, it was false.

I assured my daughter, on Monday, that I would be at her wedding on Saturday. Every morning from Tuesday to Saturday, at 8.00, she phoned me to remind me of my promise. Each time I repeated that I would be there on the Saturday. And so I was. At 8.00 on Sunday the phone woke me: I groggily picked it up, heard my daughter's voice, and without thinking said, rather huffily:

---

[48] *nec ei qui dicunt immutabilia esse quae futura sint nec posse verum futurum convertere in falsum fati necessitatem confirmant sed verborum vim interpretantur.*

If I've told you once I've told you five times—I'll be there on Saturday.
I asserted the same assertible for the fifth time. The first four times it was
true. The fifth time it was not.

At 2.00, the doctors gathered round his bed and offered their melancholy
diagnosis:

Henry will very soon be dead.

The afternoon dragged on. They repeated the diagnosis at 3.00, and at 4.00.
Preoccupied with the question of their fees, they did not notice that Henry
had snuffed it, and at 5.00 they again intoned:

Henry will very soon be dead.

They said the same thing about the future four times: false, false, true, false.

Such cases seem to show that about the future Chrysippus was right and
Diodorus wrong. But there is a difficulty. Chrysippus, like Diodorus, holds
that some assertibles about the future are immutable. He agrees that, for
example,

the sense of 'Elizabeth II will die' is such that, although it is said about the future,
yet it cannot turn into a falsity—for it is said about a man, and it is necessary that
men die.

(Cicero, *fat* ix 17)[49]

Exactly how and when Her Majesty will die are matters uncertain: and future
assertibles which bear upon such details may change their truth-value. But
even Queens are mortal; all mortals must die; and so the assertible that

Elizabeth II will die

is true now and immutably true.

That was Chrysippus' view. But what happens to the assertible once the
Queen is dead? If, after the Queen's death, you utter the sentence

Elizabeth II will die,

then surely you have asserted something, namely that the Queen will
die. Clearly what you have asserted is not true. But if it is not true,
then—according to Chrysippus—it is false.

There is a Chrysippean answer—of a sort—to that difficulty. The Stoics
had a cyclical theory of history. For them, the world's great age was always
beginning anew, and in each new cycle things happened just as they had
happened in every previous cycle. So even after her death,

Elizabeth II will die

---

[49] *nam morietur Scipio talem vim habet ut quamquam de futuro dicitur tamen id non possit
convertere in falsum. de homine enim dicitur, cui necesse est mori.*

remains true—to be sure, she will have to be born again before she dies, but she will be born again. *Hic jacet Elizabetha regina olim reginaque futura.*

To be sure, the cyclical theory of history is a bizarre fantasy; and no doubt it has even less right than the theory of fatalism to be admitted into a discussion of logical matters. Moreover, for a variety of minor reasons, I am inclined to be sceptical of the suggestion that Chrysippus appealed to this aspect of his physics, or metaphysics, in order to surmount a logical obstacle.

However that may be, we do all speak often enough as though truth-bearers change their burden; and there are numerous everyday examples—or apparent examples—of the phenomenon. Diodorus' claim that all truth and all falsity is immutable appears to knock against the evident facts. And yet it is hard to believe that his claim is merely an antique eccentricity; for the more you sniff at the supposed changelings, the stronger the smell of fish.

SAYINGS WHICH CEASE TO EXIST

In a passage in the *Categories* Aristotle searches for a feature proper to substances—a feature, that is to say, which holds of every substance and of nothing else. After rejecting a few candidates, he comes up with the idea that

especially proper to substances seems to be the capacity to receive contraries while remaining one and the same in number.

(*Cat* 4a10–11)[50]

After all (he observes), a man, who is a substance, may be now pale and now tanned; but a colour, which is not a substance, cannot be now white and now black, and an action, which is not a substance, cannot be now good and now bad. In other words, substances can change and non-substances cannot.

Or is that so? Aristotle acknowledges that there seem to be exceptions to his claim—that there seem to be cases in which non-substances change. In point of fact, dozens of apparently solid counterexamples immediately spring to mind. Actions, for example, although perhaps they do not change from good to bad, surely do change in all sorts of other ways: a lecture may be witty for ten minutes and thereafter as dull as a sermon; an argument may start out polite and turn into a brawl; and so on. But Aristotle does not consider such cases. Rather, he has this to say:

---

[50] μάλιστα δὲ ἴδιον τῆς οὐσίας δοκεῖ εἶναι τὸ ταὐτὸν καὶ ἓν ἀριθμῷ ὂν τῶν ἐναντίων εἶναι δεκτικόν.

That feature is never found in the case of anything else—unless you were to object by urging that sayings and opinions receive contraries; for the same saying seems to be true and false—e.g. if the saying that someone is sitting is true, then when he has stood up this same saying will be false. So too with opinions: if someone opines truly that someone is sitting, then when he has stood up he will opine falsely, if he retains the same opinion about him.

(Cat 4a21–28)[51]

Sayings and opinions are not substances. But they change, they 'receive contraries'. And they do so inasmuch as they change their truth-value.

Aristotle proceeds to argue that sayings and opinions are not genuine counterexamples to his claim. First, he says, you might accept that sayings and opinions do in a way receive contraries—but deny that they do so in the same way as substances do. After all, substances receive contraries in virtue of a change in themselves: opinions and sayings do so in virtue of a change in something else. Or else, secondly, you might deny that sayings and opinions receive contraries. They do indeed turn from true to false and *vice versa*; but when such changes take place, nothing actually happens in or to the sayings and opinions, which therefore do not receive anything.

Those two rejoinders have seemed less than compelling. But at least they show that Aristotle never thought of denying that sayings and opinions change their truth-value: what he denied is that the saying or opinion which thus changes thereby receives a contrary, or thereby receives a contrary in the way in which a substance may receive a contrary.

Aristotle's two rejoinders were criticized in antiquity. Simplicius, who describes and attempts to rebuff the criticisms, himself opts for the second of the two rejoinders (*in Cat* 118.26–119.16). But before so opting he reports, without comment, a third possible rejoinder to the objection that sayings and opinions receive contraries inasmuch as they change their truth-value:

It is also possible to argue in this way. The saying said first is not the same in number as the second—and that according to Aristotle himself. For (he says) it has been said and it will not be possible to recapture what has been said. For sayings are among those items which are in motion over a period (that is why they do not have positions). Thus the saying which was first said, and which was true, is the same in

---

[51] ἐπὶ δὲ τῶν ἄλλων οὐδενὸς φαίνεται τὸ τοιοῦτον εἰ μή τις ἐνίσταιτο τὸν λόγον καὶ τὴν δόξαν φάσκων τῶν τοιούτων εἶναι· ὁ γὰρ αὐτὸς λόγος ἀληθής τε καὶ ψευδὴς εἶναι δοκεῖ, οἷον εἰ ἀληθὴς εἴη ὁ λόγος τὸ καθῆσθαί τινα, ἀναστάντος αὐτοῦ ὁ αὐτὸς οὗτος ψευδὴς ἔσται. ὡσαύτως δὲ καὶ ἐπὶ τῆς δόξης· εἰ γάρ τις ἀληθῶς δοξάζοι τὸ καθῆσθαί τινα, ἀναστάντος αὐτοῦ ψευδῶς δοξάσει τὴν αὐτὴν ἔχων περὶ αὐτοῦ δόξαν.

species with the second, which was false, and not the same in number as was said of substances. And opinions are internal sayings, they too existing over a period—and the same will be said about them.

(in Cat 118.18–25)[52]

Simplicius found this in an earlier commentary on the *Categories*—no doubt in Porphyry's long and lost commentary addressed to Gedalius.

Now this third rejoinder—unlike Aristotle's two—does deny that sayings and opinions change their truth-values. Moreover, it does so by appealing to Aristotelian doctrine. For it paraphrases a later passage in the *Categories*:

Similarly with sayings: no part of them remains—they have been said, and it is not possible to recapture them. Hence their parts have no position inasmuch as none of them remains.

(Cat 5a33–36)[53]

Sayings, in the *Categories*, are utterances: more precisely, they are utterings or meaningful sound sequences. Hence they are events; and events do not repeat themselves—once they have happened, it is not possible to recapture them. Thus—according to the third rejoinder—Aristotle's example imagines two sayings of

Socrates is sitting;

and the two sayings are two different items—two different events. No doubt it is true that the two sayings have different truth-values, that the second is false and the first true. But that does not show that anything has changed: it shows only that two different things have two different characters. What goes for sayings goes also for opinions; for opinions—here the rejoinder tacitly invokes a familiar Platonic suggestion—are nothing but internal sayings, the soul talking to itself.

It will be objected that the rejoinder scarcely works for opinions. After all, and *pace* Plato, opinions are not events: they are states of mind which persist, not mental events which occur. That objection in turn will be countered thus: opinions—the Greek word is 'δόξαι'—here, as so often in Greek

---

[52] ἔστιν δὲ καὶ οὕτως ἐπιχειρῆσαι· οὐκ ἔστιν εἷς κατ᾽ ἀριθμὸν ὁ πρότερος ῥηθεὶς λόγος τῷ δευτέρῳ καὶ κατ᾽ αὐτὸν τὸν Ἀριστοτέλη· εἴρηται γάρ, φησί, καὶ οὐκέτι ἔσται τὸ ῥηθέν λαβεῖν. τῶν γὰρ κατὰ διέξοδον κινουμένων ἐστὶν ὁ λόγος, καὶ διὰ τοῦτο οὐδὲ τῶν θέσιν ἐχόντων ἐστίν· ὥστε τῷ εἴδει ὁ αὐτὸς γίνεται ὁ πρότερος ῥηθεὶς τῷ δευτέρῳ, ὁ ἀληθὴς τῷ ψευδεῖ, καὶ οὐχὶ τῷ ἀριθμῷ, ὡς εἴρηται ἐπὶ τῆς οὐσίας. καὶ ἡ δόξα δὲ λόγος ἐστὶν ἐντός, ἐν διεξόδῳ καὶ αὐτὴ ὑπάρχουσα, καὶ τὰ αὐτὰ ἂν καὶ περὶ αὐτῆς λέγοιτο.
[53] καὶ ὁ λόγος δὲ ὡσαύτως· οὐδὲν γὰρ ὑπομένει τῶν μορίων αὐτοῦ, ἀλλ᾽ εἴρηταί τε καὶ οὐκ ἔστιν ἔτι τοῦτο λαβεῖν· ὥστε οὐκ ἂν εἴη θέσις τῶν μορίων αὐτοῦ, εἴγε μηδέν ὑπομένει.

philosophical writings, are to be construed as judgements; judgements, or acts of judging, are events; and the events may plausibly be characterized as internal sayings. Well, perhaps that is right; but whether or not judgements or judgings offer a counterexample to the thesis which Aristotle is defending in the *Categories*, beliefs surely do so. The third rejoinder may deal with opinions if opinions are construed as judgements: it cannot deal with opinions if opinions are construed as beliefs.

There is a second objection. The rejoinder supposes that there are two sayings of 'Socrates is sitting', and urges that the second is a different saying from the first. But the supposition is not, or not clearly, present in Aristotle's text; and in any event it is not necessary to the counterexample. The rejoinder takes the question to be this: What is the truth-value of the saying 'Socrates is sitting' when you repeat it now that he has stood up? And the rejoinder answers that you could not, in principle, repeat it: anything you may now say will be another saying. But the pertinent question is rather this: What is the truth-value of the saying 'Socrates is sitting', which you said an hour ago when he was in fact sitting, now that Socrates has stood up? Surely it has ceased to be true? Surely it is now false?

True, the saying is over, and it cannot be repeated. The French may beat the All Blacks again—but they cannot repeat that celebrated victory. There may be future raptures—but you can't ever recapture the first, fine, careless one. Nonetheless, that victory, and that rapture, continue to have things true of them. We continue to talk about past events—that is what history is all about. And events may change their character after they are over: in July 1916 the Battle of Waterloo ceased to be the bloodiest battle in British history; and—who knows?—that victory in the semi-final may one day cease to be the most glorious exploit in the annals of French rugby.

But is it really the case that the old saying—the saying 'Socrates is sitting' which you said an hour ago—changed its truth-value when Socrates stood up? Did it then cease to be true? And if it ceased to be true, did it become false? Anyone who was minded to return a negative answer to those questions might seek help from the Stoa. For if Aristotelian sayings—unlike numbers, say, or some varieties of modern propositions—are not eternal items, then neither are Stoic assertibles. Stoic assertibles are not ephemeral; but they do not all last for ever—some of them perish. Alexander reports a Stoic contention:

That Dio has died may at some time become true, but 'This man has died' cannot. For when Dio is dead, the assertible 'This man is dead" perishes, there no longer being anything to receive the demonstrative—for demonstration is of something living and about something living.

(in APr 177.30–33)[54]

The assertible which you might express by way of the sentence

    This man has died

only exists during the life-time of the man to whom the demonstrative 'This man' refers. When the man dies, the assertible perishes with him. In general, assertibles expressed by sentences which contain demonstratives exist only so long as the items demonstrated exist.

That particular example of a perishing assertible may or may not persuade. But there is nothing peculiar about the notion that assertibles may perish—nor about its twin, the notion that assertibles may be born. For to say that an assertible may perish is to say that there is something which can be asserted now but may not be assertible later on; and to say that an assertible has come into being is to say that there is something you can assert now and could not assert before. And there are any number of things which can be asserted now but could not have been asserted in the past, and any number of things which cannot be asserted now but will become assertible in the future. Aristotle could not have asserted that Sir David Ross would one day edit the *Metaphysics*; and there are doubtless similar things which Sir Anthony Kenny cannot now assert. Aristotle could have asserted of this or that pupil that he was a lazy dog—we can no longer do so. Doubtless something similar goes for Sir Michael Dummett.

Assertibles are not eternal items; and an assertible has a truth-value—so the Stoics insist—only so long as it is there to have one. But why should that be so? Take an assertible which Chrysippus himself considered, namely the assertible that

    Cypselus will reign at Corinth.

No one could have asserted that before the birth—or at any rate, before the conception—of Cypselus; for before that time no one could have named or referred to Cypselus: the name 'Cypselus' was empty, and there were no other names for the future tyrant—there could not have been. Nonetheless—and according to Chrysippus himself—it was true a thousand years before the

---

[54] ... τῷ δύνασθαί ποτε ἀληθὲς γενέσθαι τὸ τεθνηκέναι Δίωνα, τὸ δὲ τέθνηκεν οὗτος ἀδύνατον· ἀποθανόντος γὰρ Δίωνος φθείρεσθαι τὸ ἀξίωμα τὸ οὗτος τέθνηκε μηκέτ' ὄντος τοῦ τὴν δεῖξιν ἀναδεχομένου· ἐπὶ γὰρ ζῶντος καὶ κατὰ ζῶντος ἡ δεῖξις.

event that Cypselus would reign at Corinth. So an assertible was true at a time when it did not exist.

Chrysippus took a different view; and what he actually said about Cypselus was that

it was not necessary for Cypselus to reign at Corinth, even though that had been decreed a thousand years earlier by an oracle of Apollo.

(Cicero, *fat* vii 13)[55]

Apollo had decreed the reign long before Cypselus' birth: that is to say, on Chrysippus' view it was assertible, long before Cypselus' birth, that Cypselus would reign at Corinth.

Perhaps Chrysippus took that line because of his view about the meaning of proper names? They indicate proper qualities, or properties uniquely possessed by the individual whose name they are; and with a bit of juggling, that view may be used to show that 'Cypselus' may occur in the expression of an assertible even when the word has no referent. So consider a demonstrative sentence:

This man will reign at Corinth.

According to Alexander's Stoics, it is only during Cypselus' life-time that that sentence can be used to assert something about him. Of course, at other times that same sentence may be used to make other assertions about other items; and at other times other sentences may be used to say of Cypselus what that sentence then said of him. But although the sentence

Cypselus will reign at Corinth

may be used to say of Cypselus just what

This man will reign at Corinth

was used to say of him, the two sentences do not say the same thing, do not express the same assertible. And in fact no sentence can be used before Cypselus' birth or after his death to say what

This man will reign at Corinth

was used to say during Cypselus' life-time.

So no one could have made such an assertion a thousand years before Cypselus' birth. (And no one can make it now.) Yet surely, existent or not, the assertible was true a thousand years before Cypselus' birth? Suppose that one of Cypselus' school chums pointed at him and said:

This man will reign at Corinth.

---

[55] ... *neque necesse fuisse Cypselum regnare Corinthi, quamquam id millensimo ante anno Apollinis oraculo editum esset.*

He thereby asserted something true; and was it not true before he asser-
ted it—and true before it could have been asserted? The question is not:
Would it have been true had it been asserted a thousand years ago? But rather:
Was it true a thousand years ago?

Return to the example which Alexander cites, and imagine the following
conversation. 'Have you heard that Dio is dead?'—'What, at last? So what I
said yesterday is now true.'—'Oh, you said yesterday that Dio was dead, did
you?'—'Well, not quite.'—'What did you say, then?'—'I'm afraid I can't
say it again; though I can tell you that I said it by uttering, in Dio's presence,
the sentence 'This man is dead.''—'Yes, I see—you're right: what you said
yesterday and can't say today was false when you said it and is true now that
you can't say it.'

That is surely what the Stoics should have said. But it is not what they
did say. The argument which Alexander reports presupposes that, after Dio's
death, the assertible which the sentence

This man is dead

once expressed does not become true. But it is not still false—after all, the
man is dead. So it is neither true nor false. That, I take it, was the Stoic view
of the matter. It might appear to run against Chrysippus' thesis that every
assertible is either true or false. But it does not do so. For it does not imply
that you can assert at a given time something which at that time is neither
true nor false.

The Stoic view about assertibles may be adapted to Aristotelian sayings: a
saying is either true or false only so long as it exists, or during its occurrence:
once it ceases to exist, or once it is over, it has no truth-value. If I say at
12.00 that Socrates is sitting, and he is sitting, then what I say is true then:
an hour later, when he stands up, the saying does not become false—it does
not exist and so it has no truth-value. It does not follow that there are any
sayings which are neither true nor false, or that you can say at a given time
something which at that time is neither true nor false.

Allow all that: cannot Aristotelian sayings nevertheless change their truth-
value? Perhaps a very long saying said very slowly might change its truth-value
while it was occurring? Perhaps; but it seems more plausible to suggest that a
saying does not acquire a truth-value until it is complete—so that no saying
is ever true or false for a period of time. Telling the truth—like winning a
race or beating the All Blacks—is an instantaneous affair.

That argument purportedly shows that Aristotelian sayings, interpreted
as a passage in the *Categories* suggests that they should be interpreted,

cannot—*pace* Aristotle—change their truth-value. In that case, it shows something—but not very much. It does not, for example, show anything about Aristotelian opinions; and it does not show anything about Stoic assertibles, which are not ephemeral items. Moreover, it may be doubted whether it really shows anything about Aristotelian sayings; for it may be doubted that the passage in the *Categories* matches Aristotle's usual conception of what a saying is. In other words, nothing said thus far gives any reason to reject the commonsensical notion that truth-bearers—sayings, assertibles, opinions ... —may, and sometimes do, change their truth-values.

And yet there is a still a strong smell of fish in the air. I said nonchalantly that, after Dio's death, the assertible which was once expressed by the sentence

This man is dead

cannot continue to be false; for the man is dead. But that is at best dubious. After all, what was it that was once asserted by an utterance of the sentence

This man is dead?

Well, it was then asserted, of a certain object of demonstration, that it was then dead. It was false then that the object was then dead; and it is false—still false—that it was then dead. If the Stoics are right, then you can't now say again what you then said. But, for all that, what you then said then is still false. The same goes for the assertion that Dio is dead. After all, what I asserted then was not that Dio is now dead but that Dio was then dead; and it is false—still false—that Dio was then dead.

The doctors stood around the bed of His Majesty. At 5.00 they issued a communiqué: along the wires the electric message came

He is no better—he is much the same.

An hour later a similar telegram—the wording was exactly the same—came from the same source. The first message said something true, the second said something false. Should we infer that an assertible has changed its truth-value? Well, only if the two telegrams passed on the same message or said the same thing; only if the second merely confirmed or repeated the first. Did it? No—or at least, not necessarily and not normally. The first message, wired at 5.00, asserted that Edward VII was then much the same. The second message asserted something different—it asserted something about the King's state of health at 6.00, not at 5.00. (Imagine that the second telegram came a day later, a week later, a decade later ... : it's evident that, special conditions apart, those messages are not repetitive.) What the first telegram said is still true at 6.00; for the King's state of health at 5.00 has not changed—how could it have done? What the second telegram says is false—but that has no bearing on the truth-value of the first telegram.

That, I hope, sounds rather persuasive. But *autre temps, autres morts*. The *Times* published in its obituary columns a notice which began thus:

Marley is dead, dead as a doornail.

The report was premature: Marley was merely moribund. It was an honest mistake; and the honest obituarist repeated it again and again. For his phone rang all morning, and each time he confirmed that, yes, Marley, alas, had popped his clogs. And at the evening press conference he declared:

Marley is dead—that's what *The Times* announced. That's what I've been telling callers all day long: and I repeat it again now: Marley is dead.

By the time of the press conference, Marley had expired. The assertible which *The Times* printed and which the obituarist repeated was false at the time of going to press, and remained false during most of the day; but at the end it came true. And in the same way, the belief which the honest obituarist precociously formed and obstinately clung to was false at first and then turned true.

If you want to deny that conclusion and hold that assertibles and beliefs do not change their truth-values, then you must deny that the obituarist kept on repeating the same assertion and you must deny that he retained one and the same belief. Such denials might seem audacious to the point of folly. But perhaps you might be eased into them by reflecting along the following lines.

Suppose I say this to you: 'I think that the Prime Minister is an unprincipled scoundrel. I have thought so, unwaveringly, for some fifty years. But now I fear that my belief has perhaps sometimes been false—perhaps one or two of the PMs I have lived through were principled scoundrels.' If I say that, you know what I mean; but you may well think that I have expressed myself ineptly, or even misleadingly, insofar as I imply that I have maintained one belief unchanged for half a century. Perhaps I have frequently muttered some such sentence as

What a swine the PM is.

But there is no reason to think that each time I uttered the sentence I said the same thing or confessed the same belief. For what I said when I uttered the sentence was said of a string of different ministers; thus although I always said the same thing of some item—namely that it was an unprincipled scoundrel—I did not always say it of the same thing so that I did not always say the same thing.

If that is so, then why not say something similar about the reports of Marley's death? The obituarist repeated the sentence 'Marley is dead'; but he did not repeat himself—he did not say the same thing again and again. For what he said, he said at different times. At each new PM, I believed something new. At each new time, the obituarist said something new.

SENTENCES

Such considerations are advanced to show—against the ancient consensus—that even if truth-bearers bear their truth-values at times and for periods, nevertheless they cannot change their burden. But the answer to the question 'Can truth-bearers change loads?' depends, in part at least, on what items bear truth-values. Various different items are ordinarily spoken of as being true or false—statements, for example, or judgements, or opinions. And different philosophers have taken truth and falsity to belong, or to belong primarily, to different items.

A philosopher who inclines to take sentences as truth-bearers will surely take truth to be timed and will allow truth-bearers to change their truth-value. If it is the sentence

It's Monday

which is to be assessed as true or false, then it is true every Monday and false every other day of the week. The sentence changes its truth-value with monotonous regularity.

Now if sentences may bear different truth-values at different times, they may also bear different values in different locations. For example, the sentence

On Christmas Day 2003 it snowed

was true in Moscow but not in Majorca. And not only at different times and in different locations but also in different mouths and before different audiences. Thus

I smoke Dunhill Standard

was true in the mouth of Bertrand Russell but false in that of A. J. Ayer; and

You dropped the winning goal

is true if addressed to J. Wilkinson and false if addressed to M. Johnson.

And so on. If sentences take truth-values, then they take them relative to this, that, and the other item. They take truth-values at various indexes (to use a modern jargon); and at different indexes they may take different values. One of the indexes is the index of time. If a sentence has one value at one time index and another at another, then it changes its truth-value. But that is just a special case of a more general phenomenon. A sentence may be here, now, and to him true; there, now, and to him false; here, then and to her true; and so on.

All that has suggested—though it does not of course entail—that the predicates ' … is true' and '… is false' are best construed as relational. 'That sentence is true' is either ill-formed or else elliptical: just as 'Socrates is taller', if it is to say anything at all, must be understood as elliptical for something of the form 'Socrates is taller than so-and-so', in the same way 'That sentence is true' must be understood as elliptical for something of the form 'That sentence is true at such-and-such indexes.'

The idea of indexing is not remote from ancient thought. When Aristotle formulates what he calls 'the most firm principle of all', or the principle of non-contradiction, he writes:

It is impossible for the same thing to hold and not to hold at the same time of the same item in the same respect—and let us suppose added all the other qualifications which we might add in view of the logical difficulties.

(*Met* 1005b19–22)[56]

There are other similar passages. Aristotle's appeal to 'qualifications' is tantamount to an appeal to indexing.

Again, the notion that truth and falsity are relational items is not foreign to ancient thought—think of Protagoras. (Or rather, think of Plato's presentation of one version of Protagoreanism.) Nonetheless, no ancient text, so far as I know, suggests that we should or might construe '… is true' and '… is false' as relational predicates in the way which I have just described. Pythons grow; but no one imagined that size was therefore a relation between a body and a time, or that '… is a foot long' should be understood as elliptical for '… is a foot long at such-and-such a time'. Truth-bearers were thought to be capable of changing their truth-value; but no one imagined that truth was therefore a relation between a saying and a time, or that '… is true' should be understood as elliptical for '… is true at such-and-such a time'.

That python will be two metres long next month.

That remark was true when you made it.

Those sentences do not combine pairs of singular terms ('that python' and 'next month', 'that remark' and 'when you made it') with two-placed predicates ('… is two metres long at—' and '… is true at—'). Rather, each

[56] τὸ γὰρ αὐτὸ ἅμα ὑπάρχειν τε καὶ μὴ ὑπάρχειν ἀδύνατον τῷ αὐτῷ καὶ κατὰ τὸ αὐτό (καὶ ὅσα ἄλλα προσδιορισαίμεθ᾽ ἄν, ἔστω προσδιωρισμένα πρὸς τὰς λογικὰς δυσχερείας).

puts together a singular term, a one-placed predicate, and an adverbial phrase. That is how the ancients would have parsed the things, had they thought of the matter; and it is how any grammarian would parse the things—any grammarian, I mean, who was not antecedently persuaded that the syntax of contemporary predicate logic is all we know on earth and all we need to know.

But enough of that. In any event, ancient truth-bearers were thought to change their truth-values from time to time, but not to take different values in different parts of the world, or in different mouths, or in different public contexts. If I now say that it's a fine summer's day, then—according to the common ancient understanding—the saying or the assertible which I say may be true today and false tomorrow; but it cannot be true in Oxford and false in Paris, nor true when I say it and false when you do. Or rather, it seems never to have crossed any ancient mind that truth-values might vary along such dimensions.

If the ancients restricted their attention to one index, the index of time, was that not merely arbitrary? Let truth-values change from time to time if you will—but in that case, consistency requires you to let them vary from place to place and from person to person. Modern sentences are like that: they have truth-values at various indexes. Modern propositions, on the other hand, generally have truth values absolutely: they are true or false full stop—they are not true here and there, false now and then. Stoic assertibles and Aristotelian sayings are betwixt and between, they sit on the logical fence—perhaps that is why they stink of fish?

Well, fish aren't usually found near fences—and anyway, what's wrong with sitting on a fence? Suppose that someone says

It's cold here

at noon and then again ten minutes later: then surely (special circumstances apart) he has repeated himself, he has said the same thing twice; and if at 12.15 you ask him if he's warm enough, he may reasonably reply: 'No—it's cold here, as I've already said twice.' Suppose, on the other hand, that I produce the sentence

I smoke Dunhill Standard

and that, in the next room and at about the same time, the Archbishop of Canterbury produces the very same sentence, with an equally assertive intent: then it is plain that we haven't said the same thing as one another—the Archbishop may have echoed my words but he did not say what I said. True, he said of himself just what I said of myself. But if the same thing is said of two different items, then two different things are said.

What is, or can be, asserted by the uttering of a sentence is fixed in part by the reference of any referential expressions in the sentence; and where there is a different reference, there there will be a different assertible. Two utterances of

He's a confounded liar

will say the same thing only if the expression 'he' refers to the same item on each occasion. So the two imagined utterances of

I smoke Dunhill

say different things inasmuch as the expression 'I' refers to two different items on the two different occasions. On the other hand, the several imagined utterances of

It's cold here

all said the same thing; for the expression 'here'—the only referring expression in the sentence—was supposed to refer to the same thing on each occasion.

Those last remarks are anything but profound. But they may recall the sort of style in which we habitually speak of the repetition of sayings and of the differences among them. The style is a fence-straddling style; and it suggests that there may be some difference between time indexes, at least when they are carried by the tense of a verb, and other indexes.

TRUTH, TIME, AND PLACE

But perhaps the difference is trifling, if not illusory. Compare time and place, for example.

At mid-day in Oxford it was drizzling. Glancing out of the window, I uttered the banal sentence

It's raining as per bloody usual,

thereby asserting that it was raining. 'So it is', my wife replied.—'How do you know?'—'I'm looking out of the window, of course.' My wife was in the Indre, and I was telephoning her: she was joking. The fact that what she said was a joke indicates that by uttering the banal sentence I asserted something about the Oxford weather. She might have made the same remark had I said

It's raining here;

and then it would have been plain that I was saying something about the Oxford weather—for the expression 'here' refers explicitly to a place, and in most standard circumstances to the place where its user finds himself.

Not that 'It's raining' means the same as 'It's raining here.' At any rate,

If it's raining, bring your umbrella

and

If it's raining here, bring your umbrella

may be used to express two very different pieces of advice. Nonetheless, when

It's raining

is used to assert that it's raining, then (bizarre circumstances apart) it asserts what could equally well be asserted by

It's raining here.

Since utterances of 'It's raining here' which are made at different places may express different assertibles or make different assertions, so too must it be with utterances of 'It's raining.' The truth-value of the sentence may vary from place of utterance to place of utterance; but the sentence will then express different assertibles in the different places—there is no assertible which bears one truth-value here and another there.

If that is so for place, is it not also so for time? If when I utter, at mid-day in Oxford,

It's raining

I say of Oxford, and not just in Oxford, that it's raining there, then don't I also say of mid-day, and not just at mid-day, that it's raining then? And although 'It's raining' does not mean the same as 'It's raining now', nonetheless when it is uttered to make an assertion then (bizarre conditions apart) it will make the very assertion which would be made by an utterance of that second sentence.

It might be objected that such a view has absurd consequences, that if it is right, then every time I utter, assertively, 'It's raining' I say something different; and if I believe what I say, then each assertive utterance reports a new belief. I can't, literally, go on believing that it's raining: I can, at best, have a dense sequence of beliefs, each of which I might express by uttering the sentence 'It's raining.'

That is indeed absurd. But it is not a consequence of the view I have sketched. It is not true that every time I utter the sentence

It's raining

I express a different assertible; for it is not true that every time I say

It's raining now

I express a different assertible. The word 'now' does not refer to a different time on each successive use. It refers, in most standard uses, to the present. But the present—despite what some ancient grammarians and philosophers claimed—is not necessarily an instant, a durationless flash, the temporal counterpart of a geometrical point. The present comes in longer and shorter stretches, as long and as short as you like; and the word 'now' is elastic enough to preserve its reference for minutes or days or decades. 'Last month it was sunny, but now it's raining'; 'Yesterday it was sunny, but now it's raining'; 'Two minutes ago it was sunny, but now it's raining.' Something similar holds, of course, for place. Just as 'now' refers to the present time, so 'here' refers to the present place; and 'here' has the same sort of elasticity as 'now'. 'It's fine in Australia, but it's raining here'; 'It's fine in the *midi* but it's raining here'; and so on.

Such reflections may appear to support the view that sayings and assertibles and beliefs may change their truth-value. For the past ten years I have constantly believed, and occasionally asserted, that I live in France. I have retained, unaltered, a single belief; and whenever I expressed that belief by uttering the sentence 'I live in France now' I asserted the same assertible. Suppose that it were otherwise, and that I have held and asserted a succession of different beliefs. Then how many beliefs have I held? Have I acquired a new belief about my whereabouts once a year? once a month? once a minute? Those questions seem to admit no answers; and that seems to imply that there is no succession, no plurality, of different beliefs.

In fact—and here the story becomes fictitious—in fact, I have not lived in France throughout the past ten years: five years ago, and quite unknown to us in the Indre, Andorra conquered and temporarily annexed France—so that for three weeks, until the Andorrans withdrew, I lived in Andorra. So for ten years I have stuck tenaciously to a single belief—the belief that I live in France—and that belief was first true and then false and then true again.

Now whatever force such a fantasy argument may have, it will not separate time and place. For consider the sentence

There's enough light to read by.

Suppose that it is uttered, at one and the same time, in the centre of Chamonix and on the summit of Mt Blanc. You might well be inclined to say that if the sentence was used to make an assertion in each of those two places, then it was used to make two different assertions, one of them referring to the conditions in the valley and the other to the conditions on the summit. But on the occasion I am thinking of, there was an unbroken chain of torch-bearers, each stationed a few yards from his neighbour, stretching from Chamonix to the summit, and celebrating the first ascent of the mountain. Suppose, then, that each member of the chain noticed, with interest, that there was enough light to read by; and that they each, at about the same time, assertively uttered the sentence

There's enough light to read by.

How many different things were asserted? Was there a different assertible every ten yards, or every hundred yards, or every mile? Such questions cannot be answered—and we should therefore settle for a single assertion. And evidently, if the example is suitably rigged, the assertible may have one truth-value in one place and the other in another.

Those coupled fantasies suggest that, *pro tanto*, time and place are on a par; but they do not force the conclusion that one and the same assertible may have different truth-values at different times and in different places.

First, there is something wrong with the argument itself. If Simone is in Chamonix and Max is on the summit, and each says, pretty well simultaneously,

It's light enough to read by

then—unusual circumstances apart—they will plainly have said two different things. For had each said

It's light enough to read by here,

they would have said different things. ('It's light enough to read by here', says Max into his mobile: 'Here too', replies Simone.) Suppose now that the space between Chamonix and the summit is filled by a line of mountain guides, shoulder to shoulder, and that at about the same moment each exclaims

It's light enough to read by.

That surprising fact might have many effects—but it could not bring it about that Max and Simone had, after all, said the same thing as one another.

But in that case—this was the nub of the argument—an embarrassing question arises: Exactly how many distinct things were said between the summit and Chamonix? Since—it was alleged—no answer can be given to such a question, we should settle for the view that there is but a single assertion in the case. But that is an absurd inference: if there is no answer to the question 'How many?', it does not follow that 'One' is the best answer—it follows that 'One' is a false answer. In any case, there is surely at least one true answer to the question, namely 'At least one, and at most as many as there were asserters.' Further than that, there is nothing to say in a general way. But then why should there be? Different cases may call for different answers; and in some cases, any answer will be more or less arbitrary (and what is wrong with that?).

What goes for the guides of Chamonix goes, *mutatis mutandis*, for the beliefs of the French metic.

Here is a second remark about those cases. An American simultaneously phoned a friend in Paris and a friend in Rome and asked each: 'What's the weather like in Europe?'. It was raining in Paris and fine in Rome. The honest Roman answered 'It's glorious summer weather—just right for a visit to Europe', and the subtle Parisian murmured 'Wonderful, wonderful—just the weather for a visit to Europe.' They answered the same question, and they gave the same answer: they made the same assertion, each said the same assertible. So was not one and the same assertion true in Rome and false in Paris? Well, what colour is a zebra? White? No. Black? No. A zebra is black and white, in stripes. So, too, for the European weather. The right answer to the American question was: 'Fine in parts and rainy in parts.' The answer 'Fine' was, at best, true in parts, a curate's egg; and anyone who dislikes the notion of partial truth will insist that the answer 'Fine' was false.

So too with time. On Wednesday, someone asked me what the weather was like this week. It was raining hard on Wednesday, and so I said: 'It's raining.' Someone else asked me the same thing on Thursday, when the sun was shining. Wishing to discourage him from coming to Paris, I said: 'It's raining.' I answered the same question twice, and I gave the same answer each time—I said one assertible on two occasions. Was that assertible true on Wednesday and false on Thursday? No: it was, at best, true in parts—that is to say, it was false.

In general, where at first blush it seems plausible to find a single assertible which has different truth-values at different times or in different places, at second blush things are seen to lie otherwise: either there is a single assertible, and it is false, or else there are two or more assertibles with different truth-values. Sometimes the one option commends itself, sometimes the other, and sometimes the choice appears to be arbitrary. But it is never obligatory to opt for a change of truth-value.

When the doctors prognosticate repeatedly about Henry, have they asserted one thing several times or have they made a succession of different assertions? It all depends. Suppose that you ask, at 4.00, about Henry's prospects and they say, tetchily,

We've already told you twice that he's on the way out:

then they have repeated themselves. Suppose they reply, apologetically,

This time we're sure: he's not long for this world:

then they have said something new.

If they have not repeated themselves, then there is no question of any assertible changing its truth-value. So suppose that they have repeated themselves. Could their assertible have been first false and then true? Imagine that Henry died at 4.05: was the assertible not false on the first couple of occasions and true on the third? No: the doctors simply have a generous idea of how soon is soon.

But it must be allowed that there are some cases which resist this sort of treatment. When I assured my daughter on the Sunday morning that I'd be there on Saturday, I repeated myself—at least, I took myself to be repeating myself—for the nth time. Yet what I had earlier said was true and what I said on Sunday was false. The doctors, failing to notice that Henry had died, assert for the third time that he will very soon be dead. They repeat themselves. What they said on its three occasions of utterance was true, then true, then false.

Of course, there is something strange about those cases. In May 2004 I reminded a Parisian friend that the Queen of England would pay a State visit to France in 2004. He said that Her Majesty had already done so—in April. I had muddled things up. It wasn't a linguistic muddle—it wasn't as though (to take an example from Apollonius Dyscolus) I had said 'Her Majesty will be here yesterday.' In any event, in uttering the sentence 'Her Majesty will make a State visit this year', surely I made an assertion? And surely I didn't make a true assertion. (For I said something about the future, and what I said did not come to pass.) Did I make a false assertion? You might be reluctant to say Yes—or at least, to say Yes and nothing more. But you must either say that I made a false assertion or else that I made an assertion which was neither true nor false.

The strangeness of the two cases I have just rehearsed, in which assertibles allegedly change their truth-values, derives from the fact that when they are alleged to be false their alleged falsity is like the alleged falsity of my remark about the State visit. Perhaps the assertions are indeed false but are not repetitions of the earlier assertions? The doctors and I took ourselves to be repeating ourselves—in fact we were saying something new. Or perhaps the assertions are true rather than false? They are, as it were, dislocated—but they are dislocated truths. Or perhaps nothing was asserted at all? Suppose I had said to my daughter on Sunday morning

I promise to be there on Saturday.

Would I have made a promise? You might well say No. So when I said

I'll be there on Saturday

why think that I have made an assertion?

Whatever is to be said about such examples, they are rare and exotic; and you should not build an ornithological theory on the basis of a few rare birds.

DOUBLE TIME

The queer cases aside, are not time and place on the same footing so far as truth and falsity are concerned? There is a consideration which I have thus far suppressed and which appears to differentiate pertinently between temporal indexing and spatial indexing—and indeed between time and any other index.

Any sentence which appears to express a located truth (or falsity) seems to be equivalent to—or just a funny way of saying the same as—some sentence which expresses an unlocated truth (or falsity). For example,

It's true here that the hornbeams are breaking

is only an odd way of saying that

It's true that the hornbeams are breaking here.

In general, it is true (or false) at such-and-such a location that so-and-so if and only if it is true (or false) that so-and-so at such-and-such a location. Any locative adverb attached to the prefix 'It is true (false) that...' may be removed from the prefix into the 'that' clause. And the 'that' clause is plainly its proper home.

The same does not go for temporal adverbs. To be sure, in some cases you may shunt without change of sense. For example,

It's still true that Balliol is the centre of the turning world

seems to be equivalent to

It's true that Balliol's still the centre of the turning world.

But there is no general equivalence of that sort; and that is because the 'that' clause may itself contain a temporal adverb. If you try to shunt the adverb in

It's true now that it's Monday tomorrow

you get:

It's true that it's now Monday tomorrow.

That is a barbarism; for a single clause cannot coherently contain two mutually inconsistent temporal adverbs.

Just as there is no place for two such temporal adverbs in the 'that' clause, so the 'that' clause cannot contain two distinct time-indicating tenses. If the tense of the verb in 'It's true that...' has a temporal sense, and if you try to shunt it into the subordinate clause, then you will have a clause with a time too many.

Locative indexes are in this respect different from temporal indexes. To be sure,

It's true that it's raining here there
is odd in the same way as

It's true that it's now Monday tomorrow
is odd. Doubling up incompatible places is as bad as doubling up incompatible times. But there is a difference. For whereas

It's true now that it's Monday tomorrow
is perfectly intelligible,

It's true here that it's raining there
is simple nonsense. In other words, sentences of the form 'It's true that such-and-such' allow only one locative index (or one compatible set of locative indexes); but they allow two distinct temporal indexes.

I think that there is a pertinent difference there between time and place; but the argument I have just rehearsed limps—indeed, it limps with both feet.

First look at the temporal foot. Perhaps the sentence

It's true that it's now Monday tomorrow
looks rum—not the sort of thing any true-born Englishman would readily utter. But looks are deceptive. 'Is it my birthday tomorrow?' asks the infant, again and again. 'Not yet, not yet' is the parental reply—until at last:

Yes—*now* it's your birthday tomorrow.
There's nothing odd about that, even though a single clause contains a pair of conflicting temporal indicators.

Nor—more evidently—is there any general difficulty about shunting a time-indicating verbal tense from a prefix into a subordinate clause: after all, the verb in the clause may thereby come to have a compound tense. If you push a future into a perfect, for example, you get a future perfect, so that the sentence

It'll soon be true that we've been married forty years,
in which the first verb refers to the future and the second is in the past tense, may be deemed equivalent to

It's true that we'll soon have been married forty years,
where the first verb has a timeless present tense and the second verb is in the future perfect. Or again, there is the future imperfect:

It was always true that he'd come to a sticky end
is equivalent to

It's true that he was always going to come to a sticky end.
There are other compound tenses on offer; and more can be manufactured *ad lib*.

(I use 'compound tense' loosely: English—unlike Greek and Latin—has no genuine compound tenses. What Greek and Latin do by compounding, English does by calling in auxiliaries: 'will have been married' is a sequence of four verbs, not a single compound verb. But that does not affect the point at issue.)

Nevertheless, if compound tenses may coherently unite incompatible time indications, how can doubled temporal adverbs fail to perturb when they are inconsistent with one another? Why does the inconsistency not make the sentences themselves inconsistent? The answer, I suppose, is that the two adverbs are not competing for the same grammatical position: while one of them is a genuine adverb, which modifies the finite verb in the sentence, the other is a sentential adverb, which governs the whole of the sentence to which it is attached. The syntactic structure of

Now it's your birthday tomorrow

is like the structure of

At last, it's your birthday tomorrow

or

Mercifully, it's your birthday tomorrow.

The structure might be indicated thus:

Now [it's your birthday tomorrow].

That is to say, when you shunt an adverb into the subordinate clause, it becomes—sometimes at least—a sentential adverb.

If a shunted adverb does not make for a complex or double adverb, then should not something similar happen when a tense is shunted into the subordinate clause? Suppose I say:

One day it will be true that there will be a sea-battle tomorrow.

Shunting (both of the adverb and of the tense) produces

It's true that one day there will be going to be a sea-battle tomorrow.

You may call 'will be going to be' a future future if you like. But perhaps the correct way to parse the clause is this:

FUT [there will be a battle tomorrow]

—where 'FUT' represents a free-floating future tense, or rather a free-floating future time-indicator.

But tenses and time-indicators do not float free: they need a verbal anchor. And so the tense or time-indicator must be supplied with a verb. Fortunately, there is a familiar dummy to hand: 'be the case that'. So

FUT [there will be a battle tomorrow]

becomes

It will be the case that there will be a battle tomorrow.

And so on. Now if that is right, are not time and place, despite the phenomenon of double time, on a par? For timed truth may be eliminated in much the same way as located truth was eliminated. Just as

It is-PLACED true that so-and-so

is equivalent to, and a poor substitute for,

It is-PLACELESS true that so-and-so PLACED,

so

It is-TIMED true that so-and-so

is equivalent to

It is-TIMELESS true that it is-TIMED the case that so-and-so.

And to make it perfectly clear that the ascription of truth is timeless, why not eliminate the tensed verb in the sentential prefix 'It is true that ...' and rewrite 'It is-TIMELESS true that ...' as 'Truly, ...'?

Allow all that to be true: is there not still a difference between time and place? For whereas there are doubled times, surely there are no doubled places. Of course, if that is so, it doesn't imply that there is a further difference between time and place, or that assertibles and say-ings may carry different truth-values at different times but not at different places. For nothing at all is implied about the possibility of change in truth-value. Nonetheless, it does seem to follow that—in at least one respect—time indexing is different from place indexing; and to that extent the ancient prejudice which put time and place in distinct com-partments.

And yet not even that seems to be true.[57] Consider again the other, spatial, foot. I said that the sentence

It's true that it's raining here there

is mere nonsense; and perhaps it is. But double places are not, in general, absurdities. Take

It's true here that it's raining 50 km to the south.

That seems to be perfectly respectable—and so does, say,

It's true in Paris that Oxford is a long way away.

Things of that sort can be invented at the drop of a hat. And if you want, you can do some shunting on them, to produce

It's true that, here, it's raining 50 km to the south

---

[57] For what follows I am indebted to Susanne Bobzien.

It's true that, in Paris, Oxford is a long way away
Place and time limp along foot in foot.

CHANGE AND CAUSATION

If truth is not timed, then truth-bearers cannot change their truth-values, and much of the little which ancient philosophers say or imply about truth and falsity is wrong. Some critics have urged that things are even worse than that: there is an inconsistency within the ancient texts—or at least, there is an inconsistency within Chrysippus' thought. For he cannot coherently both maintain his causal account of truth and falsity and also allow that some assertibles change their truth-value. Take the sentence

Nine bean-rows will I plant there,
and suppose—in line with Chrysippus' notions—that in uttering that sentence I might assert something which is true in March and false in May. (I planted the things in April, and I have no intention of doing anything like that again.) Then, according to Chrysippus, in February—and indeed at any and every earlier time—the world contained causal harbingers of the truth of the assertible and also causal harbingers of its falsity. And that is absurd.

Worse, inasmuch as there were, in February, causal harbingers of the future planting, then it was true in February that I would plant the beans, and inasmuch as there were, in February, causal harbingers of my planting no more, then it was false in February that I would plant the beans. So it was both true and false, in February, that I would plant the nine rows. And that is not merely absurd—it is a contradiction.

But it isn't. There were, in February, causal harbingers of the fact that, at some time in the future, I would do some serious gardening; and there were, in February, causal harbingers of the fact that, at some time in the future, I would lay down my spade for ever. Hence

It was true in February that at some later time I would plant beans, and also

It was true in February that at some later time I would not plant beans. There is no whiff of contradiction there, and Chrysippus is innocent of the charge brought against him.

But innocence is bought at a price, and Chrysippus will be presented with a steep bill. The Stoics, according to Sextus, say that opposites are items the one of which exceeds the other by a negation. For example

It is day—It is not day.

For the assertible 'It is not day' exceeds 'It is day' by a negation, namely 'not', and is for that reason opposite to it.

(*M* VIII 89)[58]

So the two assertibles

I will plant beans,

and

I will not plant beans

form an opposed or contradictory couple; and two contradictory assertibles cannot both be true at the same time. But those two assertibles can both be true at the same time.

The case of the once and future bean-planter is not in the least *recherché*—nor is the point which it makes peculiar to future assertibles. Suppose that you ask me if I was in France last month: I shall answer truly Yes. Suppose you ask me if I was in England last month: I shall again answer truly Yes. But when I'm in England I'm not in France, so it seems that I have implicitly asserted that

I was in France last month and I was not in France last month.

So I have contradicted myself.

When the Parisian said to the American that the weather in Europe was fine, then he intended to assert—mendaciously—that it was fine throughout Europe. When I say that I was in France last month, then if I mean to assert that I was there throughout the month, I contradict myself if I also assert that I was in England last month. But if—what is far more likely—I mean to say that I was in France at some time in the last month, then there is no contradiction in the air. For what I have implicitly asserted is that

> Some time during last month I was in France and some time during last month I was not in France.

That has the general form:

Something is such-and-such and something is not such-and-such,

and that is not a contradictory form.

---

[58] φασὶ γὰρ ἀντικείμενά ἐστιν ὧν τὸ ἕτερον τοῦ ἑτέρου ἀποφάσει πλεονάζει, οἷον ἡμέρα ἔστιν—οὐχ ἡμέρα ἔστιν. τοῦ γὰρ ἡμέρα ἔστιν ἀξιώματος τὸ οὐχ ἡμέρα ἔστιν ἀποφάσει πλεονάζει τῇ οὐχί, καὶ διὰ τοῦτ᾽ ἀντικείμενόν ἐστιν ἐκείνῳ.

In the case of the European weather, I claimed that either one thing was asserted and it was false or else two different things were asserted and one was true and the other false. In the case of my joint residence in France and England, I suggest, something similar is to be said.

It is tempting—perhaps it is even true—to suggest that there is a sort of syntactical ambiguity in

I wasn't in France.

On the one hand, it might be construed as the result of putting

I am not in France

into the past, thus:

PAST [I am not in France]

On the other hand, it might be construed as the result of negating

I was in France,

thus

Not [I was in France].

In other words, its structure might be analysed as

PAST [not [I am in France]]

or as

Not [PAST [I am in France]]

The latter, but not the former, contradicts

I was in France

—both in fact and in Stoic theory. It is the former, not the latter, which I intended to assert.

In the course of a long and convoluted discussion of negation, Alexander reports that—according to his unnamed adversaries—

'Socrates died' has two senses: in one, it is compounded from the name 'Socrates' and the verb 'died', and in that sense it is false; in the other, it is inflected as a whole from 'Socrates dies', and in that sense it is true.

(*in APr* 403.14–18)[59]

Past assertibles, according to the view which Alexander reports and rejects, have two construals, and there is a difference of sense between the two which may induce a difference of truth-value.

Socrates died

may be construed as

---

[59] τὸ δὲ λέγειν ὅτι τὸ Σωκράτης ἀπέθανε διττόν ἐστιν, ἐν μέν, ὃ σύγκειται ἐξ ὀνόματος μὲν τοῦ Σωκράτης ῥήματος δὲ τοῦ ἀπέθανεν, ὃ καὶ ψεῦδός ἐστιν, ἄλλο δέ, ὃ ἐγκέκλιται ὅλον ἀπὸ τοῦ Σωκράτης ἀποθνήσκει, ὃ καὶ ἀληθές ἐστιν, οὐχ ὑγιῶς λέγουσι.

PAST [Socrates [dies]]
or else as
   Socrates [PAST [dies]]
That is at least comparable to the suggestion about
   I wasn't in France
which I have just canvassed. Chrysippus and his followers ought to have
offered some reflections along those lines. Perhaps they did.

   But if Chrysippus follows, or should follow, that line of thought, will he
not discover another threat to the possibility of changing truth-values? Return
to Innisfree. The idea was something like this: what I may assert by uttering
   I shall plant nine bean-rows,
was true in March and false in May. But if it is false in May, then in May
   I shall not plant nine bean-rows
is true. But that assertible—or so I have just argued—was true well before
May: it did not need to wait in order to become true, and it did not change
its truth-value.

   That conclusion may sound plausible; but Chrysippus need not accept it.
For what exactly is supposed to become true in May, when
   I shall plant nine bean-rows,
becomes false? Well, of course, it is:
   I shall not plant nine bean-rows.
But that may be parsed in two ways:
   Not [FUT [I plant beans]]
and
   FUT [not [I plant beans]].
What was true all along was the latter, not the former. What becomes true in
May, according to Chrysippus, is the former and not the latter.

   The suggestion that negated future assertibles may be taken in either of two
ways does not provide a new reason for denying—against Chrysippus—that
they may change their truth-value. Rather the contrary. But the old reasons
remain.

TWO PRINCIPLES OF DEFLATION

Before I turn, at last, to my third question—How did Chrysippus try to
persuade us to accept his bivalent thesis?—there is one other topic to be
addressed. Most philosophers who have thought about truth have espoused
some such principle as:

It is true that so-and-so if and only if so-and-so.
The principle has a common-law partner:
It is false that so-and-so if and only if not so-and-so.
I shall call those two propositions the principles of deflation; for if the principles are taken as definitions, or as tantamount to definitions, then they represent what has been called the deflationist theory of truth and of falsity. (Or the redundancy theory—but the word 'redundant' is inept.) Of course, you may subscribe to the principles without thinking that they have a definitional status.

There are adumbrations of the principles in Plato. For example, in the *Cratylus* there is this little exchange:

—Now tell me, you talk of saying what is true and of saying what is false?—I do.—Then there are true sayings and false sayings?—Certainly.—Now isn't a saying true if it says what is as it is and false if it says what is as it isn't?—Yes.

(*Crat* 385B)[60]

A saying is true if and only if things are as it says they are, false if and only if things aren't as it says they are.

In his essay on truth in Book Theta of the *Metaphysics*, Aristotle claims, *inter alia*, that

on the side of the objects this [viz being true or false] lies in their being compounded or divided, so that he who thinks that what is divided is divided and what is compounded compounded thinks truly, and he who holds things contrarily to the objects thinks falsely.

(*Met* 1051b1–5)[61]

Setting aside the notions of composition and division, which are inessential to the argument and incoherent in themselves, and supposing that Aristotle intends to offer an equivalence rather than a simple conditional, we shall arrive at something like this:

Someone thinks truly if and only if he thinks that so-and-so and it is the case that so-and-so,

and:

---

[60] —φέρε δή μοι τόδε εἰπέ· καλεῖς τι ἀληθῆ λέγειν καὶ ψευδῆ;—ἔγωγε.—οὐκοῦν εἴη ἂν λόγος ἀληθής, ὁ δὲ ψευδής;—πάνυ γε.—ἆρ' οὖν οὗτος ὃς ἂν τὰ ὄντα λέγῃ ὡς ἔστιν, ἀληθής· ὃς δ' ἂν ὡς οὐκ ἔστιν, ψευδής;—ναί.

[61] τοῦτο δ' ἐπὶ τῶν πραγμάτων ἐστὶ τῷ συγκεῖσθαι ἢ διῃρῆσθαι, ὥστε ἀληθεύει μὲν ὁ τὸ διῃρημένον οἰόμενος διῃρῆσθαι καὶ τὸ συγκείμενον συγκεῖσθαι, ἔψευσται δὲ ὁ ἐναντίως ἔχων ἢ τὰ πράγματα. (This sentence is part of the antecedent of a complicated 'since' sentence; but it is affirmed.)

Someone thinks falsely if and only if he thinks that so-and-so and it is not the case that so-and-so.

A similar pair of equivalences may be dug out of a passage in the *Categories* which has already been cited in another context:

That there is a man converts, in respect of implication of being, with the true saying about it; for if there is a man, then the saying by which we say that there is a man is true; and the converse too: if the saying by which we say that there is a man is true, then there is a man. But the true saying is not in any way cause of the being of the object: rather, the object seems to be in a way cause of its being true—for a saying is said to be true or false by virtue of the object's being or not being.

(*Cat* 14b14–22)

That is to say:

A saying is true if and only if in uttering it you may say that so-and-so, and it is the case that so-and-so.

And—implicitly—

A saying is false if and only if in uttering it you may say that so-and-so and it is not the case that so-and-so.

In other words, the *Categories* does for saying what the *Metaphysics* does for thinking.

Those Aristotelian propositions are not the principles of deflation. But they are neighbouring principles, and they suggest that Aristotle would have accepted the two principles of deflation. A few further Aristotelian passages could be added to complete the dossier (I shall quote one of them later on); and together they present what is sometimes called Aristotle's theory of truth. It may be doubted if they are sufficiently meaty to merit the name of a theory; but that is another matter.

Later ancient philosophers scarcely go beyond Aristotle. Epicurus, for example,

said that all perceptibles are true and existent—for there was no difference between saying that something is true and saying that it holds. Hence it is that, delineating the true and the false, 'True', he says, 'is what is as it is said to be', and—he says—'false is what is not as it is said to be'.

(Sextus, *M* VIII 9)[62]

---

[62] ὁ δὲ Ἐπίκουρος τὰ μὲν αἰσθητὰ πάντα ἔλεγεν ἀληθῆ καὶ ὄντα. οὐ διήνεγκε γὰρ ἀληθὲς εἶναί τι λέγειν ἢ ὑπάρχον· ἔνθεν καὶ ὑπογράφων τἀληθὲς καὶ ψεῦδος, ἔστι (φησίν) ἀληθὲς τὸ οὕτως ἔχον ὡς λέγεται ἔχειν, καὶ ψεῦδός ἐστι (φησί) τὸ οὐχ οὕτως ἔχον ὡς λέγεται ἔχειν.

There is no difference between being true and being, or between being true and holding—no difference, we may say, between being true and being the case. It seems that Epicurus is suggesting that

It is true that so-and-so when and only when it is the case that so-and-so.

Moreover, he is suggesting that deflationary equivalence, if not as a definition of truth, then at least as a quasi-definition or delineation.

But on a closer look, it will be seen that the text does not express the equivalence; for it alludes, and the equivalence does not allude, to the way in which something is said to be. A very close look—a myopic look—suggests that the text says this:

It is true that so-and-so if and only if it is said to be the case that so-and-so and it is the case that so-and-so.

That entails that if it is true that so-and-so then someone has said that so-and-so—and hence that there are no untold truths. But that is absurd; and presumably Epicurus said, or meant, or meant to say, something more like this:

It is said truly that so-and-so if and only if it is said that so-and-so and it is the case that so-and-so.

That is close to Aristotle, and it suggests that Epicurus, like Aristotle, would have accepted the principles of deflation.

No surviving text ascribes to Chrysippus any view about truth and falsity; but Sextus does say something about the Stoics in general:

The Stoics say that some perceptible items and some thinkable items are true, the perceptible items being so not directly but by reference to the thinkable items associated with them. For according to the Stoics, what holds and is opposed to something is true and what does not hold and is opposed to something is false—and that, being an incorporeal assertible, is a thinkable item.

(*M* VIII 10)[63]

The purpose of the passage is to argue that, for the Stoics, the primary bearers of truth-values are not perceptible objects but thinkable items. The argument, in the case of truth, might be put like this:

If something is true, then it holds and is opposed to something.
If something holds and is opposed to something, then it is an assertible.

---

[63] οἱ δὲ ἀπὸ τῆς Στοᾶς λέγουσι μὲν τῶν τε αἰσθητῶν τινὰ καὶ τῶν νοητῶν ἀληθῆ, οὐκ ἐξ εὐθείας δὲ τὰ αἰσθητά, ἀλλὰ κατ᾽ ἀναφορὰν τὴν ὡς ἐπὶ τὰ παρακείμενα τούτοις νοητά. ἀληθὲς γάρ ἐστι κατ᾽ αὐτοὺς τὸ ὑπάρχον καὶ ἀντικείμενόν τινι, καὶ ψεῦδος τὸ μὴ ὑπάρχον καὶ ἀντικείμενόν τινι· ὅπερ ἀσώματον ἀξίωμα καθεστὼς νοητὸν εἶναι.

Assertibles are thinkable items.

Hence: If something is true, then it is a thinkable item.

It is a strange piece of reasoning, not least because its conclusion appears to be far stronger than the Stoics want. I suppose that it was invented by Sextus (or rather, by his sceptical source). But no doubt it was put together from Stoic cloth.

In any event, it is only the first premiss of the argument which concerns me here. I have stated it thus:

If something is true, then it holds and is opposed to something.

But the Greek text—or rather, my translation of the Greek text—says 'What holds and is opposed to something is true'; and that seems to state not the premiss of the argument, but rather its converse—namely:

If something holds and is opposed to something, then it is true.

However, that proposition will not serve the needs of the argument; and I suppose that Sextus' Greek in fact means to express neither of the two conditional propositions on the table but rather the equivalence which amounts to their conjunction, thus:

Something is true if and only if it holds and is opposed to something.

(A more accurate and less idiomatic English translation would run: 'True is what holds and is opposed to something...'.) If the remark about truth is an equivalence, then so too is the parallel remark about falsity; and Sextus doubtless means to suggest that the equivalences—which he repeats with only the most trivial of variations at *M* VIII 85 and 88—are definitions, or at least delineations, of what truth and falsity, according to the Stoics, really are. However that may be, the first premiss of the argument at *M* VIII 10 follows immediately from the equivalence about truth.

But what does the first premiss mean? I think that the two conjuncts in its consequent are logically independent of one another: in other words, if something holds, it does not follow that it is opposed to something; and if something is opposed to something, it does not follow that it holds. The second of those two independences is actually in the text; for since what is false is opposed to something and yet does not hold, being opposed to something does not imply holding. The first of the two independences is not in the text; and you might coherently imagine that being opposed to something was not an independent item but rather a presupposition of holding (and also of not holding)—a presupposition which, for some reason or another, the Stoics wanted to make explicit. But although that is coherent,

I cannot invent any plausible reason for thinking it to be true; and so I suppose that holding and being opposed to something are two independent conditions.

Take, then, take the second of the two conditions, 'it is opposed to something'. The word '*ἀντικείμενον*' in Greek may be used as generously as 'opposite' in English: the best translation is perhaps 'counterpart'. But the Stoics, as I have already noticed, also gave the word a restricted sense: two items are opposites—according to their stipulative definition—if and only if one of them is the other prefixed by a governing negation; if and only if one of them says that so-and-so and the other says that it is not the case that so-and-so. It is reasonable to think that the term 'opposite' bears that Stoic sense in our text. In that case, something is opposed to something if and only if it is a complete sayable of some variety. Thus the second conjunct will ensure that any truth is a sayable, and a complete sayable. But it will not ensure that it is an assertible; for the complete sayable might be an oath or a question or a command, and so on.

The first conjunct, 'it holds [*ὑπάρχει*]', ought then to pick out assertibles from other complete sayables. The verb 'hold' has several pertinent uses. Thus both the Aristotelians and the Stoics, despite the differences between their respective views of predication, will say that a predicate holds of its subject. Again, the verb can be used of propositions or assertibles, so that the proposition or assertible that Socrates is seated holds just when Socrates is seated. At first glance, those familiar facts lead to an embarrassment. For on the one hand, the usage in which 'hold' is said of predicates cannot be relevant to the premiss of the Sextan argument inasmuch as we need something to distinguish assertibles from other complete sayables; and on the other hand, the usage in which 'hold' is said of assertibles would make the second conjunct in the premiss otiose.

But the embarrassment can be avoided. Although the verb 'hold' has two uses, it does not have two senses, one of them a relational sense which applies to predicates and their subjects and the other an absolute sense which applies to assertibles. The verb 'hold' is syntactically multi-placed: you may say 'x holds' and also 'x holds of y' (and perhaps 'x holds of y for z', and so on). But despite its different syntaxes, the verb 'hold' has a single sense. Thus 'it holds' may be said both of complete sayables and also of incomplete sayables. And since the only complete sayables which hold (or fail to hold) are assertibles, 'it holds' in our text will serve to separate assertibles from other complete sayables.

The function which—if I am right—is performed by the condition 'it is opposed to something', might be performed in various other ways; and if the crucial thing is to ensure that the equivalences advert both to holding and to complete sayables, then perhaps the simplest and least misleading way of expressing them is this:

It is true that so-and-so if and only if it holds that so-and-so.

It is false that so-and-so if and only if it does not hold that so-and-so.

Those two propositions are very close to my two principles of deflation—closer than anything in Aristotle or in Epicurus.

They are not quite the same as the principles. The principle for truth was

It is true that so-and-so if and only if so-and-so.

The corresponding Stoic proposition is

It is true that so-and-so if and only if it holds that so-and-so.

The Stoic proposition has 'holds that so-and-so' where the principle has the simple 'so-and-so'. The propositions which I ascribed to Aristotle and to the Epicureans similarly had 'it is the case that so-and-so' rather than just 'so-and-so'. The difference is not a trifle, and the presence of the dummy verbs 'hold' and 'be the case' is not pleonastic.

For the deflationary principles, as I have formulated them, tacitly suppose that truth and falsity are not timed. What happens to the principles if that supposition is rejected? One easy suggestion is this: perhaps the time in the prefix 'It is true that ... ' is simply picked up by the time in whatever sentence replaces 'so-and-so'? In that case, a past instance of the first principle will be

It was true that polygamy was deemed a sin if and only if polygamy was deemed a sin.

A future instance:

It will be true that I shall plant nine bean-rows if and only if I shall plant nine bean-rows.

And so on.

But the principle will then lose its universality, since it will yield nothing of the forms

It will be true that polygamy was deemed a sin if and only if ...

or

It is true that I shall plant nine bean-rows if and only if ...

In general, if the principle supposes that the time in 'It is true that ...' picks up the time in 'so-and-so', then the principle will not apply to any cases in which those two times differ.

A second suggestion invites us to ignore any differences of time in 'It is true that …'. Let the principle say something like:

When and only when it is true that so-and-so, then so-and-so.

In that case,

It will be true that polygamy was deemed a sin if and only if polygamy was deemed a sin

and

It is true that I shall plant nine bean-rows if and only if I shall plant nine bean-rows.

But then on this second suggestion the principles will rule out any possibility of a change in truth-values. Given that

It was true that so-and-so if and only if so-and-so

and

It will be true that so-and-so if and only if so-and-so,

then it follows that

It was true that so-and-so if and only if it will be true that so-and-so.

That argument is readily generalized to cover the present as well, and it is readily transferred from 'It is true that …' to 'It is false that …'.

That second suggestion, which outlaws change in truth-value, has sometimes been ascribed to Carneades. According to Cicero—in a passage which I have already quoted—Carneades asked:

What could the god himself have looked at in order to predict that Marcellus—the Marcellus who was three times consul—would die at sea? That was indeed true from all eternity, but it had no active causes.

(*fat* xiv 32)

Carneades rejects the Chrysippean view that it is true at a given time that such-and-such if and only if there are, at that time, causal harbingers or causal traces that such-and-such—eternal truth does not require eternal chains of causation. So surely he is suggesting that, say,

It was true that Marcellus will die at sea if and only if Marcellus will die at sea,

It is true that Marcellus will die at sea if and only if Marcellus will die at sea,

and

It will be true that Marcellus will die at sea if and only if Marcellus will die at sea.

After all, what else could he have had in mind?

Well, there is something else which he could have had in mind. Instead of the three equivalences which I have just offered him, he might have proposed:

It was true that Marcellus will die at sea if and only if Marcellus was going to die at sea,

It is true that Marcellus will die at sea if and only if Marcellus is going to die at sea,

and

It will be true that Marcellus will die at sea if and only if Marcellus will be going to die at sea.

So construed, Carneades' proposal does not exclude change in truth-value.

The same proposal—which amounts to a third suggestion for adapting the deflationary principles to timed truth-values—may be advanced more conveniently and more perspicuously if we return to the Stoic formulation:

It is true that so-and-so if and only if it holds that so-and-so.

For the dummy verb 'hold' carries, trivially, a tense, and the tense may be taken (non-trivially) to indicate a time. We may then say, simply enough, that the time indicated by 'It is true that ...' marches with the time indicated by 'it holds that ...': the time indicated by 'so-and-so' is irrelevant—and there is no need to look for subtle modifications of the tense of the verb in 'so-and-so'.

And so it may be concluded that the two ancient principles of deflation could be stated as follows:

It is true at a given time that so-and-so if and only if it holds at that time that so-and-so.

It is false at a given time that so-and-so if and only if it does not hold at that time that so-and-so.

Those principles were accepted by Plato, by Aristotle, by Epicurus, by the Stoics; and no doubt by everyone else. Not that they were argued for or advanced in triumph—rather, they were presuppositions which went without argument and generally without saying.

Why so? The modern principles of deflation, it is true, are generally taken to be evident: to be sure, the semantic paradoxes require them to be formulated with more circumspection than I have accorded them; to be sure, there is a dispute about whether or not the deflationary principles serve to define truth and falsity. (It is true that so-and-so if and only if so-and-so: is that really all ye know on earth and all ye need to know?) But such details apart, who could question the principles? Who could conceivably suggest that perhaps it is raining and yet not true that it's raining, or that perhaps it is true that it is raining and yet it's not raining?

But suppose that you are dubious about bivalence: then won't you be equally dubious about the principles of deflation? You will no doubt accept conditional versions of the principles, namely:

> If either it is true that so-and-so or it is false that so-and-so, then it is true that so-and-so if and only if so-and-so and it is false that so-and-so if and only if not so-and-so.

But what if it is neither true nor false that so-and-so? Suppose, for example, you think that certain sorts of vague assertible have no truth-value—that such items are assessed by criteria different from the canons of truth and falsity. Then you will deny, say, that
> It is true that France is a hexagon
and you will nonetheless happily assert that
> France is a hexagon.
You might, if you were audacious enough, assert that
> France is a hexagon—but it's not true that France is a hexagon.
A sceptic about bivalence is not obliged to follow that road; but it seems to me to be a road which he might naturally think to follow—and it is not an evident cul-de-sac.

That being so, why did no ancient adversary of bivalence think to reject the deflationary principles? Well, the ancient versions of those principles—or at any rate, the items which I have just offered as the ancient versions—do seem to be trivially true, and to be entirely neutral as far as bivalence is concerned. For if, doubting bivalence, you want to distinguish between
> France is a hexagon
and
> It is true that France is a hexagon,
then you will also want to distinguish between
> France is a hexagon
and
> It is the case that France is a hexagon.

And—even more clearly—if you want to distinguish between
    I shall plant the beans
and
    It is true that I shall plant the beans,
then you will also want to distinguish between
    I shall plant the beans
and
    It is the case that I shall plant the beans.
In other words, you are likely to treat 'It is true that …' and 'It is the case
that …' (or 'It holds that …') in the same way; so that you will have no reason
to deny the principles of deflation.

Or rather, you will have no reason to deny the principle of deflation for
truth. As for its partner—

> It is false at a given time that so-and-so if and only if it does not hold at
> that time that so-and-so

—the same argument does not go through in quite the same way. But I shall
return a little later to the deflation of falsity.

AN ARGUMENT FOR BIVALENCE

Chrysippus strained his sinews to defend his thesis that every assertible is
either true or false. How did he do so? It is reasonable to suppose that Cicero is
referring metaphorically to some Chrysippean arguments, and hence reasonable to suppose that Chrysippus argued, and argued forcefully and in several
fashions, for his thesis. It would be pleasant to know what those arguments
were, and what—if anything—they proved. But Cicero keeps quiet, and no
other ancient text ascribes any pertinent argument to Chrysippus.

No doubt much of Chrysippus' effort was negative. He thought that
he could show that the truths about human freedom do not conflict with
bivalence; he hoped to solve the paradox of the Liar and the paradox of
the Sorites without supposing that certain assertibles are neither true nor
false. Such efforts were certainly sinew-stretching, and they might properly
be regarded as part of a general defence of bivalence. But did Chrysippus also
go on to the attack? Did he produce arguments in favour of bivalence?

It is not easy to find a good argument in favour of the thesis—if only
because, as Cicero put it, the thesis is a foundation of dialectic. For example,
Cicero himself argues against the Epicurean rejection of bivalence as follows:

If some assertible is neither true nor false, then certainly it is not true. But if it is not true, how can it not be false? And if something is not false, how can it not be true?

(fat xvi 38)[64]

Whatever the pedigree of that little argument, it will win no prizes at Crufts.

There is another ancient argument which seems a little more robust: it seeks to derive the principle of bivalence from the principles of deflation together with a law of the excluded middle. The origins of the argument have been sought in a passage in Book Gamma of Aristotle's *Metaphysics*:

Again, it is not possible for there to be anything between a contradictory pair—rather, it is necessary either to affirm or to deny one thing (whatever it may be) of one thing. That is clear if we first determine what is the true and false. For to say that what is is not or that what is not is is false, and to say that what is is or that what is not is not is true; so that he who says that it is or is not will speak truly or will speak falsely. But what is not said not to be or to be, neither is what is not.

(Met 1011b15–18)[65]

The passage is in parts baffling; but it is at least clear that it contains both a law of excluded middle and also a principle of bivalence. Moreover, if we may rely on the inferential particle in 'so that he who says ...', Aristotle appears to offer—as it were incidentally—an argument in favour of bivalence. But the argument is anything but plain; and in any event, the primary concern of the text is to commend the law of excluded middle, not to argue for bivalence. In other words, Aristotle argues to, and not from, the law.

However that may be, the ancient argument which I have in mind—whatever its first origins—appears clearly and distinctly in Simplicius' commentary on Aristotle's *Categories*. The Aristotelian text under discussion is this:

Items which are opposed as affirmation and negation evidently are opposed in none of the previously mentioned ways; for in their case alone it is necessary that always one of them should be true and one false.

(Cat 13a37–b3)[66]

---

[64] *si enim aliquid in eloquendo nec verum nec falsum est, certe id verum non est. quod autem verum non est qui potest non falsum esse? aut quod falsum non est qui potest non verum esse?*

[65] ἀλλὰ μὴν οὐδὲ μεταξὺ ἀντιφάσεως ἐνδέχεται εἶναι οὐθέν, ἀλλ' ἀνάγκη ἢ φάναι ἢ ἀποφάναι ἓν καθ' ἑνὸς ὁτιοῦν. δῆλον δὲ πρῶτον μὲν ὁρισαμένοις τί τὸ ἀληθὲς καὶ ψεῦδος. τὸ μὲν γὰρ λέγειν τὸ ὂν μὴ εἶναι ἢ τὸ μὴ ὂν εἶναι ψεῦδος, τὸ δὲ τὸ ὂν εἶναι καὶ τὸ μὴ ὂν μὴ εἶναι ἀληθές, ὥστε καὶ ὁ λέγων εἶναι ἢ μὴ ἀληθεύσει ἢ ψεύσεται· ἀλλ' οὔτε τὸ ὂν λέγεται μὴ εἶναι ἢ εἶναι οὔτε τὸ μὴ ὄν.

[66] ὅσα δὲ ὡς κατάφασις καὶ ἀπόφασις ἀντίκειται, φανερὸν ὅτι κατ' οὐδένα τῶν εἰρημένων τρόπων ἀντίκειται· ἐπὶ μόνων γὰρ τούτων ἀναγκαῖον ἀεὶ τὸ μὲν ἀληθὲς τὸ δὲ ψεῦδος αὐτῶν εἶναι.

Aristotle distinguishes four sorts of opposites or counterparts. Contradictory opposition, which holds (in principle) between an affirmation and a corresponding negation has this special characteristic: if two items are contradictory opposites, then (in an ancient jargon) they 'divide truth and falsity'—at any given time, exactly one of them is true and exactly one of them is false.

In his commentary Simplicius reports an objection which had been advanced against that Aristotelian claim:

> Here too Nicostratus finds fault, saying that it is not a property of contradictory opposites to divide the true and the false; for it does not hold of them alone, nor of all of them. Not of them alone since of jurative and abjurative sayings too it holds that necessarily one of them is the case (e.g. 'By God, I did it', 'By God, I didn't do it'); and the same holds for admiratives ('How beautiful is the Piraeus') and for reprehensives (e.g. 'He is wicked', 'He is not wicked'). Hence it does not hold of contradictories alone. Nor yet of all of them, he says. For propositions with a future inflection are, because of the nature of the contingent, neither true nor false—for neither 'There will be a sea-battle' nor 'There won't be' is true, but whichever happens to turn out.
>
> (*in Cat* 406.6–16)[67]

Simplicius then replies—or reports a reply—to Nicostratus. The reply divides into two halves, one half devoted to each of the two criticisms made by Nicostratus. Although only the second half is strictly pertinent to the present business, I shall spend a moment on the first half, which addresses the claim that 'dividing truth and falsity' is not peculiar to affirmation and negation.

The first part of the reply, ascribed to an anonymous 'they', begins by remarking that in the *Categories* the division of truth and falsity is invoked only to distinguish the opposition of affirmation and negation from the other oppositions which Aristotle is there discussing, so that Nicostratus' appeal to oaths and the like is irrelevant. That is correct. For Aristotle is not there concerned to distinguish assertions from other types of saying but to distinguish contradiction from other types of opposition: when he says 'of them alone' he means 'of contradictories alone among oppositions'.

---

[67] ὁ δὲ Νικόστρατος αἰτιᾶται κἀνταῦθα, λέγων μὴ ἴδιον εἶναι τῶν κατὰ ἀντίφασιν ἀντικειμένων τὸ διαιρεῖν τὸ ἀληθὲς καὶ τὸ ψεῦδος. οὔτε γὰρ μόνοις οὔτε πᾶσιν αὐτοῖς ὑπάρχει· οὐ μόνοις μέν, ὅτι καὶ τοῖς ὀμοτικοῖς καὶ τοῖς ἀπομοτικοῖς λόγοις ὑπάρχει τὸ ἐξ ἀνάγκης θάτερον, οἷον νὴ τὴν Ἀθηνᾶν ἔπραξα τάδε· οὐ μὰ τὴν Ἀθηνᾶν οὐκ ἔπραξα. ἀλλὰ καὶ τοῖς θαυμαστικοῖς, φησί, τὸ αὐτὸ ὑπάρχει· ὡς καλός γε ὁ Πειραιεύς· καὶ τοῖς ψεκτικοῖς, οἷον φαῦλός ἐστιν, οὐ φαῦλός ἐστιν. οὐκ ἄρα μόνοις ὑπάρχει τοῖς κατὰ ἀντίφασιν τοῦτο. ἀλλ' οὐδὲ πᾶσιν, φησίν. αἱ γὰρ εἰς τὸν μέλλοντα χρόνον ἐγκεκλιμέναι προτάσεις οὔτε ἀληθεῖς εἰσιν οὔτε ψευδεῖς διὰ τὴν τοῦ ἐνδεχομένου φύσιν· οὔτε γὰρ τὸ ἔσται ναυμαχία ἀληθὲς οὔτε τὸ οὐκ ἔσται, ἀλλ' ὁπότερον ἔτυχεν.—It seems likely that a negative admirative has dropped from the text.

But although that is enough to deflect Nicostratus' objection, Simplicius' anonymous respondents nevertheless add a second consideration. The second consideration goes like this:

Apart from that, they say, the point has been resolved long ago in the commentaries on the definition of the assertible which determines an assertible as that which is true or false. For a jurative cannot be true or false. Rather, it is reasonable to think that keeping an oath and perjuring yourself are found among oaths and that being true and being false cannot be found among them—not even if someone swears about what is true or false. ... But let us grant that those resolutions depend on Stoic subtlety.

(*in Cat* 406.20–28)[68]

Nicostratus' respondents indulge in Stoic subtleties, so that—in Simplicius' view—the Stoa comes to the rescue of the Lyceum. Were the respondents Stoics who determined to defend Aristotle on this point because on this point Aristotle had anticipated a Stoic thesis? Or were they Aristotelians who were happy to borrow a good argument from the Stoics?

However that may be, we happen to know something of what the Stoics said on the matter of oaths.

Cleanthes said that anyone who swears either keeps his oath or perjures himself at the time at which he swears. For if he swears as one who will fulfill what he swore, he keeps his oath, and if as one who has the intention not to fulfill it, he perjures himself.

Chrysippus said that swearing truly differs from keeping an oath and perjuring yourself differs from swearing falsely. If someone swears, then on the occasion on which he swears he certainly either swears truly or swears falsely; for what is sworn by him is either true or false since it is in fact an assertible. But anyone who swears does not certainly, at the time at which he swears, either keep his oath or perjure himself—unless the time to which the oath has reference is present. For just as someone is said to keep a contract or to break a contract not when he contracts but when the time specified in the agreement is present, so you will be said to keep an oath and to perjure yourself when the occasion arrives at which you agreed that you would fulfill your oath.

(Stobaeus, *ecl* I xxviii 17–18)[69]

[68] χωρὶς δὲ τούτων, φασίν, πάλαι λέλυται ταῦτα ἐν ταῖς ἐξηγήσεσιν τοῦ ὅρου τοῦ ἀξιώματος τοῦ ἀφοριζομένου τὸ ἀξίωμα ὅ ἐστιν ἀληθὲς ἢ ψεῦδος. οὐδὲ γὰρ τὸ ὁμοτικὸν οἷόν τε ἀληθὲς εἶναι ἢ ψεῦδος, ἀλλ' εὐορκεῖν μὲν ἢ ἐπιορκεῖν ἐν τοῖς ὅρκοις εἰκός, ἀληθεύειν δὲ ἢ ψεύδεσθαι ἐν αὐτοῖς οὐχ οἷόν τε, κἂν περὶ ἀληθῶν ὀμόσῃ τις ἢ ψευδῶν. ... ἀλλ' αὗται μὲν ἀπὸ τῆς Στωϊκῆς ἀκριβείας ἔστωσαν αἱ λύσεις.
[69] Κλεάνθης ἔφη τὸν ὀμνύοντα ἤτοι εὐορκεῖν ἢ ἐπιορκεῖν καθ' ὃν ὄμνυσι χρόνον. ἐὰν μὲν γὰρ οὕτως ὀμνύῃ ὡς ἐπιτελέσων τὰ κατὰ τὸν ὅρκον, εὐορκεῖν· ἐὰν δὲ πρόθεσιν ἔχων μὴ ἐπιτελεῖν, ἐπιορκεῖν. Χρύσιππος διαφέρειν ἔφη τὸ ἀληθορκεῖν τοῦ εὐορκεῖν καὶ τὸ ἐπιορκεῖν τοῦ ψευδορκεῖν· τὸν μὲν ὀμνύντα καθ' ὃν ὀμνύει καιρὸν πάντως ἢ ἀληθορκεῖν ἢ ψευδορκεῖν·

Stobaeus is paraphrasing rather than citing; but there is no reason to think that the paraphrase is inaccurate; and despite the jargon the main point made by Chrysippus is simple.

The subject is swearing—or rather, promising on oath. (The oaths in question concern the swearer's future behaviour—not the past or the present or any other aspect of the future.) Chrysippus urges that it is one thing to promise truly or falsely, another to keep or break your promise. That is so because the two things are chronologically distinct. On Monday I swore by the nine Gods to be at your wedding on Saturday; and on Saturday, there I was. I promised truly on Monday. I kept my promise on Saturday.

Cleanthes appears to suppose that whenever you make a promise, either you keep it or else you break it. In that case, since every promise is either truly promised or falsely promised, it seems to follow that I swear truly if and only if I keep my oath and I swear falsely if and only if I perjure myself. But that consequence is false. If I break a promise, then I promised falsely. But I may promise falsely without breaking a promise—perhaps I failed to turn up at the wedding because I had been kidnapped by pirates, or because I had died of cirrhosis of the liver. Again, if I keep a promise, then I promised truly. But I may promise truly without keeping my promise—perhaps I turned up on Saturday because I had been drugged and dragged along, or because I thought that it was Sunday. As for Chrysippus, there is nothing in the text which implies that, in his view, you promise truly if and only if you keep your oath.

In any event, Chrysippus certainly held that whatever I swear is, when I swear it, either true or false—for what I swear is an assertible. It might then seem that Chrysippus disagreed with those Stoics or Stoically minded Peripatetics who urged, against Nicostratus, that juratives are neither true nor false; after all, if whatever I swear is either true or false, then surely all juratives are either true or false? But that is not so. A jurative is a complete sayable by saying which you may swear something. For example, what Pétain said when he uttered the phrase

Parbleu, ils ne passeront pas

τὸ γὰρ ὀμνύμενον ὑπ᾽ αὐτοῦ ἢ ἀληθὲς εἶναι ἢ ψεῦδος, ἐπειδὴ ἀξίωμα τυγχάνει ὄν· τὸν δὲ ὀμνύντα μὴ πάντως καθ᾽ ὃν ὀμνύει χρόνον ἢ εὐορκεῖν ἢ ἐπιορκεῖν, ὅτε μὴ πάρεστιν ὁ χρόνος εἰς ὃν ἡ ἀναφορὰ τῶν ὅρκων ἐγίγνετο. ὃν τρόπον γὰρ λέγεσθαί τινα εὐσυνθετεῖν ἢ ἀσυνθετεῖν οὐχ ὅτε συντίθεται ἀλλ᾽ ὅτε οἱ χρόνοι ἐνίστανται τῶν κατὰ τὰς ὁμολογίας, οὕτω καὶ εὐορκεῖν τις καὶ ἐπιορκεῖν ῥηθήσεται ὅταν οἱ καιροὶ παραστῶσι καθ᾽ οὓς ὡμολόγησεν ἐπιτελέσειν τὰ κατὰ τοὺς ὅρκους.

was a jurative. And that—the jurative itself—is neither true nor false. But the jurative is not what Pétain swore: what he swore was that the Boche would not break through, and

The Boche will not break through

is an assertible, not a jurative. As an assertible, it had (according to Chrysippus) a truth-value—and in fact, it was true.

In a similar way, those complete sayables which the Stoics called hypotheticals are neither true nor false—even though what you hypothesize by saying a hypothetical is either true or false. The hypothetical

Suppose that there is a highest prime number

is neither true nor false. The hypothesis which you hypothesize by saying that hypothetical, namely

There is a highest prime number

is an assertible, and it has a truth-value—it is false. Let it be added that by saying

Suppose that there is a highest prime number

you do not make a false assertion; for although you say a false assertible, you do not assert it—or anything else. The same is true of oaths: when Pétain swore, he asserted nothing—although he said an assertible.

I turn now to the second part of Simplicius' reply to Nicostratus—the reply to his claim that not all assertibles are either true or false. It is a curious piece of text. Simplicius first states the opinion of the Stoics, who hold that all assertibles, including those about the future, are either true or false. So in the second part of the reply as well as in the first, the Stoics ride to the rescue of the besieged Peripatetics. But next Simplicius gives the view of the Peripatetics themselves. According to them, he says,

what is stated about the future is not yet either true or false but will be such or such.

(*in Cat* 407.12–13)[70]

The Peripatetics are evidently invoking a thesis which they found in chapter 9 of the *de Interpretatione*; but in doing so, they scarcely appear to answer Nicostratus: on the contrary, they appear to express their agreement with him, and their disagreement with the Aristotle of the *Categories*. Nicostratus attacks Aristotle. The Stoics defend Aristotle. The Peripatetics fight alongside Nicostratus.

---

[70] ὅσα δὲ περὶ τοῦ μέλλοντος ἀποφαίνεται, ἤδη μὲν οὐκ ἔστιν ἢ ἀληθῆ ἢ ψευδῆ, ἔσται δὲ ἢ τοῖα ἢ τοῖα.

But that is not what the Peripatetics meant to be doing (nor what Simplicius took them to be doing). Rather, they urged—against Nicostratus—that future contingent propositions do divide truth and falsity: they do so inasmuch as, although they may not now be either true or false, they will at some time be either true or false. In other words, the Peripatetics—these Peripatetics, whoever they may be—propose a principle of bivalence which is significantly different from the Chrysippean thesis. Whereas Chrysippus argues that

> Whenever it can be asserted that so-and-so, either then it is true that so-and-so or then it is false that so-and-so,

the Peripatetics in effect suggest that

> If it can ever be asserted that so-and-so, then at some time either it is true that so-and-so or it is false that so-and-so.

Chrysippus' thesis entails but is not entailed by their thesis. And they implicitly reject Chrysippus' thesis inasmuch as, according to them, it does not hold for all future assertibles. (Perhaps it does not hold for all past assertibles either?)

That is a highly forced way of interpreting what Aristotle says in the *Categories*; but it is an ingenious way of reconciling the *Categories* with the *de Interpretatione*.

In any event, it is the Stoic argument which is the meat of the matter. Simplicius takes the Stoics to be defending Aristotle against Nicostratus; and he might be taken to suggest that some Stoics actually said: 'Nicostratus is wrong and Aristotle right.' Perhaps they did; or perhaps, at any rate, some Stoics, commenting on the *Categories*, said that Aristotle was right there—and wrong in the *de Interpretatione*. But in truth there may be no more behind Simplicius' text than the indubitable fact that the Stoics affirmed that every assertible is either true or false.

Here, then, is the passage of Simplicius' text which reports the Stoic view:

As for contradictions bearing on the future time, the Stoics offer the same assessment as they do for the other cases: as with opposites about present and past items, so too (they say) with futures—for future opposites and their parts. For either 'It will be' is true or 'It will not be', if they must be either true or false (for, according to them, futures are determined); and if there will be a sea-battle tomorrow, it is true to say that there will be; and if there will not be, it is false to say that there will be. But either there will be or there will not be. Therefore each is either true or false.

(in Cat 406.34–407.5)[71]

Simplicius is not citing Chrysippus. He is not citing—and he does not even purport to be paraphrasing—any Stoic text. Rather, he purports to document a Stoic opinion and a supporting Stoic argument.

The argument is in parts obscure and puzzling; but the gist of it is presented in the last few lines of the passage, and it seems to run like this:

> Either there will be a sea-battle tomorrow or there will not be a sea-battle tomorrow.
>
> If there will be a sea-battle tomorrow, then it is true that there will be a sea-battle tomorrow.
>
> If there will not be a sea-battle tomorrow, then it is false that there will be a sea-battle tomorrow.
>
> Therefore either it is true that there will be a sea-battle tomorrow or it is false that there will be a sea-battle tomorrow; and either it is true that there will not be a sea-battle tomorrow or it is false that there will not be a sea-battle tomorrow.
>
> Therefore either it is true that there will be a sea-battle tomorrow or it is true that there will not be a sea-battle tomorrow.

The argument does not turn upon the particular example of the sea-battle, so that the Stoics may infer a universal conclusion about all future assertibles. Moreover, the argument does not turn upon the fact that the example is a future assertible, so that the Stoics may infer—or might have inferred—an unrestricted conclusion about all assertibles whatsoever. In other words, the argument promises an entirely general proof of a principle of bivalence.

Simplicius' presentation of the argument carries some spare flesh—flesh which is spare in my present context; and its bones may be represented as follows:

> Either so-and-so or not so-and-so

---

[71] περὶ δὲ τῶν εἰς τὸν μέλλοντα χρόνον ἀντιφάσεων οἱ μὲν Στωϊκοὶ τὰ αὐτὰ δοκιμάζουσιν ἅπερ καὶ ἐπὶ τῶν ἄλλων. ὡς γὰρ τὰ περὶ τῶν παρόντων καὶ παρεληλυθότων ἀντικείμενα, οὕτως καὶ τὰ μέλλοντα αὐτά τε, φασίν, καὶ τὰ μόρια αὐτῶν· ἢ γὰρ τὸ ἔσται ἀληθές ἐστιν ἢ τὸ οὐκ ἔσται, εἰ δεῖ ἤτοι ψευδῆ ἢ ἀληθῆ εἶναι (ὥρισται γὰρ κατ' αὐτοὺς τὰ μέλλοντα). καὶ εἰ μὲν ἔσται ναυμαχία αὔριον, ἀληθὲς εἰπεῖν ὅτι ἔσται· εἰ δὲ μὴ ἔσται, ψεῦδος τὸ εἰπεῖν ὅτι ἔσται· ἤτοι δὲ ἔσται ἢ οὐκ ἔσται· ἤτοι ἄρα ἀληθὲς ἢ ψεῦδος θάτερον.

If so-and-so, then it is true that so-and-so
If not so-and-so, then it is false that so-and-so
Hence either it is true that so-and-so or it is false that so-and-so

The argument looks pretty promising. Surely it is valid—cannot its validity readily be proved in standard modern logic? Its first premiss is a law of excluded middle—and who will deny that law? Its two other premisses are immediate consequences of the principles of deflation—and those principles, or items very like them, were generally accepted in antiquity.

True, the conclusion of the argument is not, as it stands, the Chrysippean principle of bivalence: it doesn't allude to assertibles, and it doesn't time the truth and falsity which it introduces. But that is readily dealt with. A simple modification to the argument will replace its first premiss by, say,

If it is assertible that so-and-so, then either so-and-so or not so-and-so.

The second and third premisses may be adapted along the lines suggested by the Stoic deflationary propositions. After a little polishing, the argument will look something like this:

Whenever it is assertible that so-and-so, either it then holds that so-and-so or it does not then hold that so-and-so.
Whenever it holds that so-and-so, it is then true that so-and-so.
Whenever it does not hold that so-and-so, it is then false that so-and-so.
Therefore whenever it is assertible that so-and-so, either it is then true that so-and-so or it is then false that so-and-so.

The second and third premisses are no longer the principles of deflation—but they are their ancient counterparts (and so much the better for that). The first premiss is no longer the law of excluded middle—but can hardly seem less evident than the law of excluded middle.

The argument, I said, looks to be valid; and you might think to establish its validity along the following lines:

Suppose that at t it is assertible that P.
Then—by the first premiss—there are two possible cases: either at t it holds that P or at t it doesn't hold that P.
Take the first case: then by the second premiss it's true at t that P—and hence, trivially, it's either true at t that P or false at t that P.
Take the second case: then by the third premiss it's false at t that P—and hence, trivially, it's either true at t that P or false at t that P.
So in any case it's either true at t that P or false at t that P.

That argument is impeccable—so long as the 'either … or …' in it is taken to indicate an inclusive disjunction. But Chrysippus' thesis uses an exclusive disjunction, and if the 'either … or …' is construed exclusively, then the argument is not valid. I said that 'it's true at t that P—and hence, trivially, it's either true at t that P or false at t that P.' That is right if 'either … or …' is inclusive, wrong if it is exclusive.

If the argument is to conclude to the Chrysippean thesis, in which the disjunction is exclusive, then it is necessary either to modify the second and third premisses, or else to add a further premiss or premisses. Now in fact it is easy enough to make suitable modifications or additions—and to do so without introducing any suspect matter into the argument. But the argument then becomes rather complicated, and the complications may confuse or disguise the crucial issue. So I shall suppose that the disjunctions in the argument are to be construed as inclusive. The argument is then uncontroversially valid. True, its conclusion is not the Chrysippean thesis itself; but it is one part of the Chrysippean thesis—and the more controversial part.

The Chrysippean thesis holds both that assertibles must have one truth-value and also that they can't have two. The second part of that conjunction was hardly disputed. True, we happen to know that Chrysippus wrote an essay *Against those who think that items are both true and false* (Diogenes Laertius, VII 196).[72] The position of this item in the catalogue of Chrysippus' writings suggests that it was connected to the paradox of the Liar; and the title suggests that some people had attempted to resolve the paradox by claiming that some assertibles might be both true and false (at the same time). But we hear nothing more about that heroic claim, and speculation is pointless. In any event, it is plain that Chrysippus' chief adversaries, and his most potent adversaries, claimed not that assertibles might be both true and false but that they might be neither true nor false. And against those adversaries an argument to an inclusive disjunction would have done the trick.

A RETORT

What is the value of the argument? How might, or how should, an Epicurean have reacted to it? Turn again to the Epicurean texts on bivalence. There are

---

[72] Πρὸς τοὺς νομίζοντας καὶ ψευδῆ καὶ ἀληθῆ εἶναι.—Susanne Bobzien drew my attention to this title.

four items to add to the passage from Cicero's *On Fate* which has already been quoted—but which I shall repeat for convenience:

Chrysippus strains every sinew to persuade us that every assertible is either true or false. For just as Epicurus feared lest, should he concede this, he would have to concede that whatever happens happens by fate (for if one or the other is true from eternity, then it is already fixed; and if it is fixed, then it is necessary—so that he thinks that both fate and necessity are confirmed in this way) ...

(*fat* x 21)

One of the four items to be added confirms the message of that text:

It is just as immutable that <Cato> will come <to the Senate> when it is true that he will as it is that he came. ... And it must be allowed that if this assertible—
    Hortensius will come to Tusculum
—is not true, then it follows that it is false. And they want neither of those things.

(*fat* xii 28)[73]

It is the Epicureans who 'want neither of those things': first, they do not want an immutable future; and secondly, they will not allow that if an assertible is not true then it is false. It is clear from the context that Cicero means to ascribe to the Epicureans the thesis which he ascribed to Epicurus in the earlier passage at x 21.

There is a further pertinent passage from *On Fate*; but it is better to leave it to the end. So I take next a passage from the *Lucullus*:

The Stoics cannot get Epicurus, who despises and ridicules the whole of logic, to concede that what we express thus—
    Either Hermarchus will be alive tomorrow or he will not be alive
—is true, although the logicians establish that everything which is disjoined in the manner of either Yes or No is not only true but necessary. Notice how cunning is the man whom they think to be slow. For, he says, if I allow that one or the other is necessary, then it will be necessary tomorrow either that Hermarchus is alive or that he is not alive. But there is no such necessity in the nature of things.

(*Luc* xxx 97)[74]

---

[73] *et tamen tam est immutabile venturum cum est verum quam venisse. ... etenim erit confiteri necesse si hoc enuntiatum, veniet in Tusculanum Hortensius, verum non est, sequitur ut falsum sit. quorum isti neutrum volunt.*

[74] *etenim cum ab Epicuro qui totam dialecticam et contemnit et irridet non impetrent ut verum esse concedat quod ita effabimur, aut vivet cras Hermarchus aut non vivet, cum dialectici sic statuant omne quod ita diiunctum sit quasi aut etiam aut non non modo verum esse sed etiam necessarium, vide quam sit catus is quem isti tardum putant. si enim, inquit, alterutrum concessero necessarium esse, necesse erit cras Hermarchum aut vivere aut non vivere. nulla autem est in natura rerum talis necessitas.*

The passage switches disconcertingly from truth to necessity; but if we disregard that, we may affirm that, according to Cicero, Epicurus denies that
Either so-and-so or not so-and-so
is in all cases true. He does so because he supposes that if it is true that either so-and-so or not so-and-so, then either it is true that so-and-so or it is true that not so-and-so. But
Hermarchus will be alive tomorrow
is a future contingent—today, it is neither true nor false. Hence
Hermarchus will not be alive tomorrow
is, today, neither true nor false. Hence

Either Hermarchus will be alive tomorrow or Hermarchus will not be alive tomorrow

is not true.

A further passage is found in a section of the *Nature of the Gods* in which Cicero conducts a rapid discussion of fatalism and similar notions.

Epicurus does the same against the logicians who agree that in all disjunctions in which either Yes or No is posited one or the other is true. Fearing lest if he conceded that
Either Epicurus will be alive tomorrow or he will not be alive
was of that sort, then one or the other would be necessary, he denied that the whole item
Either Yes or No
was necessary.

(*nd* I xxv 70)[75]

This text too switches from truth to necessity; and in any event it is plain that Cicero means to ascribe to Epicurus the theses which he ascribes to him in the *Lucullus*.

Those two texts add material which is not present in the passage from *On Fate*. But the new material is readily appended to the old. There are three items to consider. First, Epicurus plainly imagines that assertibles which lack truth-value go in pairs: if a given assertible lacks a truth-value, then so does its contradictory negation. That is hardly astonishing. After all, if it is not fixed that there will be a festival at Aix next year, then it is not fixed that

---

[75] *idem facit contra dialecticos. a quibus cum traditum sit in omnibus diiunctionibus in quibus aut etiam aut non poneretur alterum utrum esse verum, pertimuit ne si concessum esset huius modi aliquid aut vivet cras aut non vivet Epicurus alterutrum fieret necessarium, totum hoc aut etiam aut non negavit esse necessarium.*

there will not be a festival at Aix next year. Or rather, what is not fixed is precisely whether or not there will be a festival. More generally, if it is true that not so-and-so, then it is false that so-and-so, and if it is false that not so-and-so, then it is true that so-and-so. Hence if it is neither true nor false that so-and-so, then it is neither true nor false that not so-and-so.

Secondly, Epicurus maintains that 'disjunctions in which either Yes or No is posited' are not, all of them, true. In other words, he rejects the law of excluded middle, holding that there are some cases in which

Either so-and-so or not so-and-so

is not true. Doubtless, Epicurus proposes that if it is not true that so-and-so and not false that so-and-so, then it is not true that either so-and-so or not so-and-so. If it is not now true that there will be a festival at Aix and not now false that there will be a festival at Aix, then it is not now true that either there will be a festival at Aix or there won't be a festival at Aix.

Does Epicurus think that, in that case, it is now false that either there will be a festival at Aix or there won't be a festival at Aix? Or does he rather think that it is now neither true nor false that either there will be a festival or there won't be a festival? The texts do not determine an answer.

Thirdly, Cicero implies that Epicurus' rejection of the law of excluded middle took place in a certain argumentative context: he rejected

Either so-and-so or not so-and-so

because he took it to entail

Either it is true that so-and-so or it is true that not so-and-so.

Now it is true that not so-and-so if and only if it is false that so-and-so, so that Epicurus presumably took

Either so-and-so or not so-and-so

to entail

Either it is true that so-and-so or it is false that so-and-so.

In short, Cicero implies—perhaps correctly—that Epicurus was worried by an argument which led from a law of excluded middle to a principle of bivalence.

There is one further item in the Epicurean dossier. It is another passage from *On Fate*:

So, *pace* Epicurus, it is necessary that one is true and one false, so that

Philoctetes will be wounded

was true all eternity ago and

He will not be wounded

false. Unless of course we want to follow the doctrine of the Epicureans when they say that such assertibles are neither true nor false—or else, when that shames them, they say, yet more shamingly, that disjunctions from contraries are true but that neither of the assertibles in them is true.

(fat xvi 37)[76]

According to this text, the Epicureans say one thing; and then when that shames them, they say something different—and which in fact is even more shaming. They adopt one position and then abandon it for another.

The first position, as Cicero describes it, seems to be nothing other than the rejection of bivalence: 'such assertibles are neither true nor false'. The second position is this: 'disjunctions from contraries are true but ... neither of the assertibles in them is true'—that is to say, some disjunctions of the form 'Either so-and-so or not so-and-so' are true even though it is not true that so-and-so and not true that not so-and-so. If the first position was abandoned in favour of the second, then the story goes something like this: The Epicureans couldn't stomach fatalism, so they rejected bivalence. But they found that rejection too shameful; so they re-admitted bivalence and claimed instead that there are true disjunctions no disjunct of which is true. Alas, the second position is even more shaming than the first.

That story is intelligible, but I wonder if it is the story which Cicero really means to tell? If so, then in the second position, the Epicureans accept bivalence. They also hold that, in some cases, it is true that either so-and-so or not so-and-so, and not true that so-and-so and not true that not so-and-so. It follows, trivially, that they hold that in some cases it is not true that so-and-so and not true that not so-and-so. But if that is so, then they must deny that if it is false that so-and-so then it is true that not so-and-so. For suppose that

If it is false that so-and-so, then it is true that not so-and-so.
Then

If it is not true that not so-and-so, then it is not false that so-and-so.
Hence if

In some cases it is not true that so-and-so and not true that not so-and-so, then

In some cases it is not true that so-and-so and it is not false that so-and-so.
That is to say, bivalence does not hold.

---

[76] *ex iis igitur necesse est invito Epicuro alterum verum esse alterum falsum, et sauciabitur Philocteta omnibus ante saeculis verum fuit, non sauciabitur falsum. nisi forte volumus Epicureorum opinionem sequi qui tales enuntiationes nec veras nec falsas esse dicunt aut, cum id pudet, illud tamen dicunt, quod est impudentius, veras esse ex contrariis diiunctiones sed quae in his enuntiata essent eorum neutrum esse verum.*

Perhaps what makes the second position even more shaming than the first is precisely the fact that it commits the Epicureans to denying that

If it is false that so-and-so, then it is true that not so-and-so?

Cicero does not say so: he does not hint at any difficulty with the relationship between 'false that so-and-so' and 'true that not so-and-so', and his text indicates that the greater shame is simply the claim that there may be true disjunctions in which no disjunct is true. So I incline to think that the story which I extracted from Cicero's words is false—and that it is not the story which Cicero means to tell. Let us say that Cicero has compressed his account.

The situation is rather this. There are three propositions around which the Epicureans circle. First, there is the denial of bivalence, which may be expressed roughly thus:

In some cases it is neither true that so-and-so nor false that so-and-so.

The Epicureans consistently held on to that point—which is indeed the very centre of the position. Secondly and thirdly, there are these propositions:

(1) In some cases it is not true that either so-and-so or not so-and-so.

(2) In some cases it is true that either so-and-so or not so-and-so but not true that so-and-so and not true that not so-and-so.

The adjunction of (1) to the central point produces the first of the two positions which Cicero ascribes to the Epicureans. The adjunction of (2) to the central point produces the second.

The two propositions (1) and (2) are consistent with one another, so that the Epicureans might have upheld both at once. Cicero implies that they did not do so: rather, (1) and (2) were embraced as two different ways of getting round a single obstacle. Cicero says that the Epicureans took the second way to be less shaming than the first; but I guess that that is Cicero's invention: I doubt if the Epicureans found either position more shameful than the other—I doubt if they found either position shameful. I guess, too, that the two alternative positions were put forward by the Epicureans, in a familiar Epicurean ploy, as multiple explanations: 'Maybe it's (1) and maybe it's (2). We can't tell, and we don't care: what matters is that there is an explanation, not what the explanation is.'

However that may be, what was—or might, or should, have been—the Epicurean response to the argument for the Chrysippean thesis which was presented in the previous section? The argument went like this:

Whenever it is assertible that so-and-so, either it then holds that so-and-so
or it does not then hold that so-and-so.
Whenever it holds that so-and-so, it is then true that so-and-so.
Whenever it does not hold that so-and-so, it is then false that so-and-so.
Therefore whenever it is assertible that so-and-so, either it is then true that
so-and-so or it is then false that so-and-so.

According to the first of the two Epicurean positions, the first premiss of the
argument is false; for there are any number of cases in which an assertible
neither holds nor fails to hold. For example, I can now assert that

I must down to the seas again.

But it neither now holds that I will go down to the sea nor now does not
hold that I will go down to the sea: for the moment my future sea-faring is
in the air.

There could scarcely be a simpler reply to the Stoic argument. Is the
reply not only simple but also reasonable? Well, if the Epicureans simply
deny the law of excluded middle and then shut up, they will not persuade
us that they are serious philosophers. After all, they deny something which
logicians take to be a fundamental principle of logic; and they owe us—and
themselves—some sort of explanation or justification for their denial. More
particularly, they need a reply to the following objection: 'A disjunction—I
mean, an inclusive disjunction or a quasi-disjunction—announces that at
least one of its disjuncts holds, and a negation of an assertible holds if
and only if the assertible does not hold. So consider any Either Yes or No
assertible—say

Either the sedge has withered from the lake or the sedge hasn't withered
from the lake.

That holds if and only if at least one of its disjuncts holds. Suppose that
the first disjunct doesn't hold—then its negation must hold, and the second
disjunct is its negation. Suppose that the second disjunct doesn't hold—then
its negation must hold, and the first disjunct is its negation. So in any case at
least one of the disjuncts holds—and therefore the disjunction always holds.'

An Epicurean reply might run along the following lines. 'First, there is
nothing odd about the notion that a sentence may have the form 'Either so-
and-so or not so-and-so' and yet fail to be true: suppose that the so-and-so is an
imperative, or an optative, and so on. There is only an oddity when 'so-and-
so' is replaced by an assertoric sentence. Now it is true that future contingents
are expressed by assertoric sentences—and that is why our position seems at

first sight strange. But it must be remembered that the assertoric sentences in question are of a special sort—in particular, they do not express items which are, necessarily, either true or false. The remarks about disjunction and negation which were adduced to show that our view is incoherent are true enough; but they apply only to assertoric sentences which express items which are true or false; they apply to assertibles which bear truth-values, and to nothing else. The patriarchal papa says to his dithering daughter:

Make up your mind—either accept him or don't.

It would be absurd to take the remarks about disjunction and negation to indicate that 'Either accept him or don't' must be true. It is equally absurd, though less obviously absurd, to say the same about 'Either she'll accept him or she won't.'

According to the second of the two Epicurean positions, assertibles of the form 'Either so-and-so or not so-and-so' are always true. In that case, the Epicureans must accept the first premiss of the Stoic argument, namely

Whenever it is assertible that so-and-so, either it then holds that so-and-so or it does not then hold that so-and-so.

And in that case they must reject either the second premiss or the third premiss or both. What would or should they have rejected? And could they coherently have done so?

Cicero thinks it positively shameful to declare that a disjunction may be true even if neither of its disjuncts is true—after all, that goes against the very definition of a disjunction. So at the very least, the Epicureans must explain how they can understand disjunctions other than in accordance with the orthodox definition. No Epicurean explanation survives, and perhaps none ever existed. But it is not difficult to conjure something up—for example, this:

An inclusive disjunction is true if and only if not all of its members are false.

Any proposition of the form 'Either so-and-so or not so-and-so' will then be true, whether the so-and-so has a truth-value or not.

How, in the second position, would the Epicureans have defended themselves against the Stoic argument? Here too we have no texts. Here too it is not difficult to propose something. The two premisses in question are the consequences of the two principles of deflation:

Whenever it holds that so-and-so, it is then true that so-and-so,
and

Whenever it does not hold that so-and-so, it is then false that so-and-so.
The Epicureans in the second position must reject at least one of those
propositions. I have already suggested that they did not reject, and scarcely
could have rejected, the deflationary principle for truth; and so they must
have accepted the former of those two premisses. And I think it's a racing
cert that the Epicureans rejected—or would have rejected—the latter.

If it is now true that there will be a naval engagement next week, then
there must be something now in place which now ensures that there will be
such an engagement—there must be a present cause of that future event.
Similarly, if it is now false that there will be a naval engagement next week,
then there must be something now in place which now prevents any such
future engagement—there must be a present inhibiting cause. And surely if
it is now the case that there will be an engagement, then it is now true that
there will be an engagement, so that there is now a present cause of the future
engagement.

Suppose that it is not now the case that there will be an engagement
next week. In that case, there is not now a cause which ensures such an
engagement. Does it then follow that there is a present cause which inhibits
such an engagement? Not at all; for as far as future naval engagements are
concerned there may be as yet no causes present, one way or the other. Thus

Whenever it does not hold that so-and-so, it is then false that so-and-so
is not true. It is not true—to put the matter generally and roughly—because
there are not always causes in place for everything.

Even if all that is true, it may be murmured, the Epicureans have not
gained the battle; for there is another way of taking the questionable premiss
of the argument: instead of

Whenever it does not hold that so-and-so, it is then false that so-and-so
read

Whenever it holds that not so-and-so, it is then false that so-and-so.
The replacement premiss, I suppose, is true—or at any rate, it would have
been accepted by my hypothetical Epicureans.

But accepting it is not fatal. For if the third premiss is thus revamped,
then either the argument becomes invalid or else the first premiss must be
similarly revamped. To secure validity, the first premiss must become:

> Whenever it is assertible that so-and-so, either it then holds that so-and-so
> or it then holds that not so-and-so.

And the Epicureans have no reason to accept that proposition.

Many modern philosophers will be unimpressed by the Epicurean argument, or by the argument which I have just offered to the Gardeners. For, like Carneades, they do not think much of the suggestion that truth and falsity must be underwritten by causes: it is now true that I shall be in Paris tomorrow (if it is now true that I shall be in Paris tomorrow) not because there is now some determinate and determining cause of my being there tomorrow but simply because I shall be there tomorrow. But Chrysippus could not have taken that dismissive line. Rather, he must have appealed to his fatalism: it is thanks to destiny that every assertible is at every moment of its existence either true or false; for it is the permanent presence of fatal causes which underwrites the truth or the falsity of any assertible at any time.

Epicurus and Chrysippus disagree on a fundamental principle of logic. The disagreement is undergirded by a disagreement on a fundamental principle of physics.

2. Predicates and Subjects

PREDICATES IN ANCIENT GRAMMAR

When Frege decided to ditch subjects and predicates and to make a new life with arguments and functions, he claimed that subjects and predicates were among those several unhealthy notions which grammar had foisted upon logic. He did not affirm that subjects and predicates were items like phlogiston and the luminiferous ether; but he was sure that they were, at best, items for the grammarian's eyes only. That is perhaps the only view which Frege shared with Nietzsche.

When—a few decades later—de Saussure first delivered his Genevan course on general linguistics, he began by urging his pupils to forget the distinction between subjects and predicates. The distinction is alien to linguistics: it is one of the several impertinent notions which logic has foisted upon grammar. No doubt subjects and predicates have some logical utility; but they are of no use or interest to the grammarian.

Every schoolboy once knew that in a sentence such as

Every valley shall be exalted

exaltation, or perhaps future exaltation, is predicated, affirmatively and universally, of a certain subject—namely, of valleys. That traditional parsing was, according to Frege, imposed on logic by grammar; and according to de Saussure, it was foisted on grammar by logic. If we take a long view of the matter, Frege was wrong and de Saussure right.

For subjects and predicates are ancient animals; and they are animals which were reared by the ancient logicians, not by the ancient grammarians. They were not reared in secret; nor were they particularly delicate creatures, or particularly exotic. Their language was readily mastered. Latin logicians used the verbs '*subiacere*' and '*praedicere*' for 'to be subject' and 'to predicate' (although '*declarare*' was at first preferred for 'to predicate'), and their Greek masters used '*ὑποκεῖσθαι*' and '*κατηγορεῖν*'. The pairs of verbs, in Latin and in Greek, had produced little families of adjectives and nouns; and they had various compound relations. The ancient grammarians might easily have adopted subjects and predicates. In fact they hardly ever mentioned them.

The Latin *Institutions* of Priscian gave the mediaeval West its grammar. Not once in the eighteen books of that work does Priscian discuss predication; and the words '*subjectum*' and '*praedicatum*' and the like are as rare in his *Institutions* as they are in the writings of his Latin predecessors. In Greek, the fundamental grammatical text was, or came to be, the *Art of Grammar* falsely ascribed to Dionysius Thrax, a pupil of the great Aristarch. In the *Art* predication is not mentioned, and the words 'κατηγορεῖν' and 'ὑποκεῖσθαι' and their relatives never appear. The ancient commentaries on the *Art*—which, though late and repetitive and confused, together constitute a large portion of our evidence for ancient grammatical theory—show no interest in subjects and predicates.

Once or twice, it is true, the commentaries speak in passing of predication. They do so, for example, in their definition of 'genus', which they lifted from Porphyry's *Introduction* (scholiast to Dionysius Thrax, 117.1–5). Again, we learn that

the infinitive is also called predicative because it is predicated of the objects which are named by it.

(scholiast to Dionysius Thrax, 400.24–26)[1]

Or again,

some people call adjectives predicatives because they are always predicated of proper names or of appellatives. For just as adverbs are necessarily attached to verbs, so adjectives are attached to names.

(scholiast to Dionysius Thrax, 233.24–25)[2]

But such things have little but the name in common with what the logicians thought of as predication: as the second of the two citations shows, 'be predicated of' means no more than 'be attached to'.

With Apollonius Dyscolus the case appears to be different—and Apollonius was the best grammarian of antiquity. For the words 'subject' and 'predicate', together with their congeners, are found fifty odd times in his surviving works. Yet if the verb 'κατηγορεῖν' is found in his writings, it is rarely used to connote predication; and although 'ὑποκείμενον' is not uncommon, it never pairs with 'κατηγορούμενον' and never means 'subject'.

---

[1] ἡ ἀπαρέμφατος καλεῖται καὶ κατηγορική· κατηγορεῖται γὰρ τῶν πραγμάτων ἃ δι' αὐτῆς ὀνομάζεται.

[2] τὸ ἐπίθετον τοῦτο κατηγορικὸν ὑπ' ἐνίων καλεῖται διὰ τὸ πάντῃ κατηγορεῖν κυρίων ἢ προσηγορικῶν· ὡς γὰρ τὰ ἐπιρρήματα τοῖς ῥήμασι πάντως συναρτᾶται, οὕτω καὶ τὰ ἐπίθετα τοῖς ὀνόμασιν.

To establish those negative points would require a tedious survey. But it may be instructive, or at least diverting, to look at a few passages.

I start with '*ὑποκείμενον*', for which the right translation is usually not 'subject' but simply 'thing' or 'item'. Sometimes, the word means 'thing <as opposed to expression>': for example, *synt* III 10 [275.6–9]. Often, it means 'item <in question, on the table, before us>': there is a very good case at *pron* 33.5. Most often it means 'item <indicated by the name in question>': there is a clear example at *conj* 216.1—where '*ὑποκειμένη*' picks up '*δηλούμενον* [indicated]' a few lines earlier. In a similar vein, the object of a transitive verb is called its *ὑποκείμενον* (e.g. *synt* III 149 [396.4–8]; 160 [407.2]; 177 [422.15]).

Again, in the Homeric line 'Zeus gave it to Hector to wear on his head', Apollonius says that 'three *ὑποκείμενα* are thought of'—Zeus, Hector, and Hector's head (*synt* II 111 [211.17–212.3]): it is not that the sentence has three distinct subjects but that it refers to three distinct items. Or again:

Often in the case of names which are of a single *ὑποκείμενον* there is a double inflection: Νέα πόλις, Νέας πόλεως.

(*pron* 60.14–15)[3]

Apollonius is speaking of compound names which refer to a single object. Finally, a longer passage:

By way of a nominal construction we seek the substance of the *ὑποκείμενον* (for pronouns only manifest the substance—although their deictic force comments on the attendant features—and that is why they extend to every *ὑποκείμενον*), whereas by a pronominal construction we grasp the substance but not its proper quality which goes along with the imposition of the name.

(*synt* I 119 [101.12–102.3])[4]

That is to say, a name shows what sort of thing is the item to which it refers: a pronoun, although it indicates such attendant features as number and gender, serves merely to identify the item—and so may be used to identify any item.

Where the traditional schoolboy will say that, in the line from the *Messiah*, exaltation is the predicate and its subject is valleys, Apollonius will note

---

[3] πολλάκις καὶ ἐπ᾽ ὀνομάτων καθ᾽ ἑνὸς ὑποκειμένου δύο κλίσεις γίνονται· Νέα πόλις, Νέας πόλεως ...

[4] διὰ μὲν τῆς ὀνοματικῆς συντάξεως τὴν οὐσίαν ἐπιζητοῦμεν τοῦ ὑποκειμένου (ταύτην γὰρ μόνον αἱ ἀντωνυμίαι ἐμφαίνουσι, τῆς ὑπ᾽ αὐτῶν δείξεως συνεξηγουμένης τὰ παρεπόμενα, ἔνθεν ἐπὶ πᾶν ὑποκείμενον συντείνουσιν), διὰ μέντοι τῆς ἀντωνυμικῆς συντάξεως τῆς μὲν οὐσίας ἐπιλαμβανόμεθα, τῆς δὲ ἐπιτρεχούσης ἰδιότητος κατὰ τὴν τοῦ ὀνόματος θέσιν οὐκέτι.—It is hard to believe that the text is sound; but its difficulties do not matter here.

that the ὑποκείμενον of the word 'valley' is a valley—and that is always its ὑποκείμενον, wherever it may appear in a sentence and whether a traditional logician would count it as a subject or as a predicate.

In a few Apollonian texts it is initially tempting to think that the word 'ὑποκείμενον' does mean 'subject' in the logician's sense of the word. For example,

Seeking the existence of some ὑποκείμενον, we say 'Who is moving? Who is walking? Who is talking?'. The movement, the walk, the talk, are clear—the active person remains unclear.

(synt i 31 [29.1–4])[5]

Surely he means that we've got the predicate and are now looking for a subject? I doubt it: there is no mention of predicates in the passage; and there is no reason to think that 'ὑποκείμενον' means anything more than 'object' or 'item'. Apollonius doesn't mean that we have found a predicate—say, 'is walking'—and are now looking for a subject to make an honest sentence out of it. He means that we grasp that someone's walking and wonder who.

Again, there are half-a-dozen occurrences of 'ὑποκείμενον'—but none of 'κατηγορούμενον'—in a short argument in *Pronouns* where Apollonius contends, against unnamed adversaries, that the words 'τηλικοῦτος' and 'τοιοῦτος' ('as big as that', 'like that') are not compound pronouns but simple names. The adversaries claim, *inter alia*, that those two expressions,

being names which indicate a similarity, are agreed to establish a reference to their ὑποκείμενα.

Apollonius has a brisk reply:

That is perfectly silly; for what is shown by a pronoun does not apply to something else—it is itself the ὑποκείμενον both in gender and in number. Looking at a lake, you will say 'The Nile is as big as that'.

(pron 30.23–31.3)[6]

---

[5] ὑπαρξίν τινος ὑποκειμένου ἐπιζητοῦντές φαμεν τίς κινεῖται; τίς περιπατεῖ; τίς λαλεῖ; προδήλου μὲν οὔσης τῆς κινήσεως, τῆς περιπατήσεως, τῆς λαλιᾶς, τοῦ δὲ ἐνεργοῦντος προσώπου ἀδήλου καθεστῶτος.

[6] ἄλλως τε καὶ ὁμοιώσεως ὄντα ὀνόματα τῶν ὑποκειμένων ἐδόκει δεῖξιν παριστάνειν. ὅπερ ἄγαν ἐστὶ ληρῶδες. τὸ γὰρ δεικνύμενον δι' ἀντωνυμίας οὐκ ἐπ' ἄλλου συντείνει, αὐτὸ δὲ τὸ ὑποκείμενον καὶ κατὰ γένος καὶ κατὰ ἀριθμόν. ἀφορῶν γάρ τις εἰς λίμνην φήσει τηλικοῦτον εἶναι τὸν Νεῖλον.

The argument is obscure and has excited some controversy. In addition, like so many arguments in Apollonius, it appears to conflate an object of reference, the lake, with a term which refers to it.

What Apollonius means is, I think, this: If, looking at a lake, you say 'The Nile is as big as that [τηλικοῦτος]', the expression 'as big as that' agrees in gender and in number with the word 'Nile'. But what the expression 'as big as that' refers to or demonstrates is the lake and not the Nile. Were 'as big as that' a pronoun or a pronominal expression, it would agree with what it demonstrates (in the example, it would be feminine, to agree with 'lake'). Evidently, the word 'ὑποκείμενον' does not here mean 'subject <of the sentence>'. For, according to Apollonius's usage, in 'The Nile is as big as that' the ὑποκείμενον—the ὑποκείμενον of 'as big as that'—is the lake. It is not the Nile.

So much for 'ὑποκείμενον'. Nowhere does the term indicate, let alone mean, 'item <which is subject rather than predicate>'. The dossier on 'κατηγορεῖν' supports a parallel conclusion. Thus:

An adverb is an expression which does not inflect and which predicates of the inflections of verbs, either universally or particularly, without which it will not close up a thought.

> (*adv* 119.5–6)[7]

And the opening pages of Apollonius' essay purport to show that 'adverbs predicate of verbs' (122.33–34). An ancient commentator remarks of the passage that

'predicates' means 'is placed', so that it runs 'is placed on the inflections of verbs'—since the philosophers call adverbs too predicates.

> (scholiast to Dionysius Thrax, 95.18–20)[8]

We need not crack our heads over the last clause—it is enough to note that 'predicate' means 'modify' or 'be attached to'.

Elsewhere, and similarly, Apollonius will say that

the expressions 'τῶν', 'τοῖν' and the like are not predicated of a single gender

> (*synt* i 40 [36.8–9])[9]

---

[7] ἔστιν οὖν ἐπίρρημα μὲν λέξις ἄκλιτος, κατηγοροῦσα τῶν ἐν τοῖς ῥήμασιν ἐγκλίσεων καθόλου ἢ μερικῶς, ὧν ἄνευ οὐ κατακλείσει διάνοιαν.

[8] κατηγοροῦσα ἀντὶ τοῦ τιθεμένη, ἵν' ἦ τὸ ἑξῆς οὕτως, τιθεμένη κατὰ τῶν ἐν τοῖς ῥήμασιν ἐγκλίσεων, ἐπειδὴ καὶ τὸ ἐπίρρημα κατηγόρημά φασιν οἱ φιλόσοφοι.

[9] τὸ τῶν ἢ τοῖν ἢ ἄλλο τι τοιοῦτον οὐχ ἑνὸς γένους κατηγορεῖται.

—that is to say, they are not applied to names of one gender only. Or again, he notes that

'ἄλλοι' will always take an article when it embraces the whole of the predicated plurality

(*synt* I 63 [53.18–19])[10]

—that is to say, when it embraces all the items to which it is applied.

In several texts, 'κατηγορεῖν' is coupled with, and is evidently a variant upon, 'σημαίνειν' or 'signify'. For example,

it is clear that <the adverb> 'κύκλῳ' signifies a spatial relation not because it is a derived form but rather insofar as 'κύκλος' too predicates of a spatial relation.

(*adv* 204.16–18)[11]

He does not mean that in a sentence such as 'That figure is a circle' you predicate a spatial relation of something. He means that the adverbial phrase 'in a circle', like the name from which it derives, signifies a certain spatial relation.

Again, infinitives are names and

in appropriate sayings they may take an article, since a nominal predication of the object is presented.

(*adv* 129.20–21)[12]

That is to say, an infinitive may signify an object in the way in which names do. And here is a passage from Herodian, Apollonius' son:

Words of more than three syllables which end in -αλιος are proparoxytone—unless they are predicated of birds.

(*pros cath* 123.5–6)[13]

That is, unless they are names of birds.

I find only one place—apart from a few passages in which Apollonius reports certain Stoic views—in which a member of the 'κατηγορεῖν' family might plausibly be deemed to signify predication. Of the word 'τις' he asks:

---

[10] πάντοτε οὖν τὸ ἄλλοι συνέξει τὸ ἄρθρον ἡνίκα τοῦ κατηγορουμένου πλήθους ὅλου ἐστὶν ἐμπεριληπτικόν.

[11] καὶ δῆλον ὅτι τὸ κύκλῳ οὐ διὰ τῆς παραγωγῆς τὴν εἰς τόπον σχέσιν σημαίνει, ἀλλὰ καθὸ καὶ τὸ κύκλος κατηγορεῖ σχέσεως τοπικῆς.

[12] ... κατὰ τοὺς δέοντας λόγους ἄρθρου ἐστὶ προσδεκτικά, ἐπεὶ ἅπαξ παρυφίσταται ὀνοματικὴ κατηγορία τοῦ πράγματος.

[13] τὰ εἰς αλιος ὑπερτρισύλλαβα προπαροξύνεται, εἰ μὴ ὀρνέου κατηγοροίη.

How is it that, although it is a monosyllable, it is not lengthened, as names are?—Well, that is a predicate of an expression and not of what is thought by way of the expression.

(pron 27.25–26)[14]

Apollonius means that if I say, for example,

Dogs has a short O

then having a short O, or 'has a short O', applies to the expression 'dogs' and not to the canine beasts. Certainly, in that passage 'κατηγόρημα' could signify 'predicate'; and yet even there it is plain that Apollonius means no more than that having a long O holds of the word and not of the animal.

In sum, Apollonius uses the word 'ὑποκείμενον', but he does not use it to mean 'subject'; and he uses the word 'κατηγόρημα', but he does not use it to mean 'predicate'.

Let it be added that Apollonius' way with these words is not idiosyncratic; nor is it peculiar to the grammarians. On the contrary, it can be paralleled in many other texts—among them philosophical texts, and even Peripatetic philosophical texts.

I end this resolutely negative argument by returning to a Latin author. For Martianus Capella's account of the liberal arts—the *Marriage of Philology and Mercury*—indicates the ancient state of things as clearly as you might wish. In Book III, which is given to grammar, subjects and predicates are not noticed. In Book IV, on dialectic or logic, Capella promises to explain 'what is the subject part of a sentence and what the predicative [*declarativa*]' (341), and also to indicate 'what a predicative [*praedicativus*] syllogism is' (343). He duly does so; and in addition he offers an account of 'the ten predications' (see 383). All this is part of his account of Aristotelian logic; and nothing is plainer than that in Capella's mind predication is not a matter for grammarians and is a matter for logicians.

Some historians of ancient grammar have lamented the fact that it ignored subjects and predicates; and they have tried to explain how such lamentable ignorance could have come about. In truth, there is nothing to lament, and nothing to explain.

---

[14] πῶς οὖν οὐ τείνεται μονοσυλλαβοῦν ὡς τὰ ὀνόματα; τοῦτο φωνῆς κατηγόρημα, οὐ τοῦ νοουμένου ἀπὸ τῆς φωνῆς.

PREDICATES AND VERBS

The first and original home of subjects and predicates was logic. More particularly, it was Aristotelian logic; and the distinction between subject and predicate had nothing to do with grammar. That is the well-rounded truth. But it requires a couple of riders.

The first rider concerns the Stoics. It is best introduced by way of a grammatical text which I have so far held under wraps:

It is disputed whether the present work [i.e. the *Art of Grammar*] is genuinely by Dionysius Thrax. Some have argued as follows … And that there are two men is also shown by their definitions of the verb. For our author defines the verb as follows: A verb is a caseless expression which accepts times and persons and numbers, and indicates an activity or a passivity; but Dionysius Thrax, as Apollonius says in *The Verb*, defines the verb in this way: A verb is an expression which signifies a predicate.

(scholiast to Dionysius Thrax, 161.6–10)[15]

The *Art* ascribed to Dionysius defines the verb in one way—and the scholiast cites from §13 [46.4–5]. Dionysius himself—according to Apollonius—defined it in another way. Perhaps the commentator who cites Apollonius' *Verb* (a work lost to us) was muddled? Perhaps Apollonius was mistaken? Perhaps Dionysius changed his mind about the verb, or offered two different but compatible definitions? Such things are ever possible. But in fact the commentator and Apollonius were doubtless both right; and on this point the *Art* ascribed to Dionysius—whatever its date and its origins—differed from the *Art* written by Dionysius.

In any event, the real Dionysius Thrax said that verbs signify predicates. His view found its way into the Byzantine encyclopaedias:

A purely verbal expression is called a verb (e.g. strike, write), when it is said purely and alone. What is signified by a purely verbal expression is called a predicate.

(*Suda*, s.v. ῥῆμα)[16]

---

[15] περὶ δὲ τοῦ εἰ ἔστι γνήσιον τὸ παρὸν σύγγραμμα Διονυσίου τοῦ Θρᾳκὸς ἠμφισβήτηται· ἐπεχείρησαν γάρ τινες οὕτως εἰπόντες ὡς … ὅτι δὲ ἄλλος ἐστὶν ἐκεῖνος καὶ ἄλλος οὗτος, δηλοῖ καὶ ὁ παρ' ἀμφοτέρων ὁρισμὸς τοῦ ῥήματος· οὗτος μὲν γὰρ οὕτως τὸ ῥῆμα ὁρίζεται· ῥῆμά ἐστι λέξις ἄπτωτος, ἐπιδεκτικὴ χρόνων τε καὶ προσώπων καὶ ἀριθμῶν, ἐνέργειαν ἢ πάθος παριστᾶσα. ὁ δὲ Διονύσιος ὁ Θρᾷξ, ὥς φησιν Ἀπολλώνιος ἐν τῷ Ῥηματικῷ, οὕτως ὁρίζεται τὸ ῥῆμα· ῥῆμά ἐστι λέξις κατηγόρημα σημαίνουσα.

[16] ῥῆμα λέγεται ἡ ἁπλῶς ῥηματικὴ φωνή, οἷον τύπτω, γράφω, ἁπλῶς μόνον λεγόμενον· τὸ δὲ ἐκ τῆς ἁπλῶς ῥηματικῆς φωνῆς σημαινόμενον κατηγορία καλεῖται.

And it seems at first sight reasonable to link the view to Aristotle, who says that

a verb ... is a sign of items which are said of something else.

(*Int* 16b6–7)[17]

Since an item which is said of something is an item which is predicated of something, Aristotle holds that verbs are signs of predicates—and that is just the view of Dionysius. Nonetheless, most scholars will deem that the Dionysian view is of Stoic rather than Aristotelian inspiration.

The situation is in fact rather murky. The Stoics certainly did connect verbs and predicates; but according to the testimony of the grammarians they did not do so in the Dionysian way. Thus one commentator assures us that

the Stoic philosophers ... list the parts of sayings as follows: first, name; secondly, appellation; thirdly—and together—verb and participle, saying that a verb is a predicate and that a participle is an inflection of a verb (i.e. a derivative of a verb).

(scholiast to Dionysius Thrax, 356.7–12)[18]

The commentators on the Dionysian *Art* often draw on Apollonius, and sometimes mangle him. They probably do so here. For according to Apollonius,

every infinitive is a verbal name—after all, the Stoics call it a verb, while 'walks' or 'writes' (and also their inflections) they call predicates or accidents.

(*synt* I 50 [43.14–44.1])[19]

Aristotle claims that verbs signify predicates, and Dionysius defined the verb as an expression which signifies a predicate. The Stoics are said to have held a different view: verbs, according to them, actually are predicates—or at any rate, the finite verbal forms are predicates.

That is what the grammarians report. And there is indirect support, of a sort, in a philosophical text. Plutarch, writing about what Plato called primary sayings, states that such a saying is an assertible

---

[17] ῥῆμα δέ ἐστι ... τῶν καθ' ἑτέρου λεγομένων σημεῖον.

[18] οἱ γὰρ Στωϊκοὶ φιλόσοφοι ... καταλέγουσιν οὕτω τὰ μέρη τοῦ λόγου· πρῶτον ὄνομα, δεύτερον προσηγορία, τρίτον ὑφ' ἓν ῥῆμα καὶ μετοχή, τὸ μὲν ῥῆμα κατηγόρημα λέγοντες, τὴν δὲ μετοχὴν ἔγκλιμα ῥήματος, ὅ ἐστι ῥήματος παραγωγή.

[19] πᾶν ἀπαρέμφατον ὄνομά ἐστι ῥήματος, εἴγε καὶ οἱ ἀπὸ τῆς Στοᾶς αὐτὸ μὲν καλοῦσι ῥῆμα, τὸ δὲ περιπατεῖ ἢ γράφει κατηγόρημα ἢ σύμβαμα, καὶ ἔτι τὰς ἀπὸ τούτων ἐγκλίσεις.

which is composed of a name and a verb, which the logicians call a case and a predicate.

(quaest Plat 1009c)[20]

In the simple sentence or primary saying
    Edward lives
'lives' is verb and predicate (and 'Edward' is name and case). Plutarch does not refer specifically to the Stoics; but the terminology he uses was used by the Stoics, and it is reasonable to suppose that among his anonymous logicians were the Stoic logicians. So Plutarch may be taken to imply that the Stoics took verbs to be predicates.

Nonetheless, the view that, for the Stoics, verbs and predicates were one and the same thing is contradicted by most of our more philosophical sources. The account of Stoic logic in Diogenes Laertius includes this remark:

Predicates are classed among the deficient sayables ... A predicate is what is stated of something, or an object constructible about some item or items (as Apollodorus says), or a deficient sayable constructible with a nominative case to make an assertible.

(vii 63–64)[21]

Stoic predicates—according to that account—are not verbs. For they are not linguistic items at all: rather, they are a sort of sayable. By uttering the sentence
    The king was in his counting-house
I may assert something, namely that the king was in his counting-house. I may also (and of course at the same time) say something of the king—that he was in his counting-house, and of the king's counting-house—that the king was in it, and of the pair of them—that the former was in the latter. What I thereby assert of one of the items, or of the pair of items, is a predicate.

Verbs, according to the Stoa, are bodies: they are pieces of hammered air. Sayables, among them predicates, are incorporeal. Far from being identical with one another, verbs and predicates are as different as two Stoic items can be.

---

[20] τοῦτο δ' ἐξ ὀνόματος καὶ ῥήματος συνέστηκεν, ὧν τὸ μὲν πτῶσιν οἱ διαλεκτικοὶ τὸ δὲ κατηγόρημα καλοῦσιν.

[21] ἐν μὲν οὖν τοῖς ἐλλιπέσι λεκτοῖς τέτακται τὰ κατηγορήματα ... ἔστι δὲ τὸ κατηγόρημα τὸ κατά τινος ἀγορευόμενον ἢ πρᾶγμα συντακτὸν περί τινος ἢ τινῶν, ὡς οἱ περὶ Ἀπολλόδωρόν φασιν, ἢ λεκτὸν ἐλλιπὲς συντακτὸν ὀρθῇ πτώσει πρὸς ἀξιώματος γένεσιν.

Scholars generally—and no doubt correctly—suppose that Diogenes Laertius is right and Apollonius wrong, or else that Diogenes represents the standard Stoic view and Apollonius at best a minor heterodoxy. But if, *pace* Apollonius, Stoic predicates are not verbs, they are nonetheless closely connected to verbs; for according to Diogenes Laertius,

a verb is a part of sayings which signifies an incomposite predicate (as Diogenes says), or (as others say) an element of sayings which has no cases and which is constructible about some item or items—e.g. write, talk.

(VII 58)[22]

The second of those two definitions mimics one of the Stoic definitions of the predicate, and the first definition explains verbs in terms of predicates. Thus Stoic verbs and predicates are not identical; nor do they even pair off one against one—for not all predicates are signified by verbs. Nonetheless, there is a connexion: verbs signify a certain type of predicate—and that establishes a link between grammar and logic, or (to use the Stoic jargon) between the theory of signifiers and the theory of signifieds.

The Stoics wrote much about predicates—we hear of monographs *On Predicates* by Cleanthes, by Sphaerus, by Chrysippus (Diogenes Laertius, VII 175, 178, 191). Scholars like to suppose that they were inspired by the Megaric philosopher, Clinomachus of Thurii,

who was the first to write about assertibles and predicates and the like.

(Diogenes Laertius, II 112)[23]

But the nature and the extent of the influence are matters of conjecture, since all we know about Clinomachus is contained in the sentence I have just cited.

However that may be, the Stoics put their predicates to work. The items had a significance in Stoicism outside logic—notably in the theory of causation and in the theory of action. Within logic, the Stoics classified simple assertibles by reference to their predicational structure:

A predicative assertible is one composed of a nominative case and a predicate, for example
    Dio walks;
a predicatory assertible is one composed of a demonstrative nominative case and a predicate, for example

---

[22] ῥῆμα δέ ἐστι μέρος λόγου σημαῖνον ἀσύνθετον κατηγόρημα, ὡς ὁ Διογένης, ἤ, ὥς τινες, στοιχεῖον λόγου ἄπτωτον, σημαῖνόν τι συντακτὸν περί τινος ἢ τινῶν, οἷον γράφω, λέγω.

[23] Κλεινόμαχος ... ὁ Θούριος, ὃς πρῶτος περὶ ἀξιωμάτων καὶ κατηγορημάτων καὶ τῶν τοιούτων συνέγραψε.

This item walks;

and an indeterminate assertible is one composed of an indeterminate particle (or indeterminate particles) and a predicate, for example

Someone walks.

(Diogenes Laertius, VII 70)[24]

In addition, the Stoics distinguished among various types of predicate:

Of predicates, some are upright, some supine, some neither. Upright are those which are construed with one of the oblique cases to produce a predicate (e.g. hears, sees, talks). Supine are those which are construed with a passive particle (e.g. am heard, am seen). Neither are those which are neither way (e.g. to think, to walk).

(Diogenes Laertius, VII 64)[25]

The fragments of Chrysippus' *Logical Investigations* show that he had engaged in reflection more detailed and more refined than anything which is to be found in the Peripatetic texts on predication. For example:

If there are plural predicates, then there are plurals of plurals *ad infinitum*. But that is certainly not so. So not the first.

(PHerc 307, II 21–26)[26]

Chrysippus did not deny the existence of plural predicates—rather, there was a little argument which threatened their coherence and which he had to refute.

It is plain that there is the closest connection between many of those logical notions and certain corresponding grammatical notions. A supine predicate, for example, is one which takes a passive particle to make a predicate. A passive particle is a preposition of agency—'by', for example; and the Stoics mean to say that S is a supine predicate if and only if S + 'by' + C (where C is an oblique case) is a predicate. That is not, in principle, a grammatical comment; for it concerns sayables, not expressions. But it is presented in a grammatical terminology, and it is—or so I should say—unintelligible

---

[24] κατηγορικὸν δέ ἐστι τὸ συνεστὸς ἐκ πτώσεως ὀρθῆς καὶ κατηγορήματος, οἷον Δίων περιπατεῖ· καταγορευτικὸν δέ ἐστι τὸ συνεστὸς ἐκ πτώσεως ὀρθῆς δεικτικῆς καὶ κατηγορήματος, οἷον οὗτος περιπατεῖ· ἀόριστον δέ ἐστι τὸ συνεστὸς ἐξ ἀορίστου μορίου ἢ ἀορίστων μορίων καὶ κατηγορήματος, οἷον τὶς περιπατεῖ ...

[25] καὶ τὰ μέν ἐστι τῶν κατηγορημάτων ὀρθά, ἃ δ' ὕπτια, ἃ δ' οὐδέτερα. ὀρθὰ μὲν οὖν ἐστι τὰ συντασσόμενα μιᾷ τῶν πλαγίων πτώσεων πρὸς κατηγορήματος γένεσιν, οἷον ἀκούει, ὁρᾷ, διαλέγεται· ὕπτια δ' ἐστὶ τὰ συντασσόμενα τῷ παθητικῷ μορίῳ, οἷον ἀκούομαι, ὁρῶμαι· οὐδέτερα δ' ἐστὶ τὰ μηδετέρως ἔχοντα, οἷον φρονεῖν, περιπατεῖν.

[26] εἰ πληθυντικά ἐστιν κατηγορήματα, καὶ πληθυντικῶν πληθυντικά ἐστι μέχρι εἰς ἄπειρον· οὐ πάνυ δὲ τοῦτο· οὐδ' ἄρα τὸ πρῶτον.

unless it is regarded as a perverse way of expressing a piece of grammar: an expression E expresses a supine predicate if and only if E + 'by' + N (where N is a name) is a verbal formula. (And V is a verbal formula if and only if N + V is a sentence.)

So in the Porch, logic and grammar saunter hand-in-hand; and it is tempting to infer that predicates—despite all the negative evidence which I have taken from the grammarians—were in fact quite at home, in the ancient world, in the house of grammar.

Moreover, Dionysius Thrax—the real Dionysius, who defined verbs as expressions which signify predicates—surely took his notion of the verb from the Stoics. True, if you look at the verb in isolation, you might conclude that he took over something which was common to Peripatetics and Stoics—that his verb had a philosophical pedigree but not a specifically Stoic pedigree. But the grammatical commentator who reports Dionysius' definition of the verb and notes that it differs from the definition found in the *Art* also remarks, as further evidence for the inauthenticity of the work, that

the technical writers refer to Dionysius Thrax and say that he separated appellations from names and connected pronouns to articles, whereas the technical author of the *Art* knows appellations and names as a single part of sayings ... and he recognizes articles and pronouns as two parts of sayings and not as one.

(scholiast to Dionysius Thrax, 160.25–31)[27]

The real Dionysius Thrax distinguished between names and appellations, or between proper and common nouns; and he did not distinguish between articles and pronouns. On both points he took the same view as the Stoics, and on both points—it is plausible to think—he was following the Stoics. So we shall reasonably conclude that when he defined a verb as an item which signifies a predicate he was again following the Stoics (rather than following Aristotle, or a general philosophical tradition, or his nose).

However that may be, the case of Dionysius shows that we must qualify the claim that the distinction between subjects and predicates had nothing to do with ancient grammar: at least one ancient grammarian appealed to predicates in one of his grammatical definitions, and that definition had a philosophical and a logical origin.

---

[27] οἱ τεχνικοὶ μέμνηνται Διονυσίου τοῦ Θρᾳκὸς καὶ λέγουσιν ὅτι διεχώριζε τὴν προσηγορίαν ἐκεῖνος ἀπὸ τοῦ ὀνόματος καὶ συνῆπτε τῷ ἄρθρῳ τὴν ἀντωνυμίαν· ὁ δὲ παρὼν τεχνικὸς τὴν προσηγορίαν καὶ τὸ ὄνομα ἓν μέρος λόγου οἶδεν ... καὶ τὸ ἄρθρον καὶ τὴν ἀντωνυμίαν δύο μέρη λόγου γινώσκει, καὶ οὐχὶ ἕν.

But Dionysius does not mention subjects—he invokes the notion of a predicate and not the twin notion of a subject–predicate sentence. Moreover, Dionysius' view had no echo in the later grammatical tradition; and although some scholars have argued that Stoic logic had a massive influence on ancient grammatical theory, as a matter of fact Stoic predicates did not move any grammarian after Dionysius. In any event, the notion of predication which came to dominate mediaeval and modern logic, and against which Frege and de Saussure rebelled, owes nothing to Stoicism—it is wholly Peripatetic.

NAMES AND VERBS IN ARISTOTELIAN LOGIC

The second rider to the well-rounded truth which excludes subjects and predicates from ancient grammar is concerned with Peripatetic predication.

The study of logic in late antiquity had a fixed structure, and the structure was determined by the uncontroversial observation that inferences or syllogisms are compounds of propositions, and propositions compounds of terms. To that observation was annexed the general claim that you cannot rationally study an item until you have first studied its constituent parts. It was concluded that in studying logic you should begin with terms, then move up to propositions, and finally tackle syllogisms and their various species. Now by some pre-established harmony, Aristotle's *Organon*—the *summa* of later Greek logic—is ideally adapted to that conclusion. For in the *Organon* there comes first the *Categories*, which discusses terms, then the *de Interpretatione*, which deals with propositions, next the *Prior Analytics*, which elaborate a general theory of the syllogism, and finally the *Posterior Analytics* and the *Topics* and the *Sophistical Refutations*, which handle the different sorts or species of syllogism.

And so it was that, in late antiquity—and for fifteen hundred years thereafter—every student of logic, once he had conned Porphyry's *Isagoge* or *Introduction*, began with the *Categories*, then read the *de Interpretatione*, and so on. The argument which underlay that pedagogical practice is frail: why, after all, should we study the parts of a chain-saw before we wonder at the chain-saw as a whole? And as for the *Organon*, it is one of the stranger constructions in the history of philosophy. Nothing in the central part of the *Categories* prepares the way to the later books of the *Organon*. The *de Interpretatione* neither builds on the *Categories* nor lays the foundations for the *Analytics*. The *Analytics* has no use either for the *Categories* or for the *de Interpretatione*. The *Organon* was jerry-built—and jerry-built long after Aristotle's day. It is the ricketiest of constructions. Yet how it lasted.

However that may be, syllogisms are indeed sequences of propositions—of the propositions which constitute their premisses and their conclusion. And propositions are indeed composed of terms; for, as Aristotle puts it,

I call a term that into which a proposition dissolves—I mean what is predicated and that of which it is predicated—when to be or not to be is added.

(*APr* 24b16–18)[28]

The *Categories* does not use the word 'term'; but it certainly says something about predication and predicates, and it was for that reason taken for an introduction to the theory of terms. Now between the *Categories* and the *Prior Analytics* comes the *de Interpretatione*. Students were instructed to find in that essay a theory of the proposition. In fact, they must have noticed that, after its opening paragraph, the essay begins not with an account of propositions but with some rapid remarks about names and verbs. Names and verbs seem to be presented as parts or elements of propositions. We know that terms are the elements of propositions. So must there not be some close liaison between terms—or subjects and predicates—on the one hand and names and verbs on the other?

A connection is indeed frequently signalled in the ancient texts. Alexander is brisk:

The terms in a simple proposition are name and verb.

(*in APr* 14.28–29)[29]

Galen says of predicative propositions that

the parts from which they are constructed we call terms, following the old usage—for example, in 'Dio walks', they are Dio and walking, and we take Dio to be the subject term and to walk the predicate. So when a proposition is made of a name and a verb, that is how the terms should be distinguished.

(*inst log* ii 2–3)[30]

---

[28] ὅρον δὲ καλῶ εἰς ὃν διαλύεται ἡ πρότασις, οἷον τό τε κατηγορούμενον καὶ τὸ καθ' οὗ κατηγορεῖται, προστιθεμένου τοῦ εἶναι ἢ μὴ εἶναι. After 'προστιθεμένου' the manuscripts have 'ἢ διαιρουμένου'; but 'or divided' (or 'or removed') makes little sense.

[29] εἰσὶ δὲ ὅροι ἐν ἁπλῇ προτάσει ὄνομα καὶ ῥῆμα.

[30] τὰ μέρη δὲ ἐξ ὧν σύγκεινται καλοῦμεν ὅρους ἑπόμενοι τῇ παλαιᾷ συνηθείᾳ· οἷον ἐν τῇ Δίων περιπατεῖ τόν τε Δίωνα καὶ τὸ περιπατεῖν, ὑποκείμενον ὅρον τὸν Δίωνα, κατηγορούμενον δὲ τὸ περιπατεῖν λαμβάνομεν. ὅταν μὲν οὖν ἐξ ὀνόματος ᾖ καὶ ῥήματος ἡ πρότασις, οὕτω χρὴ διαιρεῖν τοὺς ὅρους.—That is Kalbfleisch's text: it cannot be right; but whatever words Galen may have written, his meaning is not in doubt.

And Apuleius:

A proposition, as Plato says in the *Theaetetus*, consists of at least two of the parts of sayings, a name and a verb—for example:
Apuleius talks.
... Further, of those two aforesaid parts, one is called subject or subjective (as Apuleius) and the other declarative (as talks).

(*int* iv [191.16–192.8])[31]

'Dio walks' and 'Apuleius talks' each consists of a name and a verb. In each, the name is the subject and the verb the predicate.

The view persisted. It is summed up by Martianus Capella when he says that

a proposition has two parts: the one which consists in the name is subject, the one which consists in the verb is predicate.

(iv 393)[32]

And in Ammonius you may read this:

Those items which signify a nature or a person or an activity or a passivity or some combination of person with activity or passivity—all those Aristotle divides into names and verbs. He calls verbs those which are timed or which are predicated in propositions, and names those which are without time or which supply the need for subjects.

(*in Int* 12.16–20)[33]

Predicates and verbs are one, subjects and names are one.

Of course, no ancient philosopher really meant to say that every sub-ject–predicate proposition answers to a name–verb sentence, the subject being the name and the predicate the verb—that was quite clearly false. Rather, they meant to parrot Plato. Apuleius refers to the *Theaetetus*. (For '*in Theaeteto*' is the text which lies behind the nonsense transmitted by the manuscripts.) But he has confused the *Theaetetus* with the *Sophist*, in which Plato says this:

---

[31] *ceterum propositio, ut ait in Theaeteto Plato, duabus paucissimis orationis partibus constat, nomine et verbo, ut Apuleius disserit ... porro ex duabus praedictis partibus altera subiectiva nominatur velut subdita, ut Apuleius; altera declarativa, ut disserit.*

[32] *nam sunt proloquii partes duae: quae in nomine subiectiva dicitur, quae in verbo declarativa.*

[33] τὰ μὲν οὖν φύσεων ἢ προσώπων ἢ ἐνεργειῶν ἢ παθῶν ἢ ποιᾶς συμπλοκῆς προσώπου πρὸς ἐνέργειαν ἢ πάθος σημαντικὰ πάντα ὁ Ἀριστοτέλης εἰς ὀνόματα διαιρεῖ καὶ ῥήματα, τὰ μὲν κατὰ χρόνον λεγόμενα ἢ κατηγορούμενα ἐν ταῖς προτάσεσι ῥήματα καλῶν, τὰ δὲ ἄνευ χρόνου λεγόμενα ἢ τὴν χρείαν συμπληροῦντα τῶν ὑποκειμένων ὀνόματα.

—When someone says A man learns, you say that that is a saying of the smallest and primary sort?—Yes.—Yes, for it thereby shows something about what is, or is coming to be, or has come to be, or will come to be; and it doesn't just name but it achieves something, linking verbs to names.

(*Sophist*, 262cd)[34]

The primary and simplest propositions divide into name and verb; and it is in these cases—the elementary and the paradigmatic cases—that the later tradition declared the division into subject and predicate to be the same as the division into name and verb.

So consider some simple sentence—for example:

Bugles sang.

There is a verb there, and a name. The name is represented by the word 'bugles' and the verb by 'sang'. (But the name in the sentence is perhaps 'bugle' rather than 'bugles'; and the verb is perhaps 'sing' or 'to sing' rather than 'sang'.) There is also a subject and a predicate; and 'bugles' represents the subject, 'sang' the predicate. More generally, the simplest sentences consist of a single name and a single verb; they also consist of a subject and a predicate; and the subject is the name, the predicate the verb.

Here, then, is a clear case in which grammar and logic interacted with one another. But it is less clear whether grammar imposed itself on logic (as Frege grumbled) or logic on grammar (as de Saussure alleged). Indeed, you might be inclined to think that there was no imposition in either direction—merely a conflation. And a harmless conflation. For if the thesis about the simplest of sentences was sometimes carelessly advanced as though it applied to all sentences, and although such carelessness is deplorable, the thesis itself seems modest, and innocuous.

But it is false—or at least, any Peripatetic is obliged to judge it false. For in Aristotelian logic, subjects and predicates are homogenous, in the following sense: any item which may function as a predicate may function as a subject, and *vice versa*. That fact is a presupposition of the conversion rules of Aristotelian syllogistic, and the rules are a fundamental part of the syllogistic. Names and verbs, on the other hand, are heterogeneous: the slot occupied by a verb may not be occupied by a name, nor *vice versa*. If you interchange the name and the verb in

---

[34] —ὅταν εἴπῃ τις ἄνθρωπος μανθάνει, λόγον εἶναι φῂς τοῦτον ἐλάχιστόν τε καὶ πρῶτον;—ἔγωγε.—δηλοῖ γὰρ ἤδη που τότε περὶ τῶν ὄντων ἢ γιγνομένων ἢ γεγονότ- ων ἢ μελλόντων, καὶ οὐκ ὀνομάζει μόνον ἀλλά τι περαίνει, συμπλέκων τὰ ῥήματα τοῖς ὀνόμασι.

Bugles sang

you will get

Sang bugles,

or something similar; and such items are ill-formed. (To be sure, you might meet them in a piece of English; but then you would read them as poetic inversions.) Again, if you replace the verb by a name or the name by a verb you get ungrammatical nonsense, such as

Bugles trumpets

or

Blared sang.

But if you interchange the subject and the predicate of a proposition, the result—whether true or false—is well-formed. Likewise, if you replace the subject by a predicate—by an item which is a predicate in some other proposition—or the predicate by a subject—by an item which is a subject in some other proposition—then the result is again well-formed.

Since that is so, the predicate in

Bugles sang

is not 'sing' or 'to sing' or 'sang'. But then what is it? In the case of a sentence like

Hopes are dupes,

the question is readily answered: the two terms are 'hope' and 'dupe'. They are linked by the copulative 'is' which itself is not a term. The terms are homogeneous inasmuch as

Dupes are hopes

is well-formed. So the question may be put like this: How are we to find in

Bugles sang?

something like the copulative 'is'?

The traditional answer to that question is this: The copulative 'is' is already present in the sentence—potentially. Thus Ammonius remarks, of an Aristotelian thesis about negation, that

he shows this in the case of propositions which have 'is' potentially—for example, in the case of 'A man walks', he analyses 'walks' into the participle and 'is', and he leaves us to deduce that if in the case of the analysed proposition which has 'is' actually we make the negation by tying the denial to 'is', then in the case of the proposition which has 'is' potentially we shall have to tie the negative particle to the part of the proposition which contains 'is'.

(in Int 222.18–24)[35]

Aristotle actually said that

there is no difference between saying that a man walks and that a man is walking.

(Int 21b9–10)[36]

Aristotle's phrase 'there is no difference' is vague; but the later tradition not unreasonably took him to mean that 'A man is walking' makes actual or explicit what is merely potential or implicit in 'A man walks.'

There is no reason to question the equivalence which Aristotle and his followers proclaim—although it is perhaps worth insisting that the claim does not concern the English continuous present (for which, of course, it would be quite false) but rather a certain Greek paraphrastic idiom. So (the Greek for) 'sang' means the same as (the Greek for) 'was singing'; and in general 'VERBS' means the same as 'is VERBing'.

Aristotle makes the point again in the *Metaphysics*:

There is no difference between 'A man is ailing' and 'A man ails', nor between 'A man is walking' (or 'cutting') and 'A man walks' (or 'cuts'); and similarly in the other cases.

(Met 1017a27–30)[37]

Alexander comments thus:

He states that 'A man is ailing' signifies nothing other than 'A man ails'—i.e. the 'is', which is constructed with illness signifies nothing other than the holding of illness. Similarly in the case of 'walking', it signifies the holding of walking, in the case of 'cutting', it signifies the holding of cutting, and likewise in all cases. For as he said in

---

[35] τοῦτο οὖν καὶ ἐπὶ τῶν δυνάμει τὸ ἔστιν ἐχουσῶν οὕτως ἔχον ἐπιδείξας, οἷον τῆς ἄνθρωπος βαδίζει, τῷ ἀναλῦσαι τὸ βαδίζει εἰς τὴν μετοχὴν καὶ τὸ ἔστι καὶ καταλιπεῖν συλλογίζεσθαι ἡμῖν ὡς εἰ ἐπὶ τῆς ἀναλελυμένης προτάσεως καὶ ἐνεργείᾳ τὸ ἔστιν ἐχούσης αὐτῷ τῷ ἔστι συμπλέκοντες τὴν ἄρνησιν ποιοῦμεν τὴν ἀπόφασιν, δεήσει καὶ ἐπὶ τῆς κατὰ δύναμιν αὐτὸ ἐχούσης τῷ περιέχοντι αὐτὸ μορίῳ τῆς προτάσεως τὸ ἀποφατικὸν μόριον συμπλέκειν.

[36] οὐδὲν γὰρ διαφέρει εἰπεῖν ἄνθρωπον βαδίζειν ἢ ἄνθρωπον βαδίζοντα εἶναι.

[37] οὐθὲν γὰρ διαφέρει τὸ ἄνθρωπος ὑγιαίνων ἐστὶν ἢ τὸ ἄνθρωπος ὑγιαίνει, οὐδὲ τὸ ἄνθρωπος βαδίζων ἐστὶν ἢ τέμνων τοῦ ἄνθρωπος βαδίζει ἢ τέμνει· ὁμοίως δὲ καὶ ἐπὶ τῶν ἄλλων.

the *de Interpretatione*, in itself it is nothing, but it co-signifies a sort of composition which cannot exist without the items composed.

(*in Met* 371.30–36)[38]

If I say
    Bugles sing,
that signifies nothing other than
    Bugles are singing,
and there the verb 'are' signals that the activity of singing, which the participle 'singing' expresses, holds or is predicated of bugles.

But what good does that do us? After all, the analysis in terms of copula and participle does not introduce the desired homogeneity:
    Singing are bugles
—just like 'Sang bugles'—is either a poetical inversion or nonsense. Well, in Greek things are different. Or rather, with a little juggling they come to be different. And after all, a little juggling works wonders in English too. Translate Aristotle's analysed proposition not as 'A man is walking' but as 'A man is an item which walks.' In general, suppose that 'VERBS' means 'is an item which VERBS'. Then 'sang' means the same as 'is an item which was singing': it is, as it were, an amalgamation of a copulative 'is' and the nominal phrase 'an item which was singing'. The homogeneity is now guaranteed: any nominal phrase of the form 'an item which ...' may function in the subject place of a sentence and also in the predicate place. After all, bugles are bugles, and items which sang are items which sang.

To be sure, the copulative 'is' requires scrutiny. Is it—for example—a genuine verb which indicates a time? If not, then what is it? If so, then why not parse 'Bugles sang' as 'Bugles were singing items'? Why, in other words, should the copulative connector not indicate both a connection and a time of connection? That question will turn up briefly in a later context. Here it can be left to one side.

In the light of that, what is the relation between names and subjects, verbs and predicates? Or between Aristotelian grammar and Aristotelian logic? A partial answer to the question might run like this: In the simplest of sentences, which consist of one name and one verb, the name will be, or will correspond

---

[38] παρέθετο τὸ μηδὲν σημαίνειν ἄλλο τὸ ἄνθρωπος ὑγιαίνων ἐστὶν ἢ τὸ ἄνθρωπος ὑγιαίνει, τουτέστι τὸ ἔστιν, ὃ ἐπὶ τῇ ὑγείᾳ συντέτακται, μηδὲν ἄλλο ἢ τὴν τῆς ὑγείας ὕπαρξιν σημαίνει· ὁμοίως καὶ ἐπὶ τοῦ βαδίζων τὴν τῆς βαδίσεως, καὶ ἐπὶ τοῦ τέμνων τὴν τῆς τομῆς, καὶ ἐπὶ πάντων ὁμοίως. ὡς γὰρ εἶπεν ἐν τῷ Περὶ ἑρμηνείας, αὐτὸ μὲν οὐδέν ἐστι, προσσημαίνει δὲ σύνθεσίν τινα, ἣν ἄνευ τῶν συγκειμένων οὐχ οἷόν τε εἶναι.

to, the subject. No more adventurous or less partial answer will be both true and informative.

Antiquity did indeed offer a wholly general answer—but it is wholly boring. Ammonius explains that Aristotle uses the word 'verb' in three ways: it may mean pretty well what we and the ancient grammarians normally mean by 'verb'; it may designate a present indicative of what we and the ancient grammarians normally mean by 'verb'; and it may signify

> any expression which makes a predicate in a proposition; so that in this sense 'beautiful' and 'just' and 'white' and 'animal', when they are taken as predicated, are called verbs, which is not so in either of the two earlier senses.
>
> (in Int 53.5–8)[39]

So verbs and predicates are one and the same thing—provided that you take 'verb' to mean 'predicate' (and hence classify names as verbs). Whether or not Ammonius is right to discover such a use of the word 'verb' in the text of Aristotle, it is evident that the discovery can be of no substantive interest.

PORPHYREAN PREDICATES

Aristotelian subjects and predicates are mutually correlative items (in Greek, they are ἀντιστρέφοντα), names and verbs are not. A subject is a subject for a predicate and a predicate is a predicate of a subject. A name is not a name for a verb and a verb is not a verb of a name. Again, a predicate is a predicate of a subject in a proposition: a verb is not a verb of a name in a sentence—it is a verb full stop. (Names, of course, are relational items inasmuch as a name is a name of something. So they have their correlatives; but the correlative of a name is the item which it names, not a verb with which a sentence may associate it.) That correlativity not only distinguishes subjects and predicates from names and verbs: it also distinguishes Aristotelian predicates from Stoic predicates (and from the predicates of contemporary logic).

So subjects and predicates are relational items, and predication is a two-placed relation: 'x is predicated of y'. Subjection, in that case, is also and of course a two-placed relation: 'x is subjected to y'. Subjection is the converse of predication: x is subjected to y if and only if y is predicated of x. A

---

[39] ... ἢ πᾶσαν φωνὴν κατηγορούμενον ἐν προτάσει ποιοῦσαν, ὥστε κατὰ τοῦτο τὸ σημαινόμενον τὸ καλὸς καὶ δίκαιος καὶ λευκὸς καὶ ζῷον, ὅταν κατηγορούμενα ληφθῇ, ῥήματα λέγεσθαι, ὅπερ κατ' οὐδέτερον ἦν τῶν προτέρων σημαινομένων.

predicate is whatever is predicated of something—that is to say, 'x is a predicate' means 'x is predicated of something'; and a subject is whatever is subjected to something—'x is a subject' means 'x is subjected to something'. (In the same way, 'x is a parent' and 'x is a child' mean 'x has some offspring' and 'x is offsprung from something'.) It is sometimes said that you cannot coherently speak of subjects and predicates *simpliciter*—that you cannot ask, say, if the term 'llama' is a predicate or not. After all, a subject is always a subject of something, and a predicate a predicate of something. That is true; but it is a half truth: you can coherently ask of an item if it is a predicate, or a subject, just as you can coherently ask of an item if it is a parent, or a child.

'x is predicated of y' is a passive construction. In speaking of predication Aristotle and his successors most often use the verb 'κατηγορεῖν', in the passive. It is followed by a genitive, or by 'κατά' + genitive: 'τὸ Α κατηγορεῖται (κατὰ) τοῦ Β'. There are other locutions; and often enough, especially in technical expositions, the verb is elided, so that 'τὸ Α τοῦ Β' means 'A is predicated of B'. (In speaking of subjection the Peripatetics use 'ὑποκεῖσθαι', which takes a dative: 'τὸ Α ὑποκεῖται τῷ Β'. Other formulas are found; but they are rare—and in fact 'ὑποκεῖσθαι' is itself far rarer than 'κατηγορεῖσθαι'.) The verb 'predicate' also has an active use, in Greek as in English. Thus you may say that a sentence, or a proposition, predicates one item of another; and you may say that a speaker, or a thinker, predicates something of something. Very roughly speaking, a sentence or a speaker predicates x of y if and only if what it or he says is true if and only if x is predicated of y. And we may suppose that a speaker or thinker predicates x of y if and only if he produces or entertains a sentence or a proposition which predicates x of y. A predicable, you might then say, is something which a sentence or a speaker might predicate of something, and a subjectible is something which a sentence or a speaker might subject to something. In Peripatetic logic, an item is a predicable if and only if it is a subjectible. That is another way of expressing the homogeneity of subjects and predicates.

If predication is a two-place relation it invites a few elementary questions: Is it a reflexive relation? Is it symmetrical? Transitive? And so on. If you can't answer such questions, then you haven't got the second idea about the relation. But in the case of predication the matter is better postponed.

For first, I want to raise the following question: What sorts of things are subjects and predicates? What are the relata of the relation of predication? If x is predicated of y, then what kind of items must x and y be? The preceding pages have vacillated, and the matter demands examination.

It was much discussed in late antiquity, and it was discussed in a particular context. For the term 'predicate' first met the student philosopher in the pages—or more precisely, on the title-page—of the first component of the Peripatetic *Organon*. The title under which that little essay generally goes in English, namely '*Categories*', is not a translation but a quasi-transliteration of the standard Greek title; and that title, 'Κατηγορίαι' means '*Predications*'. (Latin writers generally used '*Praedicamenta*'.) As ancient scholars saw things, the words 'subject' and 'predicate' were technical terms of Peripatetic logic. To be sure, the words in question were not Aristotelian neologisms; for Aristotle was not a great neologizer. But Aristotle had given them new senses, and the senses needed explanation. No doubt the terminology had ventured beyond the borders of Aristotelianism; but nonetheless, it was at bottom Peripatetic, and it had to be mastered—or at any rate, first approached—within the context of the Peripatetic philosophy. It needed explaining as soon as a student opened the *Predications*—and where better to look for the elements of an explanation than in the essay itself?

So what—according to the *Predications* or *Categories*—are predicates and subjects? An ancient commentator on the essay would first tell you that Aristotle took the term 'κατηγορεῖν' from the law-courts, where it meant 'to accuse (someone of something)' or 'to impute (something to someone)'. The imputation went in the accusative, the imputee in the genitive. So an indignant Demosthenes refers to an enemy as

he who, o earth and gods, imputes philippism to me ...

(*cor* 294)[40]

The imputation or predicate is philippism, the imputee or subject is Demosthenes.

Next, the ancient commentator would remind you that there are in principle three possible answers to the question 'What are predicates?': 'They are words'; 'They are thoughts'; 'They are things.' He would explain how each answer was confronted by insuperable objections—and then he would pull a rather tatty rabbit from his hat: 'Predicates are words insofar as they are used to signify things by way of thoughts.' So each of the three possible answers is partially correct.

---

[40] ὃς γὰρ ἐμοῦ φιλιππισμόν, ὦ γῆ καὶ θεοί, κατηγορεῖ ...

The rabbit was generally fathered on Porphyry. Here is a passage from Dexippus' set of questions and answers on the *Categories*—a work which is largely cribbed from Porphyry:

The predicates are not the entities themselves but the expressions which signify the thoughts and the objects. When they say
    Animal is predicated of man
they say that the expression significant of animal—which is the name animal—is predicated of the thought signified by the expression man and of the object which is subject to that thought; for being predicated is a property of significant utterances which signify thoughts and objects.

(*in Cat* 10.25–32)[41]

Animals are not predicated, nor are thoughts of animals or the concept of an animal: what is predicated is the word 'animal'. But not every word can be predicated: not the word 'blityri', for example, because though it is a word, it has no sense; not the words 'often' or 'and' or 'through', for example, because although they are words endowed with senses, they do not signify anything. (What does that mean? An answer will emerge in a later context.)

The question 'What sort of item is a predicate?', and hence Dexippus' answer to it, were developed in terms of a sketchy semantic theory which ancient scholars discovered in the first few lines of Aristotle's *de Interpretatione*. According to that theory, the word 'animal' stands for or means, primarily, the thought or concept of an animal—or perhaps the thought or concept of an animal which is in the soul of the man from whose mouth the word 'animal' emerges. That thought or concept fortunately resembles animals or an animal. And so the word 'animal' signifies, derivatively, animals.

But is not that theory quite ridiculous? And must not any account of predication which is based upon it be hooted or booted off the philosophical stage? Yes; and No. For although the Porphyrean account of predication was conceived and presented in terms of a certain set of semantic ideas, and although those ideas—whether or not they are Aristotelian—are indeed laughably inept, nonetheless the account of predication is in fact independent of the ideas. After all, the account amounts (so far) to no more than this:

---

[41] οὐκ αὐτὰ οὖν τὰ ὄντα αἱ κατηγορίαι, ἀλλ' αἱ σημαίνουσαι λέξεις τὰ νοήματα καὶ τὰ πράγματα. ὅταν γὰρ λέγωσι τὸ ζῷον κατὰ τοῦ ἀνθρώπου κατηγορεῖται, λέγουσιν ὅτι ἡ σημαντικὴ λέξις τοῦ ζῴου, ἥτις ἐστὶ τὸ ζῷον ὄνομα, κατὰ τοῦ σημαινομένου νοήματος ὑπὸ τῆς ἄνθρωπος λέξεως καὶ τοῦ ὑποκειμένου τούτῳ πράγματος κατηγορεῖται· τὸ γὰρ κατηγορεῖσθαι τῶν σημαντικῶν φωνῶν ἦν ἴδιον, αἳ σημαίνουσι τὰ νοήματα καὶ τὰ πράγματα.

predicates are a sort of significant expression. To that you may attach whatever theory of signification pleases you—or no theory at all.

However that may be, the Porphyrean account of predication was generally—if not universally—accepted in late antiquity. And of course it must have commended itself to anyone who thought that, at least in the simplest cases, the predicate of a sentence is its verb; for verbs are significant expressions. But if the Porphyrean account triumphed in antiquity, not many modern Aristotelians will be found to support it. After all, it goes flatly against numerous texts in which Aristotle clearly takes predicates to be something other than expressions.

Here are a couple of familiar examples, the first from the *de Interpretatione* and the second from the *Prior Analytics*:

> Of objects, some are universal and some particular—by universal I mean such as can be predicated of several items and by particular such as cannot (for example, man is a universal and Callias a particular).
>
> (*Int* 17a38–b1)[42]

Objects, or πράγματα, come in two sizes, and what makes the difference is their predicability: that is to say, here it is objects and not expressions which are supposed to be predicated. Or again:

> Of all the things which there are, some are such that they are not predicated truly and universally of anything else (e.g. Cleon, Callias—whatever is individual and perceptible) but other items are predicated of them (each of the two, after all, is a man and an animal). Other things are themselves predicated of other items and yet nothing else is earlier predicated of them. Yet further things both are themselves predicated of other items and have other items predicated of them (e.g. man of Callias and animal of man).
>
> (*APr* 43a25–32)[43]

Aristotle is classifying 'the things which there are'—entities or τὰ ὄντα: it is among existent things, and not among expressions which apply to existent things, that he locates predicates.

---

[42] ἐπεὶ δέ ἐστι τὰ μὲν καθόλου τῶν πραγμάτων τὰ δὲ καθ' ἕκαστον—λέγω δὲ καθόλου μὲν ὃ ἐπὶ πλειόνων πέφυκε κατηγορεῖσθαι, καθ' ἕκαστον δὲ ὃ μή, οἷον ἄνθρωπος μὲν τῶν καθόλου Καλλίας δὲ τῶν καθ' ἕκαστον.

[43] ἁπάντων δὴ τῶν ὄντων τὰ μέν ἐστι τοιαῦτα ὥστε κατὰ μηδενὸς ἄλλου κατηγορεῖσθαι ἀληθῶς καθόλου (οἷον Κλέων καὶ Καλλίας καὶ τὸ καθ' ἕκαστον καὶ αἰσθητόν), κατὰ δὲ τούτων ἄλλα (καὶ γὰρ ἄνθρωπος καὶ ζῷον ἑκάτερος τούτων ἐστί)· τὰ δ' αὐτὰ μὲν κατ' ἄλλων κατηγορεῖται, κατὰ δὲ τούτων ἄλλα πρότερον οὐ κατηγορεῖται· τὰ δὲ καὶ αὐτὰ ἄλλων καὶ αὐτῶν ἕτερα (οἷον ἄνθρωπος Καλλίου καὶ ἀνθρώπου ζῷον).

So the Porphyrean account of predication, whatever its philosophical credentials, is not a faithful account of Aristotelian predication.

Before I answer, on Porphyry's behalf, that seemingly definitive objection, there is another and less daunting obstacle which needs to be confronted. Dexippus says that in

Animal is predicated of man

the predicate 'is predicated of the thought signified by the expression man and of the object which is subject to that thought'. There the phrase 'the object which is subject to that thought' gives the Greek 'τὸ ὑποκείμενον τούτῳ πρᾶγμα'—and that looks for all the world as though it is just a longwinded way of saying 'the subject'. In any event, whereas Dexippus insists that predicates are expressions, the items of which they are predicated are said to be not expressions but thoughts or objects. There are any number of ancient texts in which it is taken for granted that you predicate things of objects and not of expressions, and hence that subjects are objects and not names of objects (except, of course, in the special case in which the object is itself a name).

And after all, the subject of a sentence is surely what the sentence is about, and sentences are generally about things rather than about their names:

Charlie is me darling

says something about a prince, not about his Christian name. True, you can talk about significant expressions, for example:

Constantinople is a very long word

is about the name of a city and not about a city. But just as it is not Charlie but the name 'Charlie' which is a part of the sentence

Charlie is me darling,

in the same way—or so the logicians assure us—it is not the name of the city but a name of that name which features in the sentence

Constantinople is a very long word.

And apart from a few oddities—such as

'Sentence' is the last word in this sentence

—sentences are not about their own parts.

So, if Dexippus is right, then on the Porphyrean account of predication, subjects are one sort of thing and predicates another. But in that case it cannot be a true account of Aristotelian predication: it breaks on the fact that Aristotelian subjects and Aristotelian predicates are homogenous: any item which is a predicate may also be a subject, any item which is a subject may also be a predicate.

That is indeed an obstacle to Porphyry's account—or to the Dexippan version of the account; but it is not an insuperable obstacle. For there are several ways of surmounting it. You might, for example, construe a term not as an expression but rather as an ordered pair consisting of a significant expression and its extension.[44] Then if x is <'A', A> and y is <'B', B>, x is predicated of y if and only if 'A' holds good of B. Needless to say, there is nothing like that in any ancient text. Rather, an ancient Porphyrean would maintain that, just as predicates are significant expressions, so too are subjects. Such a view is present in all those authors who claim that, at least in the simplest cases, it is names which are the subjects of sentences. And there are several ancient texts in which it is explicitly stated that the subject of this or that proposition is an expression. No doubt it is, so to speak, natural to think of a subject—especially if it is called a ὑποκείμενον or underlying item—as if it were something external to the sentence in which it receives a predicate; and the ancients frequently fell into that natural way of thinking. But it was a fall: their theory virtually required them to take subjects to be expressions—and when they thought about the matter, they did.

In that case, does it not follow that all predicative sentences are about significant expressions? And is that not absurd? It is absurd; but it does not follow. What follows is that a subject of a sentence is not an item about which the sentence has something to say: at best, it is a significant expression which indicates an item about which the sentence has something to say.

But if the requirement of homogeneity may be met by insisting that subjects as well as predicates are significant expressions, what about the first of the two objections to Porphyry's account—the objection that it doesn't fit the Aristotelian texts? It must now appear even more formidable; for if it is hard to accommodate linguistic predicates to the texts, surely it is even harder to accommodate linguistic subjects? When, for example, Aristotle distinguishes in the *Categories* between items which are said of a subject and items which are in a subject, the subjects are not expressions. White, he says, is in a subject—namely, a body. He does not mean that the word 'white' is in the word 'body', but that the colour white is in that bag of bones.

Porphyry was aware of the objection. The very posing of the question 'What sort of item is an Aristotelian predicate?' suggests that the matter is not immediately clear; and Porphyry knew that the various candidate answers

---

[44] This possibility was brought to my attention by Otto Bruun.

could each appeal to textual evidence. Here, then, is his brief answer to the objection:

—If the work is about significant utterances, how does it come about that the whole of the later discussion is about objects?
—Because expressions, like announcers, announce the objects, and they take their differences from the objects which they announce.

                                                        (*in Cat* 58.21–24)[45]

Since expressions take their pertinent differences from, or are classified according to, the sorts of object which they signify, you may easily talk about predicates as though they were not the expressions which signify objects but the objects which are signified by expressions. So although Aristotle does often talk of predicates as if they were objects, that is no objection to Porphyry's thesis that predicates are expressions; for objects are, or can be called, predicates just insofar as their names are predicates. Is white—the colour white—predicated of a well-laundered shirt? No, of course not; for predicates are expressions and the colour white is not an expression. And yet also Yes, if you like—you may say that the colour is predicated of the shirt inasmuch as the expression 'white' is predicated of the shirt (or of 'the shirt') and the expression 'white' signifies the colour white.

Well, it will be said, there argues a commentator desperate to defend his own interpretation against a definitive textual objection. True. But there are definitive textual objections to any interpretation. After all, Porphyry has—and produces—impeccable evidence in favour of his own interpretation and therefore against any rival account. He points out, for example, that

if Aristotle had been talking about objects, he would not have said 'Either they signify substances …': objects do not signify—they are signified.

                                                        (*in Cat* 57.10–12)[46]

Porphyry is right—and he can cite half a dozen other passages in the same direction.

The textual situation looks like this. Most of the numerous passages in which Aristotle discusses or alludes to subjects and predicates offer no clear

---

[45] —ἀλλὰ πῶς, εἰ περὶ φωνῶν σημαντικῶν ἐστιν ἡ πραγματεία, ἐν τοῖς ἑξῆς περὶ τῶν πραγμάτων ὁ πᾶς αὐτῷ γεγένηται λόγος;—ὅτι αἱ φωναὶ ἀγγέλῳ ἐοικυῖαι τὰ πράγματα ἀγγέλλουσιν, ἀπὸ δὲ τῶν πραγμάτων ὧν ἀγγέλλουσι τὰς διαφορὰς λαμβάνουσιν.

[46] εἰ γὰρ περὶ πραγμάτων ἦν αὐτῷ ὁ λόγος, οὐκ ἂν εἶπεν τὸ ἤτοι οὐσίαν σημαίνει· οὐ γὰρ σημαίνουσι τὰ πράγματα ἀλλὰ σημαίνεται.

answer one way or another to the question 'What sort of item is a predicate?'.
(You wouldn't expect the texts to do so.) Several texts quite plainly indicate
that Aristotle took objects, and not significant expressions, to be predicates
and subjects. Several texts quite plainly indicate that Aristotle took significant
expressions, and not objects, to be subjects and predicates. That is to say,
Aristotle was muddled or inconsistent when he thought about the status of
predicates and subjects; or rather (what comes in the end to the same thing),
Aristotle probably never thought very long about the status of the things.

Anyone who determines to think about the matter on Aristotle's behalf
will be confronted by a number of pertinent considerations of very different
sorts. One such consideration starts from Dexippus' example,

Animal is predicated of man.

There the first word represents the predicate and the last the subject. The
particular example is taken from the *Categories*; but it occurs again and again
in the *Analytics*; and in general, when the *Analytics* offers illustrative terms
they are usually conveyed by words like 'animal', 'man', 'white', ... Roughly
speaking, they are conveyed by words which will make a verbal phrase when
they are prefixed by 'is (a)'.

Dexippus' illustrative sentence, and sentences like it, are so much part of
the jargon of traditional logic that we are inclined to think that we understand
them. But what on earth does

Animal is predicated of man

mean? The sentence—or at least, its English version—looks ungrammatical,
or babu. Perhaps it is comparable to

Animal is eaten by man

—which might just be construed as an off-colour way of saying that some
or all animals are used as human fodder. The Greek, in fact, admits that
construal less unwillingly than the English; for in the Greek the word 'animal'
is preceded by the definite article ('τὸ ζῷον'), and in Greek as in English the
definite article may indicate universality ('The triangle has an angle-sum of
180°'). In that case, Dexippus' sentence means that every animal is predicated
of man.

But that interpretation cannot be correct. You can do all sorts of things to
animals, legal and illegal; but one thing you can't do is predicate them. It is
terms which are predicated, and animals are not terms. And if that objection
is deemed unsatisfactory, then recall that

Animal is predicated of man

is supposed to convey a truth. Now

All animals are predicated of man

presumably entails that

Zebras are predicated of man.

And that—whatever it may mean—is surely not true.

Rather, if the Dexippan sentence is to be understood, then its first word must be taken as a singular term. Perhaps, then, 'animal' stands for 'animality', or for 'being an animal', or for 'to be an animal', or for some other such abstract expression? After all, it was philippism—or being a partisan of Philip—which was so scandalously imputed to or predicated of Demosthenes. That construal fits well with some of the Aristotelian texts, and it is in many ways attractive. When I say that Jeoffry is grey, I say something of him, namely that he is grey; that is to say, I predicate being grey of him—or I predicate greyness of him. Such things trip neatly off the tongue.

But the construal has its drawbacks. First, and most obviously, it is difficult to see why Aristotle should have written 'animal' and 'white' and the like if he really meant 'animality' and 'being white' and the like.

Secondly, the requirement of homogeneity will not be met unless subjects as well as predicates are taken as abstract objects. So the sentence

Animal is predicated of man

will come out as, say,

Animality is predicated of humanity.

But what could that mean? Like the Platonic sentence

Man participates in animality,

the Aristotelian sentence

Animal is predicated of man

is intended somehow to reveal the truth, or an aspect of the truth, which is conveyed by the ordinary sentence

Men are animals.

But, like the genuine Platonic sentence, the pseudo-Aristotelian sentence

Animality is predicated of humanity

is at best an inflated and an obscure way of saying that men are animals.

The Porphyrean account of predication takes the first word of the Dexippan sentence as a singular term—it is a name of an expression. In

Animal is predicated of man

the word 'animal' occurs autonomously; and that is, of course, a perfectly normal piece of English (and of Greek). Homogeneity then requires the same treatment for 'man'; but, again, that does not unduly force the Greek.

I do not claim (and neither did Porphyry) that the Porphyrean account represents what Aristotle said; I do not claim (though Porphyry did) that it represents what Aristotle really meant to say or what he ought to have said. Rather, I make a doubly conditional claim, thus: if, first, the homogeneity requirement is to be met and subjects and predicates are to be items of the same sort, and if, secondly, the general notion of predication is to be understood in the same way in the *Categories* and in the *Analytics* (and throughout the *Organon*), then the Porphyrean account of predication is at least as good as any other account. The two conditions are not independent of one another. If the second condition is met and predication is uniform across the *Organon*, then the first condition must also be met; for the syllogistic of the *Analytics* demands homogeneity. The second condition will be accepted—insisted upon—by anyone who takes the *Organon* to constitute a unified treatment of logic. And even for those of us who know that the *Organon* was a botch, the second condition must be at least mildly enticing: after all, Aristotle never indicates that he changed his mind about predication, or that he worked with different conceptions of predication in different contexts.

PROBLEMS FOR PORPHYRY

Predication is a relation between a pair of terms in a proposition; and, on the Porphyrean account of the matter, terms and propositions are linguistic items, so that predication is a relation between a pair of expressions in a sentence. In the sentence

Full fathom five thy father lies,

something is said of something, a term is predicated of a term, the expression 'an item which lies five fathoms deep' is predicated of the expression 'thy father'. So the sentence might be compared to what I shall call its Porphyrean partner, namely

'an item which lies five fathoms deep' is predicated of 'thy father'.

In general, any sentence in which something is said of something will have a Porphyrean partner which says what item it says of what item.

What is the relation between a sentence and its Porphyrean partner? Inasmuch as the partner purports to analyse the sentence, or to make explicit what the sentence leaves implicit, you might be tempted to think that the two things must be very close to one another; more particularly, you might be tempted to think that a Porphyrean partner ought to have the same structure as its mate, and that it ought to be logically equivalent to its mate. But it looks as though a Porphyrean partner has a different structure from its mate—it is explicitly relational whereas its mate is not. And it looks as though a Porphyrean partner is not equivalent to its mate—it implies various things about linguistic expressions whereas its mate does not. There are, it seems, two problems for Porphyry: they indicate that Porphyrean partners are too distant from their mates, and they thereby suggest that the Porphyrean account of predication must be called into doubt.

As far as identity of structure goes, it has been pointed out that Porphyrean partners, like their mates, have a subject–predicate structure or say something of something. Thus the sentence

'an item which lies five fathoms deep' is predicated of 'thy father'

predicates 'an item predicated of 'thy father'' of ''an item which lies five fathoms deep''. In general, any sentence of the form 'x is predicated of y' says something of something: it predicates 'an item predicated of y' of 'x'. But that observation does not go very far—indeed it hardly leaves the starting-gates. For the problem is not that the Porphyrean partner lacks a structure which its mate possesses: rather, it is that the partner has a structure which its mate lacks. The Porphyrean partner has a relational structure—insofar as predication is a two-placed relation. The sentence

Full fathom five thy father lies

is not relational (or at any rate, it is not relational in the pertinent way). A Platonist might demur, alleging that the real form of the sentence comes out from a paraphrase such as

Thy father participates in being-at-a-depth-of-five-full-fathoms

But that way madness lies, and an infinite regression.

In any case, there is a far better way of dealing with the matter. It is true that the Porphyrean sentence

'an item which lies five fathoms deep' is predicated of 'thy father'

has a relational structure. And from that indisputable fact we are invited to infer that, if the partnership is genuine, then its mate

Full fathom five thy father lies,

must also have a relational structure. But why make the inference? Here is a rough parallel. In the sentence

The weeping Pleiads wester and I lie down alone,

'the weeping Pleiads wester' is conjoined with 'I lie down alone'. Now the sentence

'the weeping Pleiads wester' is conjoined with 'I lie down alone' expresses a relation—and a relation between two linguistic items. Must we infer that

The weeping Pleiads wester and I lie down alone

also expresses a relation between two linguistic items? Of course not: how can we infer something evidently false from two palpable truths? The moral is this: a sentence which explicates the structure of a given sentence need not itself have the structure which it explicates. Why ever think that it ought to?

This point, or something fairly close to it, was acknowledged in antiquity. According to Alexander,

the later thinkers, attending to expressions and not to meanings, deny that the same thing comes about when terms are replaced by equipollent expressions. For although 'If A, B' means the same as 'B follows A',

they claim that those two sorts of expression have different logical characters (*in APr* 373.29–32).[47] The claim made by the later thinkers will be addressed in a later chapter. Here I cite the passage to show that Alexander took two sentences with very different syntactical structures to have the same sense.

Alexander's remark is echoed in Apollonius Dyscolus, who reports that

Trypho says that items which are replaced do not necessarily fall into the same species—the verb 'follows' is replaced by the connector 'if':

Its being light follows its being day

—that is the same as

If it is day, it is light.

(*conj* 220.7–10)[48]

The point is not made very cleanly; but the general message is plain. Nor is it an isolated remark. Elsewhere, where he is arguing against the suggestion that articles are a form of pronoun, Apollonius has this to say:

It is feeble to say that articles are used in place of pronouns and for that reason form a single part of sayings with them. For first, it is not the case that if one item is taken in place of another, then it is for that reason the same as it. ... The conditional connector 'if' has the same force as the verb 'follows':

---

[47] οἱ δὲ νεώτεροι ταῖς λέξεσιν ἐπακολουθοῦντες οὐκέτι δὲ τοῖς σημαινομένοις οὐ ταὐτόν φασι γίνεσθαι ἐν ταῖς εἰς τὰς ἰσοδυναμούσας λέξεις μεταλήψεσι τῶν ὅρων. ταὐτὸν γὰρ σημαίνοντος τοῦ εἰ τὸ Α, τὸ Β τῷ ἀκολουθεῖν τῷ Α τὸ Β, ...

[48] καί φησι Τρύφων ὡς οὐ πάντως τὰ μεταλαμβανόμενα εἰς τὸ αὐτὸ εἶδος ἐπάγεται. τὸ ἀκολουθεῖ ῥῆμα μετάληψιν ἔχει τὴν εἰς τὸν εἰ σύνδεσμον· ἀκολουθεῖ τῷ ἡμέραν εἶναι τὸ φῶς εἶναι· ἴσον γὰρ τῷ εἰ ἡμέρα ἐστί, φῶς ἐστίν.

Its being light follows its being day.
If it is day, it is light.

(*pron* 7.8–15)[49]

A couple of sentences may have the same force or sense and yet display different syntactical structures.

The conditional sentence

If it is day, it is light

says that 'It is light' follows from 'It is day', so that it has what I may call an Apollonian partner, namely

'It is light' follows from 'It is day'.

Every conditional sentence has its Apollonian partner. The partner has a relational structure, being of the form 'x follows from y'. The conditional sentence itself does not have a relational structure. Apollonius rightly finds nothing odd about that; and we should find nothing odd about the fact that Porphyrean partners are relational while their mates are not.

That is surely true; and it is perhaps quite uncontroversially true that equivalent sentences need not have all their structures in common. But the second problem for Porphyry remains; for surely a Porphyrean partner and its mate are not logically equivalent to one another? (Nor, come to that, do Apollonian partners and their mates form logically equivalent couples.) The sentence

Full fathom five thy father lies

does not imply anything about any relations between significant expressions, whereas the Porphyrean partner,

'an item which lies five fathoms deep' is predicated of 'thy father'

entails that at least one linguistic expression is predicated of another linguistic expression. The Porphyrean sentence is true only if the expression "thy father" designates something—and designates a linguistic expression. Its mate is true only if 'thy father' designates something (and designates a man); but the truth of the mate does not require that "thy father" designate anything—indeed, it does not require that there be such an expression as "thy father". Two sentences which have different implications are not equivalent to one another. So a Porphyrean partner is not equivalent to its mate. (Nor is an Apollonian partner equivalent to its mate.)

---

[49] κἀκεῖνο δ' εὔηθες τὸ λέγειν ἄρθρα ἀντὶ ἀντωνυμιῶν καὶ διὰ τοῦτο ἓν μέρος λόγου. πρῶτον οὐκ εἴ τι ἀντί τινος παραλαμβάνεται, εὐθέως ταὐτὸν ἐκείνῳ ἐστίν. ... καὶ ὁ εἰ συναπτικὸς ἰσοδυναμεῖ τῷ ἀκολουθεῖ ῥήματι· ἀκολουθεῖ τῷ ἡμέραν εἶναι καὶ φῶς εἶναι—εἰ ἡμέρα ἐστί, φῶς ἐστί.

It is tempting to reply to that argument along the following lines. Philosophers of a certain persuasion have long been fond of what they call T-sentences. The 'T' stands for truth. The familiar example of a T-sentence is

'Snow is white' is true if and only if snow is white.

The general form of a T-sentence is this:

S is true if and only if P.

Such equivalences are the theorems of the only respectable theory of truth, and they form the heart of the only serious theory of meaning.

Now the pertinent Shakespearean T-sentence guarantees that

Full fathom five thy father lies

is equivalent to

'Full fathom five thy father lies' is true.

But that is equivalent to

'item which lies five fathoms deep' is true of what 'thy father' is true of.

And that, in turn—to anticipate a later contention—is equivalent to

'item which lies five fathoms deep' is predicated of 'thy father'.

So the Porphyrean partner is in fact demonstrably equivalent to its mate.

Of course, anyone who rejects the equivalence will hesitate at the very first step in the argument. After all,

'Full fathom five thy father lies' is true

entails that there exists at least one sentence, whereas the Shakespearean line does not—so those two items are not equivalent. And quite generally, T-sentences do not express logical equivalences; that familiar proposition,

'Snow is white' is true if and only if snow is white

is true; but it is not a truth of logic—still less, despite what tiros often incautiously think, is it an empty tautology: it is a contingent truth, an empirical truth, a truth which is underwritten by certain facts about English usage.

That is the indisputable truth about T-sentences. But it is something which should hearten rather than depress the Porphyreans. They may, after all, claim that the equivalence

'an item which lies five fathoms deep' is predicated of 'thy father' if and only if full fathom five thy father lies

is not a logical but an empirical truth, which has the same status as the T-sentence

'Full fathom five thy father lies' is true if and only if thy father lies full fathom five.

There is no reason why the Porphyreans, or anyone else, should want more than that.

COMPLEX PREDICATIONS

However all that may be, the ancient commentator on the *Categories*, will state, with a bow to Porphyry, that predicates are significant expressions. But significant expressions come in several varieties, and the commentator will next ask what sort of expressions predicates are. To that question there was a standard answer: Predicates are simple significant expressions. In discussing predicates of quantity and the difficulty of finding any genuine examples of the things, Plotinus observed that

after all, three oxen are not a quantity—rather, their number is. For three oxen are thereby two predications—and in the same way a line thus-and-so long is two predications, and a surface thus-and-so large is two.

(*enn* vi i 4.[17–20])[50]

When the poet, contemplating the infant's grave, cries
       'Tis three feet long and two feet wide
surely he has predicated something of something? And if predicates are significant expressions, then presumably he has predicated 'three feet long and two feet wide' of something. According to Plotinus, that is not so; or at any rate, it is not so strictly speaking. For although in uttering
       'Tis three feet long and two feet wide
the poet has indeed done some predication, he has predicated several items rather than one. Perhaps it is evident that he has predicated both 'three feet long' and also 'two feet wide'. But Plotinus will go further than that. At any rate, if 'three oxen are thereby two predicates', then 'three feet long' must be two (or three) predicates; so that in saying
       'Tis three feet long
the poet predicates both 'three feet' and also 'long' of something—or perhaps he predicates 'three' and 'feet' and 'long' of something.

      That, for several reasons, is what we might call moderately satisfactory only. And since Plotinus was absolutely right when he argued that predicates

---

[50] ἐπεὶ οὐδὲ τοὺς τρεῖς βοῦς ποσόν, ἀλλὰ τὸν ἐπ᾽ αὐτοῖς ἀριθμόν· βόες γὰρ τρεῖς δύο κατηγορίαι ἤδη. οὕτως οὖν καὶ γραμμὴ τοσήδε δύο κατηγορίαι, καὶ ἐπιφάνεια τοσήδε δύο.

in the Aristotelian class of quantity are puzzling items, let me turn to a different poet and an easier sort of example:

The mouse is a creature of great personal valour.

There—Plotinus would have urged—are (at least) two predicates; for the sentence, or its user, predicates (at least) two different things of 'mouse', namely 'creature' and 'of great personal valour'. Why so? Why not say that the predicate is 'creature of great personal valour', or 'brave beast'? The answer lies in the *Categories*. There Aristotle distinguishes ten types or classes of predicate. The division was taken to be exhaustive and exclusive: an item is a predicate if and only if it is a member of exactly one of the ten classes. (In truth, there were rumblings about exclusivity—but they do not concern the present point.) But 'brave beast' belongs to none of the ten classes. True, 'brave' is a predicate in the class of quality, and 'beast' is a predicate in the class of substance; but 'brave beast' is neither in quality nor in substance—nor anywhere else. Hence it is not a predicate; that is to say, it is not one predicate but several predicates.

Then what is to be done with such items? They cannot simply be disregarded by the logician. After all, they may occur in seemingly decent Aristotelian syllogisms:

The mouse is a creature of great personal valour, and brave beasts die young—so there are no old mice.

So, as well as being two predicates, 'brave beast' is perhaps also, in a way, a single predicate—a single complex predicate? Aristotle once or twice mentions what he calls conjoined predicates. For example:

That this holds of that, and that this is true of that, should be taken in as many ways as the predications have been divided—and those either with a certain qualification or simply, and again either simple or conjoined. Similarly for not holding. We must look into that and distinguish it better.

(*APr* 49a6–10)[51]

Alexander comments as follows:

And again, they should be predicated either simply and without composition—i.e. a single item which belongs to a single predication—or else conjoined and combined. For

---

[51] τὸ δ' ὑπάρχειν τόδε τῷδε καὶ τὸ ἀληθεύεσθαι τόδε κατὰ τοῦδε τοσαυταχῶς ληπτέον ὁσαχῶς αἱ κατηγορίαι διῄρηνται· καὶ ταύτας ἢ πῇ ἢ ἁπλῶς, ἔτι ἢ ἁπλᾶς ἢ συμπεπλεγμένας· ὁμοίως δὲ καὶ τὸ μὴ ὑπάρχειν. ἐπισκεπτέον δὲ ταῦτα καὶ διοριστέον βέλτιον.

Socrates is a man

has a single predicate, while

Socrates is a white man

or

Socrates talks sitting down

are compound and conjoined. ... Aristotle discusses this in the *de Interpretatione*, and Theophrastus—at greater length—in his *On Affirmation*.

(*in APr* 367.3–14)[52]

We do not know what Theophrastus said on the matter. As for Aristotle, Alexander is thinking of a passage in Chapter 11 of the *de Interpretatione* which obscures rather than illuminates.

Nonetheless, compounded predicates are recognized in the Peripatetic tradition, and a few later texts discuss the issue. It was generally supposed that conjunction is the paradigmatic way of producing a compound predicate. Such conjunction may be done either with or without a conjoining particle. If I say

Al Burlap was tough and brawly,

the conjunctive predicate 'tough and brawly' is formed by placing 'and' between two simple predicates. If I add

He was a fork-lift-truck-driving man,

the conjunctive predicate 'fork-lift-truck-driving man' is formed without the aid of such a connector. Now in principle, a conjunctive predicate is no more than the conjunction of two or more simple predicates, so that the predication of a compound predicate may be construed as the conjunction of two or more predications of simple predicates. Thus

Al Burlap was tough and brawly,

is equivalent to, or perhaps even an abbreviated form of,

Al Burlap was tough and Al Burlap was brawly.

So, in a straightforward way, the compound predicate 'tough and brawly' is, as Plotinus would have put it, two predicates.

Some compound predicates may indeed be analysed after that conjunctive fashion. But it must be avowed that the analysis does not greatly help the Aristotelian logician. The mouse syllogism used the compound predicate 'brave beast'; and you might allow that 'So-and-so is a brave beast' is equivalent

---

[52] ἔτι δὲ ἢ ἁπλῶς τε καὶ ἄνευ συνθέσεως κατηγορητέον, τοῦτ' ἔστιν ἕν τι καὶ μιᾶς κατηγορίας, ἢ συμπεπλεγμένα τε καὶ συγκείμενα· ἡ μὲν γὰρ Σωκράτης ἄνθρωπός ἐστιν ἁπλοῦν ἔχει τὸ κατηγορούμενον, ἡ δὲ λέγουσα Σωκράτης ἄνθρωπος λευκός ἐστιν ἢ Σωκράτης καθήμενος διαλέγεται σύνθετόν τε καὶ συγκείμενον. ... καὶ αὐτὸς μὲν ἐν τῷ Περὶ ἑρμηνείας, ἐπὶ πλέον δὲ Θεόφραστος ἐν τῷ Περὶ καταφάσεως, περὶ τούτων λέγει.

to, or even an abbreviated form of, 'So-and-so is brave and so-and-so is a beast'. In that case, the first premiss of the syllogism,

The mouse is a creature of great personal valour

or

Mice are brave beasts,

is equivalent to, or even synonymous with,

Mice are brave and mice are beasts.

But for the second premiss,

Brave beasts die young

No comparable equivalence is forthcoming—certainly, the premiss is not equivalent to:

The brave die young and beasts die young.

So the conjunctive analysis cannot justify the mouse syllogism.

In any event, there are innumerably many complex predicates to which the conjunctive analysis does not apply. The complex predicate 'fork-lift-truck-driving man' is not an ordinary conjunction of simple predicates; and although Aristotle knew nothing about fork-lifting, he more or less recognized the point which it here illustrates. For he remarks that

of man it is true to say animal separately and biped separately—and also as one. Also man and pale, and those two as one. But it is not the case that if he is a shoe-maker and good, he is a good shoe-maker.

(*Int* 20b33–36)[53]

Some compound predicates are conjunctive, or equivalent to conjunctions, and others are not.

Socrates is a pale man

is equivalent to the conjunction of

Socrates is pale

and

Socrates is a man.

But

Simon is a remarkable old cobbler

is not equivalent to the conjunction of

Simon is remarkable,

Simon is old,

---

[53] κατὰ γὰρ τοῦ ἀνθρώπου ἀληθὲς εἰπεῖν καὶ χωρὶς ζῷον καὶ χωρὶς δίπουν, καὶ ὡς ἕν, καὶ ἄνθρωπον καὶ λευκόν, καὶ ταῦθ' ὡς ἕν· ἀλλ' οὐχί, εἰ σκυτεὺς καὶ ἀγαθός, καὶ σκυτεὺς ἀγαθός.

and

Simon is a cobbler.

True, the text which I have quoted does not say exactly what I have just said; nonetheless—as I cautiously put it—Aristotle more or less acknowledges the point that complex predicates are not always conjunctive.

There is a deeper difficulty. In principle, the simple predicates are all and only those which belong to one of Aristotle's ten classes of predicate. Every other predicate is complex—that is to say, it is somehow formed from the simple predicates by means of various operations which Aristotle once thought he ought to look into. But what sort of complexity and what sort of simplicity are in play? Evidently, the notions in question are semantic; and a first shot at explaining complexity might look like this: A predicate is complex if and only if its meaning is determined by the meaning of its simple components (and by the nature of the composition which unites them). So 'remarkable old cobbler' is complex inasmuch as its sense is fixed by the senses of its three parts.

Then consider the technical term 'featherweight'. It is surely simple, according to the account I have just sketched; for although it is, in an innocuous sense, compounded from the words 'feather' and 'weight', the meanings of those terms do not fix the meaning of 'featherweight'. So perhaps it is a simple predicate—in the Aristotelian class of quantity? But the word 'featherweight' is defined thus: A featherweight is a boxer who weighs between 8st 6lb and 9st if he is professional and between 8st 7lb and 9st if he is amateur. There is complexity enough there; and it is an *ad hoc* and accidental complexity—few will persuade themselves that the term is nevertheless a simple member of one of the ten Aristotelian classes.

There is no need to resort to fisticuffs to make the point. Let me invent the word 'robbler' and define it thus: A robbler is a remarkable old cobbler. The term 'robbler' is a simple expression inasmuch as it has no semantically active parts. But it does not belong to an Aristotelian class—it is, in Plotinian terms, three predicates.

So 'robbler' and 'featherweight' must be complex predicates: if their complexity is not found on the surface, then it is revealed by their definitions. That might suggest that an expression is complex, in the pertinent sense, if and only if it is definable. For it is the definitions of 'robbler' and of 'featherweight' which furnish the several predicates which together compose and account for the complexity of the terms which they define. In itself that is a sensible sort of notion; but it has disastrous consequences for Aristotle.

For it determines that the word 'man', for example, is complex: the word may have no evident parts to it; but it is definable—as 'rational mortal animal' (*vel sim*)—and for that reason it is complex. If that line of inquiry is pursued, it will turn out that—if Aristotle's theory is true—there are exactly ten simple predicates: 'substance', 'quantified item', 'qualified item', and so on. Now some ancient texts do indeed hint at that conclusion; but it does not answer to anything in Aristotle—or in Plotinus, or in Porphyry.

Aristotelians thus need to distinguish the simplicity of 'man' from the complexity of 'featherweight'. They thought to do so by declaring that the former, but not the latter, signifies 'one thing'—that it signifies some single or unified item. The definitional formula for 'man', namely 'rational mortal animal', is semantically complex; but the term and its definition signify a unity and for that reason, or in that sense, the term is not complex. The definitional formula for 'featherweight' not only is complex: in addition, it signifies a plurality, or at least a non-unity—featherweights tend to crack up. But under what conditions does a term or a formula signify a unity? Not even Aristotle managed to give a satisfactory answer to the question.

As Plotinus mercilessly demonstrated, the Aristotelian classification of predicates—the so-called 'doctrine of the categories'—is a quagmire; and any account of predication which is built upon that doctrine must wobble. If you take the *Categories* to be the first part of a unitary *Organon*, and if you suppose that the 'doctrine of the categories' prepares the ground for the 'doctrine of the syllogism' which the *Prior Analytics* presents, then you are up the creek—and paddleless.

Happily, the central part of the *Categories*, in which the 'doctrine of the categories' is developed, has nothing to do with the logic of the *Analytics*. Of course, Aristotle's syllogistic is essentially tied to the concept of predication; for the argument forms which it examines are fixed by a certain logical structure, namely the subject–predicate structure. But nothing in the syllogistic requires, or even suggests, any classification of predicates: that a predicate is substantial or qualitative, relational or a matter of *habitus*—all that is of supreme indifference to the syllogistic. There is no difference whatever, from a syllogistic point of view, between 'Every man is an animal', where the predicate is substantial, and 'Every man is less than ten feet tall', where the predicate is quantitative.

I do not mean that no classification of predicates could be of pertinence to any theory of inference. I do not even mean that Aristotle's classification of predicates has no logical interest. I mean, simply and indisputably, that the

Aristotelian classification of predicates has no bearing upon the Aristotelian theory of inference.

If the syllogistic does not require, or even invite, any classification of predicates, neither does it require, or even suggest, that a predicate must be simple or that it must belong to one or other of the ten Aristotelian classes. As far as syllogisms are concerned, there is no difference at all between 'man' and 'featherweight', between 'ape' and 'fork-lift-truck-driving man', between 'finch' and 'soprano who sings Schubert like an angel'. Indeed, Aristotelian syllogistic need not even be cowed by the monster predicates which modern logicians like to breed. The formula '... is such that it is identical to itself and in Manchester it never rains on Bank Holiday Mondays' is a perfectly acceptable predicate in modern logic; for it is an expression which may legitimately occupy the place of the 'F' in inferences of the sort:

F(Socrates): so F(something).

By the same token 'an item such that it is identical to itself and in Manchester it never rains on Bank Holiday Mondays' is a perfectly acceptable Aristotelian predicate; that is to say, it is an expression which may feature alongside such quotidian items as 'man' and 'animal' in an Aristotelian syllogism.

'SOMETHING OF SOMETHING'

If predicates and subjects are expressions, how shall we determine, in the case of a given sentence or proposition, what is a subject for it and what a predicate? In the *Prior Analytics* Aristotle explains that

a proposition is a saying which affirms or denies something of something.

(*APr* 24a16–17)[54]

In the *de Interpretatione* there is something rather more elaborate:

Of these [sc. assertoric sayings] some are simple assertions, namely those which say something of something or something from something, and some are composed from them, namely those which are thereby compound sayings.

(*Int* 17a20–22)[55]

---

[54] πρότασις μὲν οὖν ἐστι λόγος καταφατικὸς ἢ ἀποφατικός τινος κατά τινος.
[55] τούτων δ' ἡ μὲν ἁπλῆ ἐστιν ἀπόφανσις, οἷον τι κατά τινος ἤ τι ἀπό τινος, ἡ δ' ἐκ τούτων συγκειμένη, οἷον λόγος τις ἤδη σύνθετος.

The propositions of the *Analytics* seem to be identical with the simple assertions of the *de Interpretatione*—on the plausible assumption that to deny something of something is the same thing as to say something from something. So in predicative sentences, something is said of something, τι κατά τινος—and the first something corresponds to a predicate, the second to a subject.

In that case, if we want to determine subject and predicate in a proposition, we might apply the 'something of something' test. That is to say, we might ask: What, here, is said of what? Take again

Bugles sang.

What does that sentence say of what? Or rather, if someone utters such a sentence, what does he say—or what can he be saying—of what? Well, it is pretty clear that the sentence, or an appropriate utterer of the sentence, says or may say of bugles that they sang. And in that case we shall identify 'an item which sang' as a predicate in the sentence and 'bugle' as a subject.

That banal idea invites two simple comments, and two less simple reflections.

The first comment is this: the 'something of something' test will allow predicates of any degree of linguistic complexity. (The same goes, of course, for subjects.) 'Fork-lift-truck-driving man' will make an impeccable predicate (and an impeccable subject). Or take this relatively complex sentence:

Love is not love which alters where it alteration finds or bends with the remover to remove.

What does the sentence—or what did Shakespeare—say of what? Surely it or he said something of love, namely that it doesn't alter &c; so that 'love' will be a subject and 'an item which doesn't alter &c' a predicate.

In the *de Interpretatione* Aristotle distinguishes between simple and compound sayings, and his words imply that the distinction is exclusive. But consider the sentence:

If young hearts were not so clever, oh, they would be young forever.

That is surely a compound sentence; equally surely, it, or its utterer, says something of something: it says of young hearts that, were they not so clever &c. The familiar sentence which begins with 'If you can keep your head' and continues for some twenty lines before it reaches 'you'll be a man, my son', also says something of something.

I do not suppose that Aristotle had imagined examples of that sort. Nonetheless, it is clear that the distinction he makes in the *de Interpretatione* ought to be construed not as a distinction between sorts of proposition but as a distinction between certain propositional forms; and it is clear, too, that when the *Analytics* limits propositions to what the *de Interpretatione* calls simple assertions, it thereby excludes few propositions (if any) from its domain.

The second comment: the items which are predicate and subject in a sentence need not, themselves, be literally parts of the sentence. The simple sentence 'Bugles sang' perhaps contains the expression 'bugle', which is a subject for it; but it certainly does not contain the expression 'an item which sang', which is a predicate in it. In general, if a simple sentence has the form 'So-and-so VERBS', then the expression 'VERBING' or 'an item which VERBS' will be a predicate for it—and those expressions do not literally appear in it.

The point was made—or at least half made—by Aristotle in wholly general terms:

We say, without qualification, of all cases that the terms should always be set down according to the names of the words—e.g. man or good or opposites—not of man or of good or of opposites—but that the propositions should be taken in accordance with the cases of each word.

(*APr* 48b39–49a2)[56]

The remark is obscure (and my translation perhaps exaggerates some of its obscurities); and the concrete applications which Aristotle proceeds to offer are curious. But what Aristotle means is this: in setting out the terms of a proposition—in designating predicate and subject—we should always use the nominative case; in setting out the proposition, we should use whatever case is grammatically appropriate. One of the terms of a sentence may be 'opposites' (nominative plural), while the sentence itself contains 'of opposites' (genitive plural).

The first of the two reflections I promised takes its start from that last remark. If a subject and a predicate of a sentence need not be literally parts of the sentence, then how are they related to the sentence? Must they not at least have, as it were, a representative in the sentence, as 'an item which sang' has 'sang' to represent it? That is so in all the examples which Aristotle gives, and the text which I have just cited implies that it must always be so. Nevertheless, various cases suggest themselves in which it is tempting to find

---

[56] ἁπλῶς γὰρ τοῦτο λέγομεν κατὰ πάντων ὅτι τοὺς μὲν ὅρους ἀεὶ θετέον κατὰ τὰς κλήσεις τῶν ὀνομάτων, οἷον ἄνθρωπος ἢ ἀγαθόν ἢ ἐναντία, οὐκ ἀνθρώπου ἢ ἀγαθοῦ ἢ ἐναντίων, τὰς δὲ προτάσεις ληπτέον κατὰ τὰς ἑκάστου πτώσεις.

subjects and predicates from beyond the confines of their sentences. Here are three sorts of example.

The first is the most extreme. In answer to the question 'What happened in London yesterday evening?' I might utter the sentence

A nightingale sang in Berkeley Square

and thereby say of a certain summer evening that it was such that..., or of London that it was such that... If that is so, does not the 'something of something' test make 'yesterday evening', and 'London', subjects for the sentence? But those two alleged subjects have no representative of any sort in their sentence. You might urge that the test will declare them subjects if it refers to utterers, but that it will not do so if it refers to sentences. For although an utterer of the sentence 'A nightingale sang...' might use it—might very well use it—to say something of London, surely the sentence itself does not say anything of London. (But why not? After all, it says something of Berkeley Square—and isn't that a decent way of saying something about London?)

The second sort of example may be illustrated by Duncan's remark:

He was a man in whom I placed the most absolute trust.

Duncan thereby said of the Thane of Cawdor that he had trusted him; and the sentence—or at least, a certain occurrence of the sentence—says something of the Thane. So the 'something of something' test makes 'the Thane of Cawdor' a subject for the sentence. It is true that 'the Thane of Cawdor' has a representative in the sentence, namely the expression 'he'; but the relation between 'the Thane of Cawdor' and 'he' is not at all the same as the relation between 'sang' and 'an item which sang'.

Thirdly, consider cases in which the language changes. When you sing

Und der Haifisch, der hat Zähne,

you surely say something of sharks, namely that they have teeth; and the sentence, equally surely, says of sharks that they have teeth. So 'shark' is a subject for the sentence and 'an item which has teeth' is a predicate in it. Yet those two English expressions do not appear in the German sentence. To be sure, they have their representatives—in the expressions 'der Haifisch' and 'hat Zähne'. But again, they are not representatives in the way in which 'sang' represents 'an item which sang'.

Or perhaps the expression 'shark' does occur in the German sentence? Is it not true that in his *Analytics* Aristotle uses the word 'syllogism' I don't know how many times? It would be at best a weak joke to say: 'On the contrary, he never uses it—nor any other English word.' Is it not true that Frege took pains to distinguish between the sense and the reference of the singular term 'The Morning Star'?—'No he didn't: he was exclusively concerned with the sense and reference of a German word.'

The ancient texts, needless to say, do not consider—let alone resolve—such conundrums. But the main point which I want to make here is both ancient and true: even when, on the Porphyrean account, subjects and predicates are taken to be significant expressions, there is no reason to think that the expressions must be literally parts of the sentences of which they are subjects and predicates—and there is every reason to think that they are not always such parts.

That brings me to a second reflection. Ancient logicians and modern scholars commonly speak of the subject and the predicate of a sentence or proposition, as though every sentence or proposition which exhibits a subject–predicate structure had a single determinate subject and a single determinate predicate. But in fact, as some of the examples have already hinted, the 'something of something' test will accommodate a plurality of subject–predicate analyses. In uttering

When beggars die there are no comets seen,

what may I say of what? Pretty plainly, I may say something about beggars—that their deaths are not marked by the appearance of comets. Equally plainly, I may say something about comets—that they do not mark the deaths of beggars. Slightly less evidently, I may say something about deaths—that when they are beggarly, they are not marked by comets. And a little ingenuity will elicit other potential subjects and predicates in that not very complicated sentence. It is not that sometimes I may say one of those things and sometimes another. True, if I produce the sentence in the course of a lecture on astrology, it will be natural to remark that I thereby said something about comets. And so I did—but I also, and in the same breath, said something about beggars, and deaths, and God knows what else.

That sentences admit multiple analyses, and that one analysis may be pertinent to one inferential context and another to another—those are commonplaces of modern logic. They were not commonplaces of ancient or of traditional logic. Indeed, they were not recognized by ancient logicians—with the possible exception of a handful of texts which I shall discuss in a later context. Nonetheless, it is worth insisting on the fact that nothing in the Aristotelian theory of predication excludes multiple predicative analyses.

STYLES OF PREDICATION

The slanderer who predicated philippism of Demosthenes did so inasmuch as he said of Demosthenes that he philippized. Similarly, the sentence, or an utterer of the sentence

The world is too much with us

predicates 'an item which is too much with us' of 'the world' inasmuch as it or he thereby says of the world that it is too much with us. But if the sentence

Demosthenes philippizes

predicates 'an item which philippizes' of 'Demosthenes', it does not follow—and according to Demosthenes it was not true—that 'item which philippizes' is predicated of 'Demosthenes'. So a sentence or an utterer may predicate something of something without its thereby being the case that the something is predicated of the something.

That sounds odd—if not downright contradictory. In any event, it forces the following question: If when someone predicates x of y, it does not follow that x is predicated of y, then what exactly is it for x to be predicated of y?

The Aristotelians often use the verb 'ὑπάρχειν' (+ dative)—'hold of' or 'apply to' or 'belong to'—as equivalent to 'κατηγορεῖσθαι' (+ genitive). More precisely, it is clear that, at any rate in the *Analytics*, x is predicated of y if and only if x holds of y. The Stoics also connected predication—their notion of predication—to holding or belonging: Chrysippus

says that only the present holds: the past and the future subsist but do not hold—except in the way in which some predicates hold, namely those and only those which are attributed—e.g. to walk holds of me when I am walking and does not hold when I am sitting or lying down.

(Stobaeus, *ecl* I viii 42)[57]

A Stoic predicate is not an expression but an item sayable by way of an expression; but, like an Aristotelian predicate, such an item, when it is predicated, holds of what it is predicated of.

---

[57] μόνον δ' ὑπάρχειν φησὶ τὸν ἐνεστῶτα [sc. χρόνον], τὸν δὲ παρῳχημένον καὶ τὸν μέλλοντα ὑφεστάναι μέν, ὑπάρχειν δὲ οὐδαμῶς, εἰ μὴ ὡς καὶ κατηγορήματα ὑπάρχειν λέγεται μόνα τὰ συμβεβηκότα, οἷον τὸ περιπατεῖν ὑπάρχει μοι ὅτε περιπατῶ, ὅτε δὲ κατακέκλιμαι ἢ κάθημαι οὐχ ὑπάρχει.—Text and translation are doubtful in parts; but the doubts do not affect the point for which I cite the passage.

An expression holds of, or belongs to, something if and only if it is true of it; and that suggests that predication is best explained in terms of truth—that is to say, in terms of something's being true of something. A first version of the suggestion—which is neither eccentric nor exciting—amounts to this:

x is predicated of y if and only if x is true of what y is true of.

'An item which sang' is predicated of 'bugle' inasmuch as 'an item which sang' is true of what 'bugle' is true of—and hence inasmuch as bugles are items which sang, or bugles sang. The sentence, or an utterer of the sentence,

Bugles sang

predicates 'an item which sang' of 'bugle' inasmuch as what it or he says is true if and only if 'an item which sang' is in fact predicated of 'bugle'.

But that explanation cannot capture the notion of predication which governs the *Analytics*. For consider this sentence:

And no bird sings.

What is there predicated of what? The right answer to that question, within the context of Aristotle's logic, is this: 'singing item' is predicated of 'bird'. But although the sentence predicates 'singing item' of 'bird', it is not true if and only if 'singing item' is true of what 'bird' is true of. Quite the contrary. How, then, is 'singing item' predicated of 'bird'? Well, it is predicated of it in a certain style—and the style's the thing. (The point still holds, *mutatis mutandis*, if you reject the Porphyrean view which makes subjects and predicates expressions. For then you will say that in

And no bird sings

singing is predicated of bird.)

Predication—despite what I have so far been pretending—is not in fact a two-place relation which might hold between, say, 'singing item' and 'bird'. Certainly, predication is a matter of two-placed relations; but the formula 'x is predicated of y' does not itself express a two-placed relation. Rather, the two-placed relations involved in predication are expressed by formulas of the sort 'x is predicated-in-style-*S* of y'. So if we ask, what, in general, are the truth-conditions for sentences of the form 'x is predicated of y', then we shall receive no general answer: we shall receive a disjunction of specific answers. (To be sure, you may always define 'x is predicated of y' as 'x is predicated-in-some-style-or-other of y'.)

What are the styles of predication? They are numerous; but the ones which concern me here are the ones which bear on Aristotle's syllogistic. If we leave aside modality, which complicates matters impertinently, then a style is a combination of a quantity and a quality. Very roughly speaking, a quality indicates in what manner a predicate attaches to a subject, and a quantity indicates to how much of the subject the predicate attaches. There are two qualities: positive and negative, or affirmative and privative. There are infinitely many quantities; but Aristotle's logic restricts itself in principle to three of them and in practice to two. The three quantities are universal, particular, and indeterminate. But the indeterminate quantity is scarcely mentioned in the *Analytics*, Aristotle taking it to be equivalent to the particular quantity; and so we may confine ourselves—as the later Aristotelians generally did—to two quantities. Two qualities multiplied by two quantities give four styles of predication—or four sorts of predicative proposition.

The tradition speaks of propositions of the types A, E, I and O; and we might speak of four styles of predication A, E, I and O—universal and affirmative, universal and negative, particular and affirmative, particular and negative. An attempt to elucidate the Aristotelian notion of predication might then start from the schema:

x is predicated in style S of y if and only if, in style S, x is true of what y is true of.

And it might proceed to define the four canonical styles, along familiar lines. For example, the universal affirmative style, or style A, is explained thus:

In style A, x is true of what y is true of if and only if there is nothing of which y is true and x is not true.

Or, in Aristotle's words,

we say that something is predicated of every item when it is not possible to take any of the items of which the other will not be said.

(*APr* 24b28–30)[58]

That explication has its *ennuis*, to which I shall return in a later context. But they need not derange us here.

The other three styles may be explained along the same lines. So let us return to the withered sage. In the sentence

And no bird sings

'singing item' is indeed predicated of 'bird'; for it is predicated of 'bird' universally and negatively, or in style E. In style E, x is true of what y is true of if and only if there is nothing of which y is true and x is true. So

---

[58] λέγομεν δὲ τὸ κατὰ παντὸς κατηγορεῖσθαι ὅταν μηδὲν ἦ λαβεῖν καθ᾽ οὗ θάτερον οὐ λεχθήσεται.

No bird sings

is true if and only if there is nothing of which 'singing item' is true and 'bird' is true—that is to say, if and only if no bird sings.

THE TRANSITIVITY OF PREDICATION

Earlier I wondered whether the relation of predication was reflexive, symmetrical, transitive, and the like; and I postponed the question. The reason for the postponement should now be clear: there is no such thing as the relation of predication of which such questions can be asked. Rather, there are—in Aristotelian logic—four relations. With regard to each of the four styles of predication it may be asked whether it is reflexive, symmetrical, transitive, and so on. And, rather more excitingly, we can ask what logical links can be established among the four styles of predication. Suppose, for example, that x is A-predicated of y—does it follow that y is I-predicated of x? Or suppose that x is A-predicated of y and E-predicated of z—does it follow that y is predicated of z in some style or other?

Those questions were all asked by Aristotle and his successors—though not, to be sure, in that form. Thus Aristotle's argument in favour of what is called the accidental conversion of A-style predication is an argument that if x is A-predicated of y then y is I-predicated of x; and his proof of the validity of the second figure mood known as Camestres is a proof that if x is A-predicated of y and E-predicated of z, then y is E-predicated of z.

Or consider A-predication. It seems clear that this relation is reflexive; for x is surely true of everything of which x is true. It seems equally plain that it is neither symmetrical nor asymmetrical; for when x is true of everything of which y is true, y may or may not be true of everything of which x is true. (Let x be 'a man' and y first 'an item capable of laughter' and then 'a philosopher'.) Finally, it seems evident that the relation is transitive: if x is true of everything of which y is true, and y is true of everything of which z is true, then x is true of everything of which z is true.

The transitivity of A-style predication—of universal affirmative predication—corresponds to Barbara, the first mood of Aristotelian syllogistic; and Aristotle explicitly notices the point:

Now when three terms are so related to one another that the last is in the middle as in a whole and the middle is in the first as in a whole ... , it is necessary for there to be a perfect syllogism of the extremes. ... For if A of every B and B of every C, then it is necessary for A to be predicated of every C.

(*APr* 25b32–39)[59]

The last sentence—'For if A of every B ...'—is as clear an affirmation of the transitivity of A-predication as you could hope to find. The sentence is there, as its initial particle shows, in order to explain why from

A holds of every B

and

B holds of every C

there is a syllogism to

A holds of every C.

And arguments of that sort are syllogisms in Barbara.

Later in the *Prior Analytics*, where Aristotle is discussing the best way to select terms which stand in logical relationships to one another, he remarks that

you should not select for the universal the terms which a contained item follows—for example, for animal you should not select the terms which man follows. For it is necessary that, if animal follows man, then it also follows all those items—and those items are more appropriate to the selection for man.

(*APr* 43b29–32)[60]

Suppose that you are looking for items which 'animal' follows—that is to say, of which 'animal' is A-predicated; and suppose that you hit upon 'man' and add it to your list. You then come across 'grammarian': it is true that 'animal' is A-predicated of 'grammarian'. Nonetheless, you should not add it to your list; for 'man' too is A-predicated of 'grammarian', and you have already got 'man' on the list. 'For it is necessary that, if animal follows man, then it also follows all those items'; that is to say, generalized and schematically put:

If x is A-predicated of y, then for any z, if y is A-predicated of z, then x is A-predicated of z.

---

[59] ὅταν οὖν ὅροι τρεῖς οὕτως ἔχωσι πρὸς ἀλλήλους ὥστε τὸν ἔσχατον ἐν ὅλῳ εἶναι τῷ μέσῳ καὶ τὸν μέσον ἐν ὅλῳ τῷ πρώτῳ ..., ἀνάγκη τῶν ἄκρων εἶναι συλλογισμὸν τέλειον. ... εἰ γὰρ τὸ Α κατὰ παντὸς τοῦ Β καὶ τὸ Β κατὰ παντὸς τοῦ Γ, ἀνάγκη τὸ Α κατὰ παντὸς τοῦ Γ κατηγορεῖσθαι.

[60] οὐδὲ δὴ τῷ καθόλου ἐκλεκτέον οἷς ἕπεται τὸ περιεχόμενον, οἷον ζῴῳ οἷς ἕπεται ἄνθρωπος· ἀνάγκη γάρ, εἰ ἀνθρώπῳ ἀκολουθεῖ τὸ ζῷον, καὶ τούτοις ἅπασιν ἀκολουθεῖν· οἰκειότερα δὲ ταῦτα τῆς τοῦ ἀνθρώπου ἐκλογῆς.

And that is one way of expressing the transitivity of universal affirmative predication.

Of course it is transitive—why fuss over such a banality? Well, I fuss because the banality was officially rejected by a large part of the ancient tradition: according to that tradition, A-predication is not transitive.

To be sure, the tradition did not thereby reject Barbara—how could it have done? But it accepted only a restricted form of Barbara. Here is Simplicius on the subject:

> Having said what being of a subject is not, he now says what it is—namely, that being predicated synonymously and essentially is what being said of a subject is. And that comes about when, presenting the definitory formula of the subject, we present it through the predicate. For if someone presents what man is, he will say animal. So, when something is predicated as of a subject (e.g. man of Socrates) and something else is predicated of the predicate (and that too not accidentally but as of a subject and synonymously—e.g. animal of man), then animal will also be predicated of Socrates—for in this way we shall have the first mood of the first figure, the middle being in the major extreme as in a whole and being said of all the minor.

> (*in Cat* 51.30–52.10)[61]

According to this passage, the relation expressed by 'x is universally and affirmatively predicated essentially of y' is transitive, and supports the first mood of the first figure or Barbara. Thus the argument

> Men are animals and animals are substances—and so men must be substances

is valid; for its two premisses express essential A-predications.

But consider an argument which is apparently on all fours with it:

> Frenchmen are heavily taxed and heavy taxes make for disgruntlement—so it's not surprising that the French are so disgruntled.

There the premisses are indeed A-predications; but they are not essential A-predications—it is no part of the essence of being French that you are

---

[61] εἰπὼν τί οὐκ ἔστιν καθ' ὑποκειμένου, νῦν τί ἐστιν λέγει, ὅτι τὸ συνωνύμως καὶ ἐν τῷ τί ἐστιν κατηγορεῖσθαι, τοῦτό ἐστι τὸ καθ' ὑποκειμένου λέγεσθαι· τοῦτο δέ ἐστιν ὅταν τὸν λόγον τὸν ὁριστικὸν ἀποδιδόντες τοῦ ὑποκειμένου διὰ τοῦ κατηγορουμένου ἀποδιδῶμεν. ἐὰν γὰρ ἀποδιδῷ τις τί ἐστιν ἄνθρωπος, ζῷον ἐρεῖ. ὅταν οὖν ὡς καθ' ὑποκειμένου κατηγορῆται, οἷον ὁ ἄνθρωπος τοῦ Σωκράτους, καὶ τοῦ κατηγορουμένου ἄλλο τι κατηγορῆται καὶ αὐτὸ μὴ ὡς ἔτυχεν ἀλλ' ὡς καθ' ὑποκειμένου καὶ συνωνύμως, οἷον τὸ ζῷον τοῦ ἀνθρώπου, καὶ τοῦ Σωκράτους τὸ ζῷον κατηγορηθήσεται· ἔσται γὰρ ὁ πρῶτος τρόπος οὕτως τοῦ πρώτου σχήματος, τοῦ μέσου ἐν ὅλῳ μὲν ὄντος τῷ μείζονι ἄκρῳ, κατὰ παντὸς δὲ τοῦ ἐλάττονος λεγομένου.

rudely taxed. Since it is essential A-predications which are transitive and the predications in the argument are not essential, the argument is not valid—or at any rate, it is not a valid syllogism in Barbara.

True, Simplicius does not explicitly mention arguments the component predications of which are not essential, nor does he explicitly say that A-predication is not in general transitive. But he quite clearly commits himself to such a view, and the view was orthodox among the later commentators on Aristotle. It must sound a strange view—a perverse view. So why ever was it promoted? It was promoted because Aristotle himself was taken to have promoted it. In the *Categories*, he states that

> whenever one item is predicated of another as of a subject, everything which is said of the predicate will also be said of the subject. For example, man is predicated of an individual man, and animal of man: so animal will be predicated also of the individual man.

> (*Cat* 1b10–15)[62]

That is transitivity; but it is transitivity not for A-predication, but for the relation 'x is predicated of y as of a subject'. You might think that the phrase 'as of a subject' was an idle addition, a pleonasm—after all, how could x be predicated of y but not of y as a subject? Surely what something is predicated of simply is its subject? Perhaps—but the ancient commentators were persuaded that 'as of a subject' was anything but pleonastic.

The clearest ancient account of the matter is found in Porphyry's commentary on the *Categories*. He sets out the gist of the Aristotelian passage I have just quoted, and then he raises an objection to it:

> —But how can that be true? After all, man is said of Socrates as of a subject, and of man is predicated not only animal but also species (for man is a species). But they won't all be predicated of Socrates; rather, animal will be predicated of him but species will not—for Socrates isn't a species.
> —But look: the absurdity depends on the fact that you have mistaken what 'which is said of the predicate' means. He didn't simply say 'which is said of the predicate'; rather, inasmuch as he has just said 'whenever one item is predicated of another as of a subject', he gives us to understand 'synonymously and essentially' when he says 'everything which is said of the predicate will also be said of the subject'. For

---

[62] ὅταν ἕτερον καθ' ἑτέρου κατηγορῆται ὡς καθ' ὑποκειμένου, ὅσα κατὰ τοῦ κατηγορουμένου λέγεται, πάντα καὶ κατὰ τοῦ ὑποκειμένου ῥηθήσεται· οἷον ἄνθρωπος κατὰ τοῦ τινὸς ἀνθρώπου κατηγορεῖται, τὸ δὲ ζῷον κατὰ τοῦ ἀνθρώπου· οὐκοῦν καὶ κατὰ τοῦ τινὸς ἀνθρώπου τὸ ζῷον κατηγορηθήσεται.

example, animal is predicated of man as of a subject; for both the name of animal and its account fit man.

(in Cat 80.32–81.11)[63]

Transitivity, according to Porphyry, cannot hold unrestrictedly; for in that case we should have to accept as valid the following argument:

> Socrates is a man.
> Man is a species.
> So Socrates is a species.

And Aristotle does not in fact propose an unrestricted transitivity: it is predication-as-of-a-subject, not predication *tout court*, which he claims to be transitive. And in the fallacious argument, the predication in the second premiss is not predication-as-of-a-subject.

Predication-as-of-a-subject is taken by Porphyry to be the same as essential predication, and essential predication is taken to be the same as what he calls 'synonymous' predication, or predication in which both the name and the account (or the definition) of the predicate hold of the subject. That notion of synonymous predication derives from a later paragraph in the *Categories*:

> It is clear from what we have said that in the case of items said of a subject, both the name and the account are predicated of the subject ... But with items which are in a subject, in most cases neither the name nor the account is predicated of the subject, but in some cases nothing prevents the name from being predicated of the subject, although it is impossible for the account to be predicated of it. For example, white, which is in a subject, namely a body, is predicated of the subject—for a body is called white. But the account of white will never be predicated of a body.

(Cat 2a19–34)[64]

---

[63] —ἀλλὰ πῶς τοῦτο ἀληθές; ὁ μὲν γὰρ ἄνθρωπος κατὰ Σωκράτους λέγεται καθ᾽ ὑποκειμένου· κατὰ δὲ τοῦ ἀνθρώπου κατηγορεῖται οὐ μόνον τὸ ζῷον ἀλλὰ καὶ τὸ εἶδος· εἶδος γὰρ ὁ ἄνθρωπος. οὐ μὴν ἔτι κατὰ τοῦ Σωκράτους πάντα κατηγορηθήσεται, ἀλλὰ τὸ μὲν ζῷον κατηγορηθήσεται, οὐκέτι δὲ καὶ τὸ εἶδος· οὐ γὰρ Σωκράτης εἶδος.—ἀλλ᾽ ὁρᾷς ὅτι ἡ ἀτοπία γέγονε παρὰ τὸ μὴ ἐκδέξασθαι ὀρθῶς πῶς εἴρηται ὅσα κατὰ τοῦ κατηγορουμένου λέγεται· οὐ γὰρ ἁπλῶς εἴρηκεν ὅσα κατὰ τοῦ κατηγορουμένου λέγεται, ἀλλ᾽ εἰπὼν ὅταν ἕτερον καθ᾽ ἑτέρου κατηγορῆται ὡς καθ᾽ ὑποκειμένου δέδωκεν ὑπολαβεῖν τὸ συνωνύμως καὶ ἐν τῷ τί ἐστι τὸ τηνικαῦτα· ὅσα κατὰ τοῦ κατηγορουμένου λέγεται, τοσαῦτα καὶ κατὰ τοῦ ὑποκειμένου ῥηθήσεται. οἷον τὸ ζῷον κατὰ τοῦ ἀνθρώπου ὡς καθ᾽ ὑποκειμένου κατηγορεῖται· ἐφαρμόζει γὰρ τῷ ἀνθρώπῳ καὶ τοὔνομα τοῦ ζῴου καὶ ὁ λόγος.

[64] φανερὸν δὲ ἐκ τῶν εἰρημένων ὅτι τῶν καθ᾽ ὑποκειμένου λεγομένων ἀναγκαῖον καὶ τοὔνομα καὶ τὸν λόγον κατηγορεῖσθαι τοῦ ὑποκειμένου· ... τῶν δ᾽ ἐν ὑποκειμένῳ ὄντων ἐπὶ μὲν τῶν πλείστων οὔτε τοὔνομα οὔτε ὁ λόγος κατηγορεῖται τοῦ ὑποκειμένου· ἐπ᾽ ἐνίων δὲ τοὔνομα μὲν οὐδὲν κωλύει κατηγορεῖσθαι τοῦ ὑποκειμένου, τὸν δὲ λόγον ἀδύνατον· οἷον τὸ λευκὸν ἐν ὑποκειμένῳ ὂν τῷ σώματι κατηγορεῖται τοῦ ὑποκειμένου (λευκὸν γὰρ σῶμα λέγεται), ὁ δὲ λόγος τοῦ λευκοῦ οὐδέποτε κατὰ τοῦ σώματος κατηγορηθήσεται.

Items which are 'in a subject' are—or so the tradition uniformly supposed—accidents or accidental predicates of that subject. Predication is transitive only if both the name and the definition of the predicate hold of the subject. In accidental predication the name rarely holds of the subject and the definition never.

Consider a case in which the name of an accident is predicated of the subject and ask whether such predication is transitive. If it is, then the following argument must be valid:

Socrates is white.
White is a colour.
So Socrates is a colour.

Of course, the argument is not valid, and so transitivity does not hold for accidental predication. To be sure, Aristotle does not say that in so many words. But—so Porphyry and others thought—he is plainly committed to it; and after all—so they thought—it is true.

I will consider my Cat Jeoffry; for the English Cats are the best in Europe. Now Jeoffry is quintessentially a cat; and so, according to Aristotle, both the name 'cat' and the definition of the name 'cat' are predicated of him. Jeoffry is also tenacious of his point. But neither the name 'tenacity' nor any definition of that name is predicated of him—after all, Jeoffry is not tenacity itself. Finally, Jeoffry is of the Tribe of Tiger—but here truth must be sacrificed to the demands of the example, and I shall pretend that Jeoffry is grey. Here, according to Aristotle, the name 'grey' is predicated of Jeoffry; but the definition of that name, which must be 'colour of such-and-such a kind', is not.

That illustrates what Aristotle appears to say in the *Categories*; and it illustrates what Porphyry, and other Aristotelian commentators, took to be quite generally true. But whether or not it is Aristotelian, it is odd. In particular, what Aristotle says about

Jeoffry is grey

cannot possibly be true—and cannot possibly be true by Aristotle's own lights. The passage from the *Categories* claims that sometimes a name, but not the account or definition of the name, may be true of something. But it is a trivial truth, and a truth known to Aristotle and his successors, that a *definiens* must be true of all and only those items of which the *definiendum* is true, that *definiens* and *definiendum* must be logically equivalent. So it cannot be the case that sometimes a name, but not its definition, applies to something. If the name 'grey' is predicated of Jeoffry, then so is the definition—or an appropriate definition—of that name. That is not, or should not be, a controversial claim: it is a childish truth.

How on earth did Aristotle come to deny it? He denied it on the basis of an example—and his successors found further examples, and offered some sort of classification of them. But Aristotle's example is false.

Jeoffry is grey

is on all counts parallel to

Jeoffry is tenacious.

If the name 'grey' (or the expression 'a grey item', or the word 'greyness', ...) is predicated in the sentence of 'Jeoffry' (or of Jeoffry), then—and trivially—the definition of the name is predicated of Jeoffry. The definition of 'grey', as it appears in

Jeoffry is grey

is not 'colour of such-and-such a sort' but rather 'of such-and-such a colour'; and for Jeoffry, as for anything else, to be grey is precisely to be of such-and-such a colour.

Aristotle's example is specious. How did he come to be taken in by it? It is difficult not to think that he was misled by a simple syntactical ambiguity. In English, the word 'grey' may be either an adjective or a noun. In Greek, the word 'λευκός' is an adjective; but in the neuter singular form 'λευκόν' it functions not only as an ordinary adjective but also as a noun. When Aristotle says that 'the account of white will never be predicated of a body', then what he says is true provided that the word 'white' is construed as a noun. But then the name 'white'—when that is construed as a noun—is not predicated of body either. It is as though Aristotle were to remark that the definition of the noun 'grey' is not predicated of the grey Jeoffry. Of course it isn't—nor is the noun 'grey'.

Aristotle finds important differences among 'cat', 'tenacious' and 'grey'. He is wrong when he claims that 'grey' is interestingly different from 'tenacious'. He is also wrong when he claims that 'tenacious' is interestingly different from 'cat'. Or rather, he is wrong if that claim is interpreted as a claim about predication. Jeoffry is tenacious, according to the *Categories*, inasmuch as tenacity is in Jeoffry; it is not the case that he is a cat inasmuch as cat or catness is in him. Perhaps those claims are intelligible, and perhaps they are true. But here they interest me only insofar as they bear upon the theory of predication.

Their bearing on predication was supposed (I think) to be something like this. In

Jeoffry is a cat

there is an essential predication; and so both the word 'cat' and its definition are predicated of 'Jeoffry'. In

Jeoffry is tenacious

there is an accidental predication; and so neither the word 'tenacity' nor its definition is predicated of Jeoffry. All that—with the exception of the repeated 'and so'—is indisputable. But it does not set up a difference between being a cat and being tenacious, or between the predications in the two pertinent sentences. Just as neither the word 'tenacity' nor its definition is predicated of Jeoffry, inasmuch as Jeoffry is not tenacity, so neither the word 'cathood' nor its definition is predicated of Jeoffry, inasmuch as Jeoffry is not cathood. Just as both the word 'cat' and its definition are predicated of Jeoffry, inasmuch as Jeoffry is a cat, so both the word 'tenacious' and its definition are predicated of Jeoffry, inasmuch as Jeoffry is tenacious.

Aristotle's infelicitous remarks about 'white' provided the later comment-ators with one spurious counterexample to the transitivity of A-predication. Porphyry—in the passage I cited earlier—invokes the sentence

Man is a species.

The difficulties raised by that are different from any which might be raised by 'Jeoffry is grey'. In particular, if the word 'species' is replaced by its definition—say 'item which is ordered under a genus'—then the resulting sentence is no odder than 'Man is a species': it is perfectly plain that, however we should parse 'Man is a species', it cannot be that the word 'species' is predicated of 'man' and its definition not. Nonetheless, however we should parse 'Man is a species', it raises no difficulty for transitivity.

The central point may be brought out as follows. Here are three arguments which, in an obvious way, run parallel to one another:

(1) Jeoffry is a cat. A cat is an animal. So Jeoffry is an animal.
(2) Jeoffry is grey. Grey is a colour. So Jeoffry is a colour.
(3) Jeoffry is a cat. The cat is a species. So Jeoffry is a species.

The first argument is valid, the second and third are invalid. So although they are superficially similar, there must be some underlying difference which distinguishes (1) from (2) and (3). What is it? The ancient tradition answers as follows: 'In argument (1) both premisses are predications-as-of-a-subject; and since predication-as-of-a-subject is transitive, argument (1) is valid. In arguments (2) and (3) the two premisses are predications; but in each case one of them is not a predication-as-of-a-subject. And since predication is not in general transitive, the arguments are not valid.'

That diagnosis gives the required results in the case of the three arguments before us. But it is difficult to see how anyone who was not beguiled by the *Categories* could have thought that it was a plausible diagnosis, or that it was the only or the best way to exclude the fallacious inferences. For quite apart from anything else, it has disastrous consequences for Aristotle's syllogistic—as the passage I quoted from Simplicius well illustrates. It implies—to take another example—that the following argument,

> All men can laugh
> No crocodiles can laugh
> So no men are crocodiles

is not a syllogism in Cesare. And it thus places severe and unwarranted restrictions on the scope of the syllogistic.

In any event, a better diagnosis of the fallacies in arguments (2) and (3) is not far to seek. In argument (2), the sentence 'Grey is a colour' does not predicate 'colour' affirmatively and universally of 'grey item'. (Why not? Why shouldn't I construe it as saying that every grey item is a colour?—Well, construe it like that if you like; and argument (2) will indeed be valid—but its second premiss will be false.) Again, the sentence 'The cat is a species' does not predicate 'species' affirmatively and universally of 'cat'. (Again, if you perversely construe it in that sense, argument (3) is valid—and its second premiss is false.) And that is all there is to say—transitivity has nothing to do with the case.

That diagnosis was not unknown in antiquity. Here is a passage from Philoponus' commentary on the *Prior Analytics* which proposes it—or half proposes it.

The article and the universal determiner do not mean the same thing in propositions. For when I say

> Jeoffry is a cat, The cat is an animal,

'the cat' signifies the indivisible species of cat, in virtue of which all individual cats are called cats. But when I say

> Every cat is an animal,

I no longer take the indivisible species but rather all the individuals of which the species holds. That this is true is clear from the fact that you can say

> The cat is a species,

but not

> Every cat is a species.

Hence the fallacies:

> The swan is white
> White is a colour

So the swan is a colour.
For it is not true to say
Every white item is a colour.
For 'every' signifies the individuals which participate in white; and you can't say of
them that they are a colour. But when I say 'white', since I take the species white,
it is true to say that it is a colour. So that since the universal premiss is false, the
conclusion too is false.

(in APr 325.26–326.5)[65]

(Philoponus' examples concern men rather than cats; but in English it is
'man' rather than 'the man' which names the species.)

The gist of the matter is this. Consider the following argument:

Jeoffry is a cat
The cat is a species
So Jeoffry is a species

The definite article in the second premiss ensures that the phrase 'the cat'
designates an indivisible species. The premiss does not mean

Every cat is a species.

It does not do so because, in general, articles and determiners (or quantifiers)
do not mean the same thing. Since the second premiss does not mean that
every cat is a species, the argument is not valid—or at any rate, it is not a
valid Aristotelian syllogism.

Philoponus is fundamentally right; and he does not make any reference
to predication-as-of-a-subject, or to essential or synonymous predication.
But he is only half right; for he holds that the phrase 'the cat' designates a
species in

The cat is an animal.

That sentence is therefore not equivalent to

Every cat is an animal.

Hence the argument

---

[65] οὐ γὰρ ταὐτὸν δύναται ἐν ταῖς προτάσεσι τό τε ἄρθρον καὶ ὁ καθόλου προσδιορισμός.
ὅταν μὲν γὰρ εἴπω Σωκράτης ἄνθρωπος, ὁ ἄνθρωπος ζῷον, τὸ ὁ ἄνθρωπος τὸ ἐνοειδές τοῦ
ἀνθρώπου εἶδος σημαίνει, καθ' ὃ πάντες οἱ κατὰ μέρος ἄνθρωποι λέγονται· ὅταν δὲ εἴπω
πᾶς ἄνθρωπος ζῷον, οὐκέτι τὸ εἶδος λαμβάνω τὸ ἐνοειδὲς ἀλλὰ τοὺς καθ' ἕκαστα πάντας
οἷς ὑπάρχει τὸ εἶδος. καὶ ὅτι τοῦτο ἀληθές ἐστι, δῆλον ἐξ ὧν δυνατὸν εἰπεῖν ὁ ἄνθρωπος
εἶδός ἐστιν, οὐ μέντοι πᾶς ἄνθρωπος. ἔνθεν καὶ οἱ παραλογισμοὶ ἐκεῖνοι· ὁ κύκνος λευκός, τὸ
λευκὸν χρῶμα, ὁ κύκνος ἄρα χρῶμα. οὐκέτι γὰρ ἀληθὲς εἰπεῖν πᾶν λευκὸν χρῶμα· τὸ γὰρ
πᾶν τὰ καθ' ἕκαστα σημαίνει τὰ τοῦ λευκοῦ μετέχοντα· οὐκ ἔστι δὲ ἀληθές εἰπεῖν περὶ τούτων
ὅτι χρῶμά εἰσιν. ὅταν δὲ τὸ λευκὸν εἴπω, ἐπειδὴ τὸ εἶδος τοῦ λευκοῦ λαμβάνω, ἀληθές εἰπεῖν
ὅτι χρῶμά ἐστιν. ὥστε ἐπειδὴ ἡ καθόλου πρότασις ψευδής, καὶ τὸ συμπέρασμα ψευδές.

Jeoffry is a cat

The cat is an animal

So Jeoffry is an animal

is not a valid Aristotelian syllogism—it is just as bad as the previous argument.

But the argument surely is valid; and its second premiss surely is equivalent to

Every cat is an animal.

Several ancient texts, logical and grammatical, recognize that in Greek the definite article sometimes functions as a universal quantifier, that 'the so-and-so' sometimes means 'every so-and-so'. Philoponus has no reason—and no need—to deny that truth.

Again, when Philoponus comments on the *Categories* he follows the orthodox line. Predication-as-of-a-subject is transitive.

> What does he mean by 'as of a subject'?—'Essentially and objectually'; for if something is predicated accidentally of the predicate it is not necessarily also said of the subject.
>
> (*in Cat* 38.28–31)[66]

If x is predicated accidentally of y and y is predicated of z, it does not follow that x is predicated of z.

The passage in the *Categories* about the predication of names and their definitions is a slip on Aristotle's part. It is a fairly trivial slip—you can cut the offending lines from the text and nothing much else will need changing. Nor did the slip have any effect on anything which Aristotle said in the *Analytics*. Nonetheless, once the passage in the *Categories* was taken to convey a truth, and a doctrinal truth, and once the *Categories* became the first element in the *Organon*, the trivial slip inflated into a massive blunder. Whoever invented the *Organon* has something to answer for.

Some scholars think that the inventor of the *Organon* was Andronicus of Rhodes. Whether or not that is so, Andronicus was not misled—or not wholly misled—by the trivial slip in the *Categories*. Simplicius says:

> It should be noted that Andronicus, and also some others, say that it is not only items predicated essentially which are predicated of a subject—so too are other items: for example, 'musical' of Aristoxenus, and 'Athenian' of Socrates, and perhaps those items in predicating which of something we say that it is just what we predicate—in

---

[66] τί δὲ αὐτῷ βούλεται τὸ ὡς καθ᾽ ὑποκειμένου; τὸ οὐσιωδῶς καὶ πραγματικῶς· εἰ γάρ τι κατὰ τοῦ κατηγορουμένου κατὰ συμβεβηκὸς κατηγορεῖται, οὐκ ἀνάγκη τοῦτο καὶ κατὰ τοῦ ὑποκειμένου λέγεσθαι.

saying that Socrates walks we do not say that Socrates is walks, but we do say that he is Athenian and a philosopher. And what is predicated of those items, when we say that they are such-and-such, will also be said of the subject. For if Socrates is a philosopher and a philosopher is knowledgeable, then Socrates too will be knowledgeable. Again, they say: if a body is white and white is a colour, will a body then be a colour? Surely white signifies two things, the quality and also what is coloured? It is what is coloured which is predicated of the body (for the body is not whiteness), whereas it is the colour which is predicated of the quality (for the quality is not whitened but whiteness). Thus it is not the colour but the coloured item which is predicated of the body.

(in Cat 54.8–21)[67]

That is all we know about Andronicus' view—and the text at the very end of the passage is uncertain. Even so, it is plain that Andronicus gave a good diagnosis of Aristotle's example of 'white'. As for Andronicus' general position, Simplicius is not as clear as he might have been: plainly, he did not think much of it, and he reported it dutifully rather than excitedly.

Nonetheless, the illustrative examples suggest something like this. Andronicus agrees with Aristotle that predication is not, in general, transitive: rather, it is predication-as-of-a-subject which is transitive. But predication-as-of-a-subject is not limited to essential predication. It is found not only in the essential sentence

Socrates is a man,

but also in the accidental

Socrates is Athenian.

And surely the same goes for all predication? Not according to Simplicius' text; for the text indicates that predication-as-of-a-subject occurs with 'those items in predicating which of something we say that it is just what we predicate'. So predication-as-of-a-subject is not found in (say)

Socrates walks

—for when we say that Socrates walks we do not say that Socrates is walks.

---

[67] ἰστέον δὲ ὅτι καὶ Ἀνδρόνικος καὶ ἄλλοι δέ τινες οὐ μόνον τὰ ἐν τῷ τί ἐστι κατηγορούμενα καθ᾽ ὑποκειμένου κατηγορεῖσθαί φασιν, ἀλλὰ καὶ ἄλλα οἷον τὸ μουσικὸν κατὰ Ἀριστοξένου καὶ τὸ Ἀθηναῖος κατὰ Σωκράτους, καὶ ἴσως ἐκεῖνα ὅσα κατηγοροῦντές τινος ἐκεῖνο εἶναι λέγομεν αὐτὸ ὅπερ κατηγοροῦμεν· βαδίζειν μὲν γὰρ λέγοντες τὸν Σωκράτη οὐ λέγομεν βαδίζειν εἶναι τὸν Σωκράτη, Ἀθηναῖον δὲ εἶναι λέγομεν καὶ φιλόσοφον. καὶ ὅσα δὴ τούτων κατηγορεῖται, λεγόντων ἡμῶν ταῦτα ἐκεῖνα εἶναι, καὶ κατὰ τοῦ ὑποκειμένου ῥηθήσεται· εἰ γὰρ ὁ Σωκράτης φιλόσοφος καὶ ὁ φιλόσοφος δὲ ἐπιστήμων, ἔσται καὶ ὁ Σωκράτης ἐπιστήμων. πάλιν δέ φασιν· εἰ τὸ σῶμα λευκὸν καὶ τὸ λευκὸν χρῶμα, ἔσται καὶ τὸ σῶμα χρῶμα; ἢ τὸ λευκὸν δύο σημαίνει, τήν τε ποιότητα καὶ τὸ κεχρωσμένον, καὶ τοῦ μὲν σώματος τὸ κεχρωσμένον κατηγορεῖται (οὐ γάρ ἐστι τὸ σῶμα λευκότης), τῆς δὲ ποιότητος τὸ χρῶμα, (<οὐ γάρ ἐστιν ἡ ποιότης λελευκωμένον> ἀλλὰ λευκότης)· ὥστε οὐ τὸ χρῶμα κατηγορηθήσεται τοῦ σώματος, ἀλλὰ τὸ κεχρωσμένον.

Yet I wonder if Andronicus meant to restrict predication-as-of-a-subject in that way—or in any other way. When Simplicius says 'and perhaps those items in predicating which ...' he seems to me not to be reporting a generalization which Andronicus had made but rather to be conjecturing a generalization of his own. And the conjecture seems to me to be rather dubious, for the following reason. I have already invoked the Aristotelian thesis that 'x VERBS' and 'x is VERBING' are synonymous. That thesis was accepted—so far as I know—by all ancient Aristotelians, and there is no reason to imagine that Andronicus raised a dissident voice. So he will have known that

Socrates walks

is the same as

Socrates is a walking item.

If he thought that

Socrates is Athenian

is a predication-as-of-a-subject, then he must surely have held the same view of

Socrates is a walking item.

And in that case, every predication either is or is synonymous with a predication-as-of-a-subject, and the restriction of transitivity to predication-as-of-a-subject is no restriction at all. In short, Andronicus probably saw that all predication—that is to say, all A-predication—is transitive.

SINGULAR PREDICATION

But is there not something very wrong with the last few pages of my argument? I have said that, with the exception of Andronicus, ancient scholars endorsed the false thesis of the *Categories* according to which A-predication is not in general transitive: transitivity is a property of essential A-predication, not of A-predication itself. But the *Categories* does not speak of A-predication: it speaks of predication in general, and it makes no mention of what I have called different styles of predication.

Not only that: in addition, it seems that the argument in the *Categories* cannot be construed in terms of A-predication. For the examples of predication about which it turns include singular sentences such as

Socrates is white;

and they do not express A-predications. Indeed, according to the modern wisdom, singular sentences do not convey predications of any Aristotelian style. They convey, as we might say, singular predications; and singular predications are not recognized by Aristotle's syllogistic and hence are not Aristotelian predications at all.

Singular sentences have long been supposed to raise a problem for Aristotelian logic—or to reveal a fundamental weakness in Aristotelian syllogistic. For on the one hand, it seems evident that if x is predicated of y, then both x and y must be general terms; or, more precisely, that if x is predicated in style S of y, and S is one of the four Aristotelian styles, then both x and y must be general terms. That is implicit in the structure of the syllogistic; and although it is never discussed or examined by the ancient logicians, it is found more or less explicitly in a scattering of texts. On the other hand, Aristotle's followers and commentators—and also Aristotle himself—sometimes introduce singular sentences into syllogisms. They do so with no embarrassment. They do not hint that such items are anomalous—or worse.

Their remarkable nonchalance in this regard is explained in part—or so it is tempting to conjecture—by the influence of the *Categories*. At any rate, once you take the *Categories* and its doctrine of predication to introduce the logic of the *Analytics*, and once you think that one of the first questions to be raised about predication is the question of transitivity which is implicitly tackled in the *Categories*, then you are unlikely to imagine that there might be something untoward about singular sentences. After all, in the *Categories* it is singular sentences which provide the primary examples of predication. Thus Simplicius finds a syllogism in Barbara in the text, and he implicitly takes singular sentences to express A-predications.

So much the worse, it will be said, for Aristotle—or at least, so much the worse for many Aristotelians. True, a reference to the *Categories* may enable us to understand how they came to treat singular sentences as unproblematical. But that is only to say that we can understand how they came to make an egregious error.

Nevertheless, the matter is not quite as simple as that; and I shall finish this chapter with a few reflections on singular predication.

First, a trifling point. Say that a singular sentence is a sentence which contains at least one singular term, and that a singular term is a term which designates or refers to an individual item or object. (Proper names are singular terms, so are many pronouns, so are some phrases of the form 'the so-and-so'.) That is approximate, but approximate enough. Then can Aristotelian syllogistic accommodate singular sentences? Quite evidently it can. Here is syllogism in Barbara:

Anyone who likes *La Bohème* likes *Madama Butterfly*, and everyone who likes *Butterfly* likes *Tosca*. So anyone who likes *Bohème* likes *Tosca*.

That syllogism contains three singular terms, which designate three operas. There is nothing in the least problematical about that.

There is nothing problematical because the singular terms which occur in the syllogism are not terms of the syllogism: the syllogism turns around three A-predications, and in none of those predications is either subject or predicate a singular term. The predicate in the first premiss, for example, is 'liker of *Madama Butterfly*', and that is a general term. In other words, the question is not: Can Aristotelian syllogistic accommodate singular sentences? For of course it can. The question is rather this: Can singular terms function as subjects and predicates in Aristotelian syllogistic? Or: when a sentence which predicates x in style S of y appears as such as a component in an Aristotelian syllogism, can either x or y be a singular term?

The Aristotelians certainly took some singular sentences to have, as such, a subject–predicate form or to say 'something of something'. To establish that fact—which is in any case perhaps too evident to need establishment—it is enough to appeal to a piece of the *Prior Analytics* which I quoted earlier to illustrate a different point:

Of all the things which there are, some are such that they are not predicated truly and universally of anything else (e.g. Cleon, Callias—whatever is individual and perceptible) but other items are predicated of them (each of the two, after all, is a man and an animal). Other things are themselves predicated of other items and yet nothing else is earlier predicated of them. Yet further things both are themselves predicated of other items and have other items predicated of them (e.g. man of Callias and animal of man).

(*APr* 43a25–32)

Alexander, in his long comment on that passage, has this to say:

Individual substances are not themselves truly predicated of other items, but other items are predicated of them—for the species and genera of individual substances are predicated of them, and so also are their accidents.

(*in APr* 291.14–17)[68]

---

[68] αἱ δὴ ἄτομοι οὐσίαι αὐταὶ μὲν ἀληθῶς κατ᾽ ἄλλων οὐ κατηγοροῦνται, κατὰ δὲ τούτων ἄλλα· τὰ γὰρ εἴδη καὶ τὰ γένη τῶν ἀτόμων οὐσιῶν κατηγορεῖται αὐτῶν, ἀλλὰ καὶ τὰ συμβεβηκότα αὐταῖς.

That seems pretty clear. But there was and is some uncertainty about what exactly Aristotle meant to deny.

He denies that individuals can ever be predicated truly and universally of anything else; and he is apparently thinking of affirmative predication. So he claims that no sentence which predicates an individual term universally and affirmatively of some other term is true. That, strictly speaking, is all that he says. But is it all that he means to say? If so, then he leaves open the possibility that an individual may be predicated truly and universally and negatively of another item. For example:

No English philosopher is Socrates.

Again, he leaves open the possibility that an individual may be predicated falsely and universally and affirmatively of another term. For example:

Every philosopher is Socrates.

Again, he leaves open the possibility that an individual may be predicated non-universally of another term, whether truly or falsely and whether affirmatively or negatively. For example:

Some philosopher is not Socrates,

or

Some English philosopher is Socrates.

And finally, he leaves open the possibility that an individual might be predicated truly and universally and affirmatively of itself. For example:

Every son of Sophroniscus is Socrates;

or perhaps, more modestly,

Every Socrates is Socrates.

I say that he leaves open such possibilities. The letter of his text certainly leaves them open. But in the view of some commentators, the spirit of the text closes them off—what Aristotle in fact intended to convey by his remarks was that if x is predicated of y, then x is a general and not a singular term.

After all, if Aristotle had really meant to countenance some cases of singular predicates, why didn't he go the whole way and recognize that individuals may be predicated truly and universally and affirmatively? For if you accept

Every philosopher is Socrates

as well formed but false, then surely you must accept

Every snub-nosed Greek philosopher is Socrates

as well formed and true? But that is an item which Aristotle explicitly excludes—hence he must have intended to exclude all cases in which singular terms are predicated.

Perhaps. But I wonder if Aristotle should not, and would not, have accepted the suggestion that

Every snub-nosed Greek philosopher is Socrates

is well-formed and true. After all, the text of the *Analytics* does not definitively outlaw it. For if 'Socrates' is true of everything of which 'snub-nosed Greek philosopher' is true, then there is exactly one snub-nosed Greek philosopher, and he is Socrates. In that case, 'snub-nosed Greek philosopher' is not true of anything other than Socrates, so that although 'Socrates' is predicated truly and universally and affirmatively of 'snub-nosed Greek philosopher', 'Socrates' is not thereby predicated truly and universally and affirmatively of something other than Socrates.

However that may be, the passage from the *Analytics* is unambiguously and indisputably clear on one matter: individuals, or singular terms, may be subjects; and items—at any rate, other items—may be predicated of them. In other words, the Aristotelian conception of predication is such that you may predicate 'animal' (or animal) of 'Socrates' (or of Socrates), just as you may predicate it of 'man' (or of man).

And that indisputable fact has an indisputable corollary: since the *Analytics* requires subjects and predicates to be homogeneous, then, whatever he meant in the passage I have just discussed, Aristotle was in fact committed to the thesis that singular terms may function as predicates.

That being so, singular sentences may appear as such in Aristotelian syllogisms—that is to say, there may be syllogisms in which a premiss or the conclusion predicates x of y and either x or y is a singular term (or both x and y are singular terms). Indeed, there may be probative syllogisms which contain singular predications in that way. And Aristotle acknowledges the fact quite explicitly; for a few lines later in the *Prior Analytics* he notes that

it is not possible to prove anything of these items [i.e. of highest genera] save according to opinion—rather, you prove these of other items. Nor is it possible to prove individuals of anything else—rather, you prove other items of them.

(*APr* 43a37–40)[69]

You cannot prove that a singular item holds of some other item or items—you cannot prove it (let it be added) because it cannot be true. But you can,

---

[69] κατὰ μὲν οὖν τούτων οὐκ ἔστιν ἀποδεῖξαι κατηγορούμενον ἕτερον, πλὴν εἰ μὴ κατὰ δόξαν, ἀλλὰ ταῦτα κατ᾽ ἄλλων· οὐδὲ τὰ καθ᾽ ἕκαστα κατ᾽ ἄλλων, ἀλλ᾽ ἕτερα κατ᾽ ἐκείνων.

according to Aristotle himself, sometimes prove that x is predicated of y where y is a singular term. So a singular predication may, as such, form the conclusion of a syllogism—and hence, of course, a singular predication may form a premiss of a syllogism.

In fact, several of the examples of proofs in the *Posterior Analytics*—and also several of the examples in Galen's *Introduction*—concern singular propositions. Nor is there anything remarkable about that: Greek geometers normally proceeded by first proving a singular proposition and then generalizing it; and in a science such as astronomy it is not easy to avoid singularities.

The real difficulties begin when we ask ourselves in what style of predication singular terms may feature. For the answer to the question seems to be: In no style at all. Or rather: In none of the four styles which participate in Aristotelian syllogisms.

The point may be brought out in the following way. First, singular terms do not take quantifiers. Galen, for one, thinks that it is impossible—perhaps ungrammatical—to attach quantifiers to singular terms:

When we predicate something of Dio, it is not possible to say either all or some. But when we predicate something of some other object which can be divided—of man or tree, for example—then it must be determined in the saying whether the predicate is predicated of all of it or of some (and similarly if it is denied of all or of some).

(inst log ii 4)[70]

Something similar is found in Alexander: discussing a passage in which the status of a certain term—indicated in Aristotle's text simply by the letter 'C'—is unclear, he remarks that

if it is to universals that the determiners 'of all' and 'of none' and 'of some' and 'not of some' are annexed, as he has shown in the *de Interpretatione*, then it is plain that the term in question is universal and not individual.

(in APr 65.26–28)[71]

---

[70] ὅταν μὲν οὖν ἐπὶ Δίωνός τι κατηγορῶμεν, οὐκ ἐγχωρεῖ λέγειν οὔτε πᾶς οὔτε τίς· ὅταν δ' ἐφ' ἑτέρου πράγματος ὃ τέμνεσθαι δύναται, καθάπερ ἐπ' ἀνθρώπου καὶ δένδρου, διωρίσθαι χρὴ κατὰ τὸν λόγον εἴτε παντὸς αὐτοῦ κατηγορεῖται τὸ κατηγορούμενον εἴτε τινός· ὡσαύτως δὲ καὶ εἰ παντὸς ἢ τινὸς ἀποφάσκεται.

[71] εἰ γὰρ οἱ διορισμοί, τὸ παντὶ καὶ τὸ μηδενὶ καὶ τὸ τινὶ καὶ τὸ τινὶ μή, τῷ καθόλου προστίθενται, ὡς ἐν τῷ Περὶ ἑρμηνείας δέδεικται, δῆλον ὡς καθόλου ἐστὶν ὁ ἔσχατος ὅρος ἀλλ' οὐχὶ ἄτομος.

Aristotle has not in fact shown—or even said—anything of the sort in the *de Interpretatione*. But Alexander is presumably thinking of the passage in which it is stated that

'every' signifies not the universal but that something is universally so.

(Int 17b11–12)[72]

He reads too much into that phrase; but the thesis which he and Galen uphold and which he ascribes to Aristotle is scarcely outlandish.

True, we may say things like 'All the Campbells were massacred', and 'Every Napoleon meets his Waterloo'; but there 'Campbell' means 'member of the Campbell clan' and 'Napoleon' does not designate the Corsican adventurer. Such idioms apart, the juxtaposition of a quantifier and a proper name breeds nonsense. True, an e.e.cummings—whoops—might have written

and some of i embraces every you,

though 'I' and 'you' are singular pronouns. But poetry does not count—and in any case, the cummings' style sculpts sense from nonsense. As for items like

Every the horse I put my shirt on loses

or

Some the cat for once isn't demanding to be fed,

they are merely deformed. To be sure, we can easily understand them. But there is a lot of nonsense which we easily understand, and we do so precisely insofar as we recognize it as a deformation of a piece of sense.

Now a sentence may contribute to an Aristotelian syllogism only insofar as it makes a predication in one of the four Aristotelian styles. Galen, in the passage I have just cited, requires that there be a quantifier in every sentence which forms part of an Aristotelian syllogism: 'it must be determined in the saying whether the predicate is predicated of all of it or of some'. He does not state—and he should not be taken to mean—that (say) every universal affirmative sentence in an Aristotelian syllogism must contain the word 'every', still less that it must be an instance of the formula 'Every so-and-so is such-and-such'. For he elsewhere notices explicitly that there are several ways of determining a sentence as universal. For example, he holds that in

The mouse is a creature of great personal valour,

[72] τὸ γὰρ πᾶς οὐ τὸ καθόλου σημαίνει ἀλλ' ὅτι καθόλου.

the definite article functions as a universal quantifier. So too does the indefinite article in

A garden is a lovesome thing, God wot.

In general, there are numerous idiomatic ways of determining a sentence as universal or particular. But by one crook or another, Aristotelian sentences must be determined as universal or particular.

Those two facts—that you can't attach quantifiers to singular terms and that propositions which appear in syllogisms must be quantified—do not of course in themselves entail that singular propositions cannot appear in syllogisms. I have just urged that some singular propositions may quite decently sport quantifiers—for example,

Every snub-nosed Greek philosopher is Socrates.

Do not such things slip through a gap in the fence so that a little singularity may sneak into the syllogistic? No; for such things are blocked by the requirement of homogeneity. If 'Socrates' may function as a predicate in a syllogistic proposition, then it may function as a subject—that is homogeneity. If 'Socrates' may function as a subject in a syllogistic proposition, then it may carry a quantifier. But 'Socrates' cannot carry a quantifier.

In sum, there seems to be good reason to hold, first, that singular propositions may and do appear as such as components of Aristotelian syllogisms; secondly, that only quantified propositions may appear as components of such syllogisms; and thirdly, that propositions with singular subjects may not be quantified. But those three propositions are mutually inconsistent. What—if anything—can be done?

It is, I think, often supposed that the last two of the three propositions must be maintained. That is to say, predications in one of the four Aristotelian styles are the only matter of Aristotelian syllogistic, and the subjects of such predications are determined by quantifiers. And it is often supposed, in addition, that you simply cannot say 'Every Socrates' or 'Some Socrates' or anything else of the sort; for such phrases—given that 'Socrates' is a singular term—are nonsense, ungrammatical nonsense.

So we must reject the first of the three propositions, and insist that singular subjects cannot feature in Aristotelian syllogisms. To say that is to go against a considerable number of texts: it is not an interpretation of Aristotle but a correction. Nonetheless, it may be held to correct him in an Aristotelian way. For despite certain asides in the *Analytics* and elsewhere, the official doctrine of the *Posterior Analytics* denies that singular truths can be proved; and although that doctrine does not entail that singular subjects cannot appear in non-probative syllogisms, nothing much will be lost—and nothing at all will be lost to demonstrative theory—if singular subjects are banned from the syllogistic altogether.

Having gone that far, why not go a little further? Why not maintain that singular sentences do not manifest, as such, the structure of Aristotelian predication? Did not Frege truly claim that there is a fundamental difference—a fundamental logical difference—between

Jeoffry is grey

and

All cats are grey in the dark?

The former sentence has (among other forms) the form characteristic of singular propositions which logicians customarily represent by a formula such as

F(a).

'F' represents a one-placed predicate and 'a' a singular term; so that 'F(a)' might represent 'is grey(Jeoffry)'—which is just a funny way of writing 'Jeoffry is grey'. The latter sentence—

All cats are grey in the dark

—has (among other forms) the form characteristic of universal propositions. Logicians usually represent it by something equivalent to this:

Take anything whatever, if F(it), then G(it).

So:

Take anything you like, if it's a cat then it's grey in the dark.

Aristotelian logic does not, and cannot, distinguish between those two forms of proposition. That is the invisible worm in the bud, the Achilles' heel, the *hinc illae lacrimae*, of traditional syllogistic.

Now there can be no doubt but that it is a far far better thing to be a Fregean in logic than to be an Aristotelian. And there may be a dozen good reasons for abandoning Aristotelian syllogistic, reasons which have nothing to do with singular propositions. But a stubborn Aristotelian will not sell the pass at the first appearance of a singular subject.

If propositions with singular subjects are to be accommodated within Aristotelian logic, then either we must find quantifiers for singular subjects or else unquantified propositions—and another style, or other styles, of predication—must be allowed into the syllogistic. At first blush, the latter option is the more inviting: after all, no one is forbidden to make additions to Aristotelian syllogistic; and it would not be difficult to invent rules which specify the logical relations among different sorts of singular proposition and between singular propositions on the one hand and quantified Aristotelian propositions on the other. But to do that is hardly to accommodate singular subjects within Aristotelian logic: it is to accommodate Aristotelian logic to singular subjects.

So it is the former option—that of finding quantifiers for singular subjects—which the stubborn Aristotelian must take. And he might first appeal to a passage in the *Analytics* where Aristotle considers a couple of sophistical arguments, which he refutes by urging that each has a false premiss. (The arguments themselves need not detain us.) In the first case he says that

It is false to claim that every thinkable Aristomenes exists forever.

(*APr* 47b28–29)[73]

In the second case he says that

It is not universally true that Mikkalos is musical.

(*APr* 47b35–36)[74]

In the first case Aristotle seems prepared to affix a quantifier to something which might perhaps be a singular term, namely 'thinkable Aristomenes'; and in the second case he seems prepared to allow that a proposition with a singular subject might somehow be universally true.

Alexander's commentary on the passage is disappointing insofar as he does not take up the quantificational question. But at the end of his remarks he observes, casually enough, that

'universally Mikkalos is musical' means 'every Mikkalos is musical'.

(*in APr* 352.25–26)[75]

Apparently he sees nothing untoward in that sentence—which he simply declares to be false.

Philoponus takes a different line from Alexander on the case of Mikkalos, and he does not think that anything like 'Every Mikkalos is musical' is involved. On the case of Aristomenes—where Alexander says nothing pertinent to the present point—he has this to say:

When I say
    The thinkable Aristomenes,
I indicate the very thinkable form of Aristomenes; but if I say

---

[73] τοῦτο δὲ ψεῦδος, τὸ ἀξιοῦν πάντα τὸν διανοητὸν Ἀριστομένην ἀεὶ εἶναι.

[74] οὐ γὰρ ἀληθὲς καθόλου, Μίκκαλος μουσικός ...

[75] τὸ γὰρ καθόλου Μίκκαλος μουσικὸς τὴν πᾶς Μίκκαλος μουσικὸς σημαίνει.

Every thinkable Aristomenes,
I mean nothing other than
All the individual Aristomeneses who happen to be thinkable
—and of them it is not true to say that they exist forever.

(in APr 326.6–10)[76]

So Philoponus, like Alexander, finds nothing untoward in fastening a quantifier to a proper name.

But Philoponus fastens a plural quantifier to his proper name, and he puts the proper name itself in the plural: presumably, by 'all the individual Aristomeneses' he meant something like 'everyone who is called by the name 'Aristomenes''. Whether or not that is a good way of dealing with Aristotle's sophism, it is of no interest in the present context; for although

Every item called 'Jeoffry' is grey

is an impeccably formed predicative sentence, it is not equivalent to

Jeoffry is grey.

For on Philoponus' understanding, it is about a plurality of cats and not, or not uniquely, about Christopher Smart's best friend.

Alexander's view of Mikkalos is more promising. For it suggests that we might construe singular terms as though they were general. Why not, for example, print the word 'aristotle' with a little a, and suppose that 'Aristotle wrote the *Analytics*' is equivalent to—or perhaps short for—'Every aristotle wrote the *Analytics*'? As for the general term 'aristotle', that is perfectly intelligible: 'aristotle' is true of an item if and only if that item is Aristotle. Such a line of thought has something going for it. For example, it might invoke the fact that, in Greek, proper names regularly take the definite article: 'ὁ Σωκράτης' is good Greek for 'Socrates'. Why not construe the definite article there as a universal quantifier?

Well, in 'ὁ Σωκράτης' the article is in fact better taken as a demonstrative—like the Latin '*ille*' in '*Hector ille*'. (Something similar is true of the comparable use of the definitive article in German, say, or in Italian.) And even if we swallow a quantificational article for 'Socrates', and for proper names in general, we shall not do so for pronouns or for singular phrases such as 'the sun' and 'the moon'. If

Every aristotle shall be extolled

[76] ὅταν μὲν γὰρ εἴπω ὁ διανοητὸς Ἀριστομένης, αὐτὸ τὸ διανοητὸν εἶδος τοῦ Ἀριστομένους δηλῶ· ἐὰν δὲ εἴπω πᾶς διανοητὸς Ἀριστομένης, οὐδὲν ἕτερον λέγω ἢ πάντες οἱ καθ' ἕκαστα Ἀριστομένεις οἷς συμβέβηκε τὸ διανοητοῖς εἶναι. διὸ οὐκ ἀληθὲς ἐπὶ τούτων εἰπεῖν ὅτι ἀεί εἰσιν.

is as good as

Every valley shall be exalted,

the same can hardly be said for

Every the sun shall be extinguished.

Moreover, even if ingenuity could make something out of 'every the sun', the effort is hardly worthwhile. For there is another—and a more familiar—line of thought which is more enticing.

It too transforms singular terms into general terms; but it does so by prefixing them with some such formula as 'item which is the same as'. Thus 'Aristotle' is replaced by 'item which is the same as Aristotle', 'you' by 'item which is the same as you', 'the sun' by 'item which is the same as the sun', and so on. Singular sentences, thus treated, turn at once into indefinite sentences; and so they may then be regarded as particular predications—or, of course, you may attach quantifiers to them.

There is nothing mysterious about the general term 'item which is the same as Aristotle': it is true of an object if and only if that object is the same as Aristotle—that is to say, it is true of Aristotle and of him alone. In general, 'item which is the same as A' is true of all and only those objects which are identical with A—that is to say, it is true of A and of A alone. Then the propositions

Aristotle is wise

Some item identical with Aristotle is wise

Every item identical with Aristotle is wise

turn out to be equivalent to one another. And that equivalence is all that an Aristotelian needs in order to accommodate singular subjects within his syllogistic.

Of course, there is no need to replace 'Aristotle' by 'item which is the same as Aristotle'. Rather, the sentence

Aristotle is wise

itself is—among other things—an A-predication; for it predicates 'wise' universally and affirmatively of 'an item which is the same as Aristotle'.

In traditional manuals of logic, the paradigm example of a syllogism in Barbara was often this:

All men are mortal

Socrates is a man

Therefore: Socrates is mortal

Refined Aristotelians have urged that the traditional paradigm is not a case of Barbara at all: all three component propositions of a syllogism in Barbara must be A-predications, but the second premiss and the conclusion of the paradigm are not A-predications. Aristotelians of yet more exquisite refinement may now welcome the paradigm back into the Aristotelian fold.

An audacious conclusion now huffs at the gate: whether or not de Saussure was right about grammar, Frege was wrong about logic—wrong insofar as he suggested that subjects and predicates should be banished from logic. For singular predications are not, as Frege perhaps thought, the invisible worm of Aristotelian syllogistic; and the traditional obsession with subjects and predicates does not imply that singular propositions cannot find a place within traditional logic.

But of course, Frege was not wrong, and nothing in the preceding argument implies that he was wrong. If the sentence

Jeoffry is grey

has the form of an Aristotelian A-predication, it also has the form 'F(a)', which is the characteristically singular form of singular sentences. That form is something which Aristotelian syllogistic does not and cannot recognize. Consequently—and this is the underlying force of Frege's criticism—Aristotelian syllogistic will be unable to account for the validity of any syllogisms which turn about the peculiarities of that particular singular form. For example, Aristotelian syllogistic cannot accommodate the simple inference from

Jeoffry is grey

to

Something is grey.

And if Aristotelian logic cannot accommodate that inference, it is evidently less potent—immeasurably less potent—than its admirers have supposed.

I say that Aristotelian logic cannot accommodate the simple inference. It will be answered that the inference can be reformulated as a syllogism in Darapti, thus:

Every Jeoffry is grey.
Every Jeoffry is a thing.
Therefore, some thing is grey.

Well, you can do that if you like; and with enough ingenuity you will be able to do similar and more complicated things for similar and more complicated cases.[77] But does that show that Aristotelian syllogistic can, after all, accommodate the inferences? What are the rules of the game?

However that may be, treating singular sentences as A-predications does not suddenly transform Aristotelian syllogistic into modern predicate logic. But at least it enables Aristotelian syllogistic to formulate proofs which conclude to a singular truth. And that is not nothing.

[77] Corine Besson forced me to take note of this point.

3. What is a Connector?

SENTENTIAL CONNECTIVES

The symbolisms of contemporary logic contain certain expressions called propositional connectives or, perhaps better, sentential connectives. A sentential connective is an expression which, when suitably concatenated with one or more sentences, makes a sentence. For example, the symbol '⊃' is a sentential connective: inscribe it between any pair of sentences and the result is a sentence. Or again, '¬' is a sentential connective: inscribe it before any sentence and the result is a sentence.

Natural languages, English among them, also contain sentential connectives. For example, the word 'if' is a sentential connective: utter 'if' followed by a pair of sentences (of an appropriate sort) and the result is a sentence. The word 'if', like the symbol '⊃', takes two sentences to tango. English also contains expressions which, like the symbol '¬', take a single sentence to make a sentence. For example, write 'perhaps' followed by a sentence—or in the middle of a sentence—and the result is a sentence. So too 'mercifully', or 'necessarily'. And there are complex expressions with the same construction, among them 'It is not the case that'. Fastidious anglophones will not call such items connectives (for they do not connect one thing to another); and perhaps they are better named sentential adverbs, or 'adsentences'. But that is a matter of taste.

In the standard symbolisms of logic, every connective takes a fixed and determinate number of sentences to make a sentence. In English, there are connectives which take an indeterminate number of sentences. 'and' is the most obvious example: from 'and' and the twenty-six sentences 'A', 'B', ..., 'Z', you may make the sentence:

A, B, ..., Y, and Z.

Or 'or':

Let him go, let him tarry, let him sink, or let him swim.

But some English connectives—'if' and 'because', for example—are resolutely bigamous. Again, in the symbolisms of standard logic, the sentences which connectives connect are indicative sentences, sentences which have a truth-value (or perhaps sentences which express propositions which have a truth-value). In English, connectives may conjoin sentences of any variety—imperatives and subjunctives, optatives and interrogatives.

An expression is identified as a sentential connective inasmuch as it can take a number of sentences and make a sentence. It does not follow, and it is not true, that sentential connectives can connect nothing but sentences. Even in the symbolisms of logic, sentential connectives may connect items which are not sentences. In the formula

$(\forall x)(Fx \supset Gx)$

the sentential connective '$\supset$' links 'Fx' and 'Gx', which are not sentences. (True, logicians call such things 'open sentences'. But an open sentence is a Bombay duck.) In English, sentential connectives connect all sorts of non-sentential items. Verbs, for example, and verbal phrases: 'You've gone and done it'. Names: 'Sampras and Agassi met in the final'. Other nominal phrases: 'The good, the bad, and the ugly'. Or adverbs: 'They ran silently and very fast'. And so on—connectives may even connect connectives: 'He dined if and when he pleased'. Those examples put together items of the same syntactical sort; but connectives may also connect items of different sorts—a name and a pronoun: 'My husband and I ...'; a sentence and an adverb: 'He went to the conference, if reluctantly'.

Or do sentential connectives really do such varied work? The word 'and' certainly appears in 'They ran silently and very fast', and in that sentence it seems to connect a couple of adverbs. But why think that it is the sentential 'and'? Why not suppose that it is a homonymous adverbial connective? The answer, I suppose, is this: the sense of 'and' in

They ran silently and very fast

is fully determined by the sense it bears when it connects sentences. Roughly speaking, you understand the 'and' in

They ran silently and very fast

inasmuch as, first, you know that the sentence is synonymous with

They ran silently and they ran very fast,

and, secondly, you understand the sense of 'and' in that latter sentence. More generally, you understand the construction

ADVERB + and + ADVERB

insofar as, first, you recognize that

SENTENCE + (ADVERB + and + ADVERB)

is synonymous with

(SENTENCE + ADVERB) + and + (SENTENCE + ADVERB),

and, secondly, you understand the latter construction. (Perhaps the shorter versions are elliptical for or abbreviations of the longer? That is another question.)

Elucidations of that sort, which explain a non-sentential use of a sentential connective in terms of its sentential use, are readily available in a vast number of cases. But there are some truculent items. It may be conceded that idioms—'here and there', 'to and fro', 'heads or tails', 'now if ever', ... —are of no theoretical interest: idioms conform to no rule and are to be learned one by one. But there are also some non-idiomatic cases in which the elucidation appears to be blocked.

The arithmetical 'and', for example, resists reduction. I have in my hands a book which I once bought for seven and six; in French I count my age—I used to count my age—as *soixante-et-un*; and I think that two and two make four and neither three nor five. True, such items are unperplexing; for in arithmetical examples the word 'and' is a synonym for 'plus'. But that does not alter the fact that there are numerous cases in which 'and' functions as a connective and is not to be explicated straightforwardly in terms of sentential connection.

Again, certain verbs block a sentential elucidation: 'marry', 'quarrel', 'meet', and so on. For

Sampras and Agassi met in the final

will not be explained by way of the ungrammatical non-sentence:

Sampras met in the final and Agassi met in the final.

True, such cases are unperplexing; for

Sampras and Agassi met in the final

is synonymous with—and perhaps derives from—

Sampras met Agassi in the final.

The verb 'meet' is transitive; but some transitive verbs in English allow a transformation from 'x VERBs y' to 'x and y VERB'. In any event,

(NAME + and + NAME) + VERB

is often synonymous with

NAME + VERB* + NAME.

But that does not eliminate the counterexamples—it confirms them. For in these cases a nominal connective, 'and', is not explicable in terms of the sentential connective 'and'.

Again, ordinary verbs will sometimes take an irreducibly complex subject. Move from men's singles to mixed doubles:

Graf and Agassi and Seles and Sampras met in the final.

That gives way to

Graf and Agassi met Sampras and Seles in the final.

But the two 'and's in the new sentence cannot be removed in the same way. Rather, in such cases the connected names are comparable to collective names—or to plural pronouns or to non-distributive quantifiers: 'The Opposition voted against the motion'; 'Ils ne passeront pas'; 'All the perfumes of sweet Araby …'. (And I might have thought of the 'and' in 'All the King's horses and all the King's men …'.)

Again, adverbs or adverbial expressions will sometimes foil a sentential analysis. Thus

Either the President or the Vice-President is always awake

is not equivalent to

Either the President is always awake or the Vice-president is always awake.

And

Bach, Handel, Scarlatti and Berkeley were all born in the same year

is not equivalent to

Bach was born in the same year and Handel was born in the same year and …

Of course, in such cases—or in many of them—a logician will sniff out a skulking quantifier. Thus

Bach and Handel were born in the same year

is synonymous with

There is a year such that Bach and Handel were born in it;

and that in turn is synonymous with

There is a year such that Bach was born in it and Handel was born in it

—and there the 'and' links a couple of sentences.

But there are some adverbs and adverbial phrases which put up more resistance. For example,

Hilary and Tensing climbed to the summit together,

or

The walrus and the carpenter were walking hand-in-hand.

Those are not synonymous with the ungrammatical

> Hilary climbed together to the summit and Tensing climbed together to the summit,

and

> The walrus was walking hand-in-hand and the carpenter was walking hand-in-hand.

Nor are they easily treated on the model of the men's singles. To be sure, you might try:

> Hilary climbed with Tensing to the summit,

and

> The walrus was walking hand-in-hand with the carpenter.

And there

> (NAME + and + NAME) + VERB

goes over into

> NAME + VERB* + NAME.

But that is not very appealing; for who will think that 'climb with' or 'walk hand-in-hand with' are transitive verbs?

Better allow that the 'and' in those examples is a genuinely and irreducibly nominal connective, that it is not to be elucidated by way of the sentential 'and'. But if that is so for

> The walrus and the carpenter were walking hand-in-hand,

surely it must also be so for

> The walrus and the carpenter were walking?

After all, how could the addition of an adverb to

> The walrus and the carpenter were walking

change 'and' from a sentential to a nominal connective?

Those last examples all involve the connective 'and'. Not only that: in all of them 'and' connects names or nominal expressions. True, there are a few truculent cases which involve other connectors. For example,

> Theirs but to do or die

offers an initial resistance to sentential elucidation.[1] But at least there is a verbal infinitive there, and infinitives are quasi-sentential. In any event, the nominal connective 'and' is—or so I incline to conjecture—the only English connective which in the end successfully resists sentential domestication. That is to say, the preceding remarks—if they are not merely mistaken—say something not about connectives in general but about nominal conjunction in particular.

---

[1] The example was brought to my attention by Sabina Lovibond.

Whatever be made of all that, it seems clear that 'and' in English sometimes functions as a sentential connective and sometimes as a nominal connective, and that the latter functioning is not explicable—or at least, not always straightforwardly explicable—in terms of the former functioning. Should we infer that the word 'and' is ambiguous? That seems to me a very dubious suggestion. True, the sentence

Sampras and Agassi are in the final

is ambiguous; but the ambiguity is structural or syntactical—it is not a matter of the word 'and' having two different senses.

Then should we rather infer that the term 'and' is not a sentential connective but a connective *tout court*—that is to say, an expression which takes a number of expressions (of specifiable sorts) to make an expression (of a specifiable sort)? In that case, how is the sense of a connective *tout court* to be explained? After all, those who attempt the sentential domestication of connectives are not moved by a simple desire for tidiness, nor by an irrational preference for sentences over other walks of expression: they want their connectives to be sentential because a sentential connective is relatively easy to define.

What, for example, does 'or' mean? Well, you have mastered the sense of the sentential connective 'or'—or rather, you have mastered one of its senses—once you know that something of the form

SENTENCE + 'or' + SENTENCE

is true provided that at least one of the component SENTENCES is true. That sort of thing is at least a promising beginning of an elucidation; and it can be done for other sentential connectives. If connectives are taken to be fundamentally nominal, say, or fundamentally neutral, it is far from easy to see how to begin to explain their senses.

ARISTOTELIAN CONNECTORS

The Greek word closest in sense to 'connective' is 'σύνδεσμος'. As Quintilian remarked, the best Latin translation of the Greek is '*convinctio*' (I iv 18); but the word was normally Latinized as '*coniunctio*', and the normal Latinization slid into modern languages—so that an English grammarian will normally speak of conjunctions where an English logician will speak of connectives. I do not like 'conjunction' any more than Quintilian liked '*coniunctio*'; but I do not want to translate 'σύνδεσμος' by 'connective' and thereby, without ado, identify ancient σύνδεσμοι with modern connectives. So I shall use 'connector'.

The ancient grammarians had something to say about connectors, and some of them had rather a lot to say on the topic. But I shall start with a philosopher.

The word 'σύνδεσμος' means 'link' or 'chain' or 'bond'. Aristotle frequently used it of physical linkings (e.g. *IA* 712a1–2); and he also used it of meta-phorical bonds—'Children are thought to be a bind' (*EN* 1162a27—but he was not impressed when others spoke metaphorically of the 'bond' between body and soul: *Met* 1045b11–16). And he used the word metaphorically, a dozen times or more, in logico-linguistic contexts.

When Dionysius of Halicarnassus enumerates 'the parts of sayings, which some call elements of language' (and which we now call parts of speech), he says that

Theodectes and Aristotle and the philosophers of their time brought the number of the parts up to three, making names and verbs and connectors the primary parts of language.

(*comp verb* iv 32;[2] cf. *Dem* 48)

Similarly, Quintilian, in his brief history of the parts of speech—a history of which philosophers rather than grammarians are the protagonists—says that

the ancients, among them Aristotle and Theodectes, spoke only of verbs and names and connectors—inasmuch as they judged verbs to contain the force of a saying and names its matter (for what we say is one thing, that about which we say it is another), while they took connectors to hold names and verbs together—I know that most people call these items conjunctions, but 'connector' seems a better translation of 'σύνδεσμος'.

(i iv 18)[3]

Plato uncovered two parts of sayings, the name and the verb. Aristotle found a third part. The Stoics tracked down a few more. And eventually—according to the grammatical *1066 and All That*—the Greek grammarians reached the total of eight.

In his surviving works, Aristotle nowhere talks explicitly of the parts of sayings, and he nowhere explicitly recognizes three such parts. Scholars

---

[2] ... τῶν τοῦ λόγου μορίων, ἃ δὴ καὶ στοιχεῖά τινες τῆς λέξεως καλοῦσιν. ταῦτα δὲ Θεοδέκτης μὲν καὶ Ἀριστοτέλης καὶ οἱ κατ' ἐκείνους φιλοσοφήσαντες τοὺς χρόνους ἄχρι τριῶν προήγαγον, ὀνόματα καὶ ῥήματα καὶ συνδέσμους πρῶτα μέρη τῆς λέξεως ποιοῦντες.

[3] *veteres enim, quorum fuerunt Aristoteles quoque et Theodectes, verba modo et nomina et con-vinctiones tradiderunt, videlicet quod in verbis vim sermonis, in nominibus materiam (quia alterum est quod loquimur, alterum de quo loquimur), in convinctionibus autem complexus eorum esse iudicaverunt. quae coniunctiones a plerisque dici scio, sed haec videtur ex* συνδέσμῳ *magis propria translatio.*

suppose that the reports in Dionysius and Quintilian derive from Aristotle's lost and mysterious *Collection of the Art of Theodectes*. It may also be recalled that in the *de Interpretatione* Aristotle explicitly describes names and verbs, and also implicitly notices that Greek has connectors. But if the *de Interpretatione* uses the term 'σύνδεσμος', it offers no analysis or explanation. For that we must go to the *Poetics*—and to a part of the *Poetics* which the source of Dionysius and Quintilian either did not know or else chose to ignore.

The passage begins with a list of 'the parts of language as a whole', namely: elements, syllables, connectors, names, verbs, articulators, cases, sayings (*Poet* 1456b20–21).[4] After the list, there is a sequence of notes on its several items. The note on connectors, which is immediately followed by a note on articulators, is textually corrupt; and the corruption infects not merely the details but the whole thrust of the note—or rather, of the pair of notes. I may be allowed a brief philological digression.

Our text of the *Poetics* is based on a couple of Greek manuscripts, a mediaeval Latin translation, and an Arabic translation (which was itself founded on an earlier Syriac translation). The note on connectors is differently transmitted in each of those four witnesses, and the differences are sometimes marked. Nonetheless, it is possible to establish, with some degree of certainty, the archetype, or the text which stands behind all our witnesses (and which in point of fact is virtually identical with the text offered by one of the Greek manuscripts). It translates thus:

A connector is a non-significant expression which neither prevents nor produces a single significant expression from several expressions, being by its nature combined both at the ends and in the middle, which it is not appropriate to place at the beginning of a saying in its own right—for example μέν ἤτοι δέ. Or: a non-significant expression which is of such a nature as to produce a single significant expression from more expressions than one.

(*Poet* 1456b38–1457a5)[5]

There is evidently something awry with that (and in the last sentence I have been obliged to cheat, since the transmitted Greek makes no sense and will not translate).

---

[4] τῆς δὲ λέξεως ἁπάσης τάδ' ἐστὶ τὰ μέρη· στοιχεῖον συλλαβὴ σύνδεσμος ὄνομα ῥῆμα ἄρθρον πτῶσις λόγος.

[5] σύνδεσμος δέ ἐστιν φωνὴ ἄσημος ἣ οὔτε κωλύει οὔτε ποιεῖ φωνὴν μίαν σημαντικὴν ἐκ πλειόνων φωνῶν πεφυκυῖα συντίθεσθαι καὶ ἐπὶ τῶν ἄκρων καὶ ἐπὶ τοῦ μέσου ἣν μὴ ἁρμόττει ἐν ἀρχῇ λόγου τιθέναι καθ' αὑτήν, οἷον μέν ἤτοι δέ. ἢ φωνὴ ἄσημος ἣ ἐκ πλειόνων μὲν φωνῶν μιᾶς σημαντικὸν δὲ ποιεῖν πέφυκεν μίαν σημαντικὴν φωνήν.

The best modern edition corrects the grammar of the last sentence, so that
it reads:

… to produce a single significant expression from more significant expressions than
one.[6]

Otherwise it prints the received reading—with a note to say that it is 'corrupt
and confused'.

The passage consists of two definitions or explanations. The second, once
its grammar is repaired, is intelligible. The first is not—indeed, it is wildly
incoherent. (And the three examples it gives are very peculiar.) How did the
wild incoherence come about? The note on articulators which immediately
follows the note on connectors runs as follows (I translate the text as it is
printed in the best modern edition):

An articulator is a non-significant expression which indicates a beginning or an
end or a division of a saying—for example 'ἀμφί' and 'περί' and the rest. Or: a
non-significant expression which neither prevents nor produces a single significant
expression from several expressions, being by its nature placed both at the ends and
in the middle.

(*Poet* 1457 a6–10)[7]

That text is not completely satisfactory—in particular, the clause 'for
example … and the rest' cannot be right. Moreover, Aristotelian articulators are odd birds: the Greek grammarians do not accept them as a part of
sayings—indeed, the Greek grammarians never mention them. (They adopt
the word 'ἄρθρον', which I have here translated by 'articulator' and for which
'joint' might be a better version; but they use it to name the class of 'articles'.)
However that may be, it is not difficult to see that there has been some
textual interference between the two successive notes, and that a part of the
note on articulators has been wrongly anticipated in the note on connectors.
In that case, the note on connectors must be severely pruned—and the wild
incoherence disappears.

Something must also be done about the illustrative examples; but so far as
I can see, that is a matter of pure speculation.

Although no two scholars agree on anything to do with this text, I cannot
help thinking that Aristotle must have written something like the following

---

[6] … ἐκ πλειόνων μὲν φωνῶν μιᾶς σημαντικῶν δὲ ποιεῖν πέφυκεν μίαν σημαντικὴν φωνήν.
I.e. 'σημαντικόν' is corrected to 'σημαντικῶν'.

[7] ἄρθρον δ' ἐστὶ φωνὴ ἄσημος ἢ λόγου ἀρχὴν ἢ τέλος ἢ διορισμὸν δηλοῖ, οἷον τὸ ἀμφί καὶ
τὸ περί καὶ τὰ ἄλλα. ἢ φωνὴ ἄσημος ἢ οὔτε κωλύει οὔτε ποιεῖ φωνὴν μίαν σημαντικὴν ἐκ
πλειόνων φωνῶν πεφυκυῖα τίθεσθαι καὶ ἐπὶ τῶν ἄκρων καὶ ἐπὶ τοῦ μέσου.

text. ('Something like': I mean, something which has the same sense but does not necessarily express that sense in the same way.)

A connector is a non-significant expression which it is not appropriate to place at the beginning of a saying in its own right—for example ... Or: a non-significant expression which is of such a nature as to make a single significant expression from more significant expressions than one.

(*Poet* 1456b38–1457a5)[8]

There are several oddities in that, to some of which I shall return in another context. But the second of the two definitions appears to be intelligible, and it is the second of the two definitions which interests me here.

So according to Aristotle, an item is a connector if and only if, itself non-significant, it takes two or more significant expressions and produces a significant expression.

Connectors unify expressions. Aristotle will speak of an expression's being one 'by connectors'. When he says that, he uses the singular of the Greek word, 'συνδέσμῳ'; but in the contexts of its occurrence, that cannot mean 'by a (single) connector'; and although the formula might just perhaps mean 'by a connection', the word 'σύνδεσμος' taking an abstract sense, it is far better to suppose that it means 'by connectors'. In any event, though connectors may work alone, they also hunt in packs, and an item may be one single expression on account of a plurality of connectors.

Connectors are links or bonds; and bonds, in general, are artificial ways of producing continuity or unity. That, at least, appears to be the implication of a passage in which Aristotle speaks of

things which are naturally continuous—not by force (like items which are continuous by glue or pegs or bonds) but having the cause of their continuity in themselves.

(*Met* 1052a23–25)[9]

So an expression unified by a connector will be an accidental unity; and in an aside in the *Parts of Animals* in which he is discussing the right way to make a division, Aristotle warns that

---

[8] σύνδεσμος δέ ἐστιν φωνὴ ἄσημος ἣν μὴ ἁρμόττει ἐν ἀρχῇ λόγου τιθέναι καθ᾽ αὑτήν· οἷον ... ἢ φωνὴ ἄσημος ἢ ἐκ πλειόνων μὲν φωνῶν μιᾶς σημαντικῶν δὲ ποιεῖν πέφυκεν μίαν σημαντικὴν φωνήν.

[9] ... εἴ τι φύσει τοιοῦτον καὶ μὴ βίᾳ, ὥσπερ ὅσα κόλλῃ ἢ γόμφῳ ἢ συνδέσμῳ, ἀλλὰ ἔχει ἐν αὑτῷ τὸ αἴτιον αὑτῷ τοῦ συνεχὲς εἶναι.

if you do not take the difference of a difference, then necessarily you will make
the division continuous only in the sense in which you make a saying one by
connectors—I mean … accidentally.

(*PA* 643b17–23)[10]

The sort of unity which is secured by connectors is accidental: it contrasts
with an intrinsic or essential unity. In the *Poetics* Aristotle says that

a saying may be one in either of two ways—by signifying one item or by being
made from several items by connectors (e.g. the *Iliad* is one saying by connectors,
the definition of man by signifying one item).

(*Poet* 1457a28–30)[11]

He says virtually the same thing in the *Posterior Analytics*:

A saying may be one in either of two ways—by connectors (like the *Iliad*) or by
showing one item of one item non-accidentally.

(*APst* 93b35–37)[12]

Presumably we may generalize from sayings to expressions, so that an item is
non-accidentally one inasmuch as it means or indicates a unitary thing.

That, as in another context I have already hinted, is not very satisfactory.
But the distinction which Aristotle is attempting to draw is not illusory. Take
the expression
    It's light.
Why is that a unit? That is to say: why does that expression make a single
saying (rather than several sayings or a sequence of non-sayings)? Well, if that
question has any answer, it must be something like this: it is the meaning of
the expression 'It's light' which guarantees its unity—the semantics and the
syntax of the expression together conspire to determine its unity. Take, on
the other hand,
    If it's day, it's light.
The unity of that sentence is not determined by its meaning. Rather, it is
determined by the fact that it has the general form
    If so-and-so, then such-and-such,

---

[10] ἐὰν δὲ μὴ διαφορᾶς λαμβάνῃ τὴν διαφοράν, ἀναγκαῖον ὥσπερ συνδέσμῳ τὸν λόγον ἕνα
ποιοῦντας, οὕτω καὶ τὴν διαίρεσιν συνεχῆ ποιεῖν. λέγω δὲ … κατὰ συμβεβηκός.
[11] εἷς δέ ἐστι λόγος διχῶς· ἢ γὰρ ὁ ἓν σημαίνων, ἢ ὁ ἐκ πλειόνων συνδέσμῳ, οἷον ἡ Ἰλιὰς
μὲν συνδέσμῳ εἷς, ὁ δὲ τοῦ ἀνθρώπου τῷ ἓν σημαίνειν.
[12] λόγος δ' εἷς ἐστι διχῶς, ὁ μὲν συνδέσμῳ, ὥσπερ ἡ Ἰλιάς, ὁ δὲ τῷ ἓν καθ' ἑνὸς δηλοῦν
μὴ κατὰ συμβεβηκός.

and any expression of that form, insofar as it has that form, is a unity. In other words,

If it's day, it's light

is not one saying in virtue of anything peculiar to itself: it is one saying in virtue of a feature which it shares with indefinitely many other expressions.

Perhaps that gives some sense to Aristotle's dark distinction. But it cannot be pressed very hard without collapsing; and the distinction itself has no importance in the later history of grammar. The question of the unity of an expression will return: the distinction between accidental and essential unity will not.

In the definition in the *Poetics*, Aristotle says that connectors unite significant expressions. The term 'expression' there will in principle cover any linguistic item—from a single word to an interminable discourse. In particular, sayings count as significant expressions; and in two or three of the other passages I have quoted the items which connectors unify are indeed sayings. In the *de Interpretatione* Aristotle does not refer to connectors until he has arrived at a special sort of saying, namely the assertoric saying.

The first assertoric saying which is one is affirmation; then negation; and the rest are one by connectors.

(*Int* 17a8–9)[13]

And a few lines later the two sorts of unity distinguished in the *Poetics* are applied specifically to assertoric sayings:

An assertoric saying is one either by showing one item or by being one by connectors: many sayings are those which show many items and not one, or which are unconnected.

(*Int* 17a15–17)[14]

In those texts, it is natural to think that a saying is a sentence, so that 'λόγος' may be translated by 'sentence' (or 'statement', or the like); and so Aristotelian connectors—at any rate in his logical writings—may come to look like sentential connectives.

---

[13] ἔστι δὲ εἷς πρῶτος λόγος ἀποφαντικὸς κατάφασις, εἶτα ἀπόφασις· οἱ δὲ ἄλλοι συνδέσμῳ εἷς.

[14] ἔστι δὲ εἷς λόγος ἀποφαντικὸς ἢ ὁ ἓν δηλῶν ἢ ὁ συνδέσμῳ εἷς, πολλοὶ δὲ οἱ πολλὰ καὶ μὴ ἓν ἢ οἱ ἀσύνδετοι.

It is true that when Aristotle introduces sayings in the grammatical prologue to the *de Interpretatione*, his mind is set upon sentences. But his formal definition of 'λόγος' does not restrict the word to sentences:

a saying is a significant expression some part of which is significant in separation.

(*Int* 16b26–27)[15]

Names and verbs have been defined as significant expressions no part of which is significant in separation. A saying, then, is any significant expression which is longer than a name or a verb; and the definition, which is found again, word for word, in the *Poetics* (1457a23–24), covers far more than sentences. Not only that: neither of the two examples of unitary sayings which Aristotle gives in the *Poetics* is a sentence—the definition of man (that is to say, the *definiens* of 'man') is not a sentence but a complex predicate; the *Iliad* is not a sentence but a connected sequence of sentences. (See *Poet* 1457a28–30: the same examples are found at *Met* 1045a12–14; cf. 1030b9–19.) A definition is subsentential, a poem is supersentential: it is as though Aristotle went out of his way to indicate that not all sayings are sentences.

There are some oddities in all that—in particular, the allusion to the *Iliad* is baffling. No doubt the *Iliad* is one poem (give or take a few interpolations); but its unity as a poem presumably depends on such matters as unity of action and of character and not upon the fact that it is stitched together with connecting particles. Perhaps the *Iliad* is one saying in virtue of the fact that you can say it? 'What did he say?'—'This is what he said: 'Sing, Goddess, the wrath of Achilles …'.' But if an item is one saying provided that it can fill the blank in 'He was six foot tall in his stockinged feet, and this is what he said:—', then absolutely any string of expressions will constitute a saying. So in what sense is the *Iliad* one saying? And how do Homer's connectors make it so? I have no idea.

However that may be, it is plain that Aristotelian connectors are not conceived of as sentential connectives: they are not presented as items whose primary and fundamental rôle is the linking of sentences to one another. Rather, they are what I have called neutral connectors: they are items which take expressions and make expressions—and the expressions which they take may, for all that Aristotle says, be anything from the shortest of phrases to the longest of orations.

---

[15] λόγος δέ ἐστι φωνὴ σημαντικὴ ἧς τῶν μερῶν τι σημαντικόν ἐστι κεχωρισμένον.

DEFINING THE CONNECTOR

Connectors play no part in Aristotelian syllogistic. In Stoic logic they come into the limelight, and Stoic syllogistic turns about 'if' and 'or' and 'and'. For every Stoic syllogism contains essentially at least one non-simple assertible; and, in Sextus' words,

non-simple assertibles are those ... which are composed from a repeated assertible or from different assertibles, and in which a connector or connectors govern. Take for the moment what they call the conditional. That is composed from a repeated assertible or from different assertibles by way of the connector '*εἰ*' or '*εἴπερ*'.

(*M* viii 108–109)[16]

Sextus is speaking of 'the logicians' in general; but Diogenes Laertius confirms that what Sextus reports was Stoic doctrine (see vii 68–71). There are puzzling aspects to the report which I shall for the moment ignore. But whatever the resolution of the puzzles, Stoic interest in connectors is secure. Of course, it would be astonishing were that not so. And in fact we know that Chrysippus had written monographs on different sorts of non-simple assertibles—and, more to the present point, that at least one later Stoic had written an essay specifically on connectors.

The grammarians, too, discussed connectors, and by far the most detailed and interesting of ancient texts on the subject—of extant ancient texts—is the *Connectors* of Apollonius Dyscolus. In the opening paragraph of his monograph, Apollonius remarks that he will not 'wholly avoid the opinion of the Stoics' (*conj* 214.2–3).[17]

Some scholars have mistaken the text to declare that Apollonius will not depart in the least from the opinion of the Stoics; and many scholars who understand the text aright nevertheless claim that the grammarians' views on connectors were heavily influenced by the Stoics. That there was some influence is certain—and at the end of this chapter I shall discuss a pertinent case. But it is well to remember another passage near the start of *Connectors*, a passage in which Apollonius criticizes some of his predecessors who

---

[16] καὶ δὴ οὐχ ἁπλᾶ μέν ἐστιν ἀξιώματα τὰ ἀνώτερον προειρημένα, ἅπερ ἐξ ἀξιώματος διφορουμένου ἢ ἐξ ἀξιωμάτων διαφερόντων συνέστηκε καὶ ἐν οἷς σύνδεσμος ἢ σύνδεσμοι ἐπικρατοῦσιν. λαμβανέσθω δὲ ἐκ τούτων ἐπὶ τοῦ παρόντος τὸ καλούμενον συνημμένον· τοῦτο τοίνυν συνέστηκεν ἐξ ἀξιώματος διφορουμένου ἢ ἐξ ἀξιωμάτων διαφερόντων καὶ διὰ τοῦ εἰ ἢ εἴπερ συνδέσμου.

[17] οὐκ ἐκτὸς γινόμενοι κατὰ τὸ παντελὲς τῆς τῶν Στωϊκῶν δόξης.

used terms which are foreign to the subject rather than those pertaining to grammar, and who introduced Stoic opinions, the transmission of which is not particularly useful for the technical study of grammar.

(*conj* 213.8–10)[18]

Stoic opinions, on grammar in general and on connectors in particular, are occasionally worth heeding but more usually irrelevant or worse. Whether or not Apollonius' judgement is just, we should be wary of finding too much Stoicism in or behind his *Connectors*.

But perhaps he took his definition of connectors from the Stoics? The Stoics, according to Diogenes Laertius, explained that

a connector is a caseless part of sayings which connects the parts of sayings.

(VII 58)[19]

That explanation is in certain ways surprising, and I shall return to the surprises. For the moment, it is enough to observe that it is echoed in a number of grammatical texts. A fragment from a Greek *Art of Grammar*, which is optimistically ascribed to Trypho by the papyrus which preserves it, contains this little exchange:

What is a connector?—An expression connective of parts of sayings.

(PLitLond 182, III 106–107)[20]

And according to a commentator on the Dionysian *Art*,

Apollonius, defining the term, says that a connector is a particle which is connective of the parts of sayings.

(scholiast to Dionysius Thrax, 435.40–436.1)[21]

So Apollonius took his account of connectors, directly or indirectly, from the Stoic philosophers?

Connectors has survived in a single stained manuscript, and the text opens in mid-sentence. No doubt the lost opening pages of the essay contained an explicit definition of the term 'connector'; and it is natural to imagine that the

---

[18] ὀνόμασιν ἀλλοτρίοις προσχρησάμενοι ἤπερ τοῖς εἰς γραμματικὴν συντείνουσι, Στωϊκὰς παρεισφέρουσι δόξας, ὧν ἡ παράδοσις οὐκ ἄγαν χρειώδης πρὸς τὴν εἰς γραμματικὴν συντείνουσαν τεχνολογίαν.

[19] σύνδεσμος δέ ἐστι μέρος λόγου ἄπτωτον, συνδοῦν τὰ μέρη τοῦ λόγου.

[20] σύνδεσμος τί ἐστιν; λέξις συνδετικὴ τῶν τοῦ λόγου μερῶν.

[21] ὁ δὲ Ἀπολλώνιος ὁριζόμενός φησι σύνδεσμον εἶναι συνδετικὸν μόριον τῶν τοῦ λόγου μερῶν.

commentator I have just cited was reporting that lost definition. But in fact the commentator's note is a paraphrase of a surviving sentence in Apollonius' *Syntax*, where he remarks that

after all the parts already catalogued, we mentioned connectors which are connective of them.

(*synt* I 28 [27.10–11])[22]

As for the definition which Apollonius presumably gave in his *Connectors*, that can be recovered by another route—and it is not just a repetition of the Stoic definition.

The story is a little complicated. In the *Art of Grammar* which goes under the name of Dionysius, connectors are explained as follows:

A connector is an expression connecting thoughts, together with order, and showing the gap in the interpretation.

(20 [86.3–4])[23]

The last clause is puzzling, and I shall get it out of the way before turning to the rest of the definition.

What on earth can the last clause mean? 'Showing the gap in the interpretation'?—The word 'interpretation' here means much the same as 'expression'. But how can a connector show a gap in an expression? Perhaps the Greek text is corrupt and must be emended? A passage in Apollonius' *Connectors* has been thought to suggest as much. It is concerned with the so-called 'parapleromatic' or expletive connectors. Those particles (to which I shall return) were thought, by most ancient grammarians but not by Apollonius, to serve a purely ornamental function. According to Apollonius,

Trypho, wanting to include them too [sc expletive connectors] in his definition [sc of the connector] says: and sometimes filling up the gap in the interpretation.

(*conj* 247.23–25)[24]

That last phrase, which is a direct quotation from Trypho's lost *Art*, seems to echo the last clause of the Dionysian definition. But Trypho uses the verb 'fill up [παραπληροῦν]' where our text of the *Art* has 'show [δηλοῦν]'. Trypho's

---

[22] ἐπὶ πᾶσι δὲ τοῖς κατειλεγμένοις ὁ τούτων συνδετικὸς σύνδεσμος παρελαμβάνετο.

[23] σύνδεσμός ἐστι λέξις συνδέουσα διάνοιαν μετὰ τάξεως καὶ τὸ τῆς ἑρμηνείας κεχηνὸς δηλοῦσα.

[24] ὁ Τρύφων ἐν τῷ ὅρῳ βουλόμενος καὶ αὐτοὺς ἐμπεριλαβεῖν φησί· καὶ τὸ κεχηνὸς τῆς ἑρμηνείας ἐστιν ὅπου παραπληρῶν.

'filling up' makes eminently good sense; for what do expletive connectors do but 'fill up the gap'? (In Greek, the point is trifling; for their name, 'παραπληρωματικοί', derives from Trypho's verb 'παραπληροῦν'.) Now 'παραπληροῦν' is a compound form of 'πληροῦν [to fill]'; and 'πληροῦν' looks not unlike 'δηλοῦν' on the written page. That has suggested that what Trypho read in his copy of the Dionysian *Art* was 'filling' rather than 'showing', 'πληροῦσα' rather than 'δηλοῦσα'. And surely what Trypho read was what the author of the *Art* originally wrote? The puzzling phrase 'showing the gap' is in our texts by accident—an ancient or mediaeval copyist miscopied his exemplar, and our editions have inherited his mistake. The suggestion is apparently supported by the fact that some of the mediaeval manuscripts of the *Art* actually offer the reading 'πληροῦσα'.

The suggestion is enticing. But there are snags. First, the reading 'πληροῦσα' was unknown to the ancient commentators on the *Art*, and the supposition that it is nonetheless authentic implies a curious and implausible textual history. Secondly, Trypho cannot have modelled himself upon the extant *Art*, which was not compiled until long after his death. Thirdly, Trypho's clause was intended to capture one special, and specially recalcitrant, type of connector, whereas the Dionysian definition appears designed to fit connectors in general.

All things considered, we had best soldier on with 'showing' or 'δηλοῦσα'. Then what can it mean? The ancient commentators offered various explanations, the least bad of which proposes that the clause was intended to cope with disjunctive connectors. After all, disjunctive connectors can hardly be said to connect a thought—but might they not picturesquely be said to show up a gap in things? Perhaps. But—again—the last clause in the definition ought to say something about connectors in general and not about a particular species of connector.

Some modern scholars have taken the clause to mean that the presence of a connector reveals not an actual gap but a virtual gap—something which would otherwise have been a gap. For example, the connector 'or' shows the gap in the expression

Heads or tails?

inasmuch as that same expression minus the connector, namely

Heads tails?

has a gap in it. Other modern scholars have observed that an expression like

Heads or

is incomplete, that it is as it were followed by a gap; and they have suggested that the connector 'or' shows the gap inasmuch as its presence at the end of the incomplete expression indicates that there is a gap to be filled.

Will you buy any of those interpretations? I won't—but I have nothing better to put on the market. Happily, the matter is not grave; for although many later grammarians discussed the last clause of the Dionysian definition, none of them imitated it; and it had no significance for ancient theorizing about connectors.

With that out of the way, what about the rest of the definition? The *Art* states that

a connector is an expression connecting thoughts, together with order.

In antiquity, not even that was accepted without question. Indeed, it was roundly criticized and replaced by an improved version. The criticisms, which need not be rehearsed, suggested that the definition was gravely deficient, requiring the adjunction of several further clauses. The criticisms also suggested that it was in one respect incorrect or misleading, and that for the phrase 'thoughts' there should be substituted 'parts of sayings'. (I shall return to the latter point.) Here is the improved version in one of its variant forms:

A connector is an uninflected part of sayings, connective of the parts of sayings, with which it co-signifies, determining either order or force or both order and force.

(scholiast to Dionysius Thrax, 102.15–18)[25]

The improved definition, and variants upon it, are found in other texts, both Greek and Latin. Diomedes, for example, gives this:

A connector is an uninflected part of sayings which links the expressions and connects the force and order of the parts of sayings. For it received its name on this account—because it is inserted into a saying as a bond; for, like a chain, when introduced it binds expressions which are loose and diffuse.

(*ars gramm* I 415.13–16])[26]

The Latin definition is a close paraphrase of the Greek. And the etymological explanation—'it received its name on this account'—must have been cribbed

---

[25] σύνδεσμός ἐστι μέρος λόγου ἄκλιτον, συνδετικὸν τῶν τοῦ λόγου μερῶν, οἷς καὶ συσσημαίνει, ἢ τάξιν ἢ δύναμιν ἢ καὶ τάξιν καὶ δύναμιν παριστῶν.

[26] *coniunctio est pars orationis indeclinabilis copulans sermonem et coniungens vim et ordinem partium orationis. nam ob hoc meruit nomen quia pro vinculo interponitur orationi. laxatum enim et diffusum sermonem more catenae interposita devincit.*

from a Greek text; for it makes no sense in Diomedes' Latin. (It pays unconscious tribute to Quintilian's preferred translation of 'σύνδεσμος'.)

No one names the inventor of the improved definition. But the Greek commentators on the Dionysian *Art* generally draw heavily on Apollonius, and it is a sporting bet that they do so here. Moreover, in Book XVI of his *Institutions* Priscian offers a translation of the improved definition as his own account of what connectors are (*inst* XVI i 1 [III 93.2–3][27]); and at the beginning of Book XVII he states that

in the previous books about the parts of sayings we have for the most part followed the authority of Apollonius.

(XVII i 1 [III 107.23–24])[28]

Where Priscian's statement can be checked, it turns out to be true. So there is another reason for thinking that the improved definition of connectors derives from Apollonius.

The improved definition is not identical with the Stoic definition, which ran thus:

A connector is a caseless part of sayings which connects the parts of sayings.

(Diogenes Laertius, VII 58)

But it adopts all the clauses of the Stoic definition, and adds a few more: why not think that it was developed by reflection upon the Stoic definition?

However that may be, the Stoic definition and the improved definition differ from the Aristotelian definition (and from the modern definition of a connective) in one striking way.

PARTS OF SAYINGS?

Modern connectives connect sentences. Aristotle's connectors connect expressions. According to the Stoics, connectors connect parts of sayings; and almost all the grammarians, both Greek and Latin, echo the Stoics. In particular, the improved definition—the Apollonian definition—echoes them on that point.

It is tempting to think that in these definitions the phrase 'parts of sayings' should be taken to mean 'the parts of the connected sayings which

---

[27] *coniunctio est pars orationis indeclinabilis coniunctiva aliarum partium orationis quibus consignificat vim et ordinationem demonstrans.*

[28] *in ante expositis libris de partibus orationis in plerisque Apollonii auctoritatem secuti sumus.*

the connector produces'. A grammatical papyrus which dates from the first century A.D. says that

a connector is an expression which links the parts of interpretations.

(PYale I 25, II 54–55)[29]

That is surely intended as a variant on the standard definition; and it is readily understood to mean that a connector is an item which connects the elements in the expression of which it is a part. And I ought to confess that the phrase which I have translated by 'the parts of sayings' has the word for saying in the singular and prefixed by a definite article: perhaps a better translation is 'the parts of the saying', that is to say 'the parts of the saying <in which it occurs as a connector>'?

There is a reason to hope that such an interpretation may be the right one. The connectors which appear essentially in Stoic logic serve to connect sayings—indeed, they function as sentential connectives (or at least, as items very closely related to sentential connectives). In that case, a Stoic connector connects the parts of the saying in this sense: the saying in which a connector appears itself has parts which are sayings, and the connector serves to bind those parts together. The definition which we are considering means, in effect and at bottom, to explain connectors in terms of sentential connection.

That interpretation is tempting. But the Greeks did not read the definition in that way—nor did the Romans. 'Parts of sayings', as they took the phrase, designates what we normally call the parts of speech. (Indeed, most English translators reasonably opt for 'parts of speech'.) For example:

Note also that the grammarian puts the account of connectors last in order. And reasonably: if they are called connectors inasmuch as they connect and bind and interweave, and if the items which are bound must be furnished before the connectors are, then the grammarian could not but take them after the other parts of sayings.

(scholiast to Dionysius Thrax, 435.36–40;[30] cf. 283.24–25)

Why are connectors treated after the other parts of sayings—names, verbs, adverbs, and so on?—Because they serve to connect those parts. The same notion is implicit in Apollonius, who thinks that the parts of sayings have an

---

[29] σύνδεσμος δ᾽ ἐστὶν λέξις συνάπτουσα τὰ μέρη τῆς ἑρμηνείας.

[30] ἰστέον δὲ πάλιν ὅτι τὸν περὶ συνδέσμου λόγον τελευταῖον τέταχεν ὁ τεχνικός. καὶ εἰκότως· εἰ σύνδεσμος λέγεται παρὰ τὸ συνδεῖν καὶ συνδεσμεῖν καὶ συμπλέκειν, δεῖ δὲ πρὸ τῶν συνδέσμων τὰ δεσμευόμενα προευτρεπίζεσθαι, ἀναγκαίως μετὰ τὰ προειρημένα μέρη τοῦ λόγου παρὰ τῷ τεχνικῷ ἔσχατος παρείληπται.

intelligible order—so that, at the end of the list, 'after all the parts already catalogued, we mentioned connectors which are connective of them' (*synt* I 28 [27.10–11]).[31]

So it seems that a connector will be an item which links, say, names to names, and verbs to verbs, and so on—and perhaps also names to verbs, and adverbs to adjectives, and so on. And that is just how the definition was construed. Perhaps the clearest statement of the view comes in a late and anonymous Latin commentary on Donatus:

A connector connects two names ('Virgil and Priscian'), two pronouns ('you and I'), two verbs ('reads and writes'), two adverbs ('yesterday and today'), two participles ('reading and writing'), it even connects itself ('if and when'), two prepositions ('around and about'), two interjections ('alas and alack').

(*in Don* VIII 263.23–27)[32]

The text perhaps suggests, incautiously, that any connector may connect instances of any part of sayings; but the fundamental idea is plain: connectors connect parts of sayings inasmuch as they may link a name to a name, a verb to a verb, and so on.

When the Latin grammarians explain why connectors are needed, they standardly take a pair of pronouns:

Our sayings are, in their nature, separated and discrete, and they cannot come into connection unless by the interposition of those parts [i.e. connectors]. ... If someone says

Let you me go,

the utterance is not complete; but if you interpose 'and', you make the utterance complete.

(Pompeius, *in Don* V 264.18–22;[33] cf. Servius, *in Don* IV 418.4–14)

The Greeks used a pair of proper names rather than a pair of pronouns—they took a line from the *Iliad*, dropped an 'and' which linked two names, and remarked that the line then falls apart (e.g. scholiast to Dionysius Thrax, 283.15–19).

---

[31] ἐπὶ πᾶσι δὲ τοῖς κατειλεγμένοις ὁ τούτων συνδετικὸς σύνδεσμος παρελαμβάνετο.

[32] *coniungit enim duo nomina ut Virgilius et Priscianus, duo pronomina ego et tu, duo verba legit et scribit, duo adverbia ut heri et hodie, duo participia ut legens et scribens, et se ipsam coniungit ut si et si, duas praepositiones circum et circa, duas interiectiones heu et euax.*

[33] *naturaliter enim nostra oratio dissidens et soluta est, nec potest in conexionem venire nisi interpositis illis particulis. ... siqui dicat ego tu eamus, non est plena ista elocutio. sed si interponas et, facis plenam elocutionem.*

That being so, it is no accident that 'and' is, so to speak, the paradigmatic connector. It was so for Varro who explained what connectors are by reference to the Latin '*et*':

What we say in uttering 'Cicero and Antony were consuls', with that same 'and' we can bind together any two consuls—or, to put it more generally, any names and indeed any words.

(*LL* viii iii 10)[34]

'and' is syntactically omnivorous—had Varro taken 'if', he would have had to tell a slightly different story.

Pompeius' introduction to his example suggests that any two words need to be glued together by a connector. But of course he does not mean to say anything so daft; rather—to judge from the context—he means to say that items from the same part of sayings need connecting. So too in Greek:

What we call connectors do not connect a name and a verb (no one says: Trypho and reads), but either a name and a name or a verb and a verb (Theo and Trypho, reads and writes). For connectors are connective of items of the same sort or as if of the same sort: I and you and Apollonius.

(scholiast to Dionysius Thrax, 516.7–11)[35]

Certain words fit naturally together, they are made for one another: a name satisfies the need of an intransitive verb, an adjective attaches itself by its own strings to a name, and so on; but a name won't stick to a name, nor a verb to a verb. Inter-class bonding needs no help from outside; for items from different classes automatically cohere. Intra-class bonding is another matter.

That idea is not silly. But it is at best eccentric. After all, sayings are not themselves parts of sayings; and yet one of the primary rôles played by connectors—by the items which the Greek and the Roman grammarians classified as connectors—is the rôle of joining sayings or sentences to one another. That must have been plain to the grammarians; and it must have been utterly evident to the Stoics inasmuch as in their logic connectors play an exclusively sentential rôle.

---

[34] *sic quod dicimus in loquendo consul fuit Tullius et Antonius, eodem illo et omnes binos consules colligere possumus, vel dicam amplius omnia nomina atque etiam omnia verba.*

[35] καὶ αὐτοὶ οἱ παρ' ἡμῖν καλούμενοι σύνδεσμοι οὐ συνδεσμοῦσιν ὄνομα καὶ ῥῆμα· οὐδεὶς γὰρ λέγει Τρύφων καὶ ἀναγινώσκει· ἀλλ' ἢ ὄνομα καὶ ὄνομα, ἢ ῥῆμα καὶ ῥῆμα, Θέων καὶ Τρύφων, γράφω καὶ ἀναγινώσκω· οἱ γὰρ σύνδεσμοι ὁμοιομερῶν εἰσι συνδετικοὶ ἢ ὡς ὁμοιομερῶν, ἐγὼ καὶ σὺ καὶ Ἀπολλώνιος.

SOME OFF-BEAT CONNECTORS

Nor is the idea that connectors connect parts of speech merely eccentric: it appears to count as connectors a number of items which are surely not connectors at all. For example, the word 'from' in

The boys from Brazil

seems to connect two parts of speech—two names. But 'from' is a preposition, not a connector.

Well, the Stoic Posidonius included prepositions among connectors; and the view that prepositions are a sort of connector is frequently ascribed to the Stoics in general: according to the grammarians, the Stoics called prepositions 'prepositive connectors' and connectors 'subordinative connectors'—so, for example, the Greek commentators on Dionysius Thrax (356.13–15,[36] 519.26–32); and also Priscian (*inst* II iv 17 [II 54.20–22]; XIV ii 18 [III 34.23–25]).

The grammatical commentators rehearse a few feeble reasons in favour of the Stoic thesis, reasons which they briskly refute. Apollonius says that

the Stoics called prepositions prepositive connectors, thinking it better to name them from their peculiar construction than from their force.

(*synt* IV 5 [436.13–437.1])[37]

And a little later:

We have said that in certain other juxtapositions too the prepositions come to show a connective construction. That gave the Stoics the impulsion to call them prepositive connectors. 'On account of what is he in pain?' and 'Because of what is he in pain?' are equivalent; and 'From idleness' and 'On account of idleness' are equivalent.

(IV 27 [457.12–458.3])[38]

Semantically speaking, 'because of [διά]', which is a preposition, functions just like 'on account of [ἕνεκα]', which is a connector. Hence 'because of'

---

[36] ... ὑφ' ἓν πρόθεσις καὶ σύνδεσμος, τὴν μὲν προθετικὸν σύνδεσμον προσαγορεύοντες, τὸν δὲ ὑποτακτικὸν σύνδεσμον.

[37] ἔνθεν γὰρ καὶ οἱ ἀπὸ τῆς Στοᾶς προθετικοὺς ἐκάλουν συνδέσμους τὰς προθέσεις, ἄμεινον ἡγησάμενοι ἀπὸ τῆς ἐξαιρέτου συντάξεως τὴν ὀνομασίαν θέσθαι ἥπερ ἀπὸ τῆς δυνάμεως.

[38] ὡς μὲν οὖν καὶ κατά τινας ἄλλας παραθέσεις αἱ προθέσεις συνδεσμικῆς συντάξεως γίνονται παρεμφατικαί, λέλεκται ἡμῖν. ἐξ ὧν καὶ ἡ ἀφορμὴ εἴληπται παρὰ Στωϊκοῖς τοῦ καλεῖσθαι αὐτὰς προθετικοὺς συνδέσμους· τὸ γὰρ ἕνεκα τίνος λυπῇ καὶ διὰ τί λυπῇ ἐν ἴσῳ ἐστί, καὶ τὸ ἐκ τῆς ῥαθυμίας ἐν ἴσῳ ἐστὶν τῷ ἕνεκα τῆς ῥαθυμίας.

shows a connective construction—and that, according to Apollonius, led the Stoics to identify it as a connector.

It is an odd argument. And in any event, the Stoics had a far better reason for counting prepositions as connectors; for connectors surely are 'caseless parts of sayings which connect the parts of sayings'—and that is the Stoic definition of what a connector is. The word 'from' is caseless, and it connects 'the boys' and 'Brazil'.

Why did Apollonius disagree with the Stoics? According to the Dionysian *Art*, a preposition is

an expression preposed to any part of sayings both in composition and in construction.

(18 [70.2–3])[39]

The commentators found fault with that; and they proposed—as they usually did—something better:

A preposition is a part of sayings, uttered in one form only, prepositive to any part of sayings in juxtaposition or in composition (except when it is uttered in conversion).

(scholiast to Dionysius Thrax, 91.20–22)[40]

(Prepositions 'in composition' are verbal prefixes; prepositions are 'uttered in conversion' when they follow the expression which they govern.) There is reason to ascribe this definition to Apollonius: Priscian asserts, of his own account of prepositions, that 'I have thought that the authority <of Apollonius> is to be followed in all matters';[41] and he immediately offers a definition of 'preposition' which translates the Greek of the commentator (*inst* xiv i 1 [iii 24.7–8]). And Apollonius himself says that

while the other parts of sayings have a single construction …, prepositions have two constructions, one with names and also one with verbs.

(*synt* iv 9 [440.7–14])[42]

That is how prepositions are distinguished from connectors: prepositions can, and connectors cannot, form verbal prefixes.

And that is why, in the eyes of the grammarians, 'ἕνεκα' or 'on account of' is a connector and not a preposition. It is so classified, without a murmur, by

---

[39] λέξις προτιθεμένη πάντων τῶν τοῦ λόγου μερῶν ἔν τε συνθέσει καὶ συντάξει.

[40] μέρος λόγου καθ᾽ ἕνα σχηματισμὸν λεγόμενον, προθετικὸν πάντων τῶν τοῦ λόγου μερῶν ἐν παραθέσει ἢ συνθέσει, ὅτε μὴ κατὰ ἀναστροφὴν ἐκφέρεται.

[41] … Apollonius, cuius auctoritatem in omnibus sequendam putavi.

[42] τὰ μὲν γὰρ ἄλλα μέρη τοῦ λόγου μίαν ἔχει σύνταξιν, … αἱ μέντοι προθέσεις δύο συντάξεις ἀναδεξάμεναι, τήν τε πρὸς τὰ ὀνόματα καὶ ἔτι πρὸς τὰ ῥήματα …

the *Art* (20 [93.2]), and also by Apollonius—who has two short discussions of the word, neither of which even considers the suggestion that it might be a preposition (*synt* II 67 [174.14–175.6]; *conj* 238.22–239.8). True, Apollonius hesitates over 'χάριν', which is a synonym of 'ἕνεκα'—but only because he thinks it might be better to classify 'χάριν' as a name than as a connector (*conj* 246.28–247.20). And in general, he has no qualms about connectors which take cases—on the contrary, he claims that 'we shall show that connectors do not take more than one case' (*synt* I 85 [73.10–11]).[43]

The Apollonian definition of the connector surely ought to have been modified in order to make it clear that, unlike the Stoics, the grammarians did not wish to count prepositions as connectors. But prepositions were not the only off-beat items which were sometimes classified as connectors. The Aristotelian commentators distinguished prepositions from connectors; but they treated the copula as a connector. Simplicius puts it directly:

When I say that this is white, I say nothing other than that this has whiteness—so to be and to have have the powers of connectors.

(*in Cat* 42.22–24)[44]

In

    Barkis is willing

or

    Barkis has willingness,

'is' and 'has' are connectors. After all, they serve to connect two parts of sayings—two names.

The point is made more than once by Ammonius, who elaborates it:

Since the predicated term too in such propositions is a name (e.g. 'just') and cannot, when coupled with the subject, in itself produce a complete saying, they needed as it were a sort of bond to connect them one to the other and make the saying complete; and that is what 'is' does.

(*in Int* 160.10–14)[45]

'Man' and 'just' are each names, and a couple of names will not stick together. They need a connector, and the need is supplied, in this case, by the word

---

[43] δείξομέν τε ὡς καὶ σύνδεσμοι οὐκ ἐπὶ πτώσεις φέρονται διαφόρους.

[44] ὅταν δὲ λέγω ὅτι τόδε λευκόν ἐστιν, οὐδὲν ἕτερον λέγω ἢ ὅτι τόδε λευκότητα ἔχει· τὸ οὖν εἶναι καὶ τὸ ἔχειν συνδέσμων ἔχει δυνάμεις.

[45] ἐπεὶ γὰρ καὶ ὁ κατηγορούμενος ἐν ταῖς τοιαύταις προτάσεσιν ὄνομά ἐστιν, οἷον τὸ δίκαιος, καὶ οὐ δύναται καθ᾽ ἑαυτὸν συνδυασθεὶς τῷ ὑποκειμένῳ τέλειον ἐργάσασθαι λόγον, ἔδει αὐτοῖς ὥσπερ δεσμοῦ τινος τοῦ συνδέοντος αὐτοὺς πρὸς ἀλλήλους καὶ τέλειον ποιοῦντος τὸν λόγον, ὃ ποιεῖ τὸ ἔστι.

'is'. 'I' and 'you', the grammarians tell us, are members of the same class of expression and will not hold together: they need the glue of 'and'. So too 'man' and 'just' need the bond of 'is'.

Philoponus agrees with Ammonius that the copula is a connector; and he goes further:

Why does Aristotle say that propositions dissolve into subject and predicate alone?—We say that strictly speaking these two items—that about which the saying is and that which is said about it—are the only parts of a proposition, and that the other items which are included in a proposition play the rôle of connectors.

(*in APr* 24.30–25.4)[46]

Modal adverbs, for example, are connectors, and in

Necessarily the sun rises

the word 'necessarily' is a connector, or at least plays the rôle of a connector. Not that it is a one-placed connector: rather, in Philoponus' view, it connects—or helps to connect—the predicate term to the subject term.

There seems to be a powerful objection to that analysis. For surely 'is' and 'has' are not connectors but verbs? No, they are not verbs—or at least, they are not fledged verbs. For verbs, according to Aristotle, signify something which holds of something: 'walks', for example, signifies walking, which holds of all and only walking items. But 'is' and 'has', when they are used to copulate subject and predicate, are not like that: in

Socrates is white

the word 'white' may perhaps signify something which holds of Socrates; but the word 'is' does not.

Even so, 'is' and 'has' surely have something verb-like about them: they indicate a time (in this case, the present time), and the indicating of time is a mark of the Aristotelian verb. Now, according to the ancient commonplace, it is indeed verbs which indicate times; but it is far from evident that the copulative 'is' does so. For according to one understanding of

Socrates was pale,

the subject is 'Socrates' and the predicate is 'an item which was pale'. The word 'was' in

Socrates was pale

---

[46] τί δήποτε τὴν πρότασιν εἴς τε τὸν ὑποκείμενον καὶ κατηγορούμενον διαλύεσθαί φησι μόνους; καὶ λέγομεν ὅτι κυρίως ταῦτα τὰ δύο εἰσὶ μόνα τῆς προτάσεως μέρη, τό τε περὶ οὗ ὁ λόγος καὶ τὸ περὶ ἐκείνου λεγόμενον, ὅσα δὲ ἄλλα παραλαμβάνεται ἐν τῇ προτάσει συνδέσμου χρείαν πληροῖ.

certainly does co-signify a time, and it is—among other things—a verb. But in fact, it is an amalgam of a copula and a verb; and the verbal part of it belongs with one of the terms. You might try to make the point clear by writing, say,

Socrates is pale-in-the-past.

Similarly, of course, for

Socrates is pale

you should really write

Socrates is pale-in-the-present.

In those two pseudo-sentences, 'is' is not a verb: it signifies nothing which holds of anything, and it indicates no time. Its sole function is to link the two terms of the proposition.

That understanding of the copula was promoted among modern philosophers by some logicians. It is already present, *in nuce*, in certain ancient texts. It is not, of course, the only way in which the copula may be construed, and it is not without its problems. But that is enough of the matter here.

Here is another off-beat connector. According to Simplicius, Lucius held that

articles ... too are a sort of connector, signifying in addition gender, masculine and feminine, and doing so indefinitely.

(in Cat 64.30–65.1)[47]

The Greek feminine article 'ἡ', for example, indicates a gender—but it does so indefinitely inasmuch as it does not in itself reveal what item named or nameable by a word of feminine gender is on the table.

Why Lucius thought that articles are connectors is unclear; but his thesis may perhaps be linked with the view later taken by Priscian, according to whom what he calls subordinative articles—that is to say, certain anaphoric pronouns—are connectors (*inst* xvii viii 56 [iii 142.4–6]). Priscian here adapts—and bowdlerizes—Apollonius, who argued the point thus:

As we said, the subordinative article is attached to a verb of its own, being connected by anaphora to a preceding name, and for that reason it does not produce a simple saying in virtue of its construction with two verbs (I mean, the verb which goes with the name and the verb which goes with the article itself). The same holds for the connector 'and': it takes the preceding name as something held in common, and by knitting on another saying it necessarily also takes another verb. So

---

[47] καὶ γὰρ ταῦτα οἷον σύνδεσμοί εἰσιν τὰ γένη προσσημαίνοντες τό τε ἄρρεν καὶ τὸ θῆλυ ἀορίστως.

The grammarian who was talking was present
has the same force as
The grammarian was present and was talking.
And the nomenclature of the parts of sayings is similar—'to be dependent' and 'to be connected' are not far from synonyms.

(synt I 144 [117.12–118.8])[48]

A subordinative article, in Apollonius' view, is not a connector—but it connects.

I might mention here a few off-beat non-connectors—I mean, items which the grammarians did not classify as connectors even though they apparently ought to have done. For example, of the word 'ἵνα' Apollonius says that

this particle has three varieties, two of them connective and one of them—the one which indicates place—adverbial. When it is connective, it changes the verbs constructed with it into the so-called subordinative inflection (just as the dubitative 'ἐάν' does) ... but adverbially it retains the indicative inflection.

(conj 243.11–16)[49]

Something similar is said of 'ὅπως' (*conj* 243.26–30), and of the archaic 'ὄφρα' (244.6–8); and Apollonius held the same view about 'ἐπεί' (*synt* IV 61 [483.3–9]). So too the Latins took '*ut*' to be a connector in some of its uses and an adverb in others (e.g. Diomedes, *ars gramm* I 408.10–24); and Priscian, having classified '*quando*' as an adverb, takes pains to add that 'it is indeed also found as a causal connector' (*inst* XV vi 38 [III 88.26–27]).[50]

The words in question are all ambiguous: in certain of their senses, they are connectors; but when they mean 'when' or 'where' they are not connectors but adverbs. Yet surely 'when' and 'where' satisfy the improved definition of connectors? And in any case, is it not perverse to deny that in, say,

---

[48] ὡς ἔφαμεν, τὸ ὑποτακτικὸν ἄρθρον ἐπὶ ῥῆμα ἴδιον φέρεται, συνδεδεμένον διὰ τῆς ἀναφορᾶς τῷ προκειμένῳ ὀνόματι, καὶ ἐντεῦθεν ἁπλοῦν λόγον οὐ παριστάνει κατὰ τὴν τῶν δύο ῥημάτων σύνταξιν, λέγω τὴν ἐν τῷ ὀνόματι καὶ τὴν ἐν αὐτῷ τῷ ἄρθρῳ. ὅπερ πάλιν παρείπετο τῷ καί συνδέσμῳ· κοινὸν μὲν παρελάμβανεν τὸ ὄνομα τὸ προκείμενον, συμπλέκων δὲ ἕτερον λόγον πάντως καὶ ἕτερον ῥῆμα παρελάμβανεν. καὶ οὕτω τὸ παρεγένετο ὁ γραμματικὸς ὃς διελέξατο δυνάμει τὸ αὐτὸ ἀποτελεῖ τῷ ὁ γραμματικὸς παρεγένετο καὶ διελέξατο, ἐγγιζούσης καὶ τῆς ὀνομασίας τῶν μορίων· τὸ γὰρ συνηρτῆσθαι καὶ συνδεδέσθαι οὐ μακρὰν τῆς συνωνυμίας πέπτωκεν.

[49] διαφορὰς ἔχει τὸ μόριον τρεῖς, συνδεσμικὰς μὲν δύο καὶ ἐπιρρηματικὴν μίαν, τόπου δηλωτικήν. συνδεσμικὸν μὲν οὖν καθεστηκὸς τὰ συντασσόμενα ῥήματα μετατίθησιν εἰς τὰ καλούμενα ὑποτακτικά, καθότι καὶ ὁ ἐάν ἐπιζευκτικός ...· ἐπιρρηματικῶς δὲ φυλάσσει τὴν ὁριστικὴν κλίσιν ....

[50] *quando autem etiam et pro coniunctione causali invenitur.*

Where the bee sucks, there suck I

the word 'where' serves to connect two sentences? Does it not connect 'the bee sucks' to 'there suck I'?

That was not the view of Apollonius: he held that 'where' and 'there' were correlatives; that 'there' is evidently a local adverb; and hence that 'where' is also a local adverb. (There is a third member of the party: the interrogative local adverb 'where'.) Apollonius was not being perverse. After all, the syntax of

Where the bee sucks, there suck I

is parallel to the syntax of

Whom the gods love die young.

As Apollonius recognizes, the 'whom' in that sentence does, in a sense, connect—it has a connective syntax. But it is not a connector. The sentence may be crudely paraphrased as follows:

Take anyone you like—if the gods love him, he dies young.

The work done by 'whom' in the original sentence is divided in the paraphrase between a quantifier, 'Take anyone you like', and a connective 'if'. The word 'whom' is, as it were, a conflation of quantifier and connector. So too, in Ariel's verse, the 'where' is an amalgam of connector and quantifier.

Nonetheless, it remains true that 'where' satisfies the improved ancient definition of the connector:

A connector is an uninflected part of sayings, connective of the parts of sayings, with which it co-signifies, determining either order or force or both order and force.

(scholiast to Dionysius Thrax, 102.15–18)

Just as the definition ought to have been modified so as to exclude prepositions, so too it ought to have been modified to exclude adverbs.

ORDER AND FORCE

Even if we set aside the off-beat cases, the improved definition of connectors still looks eccentric insofar as it refers to parts of sayings. What is more, it seems also to be incoherent. For on the one hand it explicitly rules that connectors connect parts of sayings, and on the other hand one of its clauses appears to presuppose that connected items are sentential. I refer to the obscure clause which decrees that a connector determines either order or force or both order and force.

It is clear, at least, that the order must be an order among the items which the connector connects. It is clear, too, that the order must be something to do with the meaning of the connector, or with the meaning of the connected sentences. From the examples which the commentators supply something like the following idea emerges. If you want to connect a number of items by means of a connector, the order in which you take the items sometimes matters and sometimes does not matter; that is, the order sometimes makes a difference to the sense of the connected item and sometimes makes no difference. So a connector is said to determine an order if and only if the order in which the connected items are taken makes a difference to the sense. Thus if you want to connect a couple of items by way of the connector 'if', it makes a difference whether you say 'If P, Q' or 'If Q, P': 'if' determines an order. On the other hand, if you connect the same items by 'or', the order makes no difference: 'Either P or Q' says the same as 'Either Q or P'. The disjunctive connector 'or' does not determine an order.

If that is order, then what is force? What is the force which a connector may or may not determine? 'Force' translates 'δύναμις' or '*vis*', and those words—at least when they are found in grammatical contexts—most often mean 'meaning' or 'sense'. In that case, the definition appears to mean that some connectors have a meaning but do not determine an order, that some determine an order but do not have a meaning, and that some do both things. But that is close to nonsense: how could a connector determine an order unless it had a meaning? Surely it is precisely the meaning of the connector 'if' which makes it determine an order?

It is true, as we shall shortly see, that some ancient theorists did deny meaning to some, or even to all, connectors; but Apollonius certainly did not, and neither did the late grammarians. In any event, the ancient commentators explain the pertinent notion of force in a very different way. First, they observe that, just as the order which a connector determines is the order of the items which it connects, so too the force which a connector determines is the force of the items which it connects. Secondly, they explain that 'force' here means 'holding' or 'being the case'. So, for example, while the connector 'if' determines an order,

it does not also announce a force, which is the holding of the object—for the utterer is in a state of doubt.

(scholiast to Dionysius Thrax, 102.31–32;[51] cf. 283.32)

[51] οὐκέτι δὲ καὶ δύναμιν ἐπαγγέλλεται, ὅ ἐστιν ὕπαρξιν τοῦ πράγματος· διστάζει γὰρ ὁ λέγων.

And more generally Priscian remarks that a connector indicates a force
when it means that certain items hold at the same time.

(*inst* xvi i 1 [iii 92.4])[52]

The connector 'if' does not determine a force inasmuch as 'If P, Q' entails
neither that P nor that Q. The connector 'and' determines a force insofar as
'P and Q' entails that P, and also that Q.

To use the word 'force' in that sense strikes me as peculiar; but I suppose
we should accept that the commentators understood things aright—indeed,
I daresay that Priscian's explanation comes from Apollonius himself.

Thus 'if'—for the reasons given—determines an order but not a force; and
'and' determines a force but not an order. The stock examples of connectors
which determine both an order and a force are 'since' and 'because': 'Since P,
Q' does not say the same as 'Since Q, P', so that 'since' determines an order;
and 'Since P, Q' entails that P and, also that Q, so that 'since' determines a
force. Similarly for 'because'.

The improved definition of connectors requires that all connectors determine either an order or a force or both. But what about disjunctive connectors?
They do not establish an order, since 'P or Q' says the same as 'Q or P'.
Nor—according to the account on the table—do they establish a force;
for 'P or Q' does not entail that P and does not entail that Q. So the
account needs to be modified. The ancient texts are not very clear on
the matter; but they seem to suggest that a connector will be said to
determine a force if and only if it requires that at least one of the connected items holds. Although 'P or Q' does not entail that P and does not
entail that Q, it does require that at least one of the two connected items
holds—and so it does determine a force. Even so, there are—or there may
be—connectors which escape the net. Consider, say, 'Neither ... nor ... ',
or 'Not both ... and ... '. But it is not worth pursuing that hare any
further.

Rather, let me insist on a consequence of any such account of force: insofar
as connectors are defined as items which may or may not determine a force,
they are conceived of as sentential connectives. For if a connector connects x
and y, then you may ask whether or not x and y hold, whether or not it is the
case that x and the case that y. And for that to make sense, the places of 'x'
and 'y' in that schematic sentence must be taken by indicative or assertoric
sentences.

---

[52] ... *quando simul esse res aliquas significat.*

That conclusion is unwelcome; for it threatens the improved definition with inconsistency: it explicitly requires that connectors connect the parts of sayings, and it implicitly requires that connectors connect whole sayings—and whole assertoric sentences at that. The menacing inconsistency might, in principle, be warded off by one device or another; but no ancient text even hints at any such device—indeed, no ancient text even notices the menace.

Now it will be allowed that the late grammarians were—to judge by what is left of them—a pretty pedestrian lot, and that the ancient grammarian's stone was quite capable of turning gold into base metal. But Apollonius was a better alchemist. Perhaps, then, the revised definition of the connector is not, after all, Apollonian? Perhaps it is a transmuted version of the definition which Apollonius actually gave?

WHAT DO APOLLONIAN CONNECTORS CONNECT?

James Harris, the eighteenth century English savant and eccentric, remarked that

Grammarians have usually considered the Conjunction as connecting rather *single Parts of Speech* than *whole Sentences*, and that too with the addition of like with like, Tense with Tense, Number with Number, Case with Case, &c. This *Sanctius* justly explodes.

(*Hermes* [London, 1751], p. 238 n.(a))

I do not know who Sanctius was, nor how he manufactured his explosion. But Harris confidently follows Sanctius—and he goes on to assure us that, in following Sanctius, he is returning to the correct doctrine of Apollonius Dyscolus.

Harris is right when he says that most grammarians made connectors connect parts of speech; but one or two ancient texts have been thought to recognize the centrality of sentences. For example, Plutarch writes as follows in his essay on the parts of speech:

He affirms that a connector is not a part of sayings but rather a sort of connective tool—as its name suggests—and something which holds together not any items whatever but non-simple expressions.

(*quaest Plat* 1011ab)[53]

---

[53] οὐ μέρος λόγου τὸν σύνδεσμον ἀλλ᾽ ὄργανόν τι συνδετικὸν ἀποφαίνει, καθάπερ ὠνόμασται, καὶ συνεκτικὸν οὐ πάντων ἀλλὰ τῶν οὐχ ἁπλῶς λεγομένων.

Are not non-simple expressions sentences, and does not the text imply that connectors are essentially sentential? Alas, no. All that Plutarch means—as the context makes quite plain—is this: whereas rhetoricians customarily praise unconnected figures or asyndetons, logicians sometimes find connectors necessary for binding their assertibles together. Plutarch suggests, perhaps, that logicians use connectors primarily in order to connect indicative sentences. He does not suggest that that was, in general, the primary function of connectors.

Or again, the definition of connectors offered by the Dionysian *Art* has been taken to hide a sentential heart up its sleeve:

A connector is an expression connecting thoughts together with order.

Does not that mean that a connector connects one thought to another? And is not a thought the sense of a sentence? So are not Dionysian connectors defined—at least so far as the first clause in the definition is concerned—as sentential links? Alas, no. The ancient commentators do not remark upon that supposed difference between Dionysius and all the other grammarians, who make connectors connect parts of sayings. Rather, they suppose that 'connect thoughts' and 'connect parts of sayings' are two different expressions for the same thing: a connector may be said, indifferently, to connect a thought (to bring it about that a string of expressions expresses a continuous thought) or to connect the parts of sayings (to bring it about that the parts stick together to form the expression of a continuous thought).

There are a few other authors who might be adduced; but they are all, I think, equally irrelevant—all except for one man. For many modern scholars agree with James Harris and claim that Apollonian connectors are essentially sentential. Various arguments are advanced in favour of that agreeable thesis. First, the vast majority of the illustrative examples in *Connectors* show connectors linking indicative or assertoric sentences. Secondly, Apollonius often explains the sense of a connector in a way which presupposes that it makes a sentential connection. For example,

the announcement of the disjunctive connectors announces the holding of one item and the rejection of the other or others.

(conj 216.14–16)[54]

---

[54] ἡ ἐπαγγελία τῶν διαζευκτικῶν <ἑνὸς ὕπαρ>ξιν ἐπαγγέλλεται, τοῦ δ' ὑπολειπομένου ἢ <τῶν ὑπολειπομένων> ἀναίρεσιν.—The Greek text can be restored with certainty thanks to the scholiast to Dionysius Thrax, 104.28–30.

The items in question are evidently sentential in their nature; and the disjunctive connectors are thus defined as sentential links.

Thirdly, Apollonius sometimes implies—or at least seems to imply—that by their very nature connectors bind sayings or sentences. Here are two passages from *Connectors* and three from the *Syntax* which tell in that sense.

The negation when placed before a verb makes a complete saying: I'm not writing, I'm not walking. That is characteristic of adverbs. But 'or' never does that ... rather, another saying must be taken ... and that is characteristic of connectors: I'm writing or I'm talking, I'm conversing or I'm reading.

(*conj* 222.18–23)[55]

The text is lacunose, the general sense certain: the expression 'or' cannot be added to a verb to make a saying—it calls for a second saying. The second passage from *Connectors* is this:

Again, 'It is day and' is not complete: it demands another phrase—'Both it is day and it is light'. It is the same with disjunctive connectors: 'Either it is day or it is night'. So we have proved that they are connectors inasmuch as they connect phrases.

(*conj* 216.6–10)[56]

This passage uses 'φράσις' rather than 'λόγος'; but the words are synonymous.

According to the *Syntax*,

in sayings, too, the accompanying connectors sometimes unify two sayings or even more—for example, sayings constructed from conditionals or quasi-conditionals or again conjunctives. And conversely their absence dissolves the sayings, as in

We went up into the forest as you ordered, noble Odysseus.

We found in the woods fine houses built.

It should have been bound together with 'and':

And we found in the woods ...

(*synt* I 10 [11.3–10])[57]

---

[55] ἡ ἀπόφασις πρὸ ῥήματος ἐπιτασσομένη ποιεῖ αὐτοτέλειαν—οὐ γράφω, οὐ περιπατῶ. ἦν δὲ τὸ τοιοῦτον ἴδιον ἐπιρρημάτων. ὁ δὲ ἤ οὐδέποτε τὸ τοιοῦτον ἀπετέλεσε ... τοῦ δ' ἑτέρου λόγου ἐξ ἀνάγκης παραλαμβανομένου ... ὅπερ ἦν ἴδιον συνδέσμου—γράφω ἤπερ λέγω, διαλέγομαι ἤπερ ἀναγινώσκω.

[56] ἔτι δὲ οὐκ αὐτοτελὲς τὸ ἡμέρα ἐστὶ καί, ἀλλ' ἐζήτει ἑτέραν φράσιν· καὶ ἡμέρα ἐστὶ καὶ φῶς ἐστί. τὸ αὐτὸ δὲ καὶ ἐπὶ τῶν διαζευκτικῶν· ἤ ἡμέρα ἐστὶν ἤ νύξ ἐστι. καὶ ὡς μὲν σύνδεσμοι κατὰ τὸ συνδεῖν τὰς φράσεις εἰσίν, ἀπεδείχθη.

[57] ἀλλὰ κἂν τοῖς λόγοις οἱ παρεπόμενοι σύνδεσμοι ἔσθ' ὅτε ἐνοῦσι δύο λόγους ἤ καὶ πλείους, καθάπερ οἱ συνδεόμενοι λόγοι ἐκ συνημμένων ἤ παρασυνημμένων ἤ καὶ ἔτι συμπεπλεγμένων· ἤ πάλιν ἀποστάντες διάλυσιν τῶν λόγων ποιοῦνται, ὡς ἔχει τὸ ἤομεν, ὡς ἐκέλευες, ἀνὰ δρυμά, φαίδιμ' Ὀδυσσεῦ· εὕρομεν ἐν βήσσῃσι τετυγμένα δώματα καλά. ἔδει γὰρ συμπλέξαι τῷ καί· καὶ εὕρομεν ἐν βήσσῃσι.

A little later, Apollonius remarks that a simple sentence may contain all but one of the seven parts of sayings which he recognizes, for example:

The same man, slipping, fell today.
The parts of sayings are there, apart from the connector, since when that is added it will demand another saying.

(*synt* I 14 [17.4–6])[58]

The saying contains, in order of occurrence, an article, a pronoun, a name, a participle, a verb, an adverb. It does not contain a connector, and in fact you cannot provide an example of a simple saying which uses all seven parts of sayings; for one of them, the connector, necessarily introduces a second saying.

Again, to show that certain items are not connectors Apollonius urges that

no one will think this—that they are connectors—inasmuch as they do not connect the adjunction of another saying, which is characteristic of connectors.

(*synt* III 69 [334.5–6])[59]

Other passages might be adduced. Collectively, they provide strong evidence—conclusive evidence, many scholars have thought—that Apollonian connectors essentially connect sentences.

And that conclusion is strengthened by a passage which seems at first glance to refute it. In *Adverbs* Apollonius observes that

some connectors connect name and verb universally and others are particular.

(*adv* 121.12–13)[60]

That is offered as an exhaustive disjunction: connectors, in other words, connect names and verbs, some of them connecting any old names and verbs and others being more particular in their tastes. So connectors connect names and verbs: that is to say, surely, that they connect names with names and verbs with verbs, or else names with verbs—and in any event that they connect parts of sayings rather than sentences.

The text readily lends itself to that reading, and Apollonius does nothing to warn his readers against it. But it is quite certainly a false reading.

---

[58] ὁ αὐτὸς ἄνθρωπος ὀλισθήσας σήμερον κατέπεσεν· ἔγκειται τὰ μέρη τοῦ λόγου παρὰ τὸν σύνδεσμον, ἐπεὶ προστεθεὶς ἕτερον λόγον ἀπαιτήσει.

[59] οὐδὲ γὰρ ἐκεῖνό τις οἰήσεται, ὡς σύνδεσμοί εἰσιν, καθὸ οὐ συνδέουσιν ἐπιφορὰν ἑτέρου λόγου, ὅπερ ἴδιον συνδέσμων.

[60] τίνες τε ἐν τῷ καθόλου σύνδεσμοι συνδέουσιν ὄνομα καὶ ῥῆμα, καὶ τίνες εἰσὶ μερικοί.

The sentence occurs in a paragraph in which Apollonius is remarking on the primacy of names and verbs among the parts of sayings: they are the 'thematic' or fundamental parts of sayings—the other parts merely serve their needs. Now a connector may serve the needs of names and verbs by, say, making a complex sentence from a couple of simple sentences. In doing so, it 'connects name and verb'—that is to say, it connects one name-verb couple to another. That is indubitably what Apollonius meant to say; and the connectors of that passage in *Adverbs* are therefore sentential.

For almost all the grammarians, connectors officially connect parts of sayings. For Apollonius, it now appears, they connect sayings or sentences. If that is so, then the fact that Apollonius thus distinguishes himself from his colleagues must have escaped the attention of the ancient commentators. There are, admittedly, traces of the apparently Apollonian view here and there. Thus one of the commentators on the Dionysian *Art* states that

the items in question are called connectors in virtue of the fact that they connect expressions and phrases, and they are called disjunctive connectors in virtue of their meaning. For while they are connective of the whole phrase, they disjoin the objects.

(scholiast to Dionysius Thrax, 104.25–28)[61]

He is tacitly paraphrasing a passage from Apollonius' *Connectors*; but he does not notice that it is—or appears to be—quite at odds with his official view about the nature of connectors.

Apollonian connectors are sentential—or at any rate, they are essentially or fundamentally or paradigmatically sentential. That conclusion is not easily resisted—and it is, of course, logically seductive. It has certain consequences. For example, if it is accepted, then we must accuse Apollonius of carelessness when he declares at the beginning of the *Syntax* that connectors are connective of the parts of sayings. We shall also be inclined to judge that the improved definition of connectors is not, after all, Apollonian. And we may like to conjecture that the Stoics originally explained connectors as sentential connectives; that Apollonius adopted, and also elaborated, their definition; and that the other Greek grammarians, together with all the Latins, either misunderstood the definition or else deliberately modified it, and thereby introduced the notion that connectors essentially connect parts of speech, a notion which came to dominate the whole of the grammatical tradition.

---

[61] καὶ οἱ προκείμενοι οὖν σύνδεσμοι μὲν εἴρηνται ἕνεκα τοῦ συνδεῖν τὰς λέξεις καὶ τὰς φράσεις, ἕνεκα δὲ τοῦ ἀπ' αὐτῶν δηλουμένου σύνδεσμοι διαζευκτικοὶ ὠνομάσθησαν· ὅλης γὰρ τῆς φράσεως ὄντες συνδετικοὶ τὰ ἐν αὐτῇ πράγματα διαζευγνύουσιν.

APOLLONIAN SAYINGS

The argument which makes Apollonian connectors sentential depends partly on the claim that by 'λόγος'—and also by 'φράσις'—he means 'sentence'. So I must say something about Apollonian sayings.

I have already noticed that although Aristotle frequently uses the word 'λόγος' to denote sentences—and in particular, indicative sentences—his formal definition determines as a λόγος any expression whatever which is more complex than a single name or verb. The same is true of Plato, who has this to say when, in the *Cratylus*, he sets out to describe the nature of language:

So we shall apply the letters to the objects, either one by one, wherever they seem to be required, or several together, thereby making what they call syllables, and then putting syllables together, from which names and verbs are put together; and then, again, from the names and verbs we shall assemble something grand and noble and whole—just as painters compose a picture by the art of painting, so we shall compose a saying by the art of naming or speaking or whatever it is.

(*Crat* 424E–425A)[62]

We start with letters, which are the elements or atoms of language. From letters we make syllables, and from syllables words. Finally, from words we make sayings.

Letters, syllables, words, sayings—the four-tiered hierarchy described by Plato became a standard part of ancient linguistic science. It is set out, for example, on the first pages of Apollonius' *Syntax* (I 2 [2.3–3.3]), and it serves to introduce his general conception of linguistic construction. The hierarchy recognizes no level above the level of the saying, and no level between the level of the word and the level of the saying. In general, ancient grammarians recognized the four Platonic levels, and no others.

It is true that a number of ancient theorists talk about linguistic units which they call 'commas' and 'colons'; and commas and colons are more than words and less than complete sayings (and commas are shorter than colons). For example, in his brief discussion of the definition of connectors given by the Dionysian *Art*, one of the ancient commentators asks:

---

[62] οὕτω δὴ καὶ ἡμεῖς τὰ στοιχεῖα ἐπὶ τὰ πράγματα ἐποίσομεν, καὶ ἓν ἐπὶ ἕν, οὗ ἂν δοκῇ δεῖν, καὶ σύμπολλα, ποιοῦντες ὃ δὴ συλλαβὰς καλοῦσιν, καὶ συλλαβὰς αὖ συντιθέντες, ἐξ ὧν τά τε ὀνόματα καὶ τὰ ῥήματα συντίθενται· καὶ πάλιν ἐκ τῶν ὀνομάτων καὶ ῥημάτων μέγα ἤδη τι καὶ καλὸν καὶ ὅλον συστήσομεν, ὥσπερ ἐκεῖ τὸ ζῷον τῇ γραφικῇ, ἐνταῦθα τὸν λόγον τῇ ὀνομαστικῇ ἢ ῥητορικῇ ἢ ἥτις ἐστὶν ἡ τέχνη.

What does interpretation mean?—The sentence. For a connector harmonizes to itself—I mean, by means of itself—the colons and commas.

(scholiast to Dionysius Thrax, 436.34–35)[63]

The sense of that remark is less than pellucid; but one thing is plain: an ancient grammarian here refers to commas and colons, and treats them as syntactical units (which may be united by connectors).

But the commentator says nothing more on the matter; and so far as I am aware, only one other grammatical text ever mentions commas and colons. That text is found in another of the commentaries on the Dionysian *Art*—and there the commentator associates the items with the rhetoricians, who are explicitly contrasted with the grammarians (scholiast to Dionysius Thrax, 295.41–296.1). In other words, one errant passage apart, commas and colons are not treated as grammatical or syntactical units. And that is because in fact they are not grammatical or syntactical units: they are metrical units, comparable to lines of verse or to strophes or to stanzas. Hephaestion discusses them briefly in his *Handbook on Metre* (*ench* xvi 114); Dionysius of Halicarnassus mentions them in his remarks on prose rhythm (*comp verb* xxvi 213).

In short, it is true that commas and colons are linguistic units, and it is true that they are (normally, at least) more than words and less than complete sayings. But they do not, for that reason, stand between words and sayings: they do not belong to the same sort of classification as words and sayings, they have nothing to do with syntax or with grammatical theory.

So as far as ancient grammar is concerned, there is no class of items between the class of words and the class of sayings, and there is no class of items more complex than sayings. In that case, sentences will surely count among sayings—and, of course, no one has ever doubted that they do so count. But equally surely, certain types of non-sentence ought to count among as sayings—and in fact Aristotle, as I have already recorded, recognizes subsentential units (such as definitional formulas) and also supersentential units (such as the *Iliad*) as sayings. Indeed, anything from a two-word phrase to a twenty-four book poem ought to count as a saying—provided, of course, that it has some syntactical unity. Perhaps it seems curious to place *The Tempest* and 'the tempest' in the same syntactical class; but what else can you do once you have kowtowed to the four-level hierarchy?

---

[63] τί σημαίνει ἑρμηνεία; τὴν φράσιν· ὁ γὰρ σύνδεσμος τὰ κῶλα καὶ κόμματα συναρμόττει αὐτῷ, τουτέστι δι᾽ ἑαυτοῦ.

Even if they had not read their Aristotle, the grammarians can hardly have failed to notice the existence of items larger than sentences—of sequences of sentences. So what sort of unit is a sequence of sentences? Well, if you take two or more sayings and make some one item out of them, the one item must be a saying—there is nothing else for it to be. If you regard *The Tempest* as a single unit—I mean, as a single syntactical unit—then *The Tempest* is a saying. Of course, an ancient grammarian was not obliged to classify *The Tempest* as a saying; for he was not obliged to think of it as a syntactical unit of any sort. Indeed, the play surely isn't such a unit. Nonetheless, there are certain sequences of sentences which the ancient grammarians did take to be syntactical units—and those items can only be classified as sayings. (The items in question will come in for a later discussion.)

If the grammarians allow that sequences of sentences are sayings, then their class of sayings cannot be identified with the class of sentences.

Again, consider a subsentential item. In the sentence

Jehu driveth furiously

an ancient grammarian would have discovered three words (and eight syllables, and so many letters). But it is surely plain that the sentence also consists of the name 'Jehu' together with the verbal formula 'driveth furiously', which is itself composed from the words 'driveth' and 'furiously'. True, someone might try to deny that 'driveth furiously' is a proper part of the sentence; someone might try to claim that the sentence simply consists of a string of three words and that there is no structure to it apart from its string-like structure. But such an attitude is not only hopelessly inadequate from a theoretical point of view: it is also an attitude which an ancient grammarian could hardly have contemplated with approval. For the ancient grammarians insist that adverbs are 'predicated' of verbs, that they attach to verbs, that they modify verbs. In other words, they implicitly recognize that within the sentence

Jehu driveth furiously

'driveth furiously' forms a unit.

What sort of unit? Not a word; for it has parts which signify separately—and by any criterion for counting it will be deemed to consist of at least two words. So it must be a saying. There is nothing else for it to be. But if the grammarians allow that items such as 'driveth furiously' are sayings, then their class of sayings cannot possibly be identified with the class of sentences.

And nevertheless they do seem to identify sayings and sentences. No definition of the word 'saying' is explicitly ascribed to Apollonius; but there are definitions in the other grammarians, Greek and Latin. The

Greek word 'λόγος', as every schoolboy knows, is multiply ambiguous. The commentators on the Dionysian *Art* offer lengthy accounts of its several senses (e.g. 213.6–214.2; 353.27–355.15); and they are, of course, particularly interested in the sense which the *Art* defines. This is what is found in the *Art*:

An expression is a smallest part of a constructed saying. A saying is a combination of prose expressions which indicates a complete thought.

(11 [22.4–23.1])[64]

The phrase 'complete thought' is hardly precise. But it is precise enough for me here. For it is plain that a paragraph does not, as a rule, express a complete thought—rather, it expresses a string of complete thoughts; and it is quite plain that an expression such as 'driveth furiously' does not express a complete thought. So a saying, according to the *Art*, is a sentence of prose.

The commentators were not prepared to limit sayings to prose. One of them objects briskly:

This excludes verse sayings. So a saying should be defined as follows: A combination of expressions which is well-formed and which rounds off a thought.

(scholiast to Dionysius Thrax, 214.5–6)[65]

This revised definition is found in one variant of another in several Greek and Latin texts. Diomedes offers two definitions—first there is something which I do not understand and then comes a version of the commentator's Greek, thus:

A saying is a construction of words in which an outcome is composed and which ends in a closure. Some define it thus: A saying is a combination of expressions which rounds off a thought and signifies a complete object.

(*ars gramm* I 300.17–19)[66]

More significantly, Priscian comes even closer to the Greek:

A saying is a sequence of expressions which is well formed and which indicates a complete thought.

(*inst* II iv 15 [II 53.28–29])[67]

---

[64] λέξις ἐστὶ μέρος ἐλάχιστον τοῦ κατὰ σύνταξιν λόγου. λόγος δέ ἐστι πεζῆς λέξεως σύνθεσις διάνοιαν αὐτοτελῆ δηλοῦσα.

[65] τοῦτο ἐκβάλλει τοὺς ἐμμέτρους. ὁριστέον οὖν οὕτως· σύνθεσις λέξεων κατάλληλος διάνοιαν ἀπαρτίζουσα.

[66] *oratio est structura verborum composito exitu ad clausulam terminata. quidam sic eam definiunt: oratio est compositio dictionum consummans sententiam remque perfectam significans.*

[67] *oratio est ordinatio dictionum congrua sententiam perfectam demonstrans.*

Priscian habitually follows Apollonius, and here he paraphrases or translates the revised definition of what sayings are: so is it not likely that the revised definition is Apollonian? If so, then Apollonian sayings are, officially, sentences.

Now the subject of Apollonius' *Syntax* is the construction—the syntax—of what he calls complete sayings. That is what the opening words of the work announce:

> In the lectures which we have already made public an account of utterances was laid out as the matter demanded. The publication which is now to be presented will contain the construction of utterances into well-formed and complete sayings, a matter which I have decided to set out with all exactitude inasmuch as it is indispensable for the interpretation of poetry.
>
> (*synt* I 1 [1.1–2.2])[68]

If anything is a complete saying, then surely a sentence is. So, for example, in *Connectors* Apollonius notes that

> 'It is day' is complete, but 'Either it is day' is not complete.
>
> (*conj* 225.9–10)[69]

'It is day' is a sentence, 'Either it is day' is a sentence fragment. The sentence is a complete saying, the fragment is not. That example takes an indicative or assertoric sentence; but Apollonius sometimes illustrates his remarks with other sorts of sentences—with imperatives, for example, or with interrogatives—and there is no reason in the world to doubt that they too are to be reckoned among complete sayings.

Should complete sayings be identified with sentences? The identification is certainly tempting, and temptation is not a thing I like to resist. But consider the following case. 'Mimi, Mimi', sobs Rodolfo—and the curtain falls. Does *La Bohème* end with a sentence? According to Apollonius, it ends with a complete saying; for

> the vocative, being complete, demands a mark of punctuation.
>
> (*pron* 53.16)[70]

---

[68] ἐν ταῖς προεκδοθείσαις ἡμῖν σχολαῖς ἡ περὶ τὰς φωνὰς παράδοσις, καθὼς ἀπῄτει ὁ περὶ αὐτῶν λόγος, κατείλεκται· ἡ δὲ νῦν ῥηθησομένη ἔκδοσις περιέξει τὴν ἐκ τούτων γινομένην σύνταξιν εἰς καταλληλότητα τοῦ αὐτοτελοῦς λόγου, ἣν πάνυ προῄρημαι, ἀναγκαιοτάτην οὖσαν πρὸς ἐξήγησιν τῶν ποιημάτων, μετὰ πάσης ἀκριβείας ἐκθέσθαι.

[69] τὸ ἡμέρα ἐστίν αὐτοτελές, ἀλλὰ τὸ ἤτοι ἡμέρα ἐστίν οὐκ αὐτοτελές.

[70] ἡ κλητικὴ αὐτοτελὴς οὖσα στιγμὴν ἀπαιτεῖ.

And again, more expansively:

I have not forgotten that completeness is evidence for the vocative. Take 'Helicon'—if it requires a verb, that testifies to the nominative; if not, it is in the vocative case, e.g. O Helicon.

(*synt* III 119 [372.7–10])[71]

A saying is complete if it can be used to say something complete—if, in the Stoic jargon, it can be used to express a complete sayable. Having sobbed his 'Mimì, Mimì', Rodolfo has nothing more to add.

If you feel qualms about classing isolated vocatives as sentences, then you will deny that all Apollonius' complete sayings are sentences: all sentences are complete sayings, some complete sayings are not sentences.

What about suprasentential units? What about the *Iliad*? Is Homer's poem, according to Apollonius, a complete saying? There is, so far as I have noticed, nothing in the surviving texts which determines an answer to that question. But there are a few passages—which will be cited in a later context—which explicitly classify as sayings, and implicitly as complete sayings, items which we should be inclined to count as sequences of sentences rather than as sentences.

However that may be, in practice Apollonius' complete sayings virtually coincide with sentences. What, then, is the relation between a saying and a complete saying? Scholars seem generally to suppose that the phrase 'complete saying' is pleonastic, so that something is a complete saying if and only if it is a saying. In that case, Apollonian sayings will, in practice, virtually coincide with sentences.

But why suppose that the phrase is pleonastic? After all, the notion of an incomplete saying is far from absurd—and in many ways it seems to be just the sort of notion which Apollonius would and should have embraced. For the Stoics distinguish between complete sayables and incomplete or deficient sayables, among which they number predicates; and just as a complete saying—a sentence—is an expression of a complete sayable, so an incomplete saying will be an expression of an incomplete sayable. Since verbs and verbal phrases express predicates, such items as 'runs', and 'runs silently', and 'runs silently and very fast' will count as incomplete sayings.

---

[71] οὐ λέλησμαι ὅτι καὶ ἡ αὐτοτέλεια τεκμήριόν ἐστιν κλητικῆς· ἰδοὺ γὰρ καὶ αὐτὸ τὸ Ἑλικών ἐλλεῖπον μὲν ῥήματι εὐθεῖαν ὁμολογεῖ, οὐ τῇδε δὲ ἔχον κλητικῆς ἐστιν πτώσεως τὸ τοιοῦτον, οἷον ὦ Ἑλικών.

An account of incomplete sayings along those lines would be easy to develop; and it ought to have been welcomed by any grammarian. After that, you might audaciously add the notion of a more than complete saying—that is to say, of a sequence or set of complete sayings: a paragraph, or a discourse, or whatever. More than complete sayings are, it is true, a modern fancy which no ancient text comes near to fingering. But incomplete sayings could well have been antique.

Nonetheless, no surviving text of Apollonius mentions incomplete sayings; and indeed no surviving text discusses—save quite incidentally—linguistic units which fall between words and sentences. It is doubtless the lack of any contrast in the texts between complete sayings and incomplete sayings which encourages the thesis that Apollonius' phrase 'complete saying' is pleonastic. And after all, a pleonastic use of the phrase is intelligible enough: the adjective need not be construed as contrasting one type of saying with another—its function may rather be to indicate the pertinent sense of the ambiguous word 'λόγος'.

So at this stage in the inquiry it seems reasonable to conclude that in Apollonius sayings are complete sayings and complete sayings are virtually identical with sentences. In that case, Apollonian connectors—inasmuch as they call for sayings—are, at bottom, sentential connectives.

WHAT DID APOLLONIUS REALLY THINK?

But there are further texts waiting to be called upon, and they will muddy the stream.

I have already said that Apollonius construes the word 'ἕνεκα [on account of]' as a causative connector rather than as a preposition. In one of his discussions of the item he mentions the variant form 'ἕνεκεν', and comments thus:

> It is written, in a more poetic form, with an iota, like .... The connector is always applied to the genitive of an item which takes cases: On account of me, On account of him, On account of Apollonius.

> (*conj* 238.22–24)[72]

If a modern reader is surprised to find 'on account of' classified as a connector, Apollonius evidently found nothing to marvel at. Nor does he blench at saying that a connector takes a case: on the contrary, in the *Syntax* he claims that

---

[72] ποιητικώτερον μετὰ τοῦ ι λέγεται, καθότι καὶ τὸ *** ὁ σύνδεσμος πάντοτε ἐπὶ γενικὴν πτωτικοῦ φέρεται· ἕνεκα ἐμοῦ, ἕνεκα αὐτοῦ, ἕνεκα Ἀπολλωνίου.

we shall show that connectors do not take more than one case—On account of Apollonius, On account of Dionysius.

(*synt* I 85 [73.10–12])[73]

Sayings are not cased items. So Apollonius cannot consistently hold that connectors are essentially sentential and also that some connectors take cases; and he quite explicitly asserts that some connectors take cases.

As for Apollonius' illustrative examples, it is true that *Connectors* generally makes a point by citing a sentence, and an assertoric sentence at that. But it is not always so. First—as I have already remarked—there are several illustrative sentences which are not assertoric: there are imperatival examples, say (e.g. *conj* 218.6). Secondly, there are very many examples in which—at least on the surface—it is either individual words, or else subsentential complexes, which a connector connects. Here is a banal case:

The remark
   Either Apollonius will be present or Trypho
announces a temporary disjunction.

(*conj* 217.4–5)[74]

There the disjunctive connector apparently connects a name to a name, or perhaps a name to a sentence. Or again:

There is a third use of the connector '$\ddot{\eta}$' which is called declaratory—for it declares the holding of the first item and the rejection of the next: I want to be rich rather than [$\ddot{\eta}$] to be poor, I want to work rather than [$\ddot{\eta}$] to relax.

(*conj* 221.16–19)[75]

The connector 'rather than' (which in Greek has the same form as the disjunctive connector) connects an infinitive to an infinitive. It does not connect two sentences. There are a dozen or more examples of that sort in *Connectors*.

But are not the examples phantoms? A modern grammarian will insist that in

   Either Apollonius will be present or Trypho

---

[73] δείξομέν τε ὡς καὶ σύνδεσμοι οὐκ ἐπὶ πτώσεις φέρονται διαφόρους· ἕνεκεν Ἀπολλωνίου, ἕνεκεν Διονυσίου.

[74] τὸ δὲ λεγόμενον ἢ Ἀπολλώνιος παρέσται ἢ Τρύφων ὡς πρὸς καιρὸν τὴν διάζευξιν ἐπαγγέλλεται.

[75] ἔστι καὶ τρίτη διαφορὰ τοῦ ἢ συνδέσμου, ἥτις καλεῖται διασαφητική. τοῦ μὲν γὰρ προτέρου ὕπαρξιν διασαφεῖ, τοῦ δὲ ἐπιφερομένου ἀναίρεσιν· βούλομαι πλουτεῖν ἢ πένεσθαι, βούλομαι φιλολογεῖν ἢ σχολάζειν.

the connector 'Either … or …' in fact connects two sentences. The second sentence is

Trypho will be present;

the underlying form of the disjunction is

Either Apollonius will be present or Trypho will be present;

and

Either Apollonius will be present or Trypho

—or rather, its Greek translation—is the conventional abbreviation of the underlying item.

Does not Apollonius take virtually the same line on such examples? This is what he says in the *Syntax* about a parallel case:

> The so-called collective connectors take a name or a verb in common from the sayings concerned. Hence they are not punctuated, the next saying being continuous with the one before us. Let us set out examples. From ordinary speech,
>
> Both Dio walks and Apollonius
>
> takes 'walks' in common.

(synt ii 60 [170.19–171.4])[76]

In other words, the verb 'walks' is to be taken twice, once with each conjunct; and in that case 'and' in effect conjoins sentences. Apollonius himself refers to the second item as a saying.

Here Greek and English differ, inasmuch as

Both Dio walks and Apollonius

is not a decent English sentence. English will rather say

Both Dio and Apollonius walk.

The difference is not trifling. For in the English version the verb is plural, and for that reason it cannot be taken twice. Rather, the subject of the verb is the nominal conjunction 'Both Dio and Apollonius'. Nonetheless, that only means that you have to work a trifle harder to find a sentential 'and' underlying the English sentence than to find one beneath its Greek counterpart.

Yet it is not evident that Apollonius sniffed out an underlying sentential connective in his sentence. He treats the same matter again in *Pronouns*. Here is the pertinent passage:

---

[76] οἱ δὴ καλούμενοι ἀθροϊστικοὶ σύνδεσμοι ἐκ τῶν προκειμένων λόγων ἀπὸ κοινοῦ λαμ-βάνουσιν ἢ ὄνομα ἢ ῥῆμα. ἐντεῦθεν καὶ στιγμῆς ἀπροσδεεῖς εἰσιν, ὡς ἂν ἔτι ἐχομένου τοῦ προσιόντος λόγου ὡς πρὸς τὸν ὑποκείμενον. ἐκκείσθω δὲ ὑποδείγματα, ἐκ μὲν τοῦ συνήθους λόγου καὶ Διονύσιος περιπατεῖ καὶ Ἀπολλώνιος, κοινοῦ παραλαμβανομένου τοῦ περιπατεῖ.

Conjoined or disjoined items necessarily require in their continuation the same part of sayings as, or a part equipollent with, the item conjoined or disjoined, the part constructed with it being often taken in the sequel in common with the item conjoined or disjoined. For example

Both Apollonius talked

requires 'and Dionysius' or some such name—or else a pronominal item which is equipollent with a name—and it often uses 'talked' in common. Again, if it is a verb, the conjunction or the disjunction requires a verb—

Dionysius both wrote

Dionysius either wrote

You must continue with a verb—for example

and talked

or something similar, 'Dionysius' often being taken in common.

(*pron* 41.9–19)[77]

The items which are conjoined or disjoined—the items which are connected by connectors—are unambiguously identified as parts of speech; and Apollonius' argument makes no sense if the connectors are construed as sentential connectives.

The English version of his thesis looks like this: In a sentence of the form

Both X and Dionysius talked,

the 'X' must be replaced by the same part of speech as the other conjunct (or by an equipollent part of speech). Since the other conjunct is a name, 'X' here must be replaced by a name (or by a pronoun). And in the Greek version of

Both Apollonius and Dionysius talked

you may take the (singular) verb 'talked' twice, once with 'Apollonius' and once with 'Dionysius'. The fact that you take the verb twice does not suggest to Apollonius that the 'and' really connects two sentences. Rather, he implies that in

Both Apollonius talked and Dionysius talked

the 'and' connects two names, just as in

Both Apollonius talked and Apollonius wrote

---

[77] τὰ δὴ συμπεπλεγμένα ἢ διεζευγμένα κατὰ τὴν ἐπιφορὰν πάντως τὸ αὐτὸ μέρος λόγου ἀπαιτεῖ ἢ ἰσοδυναμοῦν τῷ συμπεπλεγμένῳ ἢ διεζευγμένῳ, τοῦ συντεταγμένου μέρους λόγου κατὰ τὸ ἑξῆς πολλάκις κοινοῦ καθεστῶτος τῷ συμπεπλεγμένῳ ἢ διεζευγμένῳ, οἷον τὸ καὶ Ἀπολλώνιος διελέξατο ἀπαιτεῖ τὸ καὶ Διονύσιος ἤ τι τοιοῦτον ὄνομα ἢ ἀντωνυμικόν, ὅπερ ἦν ἰσοδυναμοῦν ὀνόματι, κοινῷ τε τῷ διελέξατο πολλάκις προσχρῆται. εἰ δὲ ῥῆμα ἦν, πάλιν ἡ ἐπιπλοκὴ ἢ ἡ διάζευξις ἀπαιτεῖ ῥῆμα, καὶ ἔγραψε Διονύσιος, ἤτοι ἔγραψε Διονύσιος· δεῖ γὰρ ῥῆμα ἐπενεγκεῖν πάλιν, ἢ διελέξατο ἤ τι τοιοῦτον, κοινῶς πολλάκις νοουμένου τοῦ Διονύσιος.

the 'and' connects two verbs.

Here is a pertinent passage from *Connectors*:

Trypho says that the connector 'because' is construed both with cased items and with caseless items:
Because the sun is above the earth, it is day.
Because I walk, I move.
But in truth, matters stand thus: the connector 'because' is applied exclusively to the indicative of the verb, so that the cased items, or anything else, which are construed with it are taken in hyperbaton:
Because well I read.
The coherent form is:
Because I read well.

(*conj* 235.11–18)[78]

Trypho's view is this. On the one hand, in the sentence
Because the sun is above the earth, it is day
—or rather, in the Greek sentence
ὅτι ὁ ἥλιος ὑπὲρ γῆν ἐστίν, ἡμέρα ἐστίν
—the connector 'because' (or 'ὅτι') is construed with the cased word 'the sun' (or 'ὁ ἥλιος'). On the other hand, in the sentence
Because I walk, I move
—or rather, in
ὅτι περιπατῶ, κινοῦμαι
—the same connector is construed with the caseless verb 'I move' (or 'κινοῦμαι').

That is a bizarre piece of syntax, and Apollonius was right to reject it. But Apollonius does not reject it by denying that the connector is construed with either the verb or the name and by affirming that it is construed with the whole of the sentence which follows it. Rather, he states that 'ὅτι' is construed—and invariably construed—with a following indicative verb. Thus although you will say, for example,
ὅτι καλῶς ἀναγιγνώσκω
[Because well I read]

---

[78] φησὶ Τρύφων τὸν ὅτι σύνδεσμον καὶ πτωτικοῖς καὶ ἀπτώτοις συντάσσεσθαι· ὅτι ὁ ἥλιος ὑπὲρ γῆν ἐστίν, ἡμέρα ἐστίν· ὅτι περιπατῶ, κινοῦμαι. τὸ δὲ ἀληθές τῇδε ἔχει· ὁ ὅτι σύνδεσμος μόνως φέρεται ἐπὶ τὰ ὁριστικὰ τῶν ῥημάτων, ὥστε τὰ συντασσόμενα πτωτικὰ ἢ ἄλλα τινὰ ἐν ὑπερβατῷ λαμβάνεσθαι. ὅτι καλῶς ἀναγινώσκω· τὸ γὰρ ἀκολουθοῦν ἐστιν ὅτι ἀναγινώσκω καλῶς.

the word-order is inappropriate inasmuch as it masks the syntax: the 'coherent' or perspicuous formulation is

ὅτι ἀναγιγνώσκω καλῶς,

[Because I read well]

where it is plain that the connector attaches to the verb.

That argument shows that, in Apollonius' considered view, the connector 'because' takes not a sentence but a verb. A passage in the *Syntax* has suggested that he took this to be an idiosyncrasy of the connector 'because' (see *synt* II 66 [174.6–13]). But the passage does not imply that notion, which seems vastly implausible; and another passage from the *Syntax* clinches the issue:

Two verbs cannot make a single construction without a conjunction. This is clear from the example we have already given:
The philosopher Dio is talking
together with a second example
Being a philosopher, Dio is talking
and a third
Dio is a philosopher and is talking
Without the connector 'and' it will not be well formed:
Dio is a philosopher is talking.

(*synt* I 107 [90.5–10])[79]

Apollonius does not say that two sentences will not cohere unless there is a connector: he says that two verbs will not so cohere.

The later grammarians all suppose that connectors link parts of sayings. And although Apollonius frequently speaks of connectors as connecting sayings, and although the sayings are often sentences, nonetheless, he also speaks of connectors as connecting parts of sayings, and once at least he says that they construe with verbs. On the face of it, his remarks about the syntax of connectors, taken collectively, are confused or incoherent.

Is there some coherent theory behind or beneath the apparent confusion? Perhaps what Apollonius means is this: Connectors construe with parts of sayings, and in particular with verbs; but they connect sentences. In
Dio is walking and is talking
the connector 'and' construes with the following verb, 'is talking'; but it connects the saying 'Dio is talking' to the saying 'Dio is walking'. Perhaps

---

[79] δύο ῥήματα οὐ δύναται μίαν σύνταξιν ἐπιδέξασθαι δίχα συμπλοκῆς. καὶ σαφές ἐκ τοῦ ὑποδείγματος, τοῦ μὲν προειρημένου ὁ φιλόσοφος Δίων διαλέγεται, τοῦ δὲ δευτέρου φιλόσοφος ὢν Δίων διαλέγεται, τοῦ δὲ τρίτου φιλόσοφός ἐστι Δίων καὶ διαλέγεται· οὐ γὰρ συστήσεται δίχα τοῦ καί συνδέσμου, φιλόσοφός ἐστι Δίων διαλέγεται.

'and' connects the second saying to the first precisely inasmuch as it construes with the second verb. The two sayings won't form a unit unless something connects them. They won't do so because a couple of finite verbs won't appear together in a single unit unless some connector ties them together. If

Dio is walking Dio is talking

must be construed as two sayings rather than as one, then that is because

Dio is walking is talking

is not syntactically well formed.

If you stuff an 'and' between the pair of sayings, you get a single saying:

Dio is walking and Dio is talking.

Similarly, if you intrude an 'and' into the ill-formed sequence, you get something well formed, namely:

Dio is walking and is talking.

In each case, the 'and' construes with the verb 'is talking', it connects 'is talking' to 'is walking', and it thereby permits the appearance of the two verbs in a single saying. In each case, 'and' connects the second saying 'Dio is talking' to the first saying 'Dio is walking'.

Philosophers have sometimes wondered if we really see tomatoes, or if we only see the surfaces of tomatoes. We see both; and we see the tomatoes precisely insofar as we see their surfaces. Readers of Apollonius have wondered if, on his view, connectors really connect sayings, or if they only connect parts of sayings. They connect both; and they connect sayings precisely insofar as they connect parts of sayings.

That is a crude sketch of the only sort of explanation I can find which might bring coherence to Apollonius' account of the grammar of connectors. But it is far from clear how such a sketch might be elaborated into a picture; and it is far from clear that any such elaboration would in the end reconcile all, or even most, of the different things which Apollonius says. And of course, there is not the slightest hint in the ancient texts that Apollonius had ever dreamed of such an idea.

MULTIPLE CONNECTIONS

Aristotle's connectors connect a plurality of significant expressions from which they make one significant expression. The grammarians' connectors also link a plurality of items:

They are called connectors, not nectors, since a nector may be applied to a single item whereas a connector requires two or more.

(scholiast to Dionysius Thrax, 283.5–6;[80] cf. 20–24; 436.8–10)

'It is not the case that' and 'Necessarily' are not connectors according to the ancient account of the matter: if the modern logician counts them as one-placed connectives, the ancient grammarian thinks (not unreasonably) that the phrase 'one-placed connector' is a *contradictio in adjecto*.

The ancients and the moderns differ in another respect. Modern logic has one-placed connectives and two-placed connectives. If it does not also have three-placed connectives and four-placed connectives and ..., that is not for ideological reasons: any such items (provided that they are the sort of connective with which modern logic concerns itself) can readily be defined in terms of the two-placed items. In any event, every connective in modern logic has a fixed and determinate number of places: none can connect here a pair of items and there a trio. Ancient connectors are not like that: they are not limited each to its fixed number of places. According to the Dionysian *Art*,

conjunctive connectors are those which connect an expression which is going on endlessly.

(19 [88.3–89.1])[81]

That is opaque; but a commentator explains that

someone who says 'and I walk' posits the object; and I can say, where the order is indifferent, 'I walk and I move and I read'—and whatever else you like.

(scholiast to Dionysius Thrax, 103.3–6)[82]

The connector 'and' (which determines a force but not an order) connects as many items as you please.

Similarly Apollonius, in a passage I have already cited, observes that 'the connectors which accompany the sayings sometimes unite two or even more sayings' (*synt* I 10 [11.3–5]); and his *Connectors* applies that general remark to several particular cases. For example,

---

[80] σύνδεσμος δὲ εἴρηται καὶ οὐ δεσμός, ἐπεὶ δεσμὸς καὶ ἐφ' ἑνός, σύνδεσμος δὲ ἐπὶ δύο καὶ πλειόνων.

[81] συμπλεκτικοὶ μὲν οὖν εἰσιν ὅσοι τὴν ἑρμηνείαν ἐπ' ἄπειρον ἐκφερομένην συνδέουσιν.

[82] ὁ γὰρ λέγων καὶ περιπατῶ τίθησι τὸ πρᾶγμα· ἀδιαφόρως δὲ περὶ τὴν τάξιν δύναμαι εἰπεῖν καὶ περιπατῶ καὶ κινοῦμαι καὶ ἀναγινώσκω καὶ εἴ τι βούλει ἕτερον.

the announcement of the disjunctive connectors announces the holding of one and
the removal of the other or of the others.

(conj 216.14–16)[83]

A disjunctive connector may connect two items or three or …

How exactly does a connector manage to connect three or more items?
Earlier I offered as an example of such a phenomenon the sentence:

Let him go, let him tarry, let him sink, or let him swim.

That sentence is a disjunction. It has four disjuncts. It has a single disjunctive
connector. Surely that is a paradigm case of a connector connecting more
items than two?

No doubt it is; but it cannot be the sort of thing which the ancient
grammarians had in mind—if only because Greek and Latin do not permit
such constructions. If you want to translate the four-part disjunction into
Greek you must add a couple of connectors where English can make do with
a couple of commas.

So consider the example offered by the commentator on the Dionysian
Art:

I walk and I move and I read.

That is, I take it, meant to be a case in which the connector 'and' connects
three items. But how can that be so? Surely the sentence contains two
connectors, each of which connects two items? (The first 'and' connects 'I
move' to 'I walk', the second 'and' connects 'I read' to 'I move', or perhaps
to 'I walk and I move'.) If the connector 'and' really connects three items,
then surely there ought to be only one occurrence of the word 'and', or of the
conjunctive connector, in the sentence? So perhaps we should say that, despite
appearances, the word 'and' does indeed occur only once—but it is, as it were,
split into two parts. The underlying form of the sentence might be shown thus:

AND (I walk, I move, I read)

which in ordinary parlance comes out as

I walk and I move and I read

—or rather (in English) as

I walk, I move, and I read.

How otherwise could it be supposed that 'and' may connect three items?

That way of looking at things might be enforced by considering such turns
as 'Both … and …', 'Neither … nor …', 'Either … or …'. Take

---

[83] ἡ ἐπαγγελία τῶν διαζευκτικῶν ἑνὸς ὕπαρξιν ἐπαγγέλλεται, τοῦ δ' ὑπολειπομένου ἢ τῶν
ὑπολειπομένων ἀναίρεσιν.

Both the President and the Vice-president were crooks of the first water. That is a conjunction, and the conjunctive connector conjoins two items. What is the connector? Surely it is 'Both ... and ...': surely that is a single occurrence of a conjunctive connector, and it is, as it were, accidentally split into two parts.

The Stoic logicians habitually wrote their conjunctions with a 'Both ... and ...' or 'καί ... καί ...'; and in the same way they habitually wrote their disjunctions with an 'Either ... or ...' or an 'ἤτοι ... ἤ ...'. Those Stoic habits are not pedantic affectations: they are pieces of normal Greek. Apollonius, of course, recognizes them. So, for example, he acknowledges a 'prepositive' use of the disjunctive connector—indeed, he takes it to be the normal use of the connector 'ἤτοι'.

Nonetheless, Apollonius has nothing interesting to say about the prepositive 'Either'; and neither he nor any other ancient author ever hints at the notion of a split connector. I suppose that no one ever asked an old grammarian how many occurrences of a conjunctive connector there are in the sentence

You can't be both in Paris and unhappy.

But had one been asked, he would surely have said: 'Two—one of them prepositive'. And had he been asked the same question of the sentence

I walk and I move and I read,

he would certainly have answered 'Two', and he would have done so without embarrassment.

But ought he not to have been embarrassed? After all, if the answer is 'Two', then how can he also maintain that in some cases a single connector connects more items than two? So far as I can see, the only plausible answer to that question runs along the following lines. In the sentence

I walk and I move and I read,

the first 'and' connects 'I move' to 'I walk', and so links a pair of items; and the second 'and' connects 'I read' to 'I walk and I move'. The second 'and' therefore connects three items—inasmuch as it connects one item to a pair of items. When you couple a tenth carriage to a nine-carriage train, the coupling joins ten carriages together: it makes a train of ten carriages, not a train of one complex carriage and one simple carriage.

Perhaps that sounds plausible for 'and'; and perhaps something similar would sound similarly plausible for 'or'. But surely some connectors—'if', for example—are essentially two-placed? Well, the ancient grammarians do not distinguish between two-placed connectors and multi-placed connectors;

and what little they say on the matter tends to suggest—without ever coming straight out with it—that all connectors are in principle multi-placed. So consider this sentence:

If I'm in Germany I drink beer if I'm thirsty.

Why not say that the first 'if' is two-placed, attaching 'I drink beer' to 'I'm in Germany' whereas the second 'if' is three-placed, attaching 'I'm thirsty' to 'If I'm in Germany I drink beer'?

Finally, something similar may be said for sentences which mix their connectors. For example, in

We're in Europe or we're in Asia if we're in Turkey

the 'if' connects the saying which follows it to the two which precede it. It adds a third carriage to a two-carriage train.

The railway-train model has a certain appeal—at any rate, it has the appeal of naïveté. But it faces difficulties, some of them syntactical and others semantic. Consider, first, a syntactical point.[84] It may be introduced by way of the last illustrative example; for that sentence might be parsed in either of two ways; and if it is claimed that the 'if' connects 'we're in Turkey' to what precedes it, then it must be recognized that the connection may have either of two distinct characters. The two characters and the two parsings can be crudely indicated as follows:

[We're in Europe or we're in Asia] if we're in Turkey

We're in Europe or [we're in Asia if we're in Turkey]

Any decent theory of connectors will recognize the two parsings, and the difference between them.

The issue is a general one. True, it does not arise for conjunctive connectors. In modern logic the conjunctive connective is two-placed, so that a formula of the form

P & Q & R

is ill-formed: if you want to conjoin three items you must write either

(P & Q) & R

or else

P & (Q & R).

That might lead you to think that in English three-part conjunctions admit, in principle, three parsings, namely:

I walk and I move and I read

---

[84] Paolo Crivelli brought the point to my attention.

[I walk and I move] and I read
I walk and [I move and I read]

But the parsings make no difference: whichever way it is parsed, the conjunctive sequence says the same thing, expresses the same saying.

Things are different in the case of disjunction. Just like a three-part conjunction, a three-part disjunction such as

He's good or he's bald or he's ugly

might be parsed in any of three ways, namely:

He's good or he's bald or he's ugly
[He's good or he's bald] or he's ugly
He's good or [he's bald or he's ugly]

And here the different parsings are not indifferent. A disjunctive connector, as Apollonius puts it, 'announces the holding of one and the removal of the other or of the others' (*conj* 216.14–16), so that a disjunction is true if and only if exactly one of its disjuncts is true. That being so, the three-placed disjunction

He's good or he's bald or he's ugly

will say something different from the two-placed disjunction

[He's good or he's bald] or he's ugly.

Suppose that, as a matter of horrid fact, he's good and he's bald and he's ugly. (That's why the example is unorthodox by a letter.) Then plainly the three-part disjunction

He's good or he's bald or he's ugly

is false; for exactly none of its disjuncts is true. But consider the two-placed disjunction. Since he's good and he's bald, the disjunction

He's good or he's bald

is false. But in that case, exactly one of the disjuncts in the two-placed disjunction

[He's good or he's bald] or he's ugly

is true, namely 'He's ugly'; so the two-placed disjunction is true.

Such phenomena certainly raise questions for multi-placed connectors; but I am not sure that they raise any genuine or peculiar difficulties. No doubt the ancient grammarians should somehow have distinguished between the three-placed and the two-placed readings of

He's good or he's bald or he's ugly.

They did not do so, so far as we can tell. But nothing in their theory prohibits them from doing so. Should they not at least have told us how to determine the number of items which a connector connects in a given saying? Well, it would have been nice had they pointed out that the question is not to be answered by merely enumerating the simple sentences which are constituents of the connected sentence. But that apart, what else is there to say?

'How many items does this connector here connect?' Sometimes the answer is immediately evident—if, say, the saying contains a single connector which connects two simple sayings. Sometimes the answer is given by some turn of idiom—for example, there is no doubting the intended parsing of

Sometimes I sits and thinks and sometimes I just sits.

Sometimes the context, or general background knowledge, or simple savvy, will do the trick. I recently saw on the slate in my local brasserie:

Plat + entrée ou dessert: € 16.

I was not troubled by the formal ambiguity. That is all there is to be said, on the general level. The fact that more cannot be said should not worry a partisan of multiple connections. For two-placed connectors raise exactly similar questions, to which—outside the confines of artificial languages—there are no general answers to be had.

So much for the syntactical difficulty. Consider now a semantic point. I said that in the case of the three-part disjunction

I stand or I sit or I lie,

the first 'or' is two-placed and connects 'I sit' to 'I stand', whereas the second 'or' is three-placed and connects 'I lie' to 'I stand or I sit'. But if that is so, then the first 'or' must be taken to be semantically inert—to contribute nothing to the sense of the sentence. For if it is taken as a two-placed connector and if it is assigned its standard sense, then either the sentence must be parsed as

[I stand or I sit] or I lie,

or else it is simply ill formed.

Perhaps it is semantically inert? After all, in

Either I stand or I sit,

the word 'either' was taken to be a disjunctive connector and yet to be semantically inert. It is, so to speak, a punctuation mark—or better, an indication of disjunctive things to come. Why not say something similar about the first 'or' in

I stand or I sit or I lie?

Well, perhaps you might develop that line of thought; but there is surely a better one.

I asked how many places should be assigned to the first and to the second 'or' in the triple disjunction. If there is an answer it can only be that the pair of 'or's has, as a pair, three places. But it was a bad question. You may reasonably ask how many disjunctive connectors are present in a sentence, or how many disjuncts a sentence disjoins; but that is all there is to ask—there is no further question as to the number of disjuncts each disjunctive connectors disjoins. In

I stand or I sit or I lie

there are two disjunctive connectors, and the sentence expresses a three-part disjunction. What more is there to be known about its disjunctive nature? Nothing.

Well, its disjunctive sense is still to be explained. Earlier, following Apollonius, I suggested that a disjunctive connector announces that precisely one of the items which it disjoins is the case. That is a poor suggestion: if disjunctions are allowed to have two or three or... members, then it is better to explain what they mean in the way which Sextus adopts, namely:

A disjunction announces that one of the items in it is sound and the other or the others false (together with conflict)

(*PH* ii 191)[85]

Similarly, if you want to explain the sense of the Greek disjunctive connector, then why not say something roughly along these lines:

A sentence of the sort: '$\ddot{\eta}\tau o\iota$' + P_1 + '$\ddot{\eta}$' + $\cdots$ + '$\ddot{\eta}$' + P_n is true if and only if precisely one P_i is true.

And perhaps, after all, that is what Apollonius means when he says that

the announcement of the disjunctive connectors announces the holding of one and the removal of the other or of the others.

(*conj* 216.14–16)

CONNECTION AND UNIFICATION

Connectors connect a plurality of items. But what exactly is a connection? The two-placed sentential connectives of contemporary logic unify, in the sense that they take a couple of sentences and make a single sentence. Aristotle says that connectors unify, and that a connection is a unification—or at least, an accidental unification. The ancient grammarians also speak, occasionally, of

---

[85] τὸ γὰρ ὑγιὲς διεζευγμένον ἐπαγγέλλεται ἓν τῶν ἐν αὐτῷ ὑγιὲς εἶναι, τὸ δὲ λοιπὸν ἢ τὰ λοιπὰ ψεῦδος ἢ ψευδῆ μετὰ μάχης.

unification. But the view that connectors unify was contested in antiquity—at any rate, according to Plutarch,

there are some who think that connectors do not make a unity but that the connected discourse is an enumeration, as when rulers or days are listed one after the other.

(quaest Plat 1011c)[86]

That anonymous view is not otherwise reported; and it is hard to take seriously the notion that all connectors simply make for a sequential enumeration. But there is in principle nothing odd about the notion of a non-unifying connection.

In the *Poetics* Aristotle distinguishes between what he calls 'σύνδεσμοι' and what he calls 'ἄρθρα', or between connectors and articulators. (The standard translations give 'conjunctions' and 'articles': 'articles' is wildly misleading—and, as I have already said, Aristotle's use of 'ἄρθρον' has nothing to do with the use of the word in later grammatical texts. As for 'σύνδεσμος', 'conjunction' is infelicitious in any logical context, and we should not suppose without some ado that in Aristotle the word has the sense which it bears in later authors.) The text of the passage is corrupt—and in particular, Aristotle's illustrative examples cannot be recovered with any certainty. But it is plain that articulators serve to articulate a text without thereby unifying it.

How might that be done? Suppose you are giving a number of short reasons in favour of a proposition. You might introduce the second and subsequent reasons with the word 'again'; and Aristotle might use the word 'ἔτι'. If I write

X. Again, Y.

I have connected Y to X, but I have not made a single unified saying out of X and Y. (Why not?—Well, 'X. Again, Y' hasn't got a truth-value: each of its elements has its own truth-value.—Why not give it a truth-value, saying that it is true if and only if each of its elements is true?—That is a question to which I shall half return.) I suggest that 'again'—in that usage—is an Aristotelian articulator; and if that is on the right lines, then it is not difficult to identify further items which articulate without unifying.

The grammarians do not take up Aristotle's articulators; but some of the items which they classify as connectors Aristotle might well have classified as articulators. So you might surmise that the grammarians' connectors

---

[86] τοὺς δὲ συνδέσμους εἰσὶν οἱ μὴ νομίζοντες ἕν τι ποιεῖν, ἀλλ᾽ ἐξαρίθμησιν εἶναι τὴν διάλεκτον, ὥσπερ ἀρχόντων ἐφεξῆς ἢ ἡμερῶν καταλεγομένων.

were meant to include both Aristotle's unifying connectors and also his non-unifying articulators. And in that case, the grammarians' connectors will not always unify.

Evidence in favour of that surmise has been found in Apollonius. Of the expletive connector 'δή' he remarks that

everyone is aware that 'δή' is sometimes superfluous; but that it also often makes a transition of sayings is clear from examples such as the following … For we think of the cessation of one saying and the beginning of another.

(*conj* 251.19–23)[87]

At least one connector signals the end of one saying and the beginning of another: so if I write something of the form 'P—Q δή', I do not unify a couple of items—I hold them at arm's length from one another.

That passage has no fellow in Apollonius' surviving works; it is part of an argument, which is often strained, to show that expletive connectors are genuine connectors; and it concerns the function of 'δή' when it is working together with another connector. So even if the passage unambiguously implied that there are non-unifying connectors, we should be wary of putting much weight on it. But in fact the passage does not imply that 'δή' does not unify. Consider a parallel case. Some people had wondered how disjunctive connectors could possibly be connectors: surely they don't connect things—they disjoin or separate them. Apollonius answers thus:

The connectors in question are called connectors because they connect phrases and so possess the characteristic feature of connectors. They are called disjunctive because of what they indicate—for while being connective of the whole phrase, they disjoin the objects in it.

(*conj* 216.2–6)[88]

A disjunctive connector connects (and unifies) syntactically and at the same time it disjoins semantically. In the same way, Apollonius might have said, the connector 'δή' marks a break semantically and at the same time it constructs a unity syntactically. He might have said that—and I think he would have said it.

---

[87] ἔτι ὁ δὴ ὡς μὲν παρέλκει, παντὶ πρόϋπτον· ὡς δὲ καὶ πολλάκις μετάβασιν λόγου ποιεῖται, σαφὲς ἐκ τῶν τοιούτων … νοοῦμεν γὰρ λόγου ἔκλειψιν καὶ ἀρχὴν ἑτέρου.

[88] οἱ δὴ προκείμενοι σύνδεσμοι εἴρηνται μὲν σύνδεσμοι ἕνεκα τοῦ συνδεῖν τὰς φράσεις, ὥστε τὸ κοινὸν τῶν συνδέσμων αὐτοὺς ἀναδεδέχθαι· ἕνεκα δὲ τοῦ ἀπ' αὐτῶν δηλουμένου διαζευκτικοὶ ὠνομάσθησαν. ὅλης γὰρ τῆς φράσεως ὄντες συνδετικοί, τὰ ἐν αὐτῇ πράγματα διαζευγνύουσιν.

Apollonius speaks of unification in several different linguistic contexts. For example,

sometimes supervening accidents have produced a sort of unification—when 'τί ποτε' suffers from syncope and is unified in 'τίπτε σὺ δείδοικας...'.

(*adv* 149.10–13)[89]

Or again,

'οἶκον δέ' and 'τὸν οἶκον δέ' are not the same: 'I shall go οἶκον δέ', not 'I shall go τὸν οἶκον δέ'. Relying on such arguments, they say that such things have been unified into an adverbial derivative.

(*adv* 181.6–9)[90]

Or again,

It is not plausible, as Trypho says in his *On Prepositions*, that the prepositions are unified with the verbs and yet do not receive any inflexions externally inasmuch as, being prepositions, they ought not to have anything in front of them.

(*synt* IV 36 [464.9–12])[91]

One word is sometimes unified with another: that is to say—as all the examples make clear—two words sometimes become a single word.

Apollonius says very little about unification in *Connectors*. But the following passage which introduces the causal connector 'γάρ' or 'for' is pertinent.

The particle produces the same construction as ὅτι [or 'because'], and it has the same force. But it is different in that ... it is not taken at the beginning of the sayings but in subordination. That is why it displaces into second order the causes which are placed at the beginning when they are with prepositive connectors, and in that way the saying is true. Take examples:
   Because it is day, it is light
If we remove 'ὅτι' and add 'γάρ', the saying becomes false ...

(*conj* 239.9–15)[92]

---

[89] ἔσθ᾿ ὅτε γὰρ τὰ ἐπισυμβαίνοντα πάθη ὡς ἕνωσιν τῶν μορίων ἀπετέλει, ὅτε καὶ τὸ τί ποτε ὑπὸ συγκοπὴν πεσόντα ἤνωται ἐν τῷ τίπτε σὺ δείδοικας.

[90] οὐ μὴν ταὐτόν ἐστιν ἐν τῷ οἶκον δέ καὶ τὸν οἶκον δέ· οἶκον δέ γὰρ ἐλεύσομαι, οὐ μὴν τὸν οἶκον δέ ἐλεύσομαι. τοῖς τοιούτοις λόγοις ἐπανέχοντές φασιν ἠνῶσθαι τὰ τοιαῦτα εἰς ἐπιρρηματικὴν παραγωγήν.

[91] οὐ γὰρ ἐκεῖνο πιθανόν, καθό φησιν Τρύφων ἐν τῷ περὶ Προθέσεων, ὡς ἠνωμέναι μὲν εἰσιν αἱ προθέσεις μετὰ τῶν ῥημάτων, οὐ μὴν τὴν προσγινομένην κλίσιν ἔξωθεν ἐπιδέχονται, καθὸ προθέσεις οὖσαι οὐκ ὀφείλουσιν πρὸ αὐτῶν τι ἔχειν.

[92] τὴν αὐτὴν σύνταξιν ποιεῖ τὸ μόριον τῷ ὅτι, δύναμίν τε τὴν αὐτήν. ἔχει δὲ παραλλαγὰς ... τὸ ἐν ἀρχῇ μὴ παραλαμβάνεσθαι τῶν λόγων, ἐν ὑποτάξει δέ. διὸ καὶ κατ᾿ ἀρχὴν τιθέμενα τὰ αἴτια μετὰ τῶν προτακτικῶν συνδέσμων εἰς δευτέραν τάξιν μεθίστησι, καὶ οὕτως ἀληθεύει ὁ λόγος. ἔστω δὲ ὑποδείγματα· ὅτι ἡμέρα ἐστί, φῶς ἐστιν. εἰ ἀφέλοιμεν τὸν ὅτι καὶ προσθείημεν τὸν γάρ, ψευδὴς ὁ λόγος γίνεται.

The connectors 'because' and 'for' have the same force; but 'because' is prepositive whereas 'for' is postpositive or subordinative. That is to say,

Because it is day, it is light

is equivalent not to

It is day; for it is light

but to

It is light; for it is day.

Not everything in that passage is uncontestable; and Apollonius' analysis of 'for'—or rather, of 'γάρ'—might be questioned. But it is plain that he takes it to be a unifying connector, just like 'because'. In other words, he thinks that

It is light; for it is day.

constitutes a single unified item. True, he does not here use the word 'unify'; but he calls

It is day; for it is light

a saying, and he ascribes a truth-value to it.

We might have guessed that the word 'for' would be counted as an Aristotelian articulator, or as a connector which links without unifying. Apollonius takes it to be a unificatory expression. Was that an eccentric point of view? In his commentary on the *Analytics* Alexander tries to explain how a certain argument which is not a genuine syllogism can be pummelled into syllogistic shape. The argument is this:

A is equal to C
B is equal to C
Therefore A is equal to B

To turn that inference into a syllogism, we need to do two things: first, we must add a universal premiss; and then

we must condense the items which were assumed as two propositions into a single proposition which has the same force as the two—namely: A and C are equal to the same thing for they are equal to B.

(*in APr* 344.17–19)[93]

Now scholars generally—and understandably—take the single condensed proposition to be

A and C are equal to the same thing.

---

[93] ... τὰ εἰλημμένα ὡς δύο προτάσεις εἰς μίαν συστείλωμεν πρότασιν ἣ ἴσον ταῖς δύο δύναται· ἔστι δὲ αὕτη τὸ δὲ Α καὶ Γ τῷ αὐτῷ (τῷ γὰρ Β) ἴσον.

And having so construed Alexander, they then complain, with justice, that that proposition is not in fact equivalent to the conjunction of the two original premisses of the argument. But perhaps the complaint is misplaced, and perhaps the single proposition is meant to be:

A and C are equal to the same thing, for they are equal to B.

Apollonius would have counted that as a single saying. Perhaps Alexander did too?

However that may be, there are two further Apollonian passages to be adduced. Each of them makes a general statement. One comes in *Adverbs* and the other in the *Syntax*. In *Adverbs* Apollonius says that

connectors never signify anything on their own, but they connect sayings, ordering them consecutively and thus interconnecting and unifying them.

(*adv* 133.25–134.1)[94]

That clearly indicates that connectors always unify—indeed, it suggests that connecting is precisely a matter of unification. And in the *Syntax*:

The connectors which accompany the sayings sometimes unify two or even more sayings ... or again, being absent, make a dissolution of the sayings.

(*synt* I 10 [11.3–7])[95]

That has been read as suggesting that connectors sometimes unify and sometimes merely connect. But that is not Apollonius' meaning. The word 'sometimes' is picked up by 'again': connectors sometimes, by their presence, unify, and sometimes, by their absence, dissolve. In other words, connectors always unify.

Connectors unify—they take a number of items and they produce a single item. But a single what? There is, of course, no reason to expect any answer to that question beyond the empty 'A single expression'; for what item a connector makes will depend in part on what items it takes. Let 'and' take 'you' and 'I' to make 'you and I'. What sort of an expression is that? We might call it a pronominal phrase, or a pronominal complex; and similarly we might call 'if and when' a connective phrase, 'now if ever' an adverbial phrase, and so on. But the ancient grammarians, as I have already remarked, had no terminology for and no theoretical interest in such complex expressions

---

[94] οἱ δὲ σύνδεσμοι οὔποτε κατ᾽ ἰδίαν σημαίνουσί τι, συνδέουσι δέ τοὺς λόγους, ἑξῆς τάσσοντες καὶ οὕτως ἐπισυνδέοντες καὶ ἑνοῦντες.

[95] ἀλλὰ κἂν τοῖς λόγοις οἱ παρεπόμενοι σύνδεσμοι ἔσθ᾽ ὅτε ἑνοῦσι δύο λόγους ἢ καὶ πλείους, ... ἢ πάλιν ἀποστάντες διάλυσιν τῶν λόγων ποιοῦνται.

which are longer than a word and shorter than a sentence. On Aristotle's account of things, such items are sayings; but had the question been put, it may be doubted if he—or anyone else—would so have classified them.

Suppose, in particular, that a connector takes a number of sayings and makes one item out of them: what will the new item be? Surely, a saying. For it can hardly be anything smaller than a saying, and ancient grammar recognizes no unit larger than a saying. Any compound of sayings will be a compound saying. Then consider the following three examples:

> I came, I saw, I overcame.
> First I came, then I saw, then I overcame.
> I came, and I saw, and I overcame.

The first is a connectorless sequence of sentences; the second adds three adverbs—or perhaps three Aristotelian articulators; and in the third example, there is the connector 'and'. The third example is, on (almost) anyone's account, a single saying and a single sentence. (It is also, of course, three sentences and three sayings.) But if it is a single saying, then are not the first two examples also single sayings? For aren't the three examples just three ways of saying the same thing? When Caesar said

> *veni vidi vici*

he said something. How many things did he say? Three things, no doubt; and also, no doubt, one thing. What was that one thing? Well, in uttering that sequence of expressions Caesar said that he came and saw and overcame.

It is not evident that Apollonius would have resisted that conclusion. He apparently countenanced certain connectorless connections, as we shall see. For example, he apparently thought that

> It's day. It's night

is a disjunction, and hence a single saying. Then why should he not think that

> *veni vidi vici*

is a conjunction, and hence a single saying? Well, I suspect that he would in fact have denied that the Caesarian sequence is a conjunction. For if

> It's day. It's night

is a disjunction, then that is so inasmuch as its two elements are 'naturally' disjoined—and the elements of Caesar's remark are not naturally conjoined. (There are no natural conjuncts.) In any event, neither Apollonius nor anyone else will suppose that any sequence of sayings which is not unified by any connectors constitutes a conjunction.

The compound phrase '*tu et ego*' is a unity—a single pronominal formula—inasmuch as it functions syntactically in the same way as a pronoun does. The compound phrase 'silently and very fast' is an adverbial phrase—a single or unified adverbial phrase—inasmuch as its syntax is the syntax of the adverb. More precisely, '*tu et ego*' is a pronominal phrase because it can be embedded in a pronominal context, and 'silently and very fast' is an adverbial phrase because it can be embedded in an adverbial context. Take any sentence which contains an adverb—say:

He driveth furiously.

Remove the adverb and contemplate the shell which remains:

He driveth—.

That, I shall say, is an adverbial context. An item can be embedded in that context if and only if the result of putting it in place of the dash is grammatically well formed. So 'silently and very fast' can be embedded in

He driveth—;

for

He driveth silently and very fast

is grammatically impeccable.

An item is an adverbial formula if and only if it can be embedded in at least one adverbial context. And in general, an item is a formula of a given syntactical type if and only if it can be embedded in at least one context of that type. That is what I shall call the embedding test.

Is there a similar embedding test for sayings? Frege argued that expressions like

I came, and I saw, and I overcame

constitute a single sentence by observing that they can be negated. You can say

It's not the case that I came, and I saw, and I overcame.

That is syntactically impeccable and semantically pellucid. You cannot do the same for

I came, I saw, I overcame.

So that doesn't constitute a single sentence. Frege's negation test is a special case of the embedding test. He supposes that

It is not the case that—

is a sentential context: an item is a sentence if and only if it can be embedded in that context or in some other such sentential context. Other sentential contexts will include items like 'If—, then I'm a Dutchman', 'God knows whether or not—', 'Firmly I believe and truly that—', and so on.

Or is that a test not for sentences in general but for assertoric sentences in particular? Well, is the following item a sentential context?

—or let nature deal with the problem.

If it is, then it will ensure that, say,

Cut off the affected parts and spray with Bordeaux mixture

is a sentence. If not, not. In other words, and unremarkably, an embedding test will test for sentences in general or for assertoric sentences in particular according to whether the sentential contexts to which it appeals are determined by assertoric sentences in particular or by sentences in general.

The sentential test is a test for sayings only if sayings are sentences. There are also tests for subsentential sayings. But it is hard to think of any test for suprasentential sayings. Why—to repeat an earlier question—should the *Iliad* count as a single saying whereas the *Iliad* and the *Odyssey* together must count as two?

GLUE

So much for the grammar of connectors. What, next, of their semantics? What do connectors mean? Indeed, do they mean anything at all?

Apollonius says, negatively, that 'connectors never signify anything in their own right' (*adv* 133.25);[96] and he says, positively, that 'connectors co-signify' (*conj* 222.12–13).[97] Indeed, like prepositions and articles, connectors always co-signify (*synt* I 12 [14.1–2]). The co-signification of connectors is part of what I called the improved definition; and it is a commonplace in the later tradition. For example,

Connectors are among the expressions which co-signify. They do not signify anything in their own right but they connect a gaping thought—that is why they are called connectors. For in themselves connectors signify nothing, but when they are put in the construction they bind together what was missing or gaping or dissolved.

(scholiast to Dionysius Thrax, 284.6–10)[98]

---

[96] οἱ ... σύνδεσμοι οὔποτε κατ᾽ ἰδίαν σημαίνουσί τι.

[97] οἱ σύνδεσμοι συσσημαίνουσιν.

[98] ὁ σύνδεσμος τῶν συσσημαινουσῶν ἐστι λέξεων· οὐ γὰρ καθ᾽ ἑαυτόν τι σημαίνει, συνδεῖ δὲ διάνοιαν κεχηνυῖαν· διὰ τοῦτο γὰρ καὶ σύνδεσμος ὠνομάσθη· καθ᾽ ἑαυτὸν γὰρ ὁ σύνδεσμος οὐδὲν σημαίνει, συντασσόμενος δὲ τὰ ἐλλείποντα ἢ κεχηνότα ἢ διαλελυμένα σφίγγει.

So too in the Latin tradition, where Priscian says of connectors that

> they always co-signify, i.e. signify when connected to other items, but not by
> themselves.
>
> <div align="right">(<i>inst</i> xvii i 10 [iii 114.18–20])⁹⁹</div>

And the idea was familiar outside the grammatical tradition.

One of the questions with which Dexippus deals in his set of *Questions
and Answers* on Aristotle's *Categories* is this: 'Why, they worry, did he omit
the connectors?'—that is, why is the account of homonymy and synonymy
at the beginning of the *Categories* apt for some sorts of words but not for
others, and in particular not for connectors? After all, some connectors are
ambiguous, and an account of homonymy which can say nothing about them
is, *pro tanto*, inadequate. Here is Dexippus' answer:

> It is because, or so we claim, the utility of connectors for sayings is not primary but
> secondary, not complete but incomplete, not expressive but rather symbolic—indeed,
> connectors do not even primarily signify but rather co-signify, like the double lines
> which we write in the margin and which along with what has been written co-signify
> the finished nature of the thought while themselves in themselves signifying nothing.
> So connectors, too, co-signify along with the other parts of sayings but themselves
> in themselves are not significant—rather, they are like glue. That is why we do not
> count them among the elements of sayings but, if anything, as parts of expressions.
>
> <div align="right">(<i>in Cat</i> 32.17–26)¹⁰⁰</div>

Dexippus doubtless took the question, and his answer to it, from Porphyry.
Simplicius also took the matter over; and he added the information that the
objection which the answer addresses had been advanced by Lucius (see *in
Cat* 64.18–28). Lucius thinks that any account of significant expressions
must surely make room for connectors. Simplicius disagrees: connectors are
not—or not really—significant expressions. After all, Aristotle had said that
'a connector is a non-significant expression' (*Poet* 1456b38).¹⁰¹

---

⁹⁹ *eae enim semper consignificant, id est coniunctae aliis significant per se autem non.*

¹⁰⁰ ἀλλὰ διὰ τί τοὺς συνδέσμους παρέλιπεν ἀποροῦσιν.—ἐπειδή, φαμὲν ἡμεῖς, οὔτε προ-
ηγουμένη ἐστὶν αὐτῶν ἡ χρεία τοῦ λόγου ἀλλὰ δευτέρα, οὔτε τελεία ἀλλ' ἀτελής, οὔτε λεκτικὴ
συμβολικὴ δὲ μᾶλλον· ἀλλ' οὐδὲ σημαίνει προηγουμένως συσσημαίνει δὲ μᾶλλον, ὥσπερ
τὰς διπλᾶς εἰώθαμεν παραγράφειν, αἵτινες μετὰ τῶν γεγραμμένων μὲν συσσημαίνουσι τὸ
ἀπαρτίζον τῆς διανοίας αὐταὶ δὲ καθ' ἑαυτὰς οὐδὲν δηλοῦσι. καὶ οἱ σύνδεσμοι τοίνυν συσσημαίνουσι μετὰ τῶν ἄλλων μερῶν τοῦ λόγου, αὐτοὶ δὲ καθ' ἑαυτοὺς οὐκ εἰσὶ σημαντικοί, ἀλλ'
ἐοίκασι τῇ κόλλῃ· διόπερ οὐδὲ λόγου στοιχεῖα αὐτοὺς τιθέμεθα, ἀλλ' εἴπερ ἄρα μέρη λέξεως.

¹⁰¹ σύνδεσμος δέ ἐστιν φωνὴ ἄσημος.

The commentators were appealing to an ancient theory, ascribed to Plato and associated with Aristotle and with Theophrastus:

Insofar as they [i.e. predicates] are expressions, they involve other inquiries, which Theophrastus stirred up in his *On the Elements of Sayings* and which his followers wrote about—for example, whether names and verbs are the elements of sayings or whether articles and connectors and certain other items are so too (these are indeed parts of expressions, whereas names and verbs are parts of sayings).

(Simplicius, *in Cat* 10.23–27)[102]

There are only two genuine parts of sayings, names and verbs. All the other sorts of item which turn up in complex expressions are parts of those expressions but not parts of the sayings; they do not signify anything in themselves but co-signify; they are compared to glue and nails and dowels and the like.

The comparison with glue and nails was popular: it was exploited by Apuleius (or whoever wrote the Latin *On Interpretation*); it is one of several similar metaphors which Plutarch uses in his essay on the parts of speech (*quaest Plat* 1009F–1010D); and it is elaborated by Ammonius:

Those items which signify a nature or a person or an activity or a passivity or some combination of person with activity or passivity—all those Aristotle divides into names and verbs. He calls verbs those which are timed or which are predicated in propositions, and names those which are without time or which supply the need for subjects. Items which are used in neither of those two rôles, even if in some other fashion they are appended to the propositions (signifying that the predicate holds of the subject, or that it does not hold, or that it holds at a certain moment or in a certain manner or a certain number of times, or indicating any other relation between the two), these he claims are not strictly called parts of sayings. For just as the planks are strictly parts of a ship while the dowels and the oakum and the pitch are used for the sake of connecting the planks and unifying the whole ship, in the same way in sayings connectors and articles and prepositions and even adverbs satisfy the need for a sort of dowel and are not justly called parts—after all, when combined on their own they cannot produce a complete saying. These items, then, are not parts of sayings but parts of expressions, of which sayings are themselves parts, as he says in the *Poetics*; and they are useful for combining and constructing the parts of sayings one with another, just as a cord is useful for the artificial unification of the items corded, and glue for the items which hold together by its means—but they are

---

[102] καθὸ μὲν γὰρ λέξεις, ἄλλας ἔχουσι πραγματείας, ἃς ἐν τῷ Περὶ τῶν τοῦ λόγου στοιχείων ὅ τε Θεόφραστος ἀνακινεῖ καὶ οἱ περὶ αὐτὸν γεγραφότες, οἷον πότερον ὄνομα καὶ ῥῆμα τοῦ λόγου στοιχεῖα ἢ καὶ ἄρθρα καὶ σύνδεσμοι καὶ ἄλλα τινά (λέξεως δὲ καὶ ταῦτα μέρη, λόγου δὲ ὄνομα καὶ ῥῆμα) …

not themselves parts of the items corded or glued, nor are connectors or articles or prepositions or adverbs parts of sayings.

(*in Int* 12.16–13.6)[103]

The comparisons or metaphors are elaborated in the philosophical texts. But they are unsurprising—indeed, the metaphor of binding is present in the very nomenclature of connection—and we might expect the grammarians to exploit them. Apollonius does so, lightly and in one passage:

After the parts which we have listed we mentioned the connector which is connective of them: on its own and apart from the matter of expressions it cannot establish anything—just as the bindings of bodies are of no use if the bodies do not exist.

(*synt* I 28 [27.10–13])[104]

But the later grammarians did not adopt, let alone elaborate, the topic. Rather, they ascribed the metaphors to 'the Peripatetics' (scholiast to Dionysius Thrax, 515.19–29), or to 'certain philosophers' (Priscian, *inst* XI ii 6–7 [II 551.18–552.17]). Moreover, they sometimes argued against the aptness of the figures. Priscian, for example, has a long discussion which concludes that

it is far better to side with those who call the name and the verb principal and pre-eminent parts, and the rest their appendages.

(*inst* XI ii 7 [552.12–14])[105]

---

[103] τὰ μὲν οὖν φύσεων ἢ προσώπων ἢ ἐνεργειῶν ἢ παθῶν ἢ ποιᾶς συμπλοκῆς προσώπου πρὸς ἐνέργειαν ἢ πάθος σημαντικὰ πάντα ὁ Ἀριστοτέλης εἰς ὀνόματα διαιρεῖ καὶ ῥήματα, τὰ μὲν κατὰ χρόνον λεγόμενα ἢ κατηγορούμενα ἐν ταῖς προτάσεσι ῥήματα καλῶν, τὰ δὲ ἄνευ χρόνου λεγόμενα ἢ τὴν χρείαν συμπληροῦντα τῶν ὑποκειμένων ὀνόματα· τὰ δέ γε ἐν μηδετέρᾳ τούτων χώρᾳ παραλαμβανόμενα, κἂν ἄλλως προσκέωνται ταῖς προτάσεσι, τὸ ὑπάρχειν ἢ μὴ ὑπάρχειν ἢ πότε ἢ πῶς ἢ ποσάκις ὑπάρχει τὸ κατηγορούμενον τῷ ὑποκειμένῳ σημαίνοντα ἢ τινα ἄλλην αὐτῶν πρὸς ἄλληλα σχέσιν, οὐδὲ κυρίως ἀξιοῖ μέρη τοῦ λόγου καλεῖν· ὥσπερ γὰρ τῆς νεὼς αἱ μὲν σανίδες εἰσὶ τὰ κυρίως μέρη, γόμφοι δὲ καὶ λίνον καὶ πίττα συνδέσεως αὐτῶν καὶ τῆς τοῦ ὅλου ἑνώσεως ἕνεκα παραλαμβάνονται, τὸν αὐτὸν τρόπον κἂν τῷ λόγῳ σύνδεσμοι καὶ ἄρθρα καὶ προθέσεις καὶ αὐτὰ τὰ ἐπιρρήματα γόμφων τινῶν χρείαν ἀποπληροῦσι, μέρη δὲ οὐκ ἂν λέγοιντο δικαίως, ἅ γε μὴ δύνανται συντεθέντα καθ᾿ ἑαυτὰ τέλειον ἐργάσασθαι λόγον. λόγου μὲν οὖν ταῦτα οὐ μέρη, λέξεως δὲ μέρη, ἧς καὶ ὁ λόγος αὐτὸς μέρος, καθάπερ ἐν τοῖς Περὶ ποιητικῆς εἴρηται· καὶ εἰσὶ χρήσιμα πρὸς τὴν παρ᾿ ἄλληλα ποιὰν σύνθεσίν τε καὶ σύνταξιν τῶν τοῦ λόγου μερῶν, ὥσπερ καὶ ὁ δεσμὸς πρὸς τὴν ἐπίκτητον ἕνωσιν τῶν δεδεμένων καὶ ἡ κόλλα τῶν δι᾿ αὐτῆς συνεχομένων, ἀλλ᾿ οὔτε ἐκεῖνα μέρη τῶν δεδεμένων ἢ κεκολλημένων οὔτε σύνδεσμοι ἢ ἄρθρα ἢ προθέσεις ἢ ἐπιρρήματα τοῦ λόγου μόρια.

[104] ἐπὶ πᾶσι δὲ τοῖς κατειλεγμένοις ὁ τούτων συνδετικὸς σύνδεσμος παρελαμβάνετο, οὐδὲν δυνάμενος ἰδίᾳ παραστῆσαι χωρὶς τῆς τῶν λέξεων ὕλης, καθάπερ οἱ τῶν σωμάτων δεσμοὶ οὐκ εἰσὶ χρειώδεις ἀνυποστάτων ὄντων τῶν σωμάτων.

[105] *multo melius igitur qui principales et egregias partes nomen dicunt et verbum, alias autem his appendices.*

Connectors—along with prepositions and adverbs—may be called appendages or adjuncts to verbs and names. But they should not be likened to glue or
pitch or cord—the comparisons are diverting but they are not illuminating.

CONNECTORLESS CONNECTIONS

Are the grammarians right? The comparison was intended to explain, or to
help to explain, how connectors are 'non-significant'. Apollonius says that

Posidonius, in his *On Connectors* argues against those who affirm that connectors do
not show anything but simply connect the phrase.

(*conj* 214.4–6)[106]

Posidonius' adversaries apparently held that connectors have no semantic force.

Such an idea is perhaps suggested by Dexippus' comparison between
connectors and 'the double lines which we write in the margin': connectors
are, so to speak, punctuation marks; they indicate the articulation of a saying
but they do not contribute to what it says. The Dionysian *Art* has this to say
on punctuation marks or points:

There are three points: complete, intermediate, subpoint. A complete point is a sign
of a finished thought; an intermediate point is a sign introduced for the sake of taking
breath, and a subpoint is a sign of a thought which is not yet finished but still lacks
something.

(6 [7.4–7])[107]

The remarks on complete points and subpoints—on full stops and commas—might be developed, and the comparison with connectors elaborated.

Later texts used a large number of points and signs—Isidore enumerates
no fewer than twenty-six (*etym* I xx), one of them being the double line or
διπλῆ to which Dexippus refers. But the signs and points are not all of them
punctuation marks. The double line itself had several functions—in editions
of Plato, for example, it was used to mark 'the doctrines and opinions of
Plato' (Diogenes Laertius, III 65).[108] But there is no evidence that it was ever
used as a sign of punctuation.

---

[106] Ποσειδώνιος ἐν τῷ Περὶ συνδέσμων ἀντιλέγων πρὸς τοὺς φάσκοντας ὡς οἱ σύνδεσμοι
οὐ δηλοῦσι μέν τι, αὐτὸ δὲ μόνον τὴν φράσιν συνδέουσι ...
[107] στιγμαί εἰσι τρεῖς· τελεία, μέση, ὑποστιγμή. καὶ ἡ μὲν τελεία στιγμή ἐστι διανοίας
ἀπηρτισμένης σημεῖον, μέση δὲ σημεῖον πνεύματος ἕνεκεν παραλαμβανόμενον, ὑποστιγμὴ δὲ
διανοίας μηδέπω ἀπηρτισμένης ἀλλ᾽ ἔτι ἐνδεούσης σημεῖον.
[108] διπλῆ πρὸς τὰ δόγματα καὶ τὰ ἀρέσκοντα Πλάτωνι.

So Dexippus cannot in fact have meant to compare connectors with punctuation marks. What did he have in mind? None of the known functions of the double line seems peculiarly appropriate to a comparison with connectors; and I suppose that Dexippus took the sign as one example from many. The signs which we write in the margins do not constitute a part of the text, and yet they have no sense when divorced from the text: they are, so to speak, comments upon the text. I cannot think that such considerations help us greatly to understand the semantics of connectors—but then Dexippus only mentions the double lines *en passant* and no other ancient text adduces them in the same context.

In the first version of his artificial language, Frege introduced a special sign which he called the content-stroke and printed as a longish horizontal line. The symbol served to bind together the expressions which followed it into a judgeable whole. If I write

$2 + 2 = 4$

then those five symbols do not stick together. But write

$—2 + 2 = 4$

and everything is dandy. The initial horizontal glues together the items which follow it. Its function is purely connective, purely syntactical.

Frege's view has often seemed absurd, and for several reasons. One of the reasons is this: if the five symbols are likely to fall apart, how could the addition of a further symbol help them? The addition will simply mean that there are six items to fall apart rather than five. That is clever; but it is unpersuasive. And here at least the ancient invocation of glue is illuminating. There are two sorts of parquet flooring, floating and fixed. I ordered fixed. The *parquetier* told me that I needed glue to fix it to the floor. 'What's the use of that?', I said. 'If I buy the glue, then I'll simply have three items to fix together rather than two.' The *parquetier* was unmoved. Some ancient theorists took their cue from one of his forebears: connectors are syntactical glue, not semantic planks.

That idea might be supported by reflecting on the fact that the connecting which connectors do may also be done without them. For example, you may connect

The tenor was new to the part

and

The tenor sang like a strangled hyena

by using a relative pronoun:

The tenor, who was new to the part, sang like a strangled hyena.

Or by way of a participial clause:

Being new to the part, the tenor sang &c

Or by a prepositional construction (here, but not always, rather cumbersome):

On account of his being new to the part, the tenor sang &c

And there are other familiar devices—genitive absolutes in Greek, ablative absolutes in Latin. In such cases, the role of the connector is played by something else: the connecting is done by a purely syntactical device.

Aristotle's *Rhetoric* has a certain amount to say about the proper use of connectors. In one passage he refers to items which 'are without a connector but not unconnected' (*Rhet* 1407b38–39).[109] His example is

Having travelled, I spoke.

The saying is connected, but the connection is done by a syntactical turn rather than by the interpolation of a connector. Ammonius has something a little more elaborate:

You might wonder what we shall say about a saying which says

The sun being above the earth, it is day.

For that saying is neither simple nor yet does it seem to have needed a connector to unify it. In answer, we say that it is impossible for two complete assertions to be amalgamated to produce a single saying unless a connector is actually present. Then how could

The sun is above the earth,

which is complete, be mingled with

It is day,

which itself too is complete, without a conditional connector? But often we alter the antecedent proposition together with the connector in such a way that, although it is no longer complete with regard to assertion, nonetheless inasmuch as it contains potentially a connector (or an adverb which is in this respect equivalent to a connector) it fuses together with the consequent proposition which has remained complete. And that is so in the present case. For

The sun being above the earth

is incomplete with regard to assertion, but it contains potentially either the adverb 'when' or the connector 'if', and it expresses the same as

---

[109] ἐὰν δὲ συντόμως, ἄνευ μὲν συνδέσμου, μὴ ἀσύνδετα δέ.

When the sun is above the earth
or
If the sun is above the earth.

(in Int 68.12–26)[110]

Two complete sentences cannot become one by mere juxtaposition. But they may fuse without the aid of a connector—so long as one or other of them is transposed in a suitable way.

The point was not lost on the grammarians. Apollonius will sometimes speak of a connective power or construction, which may be possessed by items which are not connectors.

When the preposition 'διά' has a connective construction, it is used with the accusative.

(synt IV 30 [461.1–2])[111]

Or again:

A connective power accrues even to a prepositional juxtaposition:
  Because of its being day, it is light
  Because of Dionysius Apollonius was present
  From idleness vices are born
—as though 'On account of idleness'. So why is it strained to say that a connector may also effect a prepositional force?

(adv 181.32–182.3)[112]

There are connections without connectors: a preposition, or a syntactical turn, may do the same job as a connecting particle.

But something, according to Ammonius, must do the job: the mere juxtaposition of two complete sayings cannot produce a compound saying. If

---

[110] ἐπιζητήσειεν ἄν τις τί ἐροῦμεν περὶ τοῦ λόγου τοῦ λέγοντος ἡλίου ὑπὲρ γῆν ὄντος ἡμέρα ἐστίν· οὔτε γὰρ ἁπλοῦς οὗτος ὁ λόγος οὔτε συνδέσμου πρὸς τὴν ἕνωσιν φαίνεται δεηθείς. πρὸς ὃν ῥητέον ὅτι δύο μὲν αὐτοτελεῖς ἀποφάνσεις συμπλακῆναι ἀλλήλαις πρὸς ἑνὸς λόγου γένεσιν συνδέσμου χωρὶς ἐνεργείᾳ ληφθέντος ἀδύνατον· τὸ γοῦν ἥλιος ὑπὲρ γῆν ἐστιν αὐτοτελές ὂν τῷ ἡμέρα ἐστίν αὐτοτελεῖ καὶ αὐτῷ ὄντι πῶς ἂν συγκραθείη δίχα τοῦ συναπτικοῦ συνδέσμου; πολλάκις δέ γε τὴν ἡγουμένην τῶν προτάσεων ἅμα τῷ συνδέσμῳ μεταρρυθμίζομεν οὕτως ὥστε μηκέτι μὲν αὐτοτελῆ εἶναι πρὸς ἀπόφανσιν, τῷ δὲ δυνάμει περιέχειν τὸν σύνδεσμον ἢ τὸ τῷ συνδέσμῳ ἰσοδυναμοῦν κατὰ τοῦτο ἐπίρρημα πρὸς τὴν ἑπομένην τῶν προτάσεων καὶ αὐτοτελῆ μεμενηκυῖαν συμφύεσθαι, καθάπερ ἔχει καὶ ἐπὶ τοῦ προκειμένου· τὸ γὰρ ἡλίου ὑπὲρ γῆν ὄντος ἀτελὲς πρὸς ἀπόφανσιν δυνάμει δὲ περιέχον ἢ τὸ ὅτε ἐπίρρημα ἢ τὸν εἰ συναπτικὸν σύνδεσμον καὶ ταὐτὸν φθεγγόμενον τῷ ὅτε ἥλιος ὑπὲρ γῆν ἐστι καὶ τῷ εἰ ὁ ἥλιος ὑπὲρ γῆν ἐστιν.

[111] προθέσεως τῆς διά κατὰ συνδεσμικὴν σύνταξιν φερομένης ἐπ' αἰτιατικὴν ...

[112] καὶ προθετικῇ παραθέσει συνδεσμικὴ δύναμις ἐγγίνεται· διὰ τὸ ἡμέραν εἶναι φῶς ἐστι, διὰ Διονύσιον παρεγένετο Ἀπολλώνιος, ἐκ τῆς ῥᾳθυμίας αἱ κακίαι γίνονται (ὡς εἰ ἕνεκα τῆς ῥᾳθυμίας). τί οὖν βίαιον τὸ καὶ σύνδεσμον προθετικὴν δύναμιν ἀποτελέσαι;

two complete sentences are juxtaposed, then there is an unconnectedness or asyndeton (ἀσύνδετος' being the Greek for 'unconnected.') Such items were of concern to rhetoric—thus Aristotle, for example, declares that

an unconnected item has this peculiarity—many things seem to have been said at the same time. For the connector makes the plurality one, so that if it is removed it is plain that, conversely, the one will be many. That produces grandeur:
I came, I spoke, I implored.

(*Rhet* 1413b31–1414a1)[113]

In
I came, I spoke, I implored
there is not only an absence of connectors: there is no connection at all—mere juxtaposition.

But does juxtaposition never connect? A curious passage in Apollonius' *Connectors* to which I have already alluded is pertinent. Of disjuncts, he claims,

some have received a true disjunction and others have taken a non-true disjunction. The expression
Either it is day or it is night
is in a true disjunctive—for those circumstances will never come about at the same time. The expression
Either Apollonius will be there or Trypho will be
announces a temporary disjunction. The former example will be in disjunction even if it does not take a disjunctive connector
It is day, it is night.
(The one of them is true—if we speak so while it is day, then it is day.) The other is not at all so:
Trypho will be here, Apollonius will be here.
For those items are not disjoined unless they take a disjunctive connector.

(*conj* 216.16–217.10)[114]

---

[113] ἔτι ἔχει ἴδιόν τι τὰ ἀσύνδετα· ἐν ἴσῳ γὰρ χρόνῳ πολλὰ δοκεῖ εἰρῆσθαι· ὁ γὰρ σύνδεσμος ἓν ποιεῖ τὰ πολλά, ὥστε ἐὰν ἐξαιρεθῇ, δῆλον ὅτι τοὐναντίον ἔσται τὸ ἓν πολλά. ἔχει οὖν αὔξησιν· ἦλθον, διελέχθην, ἱκέτευσα.

[114] καὶ ἔστι πάλιν αὐτῶν ἃ μὲν <ἀληθῆ> τὴν διάζευξιν ἀναδεδεγμένα, ἃ δὲ οὐ<κ ἀληθῆ> τὴν διάζευξιν παρειληφότα. τὸ γὰρ λεγόμε<νον ἢ> ἡμέρα ἐστὶν ἢ νύξ ἐστιν ἐν ἀληθεῖ καθέστηκε διεζευγμένῳ· ταῦτα γὰρ τὰ καταστήματα ο<ὐδέποτε> κατὰ ταὐτὸ γενήσεται. τὸ δὲ λεγόμενον ἢ Ἀπολλώνιος παρέσται ἢ Τρύφων ὡς πρὸς καιρὸν τὴν διάζευξιν ἐπαγγέλλεται. τὸ γοῦν πρότερον ὑπόδειγμα, κἂν μὴ <λάβῃ> τὸν διαζευκτικὸν σύνδεσμον, πάλιν ἐν διαζεύξει <ἔσται>· ἡμέρα ἐστί, νύξ ἐστι. (τὸ ἕτερον ἀληθές· εἰ φαί< ημεν οὕτως> ἡμέρας οὔσης ἡμέρα ἐστί.) τὸ δὲ ἕτερον οὐ πάντως· Τρύφων παρέσται, Ἀπολλώνιος οὐ παρέσται· οὐ διαζεύγνυται γὰρ τὰ τοιαῦτα ἐὰν μὴ λάβῃ τὸν διαζευκτικὸν σύνδεσμον.

The text is difficult, and it is far from plain exactly what Apollonius wants to say. But the easiest interpretation goes like this: Some items are true or natural disjuncts, others are not. If certain items are not natural disjuncts and you wish to affirm their factual disjunction, then you must use a disjunctive connector. But if the items are natural disjuncts, then nature has already done the trick: if you use a connector, you are merely gilding the lily—to say

It's day, it's night

is to affirm a disjunction.

That sounds rum; but a later passage supports the interpretation. Apollonius is urging that the word 'ἆρα', as it is used to introduce a question, is a connector. Some grammarians had observed that if you drop the word from a sentence, what remains will be a complete sentence with the same sense:

In 'ἡμέρα ἐστίν'—I mean, interrogatively taken—nothing more is thought if 'ἆρα' is added.

(*conj* 225.12–13)[115]

In Greek, the interrogative 'ἆρα' is optional: 'Is it day?' translates indifferently as 'ἆρα ἡμέρα ἐστίν;' and as 'ἡμέρα ἐστίν;'. Such a phenomenon, the grammarians argued, can never occur with genuine connectors: drop a connector, and things alter. Apollonius replies thus:

As far as that argument goes, we shall not even allow 'ἤ' to be a connector. At least, the following are phrases

You read, you don't read

You go away, you don't go away

—but it is admitted that the phrase lacks 'ἤ'. ...

We went as you bid into the wood, great Odysseus.

We found fine houses built in the glens

—'and' is missing.

(*conj* 225.18–24)[116]

There, allegedly, are three examples of sayings from which items have been dropped without loss of syntax or change of sense: the items are 'or' and

---

[115] ἐν μέντοι γε τῷ ἡμέρα ἐστί, λέγω κατ᾽ ἐρώτησιν, οὐδὲν πλεῖον νοεῖται μετὰ τοῦ ἆρα.

[116] ἕνεκά γε τοῦ τοιούτου οὐδὲ τὸν ἤ σύνδεσμον καταλείψομεν. ἔστι γάρ που τοιαύτη φράσις· ἀναγινώσκεις, οὐκ ἀναγινώσκεις· ἀπέρχῃ, οὐκ ἀπέρχῃ. ἀλλ᾽ ὡμολογημένως λείπεται ἡ φράσις τοῦ ἤ ... ᾔομεν, ὡς ἐκέλευες, ἀνὰ δρυμά, <φαίδιμ᾽ Ὀδυσσεῦ> εὕρομεν ἐν βήσσῃσι τετυγμένα δώμ<ατα καλά> · λείποντος τοῦ καί.

'and'. If the grammarians' argument about 'ἄρα' were sound, then neither 'or' nor 'and' would be a connector—and that is absurd.

The last, conjunctive, case is perhaps less surprising than the other two disjunctive examples. Nonetheless, it is not without its perplexities; for the *Syntax* quotes the same Homeric lines in the opposite sense:

… and again, by their absence, <connectors> dissolve sayings, as in
> We went as you bid into the wood, great Odysseus.
> We found fine houses built in the glens.

For he should have conjoined it with 'and':
> And we found …

(synt i 10 [11.6–10])

The two sentences do not hold together: Homer should have used a connector. According to *Connectors*, Homer has not omitted anything: the connection, and more precisely the conjunction, is there in the text without one.

However that may be, the two disjunctive cases are surely odder. Apollonius says—at least, he appears to say—that if it is impossible that both P and Q, so that those two items are true or natural disjuncts, then if you produce one of them followed by the other you have thereby made a disjunctive utterance. Now you might perhaps persuade yourself that, in colloquial English, you can sometimes put forward a disjunction without using any connector to help you do so—

> Love me, leave me—it's all one to me.

And perhaps the same thing is possible in Greek. But only, surely, when the context—or the tone of voice, or some other external factor—somehow intimates a disjunction. If I say

> She loves me, she loves me not,

I do not make a disjunctive assertion; and yet if any items are naturally disjoined, then surely a saying and its negation are so.

There are other cases—at least in English—which are less problematical. For example, if I say

> They make smoking illegal: I emigrate

I will readily be understood to have made a conditional assertion. Or take:

> Love me, love my dog.

And so on. Perhaps such things are idioms, and so do not count? Perhaps they are elliptical, and so not genuine examples of connectorless connections?

Of course, if someone utters the words

They make smoking illegal: I emigrate,

it is perfectly correct to report what he said by saying:

He swore that he'd emigrate if they banned smoking;

and in uttering those words he surely did make a conditional assertion. But it does not follow that he did so by making a single conditional saying; and in fact he did not utter a single sentence—his words do not pass the embedding test for sentences.

Connectorless connections are interesting items; but—to return to my lost sheep—they do not begin to show that connectors have a purely syntactical function. Rather, they show that certain syntactical turns have a semantic function. The sentence

Had we but world enough and time, this coyness, lady, were no crime

is a conditional saying—it is not a conjunction, say, nor a disjunction. It contains no conditional connector; but its syntactical structure determines that it is equivalent to

If we had world enough and time, then this coyness, lady, would be no crime.

The connectorless version does not show that the connector 'if' has no sense: the version with a connector shows that the syntactical turn has a semantic function. As Ammonius put it, the connectorless version contains a connector potentially: it possesses a feature which has the potency—the force or meaning—of a connector.

Well, all that is pretty obvious. And it is pretty obvious that—whatever you think about glue and parquet—the thesis that connectors, in general, have no semantic force is false. If 'and' and 'or' have no meaning, then they do not differ in meaning; and in that case there will be no difference in meaning between

Your money or your life

and

Your money and your life.

EXPLETIVE CONNECTORS

But perhaps at least some connectors—some classes of connector—have no semantic function? The ancient grammarians distinguished several species or kinds of connector. The Dionysian *Art* lists eight:

Of connectors some are conjunctive, some disjunctive, some implicative, some quasi-implicative, some causative, some interrogative, some syllogistic, some expletive.

(20 [87.1–88.2])[117]

The last kind, the expletive connectors, proved troublesome.

They had been noticed by the philosophers. The Peripatetic Demetrius remarks that

you should use the expletive connectors not as empty additions ... but only if they contribute something to the grandeur of the saying.

(*eloc* 55)[118]

He offers some examples of the grandifying use of expletives; and he calls upon the Peripatetic Praxiphanes in his support; for

those who fill out connectors to no purpose are, as Praxiphanes says, like actors who utter this and that sound to no purpose.

(*eloc* 58)[119]

Byzantine scholars liked to claim that Praxiphanes—after Aristotle—had perfected the art of grammar (scholiast to Dionysius Thrax, 164.23–29). Perhaps one of his acts of perfection was the recognition of a class of expletive connectors? Perhaps. But it seems to me more likely that Praxiphanes was talking not about a class of expletive connectors but about expletive uses of connectors. That is to say, he thought that connectors—or certain connectors—sometimes had a purely ornamental function, and he warned speakers against overindulgence.

The Stoic Chaeremon also discussed expletive connectors. He argued—so Apollonius reports—that the items may properly be called connectors: not in virtue of their sense or syntax (for they do not have a sense, and they do not serve to connect anything) but rather in virtue of their form (for they are morphologically very much like real connectors). (See *conj* 248.1–13). Nothing else is known of Chaeremon's thesis, to whom no other text ascribes any interest in linguistic or logical matters.

---

[117] τῶν δὲ συνδέσμων οἱ μέν εἰσι συμπλεκτικοί, οἱ δὲ διαζευκτικοί, οἱ δὲ συναπτικοί, οἱ δὲ παρασυναπτικοί, οἱ δὲ αἰτιολογικοί, οἱ δὲ ἀπορηματικοί, οἱ δὲ συλλογιστικοί, οἱ δὲ παραπληρωματικοί.

[118] τοῖς δὲ παραπληρωματικοῖς συνδέσμοις χρηστέον, οὐχ ὡς προσθήκαις κεναῖς ... ἀλλ' ἂν συμβάλλωνταί τι τῷ μεγέθει τοῦ λόγου.

[119] οἱ δὲ πρὸς οὐδὲν ἀναπληροῦντες, φησί, τὸν σύνδεσμον ἐοίκασιν τοῖς ὑποκριταῖς τοῖς τὸ καὶ τὸ πρὸς οὐδὲν ἔπος λέγουσιν.

Chaeremon thought that expletive connectors have no meaning; and according to Apollonius, 'it is a prejudice of most people that the so-called expletive connectors have no signification' (*conj* 247.22–23).[120] The prejudice must seem well-grounded. For the items are defined by the *Art* as

those connectors which are introduced for the sake of metre or ornament;

(20 [96.3–97.1])[121]

that is to say, as Priscian expressed it, they 'are put in for the sake of ornament or metre and not by any necessity of sense' (*inst* xvi ii 13 [iii 102.13–14]).[122]

In general, a word is used expletively in a given expression if it can be deleted from the expression without destroying the syntax or changing the sense; and a word is an expletive *tout court* if it can be deleted from any expression which contains it without damaging the syntax or altering the sense. In that case, an expletive can have no sense, and it cannot connect anything. Hence it cannot be a connector.

Chaeremon in effect accepted the argument down to its last step. But there he stopped: although expletive connectors connect nothing, there are still good reasons for calling them connectors. That is a curious suggestion: Chaeremon admits that the expletives do not satisfy the definition of 'connector'—and he wants nonetheless to call them connectors.

Apollonius rejects the argument in its entirety. He urges at some considerable length, both in *Connectors* and in the *Syntax*, that expletive connectors have a meaning and are genuine connectors. (See *conj* 247.22–253.28; *synt* iii 127 [378.5–380.8].) His conclusion ought to be that the so-called expletive connectors are not expletives—for they cannot always be deleted; and in one passage he does appear to say just that (*conj* 250.11–12). But his considered view is that they may properly be called expletive connectors. Any connector—and indeed any part of speech—will, he claims, sometimes be used expletively. In

---

[120] παρὰ τοῖς πλείστοις ἐστὶ πρόληψις ὡς οἱ καλούμενοι παραπληρωματικοὶ σημασίαν τινὰ οὐ ποιοῦνται.

[121] παραπληρωματικοὶ δέ εἰσιν ὅσοι μέτρου ἢ κόσμου ἕνεκεν παραλαμβάνονται.

[122] *quaecumque coniunctiones ornatus causa vel metri nulla significationis necessitate ponuntur hoc nomine nuncupantur.*

This was the most unkindest cut of all

'most' is used expletively, and so is 'of all'. The expletives help out the metre, and add a certain brutal grandeur to the line; but you may delete them without destroying the syntax or damaging the sense. It does not follow, and it is not true, that the word 'most' and the phrase 'of all' are expletives. According to Apollonius, the so-called expletive connectors differ from other connectors inasmuch as they are used expletively very often. Indeed, that fact is the only thing which they all have in common—which is why they are called 'expletive'.

The class of expletives is a ragbag. Apollonius resorts to that same useful receptacle when he explains the subjunctive mood (*synt* III 126 [377.5–8]), or paronyms and verbal names (*synt* III 130 [381.5–9]), or possessives and comparatives (*conj* 253.21–28). In each case, he finds that most species of a given kind of expression are classified and named in virtue of their common semantic features; but certain items evade such ordering—so they are grouped together and named in virtue of some accident which they happen to share. The device is handy but unscientific. Apollonius ought to have divided the so-called expletive connectors among the other classes of connector—if necessary inventing a few new classes on the way.

However that may be, the quarrel over expletive connectors rumbled on. Some of the commentators on the Dionysian *Art* side with Apollonius—

expletives too signify something, just like the other connectors;

(scholiast to Dionysius Thrax, 105.31–32)[123]

others insist that

they were called expletives because they are especially set down in order to fill out the metre and also to provide a certain adornment for the discourse—for they contribute nothing to the thought.

(scholiast to Dionysius Thrax, 441.21–23)[124]

The Latin tradition, unsurprisingly, shows the same features as the Greek.

---

[123] οἱ παραπληρωματικοὶ καὶ αὐτοὶ σημαίνουσί τι, καθάπερ καὶ οἱ ἄλλοι σύνδεσμοι.

[124] παραπληρωματικοὶ δὲ ἐκλήθησαν, ἐπεὶ μάλιστα τοῦ πληρῶσαι ἕνεκεν τὸ μέτρον τίθενται μετὰ τοῦ καὶ κόσμον τινὰ παρέχειν τῷ λόγῳ· πρὸς γὰρ νόησιν οὐδὲν συντείνουσιν.

CO-SIGNIFICATION

Some theorists held, hopelessly, that connectors have no semantic force at all. Others held, less hopelessly, that some connectors—expletive connectors—have no semantic force. The enigmatic Lucius, who complained that Aristotle's account of homonymy cannot be applied to connectors, evidently thought that connectors had a meaning. So too Nigidius Figulus: at the end of an essay on the Latin connector '*quia*'—an essay which derives from that dubious Pythagorean—Aulus Gellius writes that

no one will have understood the forms and varieties of the particle which we are talking about until he has learned that it is composed and conjoined and that it does not only have a force of connecting but is also endowed with a certain determinate meaning.

(*NA* xvii xiii 10)[125]

It is sometimes said that Diodorus Cronus had argued—much earlier, and demonstratively—against the thesis that connectors signify nothing. For

Diodorus the logician thought that every utterance was significant and in proof of this called one of his own servants 'And yet' and another by another connector.

(Ammonius, *in Int* 38.18–20)[126]

The grammarians dutifully report that Diodorus made 'And yet' a name; but they do not explain what the point of the gesture was. Ammonius' explanation is guess-work, and pretty implausible guess-work. Later, Stephanus said that Diodorus intended to indicate that words do not have any meaning by nature (*in Int* 9.20–24); and his guess is rather more intelligent. But none of that matters a whit; for the anecdote is doubtless a fiction.

We are better informed about another adversary of the thesis that connectors mean nothing. Near the beginning of *Connectors*, having remarked that he will not wholly avoid Stoic doctrine, Apollonius says that

Posidonius, in his *On Connectors* argues against those who affirm that connectors do not show anything but simply connect the phrase: he says that 'ἐπιδοῦναι' differs from 'ἀποδοῦναι', and 'ἀπαιτεῖν' from 'προσαιτεῖν', and some other such

---

[125] *hanc particulam de qua dicimus nisi si quis didicerit compositam copulatamque esse neque vim tantum coniungendi habere sed certa quadam significatione factam, numquam profecto rationes et varietates istius comprehensurus est.*

[126] ... τὸν διαλεκτικὸν Διόδωρον πᾶσαν οἰόμενον φωνὴν σημαντικὴν εἶναι καὶ πρὸς πίστιν τούτου καλέσαντα τῶν ἑαυτοῦ τινα οἰκετῶν Ἀλλαμὴν καὶ ἄλλον ἄλλῳ συνδέσμῳ.

constructions (thereby showing himself to believe that prepositions and connectors are a single part of sayings).

(*conj* 214.4–8)[127]

In his essay *On Connectors*—which we know of only from Apollonius—Posidonius, like Nigidius after him, attacked the thesis that connectors merely connect and have no meaning.

His argument rests on some such principle as the following: If an expression C(X) differs in meaning from C(Y), then X differs in meaning from Y. Now '[ἐπι]δοῦναι' differs in meaning from '[ἀπο]δοῦναι'. Hence 'ἐπί' differs in meaning from 'ἀπό'. But if X differs in meaning from Y, then both X and Y have a meaning. Hence 'ἐπί' and 'ἀπό' have a meaning. But 'ἐπί' and 'ἀπό' are connectors. Hence connectors—or at least, some connectors—have a meaning. The argument depends upon the Stoic notion that prepositions—and in particular, verbal prefixes—are connectors; for Posidonius' examples turn about verbal prefixes. But that peculiarity apart, it is well adapted to showing that connectors are not meaningless signs—that they have a sense. Of course, as I have already remarked, you would have to be insane to deny that they do.

But what, or how, do connectors signify? Apollonius denies that connectors have a meaning of their own. He does not mean thereby to deny that they have a meaning. On the contrary, he will frequently say that a connector 'shows' something (δηλοῦν: e.g. *conj* 228.11–13; 229.14; 230.16), and he is not averse to mentioning the 'signification' of a connector (σημασία: e.g. *conj* 235.26; 251.28). More generally, he holds that

parts of sayings are distinguished not by their form but by their meaning;

(*pron* 67.6;[128] cf. *synt* i 77 [65.4–11]; ii 33 [150.14–15])

so that all parts of sayings must have a meaning.

The way in which the connectors have a meaning is expressed by the verb 'συσσημαίνειν' or 'co-signify'. In the *Syntax* Apollonius remarks that

connectors indicate their proper meanings in relation to the constructions or consequences of the sayings.

(*synt* i 12 [14.4–6])[129]

---

[127] Ποσειδώνιος ἐν τῷ Περὶ συνδέσμων ἀντιλέγων πρὸς τοὺς φάσκοντας ὡς οἱ σύνδεσμοι οὐ δηλοῦσι μέν τι, αὐτὸ δὲ μόνον τὴν φράσιν συνδέουσι, φησὶν ὡς διαφέρει τὸ ἐπιδοῦναι τοῦ ἀποδοῦναι, ὡς τὸ ἀπαιτεῖν τοῦ προσαιτεῖν, καὶ ἄλλας τινὰς τοιαύτας συντάξεις, ἤδη πιστούμενος ὅτι ἓν μέρος λόγου ἥ τε πρόθεσις καὶ ὁ σύνδεσμος.

[128] οὐ γὰρ φωναῖς μεμέρισται τὰ τοῦ λόγου μέρη, σημαινομένοις δέ.

[129] οἱ ... σύνδεσμοι πρὸς τὰς τῶν λόγων συντάξεις ἢ ἀκολουθίας τὰς ἰδίας δυνάμεις παρεμφαίνουσιν.

That is to say, a connector co-signifies inasmuch as its sense is determined by the constructions and consequences of the items which it connects. That is a dark saying (and the text is disputed). A passage in Priscian has been thought to shed light on it.

Some expressions, Priscian says, are incapable of producing—either on their own or in collaboration with one another—an expression with a complete sense. Prepositions and connectors are expressions of that sort:

> In fact, they always co-signify, i.e. signify when connected to other items and not in themselves. Hence their signification varies according to the force of the items with which they are connected—as '*in*' signifies one thing when it is joined to an accusative, another when it is joined to an ablative.
>
> (*inst* xvii i 10 [iii 114.18–22])[130]

Connectors, like prepositions, are ambiguous items, and their sense can only be fixed by the context in which they find themselves—for example, I shall distinguish the temporal '*cum*' from the causal '*cum*' by remarking that the latter but not the former takes a subjunctive verb in the clause which it introduces.

Some scholars have discovered in those remarks an elucidation of the notion of co-signification: an expression co-signifies, they suggest, if it is ambiguous and if the ambiguity can only be resolved—or is habitually resolved—by contextual indications. Now Priscian does indeed suggest that contextual ambiguities are somehow a consequence of co-signification; but that suggestion is not presented as an elucidation of co-signification; and it would in fact be a hopelessly inadequate elucidation. For it is not only connectors and the like which are ambiguous, and it is not only the ambiguities of such items which are habitually resolved by appeal to the context—if contextual disambiguation is a mark of co-signification, then all parts of sayings are co-significant.

The passage from Priscian is based on Apollonius. Apollonius follows his claim that prepositions 'always co-signify' by appealing to the difference in sense between '$\delta\iota\acute{\alpha}$' with the genitive and '$\delta\iota\acute{\alpha}$' with the accusative, and he then offers a parallel case involving a connector rather than a preposition—he cites a Homeric line in which the context shows that the word '$\mathring{\eta}\tau o\iota$' is to be taken in a conjunctive sense. (See *synt* i 12 [14.2–10].) Just before that comes the following paragraph:

---

[130] *eae etenim semper consignificant, id est coniunctae aliis significant per se autem non. itaque variatur earum significatio ad vim coniunctorum eis, ut in aliud significat cum accusativo iungitur et aliud cum ablativo.*

Again, among letters some are vowels which produce a sound by themselves and others are consonants which do not possess a spoken pronunciation in the absence of the vowels: you should imagine the same thing in the case of expressions. Some of them can as it were be pronounced in the same way as vowels—as you may imagine in the case of verbs, names, pronouns, adverbs ...; others are as it were consonants which wait upon vowels—that is to say, the parts of sayings which we have just listed—and cannot be pronounced on their own: thus it is in the case of prepositions, articles, connectors—such particles always co-signify.

(synt I 12 [13.1–14.2])[131]

A con-sonant has a sound: the letter 'B', for example, is not mute. But the sound can only be made if the letter is linked to a vowel, as in 'BA'. That is why it is called a con-sonant. In a similar way, a co-signifier signifies something, but its signification can only come out if it is linked with some other part of speech. That is why it is called a co-signifier.

Then consider how Apollonius in fact explains the sense of connectors. He will say, for example, that the disjunctive 'ἤ' announces the holding of one of the disjuncts and the non-holding of the others; and I have earlier suggested that the same explanation—or at any rate an extremely similar explanation—may be expressed, in a different idiom, as follows:

A sentence of the sort: 'ἤτοι' + P_1 + 'ἤ' + ... + 'ἤ' + P_n is true if and only if precisely one P_i is true.

It is not evident how such formulas will be devised for all the connectors which Apollonius discusses; and the formulas will require some gloss or rider which adapts them to cases where a connector connects items other than assertoric sentences. But the general notion is plain. It may be put like this: if you want to explain what a connector, C, means, then you must come up with something of the sort:

'X(C)' means that such-and-such.

That is to say, you do not—cannot—explain C in isolation: you explain it in a linguistic context, you explain it as a part of a larger semantic unit.

---

[131] ἔτι ὃν τρόπον τῶν στοιχείων ἃ μέν ἐστιν φωνήεντα, ἃ καθ' ἑαυτὰ φωνὴν ἀποτελεῖ, ἃ δὲ σύμφωνα, ἅπερ ἄνευ τῶν φωνηέντων οὐκ ἔχει ῥητὴν τὴν ἐκφώνησιν, τὸν αὐτὸν τρόπον ἔστιν ἐπινοῆσαι κἀπὶ τῶν λέξεων. αἱ μὲν γὰρ αὐτῶν τρόπον τινὰ τῶν φωνηέντων ῥηταί εἰσι, καθάπερ ἐπὶ τῶν ῥημάτων ἔστιν ἐπινοῆσαι, ὀνομάτων, ἀντωνυμιῶν, ἐπιρρημάτων, ...· αἱ δὲ ὡσπερεὶ σύμφωνα ἀναμένουσι τὰ φωνήεντα, τουτέστιν τὰ προκατειλεγμένα τῶν μερῶν τοῦ λόγου, οὐ δυνάμεναι κατ' ἰδίαν ῥηταὶ εἶναι, καθάπερ ἐπὶ τῶν προθέσεων, τῶν ἄρθρων, τῶν συνδέσμων· τὰ γὰρ τοιαῦτα τῶν μορίων ἀεὶ συσσημαίνει.

When the Peripatetics say that names and verbs alone are significant, they are generally taken to mean that names and verbs alone designate or refer. In

All horses are now asleep

there are five words each of which possesses a sense; but only two of them—namely 'horses' and 'asleep'—refer to anything. Or as Plutarch puts it,

> it is not the case that, just as someone who utters 'strikes' or 'is struck' or again 'Socrates' or 'Pythagoras' has in a certain way provided us with something to think of and reflect upon, so we can grasp a conception of an act or a body when someone utters 'on the one hand' or 'for' or 'about' by itself.
>
> (*quaest Plat* 1010A)[132]

That is no doubt correct, at bottom. But something must be done to explain what and how a word like 'asleep' might designate—after all, it is names which refer or designate, and 'asleep' does not look much like anything's name.

Instead of 'refer' or 'designate', try 'be true of'. In other words, suppose that to have a signification is to be true of something or some things. More precisely, say that an expression E signifies if and only if its sense is, or can be, given by way of a sentence of the form 'E is true of an item if and only if such-and-such'. Then in fact names and verbs—and names and verbs alone—signify. (Adjectives?—Yes, but in ancient grammar, adjectives are a sort of name.) As for 'asleep', its sense is given by the following truth:

'asleep' is true of an item if and only if that item is asleep.

You can't produce anything like that for 'and' or 'the' or 'quickly' or 'by'. That is to say, such words are non-significant, they do not signify. But that does not for a moment imply that they are empty marks or that they have no signification at all; for they co-signify—and their signification or co-signification must be elucidated in the way in which Apollonius elucidates the sense of the connectors.

SYLLOGISTIC CONNECTORS

The grammarians, as I said, distinguished several species or kinds of connector. The Dionysian *Art* offers a list of eight varieties. Later grammarians upped

---

[132] οὐ γάρ, ὥσπερ ὁ τὸ τύπτει φθεγξάμενος ἢ τὸ τύπτεται καὶ πάλιν τὸ Σωκράτης ἢ τὸ Πυθαγόρας ἀμωσγέπως νοῆσαί τι καὶ διανοηθῆναι παρέσχηκεν, οὕτω τοῦ μέν ἢ γάρ ἢ περί καθ' αὑτὸ ἐκφωνηθέντος ἔστιν ἔννοιάν τινα λαβεῖν ἢ πράγματος ἢ σώματος.

the ante, the Latins being particularly prodigal: after listing a dozen sorts of connector, one Latin manual remarks that

it is not possible to designate all of them by name on account of the vast number of kinds or the subtlety of the distinctions by which one differs from another.

([Asper], *ars gramm* v 553.22–24)[133]

The first three items on the Dionysian list are the conjunctive, the disjunctive and the implicative—the three sorts of connector which characterize the three sorts of compound assertibles about which standard Stoic logic revolves. The next two items on the list, the quasi-implicative and the causative, were also recognized by the Stoic logicians, even if they did not enter as such into Stoic syllogistic. It has been inferred that the classification of connectors which the *Art* offers has a Stoic origin.

The penultimate items on the list are syllogistic connectors. They are explained as follows:

Syllogistic are those connectors which are well adapted to the ἐπιφοραί and συλλήψεις of proofs. They are these: ἄρα ἀλλά ἀλλαμήν τοίνυν τοιγάρτοι τοιγαροῦ.

(20 [95.2–96.1])[134]

The six items which the *Art* presents as syllogistic connectors are all capable of appearing in syllogisms. But they will appear in two different functions: four of them may serve to introduce the conclusion of an argument (so that they answer very roughly to 'therefore' or 'so'); two of them—ἀλλά, ἀλλαμήν—will not signal a conclusion but may be used to introduce a co-assumption or supplementary premiss. Thus it seems that there are, in fact, two sorts of syllogistic connectors; and since the *Art* says that syllogistic connectors are adapted to ἐπιφοραί and συλλήψεις, presumably those two terms pick out the two sorts.

That was the view of the ancient commentators on the *Art*:

He calls ἐπιφορά the introduction of the next saying and σύλληψις the sealing and concluding of the preceding saying.

(scholiast to Dionysius Thrax, 441.8–10)[135]

---

[133] *omnes nominibus suis designari non possunt propter multitudinem generum aut subtilitatem discriminum quibus aliae ab aliis differunt.*

[134] συλλογιστικοὶ δέ εἰσιν ὅσοι πρὸς τὰς ἐπιφοράς τε καὶ συλλήψεις τῶν ἀποδείξεων εὖ διάκεινται· εἰσὶ δὲ οἵδε· ἄρα ἀλλά ἀλλαμήν τοίνυν τοιγάρτοι τοιγαροῦν.

[135] ἐπιφοράν δὲ λέγει τὴν ἐπαγωγὴν τοῦ ἑξῆς λόγου, καὶ σύλληψιν τὴν ἐπισφράγισιν καὶ συναγωγὴν τοῦ προηγησαμένου λόγου.

The commentator means that by 'ἐπιφορά' we should understand 'co-assumption' and by 'σύλληψις' 'conclusion'. Modern scholars have suggested that things are the other way about: the ἐπιφορά is the conclusion (after all, in Stoic logic, 'ἐπιφορά' is the standard term for conclusion), and the σύλληψις is the co-assumption (for which 'πρόσληψις' is the normal term). Neither of those suggestions is particularly felicitous from a linguistic point of view; and it is tempting to correct 'συλλήψεις' into 'προσλήψεις'.

There is another possibility, which is both plausible and depressing. The list of six items does indeed contain two different sorts of item. But the items are not listed according to their sort. The explanation of what a syllogistic connector is does indeed use two different terms to pick out their function or their functions. But the two terms are not ordinarily used to distinguish co-assumptions from conclusions. It seems likely that the *Art* uses the two words indifferently, and that it does not intend to distinguish two species of syllogistic connector.

However that may be, syllogistic connectors are recognized, in one way or another, by all the ancient grammarians. They occur, for example, in the Yale grammatical papyrus, in the fragments of the *Art* optimistically ascribed to Trypho, and in other papyri of the same type. Apollonius does not accord a special treatment to syllogistic connectors in what survives of his *Connectors*. But he incidentally confirms that 'ἄρα' is a syllogistic connector—'ἄρα' with a short initial alpha, that is; and he adds—what is scarcely surprising, that 'οὖν' is another syllogistic connector—'οὖν' with a circumflex, that is. (See *conj* 227.24–25; 228.13–15; 229.21–22; 254.22–23.) The commentaries on the *Art* have, in this case, pretty well nothing to add; for the two pertinent passages—65.27–34 and 105.27–30—are no more than inaccurate cribs from Apollonius.

The Greek texts are meagre. Nonetheless, on their basis, and in particular on the basis of the examples which they offer, it is reasonable to suppose that a connector is syllogistic provided that it connects one component of an argument to another—a subsequent premiss to an existing premiss (so 'ἀλλά' and 'ἀλλαμήν' in Dionysius' list) or a conclusion to a premiss (the rest of the examples). In that case, syllogistic connectors are, as I shall say, either co-assumptional or inferential. (The point of that rebarbative nomenclature will emerge in a moment.)

There is much more material in the Latin grammarians—but it is confused and confusing. It is convenient to start from the views of Cominianus.

Cominianus is known to posterity only from the pages of the *Institutions* of Flavius Sosipater Charisius, a fourth century grammarian who—it was normal practice—wrote with a pair of scissors and a pot of paste. Cominianus, according to Charisius, offered a standard definition of connectors:

a connector is a part of sayings which binds and orders thoughts.

(*inst* II xiv [I 224.24–5])[136]

He then distinguished five types of connector, according to their power or *potestas*. The word '*potestas*', which answers to the Greek 'δύναμις', clearly means 'meaning' here; and Cominianus apparently assigned meanings to connectors without embarrassment.

The fifth type of connector Cominianus called 'rational [*rationalis*]'; and although Charisius reports no explanation of what makes a connector rational, he does offer a list of examples:

quamobrem, praesertim, item, itemque, enim, etenim, enimvero, quia, quapropter, quippe, quoniam, quoniamquidem, ergo, ideo, scilicet, propterea.

(*inst* II xiv [I 225.2–4])

The list is presumably illustrative rather than complete. It contains some co-assumptional connectors—notably '*item*'—and also some inferential items—for example, '*ergo*'. So it seems likely that all the Dionysian syllogistic connectors will count as rational. But Cominianus' class of rational connectors includes examples which are not syllogistic—for example, '*enim*' and '*quia*', the Greek versions of which are causative according to the *Art*.

The later Latin grammarians mostly follow Cominianus, without saying so: they give his definition and his list of five species—so, for example, Probus (*inst* IV 143.24–144.21), Donatus (*ars gramm* II 15 [IV 388.28–389.17), Servius (*in Don* IV 418.4–30). And Pompeius pretends that that was the Latin way of doing things:

The power of connectors is divided into five species among Latin authors (among the Greeks it is variously divided). They are conjunctive, disjunctive, expletive, causal, rational.

(*in Don* v 265.16–19)[137]

---

[136] *coniunctio est pars orationis nectens ordinansque sententiam.*

[137] *potestas coniunctionum apud Latinos in quinque species dividitur (apud Graecos enim varie dividitur). sunt enim copulativae disiunctivae expletivae causales rationales.*

That seems definite enough. It is one of the rare occasions on which the Latin grammarians declare independence from their Greek masters; and it would be interesting to discover why they did so.

However that may be, the Latin story has only half been told. Having cited Cominianus, Charisius turns to Remmius Palaemon, the first and most celebrated of the Roman grammarians. Charisius begins by remarking that 'Palaemon defines them thus' (*inst* II xiv [I 225.5]). But he does not reproduce a definition—or at any rate our text of Charisius does not. Instead, after a brief remark about the position of connectors in sentences, Charisius suggests that it is now time to discuss their *potestates*. He has, of course, already done so in expounding the five species of Cominianus. But now he does so again, this time distinguishing a dozen or more species.

The list—the claim of which to derive from Palaemon has been vigorously asserted and vigorously denied—does not contain an item called 'rational'. But it does contain, as its third member, this:

Ratiocinative are these: *quare, quapropter, igitur, ergo, itaque, quando* (with a grave accent), *quatenus, quoniam, ideoque, quoniamquidem, quandoquidem, siquidem*. They are called ratiocinative because they confirm by a reason whatever has already been set down, thus:

It is light: therefore it is day.

For this has connected the reason: it is thereby light, because it is day—or it is thereby day, because it is light.

(*inst* II xiv [225.20–25])[138]

The explanation for the use of the term 'ratiocinative' is monstrous (I shall return to it); and the list of examples contains some odd items. But it looks as though ratiocinative connectors include inferential connectors and exclude co-assumptional connectors, and that they also include certain other items.

The question is complicated by the fact that the list of connectors in which the ratiocinative class comes third also includes a class which Charisius calls 'inferential [*illativae*]' ([226.3]). Their name suggests that they ought to have something to do with the rational connectors—indeed, it suggests rather strongly that they should be identified as inferential connectors. Charisius offers no definition. But he does offer a list, namely: *quamquam,*

---

[138] *ratiocinativae hae: quare, quapropter, igitur, ergo, itaque, quando (gravi accentu), quatenus, quoniam, ideoque, quoniamquidem, quandoquidem, siquidem. dictae autem sunt ratiocinativae quod quamque rem praepositam ratione confirmant in hunc modum: lucet, igitur dies est. nam hic coniunxit rationem, lucem ideo esse quod sit dies seu diem ideo esse quod sit lux.*

quamvis, etsi, tametsi. 'Although', 'even if': such items are evidently not inferential.

What is going on? Some light—not much—is shed by a comparison with Diomedes' treatment of the subject, which is in places very close to Charisius and plainly was taken from the same source. Like Charisius, Diomedes notices a class of inferential connectors which is distinct from the class of ratiocinative connectors; he gives the same four examples as Charisius does; and he ascribes the things to Pliny (*ars gramm* I 416.17–19), the reference doubtless being to the younger Pliny's work on linguistic problems.

So what was Pliny up to? His work is lost; but Priscian's *Institutions* suggests a solution to the problem. Priscian recognizes seventeen types of connector. One type is called 'adversative [*adversativae*]'. It is illustrated by six examples—*tamen, saltem*, and the four items which Pliny allegedly called inferential. (See *inst* XVI ii 10 [III 99.12–100.4].) I bet that these four, or six, examples were lifted from Pliny, and that Pliny offered them as illustrations of adversative connectors—which, of course, is just what they are. Pliny's account, examples and all, was borrowed from him by various grammar-teachers, and borrowed from them by their successors. Somewhere and somewhen the group of examples strayed, or lost its name, and had another and wholly inappropriate label attached to it.

How, it may be wondered, did the muddle come about? You might dream up a sophisticated story in answer to that question; but the right answer is this: The muddle was the result of a blundering error: someone—a careless grammarian or his careless scribe—replaced '*adversativae*' by '*illativae*'. The interminable pages of *Grammatici Latini* are crammed with splendid blunders: it is misplaced charity to interpret them out of existence, and it is misplaced ingenuity to elaborate refined explanations for their presence in the texts.

However that may be, Priscian rightly calls his six items adversative. Not that he avoids the term 'inferential'. On the contrary, the inferential connector is another one of his seventeen varieties:

Collective or rational connectors are *ergo, igitur, itaque* (when the antepenultimate is acute), *quin, alioquin, immo, utique, atqui*. For these collect by an inference what was earlier said—i.e. they confirm it by reason. ... the same connectors are also called inferential because, when other items have been set down in advance, they are inferred.

(*inst* XVI ii 12 [III 100.15–101.6])[139]

---

[139] *collectivae vel rationales sunt ergo igitur itaque (quando antepaenultima acuitur) quin alioquin immo utique atqui. hae enim per illationem colligunt supra dictum, hoc est ratione confirmant. ... dicuntur tamen eaedem illativae quod praepositis aliis inferuntur.*

'Collective', 'rational' and 'inferential' determine the same class of connectors. The word *'collectivus'* is a Latin calque on *'συλλογιστικός'*, and perhaps *'rationalis'* was intended as a translation of the same Greek word. So the Latin rational connectors were meant to correspond to the Greek syllogistic connectors.

What of the ratiocinative connectors? Priscian does not use the term; but his explanation of his collective connectors overlaps with the explanation of ratiocinative connectors which is found in Charisius and in Diomedes. That suggests that 'ratiocinative' is another translation of 'syllogistic'. It is not a bad translation. Indeed, the received text of Charisius actually contains the word *'συλλογιστικοί'* in apposition to *'ratiocinativae'*; and although I suppose that the Greek word is a gloss, it is surely a true gloss.

There is a difficulty. According to Charisius and Diomedes, these connectors 'are called ratiocinative because they confirm by a reason what has already been set down'; and Priscian says the same of his collective connectors. That is to say, you set down some item or items; you then adjoin another item; you fasten on the adjoined item by means of a ratiocinative connector; and the connector indicates that the adjoined item is a reason in favour of what goes before it. If that description of ratiocinative connectors is correct, then they are completely distinct from syllogistic connectors: a syllogistic connector introduces either a supplementary premiss or else a conclusion; a ratiocinative connector introduces an item which gives a reason, or supplies a premiss, for a thesis which has antecedently been advanced.

But the description of ratiocinative connectors is followed by an example which is supposed to illustrate to it. Here again—in Charisius' words—is the example:

It is light: therefore it is day. For this has connected the reason: it is thereby light, because it is day—or it is thereby day, because it is light.

The connector 'therefore' does not illustrate the description, and it does not 'connect the reason'. Charisius—or whoever he is copying—noticed that embarrassing fact and so replaced 'therefore' by 'because': 'It is thereby light, because it is day'. 'Because' fits the description—but then Charisius noticed that 'It is light for that reason, because it is day' is scarcely an intelligent gloss on 'It is light: therefore it is day'. He saw that something was wrong—and so he added a second paraphrase, 'It is day for that reason, because it is light', as though it were more or less the same thing.

That is a sorry mess—another blunder for which no sophisticated elucidation should be sought. In any event, logic was not the *forte* of the Latin grammarians. Priscian, it is true, was on better form when he associated the term 'inferential' with collective connectors. Nonetheless, 'inferential', on Priscian's definition, only applies to one half of his collective connectors; for it is false that all collective or syllogistic connectors mark the conclusion of an inference.

If Priscian's *'collectivus'* translates 'συλλογιστικός', what is the Greek for *'illativus'*? The answer must be: 'ἐπιφορικός'. And in fact the term is known from Apollonius. Part of his argument to the conclusion that expletive connectors have a sense runs like this:

Again, we can see that they have a sense by looking at what we call syllogistic and the Stoics inferential connectors. 'τοίνυν' consists of two expletive connectors—so too, together with 'γάρ', in 'τοιγάρτοι' and, together with 'οὖν', in 'τοιγαροῦν'. These items have the same force as 'ἄρα' with a short alpha. They are called inferential insofar as they are inferred from what has been premissed—

If it is day, it is light; but it is day: therefore it is light [φῶς ἄρα ἐστί, τοιγαροῦν φῶς ἐστί, φῶς τοίνυν ἐστί].

They are called syllogistic inasmuch as, in certain proofs, when we syllogize the conclusion we use these connectors:

You have five euros from me, and you've also got three: therefore you have eight euros [ἔχεις ἄρα ὀκτὼ δραχμάς, ἔχεις τοίνυν ὀκτὼ δραχμάς].

(*conj* 251.27–252.8)[140]

The argument is this: 'τοίνυν' certainly has a sense, for it is a syllogistic connector. It is composed of two parts, neither of which can be cancelled without changing the sense. Hence each of its parts has a sense. Hence the expletive connectors 'τοι' and 'νυν' have a sense.

Apollonius' explanation of the term 'inferential' is the same as Priscian's. But Apollonius' examples, unlike Priscian's, fit his explanation. (The same four examples are found in the Dionysian list of syllogistic connectors.) Again, Apollonius' explanation of the term 'syllogistic' makes it equivalent to

---

[140] ἀλλὰ μὴν καὶ ἐν τοῖς καλουμένοις πρὸς ἡμῶν μὲν συλλογιστικοῖς, πρὸς δὲ τῶν Στωϊκῶν ἐπιφορικοῖς ἔστι παραδέξασθαι τὴν σημασίαν αὐτῶν. τὸν τοίνυν ἐκ δύο παραπληρωματικῶν συνεστῶτα, καὶ ἔτι μετὰ τοῦ γάρ ἐν τῷ τοιγάρτοι, καὶ μετὰ τοῦ οὖν τοιγαροῦν. δύναμιν γὰρ ἔχουσιν οἱ τοιοῦτοι ἴσην τῷ ἄρα συστελλομένῳ κατὰ τὸ α. καὶ εἴρηνται μὲν ἐπιφορικοί, καθὸ ἐπιφέρονται τοῖς λελημματισμένοις· <εἰ ἡμέρα ἐστί, φῶς ἐστι,> ἀλλὰ μὴν ἡμέρα ἐστί, φῶς ἄρα ἐστί, τοιγαροῦν φῶς ἐστί, φῶς τοίνυν ἐστί· συλλογιστικοὶ δέ, καθότι ἐπί τισιν ἀποδείξεσιν, ἐπισυλλογιζόμενοι τὸ συναγόμενον, προσχρώμεθα τοῖς συνδέσμοις τοῖσδε· ἔχεις μου πέντε δραχμάς, ἔχεις δὲ καὶ τρεῖς, ἔχεις ἄρα ὀκτὼ δραχμάς, ἔχεις τοίνυν ὀκτὼ δραχμάς.

'inferential' (for the reference to 'certain proofs' must not be taken to limit syllogistic connectors to syllogisms which are in fact probative). In addition, Apollonius—and he alone—tells us that the Stoics fixed a class of inferential connectors. That they should call them inferential or ἐπιφορικοί is to be expected; for 'ἐπιφορά' was the usual term in Stoic logic for the conclusion of an argument.

In short, according to Apollonius' account of the matter, inferential and syllogistic connectors are one and the same. (They were also, according to Apollonius, sometimes called 'epilogistic'; at any rate, 'οὐκοῦν is called epilogistic by some people' (*conj* 257.18).[141] Who those people were we cannot tell; but it is difficult to think that the difference in nomenclature had any particular significance.)

What about co-assumptional connectors? They too are named in Apollonius' *Connectors*:

We have explained how and with what force the connector 'δέ' is understood. But when it takes the connector 'γέ' it means something else. For the 'γέ' in 'δέγε' is not otiose, as it is in 'ἀρά γε ἡμέρα;'. You can find the Stoics calling 'δέγε' co-assumptional. For this construction of connectors introduces sayings which come from conditionals and are reformulated—

If it is day, it is light; but [δέγε] it is day.
Since the saying comes to be in a co-assumption, such connectors are co-assumptional. The same is true of 'ἀλλά' and 'ἀλλαμήν'.

(*conj* 250.12–20)[142]

Connectors which mark a co-assumption or πρόσληψις were called, by the Stoics, co-assumptional or προσληπτικοί. (The two examples which Apollonius appends to his account, 'ἀλλά' and 'ἀλλαμήν', are two of the items in the Dionysian list of syllogistic connectors.)

And so we may tell the following history. The Stoics were the first to distinguish different classes of connectors, among them the inferential and the co-assumptional. Apollonius followed them, noticing that the grammarians generally preferred to use the word 'syllogistic' to designate the inferential

---

141 ὁ οὐκοῦν καλεῖται πρὸς ἐνίων ἐπιλογιστικός.
142 ἔτι ὁ δέ σύνδεσμος ὅπως παραλαμβάνεται καὶ ἐπὶ ποίᾳ δυνάμει ἐκτεθείμεθα. ἀλλὰ προσλαβὼν τὸν γέ ἄλλο τι ἐπηγγείλατο. οὐ γὰρ ὡς ἐν τῷ ἀρά γε ἡμέρα; παρείλκετο ὁ γέ καὶ ἐν τῷ δέ γε. καλούμενον γοῦν ἔστιν εὑρέσθαι παρὰ τοῖς Στωϊκοῖς τὸν δέ γε ὄντα προσληπτικόν. τοὺς γὰρ ἀπὸ συναφῆς λόγους εἰς σχηματισμὸν μετιόντας ἡ τοιαύτη σύνταξις ἢ τῶν συνδέσμων ὑπάγει· εἰ ἡμέρα ἐστί, φῶς ἐστιν· ἡμέρα δέγε ἐστιν. καὶ ἐπεὶ ἐν προσλήψει ἐγένετο ὁ λόγος, προσληπτικοὶ οἱ τοιοῦτοι σύνδεσμοι. τὸ δ' αὐτὸ συμβέβηκε καὶ ἐπὶ τοῦ ἀλλά καὶ ἀλλαμήν.

connectors, and that some people used 'epilogistic'. Later Greek grammarians failed to see the point of distinguishing between the inferential and the co-assumptional, and they joined the two into a single class. The members of that class they called syllogistic, either changing the sense of the word 'syllogistic' or else failing to see that its old sense was no longer apt. The Latin grammarians inherited the broad class of syllogistic connectors. On the one hand, they implicitly enlarged it yet further, by stuffing it with new and heterogeneous examples; and on the other hand, they established—quite incoherently—a separate class of inferential connectors. They then spiced up the soup with some piquant confusions of their own.

That is a sad story; and I fear that it is by and large true.

ARGUMENTS AND SAYINGS

Whatever the history of syllogistic connectors may have been, we may wonder why they were counted as connectors in the first place. Marius Victorinus, in his thoroughly traditional *Art of Grammar*, follows Cominianus' definition of the connector and also his division of connectors into five species. But when he gets to the rational connectors he has a word of his own to say:

What are the rational connectors? *ita, itaque, proinde, proin, denique.* These seem to me rather to be adverbs.

(*ars gramm* VI 203.10–14)[143]

Victorinus, for once, appears to have a point.

Consider such English words as 'therefore' and 'thus' and 'so'. They are, to be sure, sentential connectives in the generous modern use of that phrase; that is to say, they are items which take sentences to make sentences. But they are one-place connectives—and hence they are not connectors as the ancients understood that notion. They are sentential adverbs or adsentences. Moreover, they are demonstrative or indexical adsentences: 'so' means 'for that reason', where 'that' is a demonstrative adjective, and the phrase 'that reason' will (at least normally) refer back to something which has just been set down or said. So in

I think. Therefore I am.

there are two sentences, not one. The 'therefore' does, of course, connect the second sentence to the first inasmuch as it contains a reference to what the

---

[143] *rationales quae sunt? ita itaque proinde proin denique. quae magis adverbia esse mihi videntur.*

first sentence says. But it is not a two-placed sentential connector: it is an Aristotelian articulator, an item which connects without unifying.

That seems right for English; and I think it is right for Latin—at any rate, '*itaque*' looks like a sentential adverb, and an indexical one at that. In other words, Victorinus is right, against all his Latin colleagues. What about the Greeks? Are the items which the Stoics and Apollonius characterize as inferential connectors not connectors at all but rather adverbs?

Greek certainly has inferential adverbs or adsentences. For example, there are 'οὕτως', 'ταύτῃ', 'διὰ τοῦτο', … The grammarians say very little about them. Apollonius cites 'οὕτως' and 'ταύτῃ' as adverbs (e.g. *adv* 123.4, 138.20, 151.23); but he does not comment on their inferential use. His only remark on 'διὰ τοῦτο' occurs when he is arguing that the connectors 'ὅτι' and 'διότι' are not synonymous:

If you say
  διότι it is day, it is light,
'διὰ τοῦτο' is missing; but
  ὅτι it is day, it is light
is complete.

(conj 242.14–16)[144]

That rather implausible contention shows that Apollonius did not take 'διὰ τοῦτο' to be a connector; but it sheds no positive light on his opinion. The Byzantine grammarian, George Choeroboscus, has the following to say:

'διὰ τοῦτο' is a demonstrative pronoun, or rather a demonstrative adverbial or an explanatory connector. It comes from the preposition 'διά' and the pronoun 'τοῦτο'.

(epim in Psalm 58.32–34)[145]

Choeroboscus often preserves ancient wisdom; but I should not like to make anything of this particular passage.

However that may be, it is clear that if in Greek you introduce a sentence with, say, 'διὰ τοῦτο' alone, then you have an asyndeton; and if you want to avoid asyndeton you may do so easily enough by adding a connector—'δέ' or 'οὖν' or what you will—after the 'διὰ τοῦτο'. Now the items which the Greek grammarians class as syllogistic connectors are not like that at all. True,

---

[144] τὸ γὰρ οὕτω λεγόμενον, διότι ἡμέρα ἐστί, φῶς ἐστι λείπει τῷ διὰ τοῦτο· τὸ δέ ὅτι ἡμέρα ἐστί, φῶς ἐστιν αὐτοτελές.

[145] διὰ τοῦτο· δεικτικὴ ἀντωνυμία, ἢ μᾶλλον ἐπιρρηματικὴ δεικτική, ἢ σύνδεσμος αἰτιολογικός. γίνεται δὲ ἐκ τῆς διὰ προθέσεως καὶ τῆς τοῦτο ἀντωνυμίας.

you may introduce the conclusion of an argument with 'διὰ τοῦτο' and you may introduce it with 'ἄρα'; but the latter, unlike the former, does not make for an asyndeton; and so the latter, unlike the former, will not tolerate a supplementary 'δέ' or 'οὖν'.

The facts are a good deal more nuanced than that. And in any event what I have just said does not prove that the Greek inferential connectors really are connectors. Nonetheless, there are, on the one hand, pertinent differences between, say, 'ἄρα' and 'διὰ τοῦτο'; and there are, on the other hand, pertinent similarities between, say, 'ἄρα' and 'ἀλλά'. So is there anything to say against the thesis that inferential connectors are connectors?

Look first at the easier case—the case of co-assumptional connectors. Apollonius' example was this:

εἰ ἡμέρα ἐστί, φῶς ἐστί· ἡμέρα δέγε ἐστι.

In English, that is roughly:

If it's day, it's light; but it's day.

According to Apollonius, 'δέγε' links a saying to a saying. He does not explicitly say that 'δέγε' unifies, and he does not explicitly say that it makes a single saying from a plurality of sayings. But I have already argued that he takes connectors in general to unify, and that the result of unifying a plurality of sayings can only be a saying. If that is so, then Apollonius holds that 'δέγε' functions as a two-placed connector, just like 'εἰ' or 'if'.

The English 'but' is not always a sentential connector; but sometimes it is. After all, 'and' often functions as a sentential connector; and where 'and' so functions, it can be usually replaced by 'but' without syntactical abuse. For example, 'and' is indubitably a sentential connector in

He is white and he is ugly.

So how cannot 'but' be a sentential connector in

I am black but I am comely?

The case passes the embedding test—you can say, for example,

Do you know that she is black but she is comely?

(Well, you can, but you won't. But you will say, without a qualm

Do you know that she is black but comely?

And come to that, what was actually said was this:

I am black but comely, O ye daughters of Jerusalem.)

Thus if P and Q are sentences, then 'P but Q' will at least sometimes be a sentence.

Perhaps the co-assumptional use of 'but' is different? After all, it will surely be thought odd, or uncouth, to utter anything like

I know that if it's day, it's light, but it's day.

The thing is a mouthful, and it is likely to be mispunctuated and misunderstood. But is it ungrammatical? I cannot see that it is; and so I incline to think that the English word 'but' functions as a sentential connector when it is used to connect a supplementary premiss to the rest of an argument.

Is the same true of the Greek 'δέγε' and of the other items which the grammarians present as co-assumptional connectors? Is, say,

εἰ ἡμέρα ἐστί, φῶς ἐστί· ἡμέρα δέγε ἐστι

embeddable? Can it be negated, or can you say that you know or believe that ...? The answers to those questions, I take it, are Yes.

It is another question what the truth-conditions for such compound sentences are. Some will suggest that 'but' may be replaced by 'and', and 'δέγε' by 'καί' (in an appropriate position), without any change in truth-value or indeed in sense. Apollonius, however, says that 'δέγε' promises or means something other than 'δέ'. And in his view, something of the form 'P, Q δέγε' will presumably express a truth if and only if, first both P and Q are true, and secondly, Q is a supplementary premiss in an argument in which P is a preceding premiss.

What, finally, of inferential connectors, the connectors which introduce the conclusion of an argument? Consider:

εἰ ἡμέρα ἐστί, φῶς ἐστί· ἡμέρα δέγε ἐστι· φῶς ἄρα ἐστι.

There, 'ἄρα' is—according to the ancient theory—a connector. It connects the saying, 'φῶς ἐστι', to the sayings which precede it: it connects the sentence which is the conclusion of the argument to the sentences which are the premisses of the argument. The whole Greek sequence which I have just cited—two premiss-sentences and a conclusion-sentence—is therefore supposed to constitute a single saying, the structure of which might be represented as follows:

(P, Q δέγε) R ἄρα

And that is comparable to, say,

If (P and Q) then R

To be sure, no ancient text actually says as much. But I cannot see what else an ancient text could have said on the subject.

Nevertheless, if that was what the Greek grammarians wanted to say, surely they were wrong? After all, translate the Greek into English and you get this:

If it's light it's day; but it's light: therefore it's day.

That is a connected sequence of sentences—but it is not a single sentence. It cannot be embedded. For example,

I know that if it's light it's day, but it's light, therefore it's day

is not an English sentence; and it is not an English sentence in the same way and for the same reason that

I know that he came, he saw, he conquered

is not an English sentence.

That is the truth about English. What about Greek? There is a bronze answer to the question: 'English 'therefore' and Greek '*ἄρα*' are on all fours; '*ἄρα*' is not a sentential connector; and the Greek grammarians—like grammarians all over the world—were wrong about their own language.' There is a silver answer: 'English 'therefore' and Greek '*ἄρα*' are on all fours; each is a connector but not a sentential connector; and the Greek grammarians were right to make '*ἄρα*' a connector which makes sayings from sayings—so long as the made sayings are not taken to be sentences.' There is a gold answer: 'English 'therefore' and Greek '*ἄρα*' are not on all fours; '*ἄρα*', unlike 'therefore', is a sentential connector; and the Greek grammarians are victorious.'

I am inclined to think that—whatever else may be the case—'therefore' is not on all fours with '*ἄρα*'. The sentential adverb or adsentence 'therefore' is the exact English for the Greek sentential adverb or adsentence '*διὰ τοῦτο*'. There is no exact English for '*ἄρα*'. (Translators will continue to use 'therefore', and rightly so.) The nearest English is perhaps 'and therefore'. In English, 'and therefore' functions as a sentential connector. To be sure, it is a compound connector—it is compounded from a connector and an adverb; but it is still a connector, and expressions of the form 'P and therefore Q' pass the embedding test. Plainly, if 'and therefore' is a connector, it is an inferential connector. A sentence of the form 'P and therefore Q' is true if and only if P is true and, for that very reason, Q is true. One way of putting such things into Greek is by means of the formula 'P, Q *ἄρα*'.

4. Forms of Argument

SPECIES OF SYLLOGISM

Logic, in the good old days, was the art of thinking—more precisely, it was the art or science of reasoning. Logicians were supposed to consider arguments—deductions, inferences, syllogisms, what you will—and to sort them into the good and the bad, the valid and the invalid. There is an endless number of arguments, and a logician cannot survey each and every one of them. Nor would he want to. Rather, and like any other scientist, a logician is interested in the universal, in the general: he is not concerned, save incidentally, with the individual items which roam his territory but with types or kinds or classes of individuals.

Towards the end of his *Introduction to Logic*, Galen announced that

there is also another, third, species of syllogism useful for proofs, which I say come about in virtue of something relational, while the Aristotelians are obliged to number them among the predicative syllogisms.

(*inst log* xvi 1).[1]

The announcement was, I suppose, designed to shock, or at least to astound. Everyone knew that, when you did logic, there were two species of syllogism to mug up: there were the predicative syllogisms which Aristotle had put on the market; and there were the hypothetical syllogisms, which were the pride but not the property of Stoic logic. Who knew about a third species? No one—until Galen discovered and published it.

The two familiar species are apparently quite different from one another. The Greek for 'predicative' is 'κατηγορικός': the word, in this context, is usually translated by—or transliterated as—'categorical', so that histories of logic discuss categorical syllogisms and categorical syllogistic. The word 'categorical' is entrenched; but 'predicative' is the right translation: predicative syllogisms are arguments the validity of which turns on the properties of

---

[1] ἔστι καὶ ἄλλο τρίτον εἶδος συλλογισμῶν εἰς ἀποδείξεις χρήσιμον, οὓς ἐγὼ μὲν ὀνομάζω κατὰ τὸ πρός τι γενέσθαι, βιάζονται δ' αὐτοὺς οἱ περὶ τὸν Ἀριστοτέλην τοῖς κατηγορικοῖς συναριθμεῖν.

predicative propositions—that is to say, on the properties of one or other of the four styles of Aristotelian predication. The constituent propositions of a predicative syllogism—its premisses and its conclusion—are all essentially such that in them x is predicated in style S of y.

The Greek for 'hypothetical' is 'ὑποθετικός'. Like 'categorical', 'hypothetical' is a transliteration rather than a translation; and it is potentially misleading. But in this case there is, I think, no better or less misleading translation. In any event, 'hypothetical' syllogisms are arguments the validity of which turns on the logical properties of certain compound propositions—and in particular (in the standard cases), on the logical properties of conditionals and disjunctions and conjunctions. At least one of the premisses of a hypothetical syllogism is essentially compounded in one or other of those ways.

Aristotle claimed that every syllogism and every proof come about through one of the three figures of his predicative syllogistic; and some Stoics appear to have made a similar claim on behalf of their hypothetical syllogistic. The two theories might therefore appear to be rivals; and certainly, if you were a card-carrying Peripatetic, you were likely to claim—with Alexander of Aphrodisias—that the predicative syllogisms were the only kosher variety; and if you were a good Stoic you might hold the converse view.

Nevertheless, it is clear that in later antiquity both theories—or rather, derivative and simplified versions of both theories—were taught as complementary parts of the single science of logic. Galen mentions disagreements over priority, and he urges that

as far as disputes of that sort are concerned, it is no great matter whether you discover the truth or remain in ignorance. For you need to learn both sorts of syllogisms—that is what is useful. You may say that one lot is prior, or teach it to be prior, as the mood takes you—but you must not be ignorant of the others.

(inst log vii 3)[2]

Most teachers, no doubt, took the Galenic line.

Galen alone offers a third species of syllogism: it was produced as a necessary supplement to the existing two species and not as a rival to them; and if Galen once or twice seems to intimate that his relational syllogisms

---

[2] ἀλλὰ περὶ μὲν τῶν τοιούτων ἀμφισβητήσεων οὔτε εὑρεῖν οὔτε ἀγνοῆσαι μέγα· χρὴ γὰρ ἀμφότερα τὰ μέρη γιγνώσκειν τῶν συλλογισμῶν, καὶ τοῦτ᾽ ἔστι τὸ χρήσιμον, ὀνομάζειν δὲ τοὺς ἑτέρους ἢ διδάσκειν προτέρους ὡς ἑκάστῳ φίλον· οὐ μὴν ἐκείνοις γε ἀγνοεῖσθαι προσῆκεν.

are more useful than either predicative or hypothetical syllogisms, he never states that that is so—and no doubt he did not mean to suggest that it is so.

Galen discusses his third species at some length in the *Introduction to Logic*. But he mentions the matter nowhere else in his vast œuvre; and no one else in antiquity ever notices relational syllogisms. We only possess a fraction of ancient writings on logic, and it is likely enough that relational syllogisms were mentioned in some lost texts. But it is improbable that they were ever widely known; and it is certain that they never became—as Galen apparently thought they ought to become—the third part of a tripartite logic.

However that may be, Galen thought that there were three species of syllogisms, and most ancients thought that there were two. If the word 'species' is taken technically, and not as a variant on such informal terms as 'kind' or 'sort', then the ancients will have supposed that the word 'syllogism' is a generic term, and they will have divided the genus into two—or in Galen's case, three—species, each definable as 'syllogism of such-and-such a sort'. Presumably the genus itself is a species of a higher genus, the genus of argument or inference; for certainly a syllogism is a particular sort of argument. And presumably the species of syllogisms themselves divide into subspecies, and so on until we arrive at lowest items or *infimae species*.

There is any number of ways of dividing a species of arguments into subspecies, just as there is any number of ways of dividing any species into subspecies. And just as some methods of dividing animal species are appropriate for a zoologist, so some methods of dividing argumentative species are appropriate for a logician. When Alexander wants to show that the conclusion of a syllogism cannot be the same as one of its premisses, he says that 'we might learn the truth if we went through the species of syllogism'; he then mentions apodictic syllogisms, dialectical syllogisms, and eristical syllogisms, and shows that in none of the three cases can the conclusion be the same as a premiss; and he concludes thus:

If a genus exists in its own species, and if the syllogism is a genus of its species, and if in none of the species is the conclusion the same as a premiss, then it will not be so either in the syllogism in general.

(*in APr* 19.1–3)[3]

---

[3] εἰ δ' ἐστὶ τὸ γένος ἐν τοῖς εἴδεσι τοῖς αὑτοῦ, καὶ ἔστιν ὁ συλλογισμὸς γένος τῶν αὑτοῦ εἰδῶν, ἐν οὐδενὶ δὲ αὐτῶν ταὐτὸν τῷ εἰλημμένῳ τὸ ἐπιφερόμενον, οὐδ' ἂν ἐν συλλογισμῷ εἴη ὅλως.

The terms 'genus' and 'species', as Alexander's argument shows, must here be taken seriously. One way of dividing up the genus of syllogisms is by a trichotomy—apodictic, dialectical, eristic.

Alexander's trichotomy distinguishes species of syllogism according to the character of their premisses—a syllogism is eristic if its premisses falsely seem to be true, it is dialectical if its premisses are reputed to be true, and it is apodictic if its premisses actually are true (and also satisfy several other conditions). That sort of distinction might be deemed to be epistemological rather than strictly logical. There were also strictly logical divisions. Alexander, like all other Aristotelians, divided types of predicative syllogisms into what were called figures, of which there were three. And each figure was divided into a certain number of moods. The exact number of moods was contested in antiquity (and after); but all agreed that it was in principle finite and in fact pretty small—the most exuberant enumerators did not go beyond 24.

Argument, syllogism, predicative syllogism, first figure syllogism, Barbara—such a sequence of terms could then be picked off the Porphyrean tree or formal division which represents the domain of logic. As far as I know, no ancient text records such a sequence or describes such a tree. But it is the sort of thing which a logician of late antiquity would have loved.

There is at least one difficulty with it. No item can belong to two species unless one of them is subordinate to the other; and hence no item can belong to more than one lowest species. Those are trivial truths about the classificatory principles which underlie Porphyrean trees. But might not one and the same argument belong to two non-subordinate kinds, being (say) both a predicative and a hypothetical syllogism? And could not one and the same argument belong to two lowest kinds, being equally or indifferently a predicative syllogism in Cesare (say) or in Camestres? There is no discussion of the question in any surviving ancient text; but there are a few wisps of evidence on the matter.

The first wisp is found in the list of Chrysippus' logical writings which Diogenes Laertius copied down and conserved for us. It contains the following two adjacent items:

Concerning the fact that the same argument is ordered in several modes (1 book).
On what has been urged against the fact that the same argument has been ordered in a syllogistic and in a non-syllogistic mode (2 books).

(VII 194)[4]

---

[4] Περὶ τοῦ τάττεσθαι τὸν αὐτὸν λόγον ἐν πλείοσι τρόποις· α'.

Πρὸς τὰ ἀντειρημένα τῷ τὸν αὐτὸν λόγον ἐν συλλογιστικῷ καὶ ἀσυλλογίστῳ τετάχθαι τρόπῳ· β'.

We know nothing of those essays save what can be deduced from their titles.

To say that an argument is 'ordered in a mode' is tantamount to saying that it is of a certain kind or that it has a certain form. The Stoics distinguished between arguments on the one hand, and what they called 'τρόποι' or 'modes' on the other. Diogenes Laertius explains the distinction as follows:

An argument ... is something consisting of an assumption and a co-assumption and an inference, as for example:

If it is day, it is light; but it is day: therefore it is light.

... A mode is as it were a shape of an argument, as for example:

If the 1st, the 2nd; but the 1st: therefore the 2nd.

(VII 76)[5]

I shall have much more to say about modes later on; but it is plain—and it is enough to be going on with—that a mode is something like an argument-form or an argument-schema. So the first of the two Chrysippean titles must have discussed the notion that one and the same argument may have two or more forms; and the title implies—a little less strongly, it must be confessed, in the Greek than in my English—that Chrysippus accepted the notion.

If Chrysippus held that a single argument may have different forms, then—it might be inferred—he cannot have thought, or at least, cannot consistently have thought, that arguments divide into genera and species. But the inference is hasty. As far as the title goes, the different modes which order a single argument may themselves be arranged as species and genus—one of the modes may be subordinate to, or an instance of, the other. It may be helpful to look at the matter in terms of a simple example; and it is convenient to take a vacuous argument. (The Peripatetics jeered at such things, but the Stoics had nothing against them.)

So consider the empty argument:

If it is day, it is day; but it is day: therefore it is day.

What modes might that argument be ordered in? What forms might it be supposed to have? Well, a modern logician will notice that the argument has at least the following four forms or that it is ordered in at least the following four modes.

---

[5] λόγος δέ ἐστιν, ὡς οἱ περὶ τὸν Κρῖνίν φασι, τὸ συνεστηκὸς ἐκ λήμματος καὶ προσλήψεως καὶ ἐπιφορᾶς, οἷον ὁ τοιοῦτος· εἰ ἡμέρα ἐστί, φῶς ἐστι· ἡμέρα δέ ἐστι· φῶς ἄρα ἐστί. ... τρόπος δέ ἐστιν οἱονεὶ σχῆμα λόγου, οἷον ὁ τοιοῦτος· εἰ τὸ πρῶτον, τὸ δεύτερον· ἀλλὰ μὴν τὸ πρῶτον· τὸ ἄρα δεύτερον.

(a) If P, P; P: therefore P
(b) If P, Q; P: therefore Q
(c) P; Q: therefore Q
(d) P, Q: therefore R

(For the moment, I represent forms or modes in that standard schematic manner, and I suppose that the manner is understood or understandable. The questions of how to represent forms of argument and of how to understand such schematic formulas will be a major theme of the later parts of this chapter.)

The first three of those modes are valid, the fourth is not. Every argument which is ordered by (a) or by (b) or by (c) is thereby a valid argument, its conclusion following by necessity from its premisses; but an argument ordered by (d) is not thereby valid. Mode (a) is a special instance of mode (b). If Chrysippus had looked at the vacuous argument when he remarked that 'the same argument can be ordered in several modes', which of those four modes would he have had his eye on? If on (b) and (c)—if, that is to say, he would have adverted to the fact that the argument is ordered both by (b) and also by (c)—then that would be directly pertinent to the question of genera and species of syllogisms; for (b) is not a special case of (c) nor (c) of (b). But if he would have been thinking rather, say, of (a) and (b), then there would be no consequences to be drawn.

There is still the evidence of the second of the two Chrysippean titles. It suggests that someone had claimed that one and the same argument may be ordered in a syllogistic and in a non-syllogistic mode; that someone had brought objections against the claim; and that Chrysippus then defended the claim against the objections. What precisely the claim was depends on the sense which is to be given to the term 'non-syllogistic'. On one hypothesis—it is not the only one, and I am not even sure that it is the most likely one—the word means 'non-concludent' or 'invalid'. In that case, Chrysippus' second essay will have defended the thesis that one and the same argument may have both a valid and an invalid mode. The thesis is true—as is shown by the fact that the vacuous argument has among its modes both (a), which is valid, and (d), which is not. Indeed, Chrysippus might have defended a stronger version of that thesis. It is a trivial truth that every argument with n premisses exhibits, among other modes, the mode:

$P_1, P_2, \ldots, P_n$: therefore Q

That mode is invalid. So every argument—and therefore every valid argument—exhibits at least one invalid form.

Who put forward the claim which had been attacked and which Chrysippus then defended? It is tempting to guess that it was Chrysippus himself who did so—that the second of the two titles refers to an essay in self-defence; and it is very tempting to guess that the claim which Chrysippus defended had been put forward in the first of the two adjacent essays on Diogenes' list, and that it constituted the chief theme of that lost essay. In that case, the first essay did not discuss, let alone defend, the thesis that one and the same syllogism may have different and non-subordinate valid forms.

All that is hopelessly iffy. But it is enough for my present ends: the two titles do not demonstrate that Chrysippus thought that an argument could have two different and non-subordinate valid forms. Perhaps he did think so; but the titles do not prove that he did.

The other wisps of evidence to which I alluded come from Galen. Here, first, is a passage from the *Introduction to Logic*:

The syllogism will be propounded hypothetically as follows:
  If Socrates is a son of Sophroniscus, then Sophroniscus is father of Socrates.
  But Socrates is a son of Sophroniscus.
  Therefore Sophroniscus is father of Socrates.
But the construction of the reasoning will be more forceful with predicative propositions ...

(*inst log* xvi 11)[6]

I have there translated an emended text, and the emendations are anything but certain. But unless the transmitted Greek is unfathomably corrupt, one thing is plain: Galen supposes that one and the same argument may be put forward either hypothetically or predicatively. He presupposes, in other words, that an argument may belong to two distinct and non-subordinate kinds.

The passage in the *Introduction* is not isolated. In his work *On Seed* Galen argues against those scientists who deny that females produce seed. After a string of refutatory arguments, he remarks:

---

[6] ὑποθετικῶς μὲν οὕτως ὁ συλλογισμὸς ἐρωτηθήσεται· εἰ Σωκράτης υἱός ἐστι Σωφρονίσκου, Σωφρονίσκος πατήρ ἐστι Σωκράτους· ἀλλὰ μὴν ὁ Σωκράτης υἱός ἐστι Σωφρονίσκου· Σωφρονίσκος ἄρα πατήρ ἐστι Σωκράτους. κατηγορικαῖς δὲ προτάσεσι βιαιότερον ἔσται ἡ σύστασις τοῦ λογισμοῦ ...

Those considerations are enough to refute their opinion. And refutation apart, it is possible to produce a direct proof, syllogizing in two ways, both hypothetically and predicatively.

(*sem* IV 609)[7]

Galen then offers some arguments, which he duly characterizes as predicative or as hypothetical syllogisms. There are difficulties in interpreting the passage; but here too one thing is plain: Galen supposes himself to be offering a single probative argument—an argument which is now done in predicative guise and now in hypothetical.

In another of his technical treatises, on simple drugs, Galen spends a few pages on the pharmacological claim that olive-oil is astringent. Those who have advanced the claim, he alleges, have made a logical error.

For it is agreed that everything astringent is rough and that olive-oil is rough. But from these suppositions it does not follow that olive-oil is astringent, whether we make the propositions predicative or hypothetical; for nothing follows from two universal affirmatives in the second figure, and the conditional is not true of necessity. In the predicative syllogism the two premisses will be these:

Everything astringent is rough,

Every olive-oil is rough

—and from agreement on them nothing follows. As for the hypothetical premiss, which the Chrysippeans call a connected assertible, we cannot find one which is true.

(*simp med temp* XI 499)[8]

Here too—and more clearly—Galen seems to suppose that one and the same argument (admittedly a faulty argument) may be either predicative or hypothetical.

How can that be? Well, 'these suppositions', or the materials which constitute the starting-points of the faulty argument, may be made into predicative propositions and they may be made into hypothetical propositions. Thus

---

[7] ταυτὶ μὲν ἱκανὰ τὴν δόξαν ἐλέγχειν αὐτῶν. ἔστι δὲ καὶ χωρὶς ἐλέγχου τὴν ἀπόδειξιν ἐξ εὐθείας ποιεῖσθαι, διττῶς συλλογιζομένοις ὑποθετικῶς τε καὶ κατηγορικῶς.

[8] ἅπαν μὲν γὰρ ὡμολόγηται τὸ δάκνον εἶναι κερχνῶδες. ὡμολόγηται δὲ καὶ τοὔλαιον ὑπάρχειν κερχνῶδες. ἀλλ᾽ ἐκ τῶν ὑποκειμένων τούτων οὐ περαίνεται δακνῶδες εἶναι τοὔλαιον, οὔτε κατηγορικὰς οὔτε ὑποθετικὰς ἡμῶν ποιησάντων τὰς προτάσεις, τῷ μήτ᾽ ἐκ δύο καθόλου καταφατικῶν ἐν δευτέρῳ σχήματι περαίνεσθαί τι μήτε τὸ συνημμένον ἐξ ἀνάγκης ἀληθεύεσθαι. γενήσονται δ᾽ ἐν μὲν τῷ κατηγορικῷ συλλογισμῷ δύο προτάσεις αἵδε· πᾶν τὸ δάκνον κερχνῶδες, πᾶν ἔλαιον κερχνῶδες· ἐξ ὧν ὁμολογηθέντων οὐδὲν περανθήσεται. τὴν δ᾽ ὑποθετικὴν πρότασιν, ἣν οἱ περὶ τὸν Χρύσιππον ἀξίωμα συνημμένον ὀνομάζουσιν, οὐκ ἔχομεν ἀληθῆ λαβεῖν.

we agree that olive-oil is rough; and we might formulate the agreement by saying, for example,

Everything which is olive-oil is rough.

We might equally well say this:

If anything is olive-oil, then it is rough.

The first of those sentences flaunts a predicative form or a subject–predicate structure: it quite overtly expresses an Aristotelian A-predication, it straight-forwardly says of every so-and-so that it is such-and-such. The second sentence just as shamelessly displays a hypothetical form: it is a sort of conditional, it says that if thus-and-so, then so-and-thus. That being so, are the 'suppositions' on which the bad inferences build really predicative or really hypothetical? Evidently, they are really both—and of course they are really both regardless of the ways in which we choose to express them.

Since a supposition may be both hypothetical and predicative, it is easy to see how a syllogism may be both hypothetical and predicative.

It may be objected that the two sentences with which I expressed the thought about olive-oil do not in fact express the very same thought—or at any rate, that there are different thoughts there to be expressed. For from an A-predication which says 'rough' universally and affirmatively of 'olive-oil', it follows—in Aristotle's logic—that

Some olive-oil is rough.

But from the hypothetical proposition which declares something to be rough if it is olive-oil, no such consequence follows. The predicative pro-position has, as they say, 'existential import', the hypothetical does not. Hence the sentence which wears predicativity on its sleeve expresses one proposition, and the sentence which sports hypotheticality expresses another; and if I try to say neutrally that olive-oil is rough—perhaps by way of the sentence 'Olive-oil is rough'—then what I say is either ambiguous or in-determinate.

Perhaps that is correct. But if so, it constitutes an objection to Galen, not to an interpretation of Galen. For Galen plainly supposes that one and the same proposition is expressed by the two sentences.

It may be objected, secondly, that no ancient text states in so many words that one and the same argument may constitute both a predicative and a hypothetical syllogism. On the contrary, most ancient logical texts give the clear impression—without, I think, ever making a direct statement—that an argument may be either predicative or hypothetical and cannot be both at once. As for Galen, the two passages which I have quoted are the only passages which suggest that an argument may be both predicative and hypothetical; and the *Introduction to Logic* will give its readers a strong contrary impression.

All of that is quite true. Nonetheless, it is reasonable to conclude from the wisps of evidence that at least one ancient logician was at least sometimes aware that every argument is not, so to speak, confined to a single syllogistic form: an argument may, in principle, have two—or more—distinct and non-subordinate valid forms.

In that case, syllogisms cannot be arranged under species and genera. You may talk of kinds or sorts of arguments. You may not talk of species of arguments—unless, of course, you use the word 'species' in a relaxed sense.

If logicians occasionally talk about kinds or sorts or even species of arguments, they also—and perhaps more often—talk about forms of argument. Now the forms of argument in which a logician is interested can be arranged into a genuine Porphyrean tree, from which we may pick—for example—the sequence: syllogism, predicative syllogism, first figure syllogism, Barbara. That is not the same sequence as before, though it is expressed in the same words. For in it Barbara is no longer an *infima species*: it is an individual—an individual syllogistic form. No such individual belongs to more than one lowest species, and the classificatory scheme is saved. As for arguments and syllogisms—concrete, individual arguments and concrete, individual syllogisms—they are not forms, and so they do not appear on the tree at all. Rather, they have or possess or show forms. And an item may have a plurality of forms without thereby prejudicing the Porphyrean structure of the tree of forms.

If you want to talk seriously about species of syllogism, then, you had better be thinking of species of syllogistic forms, not of species of concrete syllogisms. Strictly speaking, a syllogism—according to the ancient definitions—is an argument: it has premises which are either true or false, and a conclusion which either follows or fails to follow from the premises. Barbara is not a syllogism: Barbara has no premises and no conclusion—rather, instances or cases of Barbara have premises and conclusions. Barbara is a syllogistic mood or a syllogistic form. That is perfectly clear, and it was perfectly clear to the old logicians. Nonetheless, the old logicians, Galen among them, will frequently talk of, say, 'the first syllogism in the first figure' and thereby designate the syllogistic form Barbara; and in general, they use the word 'syllogism' often enough to refer to syllogistic forms and not to concrete arguments. Indeed, I suspect that their most common use of the word 'syllogism' fails to accord with their formal definition of the word 'syllogism'. That will vex pedants;

but it is generally harmless enough—and I myself shall make no serious effort to say 'syllogistic form' rather than 'syllogism' when it is a syllogistic form I mean to talk about.

FORMAL LOGIC

The preceding remarks will, I fear, have excited no one who is not a devotee of Porphyrean taxonomy. But they have at least served to introduce the notion of form; and perhaps they have also served to suggest that all logic is—in a pretty straightforward sense—formal logic. For logic is not concerned with this or that individual concrete inference, except insofar as the individual inference is an instance of some particular form; nor yet is logic concerned with this or that general type of inference, except insofar as the general type of inference is determined by a general form.

The claim that all logic is formal might be resisted, on several grounds. One bad ground for resistance is worth mentioning inasmuch as it involves a vulgar misconception—a misconception which is, I think, common among non-logicians. It will be affirmed, and truly, that not all logic is symbolic logic: after all, no ancient logicians showed any interest in artificial symbolizations, which hardly obtruded themselves before the nineteenth century. And if not all logic is symbolic, then—it may be inferred—not all logic is formal. But the inference is invalid. For although the terms 'formal' and 'symbolic' are sometimes confounded, they have two quite different significations. Symbolic logic studies forms of inferences, so that it is a kind of formal logic. But what makes it symbolic is not that feature but rather the fact that the inferences which it studies are expressed with the help of artificial symbols: just as symbolic arithmetic uses the symbols '2', and '+' rather than the words 'two' and 'plus', so symbolic logic uses the symbols '⊃' and '∀' rather than the words 'if' and 'every'. Symbols have their advantages—sometimes they have overwhelming advantages. But logic—formal logic—is not obliged to use them.

A more serious objection to the claim that all logic is formal rests on the counterclaim that there are non-formal inferences. The mediaeval logicians recognized such things, which they called 'material consequences'. They contrasted material with formal consequences—and that contrast is the immediate origin of our modern use of the term 'formal' in connection with logic. Consider, for example, the inference:

Socrates runs.
Therefore, Socrates moves.

That is surely a valid deductive inference—it is impossible that its premiss should be true and its conclusion not true, its conclusion follows necessarily from its premiss. But—so it was urged—it is a material and not a formal consequence. Hence not all logic is formal logic.

A short answer to that objection asserts roundly that material consequences are, despite their mediaeval name, formally valid. The argument

Socrates runs.
Therefore, Socrates moves.

has several forms in common with the rather similar argument

Plato runs.
Therefore, Plato moves.

One of the common forms might be described by saying that, from a premiss which says of some item that it runs, there is an inference to the conclusion that that same item moves; or you might say that the form is this:

x runs.
Therefore, x moves.

That is a form of argument, or a mode; the form or mode is valid; and the two material consequences are valid inasmuch as they are instances of that form or mode.

That blunt reply is impeccable. But it does not end the discussion. The two material consequences, it will be allowed, are indeed valid in virtue of a certain shared form, and for that reason they may, if you like, be called formally valid. But there are forms and forms: the form in virtue of which the material consequences are valid is not a logical form; and anyone who denies that all logic is formal logic means to deny that all valid inferences are valid in virtue of a logical form. No doubt—trivially—all valid inferences are valid in virtue of some form or other; but some inferences are valid in virtue of a logical form, others in virtue of a non-logical form. Any inference of the form

x runs.
Therefore x moves.

is valid. But that form is not a logical form. Therefore logic is not exclusively formal.

That conclusion is intelligible insofar as the distinction between logical and non-logical form is intelligible—and it may be said at once that that distinction is anything but self-evident. Nevertheless, grant that there is a distinction between logical and non-logical forms, and grant that there are valid arguments which are valid in virtue of non-logical forms. Even so, it does not follow that logic is not exclusively formal. For perhaps logic does not—or even cannot—deal with non-formal inferences. That, in point of fact, was the view taken, implicitly, by ancient logicians. Material consequences are not, and cannot be, objects of scientific study.

They cannot be objects of scientific study because they are, as the Stoics put it, 'non-methodically concludent'; for whatever exactly that expression may mean, it is clear that, according to the Stoics, non-methodically concludent arguments are not possible objects of methodical study—and hence not possible objects of a science. The Peripatetics, we know, disagreed with the Stoics: according to them, the arguments which the Stoics labelled unmethodical were, or at any rate could be remodelled as, predicative syllogisms. Galen disagreed with the Peripatetic remodelling. He also disagreed with the Stoics. He held that the allegedly unmethodical arguments, or at any rate some of them, are in fact syllogisms of his third species. There are sharp differences of opinion there; but they are grounded on an underlying consensus: the Stoics, the Peripatetics, and Galen may have disagreed on the question of whether this or that particular argument was or was not formally valid; but they all agreed that logic studies formally valid arguments.

What I have just said is true. But it is also—as Aristotle would have put it—unclear, or unilluminating. It is unilluminating for two reasons. First, the notion of form which I have been bandying about needs some explanation—and so, *a fortiori*, does the notion of logical form. Secondly, although the ancients agreed that logic is formal logic, they did not formulate their agreement in those terms—indeed, they did not formulate it in any terms—and the expression 'formal logic' has no synonym in any ancient text.

SHAPES OF ARGUMENT

According to Diogenes Laertius, a Stoic mode is 'as it were a shape of an argument' (VII 76). In the same vein, Sextus refers to 'the modes and as it were shapes in which arguments are propounded' (*M* VIII 227),[9] and Galen

[9] τρόποι δὲ αὐτῶν καὶ ὡσπερεὶ σχήματα ἐν οἷς ἠρώτηνται ...

observes that 'the logicians name the shapes of arguments modes' (*inst log* vi 6).[10] The word 'shape' or '*σχῆμα*' is in fact sometimes used in more or less that sense in our texts. Sextus, for example, will say that an argument 'is valid inasmuch as it is propounded in a sound shape' (*M* VIII 413);[11] and he reports a theory which distinguished four ways in which an argument might go wrong, one of which is

on account of being propounded in an unsound shape, when the shape of the argument is not concludent.

(*PH* II 147)[12]

In that last text, it is difficult not to translate '*σχῆμα*' by 'form'.

And after all, the word '*σχῆμα*' or 'shape' was often used as a synonym, or near synonym, for '*μορφή*'; '*μορφή*' was often used as a synonym or near synonym for '*εἶδος*'; and '*εἶδος*' is the Greek for 'form'. But in the texts to which I have alluded and which are of Stoic origin or Stoic inspiration, the word 'shape', although it may in fact be co-extensive, or nearly co-extensive, with 'form', is never contrasted with 'matter'. If shapes are forms, the formal is not set against the material.

In any event, it is no surprise to find that the distinction between formal and material consequence, insofar as it has any ancient ancestors, belongs to the Aristotelian and not to the Stoic clan. After all, what is it but yet another application of that Jack-of-all-trades distinction, the distinction between form and matter, *εἶδος* and *ὕλη*? As Porphyry put it,

objects are constituted of matter and form or else have their constitution analogous to matter and form.

(*Isag* 11.12–13)[13]

Pretty well anything is an object, so that matter and form are virtually ubiquitous. Certainly, arguments are objects. So arguments consist of matter and form, or at least of something analogous to matter and something analogous to form. But what is their matter, or quasi-matter, and what their form, or quasi-form?

In the *Analytics* Aristotle does not speak of matter and form in connection with syllogisms. But he does frequently talk of the shape of a syllogism, and

[10] ὀνομάζουσι δὲ τρόπον οἱ διαλεκτικοὶ τὰ τῶν λόγων σχήματα.
[11] συνάγει μὲν διὰ τὸ ἐν ὑγιεῖ ἠρωτῆσθαι σχήματι.
[12] παρὰ δὲ τὸ ἐν μοχθηρῷ ἠρωτῆσθαι σχήματι, ὅταν μὴ ᾖ τὸ σχῆμα τοῦ λόγου συνακτικόν.
[13] τῶν γὰρ πραγμάτων ἐξ ὕλης καὶ εἴδους συνεστώτων ἢ ἀνάλογόν γε ὕλῃ καὶ εἴδει τὴν σύστασιν ἐχόντων ...

his commentators found matter and form behind his use of the word 'shape'. According to Alexander of Aphrodisias, Aristotle tells us in the *Prior Analytics*

> what a syllogism is, and what it is composed from, and how many syllogistic shapes there are, and what are the differences among them—for the shapes are like a sort of common mould: by fitting matter into them, you can mould the same form in different matters; for just as, in the case of identical moulds, the difference is made not by the form and shape of what is fitted into them but by its matter, so too is it with the syllogistic shapes.
>
> (*in APr* 6.15–21)[14]

Syllogisms have form and matter; and their forms are here identified with, or at least determined by, their shapes. Now the word '*σχῆμα*', which I have thus far translated as 'shape', is standardly rendered by 'figure' when it appears in the context of Aristotelian syllogistic. So according to Alexander, the form of a syllogism is what we customarily call its figure.

The figure of a syllogism, or its shape or form, is like a mould. A mould fixes the form of the jelly you pour into it, and when one moulded jelly differs from another, that is in virtue of its matter. So too, the figure of a syllogism determines its form, and when one figured syllogism differs from another, that is in virtue of its matter.

The Aristotelian notion of figure is perfectly well determined. The figure of a syllogism is fixed by the 'conjugation' of propositions which constitute its premisses. A conjugation is a pair of predicative propositions which have exactly one term in common. Since the common term must, in each proposition, be either subject or predicate, there are three possible types of conjugation: either the common term is once predicate and once subject, or else it is twice predicate, or else it is twice subject. Those three types of conjugation determine the three syllogistic shapes or figures: a syllogism belongs to the first figure if and only if the common term in its conjugation is once predicate and once subject; and so on.

No doubt the word '*σχῆμα*'—whether we give it as 'shape' or as 'figure'—has had its sense somewhat stretched; but the stretching was done by Aristotle and not by his commentators, and it is inoffensive inasmuch as

---

[14] ... τί ἐστι συλλογισμός, καὶ ἐκ τίνων σύγκειται, καὶ πόσα σχήματά ἐστι συλλογιστικά, καὶ τίνες αὐτῶν διαφοραί· τύπῳ γάρ τινι κοινῷ τὰ σχήματα ἔοικεν, ἐν οἷς ἔστιν ἐναρμόσαντα ὕλην εἶδός τι ἀναμάξασθαι ταὐτὸν ἐπὶ ταῖς διαφόροις ὕλαις· ὡς γὰρ ἐπὶ τῶν τύπων τῶν αὐτῶν ἡ διαφορὰ οὐ κατὰ τὸ εἶδος γίνεται καὶ τὸ σχῆμα τοῖς ἐναρμοζομένοις ἀλλὰ κατὰ τὴν ὕλην, οὕτω δὴ καὶ ἐπὶ τῶν σχημάτων τῶν συλλογιστικῶν.

the stretched sense is defined. It is easy to see how Alexander glossed 'figure' by 'form'—for the two words, as I have said, are near synonyms; and it is easy to understand how he then helped himself to the term 'matter'—for where, in Peripatetic philosophy, form intrudes, can matter be far behind? True, the words 'matter' and 'form' have now lost all contact with their origins: the matter of something is no longer its constituent stuff, the form no longer the outward shape or figure. But even in Aristotle's own writings, the couple of matter and form is often found wandering far from home; and so long as the two terms are given some clear sense in their new surroundings, no serious harm is done. (Nonetheless, some unserious harm is done; for fastidious readers will be repelled and rapid readers may be misled. And in the credit column there is a large zero.)

However that may be, matter and form occasionally turn up in that way in the later logical tradition. Here, for example, is Ammonius:

We say that in every syllogism there is something analogous to matter and something analogous to form—it is the objects themselves by way of which the syllogism is composed which are analogous to matter, and the shapes which are analogous to form—for some are in a first shape, others in a second, others in a third.

(*in APr* 4.8–12)[15]

Ammonius is in one respect slightly more cautious than Alexander: he speaks not of matter and form but of something analogous to matter and something analogous to form. After Porphyry, he supposes that only material objects have matter and form in the strict sense of the words: non-material objects—such as syllogisms—have quasi-matter and quasi-form. But he is fundamentally at one with Alexander: it is the shape of a syllogism—that is to say, the figure to which it belongs—which is, or determines, its form or quasi-form.

That, as I have said, is a clear notion, and it is a notion rooted in Aristotle's own terminology. But it is not the notion which grounds the distinction between formal and material consequence and which underlies the idea of formal logic. Formal consequences are formally valid, or valid in virtue of their form; but no syllogism is valid in virtue of its figure. An argument is valid in virtue of a given feature only if every argument which shares that feature is valid. Hence a syllogism would be valid in virtue of its figure only if every syllogism which shares that figure is valid. But that

---

[15] λέγομεν ὅτι ἐν παντὶ συλλογισμῷ τὸ μέν τί ἐστιν ἀνάλογον ὕλῃ τὸ δὲ εἴδει. ὕλῃ μὲν οὖν ἀναλογεῖ τὰ πράγματα αὐτὰ δι᾽ ὧν ὁ συλλογισμὸς πλέκεται, εἴδει δὲ τὰ σχήματα· οἱ μὲν γὰρ ἐν πρώτῳ σχήματί εἰσιν, οἱ δὲ ἐν δευτέρῳ, οἱ δὲ ἐν τρίτῳ.

is not so: every figure contains conjugations which yield no conclusion at all, and every conjugation which yields a conclusion fails to yield at least two other conclusions. The point is in any case evident; for the figure of a syllogism is determined exclusively by the relation among its premises, whereas the validity of a syllogism is a relation between premises and conclusion.

SYLLOGISTIC FORM AND SYLLOGISTIC MATTER

So the shapes or figures of the *Analytics* do not serve the distinction between formal and material consequence; and nothing else in the *Analytics* hints at it. Outside the *Analytics* Aristotle has little to say about syllogisms. But a couple of passages in the *Physics* are traditionally called upon in this context. One of them occurs in a chapter where Aristotle is discussing the place of necessity in nature:

Necessity is found in a similar sort of way both in mathematics and in what comes about by nature: since the straight is such-and-such, necessarily the triangle has angles equal to two right angles; but not since the latter, the former—rather, if not the latter, then the straight is not such-and-such. In what comes about for the sake of something, it is the other way about: if the goal will be, or is, then the earlier item will be, or is; if not, then—just as in mathematics if the conclusion is not the case then the first principle will not be the case—so here with the goal and that for the sake of which.

(*Phys* 200a15–22)[16]

At first glance, the passage seems wholly irrelevant to the question at issue: after all, it does not mention syllogisms, and it does not mention matter and form.

Against that, it is to be remarked, first, that although Aristotle specifies mathematical arguments, what he says of mathematical arguments plainly applies to syllogisms in general; and secondly, that the text explicitly invokes one of the four Aristotelian causes—the goal or final cause—and so tacitly invokes the others. And so—with a nod to Simplicius' commentary (which

---

[16] ἔστι δὲ τὸ ἀναγκαῖον ἔν τε τοῖς μαθήμασι καὶ ἐν τοῖς κατὰ φύσιν γιγνομένοις τρόπον τινὰ παραπλησίως· ἐπεὶ γὰρ τὸ εὐθὺ τοδί ἐστιν, ἀνάγκη τὸ τρίγωνον δύο ὀρθαῖς ἴσας ἔχειν· ἀλλ' οὐκ ἐπεὶ τοῦτο, ἐκεῖνο· ἀλλ' εἴ γε τοῦτο μὴ ἔστιν, οὐδὲ τὸ εὐθὺ ἔστιν. ἐν δὲ τοῖς γιγνο-μένοις ἕνεκά του ἀνάπαλιν, εἰ τὸ τέλος ἔσται ἢ ἔστι, καὶ τὸ ἔμπροσθεν ἔσται ἢ ἔστιν· εἰ δὲ μή, ὥσπερ ἐκεῖ μὴ ὄντος τοῦ συμπεράσματος ἡ ἀρχὴ οὐκ ἔσται, καὶ ἐνταῦθα τὸ τέλος καὶ τὸ οὗ ἕνεκα.

it would be fastidious to cite)—it has been imagined that according to Aristotle the goal or final cause of a syllogism is to be found not in its premisses but in its conclusion. Thence, inasmuch as the final cause is frequently identical with the formal cause, we may infer that the conclusion is the form of the syllogism—and therefore that the premisses constitute the matter.

It would be merely fantastical to draw such conclusions from the paragraph of the *Physics* which I have quoted were they not in part supported by the second of the two pertinent pieces of that work, which is part of Aristotle's account of the four types of cause. He remarks that

the hypotheses are causes of the conclusion in the sense of that from which.

(*Phys* 195a18–20)[17]

By 'hypothesis' here Aristotle presumably means 'premiss'; and 'that from which' presumably designates the material cause. So Aristotle here applies the notion of matter to the analysis or description of arguments. He does not explicitly mention form; but the term 'matter' is relational, and its correlative is 'form'. So there must be a form for which the premisses of an argument are matter: what is it? And of what item are the matter and the form matter and form?

The text seems to say that the premisses of an argument are the material cause of its conclusion. But, as Alexander saw, that notion hardly makes sense:

The premisses do not inhere in the conclusion—rather, they are productive of the conclusion: they inhere in the syllogism as a whole and have the rôle of matter in it, while the conclusion has the rôle of form.

(Simplicius, *in Phys* 320.7–9)[18]

(Simplicius is quoting from Alexander's lost commentary on the *Physics*.) The premisses not the matter of the conclusion, for the conclusion is not composed of the premisses; rather, they are the matter of the syllogism, the conclusion of which is its form. That is Alexander's view: it is unclear whether he offered it as a correction or as a charitable interpretation of Aristotle's text.

---

[17] ... καὶ αἱ ὑποθέσεις τοῦ συμπεράσματος ὡς τὸ ἐξ οὗ αἴτιά ἐστιν.

[18] αἱ δὲ προτάσεις οὐκ ἐνυπάρχουσι τῷ συμπεράσματι, ἀλλὰ τούτου μὲν ποιητικαὶ μᾶλλόν εἰσιν, ἐν δὲ τῷ παντὶ συλλογισμῷ ὑπάρχουσι καὶ ὕλης ἔχουσιν ἐν αὐτῷ λόγον, τὸ δὲ συμπεπερασμένον εἴδους.

Simplicius did not think that Alexander's view was a true interpretation of the text; but he spared no more than a single sentence to denounce Alexander and to defend Aristotle, thus:

Or perhaps the premisses are in a way in the conclusion and are one with it.

(*in Phys* 320.9–11)[19]

The suggestion is empty. As Alexander indicates, if X is matter of Y, then X inheres in Y—that is part of the Aristotelian definition of matter. Well then, Simplicius supposes, the premisses do 'in a way' inhere in the conclusion. But in what way? Simplicius does not care to tell us—and that is because there is nothing to tell.

Alexander's view is scarcely any better. You can say if you like that the premisses are the matter of the argument and the conclusion its form—and you can say the opposite, that the conclusion is matter and the premisses form. Such remarks face a dilemma: either they use the words 'form' and 'matter' in something like their original Aristotelian way, in which case what they say is trivially false; or else they use the words in some other way, in which case they are toying.

Was the view which Alexander criticized and Simplicius defended the view which Aristotle intended to advance? Perhaps it was; but the text in the *Physics* is both isolated and obscure—indeed, a glance at the immediate context shows that it is not even certain that Aristotle really means to designate the premisses as material causes. In any event, this little text scarcely helped to generate, and certainly does not help to elucidate, the later distinction between material consequence and formal consequence.

Another passage from Alexander—this time from his extant commentary on the *Topics*—is more encouraging:

Aristotle and his followers ... lay it down that dialectic is a certain syllogistic method; and they think that syllogisms do not in the least differ one from another insofar as they are syllogisms—their differences are, some of them, according to the forms of the propositions, some according to the moods and the shapes, some according to the matter with which they are concerned. The first of these differences makes some syllogisms probative—or predicative, as we call them—and others hypothetical. The second makes some perfect and others imperfect, and some in a first shape, some in a second and some in a third ... And the third—the

---

[19] μήποτε δὲ καὶ ἐν τῷ συμπεράσματι τρόπον τινά εἰσιν αἱ προτάσεις καὶ ἕν ἐστιν.

difference according to matter—makes some demonstrative and some dialectical and some eristical.

(in Top 1.19–2.16)[20]

One of the ways in which one syllogism may differ from another is in its matter. You would expect Alexander to say that another way—or rather, that the other and complementary way—in which one syllogism may differ from another is in its form. He does not do so.

Instead, he mentions two other types of differentiation: first, difference in 'the forms of the propositions', and secondly, difference in 'the moods and the shapes'. In effect, then, the matter of a syllogism is contrasted with three other items—with the shape or figure of the syllogism, with its mood, and with the form of its constituent propositions. That is a different contrast from the one made in the commentary on the *Analytics*: there the figure or shape of a syllogism was identified with its form and so made up one half of the contrast; here the figure of a syllogism is not—and cannot be—identified with its form, and figure is one of four items and not one of two. Although Alexander does not mention the form of a syllogism in this passage, nonetheless—insofar as matter carries form with it—we may properly ask what he would have taken the form of a syllogism to be. The question has a ready answer: The three items with which matter is contrasted together compose the form of a syllogism.

In fact, the three items are not independent of one another. If you specify the mood of a syllogism—declaring, for example, that it is a syllogism in Darapti—you thereby determine its figure. If you specify the figure of a syllogism—declaring, for example, that it belongs to the third figure—you thereby determine it to be a 'probative' or predicative syllogism and hence you determine the pertinent general form of its constituent propositions. So the three differences which Alexander announces—and which seem in his text to be four rather than three—reduce to a couple: the mood of a syllogism contrasts with its matter. Hence we may ascribe to Alexander the view that the matter of a syllogism is constituted by its three concrete terms and that

---

[20] Ἀριστοτέλης δὲ καὶ οἱ ἀπ' αὐτοῦ ... τίθενται μὲν αὐτὴν μέθοδόν τινα εἶναι συλλογιστικήν, ἡγούμενοι δὲ τὸν συλλογισμόν, καθ' ὃ συλλογισμός ἐστι, μηδὲν ἄλλον ἄλλου διαφέρειν, εἶναι δὲ αὐτῶν τὴν διαφορὰν τὴν μὲν κατὰ τὰ εἴδη τῶν προτάσεων, τὴν δὲ κατὰ τοὺς τρόπους καὶ τὰ σχήματα, τὴν δὲ κατὰ τὴν ὕλην περὶ ἥν εἰσιν, ὧν ἡ μὲν πρώτη διαφορὰ ποιεῖ τῶν συλλογισμῶν τοὺς μὲν δεικτικούς, οὓς κατηγορικοὺς καλοῦμεν, τοὺς δὲ ὑποθετικούς, ἡ δὲ δευτέρα καθ' ἣν τοὺς μὲν τελείους τοὺς δὲ ἀτελεῖς, καὶ τοὺς μὲν ἐν πρώτῳ τοὺς δὲ ἐν δευτέρῳ τοὺς δέ ἐν τρίτῳ σχήματι, ... ἡ δὲ τρίτη ἡ κατὰ τὴν ὕλην τοὺς μὲν ποιεῖ ἀποδεικτικοὺς τοὺς δὲ διαλεκτικοὺς τοὺς δὲ ἐριστικούς.

the form of a syllogism is constituted by its mood. Take the syllogism which might be expressed by saying that since philosophers are both intelligent and industrious, some intelligent people must be hard workers. What is its form?—Darapti. What is its matter?—'philosopher', 'intelligent item', 'industrious item'.

Not infrequently elsewhere Alexander refers to the terms of a syllogism as its matter; and a passage in the Ammonian commentary on the *Prior Analytics* has been taken to show that Alexander's teacher Herminus had done so before him:

> Herminus said that the conclusion is not always necessary but only in the case of certain matter; for if we take animal, man and walking, a necessity is inferred, but if animal, man and moving a possibility.

> ([Ammonius], *in APr* 39.31–35)[21]

Herminus was discussing a crux in Aristotle's modal logic. According to Aristotle, the following form is valid:

> Necessarily A holds of every B
> B holds of every C
> Therefore necessarily A holds of every C

According to Herminus, the modal conclusion follows only in the case of certain matter—that is to say, only in the case of certain triads of terms. (Herminus' thesis is logically inept; but the ineptitude is of no concern here.) So Herminus spoke of the matter of a syllogism, which he identified with its triad of terms.

We might reasonably hesitate to infer from this late text that Herminus had actually used the word 'matter' to characterize the terms of a syllogism. But if the inference is doubtful, the conclusion is independently plausible. For when Alexander refers to the matter of a syllogism, he gives the impression that the conceit was a commonplace—and in that case it will surely have been known to Herminus.

The later commentators, both Greek and Latin, continue the habit. They will often use 'πρᾶγμα' or 'object' instead of 'ὕλη' or 'matter'. They will sometimes contrast the matter of a syllogism with the combination

---

[21] Ἑρμῖνος δ' ἔλεγεν ἀναγκαῖον γίνεσθαι τὸ συμπέρασμα οὐκ ἀεί, ἀλλ' ἐπί τινος ὕλης· εἰ μὲν γὰρ λάβωμεν ζῷον ἄνθρωπον περιπατοῦν, ἀναγκαῖον συνάγεται· εἰ δὲ ζῷον ἄνθρωπον κινούμενον, ἐνδεχόμενον.

of the premisses—with their πλοκή or συμπλοκή or *complexio*. They will sometimes contrast the 'nature' of the premisses with their 'force' or meaning; and Latin authors will speak of the *vis terminorum*. All these are so many different ways of indicating a single contrast: the contrast between the terms of a predicative syllogism and the rest of the thing.

That, no doubt, lies at the origin of the distinction between formal and material consequence—a consequence is material if it depends on the nature or force of its terms, it is formal otherwise. But three riders need to be attached to that unoriginal claim. First, the terms 'formal inference' and 'material inference' are not, so far as I have noticed, found in any ancient text. Indeed, although the contrast between the formal and the material aspect of a syllogism is a commonplace in late antiquity, the language of form and matter is invoked to express the contrast far less often than might have been expected.

Secondly, the distinction between the two aspects of a syllogism was made within the context of predicative syllogistic; and it is not evident how it might be more widely applied. Take the hypothetical syllogism:

If Socrates is a man, he is mortal.
Socrates is a man.
Therefore Socrates is mortal.

The terms, an Aristotelian will surely be inclined to say, are clear enough: they are 'man', 'mortal' and 'Socrates'; and inasmuch as those terms constitute the matter of the argument, the form is what is left. Any non-Aristotelian will surely be inclined to take a different view: in that hypothetical syllogism, he will suggest, it is the two propositions, 'Socrates is a man' and 'Socrates is mortal', which constitute the matter; and everything else is the form; for it is the constituent propositions of a hypothetical syllogism which correspond in the appropriate way to the constituent terms of a predicative syllogism. Doubtless that is right—I mean, if you want to talk of matter and form in connection with hypothetical syllogisms, then that is the best way to go about it. But in order to explain why it is the best way, you need some general notion of the formal and material aspects of an argument.

And, thirdly, there are no such notions in the ancient texts: there is no ancient theory about the difference, in general, between material and formal inferences. Take the argument:

Socrates is a man.
Therefore Socrates is mortal.

It has as one of its forms:

    x is a man
    Therefore, x is mortal

Every argument of that form is valid. Why not say that the argument
is formally valid? A standard answer to that question, as I have already
indicated, is that the form is not a logical form, and an argument is formally
valid if and only if it is valid in virtue of a logical form. So when is a form a
logical form? There is a standard answer to that question too: a form is logical
if and only if it can be specified exclusively in terms of logical constants—of
words like 'all' and 'none' and 'if' and 'or'. And how are logical constants
distinguished from non-logical expressions? That question—which has been
much debated by modern logicians—was not raised, let alone answered, by
the ancient logicians.

Perhaps they were wise. After all, consider the syllogisms which Galen
offers us in *On Seed*. What are the formal and what the material elements
in them? If the syllogisms are construed predicatively, then their matter will
be constituted by triads of terms and their form will be everything else.
If the syllogisms are construed hypothetically, then their matter will—on
the best account—be constituted by pairs of propositions and their form
will be everything else. So what, really, is the matter and what the form of
those syllogisms? That question is entirely parallel to the question: Are the
syllogisms really predicative or really hypothetical? To which the answer was:
They are really both.

If that is right, then the matter and form of an argument are determined
relative to a way of construing the argument—or rather, relative to a system
of logic within which the argument is construed. No doubt the form of
an argument is fixed by its logical constants; but what counts as a logical
constant is itself fixed by, and in that sense relative to, a logical system.

CIRCUMSCRIPTIONS

Stoic logicians sometimes spoke of the shape of an argument. Peripatetic
logicians sometimes distinguished between the matter and the form of
an argument. And in any event, even if their terminology was fluid and
their theorizing exiguous, the ancient logicians did in fact discuss forms of
argument—after all, what else could they have discussed? If they discussed

forms, then they needed some way to present forms—some way to indicate which items they were talking about. How, then, can a form of argument be specified?

In various ways. You might, for example, offer a paradigm: 'A syllogism in Barbara is an argument like this: …'. You might present a rule of inference—a permission or an instruction: 'From this, that and the other premiss, infer such-and-such a conclusion'. Antiquity took neither of those paths. Rather, ancient logicians followed two other fashions in specifying syllogistic forms. One of them I shall call circumscriptive, in honour of Alexander of Aphrodisias, and the other I shall call schematic, for want of a better word.

In the *Prior Analytics* Aristotle introduces the first two sorts of argument which his predicative syllogistic recognizes in the following way:

When three terms are so related to one another that the last is in the middle as in a whole and the middle either is or is not in the first as in a whole, it is necessary that there is a syllogism of the extremes … For if A of every B and B of every C, it is necessary that A is predicated of every C. … Similarly, if A of no B and B of every C, that A will hold of no C.

(*APr* 25b32–26a2)[22]

The first sentence compactly describes a couple of syllogistic forms: 'when three terms …'—the sentence gives circumscriptions of the forms which we know as Barbara and Celarent. The second and third sentences comment on the two forms, and do so schematically. They do not, strictly speaking, represent the two forms schematically; but schematic representations are, as it were, implicit in them. Barbara, say, may be presented thus:

A of every B
B of every C
Therefore A of every C

Both circumscriptive and schematic specifications were also used in expositions of hypothetical syllogistic. According to Galen,

---

[22] ὅταν οὖν ὅροι τρεῖς οὕτως ἔχωσι πρὸς ἀλλήλους ὥστε τὸν ἔσχατον ἐν ὅλῳ εἶναι τῷ μέσῳ καὶ τὸν μέσον ἐν ὅλῳ τῷ πρώτῳ ἢ εἶναι ἢ μὴ εἶναι, ἀνάγκη τῶν ἄκρων εἶναι συλλογισμὸν τέλειον. … εἰ γὰρ τὸ Α κατὰ παντὸς τοῦ Β καὶ τὸ Β κατὰ παντὸς τοῦ Γ, ἀνάγκη τὸ Α κατὰ παντὸς τοῦ Γ κατηγορεῖσθαι· … ὁμοίως δὲ καὶ εἰ τὸ μὲν Α κατὰ μηδενὸς τοῦ Β, τὸ δὲ Β κατὰ παντὸς τοῦ Γ, ὅτι τὸ Α οὐδενὶ τῷ Γ ὑπάρξει.

the logicians name the shapes of arguments modes—e.g. in the case of the argument which concludes from a conditional and its antecedent to its consequent (which Chrysippus calls a first unproved), the mode is this:

If the 1st, the 2nd; but the 1st: therefore the 2nd.

(inst log vi 6)[23]

Just as Aristotle presents Barbara and Celarent first by way of circumscriptions and then—in a virtual fashion—schematically, so Galen identifies the Chrysippean 'first unproved' by a circumscription and then sets out its shape or form, which he calls a mode. A formula which represents a mode is a schematic representation of the syllogistic form which is, or is associated with, the mode.

A circumscription is a description of an argument form. The word 'circumscription', or 'περιοχή', comes from Alexander, who writes thus:

You might grasp this from the circumscription of the species of the syllogism. The circumscription of this sort of syllogism is this: The syllogism which from a disjunction and one of the disjoined items infers the opposite of the other.

(in Top 11.22–25)[24]

Alexander uses the word 'περιοχή' in the same sense in his commentary on the *Prior Analytics* (see 274.20–25). But otherwise the word seems to be unknown to science. (To be sure, it turns up three times in [Themistius]—see *in APr* 81.7; but there [Themistius] is simply copying out parts of Alexander's commentary.) It has been conjectured that Alexander's employment of the word derives from its use to mean 'summary'—as in the *Summaries of Menander's Plays* by Sellius, a.k.a. Homer (Suda, s.v. Ὅμηρος). But in truth, that latter usage is hardly widespread; and the similarity between a summary and a circumscription is not overwhelming.

However that may be, circumscriptions specify logical forms by describing them. Roughly speaking, a circumscription will say something of the form: 'From this, that and the other premiss there is a syllogism to such-and-such a conclusion.' The ancient logicians show some uniformity in their circumscriptive descriptions, and some scholars think that the Stoics, at least,

---

[23] ... οἷον ἐπὶ μὲν τοῦ ἐκ συνημμένου καὶ τοῦ ἡγουμένου τὸ λῆγον περαίνοντος, ὃν ὁ Χρύσιππος ὀνομάζει πρῶτον ἀναπόδεικτον, ὁ τοιοῦτος τρόπος ἐστίν· εἰ τὸ πρῶτον, τὸ δεύτερον· τὸ δὲ πρῶτον· τὸ ἄρα δεύτερον.

[24] τοῦτο δὴ λάβοι τις ἂν ἐκ τῆς περιοχῆς τοῦ εἴδους τοῦ συλλογισμοῦ. ἔστι δὲ ἡ περιοχὴ αὕτη τοῦ τοιούτου συλλογισμοῦ· ὁ ἐκ διαιρετικοῦ καὶ ἑνὸς τῶν ἐν τῇ διαιρέσει τὸ ἀντικείμενον ἐπιφέρων τοῦ λοιποῦ.

developed a canonical set of such things. But no ancient text, so far as I know, has any discussion of the matter.

The syllogistic circumscriptions which we find in ancient logical texts are not always satisfactory. For example, Galen circumscribes Barbara in this way:

In the case of predicative syllogisms, in the first figure there are four unproveds—first, the one which from two universal affirmatives infers a universal affirmative conclusion ...

(*inst log* viii 3)[25]

The conclusion of a syllogism in Barbara, according to Galen, will be universal and affirmative. But which universal affirmative proposition will it be? We know, from Galen's general account of the syllogistic figures, that it will predicate one of the extreme terms of the other; but Galen does not specify which of the two extremes will be predicated in the conclusion, and his circumscription is thus indeterminate between two forms, one of them Barbara and the other invalid.

Aristotle, it must be added, does not always do better than Galen. Indeed, in the passage which I cited a moment ago he does worse; for, having described the conjugations for Barbara and Celarent he simply says that 'it is necessary for there to be a syllogism of the extremes'—and that in principle leaves us with a choice among eight possibilities for each conjugation.

Those criticisms are no doubt piffling. If Aristotle's circumscription is inadequate, it does not appear alone—it is complemented by the schematic comment on the first two predicative forms, and that comment is perfectly precise and determinate. As for Galen, he was writing a textbook which you might read through with the aid of a teacher or else use as a sort of *aide-mémoire*. In any event, whether or not syllogistic circumscriptions were always in fact done well, they can in principle be done well. Barbara, for example, might be circumscribed thus:

From a first figure conjugation of a pair of universal and affirmative unmodalised propositions, there is a valid inference to a universal and affirmative unmodalised proposition in which the extreme term which in the conjugation is predicated of the middle term is predicated of the other extreme term.

That is a mouthful; but it is digestible.

---

[25] ἐπὶ δὲ τῶν κατηγορικῶν ἐν μὲν τῷ πρώτῳ σχήματι τέσσαρες εἰσιν ἀναπόδεικτοι, ὅ τε ἐκ δυοῖν καθόλου καταφατικῶν καθόλου καταφατικὸν ἐπιφέρων συμπέρασμα ...

In the case of hypothetical syllogisms, circumscription again presents no theoretical difficulty—although again, ancient circumscriptions are not always strictly adequate. Sometimes, indeed, it is not clear what are the criteria of adequacy. According to Galen,

in the case of complete conflict, there will be two syllogisms, if we assume in addition either that one of the items holds or that it does not hold and infer that the other does not hold (when the first holds) and holds (when the first does not).

(*inst log* v 3)[26]

A group of items—of assertibles or propositions—is in complete conflict if and only if exactly one of them must be true. Complete conflicts are appropriately expressed by disjunctive sentences, where the disjunction is to be understood in a strongly exclusive sense. So the two syllogisms—that is to say, the two syllogistic forms—which Galen here mentions might be circumscribed thus:

(1) From an exclusive disjunction and one of its disjuncts, there is a valid inference to the negation of its other disjunct.
(2) From an exclusive disjunction and the negation of one of its disjuncts, there is a valid inference to its other disjunct.

Those two forms, according to Galen, exhaust the inferential powers of disjunctions. Of course, there are many more—infinitely many more—valid arguments one of the premisses of which is a disjunction. Take, say:

Either he's alive or he's dead. He's alive if and only if he's breathing. So either he's breathing or he's dead.

But when Galen discusses hypothetical syllogisms, he has his mind on what were sometimes called mixed hypotheticals or syllogisms which have one complex and one simple premiss. And on that assumption, his disjunctive circumscriptions may well appear to be exhaustive.

Or rather, they may appear to be exhaustive on the assumption that the pertinent disjunctions have exactly two disjuncts. But ancient disjunctions—unlike the disjunctions of standard modern logic—were not necessarily two-placed items; and an ancient logician should want to circumscribe disjunctive syllogisms the disjunctive premiss of which may have any

---

[26] κατὰ μὲν οὖν τὴν τελείαν μάχην δύο συστήσονται συλλογισμοὶ προσλαμβανόντων ἡμῶν ἤτοι γε ὑπάρχειν ἢ μὴ ὑπάρχειν τὸ ἕτερον αὐτῶν, ἐπιφερόντων δὲ θάτερον οὐχ ὑπάρχειν μὲν ὅταν ὑπάρχῃ τὸ ἕτερον, ὑπάρχειν δὲ ὅταν οὐχ ὑπάρχῃ.

number of disjuncts. How might that be done? The obvious suggestion goes like this:

(1*) From an exclusive disjunction and one of its disjuncts, there is a valid inference to the conjunction of the negations of its other disjuncts (or to the negation of its other disjunct if there is only one other disjunct).

(2*) From an exclusive disjunction and the negation of one of its disjuncts, there is a valid inference to the exclusive disjunction of its other disjuncts (or to its other disjunct if there is only one other disjunct).

But whereas (1) and (2) perhaps exhaust the inferential possibilities for two-placed disjunctions, it is plain that (1*) and (2*) are not exhaustive for disjunctions in general. For example, from a three-membered disjunction and the negations of two of its disjuncts, there is a valid inference to the third disjunct:

Either 2^2 is greater than 2 or it is equal to 2 or it is less than 2. But 2^2 isn't equal to 2, nor is it less than 2. So it's greater than 2.

That inference is not covered by (2*)—nor, of course, by (1*).

So if exhaustivity is the aim, then (2*) must be modified. The modification might look something like this:

(2**) From an exclusive disjunction and the negations of at least one of its disjuncts (but not of all of them), there is a valid inference to the exclusive disjunction of its other disjuncts (or to its other disjunct if there is only one other disjunct).

Ought Galen to have offered (1*) and (2*) rather than (1) and (2)? Ought he to have offered (1*) and (2**) rather than (1*) and (2*)? The answer to the first of those two questions is, I am sure, Yes. The answer to the second is less evident inasmuch as the syllogisms which (2**) circumscribes may be analysed as or reduced to sets of syllogisms each of which is circumscribed by (2*).

There is another point. The circumscription which I quoted from Alexander's commentary on the *Topics* was this:

The syllogism which from a disjunction and one of the disjoined items infers the opposite of the other.

(*in Top* 11.24–25)

That answers to one of Galen's two syllogisms 'in the case of complete conflict'. Like Galen, Alexander is thinking of two-placed disjunctions, so that his circumscription matches (1). But the match is not perfect: where

Galen speaks of negations, Alexander speak of opposites. There is not merely a difference there: the two circumscriptions are not equivalent to one another. For if x is an opposite of y, then y is an opposite of x; but if x is a negation of y, then y is not a negation of x. 'So-and-so' is an opposite, but it is not a negation, of 'It is not the case that so-and-so'. Then which circumscription is right? Which is the better? What are the criteria of judgement here?

Whatever the answers to such questions, it seems plain that the circumscriptive way of specifying a syllogistic form is always available: any type of argument—or so I suppose—can in principle be clearly and distinctly circumscribed. Later ancient logicians generally preferred the circumscriptive mode. In Galen's *Introduction*, for example, and in Apuleius' *de Interpretatione*, predicative syllogisms are presented by way of circumscriptions; and although Apuleius comments on the Peripatetic and the Stoic uses of schematic formulas, and although Galen suddenly makes use of schemata when he sketches ecthetic proofs of validity, no schemata appear in their official presentations of predicative syllogistic.

But circumscriptions have certain practical drawbacks. First, it is easy to misformulate them—both Galen and Apuleius, as well as Aristotle himself, illustrate the point. Secondly, even in simple cases circumscriptions can be heavy; and the more complicated the case, the harder the circumscription is to digest. Thirdly, ancient logicians were concerned not only to set out valid syllogistic forms but also to explain or justify their validity: typically, they tried to prove the validity of one syllogistic form on the basis of another. Such proofs can be expounded in the circumscriptive mode; but the expositions are obliged to choose between imprecision and a laborious cumbersomeness.

In short, circumscription leads to circumlocution.

SCHEMATIC REPRESENTATIONS

One of the more intricate pieces of exposition in the *Prior Analytics* is the so-called *pons asinorum*. In his commentary, Alexander first sets out Aristotle's theory without using any schematic formulas. He then remarks that

Aristotle proves what we have just said by using letters—for the sake of clarity.

(*in APr* 304.32)[27]

---

[27] ἐπὶ στοιχείων ἃ προειρήκαμεν δείκνυσι σαφηνείας χάριν.

And Alexander himself sets out the theory again, this time using schematic formulas. The result, it will be agreed, is far clearer—that is to say, it is far more readily understood and assessed; and Alexander remarks that

just as a geometer will construct a diagram for the sake of clarity in his exposition,

so a logician will use letters (*in APr* 379.28–29)[28]

In a similar vein, when Sextus embarks on a discussion of a certain complex syllogism, he says that

this argument is composed from a second and a third unproved—as we can learn from an analysis, which will be more clear if we set out the exposition in the form of a mode, thus:
If the 1st and the 2nd, the 3rd; but not the 3rd; but the 1st: therefore not the 2nd.

(*M* viii 235)[29]

An analysis—roughly speaking, a proof of validity—will be more clear, or more readily followed, if it is done on modes than if it is done on arguments. In other words, the substitution of symbols for concrete terms lends clarity to the enterprise. Here Sextus alludes to the advantages of symbols over concrete terms, not over circumscriptions. But the underlying point is very similar. (And it makes not a whit of difference whether you use letters or numerals.)

Schematic representations make for clarity; and they are in at least certain respects comparable to the geometers' use of diagrams in their proofs of universal theorems. (I shall return to the comparison.) In some ways, schemata are undeniably preferable to circumscriptions. But do they—can they—do the same job as circumscriptions?

Galen, as we have seen, puts circumscriptions and schemata together in one of his accounts of certain hypothetical syllogisms. So consider his account of the second of the five Stoic unproveds:

In the case which, from a conditional and the opposite of its consequent, infers the opposite of its antecedent, ... the mode is this:
If the 1st, the 2nd; but not the 2nd: therefore not the 1st.

(*inst log* vi 6)[30]

---

[28] ὡς γὰρ ὁ γεωμέτρης ὑπὲρ σαφηνείας τῆς κατὰ τὴν διδασκαλίαν καταγραφὴν ποιεῖταί τινα ...

[29] συνέστηκε γὰρ ὁ τοιοῦτος λόγος ἐκ δευτέρου τε ἀναποδείκτου καὶ τρίτου, καθώς πάρεστι μαθεῖν ἐκ τῆς ἀναλύσεως, ἥτις σαφεστέρα μᾶλλον γενήσεται ἐπὶ τοῦ τρόπου ποιησαμένων ἡμῶν τὴν διδασκαλίαν, ἔχοντος οὕτως· εἰ τὸ πρῶτον καὶ τὸ δεύτερον, τὸ τρίτον· οὐχὶ δὲ γε τὸ τρίτον· ἀλλὰ καὶ τὸ πρῶτον· οὐκ ἄρα τὸ δεύτερον.

[30] ἐπὶ δὲ τοῦ ἐκ συνημμένου καὶ τοῦ ἀντικειμένου τῷ εἰς ὃ λήγει τὸ τοῦ ἡγουμένου ἀντικείμενον ἐπιφέροντος, ... τοιοῦτός ἐστιν· εἰ τὸ πρῶτον, τὸ δεύτερον· οὐχὶ δὲ τὸ δεύτερον· οὐκ ἄρα τὸ πρῶτον.

Take this argument: 'If she's not in Italy, then she can't be in Milan. But she's certainly in Milan—so she's in Italy.' Is that a second unproved? Yes, according to the circumscription. For 'She's in Milan' is the opposite of the consequent of the conditional premiss, and 'She's in Italy' is the opposite of its antecedent. But is the argument a second unproved according to the mode?

The modern schema which corresponds to the Stoic mode is—or seems to be—this:

If P, then Q; but not Q: therefore not P.

The concrete argument which I have just rehearsed fits the following modern schema:

If not P, then not Q; but Q: therefore P.

There are—to all appearances—two different schemata there: each embraces some but not all of the arguments which meet Galen's circumscription. If Galen's Stoic mode corresponds to the first schema, then it does not match his circumscription: the mode captures only some of the arguments which the circumscription encloses.

Or again, this is Galen's presentation of the third Stoic unproved:

So too in the case of the third (according to Chrysippus), which from a negated conjunction and one of the items in it gives the opposite of the other item, the mode is this:

Not at the same time the 1st and the 2nd; but the 1st: therefore not the 2nd.

(*inst log* vi 6)[31]

The circumscription is clear, and so is the mode. But does the mode repeat the circumscription? Consider the following argument: 'Well, I'm sure she's not in England—after all, she's in Paris, and she can't both be in England and in Paris.' Is that an example of a third unproved?

According to the circumscription, it undoubtedly is. But according to the schematic version? A contemporary logician will declare that the argument is an instance of the schema

Not (both P and Q); but Q: therefore not P.

That is a distinct schema from

Not (both P and Q); but P: therefore not Q,

---

[31] ... ὥσπερ γε κἀπὶ τοῦ τρίτου κατὰ τοῦτον, ὃς ἐξ ἀποφατικοῦ συμπεπλεγμένου καὶ ἑνὸς τῶν ἐν αὐτῷ τὸ ἀντικείμενον τοῦ λοιποῦ παρέχει, τοιοῦτος ὁ τρόπος ἐστίν· οὐχ ἅμα τὸ πρῶτον καὶ τὸ δεύτερον· τὸ δὲ πρῶτον· οὐκ ἄρα τὸ δεύτερον.

which is the schema corresponding to Galen's mode. (Let it be added that if the third unproved is stated in such a way as to allow for conjunctions with any number of conjuncts, then things get far trickier.)

Has Galen bungled? Perhaps he has miscircumscribed these two unproveds, or else given the wrong modes? I do not think so; and I think that the circumscriptions trump the schemata, at least in Galen's text—that is to say, if we want circumscriptions and schemata to match, then we must modify the schemata. But how is that to be done? Indeed, is it to be done at all?

Take a third and more testing example. In Chapter xv of the *Introduction* Galen considers syllogisms based on what the ancient logicians called παραδιεζευγμένα or quasi-disjunctions: a quasi-disjunction is true if and only if at least one of its quasi-disjuncts is true; in other words, a quasi-disjunction is what a modern logician would call an inclusive disjunction. The discussion is lengthy, complicated, and textually corrupt. But the gist of the matter is plain. Galen describes the following form of hypothetical syllogism:

> From an inclusive disjunction and the opposites of one or more of the disjuncts (but not of all the disjuncts) there is a valid inference to the inclusive disjunction of the other disjuncts (or to the other disjunct if there is only one).

That is a clear and distinct circumscription, even if it is a little lumpy. What is the mode which corresponds to it?

Well, a modern logician will first come up with the familiar schema:

Either P or Q
Not P
Therefore Q

Any instance of that schema is an example of the syllogism which Galen describes; but there are indefinitely many examples of Galen's syllogism which are not instances of the schema. Alongside the familiar schema must be set, first, the equally familiar schema:

Either P or Q
Not Q
Therefore P

And then there will be six schemata for three-placed disjunctions, among them

> Either P or Q or R
> Not Q
> Either P or R

and

> Either P or Q or R
> Not P and not R
> Therefore Q

And so on. A whole family of schemata corresponds to the single circum-scription; and this particular family has an infinite number of members—or at least, it has an indeterminately vast number of members.

No ancient text raises such issues. But where the ancient logicians appeal to circumscriptions and to schemata side by side, they tacitly presuppose that, in principle at least, the two fashions of specifying syllogistic forms pair off. Can the two fashions be made to pair off? Perhaps we should look a little more narrowly at schemata; for it might be objected to the preceding argument that it construes the notion of schematization too priggishly and that it takes an unnecessarily puritanical view of the relation between a schema and a concrete argument.

The three hypothetical circumscriptions under scrutiny invoke opposition. Opposites here are contradictories; that is to say, the term 'opposite' is to be understood in the Stoic fashion. Now according to a text which I have already cited, the Stoics

> say: opposites are items the one of which exceeds the other by a negation. For example
>   It is day—It is not day.
> For the assertible 'It is not day' exceeds 'It is day' by a negation, namely 'not', and is for that reason opposite to it.
>
> (Sextus, M VIII 89)³²

That being so, we should—strictly speaking—talk of an opposite of X rather than of the opposite of X; for every proposition which is governed by a negation will have two opposites—both
    It's day
and also

---

³² φασὶ γὰρ ἀντικείμενά ἐστιν ὧν τὸ ἕτερον τοῦ ἑτέρου ἀποφάσει πλεονάζει, οἷον ἡμέρα ἔστιν—οὐχ ἡμέρα ἔστιν. τοῦ γὰρ ἡμέρα ἔστιν ἀξιώματος τὸ οὐχ ἡμέρα ἔστιν ἀποφάσει πλεονάζει τῇ οὐχί, καὶ διὰ τοῦτ' ἀντικείμενόν ἐστιν ἐκείνῳ.

It's not not day

are opposite to

It's not day.

Now where the three circumscriptions refer to opposites, the three modes or schemata use negation; and that is one of the reasons for the mismatch. So why not replace opposition by negation in the circumscriptions? (In fact, as we have seen, Galen uses negation in his circumscription of a couple of disjunctive syllogisms.) Well, that would be a retrograde move: it would reduce the ambit of the circumscription for no good theoretical reason. Better, then, emend the modes by substituting oppositions for negations.

For example, the mode for the second unproved will be not

If the 1st, the 2nd; but not the 2nd: therefore not the 1st

but rather

If the 1st, the 2nd; opp(the 2nd): therefore opp(the 1st)

—where 'opp(X)' means 'an opposite of X'. That schema, unlike its predecessor, seems to coincide with Galen's circumscription of the second unproved.

In order to deal with the schema for the third unproved, it is not enough to replace negation by opposition. But another dodge might be called upon: why not write the mode something like this:

Not both the 1st and the 2nd; but the nth: therefore not the mth

where either $n = 1$ and $m = 2$ or $n = 2$ and $m = 1$

That dodge is suggested by a modern device—the device of subscription. With the aid of subscription, you might think to represent the syllogistic form like this:

Not both P$_1$ and P$_2$; but P$_i$: therefore opp(P$_j$)

where either i = 1 and j = 2 or i = 2 and j = 1.

(That is to say, the second premiss of any argument of that form is either the first or the second of the negated conjuncts; and the conclusion is the opposite of the other conjunct.) Such devices have sometimes been used by expositors of the Stoic logic. True, they were not used by any ancient logicians, and the use of subscripts is a thoroughly modern convention. But then the modern schemata are offered as superior replacements for the old, not as explanatory interpretations of them.

Even so, it is not easy to get them to do all the work which is required of them. How, for example, shall we find a schema to correspond to a multi-placed negated conjunction? Or a schema for Galen's quasi-disjunctive syllogism? We might start with this:

Either P_1 or P_2 or ... or P_n,

where a generous soul will claim to understand the three dots and the subscripted 'n'. But what comes next? Something like:

Not Q_1 and not Q_2 and ... and not Q_m
where $n > m > 1$ and each Q_j is identical with some P_i.

And the conclusion? Try this:

R_1 or R_2 or ... or R_k
where $k = n - m$, each R_i is identical with some P_i and no R_i is identical with any Q_j.

Perhaps that—or some variant upon it—will do the trick.

But, first, such a schematic representation loses the advantage which was claimed for schemata over circumscriptions. For that particular schema is surely far less clear—far less immediately intelligible—than the corresponding circumscription.

And secondly, is the thing really a schema at all? I shall postpone that second question for a few pages.

PREDICATIVE SCHEMATA

If problems of mismatch between schemata and circumscriptions arise in the case of hypothetical syllogisms, do they also haunt predicative syllogistic? In general, no; but they have been thought to haunt one particular predicative mood.

The first syllogistic form in Aristotle's third figure, or Darapti, is described thus by Galen:

Of the syllogisms in the third figure, the first, from two universal affirmative premisses, has a particular affirmative conclusion, being reduced—by way of conversion of the premiss on its minor term—to the third syllogism in the first figure.

(*inst log* x 1)[33]

And here is the Aristotelian original:

---

[33] τῶν δ' ἐν τῷ τρίτῳ σχήματι συλλογισμῶν ὁ μὲν πρῶτος ἐκ δυοῖν προτάσεων καθόλου καταφατικῶν ἐν μέρει καταφατικὸν ἔχει συμπέρασμα, δι' ἀντιστροφῆς τῆς πρὸς τῷ ἐλάττονι τῶν ὅρων προτάσεως ἀναγόμενος εἰς τὸν ἐν τῷ πρώτῳ σχήματι τρίτον.

There is no perfect syllogism in this figure either; but there will be a potential syllogism both when the terms are universal and when they are not universal in relation to the middle term—when they are universal, when both P and R hold of every S, that P will hold of necessity of some R. For since the affirmative converts, S will hold of some R, so that since P holds of every S and S of some R, it is necessary that P hold of some R—for there is a syllogism in the first figure.

(*APr* 28a15–22)[34]

The question is this: does the schematic specification in Aristotle match the circumscriptive specification in Galen?

True, Aristotle does not, strictly speaking, offer a schema for Darapti. Nonetheless, what he does offer is tantamount to the schema:

P holds of every S.
R holds of every S.
Therefore P holds of some R.

Any syllogism which fits that schema will also fit Galen's circumscription of Darapti. But is the converse also the case? Consider the following schema:

P holds of every S.
R holds of every S.
Therefore R holds of some P.

Any argument which fits that schema plainly fits Galen's circumscription of Darapti. But is it not a different schema from Aristotle's? And do not two separate schemata then correspond to one circumscription? If so, then in predicative syllogistic as in hypothetical syllogistic there is a mismatch between circumscriptions and schemata, even if the predicative mismatch is far less impressive.

The second of the two predicative schemata is the schema for the mood known as Daraptis. Daraptis is not mentioned in the chapter of the *Prior Analytics* in which Aristotle deals with the third figure; but it is implicitly acknowledged in a later paragraph:

---

[34] τέλειος μὲν οὖν οὐ γίνεται συλλογισμὸς οὐδ᾽ ἐν τούτῳ τῷ σχήματι, δυνατὸς δ᾽ ἔσται καὶ καθόλου καὶ μὴ καθόλου τῶν ὅρων ὄντων πρὸς τὸ μέσον. καθόλου μὲν οὖν ὄντων, ὅταν καὶ τὸ Π καὶ τὸ Ρ παντὶ τῷ Σ ὑπάρχῃ, ὅτι τινὶ τῷ Ρ τὸ Π ὑπάρξει ἐξ ἀνάγκης· ἐπεὶ γὰρ ἀντιστρέφει τὸ κατηγορικόν, ὑπάρξει τὸ Σ τινὶ τῷ Ρ· ὥστ᾽ ἐπεὶ τῷ μὲν Σ παντὶ τὸ Π, τῷ δὲ Ρ τινὶ τὸ Σ, ἀνάγκη τὸ Π τινὶ τῷ Ρ ὑπάρχειν· γίνεται γὰρ συλλογισμὸς διὰ τοῦ πρώτου σχήματος.

Since some syllogisms are universal and some are particular, all the universal syllogisms always syllogize a plurality of items, while of the particulars, the affirmative syllogize a plurality but the negative their conclusion only. For the other propositions convert, but the negative does not convert; and the conclusion predicates something of something. So the other syllogisms syllogize a plurality of items—e.g. if A has been shown to hold of every B or of some B, then it is also necessary that B hold of some A, and if of no B, then that B hold of no A—and that is different from the previous conclusion.

(APr 53a3–12)[35]

Aristotle did not enumerate the new syllogisms which can thereby be added to his system. But if we start from the fourteen forms which are recognized in chapters 4–6, then it seems that there should be a further nine. For the conclusions of Barbara, Celarent, Darii, Cesare, Camestres, Darapti, Disamis and Datisi all convert; and in addition, the conclusion of the new syllogism produced from Barbara has itself a convertible conclusion.

The principle by which Aristotle generates the new syllogisms is a true principle. In general, if

A, B, ... , W: therefore X

is a valid argument, and if

X: therefore Y

is valid, then

A, B, ... , W: therefore Y

is valid. And the principle does indeed add some new moods to Aristotle's system, moods which chapters 4–6 overlooked. For in those chapters, once Aristotle had indicated that a conjugation produced a conclusion, he never stopped to ask whether it also produced a second.

When it is applied to the three relevant moods of the first figure, the principle each time generates a new mood. Barbara is

A holds of every B
B holds of every C
Therefore A holds of every C.

Its conclusion entails, by conversion:
C holds of some A.

---

[35] ἐπεὶ δ' οἱ μὲν καθόλου τῶν συλλογισμῶν εἰσὶν οἱ δὲ κατὰ μέρος, οἱ μὲν καθόλου πάντες αἰεὶ πλείω συλλογίζονται, τῶν δ' ἐν μέρει οἱ μὲν κατηγορικοὶ πλείω, οἱ δ' ἀποφατικοὶ τὸ συμπέρασμα μόνον. αἱ μὲν γὰρ ἄλλαι προτάσεις ἀντιστρέφουσιν, ἡ δὲ στερητικὴ οὐκ ἀντιστρέφει. τὸ δὲ συμπέρασμα τὶ κατά τινός ἐστιν, ὥσθ' οἱ μὲν ἄλλοι συλλογισμοὶ πλείω συλλογίζονται, οἷον εἰ τὸ Α δέδεικται παντὶ τῷ Β ἢ τινί, καὶ τὸ Β τινὶ τῷ Α ἀναγκαῖον ὑπάρχειν, καὶ εἰ μηδενὶ τῷ Β τὸ Α, οὐδὲ τὸ Β οὐδενὶ τῷ Α· τοῦτο δ' ἕτερον τοῦ ἔμπροσθεν.

So Barbara validates Baralipton:

A holds of every B
B holds of every C
Therefore C holds of some A.

Baralipton is evidently an additional mood—if only because no existing first figure syllogism derives an I-predication from a couple of A-predications. It is easy to verify that the moods generated from Celarent and Darii (and also from Baralipton) are also new.

Things are different in the second figure. Cesare, for example, yields Cesares. Cesare is

A holds of no B
A holds of every C
Therefore B holds of no C.

Conversion of the conclusion yields Cesares, or:

A holds of no B
A holds of every C
Therefore C holds of no B

Now Cesares is not Cesare—but it is not a new mood either. For it is Camestres, the second mood of the second figure. As Galen puts it,

in the second and third figures ... one new syllogism is produced by conversion of the conclusion in the case of the first syllogism of the third figure—and in its case alone. For the first two syllogisms in the second figure convert into one another by their conclusions, and so do the third and fourth in the third figure.

(*inst log* xi 7)[36]

By conversion of the conclusion, Cesare generates Camestres, and *vice versa*; and Disamis generates Dabitis, and *vice versa*. But conversion of the conclusion does produce one new mood outside the first figure; for Darapti generates Daraptis, and Galen takes Daraptis to be a new mood.

The thesis that Daraptis is different from Darapti was disputed in antiquity. Here is Apuleius on the subject:

In the third figure, the first mood is the one which infers a particular affirmative from universal affirmatives, either directly or reflexively; for example:

---

[36] κατὰ δὲ τὸ δεύτερον σχῆμα καὶ τρίτον ... ἐκ ... τῆς τοῦ συμπεράσματος ἀντιστροφῆς ἐν τῷ τρίτῳ σχήματι κατὰ τὸν πρῶτον συλλογισμὸν γίγνεται μόνον· οἱ μὲν γὰρ ἐν τῷ δευτέρῳ σχήματι πρῶτοι δύο πρὸς ἀλλήλους ἀντιστρέφουσι τῷ συμπεράσματι, ἐν δὲ τῷ τρίτῳ δύο τρίτος τε καὶ τέταρτος.—Here 'πρῶτον' is Bocheński's correction of 'τρίτον'.

Everything just is honest
Everything just is good
Therefore something honest is good
—or
Therefore something good is honest

It makes no difference from which proposition you take the subject part since it makes no difference which you express first. Hence Theophrastus was wrong to think that, on this account, this is not one mood but two.

(int xi [207.16–24])³⁷

Apuleius thus urges that Daraptis and Darapti are one mood, not two; and he reports that Theophrastus—like Galen after him—had taken the opposite view.

Theophrastus seems to have had the majority on his side. For according to Boethius,

the third figure has six moods according to Aristotle; but some add a further mood—among them Porphyry, who was following his predecessors.

(in syll cat 813c)³⁸

The predecessors of Porphyry are Theophrastus and Eudemus, whom Boethius has just named; and the further mood is later identified as Daraptis (819ʙ—where Boethius confesses that he is not himself sure whether the third figure contains six or seven moods).

Why did Theophrastus and his followers take Daraptis to be distinct from Darapti? A passage in Alexander has been cited in evidence:

There are six syllogisms in this figure. The first of them in order is the one which, from two universal affirmatives, infers a particular affirmative conclusion by conversion of the minor proposition. It can also come about if the major proposition is converted, but in that case the conclusion too will have to be converted. That is why some added this syllogism as different from its predecessor, and say that there are seven syllogisms in this figure.

(in APr 95.25–30)³⁹

---

³⁷ *in tertia formula primus modus est qui conducit ex dedicativis universalibus dedicativum particulare tam directim quam reflexim, ut: omne iustum honestum, omne iustum bonum, quoddam igitur honestum bonum; vel sic: quoddam igitur bonum honestum. quippe non interest ex utra propositione facias particulam subiectivam quoniam non interest utram prius enunties. ideo non recte arbitratus est Theophrastus propter hoc non unum modum hunc sed duos esse.*

³⁸ *... tertia vero auctore Aristotele sex* [sc *modos habet*]; *addunt etiam alii unum, sicut ipse Porphyrius, superiores scilicet sequens.*

³⁹ ἐξ δὲ ὄντων συλλογισμῶν ἐν τούτῳ τῷ σχήματι πρῶτος μὲν ἂν αὐτῶν εἴη τῇ τάξει ὁ ἐκ δύο καθόλου καταφατικῶν ἐπὶ μέρους καταφατικὸν συνάγων κατὰ ἀντιστροφὴν τῆς

There are two proofs of Darapti—two proofs, that is, which work by way of conversion—and that fact led some people to think that there were two syllogisms.

Alexander does not mention Theophrastus by name; and it has been denied that he is thinking of Daraptis. After all, when he reports that 'some added this syllogism', the only syllogism in the offing to which he can readily be taken to refer is Darapti itself. So the anonymous men who added a seventh mood did not add Daraptis: they admitted Darapti twice over—or rather, they admitted two versions of Darapti, one corresponding to each of the two proofs.

Against that it may be said, first, that it would be strange if Alexander had said nothing about Daraptis while mentioning another—and otherwise quite unknown—way of augmenting the third figure; and secondly, that the argument which, on this interpretation, Alexander ascribes to his anonymous men is absurd: it is evident that the existence of several proofs of one item is not an indication that there are several items under proof; and anyone who denied that evidence could hardly fail to see that he would then have on his hands not only two versions of Darapti but two or more versions of every second and third figure syllogism.

So it is plausible to think that Daraptis—and Theophrastus—come into the Alexandrian picture. But how? Consider the two proofs of Darapti at which Alexander hints:

(A)

(1) P holds of every S	premiss	
(2) R holds of every S	premiss	
(3) S holds of some R	2, conversion	
(4) P holds of some R	1, 3, Darii	

(B)

(1*) P holds of every S	premiss	
(2*) R holds of every S	premiss	
(3*) S holds of some P	1*, conversion	
(4*) R holds of some P	2*, 3*, Darii	
(5*) P holds of some R	4*, conversion	

ἐλάττονος προτάσεως. δύναται δὲ καὶ τῆς μείζονος ἀντιστραφείσης γενέσθαι, ἀλλὰ δεήσει καὶ τὸ συμπέρασμα ἀντιστρέφειν· διὸ καὶ τοῦτόν τινες τὸν συλλογισμὸν προστιθέντες ὡς ἄλλον τοῦ πρὸ αὐτοῦ ἑπτά φασιν τοὺς ἐν τούτῳ τῷ σχήματι συλλογισμούς.

Each proof is a proof of Darapti—a proof based on Darii and a rule of conversion. But if proof (B) is curtailed at step (4*), then that is a proof of Daraptis. The fact that there are two proofs of Darapti persuaded Theophrastus and others to add a seventh mood to the third figure not because they thought that two proofs of Darapti made two moods out of Darapti, but because the second of the two proofs of Darapti brought Daraptis to their attention.

But if that explains how Theophrastus hit upon Daraptis, it does not explain why he took Daraptis to be distinct from Darapti. No ancient text offers any explanation of that sort; but there is an argument in Theophrastus' favour which at first blush is fetching. Apuleius notes that from the pair of premisses

Everything just is honest
Everything just is good,

you may conclude either that
Something honest is good
or else that
Something good is honest.

There, then, are two syllogisms with identical premisses but distinct conclusions. So surely they must have different syllogistic forms? If 'A, B: therefore X' and 'A, B: therefore Y' are two different valid arguments, then surely they must be valid in virtue of different forms? Hence Daraptis and Darapti are different.

One reply to that argument which an Apuleian might well consider denies that the conclusions of the two arguments are different. No doubt the sentences

Something honest is good
and
Something good is honest
are different; but they are two different ways of saying the same thing.

Such an idea has a toe-hold in the ancient texts. I have already noted that according to the Greek grammarians, some connectors indicate an order and others do not. The connector 'and' or 'καί' (or 'et'), when it makes a conjunctive sentence, signals no order. That is to say, there is no semantic difference between 'P and Q' and 'Q and P'. If that is so, then how can there be a difference between

Something is A and B

and

Something is B and A?

And if, as modern logic generally supposes,

Something A is B

means the same as

Something is A and B,

then how can there be any difference between

Something A is B

and

Something B is A?

Darapti and Daraptis have the same conclusion—they simply express their conclusions in different ways.

That idea has seduced some logicians, Frege among them. But it is not evidently correct; for it is not evidently correct that

Something A is B

means the same as

Something is A and B.

And however that may be, the idea surely did not attract Aristotle. For, first, Aristotle takes pains to prove that I-predications convert or that from

A holds of some B

you may infer

B holds of some A;

and that is enough to show that he did not take the two sentences to say the same thing. Secondly, he observes explicitly that 'A holds of no B' is not the same as 'B holds of no A' (*APr* 53a11–12); and the context indicates that he thinks the same goes for 'A holds of some B' and 'B holds of some A'.

So the conclusion of Apuleius' Daraptis is different from the conclusion of his Darapti, at least in Aristotelian eyes. Must we not then infer that the two arguments have different forms? No; for the principle according to which if a couple of arguments share premisses and differ in their conclusions then they must be valid in virtue of different forms—that principle may be alluring but it is false. The following circumscription determines a single form of argument:

From a conjunction there is a valid inference to any one of its conjuncts.

It follows that for every *n*-placed conjunction, there will be *n* syllogisms which have the same form, the same premiss, and different conclusions. Or again, take the form specified by the following schema:

P: therefore either P or Q

(where the disjunction is inclusive). Indefinitely many arguments have that form, share a premiss, and have different conclusions. Hence the general reason which suggested a distinction between Darapti and Daraptis is a bad reason.

Is there any good reason on the opposite side, any good reason to identify Darapti and Daraptis? Apuleius states that 'it makes no difference from which proposition you take the subject part'; that is to say, it makes no difference whether the conclusion is 'P holds of some R' (where 'R' is taken from 'R holds of every S') or rather 'R holds of some P' (where 'P' is taken from 'P holds of every S'). That is so, Apuleius argues, because 'it makes no difference which you take first'; that is to say, there is no difference between

P holds of every S, R holds of every S

and

R holds of every S, P holds of every S.

Apuleius' premiss is true—but it is hard to see how it supports his conclusion.

In any event, there is a better argument on his side. We have, on the one hand, Darapti:

P holds of every S
R holds of every S
Therefore P holds of some R

and on the other hand Daraptis:

P holds of every S
R holds of every S
Therefore R holds of some P

It might seem that there is a difference—the conclusions of the two forms arrange their terms in different ways. But that difference is an illusion. Consider the form which I baptize Daraptix:

R holds of every S
P holds of every S
Therefore P holds of some R.

Daraptix is the same syllogism as Daraptis—its schema is merely a notational variant on the schema for Daraptis. It is also the same as Darapti; for—as Apuleius says—the order in which the premisses are inscribed or uttered is perfectly irrelevant to the argument. If Daraptix is the same as Daraptis and also the same as Darapti, then Daraptis and Darapti are one and the same.

A more general consideration is also available. What are the identity conditions for schemata? In what circumstances is schema S the same schema as schema S*? I shall restrict the question to predicative schemata—for otherwise various irrelevant obstacles would have to be surmounted; and I say that a predicative schema S characterizes the same syllogistic form as a predicative schema S* if and only if every argument which instances S instances S* and *vice versa*. Since any argument which instances the schema for Darapti will also instance the schema for Daraptis, and *vice versa*, Darapti and Daraptis are one and the same syllogistic form.

The case of Daraptis does not, after all, show that, in predicative syllogistic, schematic representations sometimes fail to pair off with circumscriptions.

SCHEMATA AND MATRIXES

So far I have spoken of schematic representations as though they and their uses needed no explanation. But that is not so.

Look again at an example which I used earlier: 'If she's not in Italy, then she can't be in Milan. But she's certainly in Milan—so she's in Italy.' In so arguing, have I thereby done a second Stoic unproved? According to the circumscription, Yes. According to the schematic representation—or so I urged—No. For although the argument fits the schema

If not P, not Q; Q: therefore P

it does not fit the different schema

If P, Q; not Q: therefore not P;

and it is that second schema which corresponds to the mode of the second unproved. I then suggested that we might modify the schema, replacing 'not' with 'opp' and so matching mode to circumscription.

But before accepting the modification, it is worth asking why the argument fits the one unmodified schema and not the other.

A schematic representation of a syllogism is a sequence of schematic representations of propositions or assertibles. What exactly is a schematic representation of a proposition or an assertible? One way of understanding such schemata—a way which is both simple and common—takes them to be sets of what I shall call matrixes. Take any sentence. Replace it or any of its syntactically coherent parts by a symbol or by symbols—by letters, say, or numerals—and what you get is a sentential matrix. So from the sentence

Aristotle is acute and Plato is profound

you might produce replace the name 'Aristotle' by the letter 'a' and thereby produce the matrix:

a is acute and Plato is profound.

Or you might replace each of the two verbal phrases by letters and produce this:

F(Aristotle) and G(Plato)

(Shouldn't that rather be something like

Aristotle(F) and Plato(G)?

Well, there are certain standard conventions which govern the order of symbols in standard matrixes.)

So a matrix—or rather, a sentential matrix—is a sequence of symbols and words, or a sequence of symbols, which can be derived from a sentence by an appropriate replacement of words by symbols; or, equivalently, a matrix is a sequence which can be turned into a sentence by an appropriate replacement of symbols by words.

Appropriateness is syntactical appropriateness. Of the symbols which occur in matrixes, the letters 'a' and 'b' are syntactically names; 'F' and 'G' are syntactically verbs (or rather, one-placed predicates); 'P', 'Q', 'R', ... are syntactically sentences. But although the symbols have a syntax, they have no sense. The symbol 'a' names nothing, the symbol 'F' can't be used to predicate anything, the symbol 'P' expresses no thought. The choice of symbols is, of course, entirely arbitrary: you might use signs like '♣', '♦', '♥', ... ; you might use numerals; you might use anything. But letters have certain practical advantages.

Although the symbols have no sense, they are not merely syntactical devices. For the repetition of the same symbol in a matrix, or in a connected sequence of matrixes, has a significance. Suppose you start from a sentence and produce a matrix: if the same expression occurs more than once in the sentence, then it may—but need not—be replaced each time by the same symbol; but different expressions must be replaced by different symbols. The sentence

Aristotle was acute and Aristotle was profound

will therefore produce, say,

Fa and Ga

and also

Fa and Gb;

but it will not produce

Fa and Fb

nor yet

Fa and Fa.

Conversely, suppose that you start from a matrix and generate a sentence: different symbols may—but need not—be replaced by different expressions;

any symbol which occurs more than once must be replaced by the same expression each time. From

If P, then Q

you may generate

If today's Thursday, then this is Paris,

and also

If this is Paris, then this is Paris.

The latter, but not the former, of those two ventures may also be generated from the matrix

If P, then P.

The sequence of formulas

If P, then Q; it is not the case that Q: therefore it is not the case that P

is a sequence of sentential matrixes, the letters of which have the syntax of sentences. Any appropriate replacement of the letters by sentences will produce a sequence of sentences which express an argument. So the sequence of matrixes is a schematic representation of a form of argument.

Return now to the Stoics. In the formula standardly used to express the mode of the Stoic first unproved, namely:

If the 1st, the 2nd; but the 1st: therefore the 2nd

the symbols are the numerals—more precisely, they are the items of the form 'the nth'. They are syntactically sentences; and each of the three elements in the formula is a sentential matrix. So the standard expression of the mode is a schematic representation of the first unproved.

On the other hand, the revised version of the formula for the mode of the second unproved, namely

If the 1st, the 2nd; opp(the 1st): therefore opp(the 2nd)

is not a sequence of sentential matrixes. For 'opp(the 2nd)' is not a sentential matrix: you cannot generate it by starting from a sentence; nor—equivalently—can you get a sentence by replacing 'the 1st' in 'opp(the 1st)' by a sentence. Hence although that formula does, of course, represent the second unproved, and although it uses symbols to do so, it is not—on the simple and common understanding of the matter—a schematic representation of the second unproved. For it is not a set of matrixes.

Take, next, a semi-revised formula for the mode of the third unproved—a formula which denies itself 'opp' but allows subscription, namely:

Not both P_1 and P_2; but P_i: therefore not P_j.

That is a set of matrixes; and it is, as such, a schematic representation of a form of argument. But it is not a schematic representation of the third unproved; for you cannot derive it from any concrete expression of a third unproved. Nor is it a schematic representation of any other valid form of argument.

As for the quasi-disjunctive syllogism, there is not and there could not be a sequence of matrixes which corresponds to its Galenic circumscription. Any quasi-disjunctive syllogism which the circumscription captures will fit some pertinent set of matrixes or other; but there is no pertinent set of matrixes which every quasi-disjunctive syllogism fits. The circumscription corresponds to a set of sets of matrixes—an infinite set of sets—and not to a single set. Insofar as the circumscription determines a particular syllogistic form, there is at least one form which cannot be represented schematically—I mean, which cannot be represented by a single schema.

Is that an argument against schemata? Not in itself; for it shows at most that you can do some things with circumscriptions which you cannot do with schemata; and perhaps those are things which a logician does not want, or does not need, to do. Nonetheless, you might reasonably suspect that the higher degree of generalization which circumscriptions offer is a mark in their favour, from a logical point of view. After all, the infinitely many quasi-disjunctive schemata are all special cases of a general form, and the general form can only be represented by a circumscription. Again, and connectedly, you might think that the circumscription of the quasi-disjunctive syllogism has an explanatory value which the innumerable schemata do not possess: a quasi-disjunctive syllogism is valid in virtue of the fact that it fits the circumscription, not in virtue of the fact that it fits this or that quasi-disjunctive schema.

However that may be, there is a further question about schemata which ought to be raised. I start out from a familiar complaint made both by Galen and by Alexander against the Stoic logicians: the Stoics, they say, pay too much attention to forms of expression or $\phi\omega\nu\alpha\acute{\iota}$ and too little to the items which they signify—to the $\pi\rho\acute{\alpha}\gamma\mu\alpha\tau\alpha$ or $\sigma\eta\mu\alpha\iota\nu\acute{o}\mu\epsilon\nu\alpha$; they identify and classify arguments by appeal to their most superficial features. Now the circumscriptional way of identifying inferential forms neither says nor implies anything about the manner in which such forms might be expressed. The circumscription of a disjunctive form, for example, may specify that one of the premisses be a disjunction; but it will leave open the question of how a disjunction may be expressed, or may best be expressed. On the other hand, schematic representations by their very nature indicate—schematically—some particular manner of expression or other.

The schematic representation of a disjunctive syllogism, say, will necessarily contain some such matrix as

Either P or Q,

and that matrix fixes a certain form of expression.

In that case, does not a schematic representation of an argument essentially determine a certain form of linguistic expression? And if that is so, then did not Galen and Alexander have philosophical or logical reasons for preferring circumscriptions to schemata? (For they wanted to determine the form of an argument without thereby fixing any particular means of expressing it.) Moreover, will there not be another—and a more straightforward—way in which schemata and circumscriptions fail to pair off?

The argument runs like this. The circumscription of the first unproved states that from a conditional and its antecedent you may infer its consequent. The mode of the first unproved is this:

If the 1st, the 2nd; the 1st: therefore the 2nd.

So consider the following argument:

He'll be in Oxford now provided that Eurostar wasn't late. So since Eurostar wasn't in fact late, he'll be there.

Is that a first unproved? According to the circumscription, the answer is Yes. For 'He'll be in Oxford ...' expresses a conditional proposition; 'Eurostar wasn't in fact late' expresses its antecedent; and 'He'll be there' expresses its consequent. But according to the schema, the answer seems to be No. For if you start from the expression of the argument and replace expressions by symbols, you will never arrive, however ingenious you are, at the matrix which represents the mode of the first unproved.

That is an unwelcome conclusion; for whatever difficulties may attend the last four of the five unproveds, surely the mode of the first unproved ought to correspond exactly to its circumscription? One way of securing an exact correspondence calls on the Stoic account of conditional assertibles. According to Sextus,

non-simple assertibles are those ... which are composed from a repeated assertible or from different assertibles, and in which a connector or connectors govern. Take for the moment what they call the conditional. That is composed from a repeated assertible or from different assertibles by way of the connector 'εἰ' or 'εἴπερ'.

(*M* viii 108–109)[40]

---

[40] καὶ δὴ οὐχ ἁπλᾶ μὲν ἐστιν ἀξιώματα τὰ ἀνώτερον προειρημένα, ἅπερ ἐξ ἀξιώματος διφορουμένου ἢ ἐξ ἀξιωμάτων διαφερόντων συνέστηκε καὶ ἐν οἷς σύνδεσμος ἢ σύνδεσμοι

If that account is right, and if it is taken *au pied de la lettre*, then the Eurostar argument does not contain a conditional assertible—for neither the connector 'εἰ' nor the connector 'εἴπερ' appears anywhere in it. So the Eurostar argument is not, after all, a first unproved according to the circumscription; and schema and circumscription correspond.

But that makes matters worse rather than better; for it limits conditional assertibles—and hence first unproveds—to items which contain one of a pair of Greek words. Well, no doubt the text in Sextus should not be taken *au pied de la lettre*, and its linguistic chauvinism was surely unintended: we may decently suppose that when the Stoics said 'the connector 'εἰ' or 'εἴπερ'' what they meant was 'the connector 'εἰ' or 'εἴπερ', or any translation of those words in other languages'.

Even so, why limit conditional assertibles to assertibles which contain those particular connectors? After all, there are numerous ways, in most natural languages, of expressing conditional notions—why privilege one of them? The limitation may have the effect of bringing the schemata and the circumscriptions into line; but it does so by pushing on the wrong item.

There is a further point. The passage from Sextus, if it is taken strictly, implies that complex assertibles are ontological hybrids: they consist of simple assertibles, which are incorporeal items, together with connectors, which are sounds and therefore corporeal items. That is curious; and in fact most philosophers do not care for such hybrids. But perhaps the Stoics did? According to some scholars, the Stoics construed simple assertibles, such as

Dio walks

as compounded from an incorporeal predicate, to walk, and a corporeal case, namely Dio himself. And if that is right, then why should they have jibbed at introducing another form of hybridization in the case of compound assertibles? But it must be said that no Stoic text ever explicitly recognizes—let alone discusses or defends—hybridization; and it may be deemed preferable to avoid it if it can be avoided.

In the case of compound assertibles it is readily avoided. For example, why not say that an assertible is a conditional if and only if in saying it you may say that if something is the case then something is the case? Or that an assertible is a conditional if and only if it may be said by uttering a sentence of the form

If P, then Q?

ἐπικρατοῦσιν. λαμβανέσθω δὲ ἐκ τούτων ἐπὶ τοῦ παρόντος τὸ καλούμενον συνημμένον. τοῦτο τοίνυν συνέστηκεν ἐξ ἀξιώματος διφορουμένου ἢ ἐξ ἀξιωμάτων διαφερόντων καὶ διὰ τοῦ εἰ ἢ εἴπερ συνδέσμου.

Those two explanations of conditionality make use of the connector 'if'; and to that extent they may be regarded as natural elaborations of the Stoic explanation which Sextus offers. On the one hand, the connector 'if' (or its Greek translation) is invoked in the explanation of conditional assertibles. On the other hand, conditionals are not language-bound, nor are assertibles inevitably hybrids.

The matrix 'If P, then Q' may now be taken to represent a conditional assertible inasmuch as an assertible is conditional if and only if it can be expressed by an instance of the matrix. So the sentence

He'll be in Oxford now provided that Eurostar wasn't late

expresses a conditional assertible; for the assertible which it expresses may be expressed by a sentence which is an instance of the matrix 'If P, then Q'—say by the sentence

If Eurostar wasn't late, then he'll be in Oxford now.

And the Eurostar argument is a first unproved not only according to the circumscription but also according to the schematic representation. For the argument fits the mode

If the 1st, the 2nd; the 1st: therefore the 2nd

inasmuch as an appropriate replacement of the symbols by sentences will produce a sequence of sentences which might be used to express the argument.

A schematic representation of a syllogism is expressed by means of a sequence of matrixes. An argument is represented by a schematic representation if and only if it could be expressed by means of a sequence of sentences which are instances of that sequence of matrixes. A schematic representation fixes the form of an argument by reference to a form of expression; but what counts is not how the argument is in fact expressed, but how the argument may or might be expressed.

Were the Stoics to have taken that line, or something like it, then they would have been able to bring circumscriptions and schemata together—at least in the case of the first unproved. But that line is more or less the line which Galen and Alexander urge us to take—and which the Stoics, according to them, signally failed to take. Were Galen and Alexander wrong about, or unfair to, the Stoics? Most scholars think that they were not. Indeed, several scholars have thought that Galen and Alexander were quite right in their report and quite wrong in their evaluation: the Stoics did indeed attend to expressions rather than to meanings, or to syntax rather than to sense—and that is just what a good formal logician ought to do. The Stoics, according to that view, did indeed hold that an argument is a first unproved if and only if it is expressed by some substitution of sentences for symbols in the schematic formula

If the 1st, the 2nd; the 1st: therefore the 2nd.

In the same way, an argument in the modern propositional calculus is an example of *modus ponens* if and only if it is expressed by some substitution of sentences for letters in the schema

P ⊃ Q, P: therefore Q.

So the Eurostar example is not, after all, a first unproved—nor is it a case of *modus ponens*.

Then what on earth is it?

SUBSYLLOGISTIC ARGUMENTS

Well, comes the answer, it is what the Stoics called a subsyllogistic argument. Subsyllogistic arguments are not syllogisms; but each subsyllogistic argument is related in a determinate manner to a particular syllogism, and it is that fact which explains its validity.

In truth, we know little enough about subsyllogistic arguments—indeed, the word 'subsyllogistic' is found exactly twice in the surviving texts on Stoic logic. In one of them, Galen refers to

the arguments which are called subsyllogistic, being uttered by way of expressions which are equipollent with syllogistic arguments.

(*inst log* xix 6)[41]

The text is in a rotten state, and Galen offers no illustrative example. But the context of his remark implies that the Stoics—and in particular Chrysippus—had named and discussed the things.

The second passage is more expansive. Alexander is discussing Aristotle's treatment of the second figure predicative mood Baroco. Aristotle says this:

Again, if M holds of every N and does not hold of some X, it is necessary that N does not hold of some X. ... And if M holds of every N and not of every X, there will be a syllogism that N does not hold of every X—the proof is the same.

(*APr* 27a36-b2)[42]

---

[41] οἱ δὲ ὑποσυλλογιστικοὶ κληθέντες ἐν ἰσοδυναμούσαις λέξεσι τοῖς συλλογιστικοῖς λεγόμενοι.

[42] πάλιν εἰ τῷ μὲν Ν παντὶ τὸ Μ, τῷ δὲ Ξ τινὶ μὴ ὑπάρχει, ἀνάγκη τὸ Ν τινὶ τῷ Ξ μὴ ὑπάρχειν· ... καὶ εἰ τὸ Μ τῷ μὲν Ν παντὶ ὑπάρχει τῷ δὲ Ξ μὴ παντί, ἔσται συλλογισμὸς ὅτι οὐ παντὶ τῷ Ξ τὸ Ν· ἀπόδειξις δ' ἡ αὐτή.

There seem to be two syllogisms there—two Barocos, as it were. Alexander explains that the second version, which substitutes 'not of every' for 'not of some'

is of the kind which the later thinkers call subsyllogistic inasmuch as it assumes something which is equipollent with the syllogistic premiss and infers the same conclusion from it. For 'not hold of all' has replaced 'not hold of some', with which it is equipollent. But they do not call such items syllogisms since they attend to language and expression whereas Aristotle, who, where the same things are meant, looks to the meanings and not to the expressions, says that the same syllogism is inferred when the language of the conclusion is transformed in this way—provided that the conjugation is syllogistic in the first place.

(*in APr* 84.11–19)[43]

Take the following two schemata:

(A) B holds of every A   (B) B holds of every A
    B does not hold of some C   B does not hold of every C
    A does not hold of some C   A does not hold of every C

Aristotle appears to suggest that those two schemata represent two distinct syllogistic forms—after all, he gives first the one and then the other, with no apology for repeating himself. But Alexander explains that in fact—and hence in Aristotle's opinion—they are two different ways of representing one and the same syllogism, namely Baroco. Alexander also notes that, according to 'the later thinkers'—and he has no doubt got the Stoics in mind—schema (B) represents a subsyllogistic argument, which is different from the syllogistic argument which (A) represents.

Did some Stoics—perhaps some imperial Stoics—comment on the two versions of Baroco? That is perfectly possible; but Alexander does not explicitly say that they did, and he probably means to say not that the Stoics had in fact found two different arguments in (A) and (B) but rather that that is just the sort of silly thing they would do.

---

[43] τοιοῦτός ἐστιν ὁ ὑποσυλλογιστικὸς ὑπὸ τῶν νεωτέρων λεγόμενος ὁ λαμβάνων μὲν τὸ ἰσοδυναμοῦν τῇ προτάσει τῇ συλλογιστικῇ ταὐτὸν δὲ καὶ ἐκ ταύτης συνάγων· τῷ γὰρ τινὶ μὴ ὑπάρχειν τὸ μὴ παντὶ ὑπάρχειν ἰσοδυναμοῦν μετείληπται. ἀλλ' ἐκεῖνοι μὲν οὐ λέγουσι τοὺς τοιούτους συλλογισμοὺς εἰς τὴν φωνὴν καὶ τὴν λέξιν βλέποντες, ἀλλὰ Ἀριστοτέλης πρὸς τὰ σημαινόμενα ὁρῶν, ἐφ' ὧν ὁμοίως σημαίνεται, οὐ πρὸς τὰς φωνάς, τὸν αὐτόν φησι συνάγεσθαι συλλογισμὸν καὶ ἐν τῇ τοιαύτῃ τῆς λέξεως ἐν τῷ συμπεράσματι μεταλήψει, ἂν ᾖ συλλογιστικὴ ὅλως συμπλοκή.

Two further texts are customarily added to the subsyllogistic dossier. First, there is another passage from Alexander's commentary on the *Analytics*.

When the same thing is meant primarily by different expressions and is taken in the same way, the syllogism will be the same ... Now that is Aristotle's view about changes in expression; but the later thinkers attend to expressions and not to meanings, and they deny that you get the same thing when you exchange the terms for equipollent expressions. For although 'If the 1ˢᵗ, the 2ⁿᵈ' means the same as 'The 2ⁿᵈ follows the 1ˢᵗ', they say that the argument is syllogistic if the expression is taken like this:

If the 1ˢᵗ, the 2ⁿᵈ; but the 1ˢᵗ: therefore the 2ⁿᵈ

but that

The 2ⁿᵈ follows the 1ˢᵗ; but the 1ˢᵗ: therefore the 2ⁿᵈ

is not syllogistic but concludent.

(in APr 373.18–35)[44]

Alexander does not say that the later thinkers called the second of those two arguments subsyllogistic; but surely they should have done and no doubt they did.

Finally, in his account of Stoic logic, Diogenes reports that there was a distinction within the class of valid or concludent arguments between arguments which are syllogistic and arguments which are not syllogistic but merely concludent; and as an example of a non-syllogistic but concludent argument he offers this:

It is false that it is day and it is night; but it is day: therefore it is not night.

(VII 78)[45]

Diogenes does not introduce the term 'subsyllogistic'; but, again, he surely might have done so—no doubt the Stoics recognized the argument as a subsyllogistic partner of a third unproved syllogism.

The general drift of all that is clear enough; but it is surprisingly difficult to frame a clear and distinct idea of what a subsyllogism is. One first attempt at doing so runs like this: A sequence of sentences

---

[44] ὥσθ᾽ ὅταν ταὐτὰ σημαίνηται ὑπὸ διαφόρων λέξεων προηγουμένως καὶ ὁμοίως λαμβάνηται, ὁ αὐτὸς ἔσται συλλογισμός. ... Ἀριστοτέλης μὲν οὖν οὕτως περὶ τῶν κατὰ τὰς λέξεις μεταλήψεων φέρεται· οἱ δὲ νεώτεροι ταῖς λέξεσιν ἐπακολουθοῦντες οὐκέτι δὲ τοῖς σημαινομένοις οὐ ταὐτόν φασι γίνεσθαι ἐν ταῖς εἰς τὰς ἰσοδυναμούσας λέξεις μεταλήψεσι τῶν ὅρων. ταὐτὸν γὰρ σημαίνοντος τοῦ εἰ τὸ πρῶτον τὸ δεύτερον τῷ ἀκολουθεῖ τῷ πρώτῳ τὸ δεύτερον, συλλογιστικὸν μὲν λόγον φασὶν εἶναι τοιαύτης ληφθείσης τῆς λέξεως εἰ τὸ πρῶτον τὸ δεύτερον, τὸ δὲ πρῶτον, τὸ ἄρα δεύτερον, οὐκέτι δὲ συλλογιστικὸν ἀλλὰ περαντικὸν τὸ ἀκολουθεῖ τῷ πρώτῳ τὸ δεύτερον, τὸ δὲ πρῶτον, τὸ ἄρα δεύτερον.

[45] ψεῦδός ἐστι τὸ ἡμέρα ἐστὶ καὶ νύξ ἐστι· ἡμέρα δὲ ἐστιν· οὐκ ἄρα νύξ ἐστιν.

P_1, P_2, ... , P_n: therefore Q

expresses a subsyllogistic argument if and only if there is a sequence of expressions

R_1, R_2, ... , R_n: therefore S

which expresses a syllogism and is such that each R_i is either the same as or equipollent with the corresponding P_i and S is either the same as or equipollent with Q.

Thus the sequence of expressions

It is false that it is day and it is night; it is day: therefore it is not night

expresses a subsyllogistic argument inasmuch as

It is not the case that it is day and it is night; it is day: therefore it is night

expresses a syllogism (a third unproved syllogism) and 'It is false that it is day and it is night' is equipollent with 'It is not the case that it is day and it is night', while 'It is day' and 'It is night' are common to the two sequences.

What arguments are thereby identified as subsyllogistic will depend on the way in which equipollence is construed. The ancient texts give little away—indeed, ancient texts use the terminology of equipollence without ever feeling the need to explain what they mean, and often enough what they say remains crucially indeterminate. The notion is expressed by way of the verb 'ἰσοδυναμεῖν' or of the verbal phrase 'ἴσον δύνασθαι', where the '-pollence' of 'equipollence' is carried by '-δυναμεῖν' or 'δύνασθαι'. Thus equipollence amounts to equality of δύναμις. Since one common meaning of 'δύναμις' is 'meaning', equipollence might well be taken to signify equality of meaning—or synonymy. In fact, it is quite clear that, sometimes at least, equipollence amounts to synonymy; and scholars generally suppose that, in the context of subsyllogistic arguments, equipollence is synonymy.

So the first attempt at defining a subsyllogistic argument may be lightly revised, thus: A sequence of sentences

P_1, P_2, ... , P_n: therefore Q

expresses a subsyllogistic argument if and only if there is a sequence of expressions

R_1, R_2, ... , R_n: therefore S

which expresses a syllogism and is such that each R_i is either the same as or synonymous with the corresponding P_i and S is either the same as or synonymous with Q.

That definition probably requires a trifling qualification—and also a non-trifling qualification. The trifling qualification is needed in order to avoid the conclusion that every syllogism is a subsyllogistic argument. For to every sequence which expresses a syllogism there corresponds, trivially, a sequence of expressions which expresses a syllogism and the elements of which are the same as or synonymous with the sequence; for every sequence so corresponds to itself. So let us write—say—'... if and only if there is a different sequence of expressions ...' rather than simply '... if and only if there is a sequence of expressions ...'.

The non-trifling qualification is suggested by the nomenclature of the items under examination; for the word 'subsyllogistic'—or more precisely, its Greek parent—suggests that we are dealing with something not quite up to snuff, something not on the level of a genuine syllogism. But why think that a subsyllogistic argument, as it has been thus far explained, is inferior to a syllogism rather than merely a different syllogism? The notion of synonymy does not help to answer the question inasmuch as synonymy is a symmetrical relation: the fact that a subsyllogism and its syllogistic counterpart are expressed by synonymous formulas leaves them on the same level; and we need to find some asymmetry, some way of setting subsyllogisms below syllogisms. The asymmetry has been discovered in a certain theory of linguistic degeneration.

Degeneration was a notion much loved by the ancient grammarians. Language, they observed, was liable to change; language, they pessimistically observed, tended to lose its pristine purity and present itself in dirty and degenerate guises. The degeneration might be a matter of orthography, of accentuation, of grammatical form, of construction, ... But the crucial fact about degeneration was this: if X is a degenerate form of Y, then X has the same meaning as Y. Degeneration does not occur when an expression changes its sense but when a sense changes its expression. As Apollonius puts it,

every expression, in whatsoever way it has degenerated, nevertheless keeps its own meaning—nor does it change the order it imposes if it imposes an order.

(*conj* 224.11–13)[46]

Or again, and with illustrations:

Complete items retain their meaning even when they are mutilated and truncated; for degeneration affects the sounds and not the meanings. The mutilated form 'δῶ' means 'house'; 'ἐθέλω' with its epsilon truncated means the same as before; ...

(*adv* 158.13–16)[47]

---

[46] πᾶσα λέξις ὁτιδήποτε παθοῦσα ἔχει καὶ τὸ ἴδιον δηλούμενον, καὶ εἴ τινος τάξεως τύχοι, ταύτης πάλιν οὐ μετατίθεται.

[47] τὰ μέντοι ἐντελῆ ὄντα καὶ ἀποκοπτόμενα καὶ ἀφαιρούμενα φυλάσσει τὸ δηλούμενον· τῶν γὰρ φωνῶν τὰ πάθη καὶ οὐ τῶν σημαινομένων. ἀποκοπὲν τὸ δῶ σημαίνει τὸ δῶμα, ἀφαιρεθὲν τὸ ἐθέλω τοῦ ε τὸ αὐτὸ σημαίνει, ...

Degeneracy is asymmetrical: if X is a degenerate form of Y, then Y is not a degenerate form of X. But degeneracy also guarantees synonymy. In other words, it is just the thing which subsyllogistic arguments are looking for.

There is a speck of evidence that there was a formal connection between subsyllogistic arguments and linguistic degeneration. It is found in the sentence at the very end of Galen's *Introduction to Logic* which mentions subsyllogistic arguments. The sentence is corrupt, and scholars do not agree even on its general sense. On one restoration, it runs like this:

Of merely concludent arguments, we have shown that some do not form a genus of syllogisms of their own but are expressed in degenerate language—sometimes by way of a coherent transposition, and in the case of the arguments which are called subsyllogistic by being uttered by way of expressions which are equipollent with syllogistic arguments.

(*inst log* xix 6)[48]

If that restoration is roughly right, then subsyllogistic arguments are—according to Galen—one of two types of argument which are expressed degenerately.

It would be rash to rest a whole theory on those withered words of Galen. On the other hand, it is difficult not to be attracted by the suggested connection between subsyllogisticality and degeneration—if only because it is difficult to find anything else which is in the least attractive.

So the idea is this. A syllogism—a genuine syllogism—must be decked out in pristine expressions. An argument degenerately expressed may indeed say the same as a syllogism—but it will be subsyllogistic. And we may finally explicate subsyllogistic arguments as follows:

A sequence of sentences
$P_1, P_2, \ldots, P_n$: therefore Q
expresses a subsyllogistic argument if and only if there is a distinct sequence of expressions
$R_1, R_2, \ldots, R_n$: therefore S
which expresses a syllogism and is such that each P_i is either the same as or a degenerate synonym of the corresponding R_i and Q is either the same as or a degenerate synonym of S.

---

[48] ἐδείχθησαν γὰρ καὶ τούτων ἔνιοι μὲν οὐκ ἴδιόν τι γένος ὄντες συλλογισμῶν ἀλλὰ διὰ πεπονθυίας λέξεως ἑρμηνευόμενοι, ποτὲ μὲν κατ' ἀκολουθοῦσαν ὑπέρθεσιν, οἱ δὲ ὑποσυλλο-γιστικοὶ κληθέντες ἐν ἰσοδυναμούσαις λέξεσι τοῖς συλλογιστικοῖς λεγόμενοι.

The pristine expression of a negated conjunction uses the form 'It is not the case that both P and Q'. The formula 'It is false that both P and Q' is a degenerate version. That is why Diogenes Laertius' example is subsyllogistic. The pristine expression of a conditional assertible uses the connector 'if'. To use 'follow' is degenerate. That is why Alexander's example is subsyllogistic.

And—to return to the matter in hand—that is why the Eurostar argument is not a first unproved. It is not a first unproved because it is not a syllogism: rather, it is a subsyllogistic argument.

So we cannot, after all, say on behalf of the Stoics that an argument is a first unproved if and only if it might be expressed by a sequence of sentences which corresponds to the sequence of matrixes:

If the 1st, the 2nd; the 1st: therefore the 2nd.

For that suggestion turns subsyllogisms into syllogisms. Rather, we must say that an argument is a first unproved if and only if it is in fact expressed by a sequence of sentences which is derivable from an expression of the mode of the first unproved.

In that case, either the circumscription of the first unproved catches numerous arguments which are not first unproveds but subsyllogistic counterparts of first unproveds; or else the Stoics must identify conditional assertibles as those which are expressed—not, which might be expressed—by way of sentences of a certain specified type. Neither of those options is appetizing. Moreover, it is hard to see how either of them—or anything at all like them—is coherent with the rest of Stoic logic.

What, after all, is the relation between Diogenes Laertius' subsyllogistic argument:

> It is false that it is day and it is night
> It is day
> Therefore it is not night

and its syllogistic cousin:

> It is not the case that it is day and it is night
> It is day
> Therefore it is night?

There ought to be two distinct arguments there; for a syllogism can hardly be the same argument as a subsyllogism. If the arguments are distinct, then they must be distinct in their first premisses. But the first premiss of the subsyllogism is expressed by a sentence which, according to the theory before us, is a degenerate synonym of the sentence which expresses the first premiss of the syllogism. But in that case, there is one argument in front of us, not two. How could two synonymous sets of expressions express two different arguments?

Well, the Stoics apparently held that there were two arguments there, one of them a syllogism and the other subsyllogistic. Now according to the Stoics, an argument is a sequence or system of assertibles, so that this argument is the same as that argument if and only if it is the same system of assertibles. But in that case, if the Stoics are to find two arguments where Alexander found but one, they must hold that the sentences

It is false that it is day and it is night

and

It is not the case that it is day and it is night

express different assertibles. But the Stoics also hold that the meaning of an expression is what you can say by uttering it, so that the meaning of a complete indicative sentence will be the complete sayable—the assertible—which it expresses. Hence if the two sentences in question express different assertibles, they have different meanings—and the argument in Diogenes Laertius is not, after all, subsyllogistic.

In general, suppose that—as before—we have two sequences of sentences

$P_1, P_2, \ldots, P_n$: therefore Q

and

$R_1, R_2, \ldots, R_n$: therefore S

such that each R_i is either the same as or synonymous with the corresponding P_i and S is either the same as or synonymous with Q. In that case, the two sequences express exactly the same assertibles. Hence one sequence expresses a syllogism if and only if the other sequence expresses a syllogism. Hence it cannot be the case that one sequence expresses a syllogistic argument and the other a subsyllogistic argument.

If that is right, there are no such things as subsyllogistic arguments: there are—you might say—subsyllogistic ways of expressing arguments and there are syllogistic ways of expressing arguments; but if a subsyllogistic expression and a syllogistic expression express the same argument, then that argument is a syllogism. The Eurostar argument is a syllogism: it is—it ought to be counted as—a Stoic first unproved.

STOIC NUMERALS

Schematic characterizations of syllogistic forms are such familiar items that we scarcely stop to ask how we understand them. I said a little earlier that the signs and symbols which appear in matrixes are syntactically determinate but semantically inert, that they are place-holders or place-markers which do not themselves mean anything. No doubt that is true of the items in a thoroughly modern matrix. But is it also true of the signs and symbols which the ancient logicians employed? And how, in any case, did the ancient logicians themselves understand their symbols?

I begin with a passage in Apuleius' *On Interpretation*. The text contrasts Peripatetic and Stoic schemata:

Thus in the Peripatetic fashion, by the use of letters, the first unproved ... is this:
    A of every B, and B of every C: therefore A of every C.
... The Stoics use numerals instead of letters, for example:
    If the first the second; but the first: therefore the second.

(int xiii [212.4–12])[49]

It is not merely that the Stoic symbols have the syntax of sentences and represent assertibles whereas the Peripatetic symbols stand in for terms: in addition, the Stoic schemata use numerals whereas the Peripatetic schemata use letters. If in an Aristotelian text you find a sentence like 'τὸ A πάντι τῷ B ὑπάρχει', you should take the Greek capitals to indicate the first two letters of the Greek alphabet. If in a Stoic text you find something like 'εἰ τὸ A, τὸ B', you should take the Greek capitals to be the first two members of the Greek 'alphanumeric' system—more particularly, you should construe them as ordinal numerals. (One standard way of saying or writing 'The first, the second, the third, ...' in Greek was: 'The alpha, the beta, the gamma, ...') Although there is rather little positive evidence in support of Apuleius' statement that the Stoics used numerals, there is no evidence against it, and no one doubts it.

English translators of the *Analytics* invariably give 'A', 'B', 'C', ... rather than 'alpha', 'beta', 'gamma', ... ; and perhaps Aristotle wrote 'τὸ A' and the

---

[49] *ut etiam Peripateticorum more per litteras ... sit primus indemonstrabilis: A de omni B, et B de omni C, igitur A de omni C. ... Stoici porro pro litteris numeros usurpant, ut: si primum secundum, atqui primum, secundum igitur.*

like rather than 'τὸ ἄλφα' and the like. But he and his followers surely said 'τὸ ἄλφα' and the like. Perhaps the Stoic logicians wrote 'τὸ A' and the like rather than 'τὸ πρῶτον' and the like. (Galen explicitly recommends that we write numerals out in full—otherwise the scribes are bound to corrupt them. But he implies that most Greeks preferred to save a little ink and time; and later copyists usually opted for the abbreviated forms.) However that may be, the Stoics certainly said 'τὸ πρῶτον' and the like, and we should translate 'the first' (or 'the 1st') and the like.

So the mode which corresponds to the first Chrysippean unproved should be expressed not by, say,

If P, Q; P: therefore Q

but rather by

If the 1st, the 2nd; but the 1st: therefore the 2nd.

No doubt that is true—but isn't it a truth of no significance? The Stoics might just as well have expressed the mode by using letters—after all, schematic letters and schematic numerals are alike in having no sense, and so they cannot differ from one another in significance. Then why not represent the mode by

If P, Q; P: therefore Q?

Matrixes of that sort will not mislead or alienate a modern reader who has a smattering of modern logic; and they have exactly the same sense as the matrixes which employ ordinal numerals.

That is correct. But it is worth pausing to ask why the Stoics opted for ordinal numerals. We know that they sometimes employed a sort of hybrid between argument and mode, which they called a λογότροπος or 'argumode'. This is how Diogenes Laertius describes the item:

An argumode is what is compounded from both [sc from an argument and a mode], for example:

If Plato lives, Plato breathes; but the 1st: therefore the 2nd.

Argumodes were introduced so that, when the components of an argument were rather long, you did not have to state the co-assumption, which was long, and also the conclusion—rather, you could continue briefly:

But the 1st: therefore the 2nd.

(VII 77)[50]

---

[50] λογότροπος δέ ἐστι τὸ ἐξ ἀμφοτέρων σύνθετον, οἷον εἰ ζῇ Πλάτων, ἀναπνεῖ Πλάτων· ἀλλὰ μὴν τὸ πρῶτον· τὸ ἄρα δεύτερον. παρεισήχθη δὲ ὁ λογότροπος ὑπὲρ τοῦ ἐν ταῖς μακροτέραις συντάξεσι τῶν λόγων μηκέτι τὴν πρόσληψιν μακρὰν οὖσαν καὶ τὴν ἐπιφορὰν λέγειν, ἀλλὰ συντόμως ἐπενεγκεῖν· τὸ δὲ πρῶτον· τὸ ἄρα δεύτερον.

Argumodes are not mentioned by name outside this text (for the entry in the *Suda*, s.v. τρόπον, was taken from Diogenes); but the things themselves are found frequently enough elsewhere. Here is an example from Sextus:

> You can deal with what we have just said briefly by propounding the argument as follows:
> If what is apparent is apparent to everyone and signs are not apparent to everyone, then signs are not apparent.
> But the 1st.
> Therefore the 2nd.
>
> (*M* viii 242)[51]

Sextus' example makes the abbreviatory function of argumodes evident. There are also exemplary argumodes in reports of Stoic inferences; and some are found in the rare fragments of Stoic logical texts. The *Logical Investigations* of Chrysippus has this:

> If there are plural predicates, then there are plurals of plurals *ad infinitum*. But certainly not that. So not the 1st.
>
> (PHerc307, ii 21–26)[52]

Perhaps that is only a quasi-argumode insofar as Chrysippus says 'not that' rather than 'not the 2nd'? Still, there is no reason to doubt that the Stoics habitually used argumodes, and that they did so primarily for abbreviatory purposes.

So although the things are called argumodes rather than arguments, and are said to be compounded from an argument and a mode, that is slightly misleading. For argumodes are in fact arguments—arguments expressed in an abbreviated form. Sextus is right when, at *M* viii 242, he introduces his item as an argument.

How are the ordinal numerals which appear in an argumode to be understood? I guess that 'the 1st' is a referring expression; that it is short for 'the first assertible' or 'τὸ πρῶτον ἀξίωμα'; and that it refers to the first assertible in the current context—that is to say, to the assertible which, in Diogenes' example, forms the antecedent of the conditional premiss of the argument. In that case, the argumodes are not only abbreviatory but also

---

[51] ἐνέσται δὲ καὶ βραχέως τὰ προειρημένα περιλαβόντας τοιουτουσί τινας προτείνειν λόγους. εἰ τὰ φαινόμενα πᾶσι φαίνεται, τὰ δὲ σημεῖα οὐ πᾶσι φαίνεται, οὐκ ἔστι τὰ φαινόμενα σημεῖα· ἀλλὰ μὴν τὸ πρῶτον· τὸ ἄρα δεύτερον.

[52] εἰ πληθυντικά ἐστιν κατηγορήματα, καὶ πληθυντικῶν πληθυντικά ἐστι μέχρι εἰς ἄπειρον. οὐ πάνυ δὲ τοῦτο. οὐδ' ἄρα τὸ πρῶτον.

brachylogical: 'the 1st' must be taken to stand for something like 'the first assertible is the case'.

In an argumode, the ordinal numerals must have a determinate reference. A sequence such as:

If the 1st, the 2nd.
But Plato lives.
Therefore Plato breathes.

is not an argumode; for the ordinals there have no reference. (To be sure, you might readily invent a convention which determined a reference for them.)

That seems clear and unremarkable; but in fact it raises a problem for the Sextan argumode which I have just cited. The argumode was evidently intended to abbreviate a valid syllogism, namely:

If what is apparent is apparent to everyone and signs are not apparent to everyone, then signs are not apparent.
But what is apparent is apparent to everyone and signs are not apparent to everyone.
Therefore signs are not apparent.

In other words, in Sextus' argumode the formula 'the 1st' refers to 'what is apparent is apparent to everyone and signs are not apparent to everyone', and 'the 2nd' refers to 'signs are not apparent'. But then 'the 1st' and 'the 2nd' do not refer to the first and the second assertible expressed in the argument: the first assertible to be expressed in the argument is in fact 'what is apparent is apparent to everyone' and the second is 'signs are not apparent to everyone'. So doesn't the argumode abbreviate the following invalid argument?

If what is apparent is apparent to everyone and signs are not apparent to everyone, then signs are not apparent.
But what is apparent is apparent to everyone.
Therefore signs are not apparent to everyone.

Well, of course that's not the argument which Sextus means to propose; of course no reader has ever imagined that he did intend to propose it; and of course a little common savvy is enough to determine which argument an argumode is meant to present.

Nonetheless, there is a theoretical problem. The best solution—perhaps the only solution—is to stipulate the following convention: The reference of ordinal numerals in argumodes is always to simple assertibles. Thus 'the 1st' will refer to the simple assertible which is first expressed in the pertinent patch of argumentative discourse; 'the 2nd' will pick out the second simple assertible; and so on. According to that convention, Sextus' argumode in fact sets down the invalid argument. What he should have written is this:

> If what is apparent is apparent to everyone and signs are not apparent to everyone, then signs are not apparent.
> But the 1st and the 2nd.
> Therefore the 3rd.

However that may be, it is plausible to suppose that the Stoic use of ordinal numerals to articulate their modes derives from their use of ordinal numerals in argumodes rather than *vice versa*. For it is in argumodes that the numerals have their ordinary use and sense. From the argument

> If Plato lives, Plato breathes; but Plato lives: therefore Plato breathes

we engender the argumode:

> If Plato lives, Plato breathes; but the 1st: therefore the 2nd.

We then bleach the argumode of its concrete content, in the obvious way, and arrive at

> If the 1st, the 2nd; but the 1st: therefore the 2nd.

And there is a mode of the first unproved.

But the transference from argumode to mode is not without its problems.

First, consider the following argument, which I take from Galen's *Introduction*:

> If food is distributed through the body, either it is pushed or it is sucked or it is conducted or it moves by itself.
> But food is distributed through the body.
> Therefore either it is pushed or it is sucked or it is conducted or it moves by itself.

That, you will say, is a first unproved; and Galen agrees. And its mode, you will therefore say, is this:

> If the 1st, the 2nd.
> But the 1st.
> Therefore the 2nd.

But there Galen disagrees. For this is his comment on the structure of the syllogism:

In one of the modes we have the force of the first of the hypothetical syllogisms, namely:

If the 1st, either the 2nd or the 3rd or the 4th or the 5th.

Then a co-assumption:

But the 1st.

Therefore either the 2nd or the 3rd or the 4th or the 5th.

(*inst log* xv 8)[53]

It is plain why Galen says what he says. Moreover, it is a natural enough thing to say if you regard modes as argumodes bleached of their concrete content, and if in an argumode the ordinal numerals refer to the simple constituents of the complex premiss on which they depend for their interpretation. Nonetheless, what Galen says has some curious consequences.

First, there will be no such thing as the mode of the first unproved. Rather, there will be an infinite number of such modes; for either the antecedent of the conditional premiss, or its consequent, or both items, may be complex assertibles—and assertibles of any degree of complexity. Secondly, it will be natural to hold that a valid argument is not automatically valid in virtue of having the mode which it has. Any argument which matches the mode which Galen sets out at *inst log* xv 8 is, of course, valid; but its validity derives—or so, I imagine, we shall be inclined to agree—not from its matching that particular mode but rather from the fact that it is a first unproved—from the fact that it fits the standard circumscription of the first unproved.

Does Galen's text here reflect Stoic thinking? Did the Stoics allow, in practice or in principle, a multiplicity of modes for their first unproved? Galen does not say that he is following the Stoics; and it would be a gross error to imagine that everything which Galen says about hypothetical syllogisms is at bottom Stoic. Nonetheless, Galen is not alone in admitting multiplicity: there are comparable examples in other authors. Thus Sextus, having announced that the structure of a certain argument will be clearer if we conduct its analysis in terms of modes, says this:

So there are two unproveds. One of them is this:

If the 1st and the 2nd, the 3rd.

But not the 3rd.

---

[53] καθ᾽ ἕτερον γὰρ τῶν τρόπων ἡ τοῦ πρώτου τῶν ὑποθετικῶν συλλογισμῶν δύναμίς ἐστιν, οὖσα τοιαύτη· εἰ τὸ πρῶτον, ἤτοι τὸ δεύτερον ἢ τὸ τρίτον ἢ τὸ τέταρτον ἢ τὸ πέμπτον. εἶτα πρόσληψις· ἀλλὰ μὴν τὸ πρῶτον· ἤτοι ἄρα τὸ δεύτερον ἢ τὸ τρίτον ἢ τὸ τέταρτον ἢ τὸ πέμπτον.

Therefore not the 1st and the 2nd.

That is a second unproved. The other is a third unproved, thus:

Not the 1st and the 2nd.

But the 1st.

Therefore not the 2nd.

That, then, is the analysis in terms of modes.

(*M* viii 236–237)[54]

The mode of the third unproved is orthodox. The mode of the second is comparable to Galen's mode of the first unproved; and it has the same implicit consequences.

It cannot be a coincidence that both Galen and Sextus deal with modes in this way—and the way is encouraged by the existence of argumodes. So I suppose that the Stoics too had sometimes spoken in the same vein. A few pages before the passage I have just quoted, Sextus adverts to a distinction—apparently made by the Stoic logicians—between simple and non-simple unproveds. (See *M* viii 228–229.) The mode of the simple first unproved is presumably this:

If the 1st, the 2nd; but the 1st: therefore the 2nd.

Sextus' own example at *M* viii 236 will presumably be a mode of a complex first unproved. There are infinitely many other complex modes of the first unproved.

If the Stoics spoke along those lines, then they had two rather different views on the nature of modes. On the one view, the ordinal numerals in the expression of a mode may be replaced by sentences which express any assertibles whatsoever, simple or complex. According to that view, there is one mode of the first unproved, namely:

If the 1st, then the 2nd; but the 1st: therefore the 2nd.

On the other view, the ordinal numerals in the expression of a mode must be replaced by sentences which express simple assertibles. According to that view there will be not one but an infinite number of modes of the first unproved. The former view is preferred—implicitly—by modern scholars; but there are at any rate traces of the latter view in the ancient texts. There are, so far as I know, no traces of any discussion of the two views—nor even of any recognition of the fact that there are two views to discuss.

---

[54] ὥστε δύο εἶναι ἀναποδείκτους, ἕνα μὲν τοιοῦτον· εἰ τὸ πρῶτον καὶ τὸ δεύτερον, τὸ τρίτον· οὐχὶ δέ γε τὸ τρίτον· οὐκ ἄρα τὸ πρῶτον καὶ τὸ δεύτερον, ὅς ἐστι δεύτερος ἀναπόδεικτος· ἕτερον δὲ τρίτον, τὸν οὕτως ἔχοντα· οὐχὶ τὸ πρῶτον καὶ τὸ δεύτερον ἀλλὰ μὴν τὸ πρῶτον· οὐκ ἄρα τὸ δεύτερον. ἐπὶ μὲν οὖν τοῦ τρόπου ἡ ἀνάλυσίς ἐστι τοιαύτη.

The transfer of the numerals from argumodes to modes raises another question—or rather, it has another and more serious consequence; for in the course of the transfer the ordinal numerals undergo an essential transmogrification. If you take Diogenes' illustrative argumode and replace its first premiss by

If the 1st, the 2nd,

then you reach the mode of the first unproved, namely:

If the 1st, the 2nd; the 1st: therefore the 2nd.

What do the numerals mean now? They are no longer used to refer; for there is nothing to which they could refer: in 'If the 1st, the 2nd' neither ordinal has a determinate referent. More precisely, in the expression of the argumode the sense of 'the 1st' determines its referent; but in the expression of the mode the sense of 'the first' determines no referent.

That being so, you might as well give the mode by:

If the 2nd, the 1st; the 2nd: therefore the 1st.

Or, come to that, by:

If the 234th, the 19th; the 234th: therefore the 19th.

There is absolutely no difference in sense among those three schemata.

In modern propositional logic, the schema for *modus ponens* is likely to be given in something like this way:

P $\supset$ Q; P: Q.

If instead I offer

Q $\supset$ P; Q: P.

or

S $\supset$ R; S: R

you may judge me eccentric—but my schemata are impeccable. I may try something even more eccentric, and choose to represent *modus ponens* by

X $\supset$ Y; X: Z

or by

1 $\supset$ 2; 1: 2

or by

♣ $\supset$ ♥; ♣ : ♥.

All those schemata are impeccable, provided that the syntax of the symbols has been appropriately specified. It is just the same for the Stoics: instead of ordinal numerals they might have used letters—or anything else.

In other words, and whatever their history may have been, the Stoic ordinal numerals, as they were employed in expressions of the modes, have no ordinal and no numerical function. To be sure, there may still have been a point to using numerals rather than letters. Letters already had a rôle in Peripatetic logic where they represented terms; and a Stoic might have chosen numerals in order to mark the fact that his symbols differ syntactically from Peripatetic symbols. (Thus a modern logician will generally use the letters 'P', 'Q', 'R', ... for sentences and 'F', 'G', 'H', ... for predicates.) He might have done—but I doubt if he did. Rather, the use of ordinal numerals to express modes is explained by the link between modes and argumodes.

'A HOLDS OF EVERY B, ...'

Apuleius, who does not use schemata at all in his presentation of predicative syllogistic, nonetheless passes a remark on the Peripatetic use of schematic letters:

Thus in the Peripatetic fashion, by the use of letters, the first unproved [i.e. Barbara]—with the order of its premisses and their parts inverted but their force unchanged—is this:
A of every B, and B of every C: therefore A of every C.
They begin with the predicate, and therefore with the second premiss. This mood, when it is put together in what they take to be the reverse way, is this:
Every C is B; every B is A: therefore every C is A.

(*int* xiii [212.4–10])[55]

There is a comparable text in Alexander:

Aristotle uses 'of every' and 'of no' in his exposition because the validity of the arguments is recognizable by way of these formulas, and because the predicate and the subject are more recognizable when things are stated in this way, and because 'of every' is prior by nature to 'in as in a whole' (as I have already said). But syllogistic usage is normally the other way about: not 'Virtue is said of every justice' but the other way about—'Every justice is virtue'. That is why we should exercise ourselves in both types of utterance, so that we can follow both usage and Aristotle's exposition.

(*in APr* 54.21–29)[56]

---

[55] *ut etiam Peripateticorum more per litteras ordine propositionum et partium commutato sed vi manente sit primus indemonstrabilis: A de omni B, et B de omni C, igitur A de omni C. incipiunt a declarante atque ideo et a secunda propositione. hic adeo modus secundum hos pertextus retro talis est: omne C B, omne B A, omne igitur C A.*

[56] χρῆται δὲ τῷ κατὰ παντὸς καὶ τῷ κατὰ μηδενὸς ἐν τῇ διδασκαλίᾳ ὅτι διὰ τούτων γνώριμος ἡ συναγωγὴ τῶν λόγων, καὶ ὅτι οὕτως λεγομένων γνωριμώτερος ὅ τε κατηγορού-μενος καὶ ὁ ὑποκείμενος, καὶ ὅτι πρῶτον τῇ φύσει τὸ κατὰ παντὸς τοῦ ἐν ὅλῳ αὐτῷ, ὡς προείρηται. ἡ μέντοι χρῆσις ἡ συλλογιστικὴ ἐν τῇ συνηθείᾳ ἀνάπαλιν ἔχει· οὐ γὰρ ἡ ἀρετὴ

In other words, there are—at least—two ways of representing universal affirmative propositions of the sort which feature in predicative syllogisms. You may say something of the form

A is said of every B

(or 'A holds of every B', or 'A is predicated of every B', or simply 'A of every B'); and you may say

Every B is A.

Similarly for the three other styles of Aristotelian predication.

Apuleius indicates that the Peripatetics somehow prefer the former mode of expression, regarding the latter mode as inverted. Alexander remarks—no doubt more accurately—that the former mode is preferred by Aristotle in his exposition of the syllogistic, whereas the latter mode is normal syllogistic usage. He means that everyone—himself and Aristotle included—will standardly use the second mode of expression (or, I suppose, something more or less like it) in the presentation of actual syllogisms.

Why the double usage? Alexander recognizes that there is something to explain. The forms of expression which we are said by Alexander to use in our syllogistic practice—items of the form 'Every A is B', and the like—are perfectly ordinary Greek. (True, Alexander's example, 'Every justice is virtue', is not exactly household Greek ...) On the other hand, sentences of the form 'A holds of B' are rare and abnormal, and sentences of the form 'A is predicated of B' are—as Porphyry says—an Aristotelian invention. So the question for Alexander is this: Why did Aristotle, in his exposition of syllogistic theory, use 'A holds of B' or 'A is predicated of B' rather than the quotidian 'B is A'?

Alexander provides three answers to his question. Presumably they are collaborative rather than competitive. The first is pretty dubious, and the third is pretty ethereal; but the second has some force:

The predicate and the subject are more recognizable when things are stated this way.

At least this much is true: if I say something of the form

A is predicated of B

I thereby explicitly mark 'A' as a predicate and I implicitly mark 'B' as a subject. So the idea is something like this: in order to grasp the structure of a predicative piece of syllogizing, you need to determine what items in it

λέγεται κατὰ πάσης δικαιοσύνης, ἀλλ' ἀνάπαλιν πᾶσα δικαιοσύνη ἀρετή. διὸ καὶ δεῖ κατ' ἀμφοτέρας τὰς ἐκφορὰς γυμνάζειν ἑαυτοὺς ἵνα τῇ τε χρήσει παρακολουθεῖν δυνώμεθα καὶ τῇ διδασκαλίᾳ.

function as subjects and what as predicates; and the locution 'A is predicated of B'—and perhaps, by a sort of natural extension, 'A holds of B'—makes the determination child's play.

Perhaps it does. But then why use it only in setting out syllogistic theory—why not use it also in actual syllogizing? Apuleius seems to present a couple of matrixes—a couple of quartets of matrixes—for predicative sentences, and Alexander in effect does the same. One of the matrixes brings out the structure of a predicative syllogism more perspicuously than the other does. And yet in syllogistic practice the more perspicuous matrix is scarcely ever exemplified. Aristotle and his successors will normally say 'A holds of every B' or 'A is predicated of every B' when they are engaged in syllogistic theory—when, for example, they are engaged in proving the validity of a given form of argument. But Aristotle will say, with the rest of us,

Every nice girl loves a sailor

rather than anything like

Item which loves a sailor holds of every nice girl.

So too will Alexander, and Uncle Tom Cobbley. Surely that is odd behaviour on the part of logicians who believe that 'A is predicated of every B' is the most perspicuous matrix for universal affirmative sentences?

Perhaps it would be if they did—but they don't. The alleged oddity in Peripatetic linguistic behaviour depends on the claim that 'A is predicated of every B' was, in Peripatetic eyes, the most perspicuous matrix for universal affirmatives. But no Peripatetic ever actually says that 'A of every B' is a perspicuous matrix; for no ancient logician ever talks about matrixes as such. Why, then, suppose that they really took it to be a perspicuous matrix? Well, they certainly took it to be perspicuous, and isn't it a matrix?

No: 'A of every B' is not a matrix for universal affirmative propositions. It is not a matrix at all. Consider one of Aristotle's principles of conversion: E-style propositions convert, if no bird sings then no singing item is a bird, if you interchange subject and predicate in a true E-predication then the result is a true E-predication. Or, using Aristotelian letters:

If A is predicated of no B, then B is predicated of no A.

Isn't that a sentential matrix, a matrix which schematically represents the principle of conversion? No, it is not a matrix. For no replacement of the symbols 'A' and 'B' in it will produce an English sentence. Exactly the same holds of the Greek and the Latin versions of the thing. And the reason is simple and syntactical: any replacement of 'A' and of 'B' must be at once a singular term (in order to precede 'is predicated') and also a general term in order to follow 'no'). And no term is both singular and general.

That consideration is powerful; but it is not decisive. A partisan of Porphyrean predication might make an honest matrix out of the thing by adapting it to say:

> If A is predicated of nothing of which B is predicated, then B is predicated of nothing of which A is predicated.

There, both 'A' and 'B' are singular terms; and no doubt the matrix is a schematic representation of the principle of E-conversion. But 'A is predicated of nothing of which B is predicated' is not a matrix for a universal negative sentence: if you replace the letters by words, what you get is a singular affirmative sentence, not a universal negative sentence.

There is another and non-Porphyrean way of getting a matrix out of the matter. Aristotle's usage has a peculiarity which I have so far overlooked: whereas in English (and also in Latin) the syllogistic letters are merely letters and we write 'A of every B', 'B of no C', and the like, in Greek Aristotle invariably prefixes a definite article and writes 'τὸ A', or perhaps 'τὸ ἄλφα', rather than the plain 'A' or 'ἄλφα'. Why so?

Well, the phrase 'τὸ ἄλφα' is, among other things, a name for the letter alpha. The grammarians will say things like

there are twenty-four letters, from alpha to omega;

([Dionysius Thrax], 6 [9.2])[57]

and in doing so they use 'τὸ A' to name the letter alpha. But that does not help us; for when Aristotle writes 'The A of ...' he evidently does not mean to say that the Greek letter alpha is predicated of ... Then perhaps the phrase 'τὸ ἄλφα' is elliptical, and we must supply some noun with it? In Greek geometrical texts you will often find similar phrases: you will also find 'τὸ ἄλφα σημεῖον' ('the point A'), and it is evident that 'τὸ ἄλφα' is elliptical for 'the point A'. But in the case of Aristotle's syllogistic, there is no possible noun which might be understood or supplied with the letters.

Nonetheless, it seems at least to be clear that the letters 'A', 'B', 'C', ... do not have the syntax of singular terms. Perhaps 'τὸ A' is a singular term; but 'A' itself is not—rather, it has the syntax of a common noun, it is an item which, prefixed by 'is a' will make a one-placed verbal formula. That grammatical

---

[57] γράμματά ἐστιν εἰκοσιτέσσαρα ἀπὸ τοῦ α μέχρι τοῦ ω.

observation is confirmed by a further feature of Aristotelian usage. When he gives a schematic presentation of the principle of E-conversion, what he actually says—or rather, what, in all probability, he actually writes—is this:

εἰ οὖν μηδενὶ τῶν Β τὸ Α ὑπάρχει, οὐδὲ τῶν Α οὐδενὶ ὑπάρξει τὸ Β.
If the A holds of none of the Bs, then the B will hold of none of the As.

(APr 25a15–16)

Here he uses singulars ('the A', 'the B') and plurals ('the Bs', 'the As') side by side; and so it is elsewhere in the *Analytics* often enough. (How often the plural occurs is unclear: the manuscripts often vary between a singular and a plural—they do so in the passage I have just quoted; and there is often no way of deciding which reading to accept.) It is plain that there is no significant difference between the plural and the singular turn: 'holds of some B' is given indifferently by 'τινι τῶν Β ὑπάρχει' and by 'τινι τῷ Β ὑπάρχει'.

In the formula 'The A holds of none of the Bs', both Greek letters are syntactically on a level. Then why not take the formula to be a matrix? The initial answer is simple: you can't take the formula to be a matrix because no replacement of letters by appropriate expressions produces a sentence.

> The stone holds of none of the men
> The justice holds of none of the vices
> The item which hates itself holds of none of the philosophers.

Such monsters may be said to have the syntax of sentences; but they are not sentences—they are nonsense. To be sure, we can understand them; but, as I have already said, nonsense is sometimes as easy to understand as sense.

That is not the end of the business: there is yet a further linguistic fact to be exploited. Aristotle sometimes uses his syllogistic letters as part of complex formulas—he will sometimes write something of the form 'that on which the A is' or 'ἐφ' ᾧ τὸ Α'. There must be fifty or more occurrences of such items in the *Prior Analytics*. The first is this:

οἷον εἰ τὸ μὲν Α εἴη κίνησις, τὸ δὲ Β ζῷον, ἐφ' ᾧ δὲ τὸ Γ ἄνθρωπος.
E.g. if the A were motion, the B were animal, and that on which the C is were man.

(APr 30a29–30)

In that sentence there is evidently no interesting difference between the simple 'the A' and the complex 'that on which the C is'; and in fact wherever the complex formula is found it is plainly equivalent to the simple one. The complex formula sometimes takes a plural form, 'those items on which the A is', where we find the genitive rather than the dative case ('ἐφ' ὧν' rather than 'ἐφ' οἷς')—for example, *APr* 44a13.

Why does Aristotle sometimes use the complex formula when the simple formula will do just as well and twice as rapidly? It seems reasonable to hypothesize that the longer expression was the original, and that the shorter expression came into being as an easy abbreviation. So 'the A' means 'that on which the A is'—and 'the As' means 'those items on which the A is'. But what on earth is the meaning of 'that on which the A is'?

It is commonly supposed that Aristotle learned his use of letters from the geometers. (I shall return to the supposal.) Expressions of the sort 'that on which the A is' do not—so far as I have observed—occur in Euclid's *Elements*; but items very like them are found in earlier geometrical texts. Simplicius quotes a long passage of Eudemus in which he discusses Hippocrates' attempt to square the circle. Eudemus uses plenty of letters; and sometimes—not always—he uses them in the style 'that on which A is'. Here is an example:

Let there be a circle the diameter of which is that on which AB is, and its centre that on which K is. And let that on which CD is cut in half and at right angles that on which BK is.

(Simplicius, *in Phys* 64.11–17)[58]

Eudemus also uses the plural formula 'ἐφ' ὧν A' (e.g. 67.22–24). He does not here prefix his letters with definite articles. Nonetheless, it is clear that there can be no difference of sense between his 'that on which K is [ἐφ' ᾧ K]' and the Aristotelian 'that on which the K is [ἐφ' ᾧ τὸ K]'; and in fact Aristotle too sometimes drops the definite article.

It is plain that the phrase 'that on which K is' means 'the item which is labelled with the letter K'. I suppose that, among the Greek geometers, the cumbersome expression 'that on which A is' was original; and that it was later dropped in favour of the simpler 'A'. In any event, the cumbersome expression indicates how the simple expression is to be understood. It indicates how it is to be understood in geometrical texts—and also, surely, in the *Prior Analytics*. After all, Aristotle uses the same type of expressions outside the *Analytics*. It is frequent in the *Physics*, and in the other works on natural philosophy; and it

---

[58] ἔστω κύκλος οὗ διάμετρος ἐφ' ᾗ AB, κέντρον δὲ αὐτοῦ ἐφ' ᾧ K· καὶ ἡ μὲν ἐφ' ᾗ ΓΔ δίχα τε καὶ πρὸς ὀρθὰς τεμνέτω τὴν ἐφ' ᾗ BK.

occasionally crops up elsewhere—in the *Ethics* and in the biological works. And often it is used in geometrical or quasi-geometrical contexts.

In other words, and after all, the phrase 'τὸ ἄλφα' does there designate the first letter of the Greek alphabet. Not that Aristotle wants to say that the first letter of the alphabet is predicated of the second: rather, he wants to say that the items to which the first letter is attached is predicated of the item to which the second letter is attached.

With that in mind, let us return for a last time to the question of matrixes. Take the formula:

The item to which the letter A is attached holds of none of the items to which the letter B is attached:

is that a matrix? Of course not—it is no more a matrix than is, say,

The shelf to which the letter A is attached holds the dictionaries.

That is not a matrix: it is a complete sentence, and it contains no symbols at all. Similarly for the syllogistic formula: it is a sentence, not a matrix. It has, of course, a subject–predicate form (among other forms); but although it somehow stands for or represents a universal negative predication, it is not itself a universal negative predication.

Or is it a sentence? Perhaps it has the syntactical form of a sentence; but whatever does it mean? does it mean anything at all? Consider this sentence or quasi-sentence:

The item to which the expression 'stone' is attached holds of none of the items to which the expression 'man' is attached.

What does it mean? Either it is nonsense or else it is jargon. So no doubt it is jargon; and no doubt it is a jargon form of

None of the items of which 'man' is true is an item of which 'stone' is true.

That is intelligible, and it is more or less English.

But what is the point of it? Suppose you were offered this formula as a schematic presentation of the first Stoic unproved:

The 2nd follows the 1st; the 1st: therefore the 2nd.

That, you might say, is nonsense—indeed, it is hardly even grammatical. But isn't that too strict? Why not take the formula as a piece of jargon—as the jargon version of, say,

If the 1st, the 2nd; the 1st: therefore the 2nd?

Perhaps the formula might be so understood; but what could the purpose or point of the jargon possibly be? Well, it serves as an indication of a certain semantic structure; it indicates that the first premiss of a Stoic first unproved is a conditional assertible.

In a similar way, the point of writing the Peripatetic jargon is to bring a certain semantic structure to the fore, to indicate that the items which are involved in a certain syllogism have this or that predicative structure. My imagined Stoic jargon in fact has little point; for the structure which it allegedly serves to indicate will, in most ordinary uses of natural language, be sufficiently clear without its help. But that is not so with predicative structure; and an earlier chapter has noticed that the predicative structures of sentences are not always written on their surfaces.

Suppose that all that is true: it still leaves at least one thing unexplained; for if we can now understand a jargon phrase like

The item to which the expression 'stone' is attached holds of none of the items to which the expression 'man' is attached,

we cannot yet understand an item like

The item to which the letter A is attached holds of none of the items to which the letter B is attached.

We know to which items the expression 'stone' is attached—it is attached to all stones and to nothing else. But to what item or items is the letter A attached? What, in other words, are these Peripatetic letters really up to?

PERIPATETIC LETTERS

Alphas and betas and gammas crop up in the *Analytics* in various different contexts, and we are not obliged to suppose that they always have the same status. True, Aristotle never indicates that they have different statuses; but then he never comments on their status at all.

In some passages at least, the letters have a determinate sense; and it is natural to think of them as merely abbreviatory devices—like the numerals in the Stoic argumodes. Here is an example:

There will be a proof by way of this—e.g. that the planets are near by way of their not twinkling. Let planets be that on which C is, not twinkling that on which B, being near that on which A. Now it is true to say B of C; for planets do not twinkle. And A of B; for what does not twinkle is near (suppose that that has been grasped by induction or perception). Therefore it is necessary that A holds of C, so that it has been proved that the planets are near.

(*APst* 78a29–36)[59]

The three letters there stand in for the three predicates in the proof (one of which, it may be remarked, is negative). But although the letters have a fixed sense, it is at best misleading to refer to them as abbreviatory devices. After all, far from shortening the argument, the letters double its length; for Aristotle gives both a literal and a verbal version of the proof. The point of the formula 'It is true to say B of C' is not to say the same thing in fewer letters as 'Planets do not twinkle'; rather, it is to bring out the pertinent structure of 'Planets do not twinkle' in a clear and brief fashion.

Passages of this sort, in which Greek letters stand in for Greek predicative expressions, are numerous, especially in the *Posterior Analytics*. But what we rightly think of as the characteristic use of letters in the *Analytics* seems to be quite different. For example, a little later in the *Posterior Analytics*, where he is discussing certain features of negative proofs, Aristotle remarks that

again, if B holds of every A and of no C, A holds of none of the Cs.

(*APst* 82b14–15)[60]

There the letters do not appear to stand in for any particular predicative expressions. It is not merely that there are no suitable expressions in the vicinity. Also, and more importantly, it is plain that Aristotle wants to say something about terms in general and not about a particular determinate triad of terms. In other words, his letters here seem to function like the letters in an algebraical formula such as:

$$x + y = y + x.$$

That formula expresses the thought that addition is commutative. It would be foolish to wonder what particular numbers the letters 'x' and 'y' there stand for or designate.

---

[59] ἔσται διὰ τούτου ἡ ἀπόδειξις, οἷον ὅτι ἐγγὺς οἱ πλάνητες διὰ τοῦ μὴ στίλβειν. ἔστω ἐφ' ᾧ Γ πλάνητες, ἐφ' ᾧ Β τὸ μὴ στίλβειν, ἐφ' ᾧ Α τὸ ἐγγὺς εἶναι. ἀληθὲς δὴ τὸ Β κατὰ τοῦ Γ εἰπεῖν· οἱ γὰρ πλάνητες οὐ στίλβουσιν. ἀλλὰ καὶ τὸ Α κατὰ τοῦ Β· τὸ γὰρ μὴ στίλβον ἐγγύς ἐστι· τοῦτο δ' εἰλήφθω δι' ἐπαγωγῆς ἢ δι' αἰσθήσεως. ἀνάγκη οὖν τὸ Α τῷ Γ ὑπάρχειν, ὥστ' ἀποδέδεικται ὅτι οἱ πλάνητες ἐγγύς εἰσιν.

[60] πάλιν εἰ τὸ μὲν Β παντὶ τῷ Α, τῷ δὲ Γ μηδενί, τὸ Α τῶν Γ οὐδενὶ ὑπάρχει.

That the syllogistic letters typically serve to introduce a generality was noticed by Alexander.

He presents the position by way of letters in order to indicate to us that the conclusions do not come about because of the matter but because of the figure and the particular combination of propositions and the mood—it is not because the matter is such-and-such that so-and-so is syllogistically inferred but because the conjugation is such-and-such. So the letters show that the conclusion will be thus-and-so universally and always and in the case of every assumption.

(in APr 53.28–54.2)[61]

The letters indicate universality. They indicate that the argument does not turn upon its particular matter—that it does not depend for its validity on the fact that it contains those terms rather than these.

Alexander repeats the point elsewhere. No doubt he inherited it from his predecessors. Certainly he bequeathed it to his successors. Here is Philoponus:

Having shown by way of examples how each of the propositions converts, next—lest anyone should think that his account of the conversions is eased on its way by the matter of the chosen examples or by anything else, and lest it be unclear whether there are not perhaps some examples for which the stated conversions do not work—for that reason he now sets down universal rules, using letters rather than terms so that we may each of us take whatever matter we wish in place of the letters, the thesis having been shown universally and without the use of matter by way of the letters.

(in APr 46.25–47.1)[62]

But if Philoponus knows that Aristotle's letters express universality, he does not explain how they manage to do so.

There is an explanation, of sorts, in Alexander. I shall cite a long passage: in parts it is obscure, and so too is the Aristotelian text on which Alexander is commenting. Here, first, is Aristotle:

---

[61] ἐπὶ στοιχείων τὴν διδασκαλίαν ποιεῖται ὑπὲρ τοῦ ἐνδείξασθαι ἡμῖν ὅτι οὐ παρὰ τὴν ὕλην γίνεται τὰ συμπεράσματα ἀλλὰ παρὰ τὸ σχῆμα καὶ τὴν τοιαύτην τῶν προτάσεων συμπλοκὴν καὶ τὸν τρόπον· οὐ γὰρ ὅτι ἥδε ἡ ὕλη συνάγεται συλλογιστικῶς τόδε, ἀλλ' ὅτι ἡ συζυγία τοιαύτη. τὰ οὖν στοιχεῖα τοῦ καθόλου καὶ ἀεὶ καὶ ἐπὶ παντὸς τοῦ ληφθέντος τοιοῦτον ἔσεσθαι τὸ συμπέρασμα δεικτικά ἐστιν.

[62] δείξας ὅπως ἑκάστη τῶν προτάσεων ἀντιστρέφει διὰ παραδειγμάτων, ἵνα μή τις οἰηθῇ διὰ τὴν ὕλην τῶν παραληφθεισῶν προτάσεων ἢ δι' ἕτερόν τι εὐοδῆσαι αὐτῷ τὸν περὶ τῶν ἀντιστροφῶν λόγον, ἄδηλον δὲ εἶναι μή πώς ἐστί τινα παραδείγματα ἐν οἷς αἱ εἰρημέναι ἀντιστροφαὶ χώραν οὐκ ἔχουσι, διὰ τοῦτο ἐνταῦθα καθολικοὺς κανόνας παραδίδωσι τὰ στοιχεῖα παραλαμβάνων ἀντὶ τῶν ὅρων, ἵνα ἕκαστος οἵαν βούλοιτο ὕλην ἀντὶ τῶν στοιχείων παραλαμβάνοι, δειχθέντος καθολικῶς τε καὶ ἀύλως ἐπὶ τῶν στοιχείων τοῦ λόγου.

You should not think that any absurdity results from the fact that a certain item is set out; for we do not in the least make use of the fact that this is such-and-such — rather, we are like the geometer who speaks of this foot line and this straight line and this breadthless line although they are not so, but who does not use them as syllogizing from them. ... We use setting out as we also use perception, in the interest of the learner.

(*APr* 49b33–50a2)[63]

The text and the translation are in places disputed; and what Aristotle means is, even in its most general outline, contested. But Alexander himself found no general difficulties:

By 'setting out' he means making a diagram of the terms. Since in the exposition of the syllogisms he used letters instead of terms and showed which conjugations were syllogistic and which non-syllogistic by means of them, he now comments on the fact, saying that we should not suppose that because of this way of taking or setting out terms anything false or absurd results, as though it were the taking of the letters which were responsible for something's seeming to be shown or not shown to lead to a conclusion — just as often things are shown to conclude to something because of their matter, although they are not syllogistic.

'For we do not in the least make use' in taking the letters (and proof according to the logicians depends on items being thus-and-so related to one another — for it is when one is whole and another part) — we make no use of the kinship of the terms to one another so as to show the conclusion by means of that (as for example that this is a genus of that, or a property or a definition), as we would if we set down the matter. For the letters themselves are taken merely as common signs of the terms and they contribute nothing in themselves toward showing that the conjugation is concludent or non-concludent. For just as a geometer, for the sake of clarity in exposition, makes a diagram and says 'Let this be a foot line', or 'Let this be straight', but does not assume that the foot line is a foot long or that the straight line is straight and does not make any use of the diagrammed items in proving what is before him — rather, he uses them as signs which contribute nothing and introduce nothing to the *demonstrandum* (for he can prove what is before him just as well without drawing these lines and without making any use of them — rather, he takes them up in order that what he says may be easy to follow — so that the intellect, being able as it were to repose upon them, may more easily follow); in the same way, we set out letters, which themselves introduce nothing into the *demonstrandum*. For

---

[63] οὐ δεῖ δ' οἴεσθαι παρὰ τὸ ἐκτίθεσθαί τι συμβαίνειν ἄτοπον· οὐδὲν γὰρ προσχρώμεθα τῷ τόδε τι εἶναι, ἀλλ' ὥσπερ ὁ γεωμέτρης τὴν ποδιαίαν καὶ εὐθεῖαν τήνδε καὶ ἀπλατῆ εἶναι λέγει οὐκ οὔσας, ἀλλ' οὐχ οὕτως χρῆται ὡς ἐκ τούτων συλλογιζόμενος. ... τῷ δ' ἐκτίθεσθαι οὕτω χρώμεθα ὥσπερ καὶ τῷ αἰσθάνεσθαι, τὸν μανθάνοντ' ἀλέγοντες.

the inference does not depend on one of them's being A and another B or C—the same thing results if we use other letters instead of them.

This is not so in the case of

Every man is an animal.

Every item capable of laughter is an animal.

For from these it seems that it can be concluded that every man is capable of laughter. But that is because of a certain relation of these particular terms to one another, not because of the figure. For if other terms are taken in the same conjugation, nothing is concluded—say in the case of

Every man is an animal.

Every horse is an animal.

But when letters are set out, it is not like that—as Aristotle indicated by his use of different letters in the different figures. For in the case of letters, you cannot take one as whole and one as part, as in the case of animate and animal (where one is whole—animate extends further and is universal—and the other part); and again, if something else so related to animal, which was taken as a part in the first premiss 'is taken as part to whole'—e.g. man (for man is a part of animal which was a part of animate), it is from items which are thus related—that is, one of the terms being predicated and one subject in the premisses—that proofs depend. For if items have no kinship with one another, it is never possible to show that anything concludes from them syllogistically, and letters have no such relation to one another. Hence it is not because of the letters that something results or does not result. For that reason, the proofs are done by means of them. And that could not be said were we to conduct the proofs by means of the matter which we use in our syllogisms. For because of its particularities, it often appears that something is concludent when it is not.

'So that there is no syllogism'—he has made it clear that proofs done with such letters are delineations of syllogistic modes, and not themselves syllogisms. For a syllogism includes the matter about which something is proved.

(*in APr* 379.14–380.27)[64]

---

[64] ἔκθεσιν μὲν λέγει τὴν τῶν ὅρων καταγραφήν. ἐπεὶ δὲ ἐν τῇ τῶν συλλογισμῶν παραδόσει κέχρηται τοῖς στοιχείοις ἀντὶ τῶν ὅρων καὶ ἐπ' αὐτῶν δέδειχε τάς τε συλλογιστικὰς συζυγίας καὶ τὰς ἀσυλλογίστους, νῦν λέγει περὶ τούτου ὅτι μὴ παρὰ τὴν τοιαύτην λῆψιν τῶν ὅρων καὶ ἔκθεσιν ὑπολαμβάνειν χρὴ ἄτοπόν τι καὶ ψεῦδος συμβαίνειν ὡς τῆς τῶν στοιχείων λήψεως αἰτίας γινομένης τοῦ δοκεῖν δείκνυσθαί τι συνάγον ἢ μὴ δείκνυσθαι, ὡς πολλάκις δείκνυταί τινα παρὰ τὴν ὕλην συνάγοντά τι οὐκ ὄντα συλλογιστικά.

οὐδὲν γὰρ προσχρώμεθα ἐν τῇ διὰ τῶν στοιχείων λήψει (ἐκ δὲ τῶν οὕτως ἐχόντων πρὸς ἄλληλα ἡ κατὰ τοὺς συλλογιστικοὺς δεῖξις· ὅταν γὰρ τὸ μὲν ὡς ὅλον τὸ δὲ ὡς μέρος) τῇ οἰκειότητι τῇ πρὸς ἀλλήλους τῶν ὅρων ὡς διὰ τούτου δεικνύναι τὸ συναγόμενον, οἷον ὅτι τόδε τοῦδέ ἐστι γένος ἢ τόδε τοῦδέ ἐστιν ἴδιον ἢ ὁρισμός, ὥσπερ ἂν εἰ τὴν ὕλην παρετιθέμεθα· τὰ γὰρ στοιχεῖα αὐτὰ μόνον σημεῖα κοινὰ τῶν ὅρων εἴληπται οὐδὲν παρ' αὐτῶν συντελοῦντα εἰς τὸ ἢ συνακτικὴν δειχθῆναι τὴν συζυγίαν ἢ ἀσύνακτον. ὡς γὰρ ὁ γεωμέτρης ὑπὲρ σαφηνείας τῆς κατὰ τὴν διδασκαλίαν καταγραφὴν ποιεῖταί τινα καὶ λέγει

Despite the numerous oddities in those paragraphs—some of which my translation has glossed over—some things emerge clearly enough.

First, Alexander takes Aristotle to be talking about his use of letters in proving logical theses. Secondly, he thinks that there is a parallel between Aristotle's use of letters and the geometers' use of diagrams. Thirdly, he supposes that the letters stand in no logical relations to one another, and hence cannot be responsible for the validity of any inference. Fourthly, he suggests that it is for that reason that letters may be used to prove universal logical theorems.

The first point is surely a wayward interpretation of what Aristotle says in the passage under scrutiny. Nonetheless, Alexander may be offering a correct interpretation of Aristotle's use of letters, even if he attaches the interpretation to an impertinent text. In any event, it is Alexander's interpretation which concerns me at the moment.

The second point may seem equally wayward: surely the comparison at which Aristotle hints ought to be not between the logician's use of letters and the geometer's use of diagrams but rather between the logician's use of letters

ἔστω ποδιαία ἥδε ἢ ἔστω εὐθεῖα ἥδε οὔτε τὴν ποδιαίαν ποδιαίαν λαμβάνων οὔτε τὴν εὐθεῖαν εὐθεῖαν, οὐδὲ τοῖς καταγεγραμμένοις προσχρώμενος δείκνυσιν αὐτῷ τὸ προκείμενον, ἀλλὰ τούτοις σημείοις χρῆται οὐδὲν συντελοῦσιν οὐδὲ συνεισφέρουσι πρὸς τὸ δεικνύμενον (οὐδὲν γὰρ ἔλαττον καὶ μὴ καταγράψας ταύτας μηδὲ προσχρησάμενος αὐταῖς δύναται δεῖξαι τὸ προκείμενον, ἀλλ᾽ ὑπὲρ τοῦ εὖ παρακολουθῆσαι ἐν τοῖς λεγομένοις λαμβάνει ταῦτα ἵν᾽ ἔχουσά πως ἡ διάνοια ἐπαναπαύεσθαι τούτοις ῥᾷον παρακολουθῇ), οὕτως καὶ ἡμεῖς τῶν στοιχείων τὴν ἔκθεσιν πεποιήμεθα οὐδὲν ἡμῖν εἰς τὰ δεικνύμενα παρ᾽ αὐτῶν συνεισφερόντων. οὐ γὰρ παρὰ τὸ τὸ μὲν Α αὐτῶν εἶναι τὸ δὲ Β ἢ Γ ἡ συναγωγή· τὸ γὰρ αὐτὸ γίνεται, κἂν ἄλλοις ἀντὶ τούτων χρησώμεθα.

ὃ οὐ γίνεται ἐπὶ τοῦ πᾶς ἄνθρωπος ζῷον, πᾶν γελαστικὸν ζῷον· ἐκ γὰρ τούτων συνάγεσθαι δοκεῖ τὸ πάντα ἄνθρωπον γελαστικὸν εἶναι. ἀλλὰ τοῦτο διὰ τὴν τῶν εἰλημμένων ὅρων σχέσιν ποιάν πρὸς ἀλλήλους, οὐ διὰ τὸ σχῆμα· ἄλλων γὰρ ὅρων ἐν τῇ τοιαύτῃ συζυγίᾳ ληφθέντων οὐδὲν συνάγεται, ὥσπερ ἐπὶ τῶν πᾶς ἄνθρωπος ζῷον, πᾶς ἵππος ζῷον. ἐπὶ δὲ τῆς τῶν στοιχείων ἐκθέσεως οὐχ οὕτως· ὃ ἔδειξε καὶ αὐτὸς ἄλλοτε ἄλλοις χρησάμενος καθ᾽ ἕκαστον σχῆμα. οὐ γὰρ ἔστιν ἐπὶ τῶν στοιχείων ἵνα τὸ μὲν ὡς ὅλον τὸ δ᾽ ὡς μέρος ταῦτα ἵν᾽ ἔχῃ τὸ ἔμψυχον καὶ τὸ ζῷον· τὸ μὲν γὰρ ὡς ὅλον ἐστίν (ἐπὶ πλέον γὰρ καὶ καθόλου τὸ ἔμψυχον), τὸ δ᾽ ὡς μέρος. καὶ πάλιν ἂν ἄλλο τι πρὸς τοῦτο τὸ ζῷον ὃ ἦν ὡς μέρος εἰλημμένον ἐν τῇ πρώτῃ προτάσει ὡς μέρος πρὸς ὅλον ληφθῇ, οἷον ὁ ἄνθρωπος (μέρος γὰρ τοῦ ζῴου, ὃ ἦν μέρος τοῦ ἐμψύχου), ἐκ τῶν οὕτως ἐχόντων, τοῦτ᾽ ἔστιν ὡς τὸν μὲν κατηγορεῖσθαι τὸν δὲ ὑποκεῖσθαι τῶν ὅρων ἐν ταῖς προτάσεσιν, αἱ δείξεις. ἐξ οὐδενὸς γὰρ τῶν ἃ μὴ ἔχει πρὸς ἄλληλα οἰκειότητα οἷόν τέ τι δειχθῆναι συναγόμενον συλλογιστικῶς. τὰ δὲ στοιχεῖα οὐδεμίαν τοιαύτην ἔχει σχέσιν πρὸς ἄλληλα. οὔκουν παρὰ ταῦτα ἢ συμβαίνει τι ἢ οὐ συμβαίνει. διὸ καὶ ἐπὶ τοιούτων αἱ δείξεις, ὃ οὐκέτ᾽ ἐνῆν λέγειν εἰ ἐπὶ ὕλης ἡμῖν ἐφ᾽ ὧν χρώμεθα τοῖς συλλογισμοῖς αἱ δείξεις ἐγίνοντο· παρὰ γὰρ τὴν ταύτης διαφορὰν πολλάκις συνακτικόν τι φαίνεται οὐκ ὂν τοιοῦτον.

ὥστ᾽ οὐδὲ γίνεται συλλογισμός· ὅτι αἱ ἐπὶ τῶν τοιούτων στοιχείων δείξεις ὑπογραφαὶ συλλογιστικῶν εἰσι τρόπων, οὐ μὴν ἤδη συλλογισμοί, ἐδήλωσεν· ὁ γὰρ συλλογισμὸς μετὰ τῆς ὕλης ἐφ᾽ ἧς τι δείκνυται.

and the geometer's use of letters? No doubt it ought to be; but Alexander's comparison is constrained by Aristotle's text; and in fact Alexander indicates two points of comparison. First, the logical letters, like the geometrical diagrams, are not essential to the proofs: they are feather-bedding, they offer the tired intellect something to repose on. Euclid does not need his diagrams, and his proofs are not about the diagrams. Aristotle does not need his letters. Secondly, the letters and the diagrams introduce—or rather, might introduce—falsities into the presentation of the proofs; but those falsities do not infect the proofs themselves—the proofs do not trade on the falsities. When a geometer says something like 'Let the line AB be a foot long', it is absurd—according to Alexander—to object that in fact the line is not a foot long. For whether or not it is in fact a foot long is of no relevance to the proof. The geometer does not use the line for its foot length. In the same way—Alexander insinuates—when Aristotle says 'Let A be said of every B and of no C', it is absurd to object that in fact A is not so said of B and C. For whether or not in fact things are so is of no relevance for the proof. The logician does not use the actual relations which hold among his terms.

At least, that appears to be one of the things which Alexander must have had in mind in making his second point. But it is scarcely consistent with the third point, according to which the logical letters in fact stand in no relation to one another. Is A really said of every B, as Aristotle seems to assert? No, of course not—the letters 'A' and 'B' do not stand in any pertinent relation to one another, they are not items which could in principle stand in a predicative relation to one another. And that very fact constitutes one aspect of their utility. If a syllogistic form is presented by way of a concrete argument—by a paradigm, as we might say—then you might wonder if its validity did not depend upon the relations which hold among its concrete terms. If a syllogistic form is presented schematically, by way of letters, then you cannot coherently entertain such a suspicion.

The problem is this: Alexander appears to suggest, on the one hand, that Aristotle's letters mean nothing at all—that they are empty signs; and on the other hand, that the letters have a sense but that their sense is not used in the arguments in which they appear. It is hard to reconcile those two hands. In addition, it is hard to see how exactly either of them might bear upon the fourth of the four points—the claim that the letters serve to introduce generality into the proofs.

A passage in Boethius' essay *On Predicative Syllogisms*—which was firmly based upon if not literally translated from a Greek original—brings out the same difficulty. (The Latin in the only edition which I have seen is in parts ungrammatical, and I have tacitly emended it; but I cannot say that I have understood all those parts which are grammatically impeccable.)

> Whenever we speak in such a way as to set down letters instead of terms, we do so for the sake of brevity and concision. That which we want to show universally, we show by means of letters. For with terms it is perhaps inevitable that some falsity will slip in. But with letters we are never deceived. That is why we use letters for the purpose, as though we were setting down terms. But in the letters themselves no truth and no falsity may be found unless the collocation of the terms is fixed and sound. So whenever we want to show that one thing is predicated of all another, we set it out thus: let the first term be A and the second B and let A be predicated of every B. But let this be so construed as if we have set down A for animal and B for man.
>
> (*syll cat* 810CD)[65]

If you use concrete terms, then you may be misled into taking something to hold universally when in fact it holds only for a limited number of terms. If you use letters, you avoid the danger. Letters inhibit the intrusion of falsity. They do not do so because they introduce nothing but truth: they do so because they introduce neither falsity nor truth. Since 'A holds of every B' is neither false nor true, it cannot introduce falsity into an argument.

That much seems clear in the text, and it corresponds to Alexander's claim that letters stand in no pertinent relations to one another. But then Boethius adds that letters will not introduce truth and falsity unless there is a proper combination of terms. Yet if letters, in themselves, exclude both falsity and truth, then how can a proper combination of them introduce a truth? And if it can introduce a truth, then why cannot it equally introduce a falsity? Finally, Boethius says that when we say 'A holds of every B' we should construe that as though it were 'Animal holds of every man'. But if that is how we should understand 'A holds of every B', then the use of letters is not, after all, a way of escaping whatever dangers concrete terms may threaten—it is a way of hiding the fact that you are courting those dangers.

---

[65] *quotienscumque ita dicimus ut litteras pro terminis disponamus, pro brevitate hoc et compendio facimus. id quod demonstrare volumus universaliter, per litteras demonstramus. nam fortasse in terminis aliquid falsum ingerendum necesse sit: in litteris vero numquam fallimur, quoniam ad hoc utimur litteris quasi terminos poneremus. in litteris vero ipsis, nisi terminorum coniunctio per se firma valensque fuerit, neque veritas neque falsitas reperietur. quotiens igitur aliud de alio omni praedicari volumus ostendere, sic ponimus: sit primus terminus A, secundus B, et praedicetur A de omni B. hoc autem ita accipito tamquam si posuerimus A animal, B hominem.*

Take again the Aristotelian sentence which I quoted a few pages ago:

If B holds of every A and of no C, A holds of none of the Cs.

(APst 82b14–15)

That is supposed to express something universal—and to express a universal truth. But the letters it contains apparently designate nothing and apparently have no sense; and in that case the sentence in which they feature has no sense—and *a fortiori* no truth-value. It is not a sentence at all, but a schema for a sentence. So there is a dilemma: express the point in terms of concrete propositions and you will not say anything universal; chip out the concrete and you will not say anything at all. The dilemma underlies the incoherence which appears to infect the halting explanations which Alexander and Boethius propose for Aristotle's use of syllogistic letters.

Or is there really a dilemma? When an algebraist writes

$$x + y = y + x,$$

he says something true and universal, and he does so despite the fact that his 'x' and his 'y' designate nothing and have no sense of their own. He does so, we generally think, inasmuch as his letters are what the logicians call variables, and insofar as a standing convention requires his formula to be understood as though it were universally quantified. In other words, his formula is a short form of the convenient barbarism:

For any x and any y, $x + y = y + x$.

What that barbarism expresses is peculiarly difficult to express in decent English—that is why the barbarism is a boon. But it is somehow clear what the barbarism means, clear that it is a genuine sentence, and clear that it expresses a truth.

Why not say the same for Aristotle's syllogistical letters? Scholars have done so. Thus when Aristotle writes

If B holds of every A and of no C, A holds of none of the Cs,

it has been urged that we should take the letters to be variables and the sentence to carry, implicitly, a trio of universal quantifiers. In other words, it is an abbreviated version of the barbarism:

For any A, B, and C: if B holds of every A and of no C, then A holds of no C.

It is difficult to express that proposition in intelligible English—or in intelligible Greek. But it is clear what it means, and it is clear that what it says is true. And there is no mystery about how the sentence manages to say something universal in scope.

Forms of Argument

In many passages in the *Analytics* the right universal truths are found
in the text once the letters are construed as variables and read with a tacit
quantifier. True, the notion of a variable (so far as I know) is not found in
ancient logic before the sixth century; and as for Aristotle, he never produces
any sentences like the barbarous 'For any A, B and C ...'. But that is only
to say that Aristotle did not trouble to explain—perhaps he was not able to
explain—his own use of syllogistic letters.

Should we then conclude that the letters which Aristotle uses so abundantly
in his *Analytics* sometimes stand in for determinate predicates and sometimes
function as variables? Perhaps; but there are also numerous texts—and
important and central texts—in which the Greek letters appear to be neither
determinate nor variable. Here is an example:

> In the second figure, if the negative premiss is necessary, the conclusion too will be
> necessary; but if the affirmative, the conclusion will not be necessary. First, let the
> negative be necessary, and let A be possible for no B, and let it hold simply of C.
> Since the negative converts, B is possible for no A. But A holds of every C, so that B
> is possible for no C—for C is under A.
>
> (APr 30b7–13)⁶⁶

'Let A be possible for no B': what is the status of the letters in that sentence?
Does 'A' perhaps mean 'planets'? or 'plants'? or 'planes'? Aristotle does not
tell us—and is that not because there is nothing to tell? Surely the letters do
not here stand for concrete predicate expressions? But neither can they be
construed as variables which carry unspoken universal quantifiers. After all,
Aristotle does not mean:

For any A and any B, let A be possible for no B.
His proof does not depend on any such bizarre supposition. Nor, even more
evidently, when he says 'A holds of every C' does he mean to affirm that
everything holds of everything.

What is true of that text is true of all the texts in which Aristotle proves
the validity of a syllogistic form.

---

66 ἐπὶ δὲ τοῦ δευτέρου σχήματος, εἰ μὲν ἡ στερητικὴ πρότασίς ἐστιν ἀναγκαία, καὶ τὸ
συμπέρασμα ἔσται ἀναγκαῖον, εἰ δ᾽ ἡ κατηγορική, οὐκ ἀναγκαῖον. ἔστω γὰρ πρῶτον ἡ
στερητικὴ ἀναγκαία, καὶ τὸ Α τῷ μὲν Β μηδενὶ ἐνδεχέσθω, τῷ δὲ Γ ὑπαρχέτω μόνον. ἐπεὶ
οὖν ἀντιστρέφει τὸ στερητικόν, οὐδὲ τὸ Β τῷ Α οὐδενὶ ἐνδέχεται· τὸ δὲ Α παντὶ τῷ Γ ὑπάρχει,
ὥστ᾽ οὐδενὶ τῷ Γ τὸ Β ἐνδέχεται· τὸ γὰρ Γ ὑπὸ τὸ Α ἐστίν.

Perhaps, nevertheless, the letters can be taken as variables provided that the tacit quantifiers are given the broadest possible scope? We should not supply 'For any A, B, C, ...' in front of each sentence of the passage I have just quoted: rather, it should be supplied at the beginning of the whole paragraph, its scope should extend to the end of the argument. Something of that sort can indeed be done. But in order to do it successfully you must prepare the ground in one of two ways: either you must recast Aristotle's text in such a way that the sequence of sentences with which he expresses his proofs is replaced by a single complex sentence; or else you must develop a new way with quantifiers which allows them to govern units of discourse of more than one sentence in length.

You must do something like that, and you could do something like that. But why bother? After all, Aristotle's proofs—for example, the proof of Darapti which I set down a few pages ago—seem to be logically respectable in the form in which he sets them out. So ought there not to be some other way of taking his letters?

GEOMETRICAL LETTERS

There are in principle several other ways of construing Aristotle's logical letters; but the way which will first come into the mind of any commentator on Aristotle takes its inspiration from geometry. Aristotle knew his geometry; it is clear that he took some of his logical terminology from the geometers; and—as I have already suggested—it is highly plausible to think that he decided to use letters in his syllogistic because he knew how useful letters were in geometry. And of course, even if that biographical conjecture is mistaken, the geometrical use of letters might nevertheless illuminate the logical use.

There are, to be sure, some differences between Aristotelian letters and geometrical letters. For example, when Euclid writes 'τὸ A' or 'the A', that is elliptical: it stands for 'τὸ A σημεῖον' or 'the point A'. In the same way 'ἡ AB' or 'the AB' is short for 'ἡ AB γραμμή' or 'the line AB'. And so on. As often as not, the noun to which the definite article belongs will be explicit in the text. When Aristotle writes 'the A', there is no noun to be supplied. But such differences are superficial—at any rate, I shall now glance at Euclid's use of letters.

Doubtless, the Greek geometers used their letters in more ways than one; but one way is particularly striking. Here is a simple example:

On the given finite straight line, to construct an equilateral triangle.—Let the given finite straight line be AB. Then we must construct an equilateral triangle on AB. Let a circle ABC have been drawn, with centre A and radius AB, and again let a circle ACE have been drawn, with centre B and radius BA ...

(Euclid, I i)[67]

Here the individual letters pick out geometrical points. Pairs of letters pick out lines, namely the lines bounded by the two points which the letters pick out. And so on. Aristotle too uses both individual letters and groups of letters. Usually, an individual Aristotelian letter will pick out a term, whereas a pair of letters will pick out a proposition; and the formula 'AB' will normally pick out a proposition the terms of which are indicated by 'A' and 'B'.

Euclid introduces his letters without any explanation. So far as I know, his ancient commentators do not discuss them—nor suggest that there is anything about them which needs discussion. But they understood what was going on. Here is Proclus:

They usually make the conclusion in a certain fashion double—for having shown it for the given case they also infer it as a universal, running up from the particular conclusion to the universal. For because they do not make use of the peculiarities of the subjects but draw the angle or the straight line merely in order to put the given item before our eyes, they think that the same thing which was concluded in that case has been concluded for every similar case. Hence they transfer to the universal so that we may realize that the conclusion is not particular, and they make the transfer with reason inasmuch as in the proof they make use of the items set out not as *these* items but as similar to the others. For it is not insofar as the angle has such and such a degree that I divide it in two but simply insofar as it is a rectilineal angle.

(*in Eucl* 207.4–18)[68]

Not everything is perfect in that paragraph; but the main lines are discernible—and in addition, it is evident that there is at least a superficial or

---

[67] ἐπὶ τῆς δοθείσης εὐθείας πεπερασμένης τρίγωνον ἰσόπλευρον συστήσασθαι. ἔστω ἡ δοθεῖσα εὐθεῖα πεπερασμένη ἡ ΑΒ. δεῖ δὴ ἐπὶ τῆς ΑΒ εὐθείας τρίγωνον ἰσόπλευρον συστήσασθαι. κέντρῳ μὲν τῷ Α διαστήματι δὲ τῷ ΑΒ κύκλος γεγράφθω ὁ ΒΓΔ, καὶ πάλιν κέντρῳ μὲν τῷ Β διαστήματι δὲ τῷ ΒΑ κύκλος γεγράφθω ὁ ΑΓΕ.

[68] τό γε μὴν συμπέρασμα διπλοῦν εἰώθασι ποιεῖσθαί τινα τρόπον· καὶ γὰρ ὡς ἐπὶ τοῦ δεδομένου δείξαντες καὶ ὡς καθόλου συνάγουσιν ἀνατρέχοντες ἀπὸ τοῦ μερικοῦ συμπεράσματος ἐπὶ τὸ καθόλου. διότι γὰρ οὐ προσχρῶνται τῇ ἰδιότητι τῶν ὑποκειμένων, ἀλλὰ πρὸ ὀμμάτων ποιούμενοι τὸ δεδομένον γράφουσι τὴν γωνίαν ἢ τὴν εὐθεῖαν, ταὐτὸν ἡγοῦνται τὸ ἐπὶ ταύτης συναγόμενον καὶ ἐπὶ τοῦ ὁμοίου συμπεπεράνθαι παντός. μεταβαίνουσι μὲν οὖν

terminological similarity between what Proclus said there about geometry and what Alexander said about logic in the long passage which I quoted earlier.

Proclus says this: Euclid will generally first prove a conclusion about the particular lines or angles which he has set out; he will then infer the appropriate universal proposition; and he will be justified in doing so inasmuch as his proof does not depend on any peculiar features of the particular items with which it is concerned.

In systems of natural deduction, as contemporary logicians call it, there is generally a rule of universal generalization or universal introduction which looks something like this:

Given an argument concluding to 'F(a)' on the base of premisses $P_1, P_2, \ldots$, P_n, infer 'For any x, F(x)', on the basis of the same premisses—provided that the name 'a' occurs neither in 'F' nor in any P_i.

The main clause in that rule corresponds to the 'transfer' from particular to universal which Proclus describes—given a proof that some individual item is thus-and-so, we may infer that everything is thus-and-so; given a proof that F(a), we may infer that F(everything). The proviso in the rule corresponds to the idea that the geometers' proofs 'do not make use of the items set out as *those* items'. Proclus describes, in an approximate fashion, a rule of universal generalization; and Euclid argued in accordance with such a rule.

The rule makes appeal to individuals; for when Proclus speaks of particulars he means 'individual' by 'particular'. That is to say, he supposes that 'the items set out' are individual geometrical objects—lines and circles and so on. Moreover, he takes the Greek letters to designate or introduce these objects: the formula 'AB' in Euclid ɪ i, for example, is a singular term which designates an individual line.

That seems fine: you prove that a certain individual so-and-so has a given property; and because your proof does not at any point turn on the fact that it is this individual so-and-so you have chosen rather than another one, you advance a further step and infer that all so-and-sos have the property in question. So in the Euclidean proof, 'AB' designates an individual line. That is surely so—but then which individual line does it designate? The question

---

ἐπὶ τὸ καθόλου ἵνα μὴ μερικὸν ὑπολάβωμεν εἶναι τὸ συμπέρασμα. εὐλόγως δὲ μεταβαίνουσιν ἐπειδὴ τοῖς ἐκτεθεῖσιν οὐχ ᾗ ταῦτά ἐστιν ἀλλ᾽ ᾗ τοῖς ἄλλοις ὅμοια χρῶνται πρὸς τὴν ἀπόδειξιν. οὐ γὰρ ᾗ τοσήδε ἐστὶν ἡ ἐκκειμένη γωνία, ταύτῃ τὴν διχοτομίαν ποιοῦμαι, ἀλλ᾽ ᾗ μόνον εὐθύγραμμος.

receives no easy answer, and so should we not say that 'AB' designates no individual line in particular, but rather an arbitrary individual line?

In modern logic, the letters 'a', 'b', 'c', ... are often used—as I used 'a' a moment ago—as singular terms or terms which designate individuals. But they are usually taken to be a rather special sort of singular term: they are not genuine proper names but 'arbitrary names'. Some logicians urge that arbitrary names are names of arbitrary objects: 'a' does not designate Agatha or Arthur—it designates another sort of item altogether. Perhaps Euclid's 'AB' is like that? I hope not. For there are no arbitrary objects for arbitrary names to designate—no more than there are variable objects for variable names to name. In particular, there are no arbitrary lines for the name 'AB' to designate. If arbitrary names are names, or singular designating expressions, then they are names or designations of actual objects, of ordinary and determinate individuals. And the question, 'Which ordinary and determinate line does 'AB' designate?', will not go away.

If there are no arbitrary objects to designate, then why do our modern logicians use letters—'a', 'b', 'c', ... ? Why don't they use ordinary proper names or designating expressions? If 'a' is a name, then it is a name for some ordinary item. So why not use an ordinary name for the ordinary item—the name 'Aristotle', say? Well, why not? Pretend that, throughout your logic handbook, the letter 'a' is merely an abbreviation for 'Aristotle', 'b' for 'Boethius', 'c' for 'Cicero': what difference will that make? The answer is that it will make no difference at all; that is to say, an inference will be valid after your unorthodox interpretation of the letters if and only if it was valid before.

But surely—it will be said—there is some reason—beyond any reason which the advantages of brevity might bring—to make use of these letters. Even if, in principle, we might just as well use ordinary names in their stead, at least we must choose those ordinary names arbitrarily or at random. After all, if your individual is chosen with malice aforethought, then you can hardly be warranted in inferring from a singular proposition about it to a universal proposition about everything. The letters serve to indicate, or to remind, that the choice of individual is strictly arbitrary—and in that case, we may as well continue to call the things arbitrary names (on the understanding that that expression means not 'name of an arbitrary object' but 'arbitrarily chosen name of an object' or 'name of an arbitrarily chosen object').

But arbitrariness of choice is quite beside the logical point. You may pick your names out of a hat if you want to; but you may equally well choose your own particular favourites. I quite deliberately fixed on 'Aristotle', 'Boethius' and 'Cicero' a few moments ago: I didn't draw them from a hat or open my telephone book at random. But the fact that they were carefully selected rather than chosen by chance had no bearing whatsoever on the use to which they were put. If the designated objects are in fact selected at random, that does not in itself help the case at all.

Suppose that you pick a name at random out of a hat, and notice that in fact it is a name of Socrates. What a bit of luck, you think—and you go on to prove that your randomly selected individual must have a nasty inferiority complex—after all, he is snub-nosed. If you then make a universal generalization ('Everyone has an inferiority complex'), your generalization will be fallacious; and all the randomness in the world will not protect you from error. If, on the other hand, you pick Socrates after lengthy deliberation—and perhaps precisely because he is snub-nosed and you want to discriminate in favour of the nasally disadvantaged in logic if not in life—then nothing at all will go wrong—provided, of course, that in your proofs you do not invoke any feature which Socrates has and some of his mates lack. For what matters insofar as the universal generalization is concerned is not how the individual objects are chosen but how they are employed: whether the objects are called up at random or elected after the most punctilious examination, things will go well if and only if no appeal is made to any of their peculiarities or to any feature which they do not have in common with every other pertinent object.

So Euclid, as Proclus saw, designates individual objects, draws individual conclusions, and then universalizes. He draws a double conclusion: first, a singular proposition, 'F(a)'; and then a universal proposition 'F(everything)'. The second inference is legitimate not because **a** is an arbitrary individual, nor because **a** has been selected at random—it is legitimate insofar as the proof that F(**a**) does not depend on any fact about **a** which is not a fact about any other individual.

In Euclid i i, the expression 'AB' designates an individual finite straight line—a real straight line, not some ghostly or arbitrary item. If it is to function at all, it must designate some genuine line or other; and the fact that it designates a particular and determinate line does not in the least embarrass the generalization which will finally be made. Nevertheless, and again, which line does the expression designate? Why, the one which Euclid then proceeds to draw—on the sand or on the blackboard. No doubt; but which line is that? 'Surely it is the line which you see in front of you: as Proclus says, Euclid puts the given item in front of our eyes.' But that cannot be right; for you can't see geometrical lines, and the traces which you see in the sand or on the blackboard are not geometrical lines—they are pictures or portraits of geometrical lines. *Ceci n'est pas une ligne.* (If that sounds implausible, think of stereometrical diagrams: a drawing of a sphere cannot itself be a sphere. What goes for three-dimensional spheres goes for two-dimensional figures and one-dimensional lines.)

Then which line does Euclid first portray in i i? 'The line which he is constructing—after all, that is pretty well what he says.' But Euclid can no more construct or make lines than an arithmetician can construct or make numbers; and even if you think that he can make lines, by joining a couple of points together (whatever that operation might be), nevertheless he surely cannot make points—and it is points which are the primary objects of his naming. It is true that an Aristotelian philosopher might suggest that points exist potentially until they are actualized by the geometer: the geometer creates his points by thinking them—that is to say, he raises them from potentiality to actuality. But that Aristotelian notion is too bizarre to tarry over. 'Is there a mid-point on the line AB?'—'Not yet—wait till I start thinking about it ...'. Is that not absurd?

So which line is Euclid naming? Perhaps we can't tell? Perhaps he didn't know himself? After all, what matters is that he was designating some line or other—which one, as Proclus insists, does not in the least bit matter. Yet if we don't know which line he is talking about, how can we understand what he is saying? And if he himself didn't know which line he was talking about, why suppose that he was talking about any line at all?

Think of the party trick in which someone invites you to choose a number, multiply it by 5, subtract 3, square the result, ... He then tells you that you've got 999. Amazing. Suppose he conducts the game like this: 'Let's all think of a number, any number we like, between 1 and 1,000. Pick your number carefully. I've picked one of my own—I won't tell you what it is, but I'll call it 'N' for convenience. You can call yours 'M', or 'K', or 'Ned Kelly'. Now let's multiply our numbers by 5 ...'. The thing drags on. And at the end, he says: 'Finally, let's see what number we've each got: mine is 999.' And so, of course, is everyone else's. In effect, he has calculated that $f(N) = 999$; and you have calculated that $f(M) = 999$, or that $f(K) = 999$, or that $f(Ned Kelly) = 999$. And we may thence infer that for any number n between 1 and 1,000, $f(n) = 999$.

Now imagine that, a few years later, we ask our ex M.C. which number he had in mind himself, which number 'N' in fact designated. 'It doesn't in the least matter', he replies. — 'I know it doesn't matter: I ask out of idle curiosity.'—'I've quite forgotten.'—'Oh dear: then how can you still be sure that your answer was 999?' That last question is misconceived. It is necessary that 'N' designates some number; for otherwise sentences of the form 'f(N) = n' would have no sense and no truth-value. It is unnecessary to know—or to specify—what item 'N' designates in order to know the truth-value of 'f(N) = n'. I may know that that sentence is true without understanding what it means. (Salvation, Cardinal Newman thought, depends upon such things.)

So the letters in the game must designate something. But there is no need to know what they designate. Yet is it not quite absurd? Well, consider the following proof:

$\mathbf{a}^3 = \mathbf{a}.\mathbf{b}$　　　　　　hypothesis
Therefore $\mathbf{a}^3/\mathbf{a} = \mathbf{b}$
Therefore $\mathbf{a}^2 = \mathbf{b}$
Therefore if $\mathbf{a}^3 = \mathbf{a}.\mathbf{b}$, then $\mathbf{a}^2 = \mathbf{b}$
Therefore for any x and y, if $x^3 = x.y$, then $x^2 = y$

That is an ordinary hypothetical proof, which—in the manner of Euclid—first shows something about particulars and then transfers to the universal. What is the status of the hypothesis? The answer to that question depends, in part, on how we construe the letters 'a' and 'b'. Presumably each letter must designate a number; but if they designate numbers, which numbers do they designate? Perhaps 'a' designates 7 and 'b' designates 43? But who would ever hypothesize that $7^3 = 7 \times 43$? Perhaps 'a' designates 2 and 'b' designates 4? That is better—but it is a cheat; for the hypothesis has been formed in such a way as to guarantee its truth.

That line of thought—which could perhaps be put more persuasively—is misguided. The hypothesis must have a truth-value. To be sure, a hypothesis is not an assertion: in the Stoic jargon, a hypothetical is not the same as an assertible. But just as an oath is not an assertion and yet what I swear is an assertible (for I swear that such-and-such, and it can be asserted that such-and-such), in the same way a hypothesis is not an assertion and yet what I hypothesize is an assertible (for I hypothesize that such-and-such and it can be asserted that such-and-such). Hence what I hypothesize has a truth-value. Hence any designating expression which the hypothesis contains must designate some item or other. And if we suppose that, in the case before us, the items in question are the natural numbers, then 'a' and 'b' must designate some natural numbers or other.

What numbers they designate does not in the least matter. Let 'a' designate 7 and 'b' 43, if you like. On that understanding of the hypothesis—as on any other—the argument is impeccable.

Perhaps that works for numbers. But does it also work for geometrical items—and hence for the geometrical use of letters which, according to the present conjecture, may explain Aristotle's use of letters in his syllogistic? Numbers and geometrical objects differ in several fundamental ways—and there appears to be at least one pertinent difference between them. 'Think of a number.'—'O.K.'—'Which number are you thinking of?' If there is no answer to that question, then you are not thinking of a number. If you are thinking of a number, then there is a number of which you are thinking. 'Draw a straight line.'—'O.K.'—'Which line have you drawn?'. The question is bizarre; for it seems to have no intelligible answer. (It is no use saying '*That* line', pointing to the diagram; for the question was precisely 'Which line is *that*?') And certainly you do not need to be able to answer the question in order for it to be true that you have drawn a line.

However that may be, no ancient philosopher would have been embarrassed by the question: Which line? Proclus thought that Euclid makes reference to individual geometrical points and lines and figures, and that Euclid's diagrams are portraits of such entities. We do not perceive the entities; but we can grasp them by thought—by the sort of thought which grasps individual intelligible objects in the way in which perception grasps individual perceptible objects. An orthodox Aristotelian, too, would have taken Euclid to be designating real points and lines and figures—namely, the points and lines and figures which his marks in the sand roughly trace out. For even if his diagrams are not themselves geometrical items but representations of geometrical items, the items represented are physically close to their representations. Geometrical items, after all, are nothing but spatial items, so that a drawing of a circle, say, or of a triangle may in principle follow—roughly, of course—the outline of the circle or the triangle which it portrays.

LOGICAL LETTERS

Should we then suppose that the Greek letters in Aristotle's syllogistic, like the Greek letters in Euclid's geometry, typically have a particular and determinate meaning? More precisely, should we suppose that, just as in natural deduction the sign 'a' may be thought to designate, say, Aristotle, and just as in Euclidean geometry the sign 'AB' is supposed to designate *that* individual line, so too and in the same way the letters which Aristotle uses in expounding his syllogistic—the letters which he uses in the schematic presentation of syllogisms—in fact represent or specify particular predicative terms? That Aristotle's 'A' is the predicate 'animal', his 'B' is 'buffalo', and so on?

The hypothesis perhaps deserves a rather more pedantic formulation. The question is: How are we to construe the letter 'A' in such formulas as 'the A' or 'the item on which the A is'. The hypothesis is that 'the A' is the name of an expression, and in particular of a predicate—a concrete and determinate predicate of course (since there are no others). The formula

The item on which A is holds of ...

is exactly on a par with

The item of which 'aardvark' is true holds of ...

Just as 'the item of which 'aardvark' is true' designates the aardvark, so 'the item on which the A is' designates whatever it is that the A is true of. That is the hypothesis. But so expressed it is a mouthful; and there is no harm in expressing it sloppily: 'Aristotle's logical letters, in their central and characteristic use, are concrete and determinate predicate expressions.'

The hypothesis has at least one advantage: it makes for a unified interpretation of the letters in the *Analytics*. Certainly, those letters sometimes stand in for determinate predicates, sometimes function as concrete terms. So let them always stand in for concrete predicates—even if, most often, there are no concrete predicates for which they stand in. 'What did Aristotle mean by 'the A' here?'—'Who knows?'—'But then what does 'the A' mean here?'—'Whatever you like it to mean.' In the early pages of his *Begriffsschrift* Frege makes use of Greek capital letters. They represent judgeable contents, or (roughly speaking) assertibles. When a capital Greek letter first appears, Frege tells us what it means—it is a shortened form of a particular sentence. Later, he does not say what the letters mean; and he remarks in a footnote that where he doesn't gloss a letter we may give it whatever sense we please. The Greek letters must always have a sense. For if they did not have a sense—in particular, if they did not have a judgeable content—then the formulas in which they appear would be ill-formed. But what sense they have does not in the least matter.

The paragraph from Boethius' essay on *Predicative Syllogisms* which I cited a little while ago suggests such a Fregean interpretation of the syllogistical letters;

for Boethius says that when we write 'A' and 'B' we should understand those letters to mean 'animal' and 'man'. A passage in Philoponus' commentary on the *Prior Analytics* (it is the continuation of a paragraph which I have already quoted) may perhaps carry the same suggestion:

> A universal thesis is refuted by even a single example, as I have already said; but it is established either by going through all the particulars, which is infinite and impossible, or by the warrant of a universal rule. That is what Aristotle does now by means of letters, giving to each of us, as I said, full liberty in their use so that we may supply terms of whatever matter we wish instead of the letters. 'Now if A holds of no B, B does not hold of any A'. If we take winged instead of 'A' and man instead of 'B', we shall find that just as winged holds of no man, so conversely no man holds of winged.
>
> (*in APr* 47.1–10)[69]

Aristotle proves conversions by means of universal rules. The universal rules rely upon the use of letters. The letters supply the desired universality insofar as 'we have full liberty in their use so that we may supply terms of whatever matter we wish': we may take Aristotle's 'A' to mean 'animal' or 'artichoke' or 'armillary sphere'—for although the letter 'A' must mean something or other, and hence must mean something or other in particular, what it means is quite up to us. And what guarantees the universality of Aristotle's proofs is precisely the fact that the sense of the letters is up to us, that we may saddle them with any of an infinity of senses.

Or is that what Philoponus means to say? A different and more down-to-earth interpretation construes him as saying that Aristotle proves the conversions universally, that he does so by using letters, and that since the conversions are universally proved, you may apply them to any particular case you like simply by replacing Aristotle's letters with the concrete terms of your choice. In that case, Philoponus gives no account at all of the letters themselves.

The text is, I think, indeterminate between those two interpretations. But I suspect that the latter and less exciting interpretation is the more probable. As

---

[69] τὸν μὲν γὰρ καθόλου λόγον ἐλέγχει μὲν καὶ ἓν παράδειγμα, ὡς ἤδη εἴρηται, κατασκευάζει δὲ ἢ ἡ διὰ πάντων τῶν κατὰ μέρος διέξοδος, ὅπερ ἐστὶν ἄπειρον καὶ ἀδύνατον, ἢ ἡ διὰ καθολικοῦ κανόνος πίστις· ὅπερ ποιεῖ νῦν διὰ τῶν στοιχείων διδοὺς ἑκάστῳ, ὥσπερ εἴρηται, ἐπ' ἐξουσίας χρῆσθαι καὶ ὑποβάλλειν ἀντὶ τῶν στοιχείων οἵας ἂν βούληται ὕλης ὅρους. εἰ οὖν μηδενὶ τῶν Β τὸ Α ὑπάρξει, οὐδὲ τῶν Α οὐδενὶ ὑπάρξει τὸ Β· εἰ γὰρ ἀντὶ μὲν τοῦ Α λάβωμεν πτηνόν, ἀντὶ δὲ τοῦ Β ἄνθρωπον, εὑρήσομεν ὅτι ὥσπερ τὸ πτηνὸν οὐδενὶ ἀνθρώπῳ ὑπάρχει, οὕτως ἔμπαλιν οὐδεὶς ἄνθρωπος πτηνῷ ὑπάρχει.

for Boethius, I have already described that passage as muddled, and muddled it surely is.

Nonetheless, it is taken from Aristotle. For Boethius' mind is evidently on the following sentences, which come at the end of Aristotle's presentation of the non-modal conversions:

If A does not hold of some B, it is not necessary that B too does not hold of some A. For example, if B is animal and A man—for man does not hold of every animal, but animal holds of every man.

(*APr* 25a22–26)[70]

'Suppose that A does not hold of some B.'—'What on earth am I being invited to suppose?'—'Well, take it that—for example—'A' means 'man' and 'B' 'animal'.' Or again: 'Suppose that that on which A is does not hold of some of that on which B is.'—'But what is A on and what is B on?'—'Oh, it doesn't matter—let's say that A is on man and B on animal.'

That account of the syllogistic letters works rather well in many of those Aristotelian texts where the letters can scarcely function as variables and yet are not presented as stand-ins for given predicate expressions. And it also works rather well in those passages which seem to invite an interpretation in terms of variables.

Take, again, the first appearance of the syllogistic letters in the *Prior Analytics*:

When three terms are so related to one another that the last is in the middle as in a whole and the middle either is or is not in the first as in a whole, it is necessary that there is a syllogism of the extremes ... For if A of every B and B of every C, it is necessary that A is predicated of every C. ... Similarly, if A of no B and B of every C, that A will hold of no C.

(*APr* 25b32–26a2)

I cited the passage in an earlier context, claiming that the last couple of sentences implicitly suggest schematic representations of the two syllogistic forms, Barbara and Celarent, for which the first sentence provides the circum-scriptions. And so they do. But Aristotle does not simply lay the schematic sentences alongside the circumscriptions: they are linked to the circumscrip-tions by the word 'for'. In that case, they ought somehow to explain or justify

---

[70] εἰ δέ γε τὸ Α τινὶ τῷ Β μὴ ὑπάρχει, οὐκ ἀνάγκη καὶ τὸ Β τινὶ τῷ Α μὴ ὑπάρχειν, οἷον εἰ τὸ μὲν Β ἐστὶ ζῷον, τὸ δὲ Α ἄνθρωπος· ἄνθρωπος μὲν γὰρ οὐ παντὶ ζῴῳ, ζῷον δὲ παντὶ ἀνθρώπῳ ὑπάρχει.

or otherwise illuminatingly comment upon what Aristotle has just said. But what exactly is the nature of the comment?

If the letters are variables, then the schematic sentences set out or explain in a clearer or more determinate fashion what the circumscriptions have imperfectly indicated. Thus interpreted, the text paraphrases as follows: 'If you've got a first figure conjugation with two universal affirmatives, then there is always a conclusion to be inferred—I mean that, for any triad of terms A, B, C, first, if A holds of every B and B of every C, then A must hold of every C; and secondly, if A holds of no B and B of every C, then A must hold of no C.' The circumscription does not say what syllogisms are there for the picking: the schematization fills out the gap.

That, it must be allowed, is a reasonable way to read the text. After all the circumscriptions are in fact inadequate to specify a pair of syllogistic forms, and the schematic sentences do in fact succeed in making the necessary specifications. Nonetheless, there is something odd about the interpretation—quite apart from the general considerations which tell against finding variables in Aristotle. For it invites us to imagine that Aristotle first gave circumscriptions of Barbara and Celarent, that he then saw that they were inadequate, and that he decided to make up for their inadequacies by using schematic letters. Why didn't he simply repair the circumscription? After all, that is readily done. Surely he must have had something else in mind when he wheeled on his Greek letters?

Suppose, then, that we take the letters to be predicates: just as the 'a' of natural deduction names Anaximander or Anaximenes or Zeno or what you will, so the 'A' of Aristotle's syllogistic means the same as 'aardvark' or 'albatross' or 'zebu' or what you will. The schematic sentences introduce concrete terms, and so hint at—without formulating—concrete syllogisms. Aristotle first describes (imperfectly) the two syllogistic forms Barbara and Celarent; and he then says something about a couple of triads of concrete predicates. He appeals to the concrete predicates in order to justify a universal claim. In other words, Aristotle, like Euclid, takes concrete terms and then transfers to the universal.

That seems to me to be the best way to take this particular passage from the *Prior Analytics*. (How Aristotle thinks that the universal validity of Barbara and Celarent are thereby established is another matter—and a matter for the next chapter.) And it seems to me to work quite well throughout most of the *Analytics*.

'Very pretty, Mr Barnes, but you may not call it Aristotle.' I am not at all sure that it is very pretty. But in any event, pretty or plain, I do not call it Aristotle. After all, it is an attempt to answer a question which Aristotle did not raise—or at any rate, a question which is not raised in the *Analytics*. The question is: What on earth can Aristotle's syllogistic letters mean (if they mean anything at all)? It is, I think, a good question. But it is not an essential question—that is to say, Aristotle could get on with his syllogistic without worrying about it. After all, you can do very well in logic without worrying much about what your sentences mean. Indeed, you can do pretty well in logic even if your sentences mean nothing at all.

5. The Science of Logic

LOGIC AS AN ARISTOTELIAN SCIENCE?

In his *Elements* Euclid first sets down certain primary truths or axioms and then deduces from them a number of secondary truths or theorems. Before ever Euclid wrote, Aristotle had described and commended that rigorous conception of a science for which the *Elements* was to provide a perennial paradigm. All sciences, in Aristotle's view, ought to be presented as axiomatic deductive systems—that is a main message of the *Posterior Analytics*. And the deductions which derive the theorems of any science from its axioms must be syllogisms—that is a main message of the *Prior Analytics*.

What, then, is the status of logic itself? More precisely, what is the status of syllogistic or of the theory of deduction? Surely it must be a science? Surely in that case it ought to be axiomatized *à la* Euclid? At any rate, surely Aristotle thought of his own syllogistic as a science?

Well, he never says in so many words that logic is a science. Indeed, he never uses the formula 'syllogistic science', nor any near equivalent. In the *Sophistici Elenchi*, it is true, you once find the expression 'syllogistic art' (*Soph El* 172a35). But what that means is indicated by a later remark:

We undertook to discover a certain syllogistic capacity ...

(*Soph El* 183a37–38)[1]

And that remark in turn refers back to the opening sentence of the *Topics*:

The aim of this study is to discover a method on the basis of which we shall be able to syllogize ...

(*Top* 100a18–19)[2]

So the phrase 'syllogistic art' refers to a capacity or a method and not to a science.

There is something comparable in the *Rhetoric*. In one passage Aristotle refers to 'the analytical science':

---

[1] προειλόμεθα μὲν οὖν εὑρεῖν δύναμίν τινα συλλογιστικήν ...
[2] ἡ μὲν πρόθεσις τῆς πραγματείας μέθοδον εὑρεῖν ἀφ᾽ ἧς δυνησόμεθα συλλογίζεσθαι ...

What we said earlier is indeed true: rhetoric is composed of the analytical science and of the political science concerned with character.

(*Rhet* 1359b8–11)[3]

Isn't 'the analytical science' the science purveyed in the *Analytics*? No doubt; but the phrase 'analytical science' is misleading; for the earlier passage to which Aristotle refers is this:

Rhetoric is as it were an offshoot of dialectic and of the study of character, which may properly be called politics. ... Neither of those studies is a science of the facts belonging to some determinate kind: rather, they are capacities for producing arguments.

(*Rhet* 1356a25–33)[4]

So 'analytical science' in the later passage is a variant on 'dialectical capacity'; and a dialectical capacity is contrasted with a genuine science.

The English nouns 'syllogistic' and 'dialectic'—and 'logic' too—began life as Greek feminine adjectives. The Greek adjectives are often used without any accompanying noun. Sometimes in Aristotle, and often in later texts, there is no need to supply a silent noun: 'ἡ συλλογιστική' and the like mean 'syllogistic' and the like. But if you insist on discovering an appropriate noun, you have a choice: 'ἐπιστήμη' or 'science' is one option; but there are also 'τέχνη' or 'art', 'μέθοδος' or 'method', 'δύναμις' or 'capacity', and 'πραγματεία' or 'discipline'. I should guess that 'μέθοδος' is the most likely supplement, and 'ἐπιστήμη' the least likely, in those Aristotelian passages in which a supplement can plausibly be made.

If Aristotle does not affirm that syllogistic is a science, neither does he expressly deny it. He shilly-shallies. His later followers made up their minds: logic is not a science. Alexander—with his eye on the passage from the *Rhetoric* which I have just cited—has this to say:

Each of the sciences is concerned with a determinate genus of things, and it shows and apprehends, by way of principles appropriate to that genus, those items which are appropriate to the genus and hold of it in their own right. These disciplines [i.e. dialectic and rhetoric] are not like that. For neither of the two has a single genus as

---

[3] ὅπερ γὰρ καὶ πρότερον εἰρηκότες τυγχάνομεν ἀληθές ἐστιν, ὅτι ἡ ῥητορικὴ σύγκειται μὲν ἔκ τε τῆς ἀναλυτικῆς ἐπιστήμης καὶ τῆς περὶ τὰ ἤθη πολιτικῆς ...

[4] συμβαίνει τὴν ῥητορικὴν οἷον παραφυές τι τῆς διαλεκτικῆς εἶναι καὶ τῆς περὶ τὰ ἤθη πραγματείας, ἣν δίκαιόν ἐστι προσαγορεύειν πολιτικήν. ... περὶ οὐδενὸς γὰρ ὡρισμένου οὐδετέρα αὐτῶν ἐστιν ἐπιστήμη πῶς ἔχει, ἀλλὰ δυνάμεις τινὲς τοῦ πορίσαι λόγους.

subject; and whatever they show, they do not show it by way of principles appropriate to and belonging to the essence of that about which they argue.

(in Top 3.28–4.2)[5]

Dialectic fails to be an Aristotelian science for two reasons: first, it is not concerned with a single class or genus of things—as geometry is concerned with points, or zoology with animals; and secondly, it does not argue on the basis of appropriate first principles—as arithmetic argues from the axioms concerning numbers, or botany from those concerning plants. The second reason does not apply to the probative use of syllogistic, or to 'apodeictic'; but the first reason holds of syllogistic in general, and there can be little doubt but that syllogistic, in Alexander's eyes, was not a science.

But Alexander's argument seems to be muddled. Allow that any science must be concerned with some determinate genus of items: then has syllogistic—or dialectic—some such unified subject-matter? Alexander argues that it has not, inasmuch as dialectical arguments—or syllogisms in general—may bear on any subject whatsoever. It is true—and Aristotle says—that dialectic or syllogistic is 'topic neutral', that it can be applied in any and every field of inquiry. But topic neutrality is not to the point. Syllogistic is the study of syllogisms; and so long as syllogisms form a unified and a determinate genus of items, syllogistic may perfectly well be an Aristotelian science. Arithmetic may be applied in calculations about any items whatsoever, and like logic it is topic neutral. Nonetheless, it has a subject-matter of its own—numbers, or units. Similarly for syllogistic.

But if Alexander's argument is bad, his conclusion might for all that be true; and true or false, it was, I suppose, an orthodoxy among the ancient Peripatetics.

THE STRUCTURE OF PREDICATIVE SYLLOGISTIC

Yet if syllogistic was not a science, there were certain close and evident resemblances between the structure of an ideal or Euclidean science and the structure of Aristotle's syllogistic.

---

[5] οὐ γὰρ ὡς τῶν ἐπιστημῶν ἑκάστη περί τι γένος ἀφωρισμένον οὖσα τὰ οἰκεῖα ἐκείνῳ τῷ γένει καὶ καθ' αὑτὰ ὑπάρχοντα δείκνυσί τε καὶ λαμβάνει διὰ τῶν οἰκείων ἀρχῶν ἐκείνῳ τῷ γένει, οὕτως καὶ αὗται. οὔτε γὰρ ἕν τι γένος τὸ ὑποκείμενον αὐτῶν ἑκατέρα, οὔτε περὶ οὗ ἂν τὸν λόγον ποιῶνται, διὰ τῶν οἰκείων ἐκείνῳ καὶ ἐν τῇ οὐσίᾳ ὄντων αὐτοῦ δεικνύουσιν ἃ δεικνύουσιν.

Chapters 4–6 of the first Book of the *Prior Analytics* contain the formal exposition of Aristotle's predicative syllogistic—more precisely, of his non-modal predicative syllogistic. There Aristotle distinguishes between 'perfect' (or 'complete') syllogisms on the one hand and 'imperfect' (or 'incomplete') syllogisms on the other. The perfect syllogisms are the four canonical syllogisms of the first figure: Barbara, Celarent, Darii, Ferio. All the syllogisms of the second and third figures are imperfect.

Aristotle shows that the imperfect syllogisms are valid, and he does so by reducing them to, or analysing them into, the perfect syllogisms. He sometimes explicitly uses the word 'prove' of such reductive or analytical manoeuvres; and it is in any event plain that he took himself to be proving the validity of the imperfect syllogisms. For example, the following passage is evidently offered as a proof of the validity of Darapti, the first mood of the third figure:

> When both P and R hold of every S, P will hold by necessity of some S. For since the affirmative converts, S will hold of some R, so that since P holds of every S and S of some R, it is necessary that P hold of some R—for a syllogism comes about through the first figure.
>
> (*APr* 28a18–22)[6]

That argument might be set out formally as follows:

(1) P holds of every S   premiss
(2) R holds of every S   premiss
Therefore (3) S holds of some R   2, conversion
Therefore (4) P holds of some S   1, 3, Darii

That is a proof of Darapti on the basis of Darii. Darapti, then, has the status of a theorem in Aristotelian syllogistic—or at least, a status comparable to the status of a theorem—and Darii looks set to have the status of an axiom.

That in itself is enough to establish the Euclidean, or quasi-Euclidean, structure of the syllogistic. But there are two further developments which should be mentioned. The first occurs in chapter 23 of the *Prior Analytics*, where Aristotle purports to establish that

---

6 ὅταν καὶ τὸ Π καὶ τὸ Ρ παντὶ τῷ Σ ὑπάρχῃ, ὅτι τινὶ τῷ Ρ τὸ Π ὑπάρξει ἐξ ἀνάγκης· ἐπεὶ γὰρ ἀντιστρέφει τὸ κατηγορικόν, ὑπάρξει τὸ Σ τινὶ τῷ Ρ· ὥστ᾽ ἐπεὶ τῷ μὲν Σ παντὶ τὸ Π, τῷ δὲ Ρ τινὶ τὸ Σ, ἀνάγκη τὸ Π τινὶ τῷ Ρ ὑπάρχειν· γίνεται γὰρ συλλογισμὸς διὰ τοῦ πρώτου σχήματος.

every proof and every syllogism necessarily comes about through the three figures we have described.

(APr 41b1–3)[7]

What exactly Aristotle proposes to establish and what (if anything) he actually does establish, are matters of controversy. But it is indisputable that he thinks he has shown, at the very least, that a vast number of complex predicative syllogisms can be reduced to, or proved on the basis of, those syllogisms whose validity is recognized in chapters 4–6—and hence on the basis of the perfect syllogisms of the first figure.

There are no examples offered in the chapter; but it is easy to guess what sort of thing Aristotle has in mind. Consider the following complex predicative form:

> A holds of every B, B holds of every C, C holds of every D: so A holds of every D.

Is that form valid? Well, it is not a syllogistic form of the sort recognized in chapters 4–6—if only because it has too many premisses. But it can readily be shown to be valid on the basis of those forms, thus:

(1) A holds of every B	premiss
(2) B holds of every C	premiss
(3) C holds of every D	premiss
Therefore (4) A holds of every C	1, 2, Barbara
Therefore (5) A holds of every D	3, 4, Barbara

Just as the earlier proof established the validity of Darapti on the basis of Darii, so this argument establishes the validity of the complex predicative form on the basis of Barbara.

The second of the two developments I adverted to is set out in chapter 7 of the *Prior Analytics*. For there Aristotle proves—and this time he really does prove—that all the syllogisms of chapters 4–6 can be established on the basis of the first two syllogisms of the first figure, Barbara and Celarent. Since the imperfect moods of the second and third figures have already been reduced to the perfect moods of the first figure, the thesis of chapter 7 will be established once it is shown that the other two perfect moods, Darii and Ferio, can be proved on the basis of Barbara and Celarent. This is what Aristotle says:

---

[7] ... πᾶσαν ἀπόδειξιν καὶ πάντα συλλογισμὸν ἀνάγκη γίνεσθαι διὰ τριῶν τῶν προειρημένων σχημάτων.

It is possible to reduce all the syllogisms to the universal syllogisms in the first figure. ... The particular syllogisms in the first figure are indeed perfected through themselves, but it is also possible to show them by way of the second figure by bringing them to the impossible. Thus if A of every B and B of some C, then A of some C; for if of none, and of every B, B will hold of no C—we know this by way of the second figure. Similarly with the proof in the privative case: if A holds of no B and B of some C, then A will not hold of some C. For if it holds of every C and of no B, then B will hold of no C—that was the middle figure. Thus since all the syllogisms in the middle figure are reduced to the universal syllogisms in the first figure and the particular syllogisms in the first figure to the syllogisms in the middle figure, it is evident that the particular syllogisms in the first figure will be reduced to the universal syllogisms in the first figure.

(APr 29b1–19)[8]

Universal syllogisms are syllogisms with universal conclusions, particular syllogisms syllogisms with particular conclusions. Thus Darii and Ferio are reduced to Barbara and Celarent. For they are proved by way of certain second figure syllogisms which are in turn proved by way of Barbara and Celarent.

The intermediate proof for Darii can be set out like this:

(1) A holds of every B	premiss
(2) B holds of some C	premiss
(3) A holds of no C	hypothesis
Therefore (4) B holds of no C	1, 3, Camestres
Therefore (5) A holds of some C	2, 4, impossibility

That proves Darii on the basis of Camestres—which has already been proved on the basis of Celarent. Aristotle might as well—or better—have proved Darii directly from Celarent, like this:

(1) A holds of every B	premiss
(2) B holds of some C	premiss

---

[8] ἔστι δὲ καὶ ἀναγαγεῖν πάντας τοὺς συλλογισμοὺς εἰς τοὺς ἐν τῷ πρώτῳ σχήματι καθόλου συλλογισμούς. ... οἱ δ᾽ ἐν τῷ πρώτῳ, οἱ κατὰ μέρος, ἐπιτελοῦνται μὲν καὶ δι᾽ αὑτῶν, ἔστι δὲ καὶ διὰ τοῦ δευτέρου σχήματος δεικνύναι εἰς ἀδύνατον ἀπάγοντας· οἷον εἰ τὸ Α παντὶ τῷ Β, τὸ δὲ Β τινὶ τῷ Γ, ὅτι τὸ Α τινὶ τῷ Γ· εἰ γὰρ μηδενί, τῷ δὲ Β παντί, οὐδενὶ τῷ Γ τὸ Β ὑπάρξει· τοῦτο γὰρ ἴσμεν διὰ τοῦ δευτέρου σχήματος. ὁμοίως δὲ καὶ ἐπὶ τοῦ στερητικοῦ ἔσται ἡ ἀπόδειξις. εἰ γὰρ τὸ Α μηδενὶ τῷ Β, τὸ δὲ Β τινὶ τῷ Γ ὑπάρχει, τὸ Α τινὶ τῷ Γ οὐχ ὑπάρξει· εἰ γὰρ παντί, τῷ δὲ Β μηδενὶ ὑπάρχει, οὐδενὶ τῷ Γ τὸ Β ὑπάρξει· τοῦτο δ᾽ ἦν τὸ μέσον σχῆμα. ὥστ᾽ ἐπεὶ οἱ μὲν ἐν τῷ μέσῳ σχήματι συλλογισμοὶ πάντες ἀνάγονται εἰς τοὺς ἐν τῷ πρώτῳ καθόλου συλλογισμούς, οἱ δὲ κατὰ μέρος ἐν τῷ πρώτῳ εἰς τοὺς ἐν τῷ μέσῳ, φανερὸν ὅτι καὶ οἱ κατὰ μέρος ἀναχθήσονται εἰς τοὺς ἐν τῷ πρώτῳ σχήματι καθόλου συλλογισμούς.

(3) A holds of no C	hypothesis
Therefore (4) C holds of no A	3, conversion
Therefore (5) C holds of no B	1, 4, Celarent
Therefore (6) B holds of no C	5, conversion
Therefore (7) A holds of some C	2, 6, impossibility

The last steps in those two proofs, which rely on the type of inference normally called reduction to the impossible, require some explanation. It must be admitted that Aristotle never explains how a reduction to the impossible works, and that his followers have some pretty confused things to say on the matter; but in principle a satisfactory explanation can be provided.

So Aristotle's syllogistic has the structure of an axiomatized deductive science: even if, as Alexander urges, it is not itself a genuine science, it makes a good job of imitating one. The theorems, or quasi-theorems, of syllogistic include all the imperfect syllogisms which Aristotle considers and also the two particular perfect syllogisms. But they also include many more—infinitely many more—syllogisms. For the three-premissed argument which I set out a few pages ago is a theorem, and so too are its four-premissed siblings, and its five-premissed siblings, ... And in addition, there are any number of other three-premissed and four-premissed and five-premissed ... predicative syllogisms.

Historians of logic sometimes speak as though Aristotle's syllogistic were a strictly finite system embracing between fourteen and twenty-four argument forms. In other words, they take chapters 4–6 of the first Book of the *Prior Analytics*—together with a few additions—to constitute the sum of (non-modal) predicative syllogistic. That is at best misleading; for the syllogisms set out in chapters 4–6 constitute only a fraction of the syllogistic system.

Historians of logic sometimes speak as though the basis of the system—the set of axioms, or quasi-axioms, of the syllogistic—consists of the four perfect syllogisms of the first figure. Thus when later commentators speak of Aristotle's logical system they follow him in saying that all syllogisms have been reduced to the perfect syllogisms of the first figure: given those four syllogisms—or better, given Barbara and Celarent—the whole syllogistic may take to the air. That too is at best misleading. It is true that all the other predicative syllogisms can be proved on the basis of a set of axioms the only predicative syllogisms among which are Barbara and Celarent. But it does not follow from that, and it is not in fact the case, that all the other predicative syllogisms can be proved on the basis of Barbara and Celarent. It is true, in other words, that the only syllogisms you need to take as axiomatic are Barbara and Celarent. It is not true that the only axioms you need are Barbara and Celarent.

And that should have been obvious enough. After all, in chapter 3 of the first Book of the *Prior Analytics*, Aristotle himself sets out the conversions on which the majority of the proofs in chapters 4–6 will depend. Thus the proof of Darapti which I cited depends not only upon Darii but also upon the conversion rule which allows you to infer from something of the form 'A holds of every B' to the corresponding item of the form 'B holds of some A'. It is equally evident that Aristotle's syllogistic depends on some rule or principle of reduction to the impossible; and that rule itself presupposes certain further logical principles—principles of contradiction and principles of subordination, among them the thesis that a universal affirmative proposition entails the corresponding particular affirmative proposition.

The upshot is this. Aristotle's predicative syllogistic is, or can be reconstructed as, an axiomatized deductive system the axioms (or quasi-axioms) of which are two syllogistic forms, certain principles of conversion and of subordination, a principle of reduction to the impossible, and a rule of exposition or ecthesis. And the theorems (or quasi-theorems) are certain derived principles of conversion and subordination—and an infinite number of syllogisms.

That structure was implicitly acknowledged by the ancient logicians. For example, in later texts a perfect syllogism is frequently called 'primary' or '$\pi\rho\hat{\omega}\tau o\varsigma$', and also 'unproved' or '$\dot{\alpha}\nu\alpha\pi\acute{o}\delta\epsilon\iota\kappa\tau o\varsigma$'. So Galen remarks that

there are three figures for predicative propositions and several syllogisms in each of them, ... some of which are unproved and primary ...

(*inst log* viii 1)[9]

And Alexander speaks in the same voice—for example, he observes that we shall reduce imperfect syllogisms 'into one of the perfect and unproved syllogisms in the first figure' (*in APr* 24.4–5).[10] Now in the *Posterior Analytics* Aristotle had stated that any science must

---

[9] τριῶν οὖν ὄντων σχημάτων ἐν ταῖς κατηγορικαῖς προτάσεσι καθ᾽ ἕκαστον αὐτῶν γίγνονται συλλογισμοὶ πλέονες ... ἔνιοι μὲν ἀναπόδεικτοι καὶ πρῶτοι ...

[10] ... εἴς τινα τῶν ἐν τῷ πρώτῳ σχήματι τῶν τελείων καὶ ἀναποδείκτων.

depend on primary unproveds, because otherwise, not having a proof of the items, you will not know them. For to know (non-accidentally) something of which there is a proof is to have a proof of it.

(*APst* 71b26–29)[11]

The axioms or first principles of any science are primary and they are unproved. The perfect syllogisms of Aristotelian syllogistic were later characterized as primary and unproved. Evidently, such a characterization intimates, and was meant to intimate, that the perfect syllogistic forms are axioms, or quasi-axioms, for the science, or quasi-science, of syllogistic.

The perfect forms are quasi-axioms, the imperfect forms are quasi-theorems: why the cautious 'quasi'? Why not speak boldly of axioms and theorems? The axioms of a science are the fundamental truths on which the remaining truths of the science depend. Axioms are propositions, and so too are theorems. Concrete syllogisms are not propositions: they are sets or sequences of propositions. *A fortiori*, syllogistic forms are not syllogisms: neither Darii nor Darapti is a proposition, nor even a sequence of propositions—so Darii cannot be a genuine axiom nor Darapti a genuine theorem.

But that is needlessly pedantic, both on an historical and on a philosophical count. For first, some ancient theorists took expressions of the form 'X, but Y: so Z' to constitute a single saying; and when Aristotle characterized a syllogism as a λόγος in which certain things are thus-and-so, they will readily have understood the word 'λόγος' to mean 'saying' rather than 'argument'. Secondly, even if syllogisms are not propositions or sayings, why should that disqualify them from forming part of an axiomatized science? Euclid's *Elements* contains numerous theorems which are not propositions. Indeed, the very first theorem of the first Book of the *Elements* is this:

On a given finite straight line, to construct an equilateral triangle.

(i i)[12]

That is a construction; and if constructions may count as theorems, then why may not syllogisms or argument forms do so? Thirdly, it is a simple matter to construct a syllogistical science the axioms and theorems of which are honest to God propositions. For example, you might take the circumscriptions of

---

[11] ἐκ πρώτων δ' ἀναποδείκτων, ὅτι οὐκ ἐπιστήσεται μὴ ἔχων ἀπόδειξιν αὐτῶν· τὸ γὰρ ἐπίστασθαι ὧν ἀπόδειξις ἐστι μὴ κατὰ συμβεβηκός, τὸ ἔχειν ἀπόδειξίν ἐστιν.

[12] ἐπὶ τῆς δοθείσης εὐθείας πεπερασμένης τρίγωνον ἰσόπλευρον συστήσασθαι.

the perfect forms as your axioms, and then derive the circumscriptions of the imperfect forms as theorems. Or you might use schemata in one way or another—'Every syllogism which is an instance of the schema S is valid', ...

'PRIMARY UNPROVEDS'

Aristotle affirms that the principles on which scientific proofs are based must be 'primary unproveds' (*APst* 71b26). At first glance, that phrase seems pleonastic: 'primary' and 'unproved' may not be synonymous expressions; but is not an item primary if and only if it is unproved?

If an item is primary, is it unproved? Yes. An item is primary if and only if there is no item prior to it; or better: a member of a set of items is primary in the set if and only if no item in the set is prior to it. The type of priority which Aristotle here has in mind is priority in knowledge, or epistemic priority. Roughly speaking, to say that x is prior in knowledge to y is to say that x may feature as a premiss in a proof of y (whereas y cannot feature as a premiss in a proof of x). It follows that if x is primary, then it cannot be proved; for there is nothing prior to x which might feature as a premiss in a proof of x. Or better: if x is primary in a set S, then there is no proof of x which uses a member of S as a premiss.

If an item is unproved, is it primary? The answer to that question depends on how we construe the word 'unproved'—or rather, on how we construe the Greek word which I have used it to translate. That word is 'ἀναπόδεικτος'.

The word is a member of a large family of negative verbal adjectives. The members of the family are all formed from an 'alpha privative', a verbal root, and a termination in -τος: they have the construction 'ἀ-VERB-τος'. They are all systematically ambiguous, having two chief senses: 'ἀ-VERB-τος' may mean either 'unVERBable' or 'unVERBed'. The ambiguity was noticed by Aristotle, and by the Stoics after him; it is remarked upon by Galen, and by several other ancient authors. Any Peripatetic or any Stoic who used the word 'ἀναπόδεικτος' in his logical theory will presumably have realized that his words might be taken in different ways; he will presumably have intended them to be taken in one determinate way; and—if he was sensible—he will have indicated the way in which he intended them to be taken.

The ancient texts do indeed show that there was some explicit comment upon the sense of 'ἀναπόδεικτος' in logical contexts. Yet the indications which they offer are surprising. According to Sextus, syllogisms are called ἀναπόδεικτοι in two ways: those which have not been proved, and those which do not need proof inasmuch as in their case the fact that they lead to a conclusion is immediately evident. We have often shown that it is the second meaning of this appellation which holds of the items which Chrysippus lists at the beginning of his first *Introduction to Syllogisms*.

(*M* viii 223)[13]

The syllogisms to which Sextus alludes are 'the celebrated unproveds of the Stoics', and Sextus says that they were called 'ἀναπόδεικτοι' insofar as they do not need to be proved. He implies the same thing—without any explicit reference to the ambiguity of 'ἀναπόδεικτος'—in the *Outlines of Pyrrhonism*:

As far as redundancy is concerned, even the celebrated unproveds of the Stoics will turn out to be invalid—and if they are destroyed, the whole of logic is overturned. For those are the syllogisms which, they say, need no proof for their own constitution but are probative of the fact that the other syllogisms conclude.

(*PH* ii 156)[14]

And the remark is confirmed by Diogenes Laertius:

There are also some syllogisms which are unproved insofar as they do not need a proof. They are given differently by different Stoics—but Chrysippus gives five. By means of them every argument is put together.

(vii 79)[15]

There need be no doubt that the Stoic unproveds were so called—and so called by the Stoics themselves—inasmuch as they were deemed not to need proof.

Nevertheless, the sense which Sextus ascribes to the word in its Stoic use is surprising. Words of the form 'ἀ-verb-τος' do not in fact mean 'not needing to be verbed'; nor—the present case apart—does any ancient text suggest that they do. Had some Stoic logician, wittingly or unwittingly, given a new sense or ascribed an improper sense to the word 'ἀναπόδεικτος'? Philosophers do give new senses to old words; and as for the improper option, Chrysippus'

---

[13] ἀναπόδεικτοι λέγονται διχῶς, οἵ τε μὴ ἀποδεδειγμένοι καὶ οἱ μὴ χρείαν ἔχοντες ἀποδείξεως τῷ αὐτόθεν εἶναι περιφανὲς ἐπ᾽ αὐτῶν τὸ ὅτι συνάγουσιν. ἐπεδείξαμεν δὲ πολλάκις ὡς κατὰ τὸ δεύτερον σημαινόμενον ταύτης ἠξίωνται τῆς προσηγορίας οἱ κατ᾽ ἀρχὴν τῆς πρώτης περὶ συλλογισμῶν εἰσαγωγῆς παρὰ τῷ Χρυσίππῳ τεταγμένοι.

[14] ὅσον γὰρ ἐπὶ τῇ παρολκῇ καὶ οἱ θρυλούμενοι παρὰ τοῖς Στωϊκοῖς ἀναπόδεικτοι ἀσύνακτοι εὑρεθήσονται, ὧν ἀναιρουμένων ἡ πᾶσα διαλεκτικὴ ἀνατρέπεται· οὗτοι γάρ εἰσιν οὕς φασιν ἀποδείξεως μὲν μὴ δεῖσθαι πρὸς τὴν ἑαυτῶν σύστασιν, ἀποδεικτικοὺς δὲ ὑπάρχειν τοῦ καὶ τοὺς ἄλλους συνάγειν λόγους.

[15] εἰσὶ δὲ καὶ ἀναπόδεικτοί τινες τῷ μὴ χρῄζειν ἀποδείξεως, ἄλλοι μὲν παρ᾽ ἄλλοις, παρὰ δὲ τῷ Χρυσίππῳ πέντε, δι᾽ ὧν πᾶς λόγος πλέκεται.

Greek was notoriously patchy. And yet I wonder if the Stoics did not use the word in one of its proper and standard senses—namely, in the sense of 'unproved'. The five Chrysippean unproveds are the five syllogistic forms which the Chrysippean system does not prove. No doubt it does not prove them because they do not need to be proved. But it does not follow that, in calling them '*ἀναπόδεικτοι*', the Stoics meant that they do not need to be proved: they may simply have meant that they are not proved.

That is why I translate '*ἀναπόδεικτος*' by 'unproved'. If you don't like that, then you must opt for 'not needing proof'. Usually the word is translated as 'unprovable' or 'indemonstrable', and scholars standardly speak of the five Chrysippean indemonstrables where I speak of the five unproveds. Whether or not the five items are in fact, or were held to be, unprovable, the standard translation is demonstrably inaccurate—and that is a pretty good reason to reject it.

What about Aristotle? The word '*ἀναπόδεικτος*' certainly may, and certainly sometimes does, mean 'unprovable', and that may well be its sense in the phrase at *APst* 71b26 which I have so far translated as 'primary unproveds'. After all, in that passage Aristotle is out to show that the first principles of a science must be items which cannot be proved; and it is therefore rather plausible to suppose that the thesis of unprovability is expressed by the word '*ἀναπόδεικτος*'. But it does not follow that when later authors describe Aristotelian syllogisms as *ἀναπόδεικτοι* they mean that they are unprovable.

First, when Sextus distinguishes two senses in which '*ἀναπόδεικτος*' is used in logical contexts, he does not even mention the sense of 'unprovable' or 'indemonstrable'. To be sure, Sextus does not purport to list all the possible senses of the word. Nonetheless, what he says strongly suggests that he has given the senses of the word which are pertinent to the discussion of syllogisms.

Secondly, several passages which use '*ἀναπόδεικτος*' of predicative syllogisms certainly do not use it in the sense of 'unprovable'. In a passage from his *Introduction to Logic* which I have already quoted in a truncated form, Galen remarks that

there are three figures among predicative propositions, and in each of them there are several syllogisms, just as there are among hypotheticals: some are unproved and primary, some need a proof.

(inst log viii 1)[16]

---

[16] τριῶν οὖν ὄντων σχημάτων ἐν ταῖς κατηγορικαῖς προτάσεσι καθ' ἕκαστον αὐτῶν γίγνονται συλλογισμοὶ πλέονες ὥσπερ κἂν ταῖς ὑποθετικαῖς, ἔνιοι μὲν ἀναπόδεικτοι καὶ πρῶτοι, τινές δ' ἀποδείξεως δεόμενοι.

The last clause shows plainly that 'ἀναπόδεικτος' does not mean 'unprovable': the word is contrasted with 'needing a proof', and it therefore means either 'not needing proof' or (as I quixotically prefer) 'unproved'.

The same implication is found in a text with impeccably Peripatetic credentials. Near the beginning of his commentary on the *Prior Analytics*, Alexander notes that Aristotle will explain, among other things,

> which of the syllogisms are perfect and immediately knowable and not needing a proof, and which are imperfect and not unproved.

> (*in APr* 6.23–25)[17]

There is the same contrast as in Galen, so that Alexander too means 'ἀναπόδεικτος' not in the sense of 'unprovable' but in the sense of 'unproved' (or 'not needing proof').

Finally, let me cite a passage from Apuleius' *On Interpretation*. Apuleius is discussing predicative syllogistic. Like most later logicians, he finds nine syllogisms in the first figure—the four canonical syllogisms of the *Prior Analytics* and five others which Theophrastus is said to have added:

> Now of these nine moods in the first figure, the first four are called unproved—not because they cannot be proved, like the measurement of the whole of the ocean, nor because they are not proved, like the squaring of the circle, but because they are so simple and so evident that they do not need a proof.

> (*int* ix [205.21–206.5])[18]

This text is generally taken to show that Apuleius recognized three senses for the Latin term '*indemonstrabilis*'; and it is inferred that his Greek copy-text reported three senses for the Greek 'ἀναπόδεικτος'. The second and the third of Apuleius' senses correspond to Sextus' two senses. The first is the sense which we are surprised not to find in Sextus, namely 'unprovable'.

In fact, matters are not quite so simple. The received text of the passage makes no sense: there is no easy correction, and the version which I have given (and translated) is anything but certain. The corruption covers at least the words which I have rendered as 'like the measurement ... or because', and it may be more extensive. That is to say, it is not even certain that Apuleius

---

[17] ... καὶ τίνες μὲν τέλειοι τῶν συλλογισμῶν καὶ αὐτόθεν γνώριμοι καὶ οὐ δεόμενοι ἀποδείξεως, τίνες δὲ ἀτελεῖς καὶ οὐκ ἀναπόδεικτοι.

[18] *ex hisce igitur in prima formula modis novem primi quattuor indemonstrabiles nominentur, non quod demonstrari nequeant, ut universi maris aestimatio, aut quod non demonstrentur, sicut circuli quadratura, sed quod tam simplices tamque manifesti sint ut demonstratione non egeant.*

noticed three rather than two uses of the word '*indemonstrabilis*'. But I shall not insist on that point; and in any event it will rightly be urged that there probably was a threefold distinction in the text. However, is there a threefold distinction of senses? Apuleius does not say so: he says that the first four moods of the first figure are called *indemonstrabiles* because they do not need to be proved. There is no pressing need to gloss 'because' by 'in the sense that'.

In any event, one thing is plain: Apuleius does not think that first figure predicative syllogisms are called '*indemonstrabilis*' in the sense of 'unprovable'. They are *indemonstrabiles* insofar as they do not need to be proved—whether '*indemonstrabilis*' is taken to mean 'not needing proof' or simply 'unproved'.

So let me return to the question: If an item is unproved, does it follow that it is primary? Evidently not. To be sure, if something is unprovable (relative to a given set), then it is primary (relative to that set). But if something is unproved it does not follow that it is unprovable; and if something does not need to be proved it does not follow that it is unprovable.

That conclusion is hardly astounding. For Darii and Ferio are unproved in chapters 4–6 of Book One of the *Prior Analytics*, and they do not need to be proved. But they are not unprovable, nor are they primary—for they are proved in chapter 7.

ARE ANY PREDICATIVE SYLLOGISMS PRIMARY?

Orthodox Peripatetics held that some predicative syllogisms are primary and so unprovable. Boethus of Sidon, a contemporary of Strabo and a leading Peripatetic of the time, disagreed. Galen reports that

some of the Peripatetics, among them Boethus, call the syllogisms which are based on leading assumptions [i.e. certain hypothetical syllogisms] not only unproved but also primary; but they are not prepared to call primary those unproved syllogisms which depend on predicative propositions.

(*inst log* vii 2)[19]

The interpretation of the text is controversial—and Galen says nothing more about Boethus' view. But he plainly states that, according to Boethus,

---

[19] καὶ μέντοι καὶ τῶν ἐκ τοῦ Περιπάτου τινὲς ὥσπερ καὶ Βόηθος οὐ μόνον ἀναποδείκτους ὀνομάζουσι τοὺς ἐκ τῶν ἡγεμονικῶν λημμάτων συλλογισμοὺς ἀλλὰ καὶ πρώτους· ὅσοι δὲ ἐκ κατηγορικῶν προτάσεών εἰσιν ἀναπόδεικτοι συλλογισμοί, τούτους οὐκ ἔτι πρώτους ὀνομάζειν συγχωροῦσι.

no predicative syllogisms are primary: none has an axiomatic, or quasi-axiomatic, status; each can be proved. Galen also suggests—though he does not strictly imply—that Boethus recognized certain predicative syllogisms as unproved and as not being in need of proof. So perhaps Boethus agreed with Aristotle that Barbara and Celarent are unproved and do not need to be proved. He disagreed with Aristotle inasmuch as he thought that they can be proved.

How did he think to prove Barbara and Celarent? It is evident that an item may be unproved relative to one set of items—and even unprovable relative to one set of items—while being provable, and proved, relative to another set. In other words, an axiom, or quasi-axiom, of one system may be a theorem of another. So when Boethus claimed that Barbara and Celarent can be proved, perhaps he meant not that they can be proved within predicative syllogistic or relative to the set of predicative syllogisms but rather that they can be proved in some larger system of logic and relative to a larger set of syllogisms. More particularly, perhaps he meant that Barbara and Celarent can be proved within hypothetical syllogistic?

That is exactly what Galen's report has been taken to intimate: the primary syllogisms which Boethus recognized in hypothetical syllogistic will have served as axioms not only for the other hypothetical syllogisms but also for Barbara and Celarent—and hence for the whole of predicative syllogistic. And is it not pleasing to imagine that Boethus had in that way anticipated Frege? For Frege in effect claimed—and demonstrated—that by means of the first unproved syllogism of Stoic logic he could, with the aid of a handful of axioms, prove the validity of Barbara and Celarent.

Perhaps Boethus was a Fregean *avant la lettre*. But I doubt it: nothing in Galen's text really suggests as much; and there is another possibility which the rest of our evidence about Boethus tends to favour. According to that other possibility, Boethus thought that Barbara and Celarent could be proved within predicative syllogistic or relative to the set of predicative syllogisms.

How might that be? Take Celarent first; and consider Aristotle's proof of Cesare, which runs like this:

(1) B holds of no A	premiss
(2) B holds of every C	premiss
Therefore (3) A holds of no B	1, conversion
Therefore (4) A holds of no C	2, 3, Celarent

There, Cesare is reduced to, or proved on the basis of, Celarent. Now it is evident that Aristotle's argument may be run in the opposite direction, not from Celarent to Cesare but from Cesare to Celarent, thus:

(1) A holds of no B	premiss
(2) B holds of every C	premiss
Therefore (3) B holds of no A	1, conversion
Therefore (4) A holds of no C	2, 3, Cesare

If the first argument proves Cesare on the basis of Celarent, does not the second prove Celarent on the basis of Cesare? And so is not Celarent a theorem? Or rather, may we not take Celarent as a theorem and Cesare as an axiom rather than *vice versa*?

The same trick cannot be turned in exactly the same way for Barbara—if only because no other syllogism has a universal affirmative conclusion. But the trick can be turned in a different way. Here is Aristotle's proof of the validity of Baroco:

(1) B holds of every A	premiss
(2) B does not hold of some C	premiss
(3) A holds of every C	hypothesis
Therefore (4) B holds of every C	1, 3, Barbara
Therefore (5) A does not hold of some C	2, 4, impossibility

Baroco is there proved on the basis of Barbara, by reduction to the impossible. The reduction to the impossible may be run in the opposite direction, thus:

(1) A holds of every B	premiss
(2) B holds of every C	premiss
(3) A does not hold of some C	hypothesis
Therefore (4) B does not hold of some C	1, 3, Baroco
Therefore (5) A holds of every C	2, 4, impossibility

One reduction takes us from Barbara to Baroco, the other from Baroco to Barbara. If the first argument is a proof of Baroco, is not the second a proof of Barbara?

That you may argue in both directions in that sort of way is not an arcane secret of predicative syllogistic: on the contrary, it is something which Aristotle explicitly recognizes and elaborates. In the second Book of the *Prior Analytics* he offers to prove, quite generally, that everything which can be concluded directly will also be shown by way of the impossible, and everything by way of the impossible directly, through the same terms.

(APr 62b38–40)[20]

He then proves the point, elaborating in effect a set of reciprocating or counterpart arguments in which X is shown to be valid on the basis of Y and Y is shown to be valid on the basis of X. Here is an example:

Again, let it have been shown in the middle figure that A holds of every B. Then the hypothesis was that A does not hold of every B, and it was assumed that A of every C and C of every B. For in that way the impossible will come about. And that is the first figure: A of every C and C of every B.

(APr 63a25–29)[21]

The passage is done in Aristotle's best telegraphese; but from it you may readily extract an argument for the validity of Barbara—the very argument which I have just set down.

Aristotle argued for Baroco from Barbara and for Barbara from Baroco. He argued for Cesare from Celarent, and he must have seen that there was an argument from Celarent to Cesare. Two of those four arguments he took to be proofs. Two he did not. Why not? There is no explicit answer to that question in our texts; but the true answer is not far to seek. According to Aristotle, Barbara and Celarent possess a property which Baroco and Cesare lack: Barbara and Celarent are perfect, Baroco and Cesare are not. In order to qualify as an axiom or quasi-axiom, a syllogism must be perfect. Baroco and Cesare, then, cannot serve as axioms or quasi-axioms for predicative syllogistic, and there are no proofs from them to Barbara and Celarent.

But perhaps Boethus did take all four arguments to be proofs? Perhaps he thought that the argument from Cesare to Celarent proved the validity of Celarent, just as the argument from Celarent to Cesare proved that validity of Cesare? Well, he could only have thought so if he took a different line from Aristotle on perfection. And that is just what he did. According to Ammonius,

---

[20] ἅπαν δὲ τὸ δεικτικῶς περαινόμενον καὶ διὰ τοῦ ἀδυνάτου δειχθήσεται, καὶ τὸ διὰ τοῦ ἀδυνάτου δεικτικῶς διὰ τῶν αὐτῶν ὅρων.

[21] πάλιν ἐν τῷ μέσῳ σχήματι δεδείχθω τὸ Α παντὶ τῷ Β ὑπάρχον. οὐκοῦν ἡ μὲν ὑπόθεσις ἦν μὴ παντὶ τῷ Β τὸ Α ὑπάρχειν, εἴληπται δὲ τὸ Α παντὶ τῷ Γ καὶ τὸ Γ παντὶ τῷ Β· οὕτω γὰρ ἔσται τὸ ἀδύνατον. τοῦτο δὲ τὸ πρῶτον σχῆμα, τὸ Α παντὶ τῷ Γ καὶ τὸ Γ παντὶ τῷ Β.

Boethus ... held the contrary opinion to Aristotle on this matter [i.e. on the matter of perfection]. His opinion was correct, and he proved that all the syllogisms in the second and third figures are perfect. Porphyry and Iamblichus followed him, and so too did Maximus ... But Themistius the paraphrast held the contrary opinion—the opinion which Aristotle had held. These two—Maximus and Themistius—holding contrary opinions on the matter and establishing, as they thought, each his own view, the Emperor Julian acted as arbiter and gave the vote to Maximus and Iamblichus and Porphyry and Boethus. It seems that Theophrastus, who was a pupil of Aristotle himself, held the contrary opinion to him on this point.

(in APr 31.13–23)[22]

Certain aspects of that report may be doubted—for example, it may be doubted if Theophrastus really disagreed with his master about perfection. And in general, the Ammonian commentary on the *Analytics* is pretty second-rate. But the gist of its report is confirmed by an earlier text.

The text is an essay by Themistius which offers 'to answer Maximus on the reduction of the second and third figures to the first'. The essay, which survives only in Arabic translation, is in many places difficult to understand.[23] But the central point is unambiguous. For Themistius describes Maximus' position as follows:

He attempts to prove that the syllogisms in the second and third figures are perfect in themselves and do not need to be proved or to be reduced to the first figure.

(ad Max 180)

And more than once he declares that Boethus upheld the same position as Maximus.

So Boethus held—according to Galen—that no predicative syllogisms are primary. He also held—according to Ammonius and Themistius—that all predicative syllogisms, or at least, all the fourteen canonical syllogisms, are perfect. Those two theses fit snugly together. There is an argument from Cesare

---

[22] ὁ δὲ Βοηθὸς ... ἐναντίως τῷ Ἀριστοτέλει περὶ τούτου ἐδόξασεν, καὶ καλῶς ἐδόξασεν καὶ ἀπέδειξεν ὅτι πάντες οἱ ἐν δευτέρῳ καὶ τρίτῳ σχήματι τέλειοί εἰσιν. τούτῳ ἠκολούθησεν Πορφύριος καὶ Ἰάμβλιχος, ἔτι μέντοι καὶ ὁ Μάξιμος ... καὶ Θεμίστιος δὲ ὁ παραφραστὴς τῆς ἐναντίας ἐγένετο δόξης τῆς καὶ τῷ Ἀριστοτέλει δοκούσης. τούτοις οὖν τοῖς δύο, τῷ τε Μαξίμῳ καὶ τῷ Θεμιστίῳ, ἐναντία περὶ τούτου δοξάζουσιν καὶ κατασκευάζουσιν, ὡς ᾤοντο, τὸ δοκοῦν αὐτοῖς διῄτησεν αὐτὰ ὁ βασιλεὺς Ἰουλιανός, καὶ δέδωκεν τὴν ψῆφον Μαξίμῳ καὶ Ἰαμβλίχῳ καὶ Πορφυρίῳ καὶ Βοηθῷ. φαίνεται δὲ καὶ Θεόφραστος ὁ Ἀριστοτέλους αὐτοῦ ἀκροατὴς τὴν ἐναντίαν αὐτῷ περὶ τούτου δόξαν ἔχων.

[23] There is a French translation—in parts evidently unreliable—in A. Badawi, *La transmission de la philosophie grecque au monde arabe*, Études de philosophie médiévale 56 (Paris, 1987²), pp. 180–194.

to Celarent. Cesare is perfect. Therefore the argument proves the validity of Celarent. Therefore Celarent is not primary. Similarly for Baroco and Barbara.

It remains to ask why Aristotle thought that perfection was limited to the four canonical syllogisms of the first figure—and how Boethus came to disagree. And in order to tackle those questions, it will be necessary to know what the property of perfection consists in.

But before I turn to that, I must add a caution to what I have just said about Boethus. According to Ammonius, Boethus 'proved that all the syllogisms in the second and third figures are perfect'. Themistius, however, says this:

I think that Boethus claims that the moods in the second figure which do not need proof are three and not four.

(ad Max 186)

Themistius does not say which three; but there will be no doubt that the odd man out was Baroco—the only syllogism in the second figure which cannot be proved by conversion. And although Themistius says nothing on the subject, who will not guess that if Baroco was the exception in the second figure, then there was also an exception in the third figure—namely, Bocardo?

In itself, the making of such exceptions is unexceptionable. But in the present context it is unsettling. For if Barbara is to be proved within predicative syllogistic, then the proof must be based either on Baroco or else on Bocardo—no other predicative syllogism may serve as an axiom or quasi-axiom for it. But if neither Baroco nor Bocardo is perfect, then Barbara cannot be proved within predicative syllogistic.

What is to be inferred? Perhaps Boethus did not tie proof to perfection in the Aristotelian way? Perhaps he thought that there was some other way of proving Barbara, a way which did not rely on either Baroco or Bocardo? Perhaps Ammonius is right and Themistius wrong, so that Boethus held that all fourteen canonical syllogisms are perfect? I am mildly inclined to the last of those possibilities. True, Themistius is, on this issue, a more detailed and a more intelligent reporter than Ammonius. But—if we may trust the Arabic text—Themistius does not say that Boethus ascribes perfection to only three of the second figure syllogisms—he says: 'I think ... '. In other words, Themistius is here inferring rather than reporting.

PERFECTION

However that might be, what is perfection? Aristotle speaks of a syllogism's being perfect or imperfect, τέλειος or ἀτελής; and he will say of an imperfect syllogism that it can be perfected (he uses the verbs 'τελειοῦν' and 'ἐπιτελεῖν'). The Greek 'τέλειος' may mean 'complete' rather than 'perfect'; and some sentences in the *Analytics* have suggested that it was in fact completeness rather than perfection which Aristotle had in mind.

Consider, for example, the following remark which occurs in Aristotle's introduction to the moods of the second figure:

> There will be no τέλειος syllogism of any sort in this figure, but there will be a potential one both when the terms are universal and when they are not universal.
>
> (*APr* 27a1–3)[24]

The remark is repeated, virtually *verbatim*, for the third figure (*APr* 28a15–17). The contrast between 'τέλειος' and 'potential' readily suggests the following notion: a syllogism which is τέλειος is already all there, while something which is a potential syllogism is the makings of a syllogism but not yet an actual syllogism. That pile of bricks and lumber next to the concrete-mixer is a potential house: the thing next to it is a τέλειος house—not, or not necessarily, a perfect house but a complete or completed house.

The Ammonian commentary on the *Prior Analytics* has a number of things to say about perfection or completion, not all of them mutually consistent. One of the things is this:

> From what Aristotle himself says you can see that these syllogisms [i.e. the syllogisms of the second and third figures] are not imperfect, as he thinks (for their terms are perfect)—rather the terms in them are simply confused.
>
> (*in APr* 33.19–21)[25]

Cesare, for example, is not imperfect—or rather, it is not incomplete. For it has a complete set of terms: its terms are perfect—or rather complete. True, the terms are 'confused', so that you need to straighten them out by conversion; but the terms are all there, and so Cesare lacks nothing.

Plainly, Ammonius—in this passage at least—took perfection to be a matter of completeness. That is how he came to think that all syllogisms are perfect or complete; for Cesare is not an incomplete or unfinished piece of argument. And he thought that Aristotle himself should have accepted

---

[24] τέλειος μὲν οὖν οὐκ ἔσται συλλογισμὸς οὐδαμῶς ἐν τούτῳ τῷ σχήματι, δυνατὸς δ' ἔσται καὶ καθόλου καὶ μὴ καθόλου τῶν ὅρων ὄντων.

[25] ὥστε καὶ παρὰ τῶν λεγομένων παρ' αὐτῷ τῷ Ἀριστοτέλει λάβοις ἂν ὅτι οὐκ εἰσὶν οὗτοι οἱ συλλογισμοὶ ἀτελεῖς, ὡς αὐτῷ δοκεῖ (τοὺς γὰρ ὅρους τελείους ἔχουσιν), ἀλλὰ μόνον συγκεχυμένοι εἰσὶν ἐν αὐτοῖς οἱ ὅροι.

that conclusion. He was thinking of Aristotle's definition of perfection or completeness:

I call perfect a syllogism which needs nothing else apart from the items assumed in order for its necessity to be apparent.

(*APr* 24b22–24)[26]

Surely 'nothing else' means 'no other term (apart from its constitutive three)'? And surely you can make the necessity of Cesare apparent—surely Aristotle does make the necessity of Cesare apparent—without importing any extra terms?

That was Ammonius' train of thought; and it is, of course, tempting to suppose that it was also Boethus' train of thought. In other words, Boethus took Aristotle's own definition of perfection to show that all the canonical syllogisms of chapters 4–6 are perfect or complete.

Now it is true that Aristotle's proofs of the second and third figure syllogisms, which proceed by conversion or by reduction to the impossible, do not introduce any terms which are not already present in their premises. A proof may introduce extra terms; and in fact Aristotle's proofs by ecthesis do so—but proofs by ecthesis are not needed in non-modal syllogistic. Nonetheless, Ammonius has misunderstood Aristotle.

For when Aristotle says 'nothing else' he does not mean 'no other term'. Here is the text in a fuller form:

I call perfect a syllogism which needs nothing else apart from the items assumed in order for its necessity to be apparent, imperfect one which needs one or more items, which are necessary by way of the existing terms but which are not assumed in the premises.

(*APr* 24b22–26)[27]

The 'one or more items' which an imperfect syllogism needs cannot be terms; for a term cannot be 'necessary by way of the existing terms'. What, then, are they? What Aristotle has in mind emerges more clearly from a later passage:

---

[26] τέλειον μὲν οὖν καλῶ συλλογισμὸν τὸν μηδενὸς ἄλλου προσδεόμενον παρὰ τὰ εἰλημμένα πρὸς τὸ φανῆναι τὸ ἀναγκαῖον.

[27] τέλειον μὲν οὖν καλῶ συλλογισμὸν τὸν μηδενὸς ἄλλου προσδεόμενον παρὰ τὰ εἰλημμένα πρὸς τὸ φανῆναι τὸ ἀναγκαῖον, ἀτελῆ δὲ τὸν προσδεόμενον ἢ ἑνὸς ἢ πλειόνων, ἃ ἔστι μὲν ἀναγκαῖα διὰ τῶν ὑποκειμένων ὅρων, οὐ μὴν εἴληπται διὰ προτάσεων.

It is clear too that all the syllogisms in this figure [i.e. in the second figure] are imperfect; for they are all perfected when certain items are introduced—items which either inhere in the terms from necessity or are laid down as hypotheses, i.e. when we show something through the impossible.

(APr 28a4–7)²⁸

The 'certain items' which are introduced for the perfecting of second figure syllogisms are, of course, the items which those syllogisms need in order for their necessity to be apparent. The items are of two sorts: either they 'inhere in the terms' or else they are 'laid down as hypotheses'. The disjunction refers to the two methods of proof which Aristotle in fact deploys. The second disjunct explicitly refers to reduction to the impossible, in which Aristotle starts by hypothesizing that the contradictory of the conclusion holds. The first disjunct, less evidently, refers to proofs by conversion. Neither method of proof introduces—or can introduce—any term which is not already in the premisses of the syllogism. So the extra items which imperfect syllogisms need are not terms.

What exactly are they? They are sometimes characterized as operations—the operations of converting and of hypothesizing. But the text suggests rather that the items are propositions. Certainly, hypotheses are propositions and not operations; and it is easier to think of a proposition than of an operation as being inherent in certain terms. But the question is not very important: what counts is that the items are not terms.

Thus Ammonius—or rather, the sentence from the Ammonian commentary which I quoted—is wrong about completeness or perfection. Whether Boethus made the same error is a question which is better postponed. For the moment, it is enough to state that the best reason for thinking that 'τέλειος' means 'complete' turns out to be a bad reason: it seems as though 'perfect' and 'imperfect' rather than 'complete' and 'incomplete' are the words we want.

But what about Aristotle's claim that the items in the second and third figures are potential syllogisms? When Aristotle says that

there will be no perfect syllogism of any sort in this figure, but there will be a potential one when ... ,

---

²⁸ δῆλον δὲ καὶ ὅτι πάντες ἀτελεῖς εἰσιν οἱ ἐν τούτῳ τῷ σχήματι συλλογισμοί· πάντες γὰρ ἐπιτελοῦνται προσλαμβανομένων τινῶν, ἃ ἢ ἐνυπάρχει τοῖς ὅροις ἐξ ἀνάγκης ἢ τίθενται ὡς ὑποθέσεις, οἷον ὅταν διὰ τοῦ ἀδυνάτου δεικνύωμεν.

modern scholarship takes 'potential one' to be elliptical for 'potential perfect syllogism' rather than for 'potential syllogism'. The text does not mean that there are potential but not actual syllogisms in the second figure: it means that there are potentially perfect but not actually perfect syllogisms there. That is hardly what the Greek suggests; but perhaps it is right.

If it is right, it is certainly odd—it is rather as if you were to describe a theorem as a potential axiom. But that particular oddity is in any event unavoidable. For Aristotle says that

every syllogism is perfected by way of the first figure and reduced to the universal syllogisms in that figure.

(*APr* 41b3–5)[29]

Cesare, for example, is imperfect; but by means of Celarent it is perfected. Now the verb 'to perfect' means 'to make perfect', so that when Cesare is perfected, it becomes perfect—it becomes a perfect syllogism. So Cesare is, now, perfect. Indeed, all predicative syllogisms are perfect—and have been for a couple of millennia: Aristotle perfected them for us long, long ago. Perhaps most of them were imperfect before Aristotle got to them. But when, in 360 AD, the Emperor Julian decided for Boethus, he was right.

Of course, that is not what Aristotle means at all. If a syllogism is once perfect, then it is always perfect; and if it is once imperfect, then it is always imperfect. Aristotle's use of the verb 'to perfect' is, at best, misleading. To perfect a syllogism is not to make it perfect: it is to prove it on the basis of a perfect syllogism.

A syllogism is perfect if and only if its necessity is directly apparent—if and only if its validity is evident. Perfect predicative syllogisms were later described as unproved inasmuch as they do not need to be proved; and when Alexander refers to syllogisms which are 'perfect and immediately knowable and not needing a proof' (*in APr* 6.23–25), he takes those three characterizations to be distinct from but equivalent to one another. The Stoics did not use the word 'perfect' in order to characterize their own unproved syllogisms. But they might as well have done so; for according to Sextus, the Stoic unproveds do not need to be proved 'inasmuch as in their case the fact that they lead to a conclusion is immediately evident' (*M* viii 223). The unproveds are unproved inasmuch as their validity is evident—inasmuch as they are, in the Peripatetic jargon, perfect.

---

[29] ... ἅπας τε συλλογισμὸς ἐπιτελεῖται διὰ τοῦ πρώτου σχήματος καὶ ἀνάγεται εἰς τοὺς ἐν τούτῳ καθόλου συλλογισμούς.

The unproved syllogisms do not need to be proved. There are no naked needs: needs are needs for something or other. If you need something, then you need it in order to do so-and-so; and if you don't need something, then you can do so-and-so without it. Imperfect syllogisms need something which perfect syllogisms don't need: they need and don't need it for what end or purpose? A syllogism which does not need a proof does not need one inasmuch as it is immediately knowable. A syllogism which needs a proof, then, presumably needs to be proved in order to be known—that is to say, in order for its validity to be known.

Thus according to Aristotle and the orthodox Peripatetics, if you are to know that Cesare (say) is valid, then you must have a proof that Cesare is valid; but you may know that Celarent (say) is valid without having any proof that Celarent is valid. Celarent, in other words, has the property of perfection, a property which Cesare lacks. And it is a good thing that Celarent does have that property. For—still according to the Peripatetic orthodoxy—Celarent is primary and cannot be proved. So that were Celarent not also perfect, then its validity could never be known.

There is a complication to the story which I shall mention only to set aside. In his account of hypothetical syllogistic Sextus introduces a distinction among unproved syllogisms to which I have already alluded:

Again, you should know that of the unproveds some are simple and some non-simple. Simple are those for which it is immediately clear that they conclude, i.e. that the conclusion is co-introduced with the assumptions. ... Non-simple are those which are constructed from the simple and which need analysis into them in order that it may be recognized that they too conclude.

(*M* viii 228–229)[30]

The distinction between simple and non-simple unproveds is found in no other passage; and some scholars have supposed that Sextus has made a careless mistake—when he says 'of the unproved, some are simple ... ', he should have said 'of syllogisms, some are simple ... '.[31]

Perhaps there is no more than a Sextan error on display. But if Sextus is reporting aright, then the Stoics—some Stoics—distinguished

---

[30] ἔτι χρὴ γινώσκειν ὅτι τῶν ἀναποδείκτων οἱ μέν εἰσιν ἁπλοῖ, οἱ δὲ οὐχ ἁπλοῖ. ὧν ἁπλοῖ μέν εἰσιν οἱ αὐτόθεν σαφὲς ἔχοντες τὸ ὅτι συνάγουσιν, τουτέστι τὸ ὅτι συνεισάγεται αὐτῶν τοῖς λήμμασιν ἡ ἐπιφορά. ... οὐχ ἁπλοῖ δέ εἰσιν οἱ ἐκ τῶν ἁπλῶν πεπλεγμένοι καὶ ἔτι χρείαν ἔχοντες τῆς εἰς ἐκείνους ἀναλύσεως ἵνα γνωσθῶσιν ὅτι καὶ αὐτοὶ συνάγουσιν.

[31] This suggestion comes from Susanne Bobzien.

between simple unproveds, which are immediately knowable, and non-simple unproveds, which need something in order for their validity to be grasped. They need not to be proved but to be analysed.

What is an analysis? Sometimes the term 'analysis' serves to designate a proof; but—unless Sextus is in error—it cannot do so here—for in that case some unproved items would need proof. So what is an analysis? Various guesses have been made. For example, a non-simple unproved might be an unproved the logically pertinent parts of which are themselves complex assertibles. A little later—it is a passage which I have already quoted in a different context—Sextus sets down the following mode:

If the first and the second, the third
But not the third
Therefore not the first and the second

He says that it is a mode of the second unproved. (See *M* viii 236.) Perhaps it is non-simple, and perhaps you need to analyse it by grasping the structure of its complex premiss? Or again, a non-simple unproved might be a set or sequence of simple unproveds, the conclusion of each member of the set (except the final member) being a premiss for one of its successors. Such a compound syllogism would not need to be proved; but it would need to be articulated or to have its simple components marked off one from the next.

However that may be, it is plain enough—and undisputed—that when a syllogism needs a proof, then it needs it in order that its validity be known or recognized. And when a simple syllogism does not need a proof, that is because its validity is immediately knowable.

EVIDENCE

Euclid mastered geometry, and he possessed knowledge of many of the truths of that science. He grasped the truth of the theorems of geometry insofar as he proved them on the basis of the axioms of geometry. And he grasped the axioms of geometry ... in some other way. So it is for any Aristotelian science. So, *mutatis mutandis*, is it for the science or quasi-science of logic. In predicative syllogistic, you know that the imperfect syllogisms are valid insofar as you prove them to be valid on the basis of the perfect syllogisms. And you know that the perfect syllogisms are valid ... in some other way.

That is familiar, and no doubt it is even true. But it is scarcely illuminating until we are told something about the 'other way'. The point is entirely general and applies to the axioms of any science: the axioms are known; they are not known on the basis of a proof; and so they are known in some other way. But in what other way? Or perhaps rather: in what other ways? For there is no reason to think that there is only one other way, or that all the axioms of all the sciences are grasped in the same fashion—indeed, it must seem initially plausible to imagine that the axioms of the science of botany are grasped in a different way from the axioms of the science of arithmetic.

So in what other way (or ways) are the axioms or quasi-axioms of logic grasped? The Stoic logicians must surely have addressed the question; but there is virtually nothing about it in the surviving texts. Aristotle addressed the question; but he did so unostentatiously, and his followers devoted less time to the matter than they might have done. Galen too may be deemed to have addressed the question, even if he did so obliquely. But Galen's answer is controversial—and it is also bedevilled by textual uncertainties. I shall start with Aristotle.

Aristotle says that the necessity, or the validity, of perfect syllogisms is apparent or evident. Later philosophers will say the same thing about axioms in general: they are known inasmuch as they are plain or clear or patent or evident; or inasmuch as they are self-evident, or (to stay closer to the Greek phrase) evident from themselves. Equivalently, axioms and axiom-like items are said to be known from themselves, or known immediately or directly—so that perfect predicative syllogisms, as Alexander put it, are ones which are 'immediately knowable' or 'knowable from themselves' (*in APr* 6.24). And again, such items are often said to be self-warranting or self-justifying: in Galen's words:

none of the other syllogisms is unproved, nor warranted from itself.

(*inst log* viii 3)[32]

There is an extensive lexicon. But—at least at first glance—it is an unsatisfactory lexicon.

First, appeals to evidence, or to self-evidence, seem strangely vacuous. 'The answer's a lemon.'—'How do you know that?'—'Why, it's self-evident.' That hardly explains how I know that the answer's a lemon: it merely repeats, with a mallet, that I do know. Nor does the answer 'By intuition' fare

---

[32] τῶν δὲ ἄλλων οὐκέτ᾽ οὐδεὶς ἀναπόδεικτός ἐστιν οὐδ᾽ ἐξ ἑαυτοῦ πιστός.

any better. True, Aristotle's translators make him speak of intuitions; true, some modern philosophers invoke our moral intuitions, and some modern philosophers appeal to our linguistic intuitions. But suppose I say: 'I intuit that the answer's a lemon': what on earth can I mean? Either I invoke an imaginary faculty or capacity of the soul, or else I say in a fancy way 'I know—but not by way of a proof'.

Secondly, evidence or self-evidence is surely a relative and a subjective matter: what is evident to you may be obscure to me, and *vice versa*; the validity of Barbara might be obscure to a tiro and the validity of Bocardo evident to an expert. How can the science of syllogistic be constructed on such subjective sand? (A similar question may, of course, be asked of any science.)

Thirdly, if Barbara—say—is evident, then on what does its evidence rest? What feature of Barbara ensures that it is evident—or at least evident to some people—whereas Baroco is not evident at all? To appeal to self-evidence without even hinting at the locus or the basis of the evidence is to support the science of syllogistic by magic and incantation.

Commentators on Aristotle's syllogistic have discussed such issues at length; and they have proposed various interpretations of evidence or self-evidence. Here I restrict my attention to Aristotle's own proposal.

THE *DICTUM DE OMNI ET NULLO*

In order to grasp what that proposal is, we must start from a passage at the beginning of the *Prior Analytics*. The opening sentence of the work announces a programme. (The first item on the programme is dealt with at once and in half a sentence; and the programme itself—like the programme which intro-duces the *de Interpretatione*—covers not the whole work but only its preface.)

First we must say what our inquiry is about and with what it is concerned—it is about proof and concerned with probative knowledge. Next, we must define what a proposition is, what a term is, what a syllogism is, what sort of syllogism is perfect and what imperfect; after that, what it is for this to be (or not be) in that as in a whole, and what we mean by being predicated of every or of none.

(*APr* 24a10–15)[33]

---

[33] πρῶτον εἰπεῖν περὶ τί καὶ τίνος ἐστὶν ἡ σκέψις, ὅτι περὶ ἀπόδειξιν καὶ ἐπιστήμης ἀποδεικτικῆς· εἶτα διορίσαι τί ἐστι πρότασις καὶ τί ὅρος καὶ τί συλλογισμός, καὶ ποῖος τέλειος

Aristotle addresses the last two items on the programme in the following passage:

For one thing to be in another as in a whole and for the other to be predicated of all of the one is the same thing. We say that it is predicated of every when you can't take anything of which the other will not be said. And in the same way for of none.

(*APr* 24b25–30)[34]

The elucidations of 'of every' and 'of none' which Aristotle there offers are traditionally known as the *dictum de omni et nullo*. The *dictum* is not lavish with its words—and the *de nullo* part is a mere gesture.

Aristotle speaks of one item's being in another item as in a whole and of one item's being predicated of all of another item. Should we take the word 'another' seriously? If we do, then Aristotle says nothing about what it is, or might be, for something to be in itself as in a whole and nothing about what it is, or might be, for something to be predicated of all of itself. Similar questions arise in other Aristotelian contexts, and they sometimes have their importance.

Consider, for example, Aristotle's explanation of relations or relativity in the *Categories*. He says that

items are said to be relative to something when they are said to be what they are of other items or in relation to some other item.

(*Cat* 6a36–37)[35]

There we find the neutral phrase 'relative to something', followed by references to 'other items' or 'some other item'. If we insist on the introduction of the word 'other' in the second clause, and suppose that it corrects the neutral 'something', then we shall conclude that Aristotle formally excludes the possibility that an item might be related to itself. Admirers are relational items—provided that they aren't self-admirers.

Now it is true that Aristotle does not discuss such things—he never explicitly wonders whether an item may stand in a given relation to itself; and it is also true that some later philosophers made a meal of the matter. ('I was

καὶ ποῖος ἀτελής, μετὰ δέ ταῦτα τί τὸ ἐν ὅλῳ εἶναι ἢ μὴ εἶναι τόδε τῷδε, καὶ τί λέγομεν τὸ κατὰ παντὸς ἢ μηδενὸς κατηγορεῖσθαι.

[34] τὸ δὲ ἐν ὅλῳ εἶναι ἕτερον ἑτέρῳ καὶ τὸ κατὰ παντὸς κατηγορεῖσθαι θατέρου θάτερον ταὐτόν ἐστιν. λέγομεν δὲ τὸ κατὰ παντὸς κατηγορεῖσθαι ὅταν μηδὲν ᾖ λαβεῖν καθ᾽ οὗ θάτερον οὐ λεχθήσεται· καὶ τὸ κατὰ μηδενὸς ὡσαύτως.—After 'λαβεῖν' the archetype of our MSS had 'τοῦ ὑποκειμένου': Alexander did not read the formula, which is an evident gloss.

[35] πρός τι δὲ τὰ τοιαῦτα λέγεται ὅσα αὐτὰ ἅπερ ἐστὶν ἑτέρων εἶναι λέγεται ἢ ὁπωσοῦν ἄλλως πρὸς ἕτερον.

thinking of myself.'—'How can that possibly be? Surely there must be one item which is doing the thinking and another which is being thought of?') But I cannot think that Aristotle intended to exclude self-relativity—and excluded it tacitly and without a word of explanation.

The word 'other'—or some equivalent word—is often inserted where strictly speaking it is out of place. When Aristotle explains affirmations and negations in the *de Interpretatione* what he actually says is this:

> An affirmation is an assertion of something of something, a negation is an assertion of something from something.
>
> > *(Int* 17a25–26)[36]

Very often, allusions to and paraphrases of that definition will say that an affirmation says one thing of another or predicates one item of another. The 'another' is not warranted by Aristotle's definition. But it is natural to insert it; for 'something of something' is stilted and 'one thing of another' is normal. The insertion is done without malice and without meaning—and usually it is not even noticed.

So, I suppose, it is with the word 'other' in the passage on relative items; so too with *dictum de omni et nullo*: Aristotle means to be explaining what it is for something to be (or not to be) in something as in a whole; he does not mean to suggest that 'x is in y as in a whole' might mean one thing when x and y are different and another thing (or nothing at all) when they are identical.

To be in something as in a whole is the same as to be wholly subjected to it; or, more clearly, B is in A as in a whole if and only if A is predicated of every B. The terminology of wholes and parts which Aristotle uses sporadically throughout the *Analytics* is not without its interest; and in some contexts it may be not without its significance. But in the context of the *dictum* it demands no special scrutiny, and I shall say nothing about it.

The *dictum* has two parts, each of which is itself a *dictum*. First, then, the *dictum de omni*:

> We say that it is predicated of every when you can't take anything of which the other will not be said.

Aristotle's formulation is ungainly—at least in translation; and what he means will be clearer if we replace his pronouns with a couple of Aristotelian letters, thus:

---

[36] κατάφασις δέ ἐστιν ἀπόφανσις τινὸς κατὰ τινός, ἀπόφασις δέ ἐστιν ἀπόφανσις τινὸς ἀπὸ τινός.

We say that A is predicated of every B when you can't take any B of which A will not be said.

That formulation may be simplified in four ways. First, and uncontroversially, the verb 'say' in 'will not be said' is a synonym for 'predicate', so that 'will not be said' may be replaced by 'will not be predicated'. Secondly, and equally uncontroversially, the future tense in 'will not be said' is an inferential future—an idiom which is less common in English than in Greek, and which in the context of the *dictum* is naturally replaced by an English present tense. Thus ' ... is not predicated' may replace ' ... will not be said'.

The third point concerns the word 'can't' and is perhaps disputable. 'Can't' is a modal word. Nonetheless, I think that the modal element, which is very lightly indicated in the Greek, is not to be taken seriously: 'you can't take' means no more than 'you won't take'. The reason for so construing the text is this: were the modal element taken seriously, then Aristotle would not be able to distinguish, as he does distinguish, between 'A is predicated of every B' and 'A must be predicated of every B'.

Finally, and again not wholly uncontentiously, it seems to me that what counts for the *dictum* is not whether you do or don't take a B of which A isn't said but whether there is or isn't such a B to be taken. Were we to take the taking seriously, then we should have to allow that A might be predicated of every B even when there were some Bs of which A didn't hold—provided that, for some reason or other, we did not or would not or could not take those particular Bs. And that is not on the Aristotelian cards.

As a result of those four little pedantries, the *dictum de omni* can be rephrased in the following fashion. What we say is that

A is predicated of every B if and only if there isn't any B of which A is not predicated.

Alexander surely so understood the *dictum*. This is his paraphrase:

Since every predicative proposition is composed of a subject term and a predicate, the predicated term is truly said of all the subject when you cannot take any of the subject of which the predicate will not be said. For example, animal of every man—for it is not possible to take a man of whom animal will not be said.

(*in APr* 24.30–25.2)[37]

---

[37] ἐπεὶ γὰρ πᾶσα πρότασις κατηγορικὴ ἐξ ὑποκειμένου ὅρου ἐστὶ καὶ κατηγορουμένου, τότε λέγεται ὁ κατηγορούμενος κατὰ παντὸς τοῦ ὑποκειμένου ἀληθῶς ὅταν μηδὲν ἦ λαβεῖν τοῦ ὑποκειμένου καθ' οὗ οὐ ῥηθήσεται τὸ κατηγορούμενον· οἷον τὸ ζῷον κατὰ παντὸς ἀνθρώπου—οὐδένα γὰρ λαβεῖν ἔστιν ἄνθρωπον καθ' οὗ τὸ ζῷον οὐ ῥηθήσεται.

It is true that Alexander here retains the modal element and also the notion of taking; but his version of the *dictum de nullo*, which I shall cite in an instant, is enough to show that he did not mean them seriously.

If that is the first part of the traditional *dictum*, namely the *dictum de omni*, what is the second part or the *dictum de nullo*? Aristotle is allusive:

And in the same way for of none.

Had Aristotle formulated the *dictum* explicitly—had he written out what the adverb 'in the same way' promises—he must presumably have said something very like this:

We say that it is predicated of none when you can't take anything of which the other will be said.[38]

After four pedantries, that formulation would be replaced by:

A is predicated of no B if and only if there isn't any B of which A is predicated.

And that, I suppose, is the *dictum de nullo*—it is how Alexander understood it:

When you can't take any of the subject of which the predicate will be said, then 'of no' is truly said. For example, neigher of no man—for there is no man of whom neigher is predicated.

(*in APr* 25.18–21)[39]

So too Philoponus:

For example, we say that animal is predicated of every man—and there is not a man of whom animal will not be said. Similarly for 'of no': we say that man holds of no stone—and there is not a stone of which man will be said.

(*in APr* 39.11–15)[40]

What is the status of the *dicta*, or of the two parts of the *dictum*? I mean, when Aristotle says 'we say', does he intend to report the ordinary usage of us Greeks, or to indicate the special usage of us logicians or of us Aristotelians, or to stipulate a special usage for the purposes of the *Analytics*?

---

[38] λέγομεν δὲ τὸ κατὰ μηδενὸς κατηγορεῖσθαι ὅταν μηδὲν ᾖ λαβεῖν καθ᾽ οὗ θάτερον λεχθήσεται.

[39] ὅταν γὰρ μηδὲν ᾖ λαβεῖν τοῦ ὑποκειμένου καθ᾽ οὗ τὸ κατηγορούμενον ῥηθήσεται, τότε ἐστὶ καὶ τὸ κατὰ μηδενὸς ἀληθῶς· οἷον τὸ χρεμετιστικὸν κατ᾽ οὐδενὸς ἀνθρώπου—οὐδεὶς γάρ ἐστιν ἄνθρωπος καθ᾽ οὗ τὸ χρεμετιστικὸν κατηγορεῖται.

[40] οἷον λέγομεν τὸ ζῷον κατὰ παντὸς ἀνθρώπου κατηγορεῖσθαι· καὶ οὐκ ἔστι τις ἄνθρωπος καθ᾽ οὗ τὸ ζῷον οὐ λεχθήσεται. καὶ τὸ κατὰ μηδενὸς ὁμοίως· λέγομεν γὰρ τὸν ἄνθρωπον κατὰ μηδενὸς λίθου ὑπάρχειν· καὶ οὐκ ἔστι τις λίθος καθ᾽ οὗ ὁ ἄνθρωπος λεχθήσεται.

Aristotle's words do not suggest a stipulation (but that signifies little). It seems unlikely that there was, or that Aristotle thought that there was, a special logical or Aristotelian sense of words such as 'every' and 'no'. It is best to suppose that the *dictum* purports to explain what we—that is to say, we Greeks—normally mean when we say 'of every' and 'of no' and the like; that is, it purports to gloss the normal use, or perhaps a normal use, of those quantifying expressions.

Did Aristotle understand the normal use aright? That is to say, is the *dictum* true? Well, a die-hard Aristotelian ought to have doubts, and for a familiar reason. Suppose that there are no items at all of a certain sort—that there is not a single phoenix, for example. And take any predicate you like—say 'red-feathered'. Now since there are no phoenixes at all, it follows that there is no phoenix of which 'red-feathered' is not predicated. And so (according to Aristotle's definition), every phoenix is red-feathered. Again, since there are no phoenixes, there is no phoenix of which 'red-feathered' is predicated. And so (according to Aristotle's definition), no phoenix is red-feathered. Thus every phoenix is red-feathered and no phoenix is red-feathered. But surely that is impossible? Well, impossible or not, it is uncontroversially impossible in the context of Aristotle's own logic. For

Every phoenix is red-feathered

and

No phoenix is red-feathered

are contraries, and contraries cannot be true together.

That consideration is part of a familiar difficulty, or a familiar group of difficulties. The sign under which the difficulty is sold is 'Existential Import'; for it is most notoriously manifested in the so-called law of subalternation which affirms that if A holds of every B then A holds of some B. For example, if every phoenix is red-feathered, then some phoenix is red-feathered. But if some phoenix is red-feathered, then there is at least one phoenix. The law of subalternation thus requires

Every phoenix is red-feathered

to be false. The *dictum de omni* makes it true.

If the difficulty is familiar, so are the various ways of circumventing it. I shall not rehearse them here; but one or another of them must be adopted by anyone who wishes both to hold onto the *dictum* and also to accept the main theses of Aristotle's syllogistic.

Someone who is not a die-hard Aristotelian is likely to find the *dictum* puzzling for a quite different reason: far from being false, or even disputable, the *dictum* will appear to be trivial, tautologous, vacuous. Look again at the *dictum de nullo*:

A is predicated of no B if and only if there isn't any B of which A is predicated.

That is hardly an elucidation of 'of no': it merely shuffles the words around. Aristotle's formulation of the *dictum*—and in particular, his failure to formulate the *de nullo* part—hides the vacuity. But surely it is there?

Well, perhaps the *dictum* is a trifle. But if it is trivial, then it has at least one virtue—it is true.

PUTTING THE *DICTUM* TO WORK

In any event, the question which will exercise me here is another one. It is this: What use is the *dictum*? what work can it do?

Two passages in chapters 4–6 of the first book of the *Prior Analytics* invoke the *dictum*, and there are a further couple of passages in the chapters on modal syllogistic. The two passages in chapters 4–6 in effect contain four appeals to the *dictum*, as follows:

[1] If A of every B and B of every C, it is necessary that A be predicated of every C—for we have earlier said what we mean by 'of every'. [2] Similarly, if A of no B and B of every C, A will hold of no C.

(*APr* 25b37–40)[41]

[3] Let A hold of every B and B of some C. Then if being predicated of every is what we said at the beginning, it is necessary for A to hold of some C. [4] And if A holds of no B and B of some C, it is necessary for A not to hold of some C—for we have also defined what we mean by 'of no'. Hence there will be a perfect syllogism.

(*APr* 26a23–28)[42]

Item [1] is the conclusion of Aristotle's account of the first mood of the first figure—of Barbara. The particle 'for [γάρ]' suggests that the account is

[41] εἰ γὰρ τὸ Α κατὰ παντὸς τοῦ Β καὶ τὸ Β κατὰ παντὸς τοῦ Γ, ἀνάγκη τὸ Α κατὰ παντὸς τοῦ Γ κατηγορεῖσθαι· πρότερον γὰρ εἴρηται πῶς τὸ κατὰ παντὸς λέγομεν. ὁμοίως δὲ καὶ εἰ τὸ μὲν Α κατὰ μηδενὸς τοῦ Β, τὸ δὲ Β κατὰ παντὸς τοῦ Γ, ὅτι τὸ Α οὐδενὶ τῷ Γ ὑπάρξει.

[42] ὑπαρχέτω γὰρ τὸ μὲν Α παντὶ τῷ Β, τὸ δὲ Β τινὶ τῷ Γ. οὐκοῦν εἰ ἔστι παντὸς κατηγορεῖσθαι τὸ ἐν ἀρχῇ λεχθέν, ἀνάγκη τὸ Α τινὶ τῷ Γ ὑπάρχειν. καὶ εἰ τὸ μὲν Α μηδενὶ τῷ Β ὑπάρχει, τὸ δὲ Β τινὶ τῷ Γ, ἀνάγκη τὸ Α τινὶ τῷ Γ μὴ ὑπάρχειν· ὥρισται γὰρ καὶ τὸ κατὰ μηδενὸς πῶς λέγομεν· ὥστε ἔσται συλλογισμὸς τέλειος.

justified or explained by reference to what 'we have earlier said'—and what we have earlier said is, of course, the *de omni* part of the *dictum*. Item [2] does for Celarent what item [1] does for Barbara; and the introductory adverb 'similarly' suggests that just as the *de omni* part of the *dictum* can be invoked in support of Barbara, so the *de nullo* part can be invoked in support of Celarent. Item [3] is Aristotle's exposition of Darii: again the *dictum* is invoked, and again with a justificatory or explanatory function. The same is true of item [4], where it is a question of Ferio—and where it is the *de nullo* part of the *dictum* which is called upon.

The four perfect syllogisms of the first figure are thus explained, or justified, or—as I shall say—underwritten by the *dictum de omni et nullo*. But what exactly does the *dictum* underwrite? In the case of Ferio, Aristotle remarks: 'so that there will be a perfect syllogism'. It might be inferred that the *dictum* is supposed to explain why Ferio is perfect rather than imperfect; and so, more generally, to explain perfection or to justify an ascription of perfection. In other words, the *dictum* does not explain why perfect syllogisms are valid—it explains why they are perfect (or in what their perfection consists).

That argument is unpersuasive. It is not, so far as I can see, clear that the *dictum* is invoked to explain perfection rather than to explain validity; but let that pass. Suppose that the *dictum* explains perfection. That is to say, the *dictum* answers the question 'Why are Barbara and the others evidently valid?' Now you might perhaps manage to construe that question so that it was about evidence and not about validity. ('Yes, I see that Barbara is valid—but tell me why it is evidently valid.') But any such construal would be bizarre; and the question is best taken at its face value—it asks why Barbara and the rest are evidently valid.

So the state of affairs with perfect syllogisms is this: A perfect syllogism is valid; its validity is evident without appeal to any external items, and without proof; its validity is evident inasmuch as it is underwritten by the *dictum de omni et nullo*. That was Alexander's view of the matter:

All the syllogisms thus far described [i.e. the first figure syllogisms] are perfect; for, using nothing but 'of every' or 'of no', which has already been established, they have an evident validity.

(*in APr* 61.3–5)[43]

And that was Alexander's view of Aristotle's view of the matter:

---

[43] πάντες δὲ οἱ προειρημένοι τέλειοι· πάντες γὰρ τῷ κατὰ παντὸς μόνῳ ἢ κατὰ μηδενὸς προσχρώμενοι, ὅ ἐστι κείμενον, φανερὰν τὴν συναγωγὴν ἔχουσιν.

He defined a perfect syllogism as one which needs nothing else apart from the items assumed in order for its necessity to be apparent: he says that all the syllogisms he has shown in this figure are perfect since all are perfected by way of the items assumed at the beginning and already established, and they need nothing else. The items assumed at the beginning by way of which the necessity of these syllogisms is apparent are 'of every', which is equivalent to 'in as in a whole', and 'of no' and 'in no'.

(*in APr* 69.14–20)[44]

Alexander has an eccentric interpretation of the phrase 'the items assumed', which surely refers to the premisses of the perfect syllogisms rather than to the *dictum*; but that gaffe apart, he is surely right.

That conclusion may be supported by reference to the heterodox view of Boethus, who held that the canonical syllogisms—all fourteen of them, or perhaps twelve of them—are perfect. Themistius reports Boethus' view about Darapti:

He says that ... in the first mood of the third figure (in which the two extremes are said of all the middle term), when two things are said of one thing, then it is evident that each is in the other as a part. As for his formula 'in every', we must discover how he uses it ...

(*ad Max* 192)

The report clearly suggests, although it does not state, that the perfection of Darapti depended, in Boethus' book, on the *dictum de omni*. And the suggestion is confirmed by a more general remark of Themistius':

Since Boethus now turns to the third figure, let us remark on how he comes to commit sophisms concerning the number of syllogisms—sophisms which are consequences of the fact that he has explained the formula 'in every' in a way different from the one which Aristotle indicates in the *Analytics*.

(*ad Max* 192)

The matter stands thus: Aristotle finds four perfect syllogisms, and their perfection depends on their relation to the *dictum de omni et nullo*. Boethus finds fourteen—or perhaps twelve—perfect syllogisms, and their perfection

---

[44] ὡρίσατο τὸν τέλειον συλλογισμὸν τὸν μηδενὸς ἄλλου προσδεόμενον παρὰ τὰ εἰλημμένα πρὸς τὸ φανῆναι τὸ ἀναγκαῖον. φησὶ δὲ πάντας τοὺς ἐν τούτῳ τῷ σχήματι δεδειγμένους συλλογισμοὺς τελείους εἶναι, ἐπειδὴ πάντες ἐπιτελοῦνται διὰ τῶν ἐξ ἀρχῆς εἰλημμένων τε καὶ κειμένων καὶ οὐδενὸς ἄλλου προσδέονται. ἔστι δὲ τὰ ἐξ ἀρχῆς λαμβανόμενα δι' ὧν τὸ ἐν αὐτοῖς ἀναγκαῖον φανερόν ἐστιν τό τε κατὰ παντὸς ἴσον ὂν τῷ ἐν ὅλῳ καὶ τὸ κατὰ μηδενὸς καὶ ἐν μηδενί.

depends on the *dictum*. The difference between Aristotle and Boethus is to be explained—if we may trust Themistius—by the fact that Boethus gave a heterodox version of the *dictum*. Unfortunately we don't know what that version was.

So far I have mentioned the use of the *dictum* in connection with non-modal syllogistic. But it is also invoked twice in Aristotle's account of modal syllogisms—or at least, it appears to be invoked in one passage and it is often taken to be invoked in a second. Of apodictic syllogisms, or syllogisms each component proposition of which says that something holds necessarily of something, Aristotle says that

in the case of necessities things are pretty much the same as in the non-modal cases: when the terms are placed in the same way, there will be or not be a syllogism both in holding and in holding of necessity (or not holding)—except that they will differ inasmuch as holding of necessity (or not holding) is added to the terms. For the privative converts in the same way, and we shall explain 'as in a whole' and 'of every' in the same way.

(*APr* 29b36–30a3)[45]

An apodictic syllogism is valid if and only if its non-modal counterpart is valid, and the validity of apodictic syllogisms is established in the same way as the validity of their counterparts (with a couple of exceptions). The reference to the *dictum* in the passage evidently applies to the four perfect apodictic syllogisms: they, like their non-modal partners, have their validity underwritten by the *dictum de omni et nullo*. So Alexander:

'of every' and 'of no' are taken in the same way in the case of the necessary as they are in the case of the non-modal, and it is by way of them that the first figure syllogisms are shown.

(*in APr* 120.13–15)[46]

The second modal invocation of the *dictum* is more controversial. It occurs where Aristotle discusses first figure problematical syllogisms, or syllogisms all of whose component propositions say that something possibly holds of something. Here are problematic Barbara and Celarent:

---

[45] ἐπὶ μὲν οὖν τῶν ἀναγκαίων σχεδὸν ὁμοίως ἔχει καὶ ἐπὶ τῶν ὑπαρχόντων· ὡσαύτως γὰρ τιθεμένων τῶν ὅρων ἔν τε τῷ ὑπάρχειν καὶ τῷ ἐξ ἀνάγκης ὑπάρχειν ἢ μὴ ὑπάρχειν ἔσται τε καὶ οὐκ ἔσται συλλογισμός, πλὴν διοίσει τῷ προσκεῖσθαι τοῖς ὅροις τὸ ἐξ ἀνάγκης ὑπάρχειν ἢ μὴ ὑπάρχειν. τό τε γὰρ στερητικὸν ὡσαύτως ἀντιστρέφει, καὶ τὸ ἐν ὅλῳ εἶναι καὶ τὸ κατὰ παντὸς ὁμοίως ἀποδώσομεν.

[46] ... τό τε κατὰ παντὸς καὶ τὸ κατὰ μηδενὸς ὁμοίως καὶ ἐπὶ τοῦ ἀναγκαίου λαμβάνεται ὡς καὶ ἐπὶ τοῦ ὑπάρχοντος, δι' οὗ οἱ ἐν τῷ πρώτῳ σχήματι δείκνυνται συλλογισμοί.

Now when A can hold of every B and B of every C, there will be a perfect syllogism to the conclusion that A can hold of every C. This is evident from the definition; for we described 'can hold of every' in that way. Similarly if A can hold of no B and B of every C—that A can hold of no C. For for A not to be possibly predicated of what B is possibly predicated of was precisely for there to be no exceptions among the items possibly under B.

(*APr* 32b38–33a5)[47]

Then Darii and Ferio:

If one of the premisses is assumed as a universal and the other as a particular, then if the universal is on the major term there will be a perfect syllogism. For if A can hold of every B and B of some C, A can hold of some C—this is evident from the definition of 'can'. Again, if A can hold of no B and B can hold of some C, then it is necessary that A can not hold of some C. The proof is the same.

(*APr* 33a21–27)[48]

There are four perfect problematical syllogisms, and each is supported by reference—explicit or implicit—to a definition.

Alexander takes the references to be to the *dictum de omni et nullo*. Or rather, he thinks that that is plainly so in the cases of the universal syllogisms. Thus for Barbara:

'This is evident from the definition' indicates that it is clear from the definition of 'of every' that in the present conjugation a universal affirmative problematic conclusion is inferred.

(*in APr* 167.14–17)[49]

And similarly five lines later for Celarent. As for Darii and Ferio, Alexander offers two interpretations, between which he does not choose:

---

[47] ὅταν οὖν τὸ Α παντὶ τῷ Β ἐνδέχηται καὶ τὸ Β παντὶ τῷ Γ, συλλογισμὸς ἔσται τέλειος ὅτι τὸ Α παντὶ τῷ Γ ἐνδέχεται ὑπάρχειν. τοῦτο δὲ φανερὸν ἐκ τοῦ ὁρισμοῦ· τὸ γὰρ ἐνδέχεσθαι παντὶ ὑπάρχειν οὕτως ἐλέγομεν. ὁμοίως δὲ καὶ εἰ τὸ μὲν Α ἐνδέχεται μηδενὶ τῷ Β, τὸ δὲ Β παντὶ τῷ Γ, ὅτι τὸ Α ἐνδέχεται μηδενὶ τῷ Γ· τὸ γὰρ καθ᾽ οὗ τὸ Β ἐνδέχεται, τὸ Α μὴ ἐνδέχεσθαι, τοῦτ᾽ ἦν τὸ μηδέν ἀπολείπειν τῶν ὑπὸ τὸ Β ἐνδεχομένων.

[48] ἐὰν δ᾽ ἡ μὲν καθόλου τῶν προτάσεων ἡ δ᾽ ἐν μέρει ληφθῇ, πρὸς μὲν τὸ μεῖζον ἄκρον κειμένης τῆς καθόλου συλλογισμὸς ἔσται τέλειος. εἰ γὰρ τὸ Α παντὶ τῷ Β ἐνδέχεται τὸ δὲ Β τινὶ τῷ Γ, τὸ Α τινὶ τῷ Γ ἐνδέχεται· τοῦτο δὲ φανερὸν ἐκ τοῦ ὁρισμοῦ τοῦ ἐνδέχεσθαι. πάλιν εἰ τὸ Α ἐνδέχεται μηδενὶ τῷ Β, τὸ δὲ Β τινὶ τῷ Γ ἐνδέχεται ὑπάρχειν, ἀνάγκη τὸ Α ἐνδέχεσθαί τινι τῶν Γ μὴ ὑπάρχειν. ἀπόδειξις δ᾽ ἡ αὐτή.

[49] τὸ δὲ τοῦτο δὲ φανερὸν ἐκ τοῦ ὁρισμοῦ δηλωτικόν ἐστιν ὅτι τὸ συνάγεσθαι ἐν τῇ προκειμένῃ συζυγίᾳ καθόλου ἐνδεχόμενον καταφατικὸν συμπέρασμα δῆλόν ἐστιν ἐκ τοῦ ὁρισμοῦ τοῦ κατὰ παντός.

He says that this too is evident from the definition of 'can', either meaning 'can hold of every' (since 'of every' was that of which you can't take anything of which the other will not be said) ... , or else he means from the definition of the possible itself.

(in APr 169.23–30)[50]

There is much to be said for the first of those two interpretations. For if it is accepted, then Aristotle will appeal to the *dictum de omni et nullo* in the case of all the syllogisms which he recognizes to be perfect, and only in their cases. A syllogism is perfect if and only if it is underwritten by the *dictum*.

That is the line which Philoponus, for example, follows—apparently without any anxiety. But modern scholarship has not sided with him. In the case of problematical Barbara and Celarent, it is urged, Aristotle must be invoking his explanation of 'possible' when he refers to his account of 'what can hold of every', and not to his definition of 'of every' and 'of no'. As for problematical Darii and Ferio, there Aristotle clearly invokes his definition of 'possible'; but he cannot be invoking the definition in order to justify the perfection of the two syllogisms—for in fact neither syllogism is perfect (and the word 'perfect' must be cut from the received text).

The reasons for denying perfection to Darii and Ferio are frail. But there is a curiosity about Aristotle's presentation of the two particular syllogisms which has suggested that he cannot be appealing to the *dictum* in their cases. For of Ferio he says that 'the proof is the same'; and although perfect syllogisms can, of course, be proved, an appeal to the *dictum* is not at all the same thing as a proof—so that if we take the word 'proof' seriously, we should not think that Aristotle is here appealing to the *dictum*. That is a fair-seeming argument. But it should not seduce. For on any account of the passage, Aristotle supports Darii and Ferio by appeal to a definition. Such an appeal does not constitute a proof. Hence we should not take the word 'proof' seriously.

However that may be, is the validity of the perfect problematical syllogisms grounded on the *dictum* or rather on a definition of 'can'? The textual evidence tells decisively in neither direction, so that we might think to rely on logical or philosophical considerations—in which direction is the better sense found?

Well, what exactly are we looking for? The validity of perfect syllogisms, I have said, is underwritten by the *dictum*. But what exactly does that mean? It

---

[50] καὶ τοῦτο φανερόν φησιν εἶναι ἐκ τοῦ ὁρισμοῦ τοῦ ἐνδέχεσθαι ἤτοι λέγων τοῦ παντὶ ἐνδέχεσθαι (ἐπεὶ τὸ παντὶ ἦν οὗ μηδὲν ἦν λαβεῖν καθ' οὗ θάτερον οὐ ῥηθήσεται), ... ἢ τοῦ ὁρισμοῦ αὐτοῦ τοῦ ἐνδεχομένου λέγει.

seems relatively easy to give the beginnings of an answer to that question: the *dictum* underwrites the perfect syllogisms insofar as it articulates the sense of the quantifying words 'every' and 'no', or insofar as it explains what universal propositions (affirmative and negative) are; and the perfect syllogisms are valid in virtue of the sense of those quantifying words, or in virtue of the nature of those universal propositions.

No doubt the perfect syllogisms are valid in virtue of what might be called their quantificational structure. But then all predicative syllogisms are valid in virtue of their quantificational structure—that is what makes them predicative syllogisms. If that is all the *dictum* does in the way of underwriting, then it underwrites Darapti and Cesare as much as it underwrites Darii and Celarent. But that is not what Aristotle is on about: if an appeal to the *dictum* is to do the work Aristotle demands of it, then there must be a special relation between it and the perfect syllogisms, a relation which it does not have with any imperfect syllogism. What might that relation be? It may be helpful to turn briefly from predicative to hypothetical syllogistic.

THE *DICTUM DE SI ET AUT*

The mode—or one of the modes—of the first Chrysippean unproved syllogism was this:

If the 1st, the 2nd; the 1st: therefore the 2nd.

The complex premiss of a first unproved is a conditional proposition, and

of non-simple assertibles, the conditional—as Chrysippus says in the *Dialectics* and Diogenes in the *Art of Dialectic*—is one which is composed with the conditioning connector 'if'. This connector announces that the second follows the first, e.g.

If it is day, it is light.

(Diogenes Laertius, VII 71)[51]

On the basis of that text, we might invent the *dictum de si*:

One item holds if another does if and only if the one follows the other.

Or perhaps:

If P, then Q if and only if given that P it follows that Q.

The *dictum* is uncontroversially correct.

---

[51] τῶν δ᾽ οὐχ ἁπλῶν ἀξιωμάτων συνημμένον μέν ἐστιν, ὡς ὁ Χρύσιππος ἐν ταῖς Διαλεκτικαῖς φησι καὶ Διογένης ἐν τῇ Διαλεκτικῇ τέχνῃ, τὸ συνεστὸς διὰ τοῦ εἰ συναπτικοῦ συνδέσμου. ἐπαγγέλλεται δ᾽ ὁ σύνδεσμος οὗτος ἀκολουθεῖν τὸ δεύτερον τῷ πρώτῳ, οἷον εἰ ἡμέρα ἐστί, φῶς ἐστι.

It is true that there were different views about conditionals in antiquity, and at least four different analyses of the truth conditions for conditional propositions. Sextus presents the different views as rivals, and he duly uses the existence of the dispute to argue that 'true conditionals will be found to be inapprehensible' (*PH* II 110).[52] But Sextus' argument for inapprehensibility has no value; and although there is some evidence that the correct analysis of conditional propositions was indeed a matter of dispute in Hellenistic antiquity, it is plain that, in principle, each of the analyses might be correct, or useful, in certain contexts; and there is some reason to hold that Stoic authors would sometimes prefer one analysis and sometimes another.

In any event, even Sextus allows that all the analyses have something in common; for all the parties to the dispute—as Sextus characterizes them—agree on the crucial point:

All the logicians say that, in general, a conditional is sound when its consequent follows its antecedent—it is about when and how it follows that they dispute with one another and produce conflicting criteria of following.

(*M* VIII 112)[53]

The *dictum de si*, in other words, is a commonplace of ancient logic. How could it not be so?

The Stoics, so far as we know, did not appeal to the *dictum de si* in the way in which Aristotle appealed to the *dictum de omni*. But they could have done. For the *dictum de si* stands to hypothetical syllogisms as the *dictum de omni* stands to predicative syllogisms. The *dictum de si* underwrites hypothetical syllogisms to the extent that they turn about conditional assertibles. No doubt syllogisms which turn about conditionals are valid insofar as the *dictum* is true or insofar as the *dictum* explains what a conditional assertible is. But in that way, just as Aristotle's *dictum de omni* will underwrite Darii and Darapti alike, so the *dictum de si* will underwrite both the first Chrysippean unproved and also, say, the following syllogistic form:

If P, then if Q then R; Q: therefore if P, then R.

If the notional *dictum de si* is to do the work we notionally demand of it, then it must have a special relation with the first unproved which it does not have with that second syllogism.

---

[52] τὸ ὑγιὲς συνημμένον ἀκατάληπτον εὑρεθήσεται.

[53] κοινῶς μὲν γάρ φασιν ἅπαντες οἱ διαλεκτικοὶ ὑγιὲς εἶναι συνημμένον ὅταν ἀκολουθῇ τῷ ἐν αὐτῷ ἡγουμένῳ τὸ ἐν αὐτῷ λῆγον· περὶ δὲ τοῦ πότε ἀκολουθεῖ καὶ πῶς στασιάζουσι πρὸς ἀλλήλους καὶ μαχόμενα τῆς ἀκολουθίας ἐκτίθενται κριτήρια.

Does it have such a relation? Well, you might understand the *dictum* and yet deny, or at least wonder about, the validity of the second argument. You might understand, thanks to the *dictum*, the constituent elements in

If P, then if Q then R; Q: therefore if P, then R

and not thereby know whether or not the syllogism is valid. Understanding it, you may still ache to prove its validity—or to work out if it really is valid. But if you grasp the *dictum* then you cannot have doubts about the first unproved, let alone deny its validity.

If you understand what a first unproved is, then you know what a conditional assertible is—you know what a sentence of the form 'If P, then Q' announces. But you know what such a sentence announces insofar as you have grasped the *dictum de si*, so what you know is that if P then Q if and only if given that P it follows that Q. And in that case you thereby know that the first unproved is valid. If you contemplate a first unproved, and see that it has the form of a first unproved, and nevertheless are doubtful of its validity, then you do not understand what conditional assertibles are—and so you do not understand what a first unproved is.

A first unproved needs no proof insofar as it is immediately evident. It is immediately evident insofar as it cannot be understood without being accepted.

The point can be put in terms of circumscriptions—indeed, it is better so put. For although the *dictum* (as I have formulated it) gives the sense of the connector 'if', it is not really a principle about the meaning of the English word 'if'. It is a principle about the nature of conditional propositions; and you might therefore express it thus:

A conditional proposition is true if and only if its consequent follows its antecedent.

The special relation between the *dictum* and the first unproved may then be put like this. A first unproved is characterized by the circumscription:

From a conditional proposition and its antecedent there is a valid inference to its consequent.

Suppose I ask myself if such a syllogism is valid. If I understand what a first unproved is, then I understand what a conditional assertible is—namely, as the *dictum de si* has it, an assertible which is true if and only if its consequent follows its antecedent. And understanding that, I know that a first unproved is valid.

There is a form of inference which involves the relation of sameness or identity, and which can be put schematically like this:

a is the same item as b
F(a)
Therefore F(b)

The validity of that inference is evident, in this sense: anyone who understands the inference knows that it is valid; anyone who doubts the validity of the inference thereby shows that he has not understood what an identity statement is. 'So this Japrisot you go on about is actually the same bloke as Rossi?'—'Yes, and I tell you again that Japrisot wrote some marvellous books'—'So you say: do you think Rossi did so too?'

What about the other four Stoic unproveds? For the fourth and fifth of them we shall need to invent a *dictum de aut*, which will presumably read something like this:

A disjunctive assertible is true if and only if exactly one of its disjuncts is true, the rest being false.

These are the circumscriptions of the fourth and fifth unproveds in their simplest versions:

From a disjunction and one of its disjuncts there is a valid inference to an opposite of the other disjunct.
From a disjunction and an opposite of one of its disjuncts there is a valid inference to the remaining disjunct.

If you understand what a disjunction is—if you grasp the *dictum de aut*—do you thereby recognize the validity of those two forms of inference?

Surely not—if only because you need also to master the secrets of opposition. Something similar goes for the second unproved:

From a conditional and an opposite of its consequent there is a valid inference to an opposite of its antecedent.

You might have mastered the *dictum de si* and yet fail to see the validity of the second unproved—for you might master the *dictum de si* while knowing nothing about the delights of opposition. As for the third unproved, it demands even more:

From a negated conjunction and one of its conjuncts, there is a valid inference to an opposite of its other conjunct.

To grasp the validity of that inference you must have mastered conjunction, negation, and opposition.

Those contentions might be accepted, and it might accordingly be allowed that there are interesting differences between the first unproved and the other four; and it might then be claimed that, in the present context, those differences make no difference. For what counts is this: the evident validity of the unproveds resides in the fact that each is underwritten by a *dictum* or group of *dicta*; in other words, each is such that anyone who understands it thereby recognizes it to be valid.

That sounds plausible enough. But suppose you have mastered the *dictum de aut* and also some appropriate *dictum de oppositis*: have you done enough—and all that you can do—in order to grasp the validity of the fourth and fifth unproveds? It is not plain that the right answer to that question is Yes. For might you not in principle master each of the two *dicta* and yet not, so to speak, put the two masteries together? And in such a pickle, might you not understand the fourth and fifth unproveds and yet intelligibly raise doubts about them? Perhaps you might; but the ground is treacherous here—and no doubt the criteria for mastery of the *dicta* are rather marshy at the edges.

A DIFFICULTY, AND ALEXANDER'S SOLUTION

However that may be, the rough idea which I have just sketched in the case of hypothetical syllogisms may now be applied to predicative syllogisms: no doubt the *dictum de omni et nullo* underwrites, in a sense, all predicative syllogisms; but perhaps it also applies in a special way to the four perfect syllogisms of the first figure. Perhaps it is worth reformulating the *dictum* along the lines of the reformulated *dictum de si*, thus:

> A proposition which predicates A universally and affirmatively of B is true if and only if there is no B of which A is not predicated.
> A proposition which predicates A universally and negatively of B is true if and only if there is no B of which A is predicated.

It might be observed that, in those formulations, the two parts of the *dictum* look less vacuous than before—but that is of no account to my argument.

The general idea, then, is this: If you have grasped the *dictum*, you must thereby recognize the validity of the perfect syllogisms; anyone who doubts, or fails to see, the validity of a perfect syllogism thereby shows that he does not understand the pertinent sense of 'of every' and 'of no'—better, that he does not understand what universal affirmative propositions and universal negative propositions are. You might grasp the *dictum* and have doubts about Darapti or Cesare: you cannot grasp the *dictum* and have doubts about Darii and Celarent.

There is an immediate and obvious objection: how can the *dictum* possibly underwrite all four syllogisms of the first figure? (Let alone the twelve or fourteen syllogisms which Boethus took it to underwrite.) Perhaps it has a sporting chance with Barbara; for in Barbara all the predications are universal and affirmative—they all involve 'of every' and the *de omni* part of the *dictum*. So Alexander can say that

'of every', which is already established as is assumed in the premisses, is enough to show the validity.

(*in APr* 54.9–11)[54]

Perhaps the *dictum* has some slight chance of underwriting Celarent—if we appeal both to the *de nullo* part of the *dictum* and to the *de omni* part; for Celarent contains universal propositions of both varieties. So Alexander:

Aristotle says that similarly in this case the validity is recognized on the basis of 'of no' and 'of every'.

(*in APr* 55.1–3)[55]

(Well, Aristotle does not say so—but perhaps that is what he meant?) But how on earth can the *dictum* underwrite Darii and Ferio? Those two syllogisms contain particular propositions: a mastery of their universal premisses surely can't be enough to guarantee a grasp of their validity?

There are several possible answers to that desperate question. For example, we might simply deny that Darii and Ferio are perfect. After all, we could do so without wrecking Aristotle's system; for, as I have already remarked, chapter 7 of the first Book of the *Prior Analytics* proves that Darii and Ferio can be derived from Barbara and Celarent. That might be a good answer to the desperate question; but it is not an answer which an interpreter of Aristotle can offer—for in chapter 7 Aristotle still asserts that Darii and Ferio are perfect.

Secondly, then, we might reinforce the *dictum* by the addition of a couple of extra clauses—a *de aliquo* dealing with 'of some' and a *de aliquo non*

---

[54] τὸ γὰρ κατὰ παντός, ὅ ἐστι κείμενον καὶ εἰλημμένον διὰ τῶν προτάσεων, ἱκανὸν πρὸς τὴν δεῖξιν τῆς συναγωγῆς.

[55] καὶ φησὶν ὅτι ὁμοίως καὶ ἐπὶ τούτου ἐκ τοῦ κατὰ μηδενὸς καὶ ἐκ τοῦ κατὰ παντὸς γνώριμος ἡ συναγωγή.

with 'not of some'. After all, Aristotle's underlying idea seems to be that the validity of the perfect syllogisms is fixed by their quantificational structures. The *dictum*, as he presents it, treats only half of the pertinent quantificational structures: why not realize Aristotle's underlying idea by making the *dictum* complete? But Aristotle himself seems to imply that the *dictum*, as it stands, can deal with Darii and with Ferio.

How can he have thought so? Alexander implicitly offers an answer to that question. Here are his comments on Darii and Ferio:

> If B holds of some C, some of C is in B as in a whole. But A is said of every B. Therefore there is no B of which A will not be said. But C is something of B. Therefore A will be said of it. ... If something of C is in B as in a whole and B is in no A, then A will not hold of some C. For some of C is under B, and nothing of B can be taken of which A will be said. Hence A will not be said of that something of C which was something of B.
>
> (*in APr* 60.22–61.1)[56]

In support of Darii Alexander invokes the *dictum de omni*, in support of Ferio the *dictum de nullo*. But he reinforces the *dicta*—not by adding further parts to them, but by appealing to a further pair of principles.

First, in his account of Darii he says that 'if B holds of some C, some of C is in B as in a whole'. Elsewhere in his commentary Alexander indicates that he found here an equivalence rather than a one-way implication; and the equivalence is most perspicuously formulated as follows:

B holds of some C if and only if B holds of all of some C.
Secondly, Alexander's account of Ferio implies a similar thesis about 'not of some', which—again—other texts elevate into an equivalence:

B does not holds of some C if and only if B holds of none of some C.
Those two equivalences are true principles.

Consider the equivalence involved in the account of Darii. The rather odd phrase 'B holds of all of some of C' means that there is a part or subgroup of the Cs of every member of which B holds. Or in other words, that there is some X such that C holds of every X and B holds of every X. Some cats are grey. Is there an X such that every X is grey and every X is a cat? Evidently

---

[56] εἰ γὰρ τὸ Β τινὶ τῷ Γ, τὶ τοῦ Γ ἐν ὅλῳ ἐστὶ τῷ Β· κατὰ παντὸς δὲ τοῦ Β τὸ Α· οὐδὲν ἄρα ἐστὶ τοῦ Β καθ' οὗ οὐ ῥηθήσεται τὸ Α· τὶ δὲ τοῦ Β ἐστὶ τὸ Γ· κατὰ τούτου ἄρα τὸ Α ῥηθήσεται. ... εἰ γὰρ εἴη τι τοῦ Γ ἐν ὅλῳ τῷ Β, τὸ δὲ Β ἐν μηδενὶ τῷ Α, τὸ Α τινὶ τῷ Γ οὐχ ὑπάρξει. τὶ μὲν γὰρ τοῦ Γ ὑπὸ τὸ Β· οὐδὲν δ' ἐστι τοῦ Β λαβεῖν καθ' οὗ τὸ Α ῥηθήσεται· ὥστε οὐδὲ κατὰ τινὸς τοῦ Γ ἐκείνου ὃ ἦν τι τοῦ Β.

yes: grey cats are such that every one of them is grey and every one of them is a cat. So, in general, if B holds of some C, then B holds of all of some C. And it is quite clear that if B holds of all of some C, then B holds of some C.

So the first of the two equivalences is true. And the second is readily shown to be true in a similar fashion.

So look at Darii in the light of the first equivalence. The premisses of Darii are:

A holds of every B.
B holds of some C.

The equivalence allows us to replace them by the pair:

A holds of every B.
B holds of all of some C.

That pair of premisses yields, by a syllogism in Barbara:
A holds of all of some C,
which the equivalence allows us to replace by:
A holds of some C.
Thus the validity of Darii can be grounded in Barbara.

The same can be done for Ferio and Celarent.

That may seem fishy; for the second premiss of the syllogism in Barbara must be something which has the form
B holds of every X;
so we must read
B holds of all of some C
as though it were
B holds of every some C
—and that looks close to nonsense. Even if we allow that it has a sense, namely the sense given less opaquely by
B holds of all of some C,
how can 'some C' express a syllogistical term? How can a term come ready equipped with a quantifier, and then be presented with a second one? It is perhaps worth demonstrating that that objection is specious. Here is a more rigorous version of the argument which I have just rehearsed.

(1) A holds of every B   premiss
(2) B holds of some C   premiss
(3) For some X, B holds of every X and C holds   2, equivalence
    of every X

(4) B holds of every D and C holds of every D   hypothesis
(5) A holds of every D   1, 4, Barbara
(6) A holds of every D and C holds of every D   4, 5
(7) For some X, A holds of every X and C holds   6
    of every X
(8) A holds of some C   7, equivalence
(9) A holds of some C   8, existential generalization

That can readily be turned into an impeccable proof. (And something similar can, of course, be done for Ferio—when the proof will involve Celarent rather than Barbara.)

Nonetheless, that argument can scarcely be what we are looking for. The question was this: How can Darii and Ferio be justified by way of the *dictum de omni et nullo*? The answer suggested by Alexander's account of the two syllogisms was this: 'By invoking in addition a couple of equivalences'. The answer may be deemed unsatisfactory: Alexander presents arguments in favour of the validity of Darii and of Ferio, or supposed proofs of their validity; but we are not looking for a proof, and neither was Alexander—on the contrary, we are trying to see how the validity of Darii and Ferio can be grasped without proof.

Now that objection to Alexander's answer is perhaps less powerful than it may seem—and I shall return to it in a later context. But there is a second, and uncontestable, reason for rejecting Alexander's answer: it does not appeal to the *dictum* at all. To be sure, in the text we are considering Alexander quite expressly appeals to the *dictum* as well as to the equivalences; but in fact—and whatever he may have intended—the line of reasoning which his remarks suggest by-passes the *dictum* entirely. True, the *dictum* is invoked to justify Barbara and Celarent, and Barbara and Celarent are, in their turn, invoked to justify Darii and Ferio. But exactly the same may be said of, say, Datisi and Festino—and they are not, for that reason, justified by the *dictum*.

A DIFFERENT SOLUTION[57]

Alexander's way with Darii and Ferio does not meet the difficulty which they present. Perhaps a more radical solution should be sought—perhaps the *dictum* should not be interpreted in the orthodox manner in which I

---

[57] Michael Frede brought to my attention the possibilities which the following paragraphs set out.

have so far interpreted it? A heterodox interpretation has been suggested; and although, in the end, it must be rejected, it is well worth a whirl.

I start from a passage in Galen's *Introduction to Logic*. The last Chapter of the manual opens like this:

Since the Peripatetics write about what are called co-assumptional syllogisms as though they had some utility whereas I deem them to be superfluous (as I have shown in my work *On Proof*), it is appropriate to say something about them. ... One species of them is like this:

Of what this, that; but that of such-and-such: therefore this of such-and-such.

Or with names:

Of what tree, plant; but tree of plane-tree: therefore plant of plane-tree.

(*inst log* xix 1–3)[58]

Galen thinks that such co-assumptional arguments are superfluous inasmuch as they are, as he puts it, 'epitomes of predicative syllogisms and not a separate genus of them' (*inst log* xix 2).[59] (Historians of logic usually call the arguments 'prosleptic', transliterating the Greek '*προσληπτικός*' rather than translating it.)

It is hard to see why he took them to be epitomes (unless he means no more than that their characteristic expression is succinct); but a text from Alexander shows why he took them to be predicative syllogisms:

What Aristotle means is this. In propositions which contain the three terms potentially within themselves, like the ones he has just set down and, in general, the ones which Theophrastus calls co-assumptional propositions (for they in a sense contain the three terms—in 'Of all of which B, of all of that A too', the two terms which are already determined, namely B and A, in a way embrace the third term (the term of which B is predicated), save that unlike them it is not determined and evident)—in such propositions, which seem to differ only in expression from predicative propositions, as Theophrastus showed in his *On Affirmation*, he says that a proposition taken thus 'Of all of which B, of all of that A' means 'Of whatever B is said, of all of them A too is said'.

(*in APr* 378.12–23)[60]

Galen's illustrative sentence

[58] ἐπεὶ δὲ καὶ περὶ τῶν κατὰ πρόσληψιν ὀνομαζομένων συλλογισμῶν οἱ ἐκ τοῦ Περιπάτου γεγράφασιν ὡς χρησίμων, ἐμοὶ δὲ περιττοὶ δοκοῦσιν εἶναι καθότι δέδεικταί μοι κἂν τῇ Περὶ τῆς ἀποδείξεως πραγματείᾳ, προσῆκον εἴη ἄν τι καὶ περὶ τούτων εἰπεῖν. ... ἐν μὲν οὖν εἶδός ἐστι τοῖον· καθ' οὗ τόδε, καὶ τόδε· ἀλλὰ τόδε κατὰ τοῦδε· καὶ τόδε ἄρα κατὰ τοῦδε. καὶ ἐπ' ὀνομάτων· ἐφ' οὗ δένδρον, καὶ φυτόν· δένδρον δὲ ἐπὶ πλατάνου· καὶ φυτὸν ἄρα ἐπὶ πλατάνου.

[59] οἱ τοιοῦτοι συλλογισμοὶ τῶν κατηγορικῶν ἐπιτομαί τινές εἰσιν, οὐχ ἕτερον γένος αὐτῶν.

[60] ὃ λέγει τοιοῦτόν ἐστιν, ὅτι ἐν ταῖς τοιαύταις προτάσεσιν, αἲ δυνάμει τοὺς τρεῖς ὅρους ἐν αὑταῖς ἔχουσιν, ὁποῖαί εἰσιν ἃς ἐξέθετο νῦν καὶ ὅλως αἱ κατὰ πρόσληψιν ὑπὸ Θεοφράστου

Of what tree, plant

is thus an abbreviation for

Of all of which tree holds, of all of that plant holds.

Or:

For any X, if tree holds of every X, then plant holds of every X.

That, according to Theophrastus and Alexander is equivalent to the ordinary predicative proposition

Every tree is a plant.

Hence Galen's illustrative co-assumptional syllogism is no more than Barbara in disguise—and that is why Galen deems it to be superfluous.

There are also negative co-assumptional propositions—for example:

Of what tree, not animal

or

Of all of which tree holds, of none of that animal holds.

That is said to be equivalent to the standard universal negative,

No tree is an animal.

So Celarent, like Barbara, will have a co-assumptional counterpart.

The two equivalences which Theophrastus announced do for universal propositions what the two equivalences I took from Alexander do for particular propositions. Indeed, it is plausible to guess that the four equivalences formed a group, and that they were all proposed by Theophrastus. However that may be, consider the affirmative equivalence, namely:

A holds of every B if and only if for any X, if B holds of every X then A holds of every X.

Is that a true equivalence?

Suppose, first, that A holds of every B. Then if B holds of all X, A will hold of all X too—that is guaranteed by Barbara. Hence if A holds of every B, then for any X, if B holds of every X then A holds of every X. Suppose, secondly, that for any X, if B holds of every X then so too does A. Then if B holds of every B, A holds of every B. But B holds of every B. So A holds of every B. Hence if for any X, if B holds of every X then A holds of every X,

λεγόμεναι (αὗται γὰρ τοὺς τρεῖς ὅρους ἔχουσί πως· ἐν γὰρ τῇ καθ᾽ οὗ τὸ Β παντός, κατ᾽ ἐκείνου καὶ τὸ Α παντός ἐν τοῖς δύο ὅροις, τῷ τε Β καὶ τῷ Α, τοῖς ὡρισμένοις ἤδη πως περιείληπται καὶ ὁ τρίτος, καθ᾽ οὗ τὸ Β κατηγορεῖται, πλὴν οὐχ ὁμοίως ἐκείνοις ὡρισμένος καὶ φανερός), ἐν δὴ ταῖς τοιαύταις προτάσεσιν, αἳ τῇ λέξει μόνον τῶν κατηγορικῶν διαφέρειν δοκοῦσιν, ὡς ἔδειξεν ἐν τῷ Περὶ καταφάσεως ὁ Θεόφραστος, φησὶν ὅτι ἡ οὕτως λαμβανομένη ὅτι καθ᾽ οὗ τὸ Β παντός, κατ᾽ ἐκείνου παντὸς τὸ Α, σημαίνει τὸ καθ᾽ ὅσων τὸ Β λέγεται, κατὰ πάντων τούτων λέγεσθαι καὶ τὸ Α.

then A holds of every B. Add those two implicative conclusions together and you get the equivalence.

The equivalence proposed for universal negative propositions is this:

A holds of no B if and only if for any X, if B holds of every X then A holds of no X.

That too is true; and it is readily proved.

But what—if anything—have those two equivalences to do with the *dictum de omni et nullo*?

The orthodox interpretation of the *dictum de omni* takes it to say that A holds of no B if and only if no individual B fails to be an A. In other words, in

There isn't a B of which A is not predicated,

the orthodox interpretation glosses 'a B' by 'an individual B'. But suppose we take it to mean 'a part of B'—or, in Alexander's phrase, 'something of B'? In that case, the *dictum* will state that

A is predicated of every B if and only if there is no part of B (or: nothing of B) of which A is not predicated.

I shall call that the heterodox version of the *dictum de omni*.

To be sure, there is something mildly odd about that version—if only because sentences such as

There's no part of cat of which being black in the dark isn't predicated

are not instances of ordinary English. In particular, the phrase 'part of cat' is unorthodox. Unorthodox, no doubt; but not in the least mysterious about them; for the 'parts of cat' are simply the tabbies and the Siamese and the Persians and so on. Then let us take

There is no part of B of which A is not predicated

as equivalent to the co-assumptional form

For any X, if B holds of every X, then A holds of every X.

And in the light of that, we may reformulate the heterodox *dictum de omni* as follows:

A is predicated of every B if and only if for any X, if B holds of every X, then A holds of every X.

A parallel line of argument will produce a heterodox version of the *dictum de nullo*.

So what? Well, if we apply the heterodox version of the *dictum de omni* to Barbara, we shall be able to argue roughly as follows. Anyone who understands a syllogism in Barbara must understand the *dictum de omni* which determines what a universal affirmative proposition is. So anyone who understands Barbara must realize that it is equivalent to—or even identical with—the following co-assumptional syllogism:

> For any X, if B holds of every X, then A holds of every X.
> B holds of every C.
> Therefore A holds of every C.

Since no one could understand that without grasping its validity, no one can understand Barbara without grasping its validity—so that Barbara is perfectly valid.

With the aid of the heterodox version of the *dictum de nullo*, something similar can be said for Celarent. But the heterodox versions of the *dicta* do not help with Darii and Ferio. If the heterodox version of the *dictum de omni* is applied to Darii, the result is this:

> For any X, if B holds of every X, then A holds of every X
> B holds of some C
> Therefore A holds of some C

That is, of course, a valid syllogism—it is simply Darii in another guise. But it is not a co-assumptional syllogism, and it is not evidently valid. What can be done?

Well, the heterodox *dictum de omni* was first set out in the following way:

> A is predicated of every B if and only if there is no part of B of which A is not predicated.

The right-hand side of that equivalence was then reformulated as
For any X, if B holds of every X, then A holds of every X,
and the result was applied to Barbara. Why not reformulate the right-hand side of the equivalence in a different way, namely:
For any X, if B holds of some X, then A holds of some X?
That will produce a co-assumptional version of Darii, namely:

> For any X, if B holds of some X, then A holds of some X
> B holds of some C
> Therefore A holds of some C.

Everything which was said about Barbara and its co-assumptional mate can then be said about Darii. (And, again, something similar can be done for Ferio.)

That second reformulation of the heterodox *dictum de omni* will not, of course, work for Barbara—just as the first reformulation will not work for Darii. So, next, we might conjoin the two reformulations to produce something like this:

A is predicated of every B if and only if whatever B holds of, either universally or particularly, A holds of, either universally or particularly.

That might be rewritten, pedantically, thus:

A is predicated of every B if and only if both (1) for any X, if B holds of every X, then A holds of every X, and (2) for any X, if B holds of some X, then A holds of some X

That is the final version of the heterodox *dictum de omni*. When we look at Barbara, we shall take the universal part of the *dictum*, part (1). When we look at Darii we shall prefer the particular part, (2).

The final version of the *dictum de nullo* is readily produced.

Why not construe Aristotle's *dictum* in that heterodox fashion? Heterodoxy has, after all, at least one attraction: one and the same *dictum de omni* will work both for Barbara and for Darii, and one and the same *dictum de nullo* will work both for Celarent and for Ferio.

Or will it? It may be argued that this version of the *dictum* cannot deliver the goods. For example, the co-assumptional version of Barbara is—or may be regarded as—a special case of the following form of inference:

For any x, if F(x) then G(x).
F(**a**).
Therefore G(**a**).

A manual of modern logic will normally prove the validity of that form, and the proof will depend upon two distinct principles. First, a principle which looks like this:

For any x Φ(x).
Therefore Φ(**a**).

That principle licenses the inference from the first premiss of the argument to
If F(**a**), then G(**a**).
The second principle is *modus ponens*, which licenses the inference from
If F(**a**), then G(**a**)
and
F(**a**)

to

G(**a**).

That suggests—though of course it does not prove—that an understanding of the heterodox *dictum de omni* is not enough to guarantee a grasp of co-assumptional Barbara: rather, you need understand two distinct principles—armed with which you may prove that Barbara is valid.

I suspect that that is right, and hence that the heterodox *dictum* will not do its work. But that is not in itself a sufficient reason for abandoning it in favour of its orthodox counterpart. After all, if it turns out that the orthodox *dictum* cannot do its work either, then we might decide to hold on to the heterodox version as the best, or least bad, shot at interpreting Aristotle.

But in fact there are at least two good reasons for rejecting the heterodox *dictum*—I mean, for rejecting it as an interpretation of what Aristotle and his followers were up to when they tried to base the four perfect syllogisms on the *dictum de omni et nullo*. The reasons are simple enough.

First, Aristotle's Greek can hardly be construed in the way demanded by the heterodox *dictum*. Aristotle could have stated the heterodox *dictum* had he wanted to—he had the necessary linguistic resources at his disposal. We cannot plausibly read his words as a botched attempt—as his best attempt—at formulating the thing. The orthodox reading, according to which 'a B' means 'an individual B', is the straightforward reading, and the reading which Alexander took (without ever thinking of anything else). It is the right reading.

Secondly, the *dictum* is meant to offer a definition of 'of every' and 'of no'—or at any rate, it is meant to explain what 'of every' and 'of no' mean in the context of predicative syllogistic. But it is evidently hopeless to try to explain the meaning of 'of every' by offering the proposition

A is predicated of every B if and only if whatever B holds of, either universally or particularly, A holds of, either universally or particularly;

for then you will be offering to explain universal affirmative predication in terms of universal affirmative predication.

THE *DICTUM DE OMNI* AND BARBARA

So I return to the orthodox *dictum* which, in its *de omni* part, assured us that

A holds of every B if and only if there is no B of which A does not hold.

How might that principle be thought to back up any perfect syllogism? I shall restrict myself to the easy case—to the case of Barbara. It will prove quite difficult enough.

Barbara looks like this:

A holds of every B.
B holds of every C.
Therefore A holds of every C.

If you understand the constituent parts of Barbara, and if your understanding is enshrined in the *dictum de omni*, then you realize that Barbara amounts to this:

There is no B of which A does not hold.
There is no C of which B does not hold.
Therefore there is no C of which A does not hold.

Could you understand that schema without recognizing its validity?

Suppose you gaze on the schema. Then you might find yourself thinking along the following lines: 'According to the first premiss, there's no B of which A fails to hold—that's to say whatever B may hold of, A holds of. But—according to the second premiss—there's no C of which B fails to hold—that's to say, whatever C may hold of, B holds of. So there can't be any C of which A fails to hold—that's to say, whatever C may hold of, A holds of. And that's just what the conclusion says.'

That seems to be an intelligible train of thought, and a simple one: I have adopted it from Alexander, who has this to say about the validity of Barbara:

Again, if B is in A as in a whole, A is said of every B. Therefore there is no B of which A is not said. Now if you can't take a B of which A isn't said, and if C is something of B, then necessarily A will be said of C too. So the validity of such syllogisms is immediately evident, coming about and being warranted by the items established—'of every' and 'of no'—and needing nothing else from outside.

(*in APr* 54.15–21)[61]

Surely that is a train of thought which starts from the *dictum* and which indicates that and how Barbara is a valid argument form?

---

[61] πάλιν εἰ τὸ Β ἐν ὅλῳ τῷ Α, τὸ Α κατὰ παντὸς τοῦ Β· οὐδὲν ἄρα τοῦ Β ἐστὶ καθ' οὗ οὐ λέγεται τὸ Α. εἰ οὖν οὐδὲν ἔστι λαβεῖν τοῦ Β καθ' οὗ τὸ Α οὐ λέγεται, τὶ δὲ τοῦ Β τὸ Γ ἐστίν, καὶ κατὰ τοῦ Γ ἐξ ἀνάγκης ῥηθήσεται. αὐτόθεν οὖν ἐναργὴς ἡ τῶν τοιούτων συλλογισμῶν συναγωγὴ γινομένη καὶ πιστουμένη διὰ τῶν κειμένων, τοῦ τε κατὰ παντὸς καὶ τοῦ κατὰ μηδενός, καὶ μηδενὸς ἔξωθεν ἄλλου προσδεομένη.

Perhaps it is; but is it the train we want to catch? A first question concerns just what sort of thing it is. Earlier on, I objected to an Alexandrian argument in favour of the validity of Darii that it constituted a proof of Darii whereas we are looking for something which is not a proof. The same objection may be made here. Indeed, the objection may be formulated in an entirely general fashion: no argument which may be advanced to prove that Barbara is valid can represent what the *dictum* is supposed to achieve; and an argument which is advanced, and yet not advanced to prove that Barbara is valid, cannot achieve anything at all.

The general objection, as I have just formulated it, is feeble. Alexander introduces his argument in favour of the validity of Barbara by saying that

'of every', which is already established and which is taken in the premises, is enough to show the validity—that is why syllogisms of this sort are perfect and, in the strict sense, unproved.

(in APr 54.9–12)[62]

You do not prove—you do not prove in the strict sense of the word—that perfect syllogisms are valid. But, as everyone knows, there are any number of arguments which are not proofs according to the strict Aristotelian conditions on proof but which nevertheless are excellent arguments for their conclusions: they establish their conclusions, they show their conclusions, and of course they prove their conclusions—in the unstrict or ordinary sense of the word 'prove'.

In general, you can't prove axioms—or at any rate, you can't provide a proof of an axiom within the science to which it belongs. But you can argue in favour of axioms. Indeed, you can even argue in favour of what Aristotle calls the firmest axiom of all—the Law of Non-Contradiction. Naturally, there is no proof of the Law; but Aristotle offers a sequence of arguments against any attempt to deny it—and he describes what he is doing as refutatory proof of the Law. Of course,

I say that proving refutatorily is different from proving;

(Met 1006a15–16)[63]

but a refutatory proof of the Law is an argument—and might in principle be a good argument—or even a conclusive argument—in favour of the Law.

---

[62] τὸ γὰρ κατὰ παντός, ὅ ἐστι κείμενον καὶ εἰλημμένον διὰ τῶν προτάσεων, ἱκανὸν πρὸς τὴν δεῖξιν τῆς συναγωγῆς· διὰ τοῦτο καὶ τέλειοι οἱ οὕτως ἔχοντες συλλογισμοὶ καὶ κυρίως ἀναπόδεικτοι.

[63] τὸ δ᾽ ἐλεγκτικῶς ἀποδεῖξαι λέγω διαφέρειν καὶ τὸ ἀποδεῖξαι.

Our question was: How can we come to know that the perfect syllogisms are valid, given that we do not prove their validity? The Aristotelian answer to the question is: 'On the basis of the *dictum de omni et nullo*'. But what is the relation between the base and what it supports? between the *dictum* and the perfect syllogisms? Well, the relation is determined by an argument—not, to be sure, by a proof, but by an argument—which starts from the *dictum* and proceeds to Barbara. What more could we want?

Well, don't we want less? We were told that the perfect syllogisms, like any axioms or axiom-like items, do not need to be proved inasmuch as they are immediately knowable. Our question then was: How can the perfect syllogisms be known immediately? And in answer to that question we have been offered an argument. But surely no argument, whether probative or non-probative, can answer the case. For the production of an argument interposes something—namely its own premises—between knowledge and its objects. If our knowledge that such-and-such rests on an argument to the conclusion that such-and-such, then we do not know immediately that such-and-such—we know that such-and-such (if we know it at all) mediately, on the basis of our knowledge of the premises.

It is tempting to reply to that as follows: 'What, at bottom, counts is this: the axioms can be known without being proved. So let us say that the axioms do not need to be proved not inasmuch as they can be known immediately but rather—and trivially—inasmuch as they can be known non-probatively. And then let us allow that you may come to know something non-probatively in two manners: either by knowing it directly or else by catching it in a non-probative argument. And for the perfect syllogisms it is the second manner which suits.'

That is a nice reply; but it won't serve—at any rate, it won't serve in an Aristotelian context. A proof—a proof in the strict Aristotelian sense—is a cognitive syllogism:

I call a proof a cognitive syllogism, and I call a syllogism cognitive if by possessing it we know that such-and-such.

(*APst* 71b17–19)[64]

Suppose, then, that we have an argument which concludes that such-and-such, and which is not a probative argument. If it is not probative, it is not a proof. If it is not a proof, it is not a cognitive syllogism. If it is not a cognitive

[64] ἀπόδειξιν δὲ λέγω συλλογισμὸν ἐπιστημονικόν· ἐπιστημονικὸν δὲ λέγω καθ' ὃν τῷ ἔχειν αὐτὸν ἐπιστάμεθα.

syllogism, it is not a syllogism the possession of which gives us knowledge that such-and-such. The question—to repeat—was this: How do we know the axioms? If the answer is 'By an argument', then that argument must be a cognitive argument and hence a proof. But the axioms cannot be proved.

So must we not, after all, admit that either the argument for the validity of the perfect syllogisms is a proof of their validity or else it achieves nothing at all? Well, it is true that either the argument is a proof or else it cannot ground our knowledge of the validity of the syllogisms; but it is not true that either it is a proof or else it is quite useless. For the argument need not be—should not be—construed as an attempt to establish the truth of its conclusion, still less as a train of reasoning which I might follow in order to come to grasp that truth. Rather, it might be construed as an attempt to articulate the way in which a grasp of the *dictum* guarantees a grasp of the validity of the perfect syllogisms.

How do I know that Barbara is valid?—'You know it immediately, if you know it at all. That is to say, you can't understand what a syllogism in Barbara is without knowing that it is valid.'—How can that be?—'Well, if you understand what a syllogism in Barbara is, then you understand what universal affirmative propositions are—that is to say, you have mastered the *dictum de omni*. And anyone who has mastered the *dictum* grasps the validity of Barbara.'—Really? Couldn't I master the *dictum* and still doubt about Barbara?—'No; for there is a link between the *dictum* and Barbara, which can be developed like this ... '. An argument is then produced. But the argument is not an argument which takes the *dictum* as its premiss and reaches the validity of Barbara as its conclusion. It is an argument which makes plain the link between the two items and which thereby explains how a grasp of the *dictum* guarantees knowledge of the validity of Barbara.

That, I think, is the best way to understand what is going on—both in the text of Alexander and in fact. But does the argument actually do what it sets out to do? I think not.

The *dictum* allowed us to see Barbara in the following form:

There is no B of which A does not hold.
There is no C of which B does not hold.
Therefore there is no C of which A does not hold.

We were then supposed to muse along these lines: 'According to the first premiss, there's no B of which A fails to hold—that's to say whatever B may hold of, A holds of. ... '. One striking fact about that line of musing is this: it does not imply that the new formulation of Barbara which the *dictum* suggested is the way to grasp the validity of the syllogism. Rather, the musing first, as it were, translates the formula 'There's no B of which A fails to hold' into something much closer to 'A holds of every B'—which was the normal form of the thing.

A second striking fact about the musing may be brought out if we look at a first cousin to Barbara, namely:

> There's nothing which is B but not A.
> There's nothing which is C but not B.
> Therefore there's nothing which is C but not A.

It seems plain that that argument is not perfect—plain, that is, that someone might understand all its components without grasping its validity. After all, it is a relatively advanced argument in the context of modern logic: tiro logicians will meet a symbolic version of it on page 45 of their *Introduction to Logic*—it is something they will be invited to prove, not something which they are invited to grasp immediately. If that is true of Barbara's contemporary cousin, it is surely true of the argument:

> There is no B of which A does not hold.
> There is no C of which B does not hold.
> Therefore there is no C of which A does not hold.

And it is surely true of Barbara.

A syllogism is perfect if and only if its validity can be grasped without being proved. That is to say, if and only if its validity is evident. That is to say—or so Aristotle's appeal to the *dictum* suggests—if and only if anyone who understands the pertinent forms of propositions thereby knows that the syllogism is valid. But if perfection is so understood and if the *dictum* is read in the orthodox way, then not even Barbara, which is surely the most promising of the four claimants to perfection, is perfect.

Should it be concluded that the validity of the perfect syllogisms is linked to the *dictum de omni et nullo* in some fashion which has hitherto eluded us? Or that the *dictum* should be interpreted in some manner which has hitherto escaped our attention? I incline to think that the right conclusion is rather this: Barbara is not perfect. Moreover, no predicative syllogism, *pace* Aristotle and his Peripatetics, is perfect.

Are there any perfect items in predicative syllogistic? Well, at least there are candidates for perfection which seem to stand a better chance than Barbara.

For example, there are the laws or principles of conversion. The principle of E-conversion states that

A holds of no B if and only if B holds of no A.

Aristotle states the principle, and offers a concise argument in its favour. Commentators were puzzled by the argument, and critics found much to criticize. Alexander has a long discussion of the problem, in the course of which he says this:

> He shows it [i.e. E-conversion] by way of items already shown and established—I mean 'of every' and 'of no' and 'in as in a whole' and 'in no'. For it is by using these items that he shows that non-modal universal negatives convert. For it being laid down that A holds of no B, it follows—he says—that B follows no A. For if B holds of some A (that is the opposite of what is laid down, and one or the other of them must be true), let it hold of C—let C be something of A of which B holds. Then C will be in B as in a whole and will be something of it, and B is said of every C (for 'in as in a whole' and 'of every' are the same). But C was something of A, and if it is in it as in a whole, A will be said of all of it. But C was something of B. Therefore A too will be predicated of something of B. But it was laid down that A is said of no B; and to be said of no B is for there to be nothing of B of which A will be predicated.

(in APr 32.8–21)[65]

According to this passage, the principle of E-conversion depends upon—and can be shown on the basis of—the *dictum de nullo*.

Alexander's presentation is convoluted. That is in part because Alexander is an essentially convoluted chap and in part because he is commenting on Aristotle's text: his aim is not simply, nor even primarily, to indicate that E-conversion can be based on the *dictum*—rather, it is to show that Aristotle so bases it. The convolutions in Alexander's text are there because he is trying to stick close to the *Analytics* while insisting on the importance of the *dictum*. In fact, Alexander's interpretation is quixotic: there is no sniff of the *dictum* in the pertinent text of the *Analytics*—and there is more than a sniff of

---

[65] δείκνυσι δὲ διὰ τῶν ἐφθακότων δεδεῖχθαί τε καὶ κεῖσθαι· ἔστι δὲ ταῦτα τό τε κατὰ παντὸς καὶ τὸ κατὰ μηδενὸς καὶ ἐν ὅλῳ καὶ ἐν μηδενί· τούτοις γὰρ προσχρώμενος δείκνυσι τὴν τῆς καθόλου ἀποφατικῆς ὑπαρχούσης ἀντιστροφήν. κειμένου γὰρ τοῦ Α μηδενὶ τῷ Β φησὶν ἕπεσθαι τούτῳ τὸ καὶ τὸ Β μηδενὶ τῷ Α· εἰ γὰρ τὸ Β τινὶ τῷ Α ὑπάρχει (τοῦτο γάρ ἐστι τὸ ἀντικείμενον τῷ κειμένῳ, καὶ δεῖ τὸ ἕτερον αὐτῶν ἀληθὲς εἶναι), ὑπαρχέτω τῷ Γ· ἔστω γὰρ τοῦτο τὶ τοῦ Α ᾧ ὑπάρχει τὸ Β. ἔσται δὴ τὸ Γ ἐν ὅλῳ τῷ Β καὶ τὶ αὐτοῦ, καὶ τὸ Β κατὰ παντὸς τοῦ Γ· ταὐτὸν γὰρ τὸ ἐν ὅλῳ καὶ τὸ κατὰ παντός. ἀλλ' ἦν τὸ Γ τὶ τοῦ Α· ἐν ὅλῳ ἄρα καὶ τῷ Α τὸ Γ ἐστίν· εἰ δὲ ἐν ὅλῳ, κατὰ παντὸς αὐτοῦ ῥηθήσεται τὸ Α. ἦν δὲ τὸ Γ τὶ τοῦ Β· καὶ τὸ Α ἄρα κατὰ τινὸς τοῦ Β κατηγορηθήσεται· ἀλλ' ἔκειτο κατὰ μηδενὸς τὸ Α τοῦ Β· ἦν δὲ κατὰ μηδενὸς τὸ μηδὲν εἶναι τοῦ Β καθ' οὗ τὸ Α κατηγορηθήσεται.

something quite other. Nonetheless, the suggestion that E-conversion rests on the *dictum* is worth considering in its own right.

Suppose you grasp that A holds of no B. That is to say—according to the *dictum*—you grasp that there is no B of which A holds. Surely if you understand that, you thereby realize that there is no A of which B holds? If, allowing that A holds of no B, you go on to wonder whether B holds of no A, that simply shows that you have not understood what you allowed to be true. Or does it?

'No Frenchman really likes Elgar', said Morse.—'Alas, you're quite right', replied Menuisier. Morse was startled: since when had Menuisier agreed with him on anything? 'You're sure you grasp what I mean?'—'Why of course: I could go through the French population, one by one, and I wouldn't find a single Elgar-lover among them.'—'Well then,' continued Morse, 'you recognize that no true lover of Elgar is French?'.—'*Mais mon cher*, that is quite another matter, and it requires quite another research: to verify that, I should have to consider, one by one, the band of Elgar-lovers and check their passports. I shall ask the CNRS at once for an *équipe* and a generous *subside*.'

That absurd little conversation is not incoherent. And in any event, you will quite often hear someone saying something of the sort: 'No B is A, and *vice versa*'—as though the '*vice versa*' added a new point. Anyone who speaks like that presumably understands 'No B is A'—and yet has not thereby grasped the rule of conversion.

GALEN'S METATHEOREM

The rest of this chapter discusses what has been called Galen's metatheorem. The general drift of the metatheorem is uncontroversial; for Galen plainly had in mind some thesis the pith of which can be roughly described as follows:

> Syllogisms owe their force to the universal axioms to which they are subordinated.

But that is hopelessly vague; and if it is also uncontroversial, little else is. The metatheorem is known only from the last chapters of the *Introduction to Logic*. The text of the *Introduction*, which survives in a single mediaeval manuscript, is in a particularly dreadful state in its later pages; and each of the passages in which Galen states or alludes to the metatheorem is textually uncertain. The

uncertainties affect numerous minor points of detail. But quite apart from
those difficulties, many of which are insoluble, there is another more general
problem; for in different passages Galen appears to present very different
versions of his metatheorem.

In any event, what relevance has the metatheorem for the question I am
now in principle addressing? Galen does not seem to be talking specifically of
primary syllogisms or of axiom-like syllogistic forms. Rather, his metatheorem
seems to be formulated for syllogisms in general. Again, he does not seem to
be talking about our knowledge of syllogisms and their validity: rather, he
is interested in the force of a syllogism, and his metatheorem is metalogical
in nature rather than epistemological. Those points are well made, and they
must be met. But for the moment I shall swagger on regardless.

The first thing to do is to establish the scope of the metatheorem: it is a
thesis about the force syllogisms—but of which syllogisms? The business is
introduced in the third part of the *Introduction*, in which Galen describes
his own third species of syllogisms. At the very end of the discussion, Galen
remarks—according to the received text—that

> all such syllogisms should be said to belong to the genus of relational arguments and
> to the species of arguments constituted in accordance with the power of an axiom, as
> Posidonius notes when he says that he calls them concludent in virtue of the power
> of an axiom.
>
> (*inst log* xviii 8)[66]

That remark indicates that the metatheorem applies to the particular kind of
relational syllogisms which Galen has just been discussing and to which he
refers by 'all such syllogisms'. The syllogisms in question are arguments based
on proportion or analogy. Arguments 'constituted in accordance with the
power of an axiom'—that is to say, arguments for which the metatheorem
holds—are therefore a sub-species of the 'third species of syllogisms'. The
metatheorem has a very restricted scope.

But that flies in the face of everything else which Galen has said about his
metatheorem in this last third of the *Introduction*; and the received text of
xviii 8 is undoubtedly corrupt. It has been proposed that something like the
following should be read:

---

[66] τοὺς δὴ τοιούτους ἅπαντας συλλογισμοὺς τῷ γένει μὲν ἐκ τῶν πρός τι ῥητέον, ἐν εἴδει
δὲ κατ' ἀξιώματος δύναμιν συνισταμένους, ὥσπερ καὶ ὁ Ποσειδώνιός φησιν ὀνομάζειν αὐτοὺς
συνακτικοὺς κατὰ δύναμιν ἀξιώματος.

all such syllogisms should be said to belong to the genus of relational arguments and to the species of arguments <based on proportion>, being constituted in accordance with the power of an axiom ...[67]

There might be disagreement about the details of that proposal; but its general thrust must, I think, be right. And in that case the passage tells us nothing about the scope of the metatheorem.

Turn, then, from its last to its first appearance in the text of the *Introduction*. Near the beginning of his discussion of relational syllogisms Galen claims that

there is a large quantity of such syllogisms, as I said, among the arithmeticians and the calculators, and what they all have in common is the fact that they have the same constitution depending on certain axioms.

(*inst log* xvi 5)[68]

Here the phrase 'such syllogisms' refers unequivocally to the relational inferences which have just been introduced as the third class of syllogism; and at first blush you will suppose that Galen means to pick out a feature which unifies the class of relational syllogisms and distinguishes them from the predicatives and the hypotheticals.

That natural supposition appears to be falsified by a sentence in xvi 10, where the metatheorem is mentioned for the second time:

Similarly in the case of all the others, the constitution of the probative syllogisms will be in virtue of the force of an axiom ...[69]

By 'all the others' does not Galen mean 'all the syllogisms other than relational syllogisms'? In that case, the metatheorem has the widest possible scope. But although the phrase may possibly have that broad reference, the context makes it far more likely that 'all the others' is short for 'all relational syllogisms other than those I have thus far described'.

In any event, the metatheorem is certainly applied only to relational syllogisms on its third occurrence:

---

[67] τοὺς δὴ τοιούτους ἅπαντας συλλογισμοὺς τῷ γένει μὲν ἐκ τῶν πρός τι ῥητέον, ἐν εἴδει δὲ κατ' <ἀναλογίαν, κατ'> ἀξιώματος δύναμιν συνισταμένους ...

[68] πολὺ δὲ πλῆθός ἐστιν, ὡς ἔφην, ἐν ἀριθμητικοῖς τε καὶ λογιστικοῖς τοιούτων συλλογισμῶν ὧν ἁπάντων ἐστὶ κοινὸν ἔκ τινων ἀξιωμάτων τὴν αὐτὴν ἴσχειν σύστασιν ...—The MS has 'συστάσεως', which gives no grammar; and 'τὴν αὐτήν' makes dubious sense. But whatever he wrote, Galen must have meant to say that the constitution of these syllogisms depends upon axioms.

[69] ὁμοίως δὲ κἀπὶ τῶν ἄλλων ἁπάντων ἡ σύστασις τῶν ἀποδεικτικῶν συλλογισμῶν κατὰ δύναμιν ἀξιώματος ἔσται ...—The next words in the received text are a conundrum; but they do not affect the point at issue.

In the same way, syllogisms propounded in accordance with any relation whatever will have their constitution and the force of the proof warranted by a general axiom.

(*inst log* xvi 12)[70]

In short, chapter xvi of the *Introduction* suggests that the metatheorem is a thesis about relational syllogisms: whatever may underwrite predicative and hypothetical syllogisms, relational syllogisms are underwritten by axioms.

The beginning of chapter xvii, however, tells strongly—perhaps decisively—in a different direction. The state of the text is lamentable; but although the following translation is speculative with regard to most of its details, its overall sense must correspond to what Galen wrote. (That is to say, either this is more or less what Galen wrote or else we must hold up our hands in sceptical resignation.) So:

In fact, pretty well all syllogisms have their constitution warranted because of the universal axioms which are superordinate to them. That is something which I came to realize later, having stated it neither in the books *On Proof* nor in *On the Number of Syllogisms*—even though in those works I was aware of relational syllogisms and had discovered their constitution and warrant. That all probative syllogisms are probative because of the warranty of universal axioms may be learned more clearly if we survey all arguments of this sort, in whatsoever manner they are propounded.

(*inst log* xvii 1–2)[71]

According to this passage, the metatheorem applies to 'pretty well all syllogisms', or to 'all probative syllogisms': do the words mean what they appear to mean, or are we to suppose a restriction to pretty well all relational syllogisms and to all probative relational syllogisms?

Two points appear to tell against supposing any such restriction. First, the text continues as follows:

As is the case with this argument:
You say: It is day.
But you are telling the truth.

---

[70] ὡσαύτως δὲ καὶ οἱ καθ᾽ ἡντινοῦν σχέσιν ἐρωτώμενοι συλλογισμοὶ γενικῷ ἀξιώματι πιστὴν τὴν σύστασιν ἕξουσι καὶ τὴν τῆς ἀποδείξεως δύναμιν.

[71] καὶ σχεδὸν ἅπαντες οἱ συλλογισμοὶ διὰ τὴν τῶν ἐπιτεταγμένων αὐτοῖς καθολικῶν ἀξιωμάτων πιστὴν ἔχουσι τὴν σύστασιν, ὃ ὕστερόν ποτέ μοι νοηθὲν οὔτε ἐν τοῖς Περὶ ἀποδείξεως ὑπομνήμασιν οὔτε ἐν τῷ Περὶ τοῦ τῶν συλλογισμῶν ἀριθμοῦ γέγραπται—καίτοι τοὺς εἰς τὸ πρός τι συλλογισμοὺς ᾔδειμεν καὶ κατ᾽ ἐκείνας τὰς πραγματείας, εὑρηκότες τὸν τῆς συστάσεως τρόπον αὐτῶν καὶ τῆς πίστεως. ὅτι δὲ πάντες οἱ ἀποδεικτικοὶ συλλογισμοὶ διὰ τὴν τῶν καθόλου πίστιν ἀξιωμάτων εἰσὶ τοιοῦτοι, μαθεῖν ἔνεστιν ἐναργέστερον ἅπασι τοῖς ὁπωσοῦν ἠρωτημένοις λόγοις τοιούτοις ἐπιβλέψασι ...

Therefore it is day.

That sort of syllogism too is probative inasmuch as the universal axiom under which it falls is true ...

(inst log xvii 3)[72]

That is surely not a relational argument; but it illustrates the truth of the metatheorem: therefore the metatheorem is not restricted to relational arguments.

That may seem a pretty powerful consideration. Yet in fact it has no force at all. For the argument must have counted, in Galen's eyes, as a relational syllogism. True, we should not so class it; true, Galen does not explicitly so class it. But it is certainly not a predicative syllogism, and it is certainly not a hypothetical syllogism. There is no fourth species of syllogisms, and no syllogism fails to belong to a species. Hence it is a relational syllogism. If that conclusion implies that Galen's notion of a relational syllogism was pretty indeterminate, then that is an implication which there are also other grounds for accepting.

The second point which tells against supposing a restriction on the metatheorem has more force. It is this. The fact that 'pretty well all syllogisms have their constitution warranted because of the universal axioms which are superordinate to them' is something which Galen had not discovered when he wrote, as a young man, his vast work *On Proof* and its appendix *On the Number of Syllogisms*. But 'in those works I was aware of relational syllogisms and had discovered their constitution and warrant'. If Galen had discovered the constitution and warrant of relational syllogisms, then he had surely discovered that relational syllogisms owe their constitution and warrant to the universal axioms to which they are subordinated. At any rate, I cannot see what else Galen might possibly have had in mind. But in that case, the early works recognized that the metatheorem applies to relational syllogisms but did not yet recognize that it applies to all syllogisms. Hence when, in the *Introduction*, Galen says that the metatheorem applies to all syllogisms, he means all syllogisms and not all relational syllogisms.

Posidonius had used the formula 'concludent in virtue of the power of an axiom' (*inst log* xviii 8), so that the idea on which the metatheorem is based derives from him. But he used the formula—if my reconstruction of the text

---

[72] ... καθάπερ ἔχει καὶ ὁ τοιόσδε· λέγεις ἡμέρα ἐστίν· ἀλλὰ καὶ ἀληθεύεις· ἡμέρα ἄρα ἐστίν. ἀποδεικτικός ἐστι καὶ ὁ τοιοῦτος συλλογισμὸς διότι καὶ τὸ καθόλου ἀξίωμα ᾧ ὑποπέπτωκεν ἀληθές ἐστι ...

is right—to refer to a subspecies of relational syllogism. When, as a young man, Galen discovered the constitution and warrant of relational syllogisms, he generalized the Posidonian notion from the subspecies to the species. Later, he saw that the metatheorem applied to all—or to pretty well all—syllogisms.

That, I am inclined to suppose, is the story we should read into the text. It is not a revolutionary story—on the contrary, I have laboriously argued for a commonplace. But the commonplace needs an argument to support it, and its support is less robust than it is often taken to be. For it depends wholly on inferences drawn from a single passage of the *Introduction* in which the Greek is quite certainly very corrupt.

At xvii 1 Galen says that the metatheorem holds of 'pretty well all' syllogisms, and of 'all probative syllogisms'. The second formula does not imply any restriction on the theorem. It is true that here, and indeed throughout the *Introduction*, Galen speaks expressly of probative syllogisms—that is to say, of syllogisms which may serve to present proofs; but in his view an argument which is not in this sense probative is not a syllogism at all. So 'syllogism' and 'probative syllogism' are equivalent terms.

What about the qualification 'pretty well all'? Well, that may simply mean 'all'; for the adverb 'pretty well [σχεδόν]' is frequently used as a mark of modesty or caution rather than as a sign of genuine limitation. But here the adverb probably does indicate a limitation; for it is echoed a little later when Galen remarks that

most of the things which men syllogize and prove are said in accordance with the force of an axiom.

(*inst log* xvii 7)[73]

Not all but 'most of the things': then what are the exceptions?

There is an indication a little later in the text—or rather, there once was an indication. At the end of a lengthy discussion of an argument even the bare bones of which are—once again for textual reasons—wholly uncertain, the received text makes Galen remark that

'Dio always speaks the truth' is assumed in the place of the universal axiom.

(*inst log* xvii 9)[74]

---

[73] τὰ πλεῖστα γὰρ ὧν οἱ ἄνθρωποι συλλογίζονται καὶ ἀποδεικνύουσι, κατὰ δύναμιν ἀξιώματος λέγεται.

[74] τὸ δὲ πάντῃ ἀληθεύειν Δίωνα ἐν χώρᾳ τοῦ καθόλου ἀξιώματος εἴληπται.

So in this argument no universal axiom is involved: something else takes its place and performs its part. Now the proposition that Dio always tells the truth is certainly not a universal axiom. But it is utterly remote from anything which might be deemed a universal axiom, and I am unable to imagine how or why Galen could have thought that it played the rôle of a universal axiom. Despite the horrible state of the text, it is reasonably plain that, somehow or other, an explanation of the meaning of the word 'true' comes into the discussion of the argument which Galen is examining. It is therefore tempting to suppose that it was that explanation, rather than the proposition about Dio, which Galen took to play the rôle of an axiom. After all, explanations of meanings, or definitions, are, in a pretty obvious way, axiom-like; and in Aristotle's theory of scientific proof definitions feature strongly among the first principles of the sciences.

If a definition or explanation of 'true' plays the rôle of axiom in the concrete argument which Galen is discussing, then it is very tempting to suppose that the exceptions to the rule that syllogisms depend on axioms are precisely those cases in which they depend instead upon definitions. In that case, a revised version of the metatheorem would claim that every syllogism depends either on an axiom or on a definition.

However that may be, Galen certainly thought that most syllogisms, or pretty well all syllogisms, depend on the force of an axiom. He cannot, then, have supposed that no predicative syllogisms and no hypothetical syllogisms depend on axioms; and despite the textual darkness, it is reasonable to conclude that the metatheorem includes in its scope both predicative and hypothetical syllogisms.

THE SENSE OF THE METATHEOREM

So much for the scope of the metatheorem: what of its content? First, it is certain that, according to Galen, it is axioms which (somehow or other) support syllogisms. The Greek word '*ἀξίωμα*' is ambiguous in logical texts: sometimes it means 'assertible' and sometimes 'first principle'. The former use is Stoic: it originated in the Stoa, and it rarely travelled abroad. Galen does not much like it—he does not much like Stoic terminology in general—and it would be surprising had he adopted it here to express a theorem of his own. In any event, he tells us expressly that we should remember the signification of the word axiom: we decided in the present exposition so to name sayings which are self-warranted.

(*inst log* xvii 7)[75]

In other words, in the metatheorem the term 'axiom' is used in the sense of 'first principle'—in more or less the sense in which it was generally used by the mathematicians, and also (sometimes) by Aristotle.

Axioms are, of course, true. They are also self-warranting (so xvi 6 and 7, as well as the formal announcement at xvii 7). They are therefore unproved inasmuch as they do not need proof. It may be supposed—although the *Introduction* does not explicitly say so—that they are also primary inasmuch as they cannot be proved. Again, the axioms to which Galen's theorem appeals are universal propositions. (So at xvi 6, and a further eight times; and once, if the easiest emendation at xvi 12 is right, they are 'general [γενικός]'). Whether Galen thought that all axioms were universal is another matter; but the axioms which ground syllogisms—the syllogistic axioms, as I shall henceforth call them—undoubtedly are universal truths. Galen surely took the syllogistic axioms to be necessary truths; but they are certainly not, or not all, items which we should class as logical truths: among them, for example, are at least some of the axioms of Euclid's *Elements*.

One passage has been taken to show that syllogistic axioms are, all of them, conditional propositions (xvi 10). But the text is—yet again—certainly corrupt, and even the general gist is wholly obscure. Moreover, the illustrative axioms which Galen introduces into the discussion are not in general expressed as conditional propositions. Nevertheless, conditionality will come into its own at a later stage in the discussion.

There is more than one syllogistic axiom: Galen's use of the plural form proves that different syllogisms are supported by different axioms; the point is confirmed by the various examples which Galen provides; and in any event it is obvious enough. But how many syllogistic axioms are there?

Evidently, there is not one axiom for each concrete syllogism—syllogisms which share their pertinent logical forms will also share their axiom. But it is tempting to suppose that syllogistic forms and syllogistic axioms form monogamous couples: all Stoic first unproveds, say, will be supported by

---

[75] ... μεμνημένων ἡμῶν καὶ αὐτοῦ τοῦ κατὰ τὴν ἀξίωμα φωνὴν σημαινομένου· τὸν γὰρ ἐξ αὐτοῦ πιστὸν λόγον οὕτως ὀνομάζειν ὑπεθέμεθα κατὰ τὴν προκειμένην διδασκαλίαν.

one and the same axiom, and that axiom will support no syllogisms but first unproveds; there will be an axiom which serves every syllogism in Barbara and which is strictly faithful to Barbara; and so on.

In the case of relational syllogisms, that supposition may well be trivially true—for how shall we distinguish one relational form from another unless by reference to its supporting axiom? But the supposition is not trivial for predicative and hypothetical syllogisms, where the different forms are determined in advance of any application of Galen's metatheorem; and in fact the supposition is dubious. No doubt there is an axiom which answers to the first Stoic unproved, and an axiom which answers to Aristotle's Barbara. But are there also axioms corresponding to derived syllogistic forms? Is there an axiom corresponding, say, to Baralipton?

Well, if Baralipton is derived from Barbara, will not the axiom which supports Barbara thereby also support Baralipton? More generally, it must seem reasonable to suppose that axioms—which are essentially unproved— correspond to unproved syllogistic forms, and that if anything corresponds in the same sort of way to a proved form, it will be a theorem rather than an axiom. So Baralipton, say, will be subordinated to a syllogistic axiom—to the syllogistic axiom to which Barbara is subordinated; and a derived hypo- thetical syllogism will be subordinated to the axiom to which—say—the first unproved is subordinated.

It must be allowed that there is nothing in Galen's text which suggests that the metatheorem bears, so to speak, directly upon primary syllogisms and indirectly on derivative syllogisms. But I cannot see how he could have maintained that every valid syllogistic form had a private axiom to support it; and that being so, the view which I have just sketched is the obvious one to embrace.

That meets one of the two points which were raised and not met earlier: since Galen's metatheorem is about syllogisms in general and not about primary syllogisms in particular, how is it pertinent to the present concerns? The answer is: fundamentally—but never explicitly—the metatheorem concerns primary syllogisms.

The next question: Is each syllogistic form supported by a single axiom? Galen's illustrative examples never appeal to a plurality of axioms; he often uses the singular in referring to the axiomatic backing of a syllogism (*inst log* xvi 10, 11; xvii 3, 7; xviii 6); and he says, introducing a new species of relational argument that, in these cases too, the syllogism will be in accordance with one of the axioms.

(*inst log* xvi 10)[76]

Such facts suggest that, according to the metatheorem, each syllogistic form has a single axiom behind it.

On the other hand, if Baralipton does not possess an axiom of its own, insofar as it depends on Barbara, it might seem plausible to think that it in fact rests on a pair of axioms. For the standard proof of Baralipton depends on Barbara and a principle of conversion. If the conversion rule has the status of an unproved rule of inference, then perhaps it too will be backed by an axiom; and in that case Baralipton will been underwritten by two axioms—namely, the axiom which underwrites Barbara and the axiom which corresponds to the principle of conversion. More generally, derived forms will depend on a plurality of axioms. Nothing in Galen's text strictly excludes that possibility. But nothing in the text remotely hints at it, and it is doubtless miles away from anything which Galen ever dreamed of.

The axioms underwrite or support their syllogisms: what sort of support do they give? I said at the start, with deliberate vagueness, that syllogisms owe their force to their associated axioms. Galen himself uses a multiplicity of linguistic turns to describe the support. Sometimes a syllogism is said to be 'in accordance with an axiom' (*inst log* xvi 10), or 'in accordance with the power of an axiom' (xvii 7; xviii 8). Once he says that certain syllogisms 'have the force of proof' by an axiom (xvi 12). But most often he expresses himself either by way of the term 'constitution [σύστασις]', or by means of the word 'warranty [πίστις]' or a cognate word. The two terms come together at xvi 12, where Galen refers either to 'the warranted constitution' of a syllogism or to 'the warrant of its constitution'. (The manuscript reading is an impossible combination of the two.) So too at xvii 2, where he refers to 'the manner of their constitution and of their warranty'.

As for 'πίστις' and its family, Galen refers sometimes to the warranty of the superordinate axioms (xvii 1—if the text is correct—and 2); that is to say, he invokes the fact that axioms are self-warranting (xvii 7). In a similar vein he notes that in the case of certain arguments the pertinent axiom 'is both thought of and believed by everyone' (xviii 6).[77] But he also refers to the warranty of syllogisms (xvii 2), and says of certain

---

[76] καὶ γὰρ ἐπὶ τούτων ὁ συλλογισμὸς ἔσται κατά τι τῶν ἀξιωμάτων.

[77] καθολικὸν δὲ καὶ κατὰ τοὺς τοιούτους λόγους ἀξίωμα νοεῖταί τε καὶ πιστεύεται πᾶσι.

syllogisms that 'their warranty is taken from certain of the universal axioms' (xviii 1).[78]

The word 'πίστις' often means 'belief', and also 'trust'. But an item which is πίστος—which is reliable or trustworthy—may be said to have πίστις (to have reliability or trustworthiness) or to be or provide πίστις for something else (to warrant it). The metatheorem, insofar as it invokes πίστις, surely means that syllogisms are reliable, or trustworthy, or warranted, in virtue of an associated axiom; and that they derive their reliability from the reliability or trustworthiness of those axioms. In what might the reliability or trustworthiness of a syllogism consist? Presumably in its validity. The syllogistic axioms, then, underwrite syllogistic validity. That unadventurous conclusion is confirmed when Galen remarks that Posidonius called certain arguments 'concludent in virtue of the force of an axiom' (xviii 8).[79] He evidently thinks that the expression is apt.

But if a syllogism is trustworthy inasmuch as it is valid, the word 'πίστις' does not, of course, mean 'validity': it means 'trustworthiness' or 'warrantability' or something of that sort. The word has an epistemological sense; and what Galen means to say is that what warrants our accepting a syllogism, what makes it right for us to trust its validity, is the axiom on which it rests, or perhaps the fact that it rests on an axiom. That being so, Galen presumably thinks that we know a syllogism to be valid insofar as we have grasped the axiom to which it is subordinated.

That meets the second of the two points which were raised earlier: the metatheorem is metalogical, not epistemological—so how can it be relevant to the present concerns? The answer is: the metatheorem has an epistemological element to it.

The σύστασις or constitution to which Galen refers is always the constitution of the syllogism in question. At xvi 5 certain syllogisms 'have the same constitution on the basis of certain axioms' (but the text is uncertain). At xvi 10, 'the constitution of probative syllogisms' is in accordance with the power of an axiom. There is a reference to 'the constitution of the reasoning' at xvi 11. I have already cited xvi 12, and xvii 2. What does the word 'constitution' mean in these passages? Or rather, what is the meaning of the Greek word 'σύστασις', which I have thus far translated by 'constitution'? .

---

[78] καὶ τούτων ἡ πίστις ἐκ τῶν καθόλου τινῶν ἀξιωμάτων εἴληπται.

[79] συνακτικοὺς κατὰ δύναμιν ἀξιώματος.

There are several possibilities, of which the most popular, I think, is 'validity'. The popularity is comprehensible—indeed, 'validity' is the very word we should most like to hear. But although the sense of 'validity' is frequently claimed for the word, and although there are one or two late texts in which the sense is at least plausible, I am inclined to doubt its existence. In any event, it is certainly not a common sense, and it is not a sense found elsewhere in Galen's writings.

The common sense of the word, as my translation has already intimated, is 'constitution': the σύστασις of a syllogism is its construction or constitution, the way in which it is put together from premisses and conclusion. And that this is the sense which the word bears in our texts is shown by two passages. First, 'the constitution of the reasoning' at xvi 11 refers to the fact that an argument is propounded as a predicative syllogism rather than as a hypothetical syllogism: it is not the validity of the syllogism but its form or constitution which is in question. Secondly, at xviii 8 Galen refers to arguments 'constituted in accordance with the force of an axiom'.[80] The participle, 'constituted' belongs to the verb of which 'σύστασις' is a nominalization; and, again, it is not validity but constitution which is in question.

If that is right, then syllogisms owe two things to their superordinate axioms: their trustworthiness, and their constitution. It is not difficult to see how an argument might owe its trustworthiness to an axiom: the argument is reliable inasmuch as the axiom is true. But how on earth might a syllogism be said to owe its constitution to an axiom?

AXIOMS AS PREMISSES

An answer to that question is suggested by the way in which Galen presents his first example of a relational syllogism. The sense of the passage is clear, and the text—for once—is well preserved:

Given that there is this universal axiom, which has its warranty from itself—namely, items equal to the same item are also equal to one another—it is possible to syllogize and prove in the way in which Euclid produced the proof in his first theorem where he shows that the sides of the triangle are equal; for since items equal to the same item

---

[80] κατ' ἀξιώματος δύναμιν συνισταμένους.

are also equal to one another, and it has been shown that the first and the second are equal to the third, the first will be equal to the second.

(inst log xvi 6)[81]

Galen alludes to the proof of the first theorem in the first book of Euclid's *Elements*—or rather, to a part of it:

Since the point A is the centre of the circle CDB, AC is equal to AB. Again, since the point B is the centre of the circle CAE, BC is equal to BA. But it has been shown that CA is equal to AB. Each of CA and CB is therefore equal to AB. But items equal to the same item are also equal to one another. Therefore CA is equal to CB. Therefore the three—CA, AB, CB—are equal to one another.

(1 i)[82]

According to Galen, 'he shows that the sides of the triangle are equal': CA, CB and AB are the sides of the triangle ABC. Again, what Galen calls 'the first' side is CA, 'the second' is CB, and 'the third' is AB. And 'it has been shown'—in the first two sentences I have just cited from the *Elements*—that CA is equal to AB and that CB is equal to AC. Galen's account of Euclid's procedure is impeccable.

In Euclid, the axiom is used as a premiss in the argument. There is nothing untoward about that: the axiom is the first of Euclid's 'common notions'; and the common notions, like the other bits and pieces which Euclid sets out before he begins his proofs, are there precisely in order to serve as premisses in proofs. Galen's account of the argument does not state clearly that the axiom is employed as a premiss; but he can hardly have imagined that Euclid employed it in any other capacity, and he must have intended to employ it in the same way himself. In other words, the argument which Galen is inviting us to consider is this:

Any two items equal to the same item are equal to one another.
CA is equal to AB.

---

[81] ὄντος γὰρ ἀξιώματος τοῦδε καθόλου τὴν πίστιν ἔχοντος ἐξ ἑαυτοῦ, τὰ τῷ αὐτῷ ἴσα καὶ ἀλλήλοις ἐστὶν ἴσα, συλλογίζεσθαί τε καὶ ἀποδεικνύναι ἔστιν ὥσπερ Εὐκλείδης ἐν τῷ πρώτῳ θεωρήματι τὴν ἀπόδειξιν ἐποιήσατο τὰς τοῦ τριγώνου πλευρὰς ἴσας δεικνύων· ἐπεὶ γὰρ τὰ τῷ αὐτῷ ἴσα καὶ ἀλλήλοις ἴσα ἐστίν, δέδεικται δὲ τὸ πρῶτόν τε καὶ τὸ δεύτερον τῷ τρίτῳ ἴσον, ἑκατέρῳ αὐτῶν ἴσον ἂν εἴη οὕτω τὸ πρῶτον.

[82] καὶ ἐπεὶ τὸ Α σημεῖον κέντρον ἐστὶ τοῦ ΓΔΒ κύκλου, ἴση ἐστὶν ἡ ΑΓ τῇ ΑΒ· πάλιν, ἐπεὶ τὸ Β σημεῖον κέντρον ἐστὶ τοῦ ΓΑΕ κύκλου, ἴση ἐστὶν ἡ ΒΓ τῇ ΒΑ. ἐδείχθη δὲ καὶ ἡ ΓΑ τῇ ΑΒ ἴση· ἑκατέρα ἄρα τῶν ΓΑ, ΓΒ τῇ ΑΒ ἐστὶν ἴση. τὰ δὲ τῷ αὐτῷ ἴσα καὶ ἀλλήλοις ἐστὶν ἴσα· καὶ ἡ ΓΑ ἄρα τῇ ΓΒ ἐστὶν ἴση· αἱ τρεῖς ἄρα αἱ ΓΑ, ΑΒ, ΒΓ ἴσαι ἀλλήλαις εἰσίν.

CB is equal to AB.
Therefore CA is equal to CB.

He took that to be a relational syllogism; and he thought that it depended for its trustworthiness and for its constitution on the axiom which appears as its first premiss.

The syllogism thus owes its constitution to the axiom in a straightforward way: the axiom is an essential part or premiss of the syllogism, the other premisses referring to special cases which fall under it. The generalization to relational syllogisms is obvious: every relational syllogism will have, among its premisses, a universal axiom, its other premisses introducing special instances which fall under its general rule.

That such was indeed Galen's view of the matter is confirmed, it seems, by other passages in the *Introduction*. Once, for example, Galen remarks of a particular relational syllogism that

the constitution of the reasoning will be more forceful with predicative propositions—there being premissed here too, of course, a universal axiom ...

(*inst log* xvi 11)[83]

The axiom is expressly said to be premissed, or put forward as a premiss of the argument. (But the passive participle 'being premissed' is a conjectural emendation of the corrupt manuscript text.) Again, the very first example in the *Introduction*—which is offered as an illustration of what a probative syllogism should look like—reads thus:

This proof is constituted from three items: first, the first one I stated, which was
    Dio is equal to Theo;
second, the one after it:
    Philo is equal to Dio;
and third, in addition to them,
    items equal to the same item are also equal to one another.
From these it will be concluded that Theo is equal to Philo.

(*inst log* i 3)[84]

The text is found on a page of the manuscript the right-hand half of which has been torn off, and only half the words which I have translated actually

---

[83] κατηγορικαῖς δὲ προτάσεσι βιαιότερον ἔσται ἡ σύστασις τοῦ λογισμοῦ, προτεινομένου δηλονότι καθόλου κἀνταῦθά τινος ἀξιώματος ...

[84] καὶ τοίνυν ἡ ἀπό[δειξις ἥδ᾽ ἐκ τριῶν συνίστα]ται, πρώτου μὲν τοῦ πρώτου ῥηθέντος, ὅπερ ἦν ἴσος ἐστὶ [Δίωνι Θέων, δευτέρου δὲ τοῦ μετ᾽ α]ὐτό Δίωνι Φίλων ἐστὶν ἴσος καὶ τρίτου πρὸς τούτοις τοῦ τὰ [τῷ αὐτῷ ἴσα καὶ ἀλλήλοις ἐστὶν ἴ]σα· περανθήσεται δὲ ἐξ αὐτῶν ἴσος

answer to any legible Greek. But the reconstruction is certainly correct in its general lines; and it is the general lines which count here: they show that Galen took his axioms to function as premisses.

That view of the function of syllogistic axioms has the great merit of being simple and intelligible; nor is it evidently foolish—after all, it answers to Euclid's actual practice. Moreover, you might conjecture a plausible origin for it. For the role which, on this view, Galen's metatheorem gives to the syllogistic axioms can hardly fail to recall the role which—according to Aristotle's *Topics*—the 'commonplaces' or τόποι hold in dialectical arguments. A commonplace, according to the most plausible view of the matter, is an abstract universal truth. Dialectical syllogisms owe their constitution to the commonplaces inasmuch as the commonplaces form their leading premisses, the other premisses adverting to special cases which fall under them. Galen knew his Aristotelian logic—and so too did that Aristotelizing Stoic, Posidonius. Galen's metatheorem is in effect a generalization to all syllogisms of the Aristotelian notion that dialectical syllogisms are constituted on the basis of commonplaces—a generalization which replaces the commonplaces by the syllogistic axioms. Perhaps Galen was inspired by the *Topics*? Perhaps Posidonius had been so inspired before him?

AXIOMS ARE NOT PREMISSES

Thus the interpretation which makes premisses of the syllogistic axioms is firmly based on the text of the *Introduction*; it fits with actual geometrical practice; and it can claim dialectical precedent. Nonetheless, it cannot be right; or at least, it is confronted by two serious difficulties.

The first difficulty is this. It is conceivable that every relational syllogism must have an axiom among its premisses—or at any rate, it is conceivable that Galen thought that every relational syllogism must have an axiom among its premisses. The argument

CA is equal to AB
CB is equal to AB
Therefore CA is equal to CB

εἶναι Θέων [Φίλωνι.—The letters inside brackets are an imaginative reconstruction of what was once on the missing half of the page.

is no doubt valid. But its validity depends on the sense of the term 'equal'—it depends (perhaps) on its matter rather than on its form. So perhaps it is not a genuine syllogism—I mean, perhaps Galen would not have taken it to be a genuine syllogism. On the other hand, the argument

> Any two items equal to the same item are equal to one another
> CA is equal to AB
> CB is equal to AB
> Therefore CA is equal to CB

surely is a syllogism—at any rate, its validity does not depend on the sense of the word 'equal' or on any other aspect of its matter.

The argument without the axiom among its premises is a relational argument, but it is not a relational syllogism. The argument with the axiom is a relational syllogism. And so it is in all cases: a relational argument with no axiom among its premises is never a syllogism; all relational syllogisms have an axiom among their premises. Now I do not think that in fact Galen ever entertained such an idea; but I allow that he could or might have done. (Whatever that means.)

Nonetheless, the idea can hardly be extended to all syllogisms. For Galen surely cannot have imagined, and quite certainly never suggests, that hypothetical syllogisms and predicative syllogisms must all always have axioms among their premises.

True, some Stoics claimed that predicative syllogisms are not really syllogisms; but they did not find predicative syllogisms wanting because their premises contained no axioms. True, Alexander—in some moods—urged that hypothetical syllogisms are not really syllogisms; but he did not claim that they fail to meet the grade because they lack an axiom among their premises.

Actually there is a passage in the commentary on the *Analytics* which has been thought to show that he did take that line; and the passage is worth an airing. Alexander is discussing this text:

Again, if, being a man, he must be an animal, and being an animal a substance, then being a man, he must be a substance. But that is not yet a syllogism—for the premises are not as we have said.

(*APr* 47a28–31)[85]

---

[85] πάλιν εἰ ἀνθρώπου ὄντος ἀνάγκη ζῷον εἶναι καὶ ζῴου οὐσίαν, ἀνθρώπου ὄντος ἀνάγκη οὐσίαν εἶναι· ἀλλ' οὔπω συλλελόγισται· οὐ γὰρ ἔχουσιν αἱ προτάσεις ὡς εἴπομεν.

The illustrative argument might be construed in more ways than one; but Alexander read it as a 'wholly hypothetical' inference, thus:

> If he is a man he is an animal.
> If he is an animal he is a substance.
> Therefore if he is a man he is a substance.

That is a valid argument, according to Aristotle; but it is not a syllogism—for 'the premisses are not as we have said'. What does Aristotle mean?

Alexander offers two interpretations of Aristotle's Delphic phrase. First, he says this:

> The premisses are not as we said they must be if there is to be a syllogism—i.e. the premisses must be universal, either both of them or at least one. And in this example neither is taken universally. But since the universal which has been omitted and the laying down of which would produce a syllogism is true, what seems to follow the items laid down seems to be true. The universal premiss is:
>> Everything which follows a certain item also follows whatever that item follows.
> ... For when the universal which we have just mentioned is assumed, and it is co-assumed that being a man he is an animal and being an animal a substance, it is concluded syllogistically that ... being a man he is a substance.
>
> (in APr 347.20–348.2)[86]

It is far from clear what syllogism—what predicative syllogism—Alexander thinks he has constructed; but it is plain, at least, that he thinks he can turn the wholly hypothetical inference into a syllogism by adding a universal premiss—and the added universal premiss might perhaps be taken for an axiom.

But Alexander then offers a second interpretation of his Aristotelian text:

> The premisses are not as we have said because they are not taken deictically or universally. There will be a syllogism if they are taken in this way:
>> Every man is an animal
>> Every animal is a substance

---

[86] οὐ γὰρ ἔχουσιν αἱ προτάσεις ὡς εἴρηται δεῖν ἔχειν εἰ μέλλοι συλλογισμὸς ἔσεσθαι· ἔστι δὲ τοῦτο τὸ δεῖν ἢ ἀμφοτέρας εἶναι τὰς προτάσεις καθόλου ἢ πάντως γε τὴν ἑτέραν. ἐνταῦθα δὲ οὐδεμία εἴληπται καθόλου. τῷ μέντοι τὴν καθόλου ἀληθῆ εἶναι τὴν παρειαμένην ἧς τεθείσης συλλογισμὸς ἔσται, ἀληθὲς δοκεῖ τὸ τοῖς κειμένοις ἕπεσθαι δοκοῦν. ἔστι δὲ ἡ καθόλου πρότασις πᾶν τὸ ἑπόμενόν τινι ἕπεται καὶ ᾧ ἐκεῖνο ἕπεται. ... ληφθέντος γὰρ τοῦ καθόλου οὗ προειρήκαμεν καὶ προσληφθέντος αὐτῷ τοῦ ἀνθρώπου δὲ ὄντος ζῷόν ἐστι καὶ ζῴου οὐσία, συνάγεται συλλογιστικῶς τὸ καὶ ... ἀνθρώπου ὄντος οὐσίαν εἶναι.

... Again, it is possible to criticize

being a man he must be an animal and an animal a substance

as not concluding syllogistically on the grounds that the premisses—'A man is an animal' and 'An animal is a substance'—are indefinite.

(*in APr* 348.15–22)[87]

On this second interpretation of Aristotle's text, the non-syllogistic argument does not need to be reinforced with a new premiss—let alone with a new axiomatic premiss: what it needs is some quantifiers.

In short, Alexander neither says nor implies that every hypothetical inference needs to be reinforced by an additional axiomatic premiss in order to become a syllogism. He holds—what is a perfectly distinct thesis—that every syllogism, predicative or hypothetical, must have at least one universal premiss.

There is a second and more fundamental difficulty with the interpretation of Galen's metatheorem which has it place an axiom among the premisses of every syllogism. If a syllogistic axiom functions as a premiss in a syllogism, then how can it also be responsible for the trustworthiness of the syllogism in which it appears? To be sure, if the syllogistic axiom is an essential premiss in a syllogism, then if it is removed what is left will not be a syllogism; and in that sense you might say that the presence of the axiom among the premisses was responsible for the warranty of the syllogism. But you might say exactly the same of any non-redundant premiss of any argument: if it is removed, then the result is not a valid argument—so that, in that sense, the warranty of any argument depends on each and every one of its premisses.

Moreover, if you were asked to account for the trustworthiness of the Euclidean argument to which Galen alludes, you would surely not appeal to the axiom which is found among its premisses—nor yet to the fact that an axiom is found among its premisses. It is true that the argument has an axiom among its premisses. But it is not that feature of it which underwrites its validity. Set the Euclidean argument alongside the following silly argument:

Any two items unequal to the same item are unequal to one another.
CA is unequal to AB.

---

[87] οὐ γὰρ ἔχουσιν αἱ προτάσεις ὡς εἴπομεν ὅτι μὴ δεικτικῶς μηδὲ καθόλου ἐλήφθησαν. ἔσται γὰρ συλλογισμὸς ἂν οὕτω ληφθῶσι· πᾶς ἄνθρωπος ζῷον, πᾶν ζῷον οὐσία. ... δυνατὸν πάλιν τὸ εἰ ἀνθρώπου ὄντος ἀνάγκη ζῷον εἶναι καὶ ζῴου οὐσίαν αἰτιᾶσθαι ὡς μὴ συλλογιστικῶς συνάγον ὅτι ἀδιόριστοι αἱ προτάσεις, ἥ τε ὁ ἄνθρωπος ζῷον καὶ ἡ τὸ ζῷον οὐσία.

CB is unequal to AB.
Therefore CA is unequal to CB.

The silly argument and the Euclidean argument are both valid, and they are valid in virtue of a valid form which they share and which might be set out schematically thus:

For any x, y, z: if xRz and yRz, then xRy
aRc
bRc
Therefore aRb

Every argument of that form is valid. Some arguments of that form—Euclid's argument, for example—may have an axiom as their first premiss. Others may have a truth which is not axiomatic. Others—like the silly argument—may have a staring falsity. All are valid, and valid for the same reason. All are trustworthy, and trustworthy for the same reason. The fact that, in Euclid's case, the first premiss is an axiom has absolutely nothing to do with the question.

There are several possible reactions to those difficulties. One of them—and not the least plausible—is despair: perhaps Galen's metatheorem is no more than a muddle, just as his 'third species of syllogism' is no more than a phantom? But if we decline to despair, then the least implausible—and the most interesting—lines to follow are those which suppose that, despite the appearances of the text, the syllogistic axioms are not meant to function as premisses in their arguments.

And the supposition is not entirely baseless. Once or twice in the *Introduction* Galen quite certainly presents syllogistic axioms as premisses of their syllogisms. But by far the greater number of his illustrative syllogisms do not count axioms among their stated premisses. You may always say that in those cases Galen leaves us to supply the missing axiomatic premiss for ourselves. But perhaps Galen did not err by omission in those cases where he left out an axiom: perhaps he erred by commission where he put the axiom among the premisses.

In any event, if the axioms are not premisses of the syllogisms whose constitution and trustworthiness they guarantee, then how do they function? One suggestion tries to have things both ways: the axioms do indeed function as premisses (as several passages show); but the syllogisms in which they function as premisses are not the syllogisms whose trustworthiness and constitution they underwrite. The Euclidean syllogism contains an axiom among its premisses. The axiom, by its position there, underwrites another syllogism, namely:

CA is equal to AB
CB is equal to AB
Therefore CA is equal to CB

That argument has no axiom among its premisses; but it is valid in virtue of the force of an axiom—namely, of the axiom which appears in the Euclidean syllogism.

The interpretation may be generalized as follows. Every syllogism is underwritten by an axiom insofar as the result of adding the axiom to its premisses produces another syllogism. In other words, if

$P_1, P_2, \ldots P_n$: therefore Q

is a syllogism, then there is an axiom A such that

$A, P_1, P_2, \ldots P_n$: therefore Q

is a syllogism; and the former syllogism is valid in virtue of the rôle of the axiom in the latter syllogism.

That suggestion has the merit of ingenuity—and several drawbacks. Among the more evident drawbacks is the fact that it introduces an infinite regression. For if Galen's metatheorem claims that every syllogism is under-written by an axiom, then the syllogism which employs the underwriting axiom as a premiss will itself be underwritten by an axiom; that second axiom will be a premiss in the syllogism which underwrites it; and so on *ad infinitum*. There are various ways in which such a regression could be blocked, or rendered harmless; but, on the whole, it seems best to decide that the underwriting axioms are not premisses at all—neither of the syllogism which they underwrite nor yet (in virtue of their office) of any other syllogism.

And after all, why should we consider such exotic suggestions? The simple suggestion is the best: a syllogistic axiom underwrites or supports a syllogism insofar as the syllogism is trustworthy because the axiom is true. Or (if you like reading letters), for any syllogism S, there is a proposition P such that it is an axiom that P and S is trustworthy because P.

CORRESPONDING CONDITIONALS

That simple suggestion in turn has its drawbacks. Most evidently, if that is what Galen means to say, then how do the syllogistic axioms secure not only the trustworthiness but also the constitution of their syllogisms?

Perhaps it will help to ask how Galen came to hit upon, or to convince himself of the truth of, his metatheorem. All he says on the matter in the *Introduction* is that the theorem will become clear to us if we consider all sorts of syllogisms. So perhaps we should not expect to find a general theoretical argument in favour of the metatheorem: we might rather hope that a survey of various syllogisms will somehow indicate the truth of the metatheorem. Such an indication might be discovered if reflection on any and every syllogism did indeed enable us to put a finger on the appropriate axioms; and it is hard to imagine how we might find ourselves capable of doing that unless we were able to discover a recipe—or perhaps several recipes—for cooking up the syllogistic axioms appropriate to any given syllogism.

Are there such recipes? In his account of Stoic logic, Diogenes Laertius notices that

of arguments, some are inconclusive and others conclusive. Inconclusive are those in which the opposite of the conclusion does not conflict with the conjunction made from the premisses.

(VII 77)[88]

Diogenes does not here explain what conclusive arguments are; but the definition is readily reconstructed: an argument is conclusive when the opposite of its conclusion conflicts with the conjunction of its premisses.

Now according to an account of conditional propositions which is generally, and correctly, associated with Chrysippus,

a conditional is sound when the opposite of its consequent conflicts with its antecedent.

(Sextus, *PH* II 111)[89]

The definition of conclusiveness implicit in Diogenes is therefore equivalent to the thesis that an argument is conclusive when the Chrysippean conditional formed from the conjunction of its premisses as antecedent and its conclusion as consequent is true. And that thesis is found a few pages later in the *Outlines of Pyrrhonism*:

---

[88] τῶν δὲ λόγων οἱ μέν εἰσιν ἀπέραντοι, οἱ δὲ περαντικοί. ἀπέραντοι μὲν ὧν τὸ ἀντικείμενον τῆς ἐπιφορᾶς οὐ μάχεται τῇ διὰ τῶν λημμάτων συμπλοκῇ.

[89] οἱ δὲ τὴν συνάρτησιν εἰσάγοντες ὑγιὲς εἶναί φασι συνημμένον ὅταν τὸ ἀντικείμενον τῷ ἐν αὐτῷ λήγοντι μάχηται τῷ ἐν αὐτῷ ἡγουμένῳ.

Of arguments, some are concludent and some inconcludent. An argument is concludent when the conditional which begins with the conjunction of the premisses of the argument and ends with its conclusion is sound.

(PH ii 137)[90]

Scholars generally ascribe that definition of concludence to the Stoics. True, Sextus does not say, in so many words, that it is Stoic. But in *Against the Mathematicians* the same definition recurs:

There is a concludent argument when, if we conjoin the assumptions and make a conditional which begins with the conjunction of the premisses and ends with the conclusion, this conditional is found to be true.

(M viii 417)[91]

That is proposed as something which 'they say' (415); and it forms part of a long exposition which is firmly and explicitly ascribed to the Stoics (396, 399, 400, 406, 407, 408, 425).

Thus according to the Stoics (this from Diogenes Laertius), an argument

$P_1, P_2, \ldots, P_n$: therefore Q

is inconclusive or invalid if and only if there is no conflict between 'not-Q' and 'P_1 and P_2 and ... and P_n'. Hence (a proper inference from this same passage in Diogenes) an argument is conclusive or valid if and only if there is conflict between 'not-Q' and 'P_1 and P_2 and ... and P_n'. Now a Chrysippean analysis of conditional propositions has it that 'If P, then Q' is true if and only if there is a conflict between 'not-Q' and 'P'. Hence (it is eminently reasonable to infer) the Stoics held that an argument

$P_1, P_2, \ldots, P_n$: therefore Q

is valid if and only if the corresponding conditional proposition

If P_1 and P_2 and ... and P_n, then Q

is true. In other words—to put it shortly—an argument is valid if and only if its corresponding conditional is true. And Sextus confirms that the thesis was indeed Stoic.

But Sextus exploits the thesis for his own ends on more occasions than one, and it is plain that he took it to be not a peculiarly Stoic idiosyncrasy

---

[90] τῶν δὲ λόγων οἱ μέν εἰσι συνακτικοὶ οἱ δὲ ἀσύνακτοι· συνακτικοὶ μὲν ὅταν τὸ συνημμένον τὸ ἀρχόμενον μὲν ἀπὸ τοῦ διὰ τῶν τοῦ λόγου λημμάτων συμπεπλεγμένου, λῆγον δὲ εἰς τὴν ἐπιφορὰν αὐτοῦ, ὑγιὲς ᾖ.

[91] οὐκοῦν ὁ μὲν συνακτικὸς τότε ἐστὶν ὅταν συμπλεξάντων ἡμῶν τὰ λήμματα καὶ συνημμένον ποιησάντων τὸ ἀρχόμενον μὲν ἀπὸ τῆς διὰ τῶν λημμάτων συμπλοκῆς λῆγον δ' εἰς τὸ συμπέρασμα, εὑρίσκηται τοῦτο τὸ συνημμένον ἀληθές.

but rather a commonplace of logic. Thus at *PH* II 249 it is invoked as a thesis belonging to 'the dialecticians'—that is to say, to logicians in general; and at *PH* II 113 and 145 it is invoked as a general test of validity—a test, so Sextus implies, accepted by all the 'dogmatic' philosophers.

Now there is at least a superficial similarity between the test and Galen's metatheorem: according to the metatheorem, a syllogism is trustworthy if and only if it is underwritten by an axiom; according to the test, an argument is valid if and only if its corresponding conditional is true.

But that is no more than a formal similarity; and we cannot identify the syllogistic axiom of a syllogism with its corresponding conditional. It is not merely that Sextus speaks of arguments in general and not of syllogisms in particular, that he does not hint—let alone state—that the conditional corresponding to an argument is an axiom, and that he says nothing in the context about the justification or underwriting of arguments. There are also positive reasons which forbid the identification. For whereas Galen's syllogistic axioms are universal, the conditional which corresponds to an argument is never universal: any universal proposition has the form 'For any x, such-and-such'; no conditional proposition has that form. And even if a corresponding conditional is somehow universalized, it will not thereby become an axiom—there are any number of universal truths which are not axiomatic.

Nonetheless, if there is any recipe for finding the axiom appropriate to a given syllogism, that recipe will surely start by considering corresponding conditionals—after all, what else could it possibly look to? Consider, then, the stock Stoic example of a hypothetical syllogism:

> If it is day, it is light.
> It is day.
> Therefore it is light.

The corresponding conditional is this:
> If if it is day it is light, and also it is day, then it is light.

Now that is not a universal proposition; nor does it look much like an axiom. But there are indefinitely many propositions which resemble it formally insofar as they are all instances of the schema:
> If if P then Q, and also P, then Q.

That schema may serve as the material for constructing a universal proposition, thus:
> For any P and Q, if if P then Q, and also P, then Q.

And if you want to avoid schematic letters, then try:

> For any pair of propositions, if if the one holds then the other does, and in fact the one holds, then the other does.

That is certainly universal, and I suppose that it is axiomatic. Is it not the universal axiom which—according to Galen—underwrites the stock Stoic syllogism?

Something similar is readily done for a standard predicative syllogism in Barbara. The stock syllogism

All men are animals.
All animals are substances.
Therefore all men are substances.

has the following corresponding conditional:

> If all men are animals and all animals are substances, then all men are substances.

That is neither universal nor an axiom. But it shares a form with countless other conditionals, namely the form:

If all As are B and all Bs are C, then all As are C.

And that schema is material for a universal truth, namely:

For any X, Y, and Z, if every X is Y and every Y is Z, then every X is Z.

You may write that without schematic letters if you prefer.

Consider, finally, a relational argument, say:

CA is equal to AB.
CB is equal to AB.
Therefore CA is equal to CB.

The corresponding conditional is:

If CA is equal to AB and CB is equal to AB, then CA is equal to CB.

That is not universal, and it is not an axiom; but it admits generalization. Thus:

For any x, y and z, if x is equal to z and y is equal to z, then x is equal to y.

Or:

> For any triad of items, if two are each equal to the third, then they are equal to one another.

Or:

Items equal to the same item are equal to one another.

That is certainly universal, and it might be taken for an axiom. And in fact, as we have seen, Galen did take it for an axiom—after all, it is the first common notion of Euclid's *Elements*.

The first part of the recipe for producing the syllogistic axiom for a given syllogism is this: construct the conditional corresponding to the syllogism and generalize it. So syllogistic axioms will not be conditional propositions, in the strict sense of that phrase; but they will be derived from conditional propositions and will have a conditional connection at their core. The sentence

> For any triad of items, if two are each equal to the third, then they are equal to one another

is not conditional; for it does not have the form
> If ... , then ...

But it is a universalized conditional—and it may be remarked that ancient logicians sometimes did classify such items as conditionals.

However that may be, the first part of the recipe will sometimes be enough to produce the appropriate axiom. But it will not always produce an axiom: it will produce one only when the syllogism on which it operates is valid in virtue of a primary form. If the form is derived, or proved, then the proposition produced by the recipe will be a theorem and not an axiom. So the recipe needs an optional second part, which goes like this: if the syllogism is not primary but derived, then its supporting axiom (or its supporting axioms) is (or are) to be found by first proving it and then applying the recipe to the items on which the proof depends.

In that way, I suppose, an axiom, or a group of axioms, can be found for each syllogism. For a universal truth can always be found; and a universal truth which corresponds in the way I have outlined to a primary syllogism will be an axiom. And if the recipe fails to work, or sometimes fails to work, then I cannot see any other general way of generating syllogistic axioms. If Galen thought that he had a way of showing that all syllogisms are underwritten by axioms, then he must have followed, at least approximately and for some of its length, the line which I have just traced.

There is rather more which could and should be said about the recipe. In addition, something needs to be added to cater for those cases in which, according to Galen, the work of a syllogistic axiom is done by an item of a different sort. (Perhaps in such cases the recipe will in fact come up with an item which might be counted a definition?) Again, it would be worth asking what is the relation between the syllogistic axioms produced by the recipe and the *dictum de omni et nullo* (and the hypothetical *dictum de si et aut*).

DO SYLLOGISTIC AXIOMS WORK?

Do syllogistic axioms, so discovered, really determine the constitution and guarantee the trustworthiness of their syllogisms? Well, you might say that the axiom

For any P and Q, if if P then Q, and also P, then Q,

determines the structure of the syllogism

If it is day, it is light
It is day
Therefore it is light

insofar as it specifies, implicitly, an argument with a conditional proposition as one premiss, the antecedent of the conditional as another, and the consequent of the conditional as the conclusion: the structure of the syllogism corresponds—trivially enough—to the structure of the axiom. In general, if the axiom answering to a given syllogism is a generalization of the corresponding conditional of that syllogism, then the constitution of the syllogism will be determined by the structure of the axiom—you will be able to read off the constitution from the structure.

That will be so for any primary syllogism. But for derived syllogisms, the case is different: the axioms which underwrite a derived syllogism will not, in general, determine its constitution. That follows from the fact that the same axioms may underwrite two different syllogistic forms. For example, Cesare and Camestres are two derived syllogisms, two different syllogistic forms; but they are underwritten—according to the present hypothesis—by the same set of axioms. Each is proved from Celarent, by the application of the principle of E-conversion. Each will therefore be underwritten by the axiom corresponding to Celarent and the axiom corresponding to E-conversion; and those axioms determine neither the constitution of Cesare nor the constitution of Camestres.

Perhaps, after all, it is better to give a restricted scope to Galen's metatheorem? Not that it should be confined to relational syllogisms, but that it should be limited in application to all and only primary syllogisms. Perhaps it should; but Galen never says so, nor even hints as much. Earlier,

I suggested that the metatheorem applies directly to primary syllogisms and indirectly to derivative syllogisms. That comes to the same thing as placing a restriction on the scope of the metatheorem; and it is perhaps a preferable way of making the point. But—as I admitted—there is no hint of that either in Galen's text.

So much for the constitutional side of the metatheorem. What of trustworthiness? In the case of primary syllogisms, you might say that the axiom guarantees the validity of the syllogism insofar as the syllogism is valid precisely because the axiom holds. (And here derived syllogisms do not, in principle, cause any special trouble: they are valid insofar as their underlying axioms are true.) You might say that—but why should I accept it if you do?

Suppose that A is the axiom answering to a primary syllogism S: then of course A is true if and only if S is valid. But the metatheorem supposes that there is also an asymmetry between A and S; for it supposes that S is valid insofar as A is true (and it is not the case that A is true insofar as S is valid). Where does the asymmetry come from?

Or rather, where do the asymmetries come from?—For there is a second asymmetrical thesis in the wings. The Peripatetic *dictum* was supposed to underwrite predicative syllogisms—or rather, perfect predicative syllogisms—in two ways: first, it explains their validity; and secondly, grasp of the *dictum* gives us a grasp of their validity:

Barbara is valid because the *dictum* is true.

I know that Barbara is valid inasmuch as I grasp the truth of the *dictum*.

Galen—so I have suggested—implicitly supposes that a syllogistic axiom will underwrite its syllogism in the same double fashion:

The Euclidean syllogism is valid inasmuch as this axiom is true.
I grasp the validity of the Euclidean syllogism inasmuch as I recognize the truth of this axiom.

So whence come those fearful asymmetries?

No doubt they depend on the fact that syllogistic axioms—like any other axioms—possess a very special character: they are self-evident, or self-warranting. In real money, that means that axioms—or at least syllogistic axioms—are warranted by the meaning of their constituent terms, or by the sense of any sentence which expresses them. For example, if you grasp the sense of the syllogistic axiom

For any P and Q, if if P then Q, and also P, then Q,
then you recognize its truth.

Now that is certainly a Galenic thought. For Galen more than once states that the axioms of any science must be anchored in the essences of the items to which they allude, and he usually adds that the essence must be determined—or at least approached—from a consideration of the sense of the terms used to express it.

But Galenic or not, the thought seems to achieve nothing at all. Earlier, I suggested that the hypothetical *dictum de si* underwrote the first Stoic unproved in the sense that anyone who grasped the *dictum* must thereby recognize the validity of the syllogism. Now I have in effect urged that the sense of Galen's metatheorem is this: anyone who grasps the *dictum* will thereby recognize the truth of the syllogistic axiom which backs up the first unproved. But why proceed to the syllogism by way of the axiom? Why not go directly from the *dictum* to the syllogism?

Again, Aristotle's *dictum de omni* is not an axiom but a definition; and it supposedly underwrites Barbara without the intervention of any axiom. The definition conveyed by the *dictum* is allegedly such that anyone who understands Barbara thereby recognizes its validity. Galen's metatheorem offers us an axiom to back up Barbara. The axiom, I have suggested, is presumably something like this:

For any triad of terms, if one holds of all of another and the other holds of all of the third, then the one holds of all of the third.

No doubt that is a truth, and perhaps it is an axiom. But insofar as it is true, its truth is underwritten by the *dictum de omni*. Perhaps the *dictum* underwrites the axiom which underwrites Barbara? Perhaps the *dictum* underwrites both the axiom and Barbara independently? In any case, it is the *dictum* which counts, not the axiom.

I have urged that the *dictum* cannot in fact do the work which is required of it, and it might be inferred that on that count the axiom must be superior. But that is not so. Rather, if the *dictum* does not work, then the proposition which was just put forward as the appropriate axiom for Barbara is not an axiom at all. For if you may master the *dictum* without thereby grasping the validity of Barbara, then you may understand the supposed axiom without thereby recognizing its truth.

Something similar may be said for the first Stoic unproved. Anyone who knows what a conditional is thereby knows that the form

If P, Q; P: therefore Q

is valid. Perhaps he also thereby knows that the conditional proposition

For any P and Q, if if P then Q and P, then Q

is true; and perhaps he thereby grasps the truth of an axiom. But so what? The appeal to an axiom seems to be otiose: a *dictum*—a definition—will attach itself directly to a syllogism, and there is no need to employ an axiom as go-between.

Perhaps there is a little more to be said on Galen's behalf? I have guessed that in his view a definition may sometimes play the role of a syllogistic axiom; and I have supposed that Galen will have accepted that the syllogistic axioms themselves depend upon definitions. But there may still be a point in introducing axioms rather than simply citing definitions. For the axioms may be taken to specify that part or aspect of the definition which is pertinent to the syllogistic form.

Consider again the fourth of the Stoic unproveds, which makes use of an exclusive disjunction; and take the syllogism:

Either it is day or it is night
But it is day
Therefore it is not night

The syllogistic axiom which lies behind that argument is—according to the recipe—this:

For any P and Q, if either P or Q and P then not Q.

Now the nature of disjunction, or the sense of 'or', determines both the truth of the axiom and the validity of the fourth unproved. But there is nonetheless point in appealing to the axiom. For although the definition of 'or' determines that any fourth unproved is a valid syllogism, it is not, so to speak, the whole of the definition which is pertinent to the validity of the syllogism. Rather, it is that part or aspect of the sense which is presented in the axiom.

6. When is a Syllogism not a Syllogism?

PLOTINUS ON LOGIC

In the third essay of the first *Ennead*, Plotinus asks

what art or method or practice leads us up to the place to which we must travel?

(*enn* I iii 1 [1–2])[1]

The piece is the twentieth of the twenty-one items which Plotinus had written before Porphyry joined his circle in 263 (*vit Plot* iv 61–62). It generally circulated under the title 'On Dialectic' (iv 18–19). It is short; and it is light—for the question which it addresses is neither intricate nor difficult to resolve.

Our destination—the place to which we must travel—is not a secret: we must ascend to the Idea of the Good. The journey has two stages: first, we must scramble from the sensible world to the intelligible world; and then we must climb up through the ranges of the intelligible world. Musicians, lovers and philosophers are all, in their own ways, equipped for undertaking the journey; but they need to prepare for it, and to prepare for it in different fashions. As for the philosopher,

to accustom him to thinking and believing about the incorporeal he must be taught mathematics, which he will accept readily inasmuch as he is a lover of learning; and, being naturally virtuous, he must be led to perfect the virtues; and after mathematics he must be given the arguments of dialectic and in sum he must be made a dialectician.

(*enn* I iii 3 [5–10])[2]

Excelsior, excelsior: the climb to the summit is done on the oxygen of mathematics—and of dialectic.

---

[1] τίς τέχνη ἢ μέθοδος ἢ ἐπιτήδευσις ἡμᾶς οἳ δεῖ πορευθῆναι ἀνάγει;

[2] τὰ μὲν δὴ μαθήματα δοτέον πρὸς συνεθισμὸν κατανοήσεως καὶ πίστεως ἀσωμάτου—καὶ γὰρ ῥᾴδιον δέξεται φιλομαθὴς ὤν—καὶ φύσει ἐνάρετον πρὸς τελείωσιν ἀρετῶν ἀκτέον καὶ μετὰ τὰ μαθήματα λόγους διαλεκτικῆς δοτέον καὶ ὅλως διαλεκτικὸν ποιητέον.

That being so, Plotinus' next question is plain: 'What is dialectic?'; and when he asks it, he adds that dialectic 'must be taught to the others too' (I iii 4 [1–2])³—that is to say, the musician and the lover, and not only the philosopher, must climb on dialectic. The addition is inelegant, inasmuch as the preceding argument gave a strong impression that dialectic was reserved for philosophers; but it is not surprising—for according to Plato,

it is the dialectical method alone which travels in this way, taking up the hypotheses, to the first principle itself.

(*Rep* 533c)⁴

If that is so, then everyone who is to ascend to the Idea of the Good must take dialectic.

The opening paragraphs of Plotinus' essay cling closely to Plato and to Platonic texts. Plotinus' answer to his question 'What is dialectic?' also clings closely to Plato. Indeed, it is a cento of allusions and paraphrases, which serve to show that dialectic

is the disposition which is capable of stating, by reason, about each item, what it is and in what it differs from other items and what it has in common with them.

(*enn* I iii 4 [2–4])⁵

And dialectic is capable of stating such things about each item 'by using Plato's division' (4 [12]).⁶ With that compass in his hands, the traveller will find his way safely through the errors of the sensible world and discover the right tracks to follow upwards in the world of Forms.

Plotinus' dialectician, then, is not exactly a logician—or at least, he is not a general logician. Rather, he is a definer and a classifier—an abstract arboriculturalist of the sort who would later educate himself in Porphyry's woods and groves. Plotinus does not dissemble the fact. On the contrary, he insists that dialectic

assigns to another art the so-called logical discipline which concerns propositions and syllogisms (just as it consigns knowledge of writing to another art)—some of those

---

³ τίς δέ ἡ διαλεκτική, ἣν δεῖ καὶ τοῖς προτέροις παραδιδόναι;
⁴ οὐκοῦν, ἦν δ' ἐγώ, ἡ διαλεκτικὴ μέθοδος μόνη ταύτῃ πορεύεται, τὰς ὑποθέσεις ἀναιροῦσα, ἐπ' αὐτὴν τὴν ἀρχήν;
⁵ ἔστι μὲν δὴ ἡ λόγῳ περὶ ἑκάστου δυναμένη ἕξις εἰπεῖν τί τε ἕκαστον καὶ τί ἄλλων διαφέρει καὶ τίς ἡ κοινότης.
⁶ ... τῇ διαιρέσει τῇ Πλάτωνος χρωμένη.

things, indeed, it deems necessary and preliminary to itself; but it passes judgement on them (as it does on everything else), and deems some of them useful and others superfluous and appropriate only to a method which is interested in such things.

(*enn* I iii 4 [18–23])[7]

Dialectic—Plotinian dialectic—is not to be identified with logic or with syllogistic any more than it is to be identified with grammar.

The fundamental difference between dialectic and syllogistic emerges a little later in Plotinus' argument. I quote an extended chunk:

Well then, is philosophy the most honourable thing? Or is dialectic the same as philosophy? Or is it a part—the honourable part—of philosophy? For certainly it mustn't be thought to be one of the philosopher's tools: it is not just empty theorems and rules—rather, it is about objects and it has the things which exist as, so to speak, its matter. It sets after them methodically, grasping the objects as well as the theorems. As for falsity and sophism, it recognizes them incidentally when someone else commits them, judging falsity to be alien to its own truths and recognizing, when it is brought forward, whatever is contrary to the rule of truth. So although it doesn't know about propositions (which, after all, are merely letters), nonetheless, insofar as it knows the truth it knows what they call propositions, and in general it knows the movements of the soul—what the soul posits and what it rejects, whether it rejects what it posits or something else, whether things are different or the same—and it attends to such items when they are presented to it, as perception does, but it leaves careful study of such things to another art which delights in them.

(*enn* I iii 5 [8–23])[8]

Dialectic is not an empty or bare subject: it deals with objects, and the things which exist are its subject-matter. Logic, on the other hand, is empty theorems and empty rules. Its propositions are just letters. That is why logic

---

[7] ... τὴν λεγομένην λογικὴν πραγματείαν περὶ προτάσεων καὶ συλλογισμῶν, ὥσπερ ἂν τὸ εἰδέναι γράφειν, ἄλλῃ τέχνῃ δοῦσα· ὧν τινα ἀναγκαῖα καὶ πρὸ τέχνης ἡγουμένη, κρίνουσα δὲ αὐτὰ ὥσπερ καὶ τὰ ἄλλα καὶ τὰ μὲν χρήσιμα αὐτῶν, τὰ δὲ περιττὰ ἡγουμένη καὶ μεθόδου τῆς ταῦτα βουλομένης.

[8] τί οὖν; ἡ φιλοσοφία τὸ τιμιώτατον; ἢ ταὐτὸν φιλοσοφία καὶ διαλεκτική; ἢ φιλοσοφίας μέρος τὸ τίμιον; οὐ γὰρ δὴ οἰητέον ὄργανον τοῦτο εἶναι τοῦ φιλοσόφου· οὐ γὰρ ψιλὰ θεωρήματά ἐστι καὶ κανόνες, ἀλλὰ περὶ πράγματά ἐστι καὶ οἷον ὕλην ἔχει τὰ ὄντα· ὁδῷ μέντοι ἐπ' αὐτὰ χωρεῖ ἅμα τοῖς θεωρήμασι τὰ πράγματα ἔχουσα· τὸ δὲ ψεῦδος καὶ τὸ σόφισμα κατὰ συμβεβηκὸς γινώσκει ἄλλου ποιήσαντος ὡς ἀλλότριον κρίνουσα τοῖς ἐν αὐτῇ ἀληθέσι τὸ ψεῦδος, γινώσκουσα ὅταν τις προσαγάγῃ ὅ τι παρὰ τὸν κανόνα τοῦ ἀληθοῦς. περὶ προτάσεων οὖν οὐκ οἶδε—καὶ γὰρ γράμματα—εἰδυῖα δὲ τὸ ἀληθές οἶδεν ὃ καλοῦσι πρότασιν, καὶ καθόλου οἶδε τὰ κινήματα τῆς ψυχῆς, ὅ τε τίθησι καὶ ὃ αἴρει, καὶ εἰ τοῦτο αἴρει ὃ τίθησιν ἢ ἄλλο, καὶ εἰ ἕτερα ἢ ταὐτά, προσφερομένων ὥσπερ καὶ ἡ αἴσθησις ἐπιβάλλουσα, ἀκριβολογεῖσθαι δὲ ἑτέρᾳ δίδωσι τοῦτο ἀγαπώσῃ.

is at best a tool for the philosopher to use, while dialectic is not a tool of his trade but a part of his expertise.

The propositions of logic are bare: they are mere letters. Plotinus is usually taken to mean that logic deals with linguistic items, with sentences, rather than with the things or facts which sentences express. But I wonder if the logician's letters are not literally letters. When Aristotle assures us that if A holds of every B and B of every C, then A holds of every C, then that is a bare rule, there is no matter to it, it is mere letters. The logician deals with schemata, with matterless forms; and so he does not deal in substantive truths.

To be sure, a dialectician recognizes such items when they present themselves to him. That is to say, a dialectician will recognize that this concrete argument is valid and that that concrete argument is fallacious: he may not know—or he may not interest himself in the fact—that this argument is a syllogism in Barbara and that argument a case of affirming the consequent; but his dialectical technique, and his familiarity with his truths, will enable him to detect falsity and fallacy.

That may seem an optimistic account of the prowess of the Platonic dialectician; for it is difficult to imagine that someone trained in Platonic divisions will thereby acquire a general competence in logical matters. It is indeed difficult—but Plotinus does not imagine that a training in division produces logical expertise. Rather, dialecticians allow that some parts of general logic must be studied—and studied as being a propaedeutic to dialectic. So dialecticians will in fact have done some general logic; and if they can unmask fallacies and recognize syllogisms, that is not because they are dialecticians and skilled in division but because they have studied logic.

The portrait of the logician is well drawn—at least insofar as Plotinus expresses the essentially formal aspect of logical study. But why does he think that logic, so understood, is merely a tool to be used by the philosopher whereas dialectic is something more? True, Plotinus does not explicitly say that logic is a tool, still less that it is nothing but a tool. But that is plainly what he implies. Moreover, if logic is a tool for philosophers, then that is because dialectic judges some parts or aspects of logic to be useful: in other words, some bits of logic help us on the ascent to the Idea of the Good. How might they do so? Might they, for example, aid the dialectician in his divisions? Perhaps; but how exactly logic might offer anything in the way of climbing-tackle Plotinus does not trouble to describe.

Even if Plotinus is right and logic is a useful dialectical tool, it will not follow that logic is nothing but a tool: perhaps it is both a tool and also a part—even an honourable part—of philosophy? After all, why should the study of bare theorems be any less honourable than the study of the things which exist? Or rather, is it not a false antithesis to set logical theorems against truths about the world? The bare theorems of the logician are truths about everything—and therefore about everything which exists.

As for dialectic, Plotinus explicitly affirms that it is not a tool but a part, and the honoured part, of philosophy. Yet for all that, he seems in fact to characterize it as a tool or instrument—and to do so as soon as he has established that it is a part:

So it is a part, the honoured part. For philosophy has other parts too—for example, it studies nature, taking help from dialectic as the other arts make use of arithmetic.

(*enn* ɪ iii 6 [1–3])[9]

Natural philosophy makes use of dialectic, just as other arts make use of arithmetic: that is to say, although dialectic is declared an honoured part of philosophy, it is also a tool of philosophy. And of course Plotinus actually introduces dialectic as a way or method, and considers it exclusively as something which helps us onward and upward; and he does nothing to explain how it might also be a valuable study in its own right—how doing long division on the model of the *Sophist* or the *Statesman* might be a worthwhile occupation quite apart from its instrumental value in aiding us to an understanding of the world of Ideas. Indeed, it is not easy to see how dialectic—Plotinian dialectic—might have anything but instrumental value for a Platonist. It is a curious fact that Plotinus himself never alludes to dialectic outside *Ennead* ɪ iii: he never breathes another word about what he there claims to be the most honourable part of philosophy. I wonder if the little essay on dialectic is anything more than lip-service to Plato?

THE STATUS OF LOGIC

However that may be, Plotinus' remarks on dialectic and logic have a larger context. Antiquity liked to divide philosophy into three parts: logic, physics,

---

[9] μέρος οὖν τὸ τίμιον· ἔχει γὰρ καὶ ἄλλα φιλοσοφία· καὶ γὰρ καὶ περὶ φύσεως θεωρεῖ βοήθειαν παρὰ διαλεκτικῆς λαβοῦσα, ὥσπερ καὶ ἀριθμητικῇ προσχρῶνται αἱ ἄλλαι τέχναι.

and ethics. No philosopher, so far as I know, ever doubted that ethics was a genuine part of his domain. A few philosophers allegedly declared themselves against physics, the subject being too deep or too elevated for merely human minds to encompass. Several philosophers, and some schools of philosophy, had their doubts about logic.

The nature and the scope of those doubts were various—and they were sometimes, it may be suspected, rather vague. When, for example, Sextus is discussing the parts of philosophy and their detractors, he observes that

Archelaus of Athens pursued physics and ethics, and with him some place Epicurus too, on the grounds that he rejected logical theory.

(*M* vii 23)[10]

Archelaus was a contemporary of Socrates: if he did not pursue logic, that was because no one had yet thought to invent the subject. But Epicurus—or so the anonymous 'some' must have thought—positively repudiated the subject. But what was it to repudiate a subject? Some scholars have supposed, radically and quite implausibly, that Epicurus did not produce—or intended not to produce, or was deemed not to have produced or not to have intended to produce—arguments in favour of his philosophical doctrines: to repudiate logic is to abjure reasoning in favour of direct insight. Other scholars have supposed, equally implausibly, that Epicurus' repudiation of logic consisted in the thesis that logic is not an independent discipline, or that the study of logical questions in abstraction from physics and ethics make no sense. And between those two sorts of repudiation there is a whole spectrum of possibilities.

Again, the term 'logic' might be taken in more ways than one. Indeed, in Greek there are three words—not one—to consider: 'λογική', 'συλλογιστική', 'διαλεκτική'. The term 'λογική' generally has a broad sense, especially when it is put on a level with 'φυσική' and 'ἠθική' and used to designate one of the three parts of philosophy; for then it is concerned with everything which pertains to λόγος—to reason and to language. If it includes everything which we might count as logic, it also embraces epistemology, and linguistics, and (sometimes at least) rhetoric. The word 'συλλογιστική' generally has a narrow sense: it means something like 'theory of inference', or perhaps, yet more narrowly, 'theory of formal deductive inference'. In other words, ancient syllogistic is roughly comparable to modern formal logic. As for 'διαλεκτική',

---

[10] Ἀρχέλαος δὲ ὁ Ἀθηναῖος τὸ φυσικὸν καὶ ἠθικόν [sc μετήρχετο]· μεθ' οὗ τινες καὶ τὸν Ἐπίκουρον τάττουσιν ὡς τὴν λογικὴν θεωρίαν ἐκβάλλοντα.

the term has different resonances in different contexts: for Plotinus—as we have seen—and for Plato, it is an honourable method, the only method which will lead to the Ideas and the really real world; in Aristotle, it is the method or practice of arguing on the basis of reputable opinions; for the Stoics, it is one of the two branches of λογική, the other being rhetoric; and in contexts which are not philosophically partisan—in Sextus, for example—dialectic is usually something like logic in a broadish sense of the word.

What, then, did Epicurus repudiate? Sextus says that, according to some, he repudiated λογική. But inasmuch as 'λογική' there names one of the three parts of philosophy, that is certainly false—to mention nothing else, there was an elaborate Epicurean epistemology. Archelaus, we may suppose, did no λογική at all. What the Epicureans lacked, or lacked interest in, was συλλογιστική—although, as Philodemus' work *On Signs* demonstrates, they had a lively interest in certain forms of inference.

Logic was a constituent part of the Stoic philosophy. (Or at least, it was a part of the orthodox Stoic philosophy; for some Stoics had had no time for logic, or for some pieces or aspects of logic.) And it is universally agreed that no Peripatetic ever repudiated logic in any sense or fashion. Nonetheless, the Peripatetics did something which the orthodox Stoics did not do, and which would not have shocked orthodox Epicureans.

Alexander opens his commentary on the *Prior Analytics* in this way:

> The study of logic or syllogistic, which is now before us and under which fall probative and dialectical and examinatory method—and also sophistical method—is a product of philosophy. Some other sciences and arts also make use of it, but they take it from philosophy, to which belong its discovery and its constitution and its most important uses. Being a product of philosophy, it seems to some people to be in addition a part of philosophy, whereas others say that it is not a part but a tool of philosophy.
>
> (*in APr* 1.3–9)[11]

Some people say this and some say that: who said what? and when? and so what?

Later texts give names to Alexander's anonymous partisans. According to Ammonius, for example,

---

[11] ἡ λογική τε καὶ συλλογιστικὴ πραγματεία ἡ νῦν ἡμῖν προκειμένη, ὑφ' ἣν ἥ τε ἀποδεικτικὴ καὶ ἡ διαλεκτική τε καὶ πειραστικὴ ἔτι τε καὶ ἡ σοφιστικὴ μέθοδος, ἔστι μὲν ἔργον φιλοσοφίας, χρῶνται δὲ αὐτῇ καὶ ἄλλαι τινὲς ἐπιστῆμαι καὶ τέχναι, ἀλλὰ παρὰ φιλοσοφίας λαβοῦσαι· ταύτης γὰρ ἥ τε εὕρεσίς ἐστι καὶ ἡ σύστασις καὶ ἡ πρὸς τὰ κυριώτατα χρῆσις. οὖσα δὲ ἔργον αὐτῆς τοῖς μὲν καὶ μέρος φιλοσοφίας εἶναι δοκεῖ, οἱ δὲ οὐ μέρος ἀλλ' ὄργανον αὐτῆς φασιν εἶναι.

the Stoics insist that logic should not only not be called a tool of philosophy—it should not even be called a subpart, but rather a part; and some of the Platonists too were of that opinion, because according to Plato logic is not a tool but a part—and a most honourable part—of philosophy. But the Peripatetics say that it is a tool and not a part.

(*in APr* 8.20–25)[12]

Ammonius' pupil Philoponus finds three rather than two parties to the dispute:

The Stoics assert outright that it is a part, co-ordinating it with the two other parts of philosophy. The Peripatetics—that is to say, Aristotle's followers—say that it is a tool. The Academics, among them Plato, plainly say that it is both a part and a tool.

(*in APr* 6.21–24)[13]

No one doubts that the Peripatetics generally took logic to be a tool and not a part of philosophy: Alexander argued for the view, which he took to be Aristotle's. The view was also found outside the Peripatetic circle: Galen supports it; it may be discovered in Epictetus' *conversazioni*; and Proclus and his set adopted it. No one doubts that the Stoics generally took logic to be a part of philosophy—although there were certainly dissident Stoics, on this as on other points of doctrine.

Philoponus insinuates that the Stoics denied that logic was a tool of philosophy—otherwise there is no contrast in his text between Stoics and Academics. But the insinuation is false, and absurd: numerous texts state or imply that logic, in Stoic eyes, was of the greatest philosophical utility. After all, the Stoics

say that dialectic was invented to be as it were the arbiter and judge of the true and the false.

(Cicero, *Luc* xxviii 91)[14]

How could such a science fail to have instrumental value? In any event, the Stoics

---

[12] οἱ μὲν Στωϊκοὶ τὴν λογικὴν οὐ μόνον ὄργανον οὐκ ἀξιοῦσι καλεῖσθαι φιλοσοφίας, ἀλλ' οὐδὲ μόριον τὸ τυχὸν ἀλλὰ μέρος. καὶ τινὲς δὲ τῶν Πλατωνικῶν ταύτης ἐγένοντο τῆς δόξης, ὅτι κατὰ Πλάτωνα οὐκ ὄργανον ἡ λογικὴ ἀλλὰ μέρος καὶ τιμιώτατον μέρος ἐστὶν φιλοσοφίας. οἱ δὲ Περιπατητικοὶ ὄργανον αὐτὴν λέγουσιν ἀλλ' οὐ μέρος.

[13] οἱ μὲν γὰρ Στωϊκοὶ ἄντικρυς μέρος αὐτὴν ἀποφαίνονται, τοῖς ἄλλοις δύο μέρεσι τῆς φιλοσοφίας αὐτὴν ἀντιδιαιροῦντες· οἱ δὲ Περιπατητικοί, τουτέστιν οἱ ἀπὸ Ἀριστοτέλους, ὄργανον· οἱ δὲ ἀπὸ τῆς Ἀκαδημίας, ὧν ἐστι καὶ Πλάτων, καὶ μέρος καὶ ὄργανον φαίνονται λέγοντες.

[14] *dialecticam inventam esse ... veri et falsi quasi disceptatricem et iudicem.*

say that the study of syllogisms is of the greatest utility; for it indicates what is probative (which contributes greatly to the correction of opinions and to their ordering and retaining) and it indicates a scientific grasp of things.

(Diogenes Laertius, VII 45)[15]

As for Philoponus' Academics, they presumably took what was in fact the Stoic view. Unless, of course, Philoponus is simply misreporting Plotinus' view of the matter—as, in a different way, Ammonius does. For where Ammonius refers to 'some of the Platonists' he is surely thinking, no doubt at a remove, of Plotinus—and he is attributing to logic the features which Plotinus denied to logic and ascribed to Platonic dialectic. I suspect that the same Plotinian text lies behind Philoponus' remarks: where Plotinus says or implies that logic is a tool and dialectic a part, Philoponus turns this into the thesis that logic was at once a tool and a part.

So all philosophers—or at any rate, all those philosophers who did not repudiate logic—supposed that the subject had an instrumental value. Sextus speaks quite generally when he remarks that

the logicians say that they have had recourse to the art of logic not simply in order to know what can be inferred from what but principally in order to distinguish truths and falsities by way of probative arguments.

(*PH* II 247)[16]

That logic is a tool was not disputed among the logicians. The question was: is logic also a part of philosophy?

When was the question first raised? Muddle and confusion are the hallmark of the late commentators, especially when it comes to historical information. But we should not succumb to the brutal charm of nihilism and declare that the whole debate on the status of logic was a myth. It is clear that the question was discussed in the Peripatetic school; it is highly probable that some other thinkers took up the issue; and it is possible that there was indeed something which might be called a debate or a dispute.

---

[15] εὐχρηστοτάτην δέ φασιν εἶναι τὴν περὶ τῶν συλλογισμῶν θεωρίαν· τὸ γὰρ ἀποδεικτικὸν ἐμφαίνειν, ὅπερ συμβάλλεσθαι πολὺ πρὸς διόρθωσιν τῶν δογμάτων καὶ τάξιν καὶ μνήμην, τὸ δ'ἐπιστημονικὸν κατάλημμα ἐμφαίνειν.—For 'τὸ δ'ἐπιστημονικόν' (Usener plus Gigante) the MSS have 'τὸ ἐπιστατικόν'.

[16] ἐπὶ τὴν τέχνην τὴν διαλεκτικήν φασιν ὡρμηκέναι οἱ διαλεκτικοὶ οὐχ ἁπλῶς ὑπὲρ τοῦ γνῶναι τί ἐκ τίνος συνάγεται, ἀλλὰ προηγουμένως ὑπὲρ τοῦ δι' ἀποδεικτικῶν λόγων τὰ ἀληθῆ καὶ τὰ ψευδῆ κρίνειν ἐπίστασθαι.

When did the matter get its first airing? The commentators ascribe a position in the debate to Aristotle; but although the ascription is not merely imaginative, there is no evidence that Aristotle had ever given the matter much thought. The Stoics, from the first, seem to have divided philosophy—or the account of philosophy—into logic and physics and ethics; and they are generally supposed to have taken the tripartition over from one or another of Plato's followers. But you may speak of logic as a part of philosophy without having wondered what its status really was. And in fact, no author earlier than Alexander unequivocally adverts to the question of status.

One text, however, may plausibly be invoked. In his account of Aristotle's philosophy, Diogenes Laertius remarks that

> to the theoretical part of philosophy there belong physics and logic—logic having been elaborated not as a part of a whole but as a tool.
>
> (v 28)[17]

That remark presupposes if not a debate at least some reflexion on our question; and although Diogenes himself is later than Alexander, the source which he used for his account of Aristotelianism was certainly earlier than Alexander—and it may well have been Hellenistic.

THE USE OF LOGIC

But of what possible interest to us can any of that old and arid stuff be?

If logic is a part of philosophy, then—as Alexander puts it—it is studied 'in order to gain knowledge of the truths which it contains in itself' (*in APr* 3.12–13).[18] If it is a tool of philosophy—and also of certain other arts and sciences—what instrumental function does it serve? No doubt it has several uses; for example,

> if logic is studied in order to exercise the mind with a view to making discoveries in the various parts of philosophy, then for that reason too it will have the status of a tool.
>
> (*in APr* 3.10–12)[19]

---

[17] τοῦ δὲ θεωρητικοῦ [sc λόγου] τόν τε φυσικὸν καὶ λογικόν, οὗ τὸ λογικὸν οὐχ ὡς ὅλου μέρος, ἀλλ᾽ ὡς ὄργανον προσηκριβωμένον.

[18] διὰ τὴν τῆς ἐν αὐτῇ ἀληθείας γνῶσιν.—The received text has 'αὐτοῖς' for 'αὐτῇ'.

[19] ἔτι εἰ σπουδάζοιτο ὡς γυμνάσιον τῆς διανοίας πρὸς τὴν εὕρεσιν τῶν ἐν τοῖς μέρεσι τῆς φιλοσοφίας ζητουμένων, καὶ οὕτως ἂν τὴν τοῦ ὀργάνου χώραν ἔχοι.

But of the various uses for logic which were or might have been mooted, one was dominant and determinant. Alexander again:

If becoming like God is the greatest good for men, and if men attain this by study and knowledge of truth, and if knowledge of truth is attained by proof, then proof will justly be deemed most honourable and most worthy of study—and so too for that reason will syllogistic, since a proof is a sort of syllogism.

(in APr 6.8–12)[20]

Proofs are syllogisms: logic or syllogistic has as its aim the production of proofs—and therein lies its utility and its instrumental value.

   Galen took the same view as Alexander. Thus, referring to certain types of argument with which—so he says—the Stoics were much occupied, he remarks that

all the construction of such syllogisms is no small waste of time on a useless object—as Chrysippus himself bears witness in his deeds; for nowhere in all his writings does he make use of such syllogisms to prove a doctrine.

(PHP v 224)[21]

If an argument cannot be called upon to formalize a proof, it is useless, and thinking about it is a waste of time. There are a dozen comparable passages in Galen's writings.

   Galen swore allegiance to no school. Alexander professed the Peripatetic philosophy; and the view which Galen and he shared was, he claimed, the view of Aristotle himself. The first words of the *Prior Analytics* are these:

First, we must say what our inquiry is about and with what it is concerned—it is about proof and concerned with probative knowledge.

(APr 24a10–11)[22]

Alexander comments:

---

   [20] εἰ δὴ τὸ θεῷ ὁμοιοῦσθαι μέγιστον ἀγαθὸν ἀνθρώπῳ, τοῦτο δ' αὐτῷ διὰ θεωρίας τε καὶ τῆς τἀληθοῦς γνώσεως περιγίνεται, ἡ δὲ τἀληθοῦς γνῶσις δι' ἀποδείξεως, δικαίως ἂν πλείστης τιμῆς ἀξιοῖτο καὶ σπουδῆς, διὰ δ' αὐτὴν καὶ ἡ συλλογιστική, εἴ γε ἡ ἀπόδειξις συλλογισμός τις.
   [21] ...πρὸς τῷ καὶ περιεργίαν εἶναι οὐ μικρὰν ἀχρήστου πράγματος ἅπασαν τὴν τῶν τοιούτων συλλογισμῶν πλοκήν, ὡς αὐτὸς ὁ Χρύσιππος ἔργῳ μαρτυρεῖ μηδαμόθι τῶν ἑαυτοῦ συγγραμμάτων εἰς ἀπόδειξιν δόγματος ἐκείνων δεηθεὶς τῶν συλλογισμῶν.
   [22] πρῶτον εἰπεῖν περὶ τί καὶ τίνος ἐστὶν ἡ σκέψις, ὅτι περὶ ἀπόδειξιν καὶ ἐπιστήμης ἀποδεικτικῆς.

At the beginning of the study he announced what its goal and aim are, namely proof and probative knowledge. Hence whatever makes no contribution to those things will not be appropriate to the study before us.

(in APr 20.24–27)[23]

The subject of the *Analytics* as a whole is the theory of proof, so that the syllogistic theory developed in the *Prior Analytics* has the theory of proof as its sole aim or goal. And Alexander inferred that, for Aristotle, logic has value just insofar as it serves the needs of proof, just insofar as philosophers and scientists may make use of logic in order to prove their theorems.

That is how the *corpus* of Aristotle's logical writings got its traditional name: logic is a tool or ὄργανον, and the *corpus* is therefore Aristotle's *Organon*. Aristotle himself certainly thought that proofs are a sort of syllogism—indeed, he defines a proof as a 'cognitive syllogism' (*APst* 71b17–18).[24] He also thought—and thought he could prove—that

it is necessary that every proof and every syllogism come about through one of the three figures we have described.

(APr 41b1–3)[25]

That is to say, the syllogistic theory which Aristotle elaborates in the *Prior Analytics* is sufficient for all the probative requirements of the sciences. So Aristotle ascribes instrumental value to logic and to syllogistic; and its instrumental value—or at any rate a part of its instrumental value—is determined by its essential contribution to the production of scientific proofs.

But it does not follow that, in Aristotle's view, the sole reason for studying logic is to satisfy the needs of probative science; and despite Alexander and his friends, it is difficult to read through the *Analytics* and imagine that their author saw no value in the work but an instrumental utility and no purpose but the production of probative structures.

However that may be, according to the utilitarian view of logic which Alexander and Galen and many others adopted, every proof is a syllogism and every syllogism is a potential proof. The point can perhaps best be put as follows.

---

[23] αὐτὸς ἀρχόμενος τῆς πραγματείας τί τέλος αὐτῆς καὶ σκοπός ἐστι προεῖπεν· ἀπόδειξις γὰρ καὶ ἐπιστήμη ἀποδεικτική· ὥσθ' ὅσα μηδέν εἰς ταῦτα συντελεῖ, οὐκ ἂν οἰκεῖα τῆς προκειμένης εἴη πραγματείας.

[24] ἀπόδειξιν δὲ λέγω συλλογισμὸν ἐπιστημονικόν.

[25] πᾶσαν ἀπόδειξιν καὶ πάντα συλλογισμὸν ἀνάγκη γίνεσθαι διὰ τριῶν τῶν προειρημένων σχημάτων.

Suppose that there is a certain form of argument, which takes us validly from premisses of this sort to a conclusion of that sort; and suppose that we wish to determine whether arguments of that form are, in virtue of having that form, syllogisms. How might the question be resolved? According to Alexander and his friends, arguments of that form are syllogisms if and only if an argument of that form may be a scientific proof. There will, of course, be innumerably many syllogisms of that form which are not proofs—syllogisms with false premisses, for example. Alexander does not make the absurd claim that an argument is a syllogism only if it is a proof; but he does claim that any syllogism must either be probative or else have probative siblings: every syllogism is valid in virtue of having a structure in virtue of which some probative arguments are valid.

A syllogism is a tool, and a tool is defined by its function: if a screw-driver is a tool for screwing and unscrewing, and this item can't screw or unscrew, then it is not a screw-driver. Or in Alexander's words:

The measure of any tool is its usefulness with regard to what is shown or produced by it—and if it is no longer useful, it is not even a tool. For an adze which is of no use to a carpenter is no longer an adze, except homonymously.

(in APr 164.31–165.2)[26]

Or again:

A syllogism is a tool; for the utility of a syllogism is to make evident, by way of known and evident items, something which is thought not to be known. ... What does not provide the utility of a syllogism is not a syllogism at all. For if a syllogism is a tool, and every tool is useful, then a syllogism is useful. ... And that a tool is useful is clear: in the case of all tools we see that when they can no longer provide their proper utility they no longer exist—for no one would call anything a lyre if it can't be used for making music nor an adze if it can't be used for carpentry. If you persist in calling by the same word items which have lost their utility, you speak homonymously—as when we talk of painted or sculpted items and speak of a stone hand. So something which does not preserve the utility of a syllogism is no longer a syllogism.

(in Top 9.22–10.6)[27]

An argumentative form which has no probative utility is not just a useless sort of syllogism—it is no sort of syllogism at all. If you insist on calling

---

[26] παντὸς γὰρ ὀργάνου μέτρον ἡ χρεία πρὸς τὸ ὑπ' αὐτοῦ δεικνύμενόν τε καὶ γινόμενον· τὸ δὲ μηκέτι χρήσιμον οὐδ' ἂν ὄργανον εἴη· τὸ γὰρ ἄχρηστον σκέπαρνον τῷ τέκτονι οὐκέτι σκέπαρνον ἀλλ' ἢ ὁμωνύμως.

[27] ... ὄργανόν ἐστιν ὁ συλλογισμός. ἔστι γὰρ πρὸς τὸ φανερόν τι ποιῆσαι μὴ δοκοῦν εἶναι γνώριμον διά τινων γνωρίμων τε καὶ φανερῶν ἡ τοῦ συλλογισμοῦ χρεία. ... ὁ δὲ μὴ παρεχόμενος τὴν τοῦ συλλογισμοῦ χρείαν λόγος οὐδὲ συλλογισμός. εἰ γὰρ ὁ συλλογισμὸς

some non-probative forms of argument syllogistic, then you merely use the word 'syllogistic' in a different sense. Hands and feet are tools for grasping and for walking with; and if a piece of stone—a part of a sculpture, say—is nonetheless called a hand or a foot, then the words 'hand' and 'foot' are used in different senses.

Alexander's reference to stone hands alludes to an Aristotelian commonplace. So, for example,

it is impossible that an item of any sort whatsoever should be a hand—for example, a bronze or a stone item—except homonymously, like a painted doctor.

(*PA* 640b35–641a1)[28]

But the commonplace is at best a half-truth; and its application to syllogisms is dubious.

Alexander, like Aristotle before him, offers a variety of cases in which an off-colour so-and-so is allegedly called a so-and-so only homonymously: rusted adzes, severed limbs, painted ladies, dead parrots, toy chain-saws, ... But the cases are not all alike. Consider the adze. True, adzes are now rarities; but my neighbour Bernard has several specimens in his workshop—he inherited them from his grandfather, who was an Alsatian. They are no longer serviceable, and some of them are irredeemably rusted. Nonetheless, they are adzes; and they are adzes in exactly the sense in which working adzes are adzes. If I say: 'Here are a couple of adzes, one of them in good working order and the other hopelessly blunted', I have not made a weak pun or indulged in a zeugma. An item which no longer functions as an adze does not thereby cease to be an adze.

In the same way, a dead parrot is a parrot. When the Norwegian blue finally fell off its perch, what lay on the bottom of the cage was a parrot—and a parrot in the ordinary sense of the word 'parrot', the sense in which the word applied to the bird before it dropped off. So too, in an Oxford museum, there is a dodo—a real dodo, though not a real live dodo.

ὄργανον, πᾶν δὲ ὄργανον χρήσιμον, ὁ συλλογισμὸς χρήσιμος· ... ὅτι δὲ τὸ ὄργανον χρήσιμον, δῆλον· ἐν πᾶσι γὰρ τοῖς ὀργάνοις ὁρῶμεν ὅταν μὴ τὴν οἰκείαν χρείαν παρέχεσθαι δύνηται ἀναιρούμενα αὐτά. οὔτε γὰρ λύραν ἄν τις εἴποι ᾗ οὐχ οἷόν τε μουσικῶς χρῆσθαι, οὔτε σκέπαρνον ᾧ μὴ τεκτονικῶς· ὁ γὰρ καὶ τὰ ἐκπίπτοντα τῆς χρείας ἔτι λέγων τῷ αὐτῷ ὀνόματι ὁμωνύμως λέγει, ὡς καὶ τὰ γεγραμμένα ἢ πεπλασμένα ὡς χεῖρα τὴν λιθίνην. οὐδὲ συλλογισμὸς οὖν ἔτι εἴη ἂν ὁ μὴ τὴν χρείαν σώζων τὴν τοῦ συλλογισμοῦ.

[28] ἔτι δ᾽ ἀδύνατον εἶναι χεῖρα ὁπωσοῦν διακειμένην, οἷον χαλκῆν ἢ ξυλίνην, πλὴν ὁμωνύμως, ὥσπερ τὸν γεγραμμένον ἰατρόν.

Of course, if you are a parrot-fancier or a carpenter you will need to be able to distinguish between serviceable adzes and adzes which no longer function, between working parrots and parrots which are no more. But there is no particular difficulty about that—and if there were, the task would become not a jot easier were we to legislate a double sense for the words 'adze' and 'parrot'.

Again, the portrait of a blinking idiot is not a blinking idiot—it is not a blinking idiot in any sense of the phrase 'blinking idiot'. Magritte illustrated that banal fact. As for a portrayed or painted idiot, he is an idiot—and an idiot in the ordinary sense of the word. No painting, not even a Holbein, is qualified to be a monarch; but one of the items portrayed by Holbein is Henry VIII—and he was a king, and not homonymously.

Toy chain-saws are different: they are not chain-saws—no more than decoy ducks are ducks or false noses noses. But that is not because they are chain-saws in a different sense of the word 'chain-saw': it is because they are toy chain-saws, and, as a general rule, toy so-and-sos are not so-and-sos. The sense of 'chain-saw' in the phrase 'toy chain-saw' is its ordinary sense.

In some cases, Alexander himself takes that sort of line. For example, certain arguments—he says—are called, perhaps with propriety, 'rhetorical syllogisms';

but such arguments are not syllogisms in the strict sense: they are rhetorical syllogisms, the phrase being taken as a whole.

(*in Top* 9.14–15)[29]

A rhetorical syllogism—according to Alexander—is like a false nose: it is not useless—any more than a false nose is useless; but it is not a syllogism—any more than a false nose is a nose. The word 'syllogism' has the same sense in 'rhetorical syllogism' as it has in 'probative syllogism'. There is no special sense of 'syllogism' in which the word is specially true of rhetorical syllogisms; and it would be entirely absurd to invent such a sense.

Another and more interesting false nose will poke into a later part of the discussion. But enough of them for the nonce. For even were Alexander right about adzes, why imagine that syllogisms are in the same case? Why, in other words, imagine that the term 'syllogism' is a functional term, on a level with 'adze' or 'parrot'? So far as I can see, there is no reason, in ordinary Greek, to think that the word 'συλλογισμός' means, or somehow must mean, 'argument useful in such-and-such

---

[29] οὐδὲ οἱ τοιοῦτοι κυρίως συλλογισμοί, ἀλλὰ τὸ ὅλον ῥητορικοὶ συλλογισμοί.

a way'; nor does Aristotle's celebrated definition of the syllogism indicate or presuppose that syllogisms are essentially functional items. To be sure, it may be important for a philosopher to be able to distinguish between syllogisms which are serviceable (to one end or another) and syllogisms which are not. But to do so is not particularly difficult; and any difficulty there may be is not one whit eased by stipulating that an argument be called a syllogism only if it is useful in a certain way or ways.

The utilitarian view of logic which makes syllogisms tools and not objects of contemplation in their own right is a stipulative view inasmuch as it depends upon—or consists in—a decision to limit the use of a certain term in a certain way. Some may think it a harmless stipulation, others a pernicious stipulation; and I have heard it called a philistine stipulation. In any event, it is surely a pointless stipulation; for Alexander and his friends could easily have expressed their utilitarianism without it. They could have said: 'You should include a given type of syllogism in your logic if and only if it is useful for proof.'

Nevertheless, the stipulation, and the utilitarianism which it proclaims, are not trifling terminological decisions: they have consequences for the study of logic. The rest of this chapter will look at three such consequences, different in kind from one another and also different in their significance.

MODAL LOGIC

One striking difference between the predicative syllogistic which Aristotle presents in the *Prior Analytics* and Stoic syllogistic (so far as we know it) is this: Aristotle considers modal syllogisms, the Stoics do not. We do not know why the Stoics, who certainly had some interest in the general phenomenon of modality, did not concern themselves with modal logic; but at the end of antiquity Boethius thought it appropriate to indicate why his own essay on hypothetical syllogisms apparently omitted certain varieties of inference:

I have judged it superfluous to inquire into the number of <propositions> determined as to their quantity, since conditionals determined in that way are not normally propounded. And in much the same way hypothetical propositions are not expressed in terms of necessity or in terms of contingency—rather, it is those which signify being the case which are chiefly introduced for use in inferences. All of them, to be sure, mean to maintain a necessary connection—those which signify being the case, those to which necessity is added, and those to which a predication of possibility is affixed (for these apply to the terms).

(hyp syll I ix 3)[30]

What Boethius means is less than plain. He clearly states that modalized hypothetical propositions are not used, or only rarely; and it is plausible to think that he drew the consequence that modal hypothetical logic is pointless. Yet the last parenthetical sentence of the passage suggests a far stronger thesis: modal operators apply to terms and not to propositions, so that while there may in principle be a modal logic of terms or a modal predicative syllogistic, there cannot in principle be a modal logic of propositions or a modal hypothetical syllogistic.

However that may be, modal predicative syllogistic was certainly developed by the Peripatetics. The modal logic of the *Analytics* is by far the most complicated and technically intricate part of Aristotle's syllogistic; and its exposition occupies about three times as much space as the exposition of the non-modal syllogistic. The modal exposition turns about apodictic propositions, or propositions which say that necessarily such-and-such, and problematic propositions, or propositions which say that possibly such-and-such. It elaborates apodictic syllogisms, every component proposition of which is apodictic, and problematic syllogisms, every component of which is problematic; and it elaborates mixed syllogisms, or syllogisms the constituent members of which have different modalities or no modality.

Not everyone appreciated modal syllogistic. It is not mentioned in Apuleius' *On Interpretation*. It is not mentioned in Galen's *Introduction to Logic*. To be sure, those two little works are introductory handbooks, and modal syllogistic is horribly difficult. But if you would not expect them to expound the ins and outs of mixed modalities, you would expect a reference to modal syllogisms or at least some sort of promissory note. After all, Galen observes more than once in the *Introduction* that the syllogisms he is discussing are 'useful for proof'; and at the end of the text he states that

---

[30] *atque ideo supervacaneum iudicavi determinatarum secundum quantitatem propositionum quaerere multitudinem, cum determinatae conditionales proponi non soleant. fere autem hypotheticae propositiones ne per necessitatem quidem vel per contingens enuntiantur, sed illae maximae in usum collectionis deducuntur quae inesse significant. omnes vero necessariam tenere consequentiam volunt, et quae inesse significant, et quibus necessitas additur, et quibus praedicatio possibilitatis aptatur (haec enim terminis applicantur).*—For '*collectionis*' the manuscripts have '*collocutionis*'; for '*applicantur*' editors have preferred the singular '*applicatur*'.

in introductions to logic, none of the useful items should be omitted—but it is not necessary to refute the superfluous items.

(inst log xix 5)[31]

If he took modal syllogisms to be instruments of proof, then how could he have failed to notice their existence in the *Introduction?*

There is a pertinent piece of evidence. It is third-hand; but it seems to be trustworthy. In a work *On Medicine,* Moses Maimonides cited a passage from al-Farabi's commentary on the *Prior Analytics,* which in turn refers to Galen's *On Proof.* Since the text is not well known, I shall cite it in full.

All this has been explained by al-Farabi, namely that Galen rejected possible syllogisms and mixed syllogisms and limited himself to non-modal syllogisms, which are called hyparctic syllogisms; and that what is useful in medicine and in the majority of the arts are possible syllogisms and mixed syllogisms. Listen, then, to al-Farabi on the subject. In his long commentary on the *Book of Syllogisms,* at the beginning of his commentary on Aristotle's introduction to the possible and to possible syllogisms, he says this. al-Farabi says:

> Matters do not stand here as Galen the doctor thought. In the book which he entitled *Book of Proof* he remarks that the study of the possible and of the syllogisms generated from it is superfluous. But if there is anyone who ought to have studied possible syllogisms, it is Galen, the doctor: in the book entitled *Book of Proof* he ought to have concentrated all his attention on possible syllogisms inasmuch as he claims that he has composed his *Book of Proof* in order for it to be of use in medicine. The syllogisms which medicine uses in its account of the parts of the art of medicine and the syllogisms which it uses to grasp the hidden diseases and their causes in each case in which it seeks a cure—all these are possible syllogisms, and there is no necessity at all in them (save in some cases which are pretty well extraneous to the art of medicine). For that reason, in the book which he entitled *Book of Proof* he ought to have spoken above all else about possible syllogisms alone, and not about hyparctic syllogisms. For if in the book he restricted himself to hyparctic syllogisms on the ground that they would be useful for proofs, in fact the hyparctic forms are not appropriate to proofs; for proofs do not come about in matter of that sort but only in necessary forms.

End of the citation from al-Farabi.[32]

The last sentence of the citation is scarcely coherent, and it may be suspected that the text once read: '... only in necessary or possible forms'. Perhaps

---

[31] κατὰ γὰρ τὰς εἰσαγωγὰς αὐτῶν οὐδὲν δεῖ τῶν χρησίμων παραλείπεσθαι, τοὺς δ' ἐλέγχους τῶν περιττῶν μὴ λέγεσθαι.

[32] Marwan Rashed generously made me a French translation of Maimonides' text. A fragment of the citation is printed in a Latin version in I. von Müller, *Galens Werk vom wissenschaftlichen Beweis,* p. 424.

the notice has suffered further and less evident damage in the course of its transmission; and certainly it would be rash to try to construct any of Galen's Greek on its base. But there is no intrinsic reason to doubt that the sentiment which the passage transmits was Galen's sentiment.

al-Farabi makes it clear that Galen rejected problematic syllogistic. The text also reports that *On Proof* restricted itself to 'hyparctic' or non-modal syllogisms; and although al-Farabi does not explicitly say that Galen regarded apodictic syllogistic and mixed modal syllogistic as superfluous, it is odds on that he took the same attitude to them as he took to problematic syllogistic. Thus the *Introduction to Logic* is neither coy nor misleading when it refrains from mentioning modal logic: Galen did not mention it there because he took it to be useless.

Modal arguments are useless for proof, and therefore there are no modal syllogisms. al-Farabi found Galen's attitude bizarre: medicine is a science of contingencies; problematic syllogistic is concerned with the contingent; and yet Galen, the leading doctor and medical theorist of his age, rejected problematic syllogistic.

The view of problematic syllogistic at which al-Farabi here hints was traditional. When he introduces the part of his modal syllogistic which deals with problematic propositions, Aristotle says this:

Let us observe that being possible is said in two senses—in one sense, coming about for the most part and not necessarily (e.g. that men go grey, or grow, or decline, or in general what holds by nature ...); and in another sense what is indeterminate.

(*APr* 32b4–10)[33]

Alexander comments thus:

He omits to exhibit the syllogisms in the figures in connexion with the latter sort of possibility not because it cannot be done but because it is useless—thereby indicating to us that in this subject we should only take up and elaborate what is useful for items which will be proved and omit the useless even if it allows certain combinations.

(*in APr* 164.23–27)[34]

---

[33] ... λέγωμεν ὅτι τὸ ἐνδέχεσθαι κατὰ δύο λέγεται τρόπους, ἕνα μὲν τὸ ὡς ἐπὶ τὸ πολὺ γίνεσθαι καὶ διαλείπειν τὸ ἀναγκαῖον, οἷον τὸ πολιοῦσθαι ἄνθρωπον ἢ τὸ αὐξάνεσθαι ἢ φθίνειν, ἢ ὅλως τὸ πεφυκὸς ὑπάρχειν ..., ἄλλον δὲ τὸ ἀόριστον ...

[34] ...παραιτεῖται τὴν ἐπὶ τοῦ τοιούτου ἐνδεχομένου δεῖξιν τῶν κατὰ τὰ σχήματα συλλο-γισμῶν, οὐχ ὡς οὐ δυναμένην γενέσθαι, ἀλλ' ὡς ἄχρηστον, ἐνδεικνύμενος ἡμῖν ὅτι δεῖ τὸ

Aristotle does not discuss arguments which use indeterminate possibility because such arguments cannot be used to prove anything. As for the former sort of possibility, which is identified with what holds for the most part,

> he promises that he will discuss the other sort because there are many arts which are conjectural and which syllogize on the basis of this sort of possibility—medicine, for example, and navigation, and gymnastics. But also and more generally, everything which is adopted on the basis of deliberation is shown by way of this sort of possibility.
>
> (*in APr* 165.8–11)[35]

There are problematic syllogisms in the case of the first sort of possibility inasmuch as some sciences prove problematic propositions of that kind: problematic syllogisms will embody proofs in medicine, and in navigation. (What gymnastical proofs Alexander might have in mind I do not care to guess.)

Alexander is not inventing: he is merely paraphrasing and illustrating the Aristotelian text on which he is commenting:

> There is no knowledge and there are no probative syllogisms about the indeterminate cases, since the middle term is disorderly; but of what holds by nature there are—and indeed our arguments and inquiries concern what is possible in this sense. As for the other sense, it is indeed possible for there to be syllogisms, but they are not usually looked for.
>
> (*APr* 32b18–22)[36]

According to Aristotle, there are two senses of 'possible'. Problematic syllogisms may be constructed around each of the senses; but in fact we generally restrict ourselves to the first sense—the sense with respect to which there are probative syllogisms. Alexander takes a harder line: there are no probative arguments which use problematic propositions of the indeterminate or disorderly sort; so there are no syllogisms which use such propositions; so the study of arguments involving indeterminate possibility has no place in logic.

In any event, Alexander—like Aristotle before him and al-Farabi after him—thinks that there are probative problematic syllogisms. He thinks

---

εὔχρηστον ἐν τῇδε τῇ πραγματείᾳ πρὸς τὰ δειχθησόμενα μόνον λαμβάνειν τε καὶ ἐξεργάζεσθαι, τὸ δ' ἄχρηστον, εἰ καὶ ἔχοι τινὰ συμπλοκήν, παραιτεῖσθαι.

[35] περὶ δὲ τοῦ ἑτέρου ἐρεῖν ἐπαγγέλλεται ὅτι πολλαὶ τέχναι στοχαστικαὶ οὖσαι ἐκ τοῦ οὕτως ἐνδεχομένου τὸ προκείμενον συλλογίζονται, ὡς ἰατρική, κυβερνητική, γυμναστική· ἀλλὰ καὶ ὅλως τὰ ἐκ τοῦ βουλεύεσθαι λαμβανόμενα διὰ τοῦ τοιούτου ἐνδεχομένου δείκνυται.

[36] ἐπιστήμη δὲ καὶ συλλογισμὸς ἀποδεικτικὸς τῶν μὲν ἀορίστων οὐκ ἔστι διὰ τὸ ἄτακτον εἶναι τὸ μέσον, τῶν δὲ πεφυκότων ἔστι, καὶ σχεδὸν οἱ λόγοι καὶ αἱ σκέψεις γίνονται περὶ τῶν οὕτως ἐνδεχομένων· ἐκείνων δ' ἐγχωρεῖ μὲν γενέσθαι συλλογισμόν, οὐ μὴν εἴωθέ γε ζητεῖσθαι.

that problematic syllogistic has a scientific application. Now that notion of the applicability of problematic syllogistic suggests a general thesis about Peripatetic modal logic. Modal syllogistic, as I have said, contains three types of syllogism: there are problematic syllogisms, there are apodictic syllogisms, and there are mixed syllogisms. Aristotle appears to tell us that problematic syllogisms will serve those sciences whose matter holds only for the most part—that is to say, the majority of the sciences which concern the world below the moon. It is therefore natural to suppose that apodictic syllogisms are designed to provide proofs for those sciences whose matter is necessary and unvarying—for the mathematical sciences, and for any science which treats the supralunary regions. There is no obvious scientific domain for mixed syllogisms, in which some constituents have one modality and some another; but an ingenious interpreter will recall that Aristotle recognizes the existence of certain subordinate sciences: thus optics, for example, stands under the mathematical science of geometry, to which it adds certain contingent axioms of its own—and the ingenious interpreter will conjecture that just as its subject-matter is a mixture of mathematics and empirically observable fact, so its logic will be a mixture of the necessary and the possible.

That general view about the application of modal syllogistic is not sketched by Aristotle himself; and Alexander says less on the matter than we might have hoped. Nonetheless, it is reasonable to think that it was an orthodox Peripatetic view: after all, any orthodox Peripatetic must do two things—he must accept and appreciate some version of Aristotle's modal syllogistic, and he must uphold the doctrine that an item is a syllogism only insofar as it is useful, and hence only insofar as it can be used to frame a probative syllogism. To advance the view which I have just sketched is the obvious way—perhaps the only way—of doing those two things.

Why did Galen reject modal syllogistic? Before that question is addressed, another Galenic text may be introduced.

A LOGICAL THEOREM

It is the only passage in Galen's surviving works which mentions modal syllogisms. It is a perplexing passage. It occurs in a section of the treatise on *Simple Drugs* in which Galen is concerned to argue that certain substances—the oak-gall and the safflower—are useful for purging the body of excessive phlegm.

At this point in the argument I should like to recall a logical theorem which was shown in the work *On Proof* and which is useful in the present context. The theorem is this. Some proofs conclude that of necessity this holds of that, others that it possibly holds; and of these latter, some transform into holding of necessity when they follow necessary principles—and that is so in the case which we have just proved. For the phlegm-like juice which is contained in oak-gall and safflower cannot be shown evidently—rather, it is what is possible or likely or contingent which holds of the argument. But since we have shown that attraction depends on similarity of essence ... , then since what is purged is phlegm, what attracts it must necessarily be phlegm-like.

(simp med temp xi 612–613)³⁷

Galen appears to be saying this: 'There are problematic syllogisms and there are apodictic syllogisms. I have just proved, by a problematic syllogism, that it is possible (or perhaps probable) that gall and safflower are phlegm-like. But I know a logical theorem which enables me to transform the problematic conclusion into an apodictic conclusion, and hence to affirm that necessarily gall and safflower are phlegm-like.'

At first sight, that is embarrassing. First, according to the testimony of al-Farabi, Galen denied that there are any problematic syllogisms (and also, in all probability, that there are any apodictic syllogisms). Secondly, he would need a magical rather than a logical theorem to infer necessity from possibility. Must we blush for Galen and move on?

Perhaps things are not quite what they seem.

First, Galen says that he cannot 'show evidently' that gall and safflower are phlegm-like—that is to say, their phlegmatic character is not revealed by smelling or tasting or otherwise perceiving them. But Galen can produce—and has produced—an argument in favour of the thesis that gall and safflower are phlegm-like. He does not set the argument out formally; but it may decently be presented thus:

Gall and safflower attract phlegm.
What attracts phlegm is phlegm-like.

---

³⁷ βούλομαι δὲ ἐπεὶ κατὰ τούτου τοῦ λόγου γέγονα, καί τινος θεωρήματος ἀναμνῆσαι λογικοῦ, δεδειγμένου κἂν τοῖς Περὶ ἀποδείξεως ὑπομνήμασιν, εἴς τε τὰ παρόντα χρησίμου. ἔστι δὲ τὸ θεώρημα τοιόνδε. τῶν ἀποδείξεων αἱ μὲν ὡς ἐξ ἀνάγκης ὑπάρχει τόδε τῷδε περαίνουσιν, αἱ δὲ ὡς ὑπάρχειν ἐνδέχεται. τούτων δὲ αὐτῶν μεταπίπτουσί τινες εἰς τὸ ἐξ ἀνάγκης ὑπάρχειν ὅταν ἀναγκαίαις ἀρχαῖς ἕπωνται, καθάπερ καὶ ἐν αὐτῷ τούτῳ τῷ νῦν ἡμῖν ἀποδεδειγμένῳ. ἐν γὰρ τῷ κόκκῳ καὶ τῷ κνίκῳ τὸν φλεγματώδη περιεχόμενον χυμὸν ἐναργῶς μὲν οὐκ ἔστι δεῖξαι, τὸ δυνατὸν δὲ καὶ εἰκὸς καὶ ἐνδεχόμενον ὑπάρχει τῷ λόγῳ. ἀλλ' ἐπειδὴ καὶ τὰς ὁλκὰς ταῖς τῶν οὐσιῶν ὁμοιότησιν ἐδείξαμεν γίγνεσθαι, ... ἐπεὶ τοίνυν τὸ καθαιρόμενόν ἐστι φλέγμα, πάντως δή που καὶ τὸ ἕλκον ἀνάγκη φλεγματῶδες ὑπάρχειν.

Therefore gall and safflower are phlegm-like.

That is, or can be construed as, a predicative syllogism in Barbara. It is not a modal syllogism. None of its component propositions carries a modal operator. In particular, its conclusion is, as we should expect, the proposition that

Gall and safflower are phlegm-like

and not the problematic proposition that

It is possible that gall and safflower are phlegm-like.

Nonetheless, it is certainly meant as an example of a proof which concludes 'that it possibly holds'.

Galen remarks that 'it is what is possible or likely or contingent which holds of the argument'. That sentence is strange, and the text may be corrupt; but I think that Galen must have meant to say that his syllogism concludes to a proposition which may—for all that the argument itself shows—hold contingently rather than necessarily. For when he says that 'it is what is possible which holds of the argument', he cannot mean that the argument concludes to something of the form 'It is possible that … '—for it does not. Nor can he mean that the argument concludes to a proposition which in fact holds contingently—for he will proceed to argue that the conclusion in fact holds of necessity. So—as far as I can see—he can only mean that the argument does not show that necessarily gall and safflower are phlegm-like. And to be sure, it does not.

Can that really be what Galen means? He distinguishes between proofs which conclude that of necessity this holds of that and proofs which conclude that possibly this holds of that. He then singles out a special case of the latter sort of proof, and says that his gall and safflower syllogism is an example of such a case. So he says of his syllogism, implicitly, that it proves 'that possibly it holds'; and that strongly suggests that he has in mind a syllogism the conclusion of which is a problematic proposition. 'Strongly suggests'?—Surely it's more than that: doesn't Galen state quite explicitly that the syllogism has a problematic conclusion? Well, I agree that that is the plain sense of his words. Nonetheless, he can't in fact have meant what the plain sense makes him mean; so I infer that he meant something else. What he meant, if I am right, is, of course, perfectly compatible with al-Farabi's report that Galen rejected problematic syllogistic.

What, then, is the logical theorem which supposedly enables Galen to conclude that gall and safflower are phlegm-like not contingently but as a matter of necessity? It is natural to suppose that the theorem must tell us that when a certain syllogism is valid, then so is another. Galen offers a hint of the content of the theorem when he claims that the transformation from possibility to necessity occurs 'when they follow necessary principles'. So why not this?

If an argument from a given set of premisses to a given conclusion is valid, then so too is the argument from the same premisses apodictically modalized to the same conclusion apodictically modalized.

Or schematically:

If 'P$_1$, P$_2$, ... , P$_n$: therefore Q' is valid, then 'Necessarily P$_1$, Necessarily P$_2$, ... , Necessarily P$_n$: therefore necessarily Q' is valid.

The suggestion that that is Galen's logical theorem has two things in its favour: first, it is a genuine theorem—it is true; and secondly, it will do the work which Galen expects his theorem to do.

For the theorem will transform Galen's first, non-modal argument into this:

Necessarily gall and safflower attract phlegm.
Necessarily what attracts phlegm is phlegm-like.
Therefore necessarily gall and safflower are phlegm-like.

In other words, a non-modal syllogism in Barbara is transformed into an apodictic syllogism in Barbara.

The apodictic syllogism is a proof only if its premisses are true. Galen says that he has elsewhere proved that attraction is a matter of similarity, and of similarity in essence. So if gall and safflower attract phlegm, then they do so in virtue of their essence: they attract phlegm essentially—and therefore necessarily. Again, Galen takes himself to have established the general thesis that

What attracts X is essentially X-like,

so that, in particular,

What attracts phlegm is essentially phlegm-like.

And that implies that

What attracts phlegm is necessarily phlegm-like.

And there are the two apodictic premisses for the apodictic Barbara.

Now as a matter of fact I do not think that what Galen had in mind was that particular logical theorem. But I shall leave Galen in suspense for a few pages: the logical theorem, whether or not it is Galen's, has an ancient history, to which a few paragraphs may be consecrated.

The logical theorem in front of us—which I shall henceforward call the Modal Theorem—will produce apodictic syllogisms quite generally from non-modal syllogisms. In particular, it will show, at a single blow, that if

X, Y: therefore Z

is a valid predicative syllogism, then so too is

Necessarily X, Necessarily Y: therefore necessarily Z.

In other words, it will establish the validity of all and only those apodictic syllogisms which Aristotle acknowledges in the *Prior Analytics*.

Aristotle in fact spends very little time on apodictic syllogisms—a bare half-page. He remarks that

in the case of necessities things are pretty much the same as in the non-modal cases: when the terms are placed in the same way, there will be or not be a syllogism both in holding and in holding of necessity (or not holding)—except that they will differ inasmuch as holding of necessity (or not holding) is added to the terms.

(*APr* 29b36–30a2)[38]

'Things are ... the same' insofar as

Necessarily X, Necessarily Y: therefore necessarily Z

is a valid predicative syllogism if and only if

X, Y: therefore Z

is a valid predicative syllogism.

True, Aristotle does not say that things are the same: he says that they are pretty much the same. But the explanation of that qualification comes in the next lines:

For the privative converts in the same way, and we shall explain 'as in a whole' and 'of every' in the same way. So in most cases the conclusion will be proved necessary

---

[38] ἐπὶ μὲν οὖν τῶν ἀναγκαίων σχεδὸν ὁμοίως ἔχει καὶ ἐπὶ τῶν ὑπαρχόντων· ὡσαύτως γὰρ τιθεμένων τῶν ὅρων ἔν τε τῷ ὑπάρχειν καὶ τῷ ἐξ ἀνάγκης ὑπάρχειν ἢ μὴ ὑπάρχειν ἔσται τε καὶ οὐκ ἔσται συλλογισμός, πλὴν διοίσει τῷ προσκεῖσθαι τοῖς ὅροις τὸ ἐξ ἀνάγκης ὑπάρχειν ἢ μὴ ὑπάρχειν.

by way of conversion, as in the case of holding. But in the middle figure, when the universal is affirmative and the particular negative, and in the third figure, when the universal is affirmative and the particular negative, the proof will not be the same.

(*APr* 30a2–9)[39]

The proofs of apodictic syllogisms will mimic the proofs of their non-modal cousins—save in the case of Baroco and Bocardo.

For in those two cases, the proofs cannot rely on the principles of conversion; and Aristotle used a proof by reduction to the impossible. That is to say, in the case of Baroco, he began his proof like this:

(1) B holds of every A   premiss
(2) B does not hold of some C   premiss
(3) It is not the case that A does   hypothesis
    not hold of some C

From those three propositions a contradiction is readily inferred: hence the negation of the hypothesis, (3), which is the conclusion of Baroco. Aristotle cannot use the very same proof for apodictic Baroco—for the simple reason that the hypothesis for apodictic Baroco would have to be not (3) but rather:

(3*) It is not the case that necessarily A does not hold of some C

The upshot is this: the apodictic syllogisms are only 'pretty much the same', not in the sense that they do not quite pair off with non-modal syllogisms, but rather inasmuch as two of them cannot be proved in the same manner as the corresponding non-modal syllogisms.

Aristotle does not advance the Modal Theorem in support of his general thesis, and Alexander does not mention the Theorem. To be sure, the Theorem does not suffice to prove Aristotle's general thesis. It will show one half of the thesis, namely that if

X, Y: therefore Z

is a valid predicative syllogism, then so too is

Necessarily X, Necessarily Y: therefore necessarily Z.

But it does not suffice to show that if

Necessarily X, Necessarily Y: therefore necessarily Z

---

[39] τό τε γὰρ στερητικὸν ὡσαύτως ἀντιστρέφει, καὶ τὸ ἐν ὅλῳ εἶναι καὶ τὸ κατὰ παντὸς ὁμοίως ἀποδώσομεν. ἐν μὲν οὖν τοῖς ἄλλοις τὸν αὐτὸν τρόπον δειχθήσεται διὰ τῆς ἀντιστρο-φῆς τὸ συμπέρασμα ἀναγκαῖον ὥσπερ ἐπὶ τοῦ ὑπάρχειν· ἐν δὲ τῷ μέσῳ σχήματι, ὅταν ᾖ τὸ καθόλου καταφατικὸν τὸ δ' ἐν μέρει στερητικόν, καὶ πάλιν ἐν τῷ τρίτῳ, ὅταν τὸ μὲν καθόλου κατηγορικὸν τὸ δ' ἐν μέρει στερητικόν, οὐχ ὁμοίως ἔσται ἡ ἀπόδειξις.

is valid, then so too is

X, Y: therefore Z.

But Aristotle himself does nothing to show the second half of his thesis; and he would have lost nothing by appealing to the Theorem for the first half.

Perhaps Aristotle simply had not thought of the Theorem? Or perhaps he thought that, despite its apparent evidence, there might in fact be something dodgy about it? The second of those suggestions *vaut le détour*.

The theorem is closely allied to a thesis which was familiar to ancient logicians. It is stated thus by Cicero:

If what is anterior in a conditional is necessary, then what is posterior too is necessary.

(*fat* vii 13)[40]

That is to say,

If necessarily P, and if P then Q, then necessarily Q.

The thesis was not undisputed; for having stated it, Cicero immediately adds that 'Chrysippus does not think that this holds in all cases'.[41] And since anyone who doubts or rejects the thesis will surely doubt or reject the Theorem, the Theorem must have been found dodgy by at least some ancient logicians.

Why did Chrysippus reject the thesis? Cicero offers no explanation; but his remark is generally glossed with the aid of a text in Alexander:

Aristotle proves that it is not possible for the impossible to follow the possible ... But Chrysippus says that nothing prevents the impossible from following the possible. He says nothing against Aristotle's proof, but he tries to show that things are not so by way of certain examples—which are not soundly put together.

(*in APr* 177.19–27)[42]

In other words, Chrysippus denied that:

If possibly P, and if P then Q, then possibly Q.

One of the two alleged counterexamples which Alexander reports has already been discussed in a different context. It is this:

If Dio is dead, then this man is dead.

---

[40] *si ... quod primum in conexo est necessarium est, fit etiam quod consequitur necessarium.*

[41] *quamquam hoc Chrysippo non videtur valere in omnibus.*

[42] Ἀριστοτέλης μὲν οὖν ὅτι μὴ οἷόν τέ ἐστι δυνατῷ ἀδύνατον ἕπεσθαι δείκνυσι ... Χρύσιππος δὲ λέγων μηδὲν κωλύειν καὶ δυνατῷ ἀδύνατον ἕπεσθαι πρὸς μὲν τὴν ὑπ' Ἀριστοτέλους εἰρημένην δεῖξιν οὐδὲν λέγει, πειρᾶται δὲ διὰ παραδειγμάτων τινῶν οὐχ ὑγιῶς συγκειμένων δεικνύναι τοῦτο μὴ οὕτως ἔχον.

According to Chrysippus, the conditional is true; its antecedent is possible; and its consequent is impossible.

If that was Chrysippus' was of dealing with the thesis which Alexander ascribes to Aristotle, then surely he would have dealt similarly with the thesis which Cicero reports. For consider the contrapositive of Chrysippus' example:

If this man is not dead, then Dio is not dead.

Chrysippus must surely hold that the conditional is true, the antecedent necessary, and the consequent not necessary. If Chrysippus is right, then the thesis which Cicero reports is false; and if the thesis is false, then the Modal Theorem which partners it is also false.

Alexander argues at length against Chrysippus; but I shall not follow him. For I doubt if Dio's death and the logical behaviour of the demonstrative phrase 'this man' have any relevance to Cicero's remark. At any rate, in the Ciceronian context Chrysippus' maverick views on demonstrative pronouns are not in the least to the point, and it is likely that Cicero has something quite different in mind.

The truth or falsity of the thesis which Cicero reports—of the thesis that

If necessarily P, and if P then Q, then necessarily Q

—depends in part on the sense of its conditional component 'If P then Q'. The point is trivial. Alexander took it; or rather, he took it in the case of the parallel thesis about possibility:

Aristotle shows that it cannot be the case that something impossible follows what is possible but that necessarily what the impossible follows is itself impossible—in the case of every necessary implication. A necessary implication is not an occasional implication, but rather one in which the consequent always follows what is taken as the antecedent. For the conditional

If Alexander exists, Alexander talks

or

If Alexander exists, he has such-and-such an age

is not true—not even if he is in fact of such-and-such an age when the proposition is said.

(*in APr* 175.34–176.6)[43]

---

[43] ... δείκνυσιν ὅτι μὴ οἷόν τε δυνατῷ τι ἀδύνατον ἀκολουθεῖν, ἀλλ' ἀνάγκη ἀδύνατον εἶναι ᾧ τὸ ἀδύνατον ἀκολουθεῖ, ἐπὶ πάσης ἀναγκαίας ἀκολουθίας. ἔστι δὲ ἀναγκαία ἀκολουθία οὐχ ἡ πρόσκαιρος, ἀλλὰ ἐν ᾗ ἀεὶ τὸ ἑπόμενον ἕπεσθαι ἔστι τῷ τὸ εἰλημμένον ὡς ἡγούμενον εἶναι. οὐ γὰρ ἀληθὲς συνημμένον τὸ εἰ 'Αλέξανδρος ἔστιν, 'Αλέξανδρος διαλέγεται, ἢ εἰ 'Αλέξανδρος ἔστι, τοσῶνδε ἐτῶν ἐστι, καὶ εἰ εἴη ὅτε λέγεται ἡ πρότασις τοσούτων ἐτῶν.—'ἑπόμενον' is Mueller's correction of the received 'εἰλημμένον'.

So that

Aristotle shows that it cannot be the case that an impossible follows a possible inasmuch as in a true conditional the consequent must follow the antecedent by necessity.

(in APr 177.19–21)[44]

What Alexander says is correct for the thesis that

> If possibly P, and if P then Q, then possibly Q.

It is also correct for the thesis that

> If necessarily P, and if P then Q, then necessarily Q.

That is to say, the two theses are true when 'If P, then Q' is construed as a necessary implication (assuming, of course, that the modal operators 'possibly' and 'necessarily' are given a normal interpretation).

There are, and in antiquity there were, other ways of construing conditional propositions. Philo of Megara, for example, proposed that a conditional is true if and only if it is not the case that both its antecedent and the negation of its consequent are true. If the thesis which Cicero reports is construed in that Philonian fashion, then it is equivalent to this:

> If necessarily P, and if it is not the case both that P and that not Q, then necessarily Q.

And that is false. (To see that it is false, take take any necessary truth for 'P' and any contingent truth for 'Q'. Thus

> Necessarily no married man is a bachelor

and also

> Aristotle was married.

Hence

> It is not the case that both necessarily no married men are bachelors and also Aristotle wasn't not married.

But it is false that

> Necessarily Aristotle was married.)

The Ciceronian context shows—or at the very least, makes it stupendously probable—that when Chrysippus denied that the thesis 'holds in all cases' he meant that it does not hold for every type of conditional connection; and—whatever we may make of Dio's death—on that point he was quite right.

---

[44] Ἀριστοτέλης μὲν οὖν ὅτι μὴ οἷόν τέ ἐστι δυνατῷ ἀδύνατον ἔπεσθαι δείκνυσι διὰ τοῦ δεῖν μὲν ἐν τῷ ἀληθεῖ συνημμένῳ ἐξ ἀνάγκης ἔπεσθαι τὸ λῆγον τῷ ἡγουμένῳ.

So the passage in Cicero's *On Fate* does not prove that Chrysippus thought that the Modal Theorem was false, or even dodgy. It shows only that he thought that it must be correctly understood. And who would have denied that?

But Dio is still dead; and if the case of this man's death does not explain anything in the Ciceronian text, it may nevertheless be pertinent to Chrysippus' attitude to the Theorem. For the case was taken by Chrysippus to show that there are exceptions to the thesis that

If possibly P, and if P then Q, then possibly Q;

and he can hardly have failed to see that the case must show equally that there are exceptions to the thesis reported by Cicero, namely:

If necessarily P, and if P then Q, then necessarily Q.

So if he also thought that

If Dio is dead, then this man is dead

is a necessary conditional, then he must have rejected the Modal Theorem—or rather, then he could not coherently have accepted the Modal theorem. Did he take that conditional to be necessary? Plainly, the sentence

If Dio is dead, then this man is dead

may be used to express contingent truths (and contingent falsehoods)—suppose that in it 'this man' refers to Theo rather than to Dio. But in Chrysippus' example, 'this man' is, of course, used to refer to Dio; and hence—or so it is plausible to think, or at least to think that Chrysippus would have thought—it is not possible for Dio to be dead and this man still alive.

However that may be, and whether or not Chrysippus found—or should have found—the Modal Theorem dubious, there is not the slightest reason to ascribe any similar doubts to Aristotle. Alexander asserts that Aristotle has shown that

If possibly P, and if P then Q, then possibly Q.

This is what Aristotle says:

First, let it be said that if, if A is the case then necessarily B is the case, then if A is possible then necessarily B too will be possible.

(*APr* 34a5–7)[45]

He then offers an argument for his claim—and he uses the claim to validate certain modal syllogisms.

---

[45] πρῶτον δὲ λεκτέον ὅτι εἰ τοῦ Α ὄντος ἀνάγκη τὸ Β εἶναι, καὶ δυνατοῦ ὄντος τοῦ Α δυνατὸν ἔσται καὶ τὸ Β ἐξ ἀνάγκης.

That being so, it is hardly likely that Aristotle—or Alexander—would have found anything dodgy about the thesis that

If necessarily P, and if P then Q, then necessarily Q.

Moreover, although I do not find the thesis in the text of the *Analytics*, the allied Modal Theorem is in fact inconspicuously announced there:

If C of D and D of F, then necessarily C of F; and if each of the two is possible, then the conclusion too is possible. So if you were to make A the premisses and B the conclusion, it will follow not only that if A is necessary then B too is necessary but also that if it is possible it is possible.

(*APr* 34a19–24)[46]

Suppose that
    A: therefore B
is a syllogism. Then so too are
    Necessarily A: therefore necessarily B
and
    Possibly A: therefore possibly B.

That is what Aristotle says: so he recognized the Modal Theorem, and he might perfectly well have used it in order to establish his apodictic syllogisms.

It is more than time to return to Galen and to his *Simple Drugs*. The Modal Theorem is a good theorem and a powerful theorem. It was stated by Aristotle; and although he did not make use of it, he could properly have done so. But what about Galen? How could he have made use of it? The theorem tells you how to generate an apodictic argument from a non-modal argument. Yet according to al-Farabi, Galen had no time for any modal syllogisms—he thought that hyparctic or non-modal syllogisms were all the syllogisms a scientist needed and hence all the syllogisms that there are. al-Farabi is reporting what Galen had said in *On Proof*; so perhaps Galen changed his mind between writing *On Proof* and compiling *Simple Drugs*? Hardly: after all, *Simple Drugs* refers explicitly to the earlier work for a proof of the logical theorem, and you will not believe that *On Proof* both rejected modal syllogistic and also offered a proof of a theorem which infers modal from non-modal syllogisms.

---

[46] εἰ γὰρ τὸ Γ κατὰ τοῦ Δ, τὸ δὲ Δ κατὰ τοῦ Z, καὶ τὸ Γ κατὰ τοῦ Z ἐξ ἀνάγκης· καὶ εἰ δυνατὸν ἑκάτερον, καὶ τὸ συμπέρασμα δυνατόν. ὥσπερ οὖν εἴ τις θείη τὸ μὲν A τὰς προτάσεις, τὸ δὲ B τὸ συμπέρασμα, συμβαίνοι ἂν οὐ μόνον ἀναγκαίου τοῦ A ὄντος ἅμα καὶ τὸ B εἶναι ἀναγκαῖον, ἀλλὰ καὶ δυνατοῦ δυνατόν.

Then is al-Farabi simply mistaken? Did Galen reject problematical syllogisms but keep his arms round apodictic syllogistic? Well, you may be attracted by such a view if you are persuaded that Galen's logical theorem is the Modal Theorem; but in fact there are pretty good reasons for thinking that it was not.

First, the Modal Theorem, as I have said, has universal scope: it will make an apodictic syllogism of any non-apodictic syllogism. Galen's logical theorem, on the other hand, is supposed to have a circumscribed domain of application; for Galen explicitly says that in some cases—and he evidently means in some cases only—the theorem allows us to move from a possible conclusion to a necessary conclusion. If the logical theorem is identified as the Modal Theorem, then we shall have to suppose that Galen somehow came to convince himself that its scope was restricted to a certain class of syllogism.

Secondly, I said that we might readily suppose the logical theorem to state something of the form: 'When such-and-such a syllogism is valid, then so too is such-and-such another syllogism.' (The Modal Theorem has that form.) But although the supposition is readily made, there is no direct warrant for it in Galen's text. Galen does not speak of transforming one syllogism into another: he speaks of showing that the conclusion of a given proof not only holds but holds of necessity. There is no explicit mention of any second syllogism, and perhaps there is no need to insert a second syllogism into the text.

Earlier, I argued that when Galen says that 'some proofs conclude that … it possibly holds', we should forget the plain sense of his words and take him to mean not that some proofs conclude to propositions of the form 'Possibly so-and-so' but rather that some proofs conclude to 'So-and-so', where—for all we yet know—it may be contingently the case that so-and-so. That is to say, the proof of possibility is simply this:

Gall and safflower attract phlegm.
What attracts phlegm is phlegm-like.
Therefore gall and safflower are phlegm-like.

It is a proof of possibility insofar as, for all that has been thus far argued, the conclusion of the syllogism may be contingently rather than necessarily true. Now if that is so, then by the same token, a proof which concludes that 'of necessity this holds of that' ought to conclude not to 'Necessarily so-and-so' but rather to 'So-and-so', where in fact, as we can show, it is necessary that so-and-so. In other words, the proof of necessity will be exactly the same as the proof of possibility, namely:

Gall and safflower attract phlegm.
What attracts phlegm is phlegm-like.
Therefore gall and safflower are phlegm-like.

It is, now, a proof of necessity insofar as we have (now) reason to think that its conclusion holds not contingently but necessarily.

If that is so, then Galen's logical theorem should not be designed to construct a new syllogism from an old syllogism, an apodictic syllogism from a non-modal syllogism. Rather, it should allow us to infer that the conclusion of the old non-modal syllogism, namely

Gall and safflower are phlegm-like,

in fact holds of necessity. Is there any such theorem? Yes. This will do the trick:

If an argument from a given set of premisses to a given conclusion is valid, then if the each of the premisses of the argument holds of necessity, the conclusion too holds of necessity.

Or schematically:

If 'P_1, P_2, ..., P_n: therefore Q' is valid, and necessarily P_1, and necessarily P_2, ..., and necessarily P_n, then necessarily Q.

When that theorem is applied to the gall and safflower syllogism, it does not produce a second syllogism: it allows us to infer that

Gall and safflower are phlegm-like

holds of necessity—given, of course, that we have established that the two premisses of the argument hold of necessity.

That interpretation of the passage from *Simple Drugs* will seem forced. It is forced. But I think that any coherent interpretation of the text—whether or not it hopes to reconcile what is there said with what al-Farabi reports about *On Proof*—will be forced.

It may also be urged that there are really no substantive differences between the Modal Theorem and the theorem which I have just put on the table. To simplify things a little, the Modal Theorem says that if

X: therefore Y

is a syllogism, then so is

Necessarily X: therefore necessarily Y;

and the other theorem says that if

X: therefore Y

is a syllogism, then if

Necessarily X

then

Necessarily Y.

Tweedledum and Tweedledee—only a pedant will discern any difference. Perhaps. But Tweedledum and Tweedledee are two distinct items; and there is some distance between them as the crow flies.

Nevertheless, I can't say that I'm enamoured of that way of dealing with *Simple Drugs*. It's just that I can find no better way of reconciling it with the report from al-Farabi.

So why not reject the report? After all—to return to the question which was earlier shelved—why ever should Galen have rejected modal syllogistic?

PROBLEMATIC SYLLOGISMS

al-Farabi gives no hint. But it has proved tempting to guess that Galen's rejection of problematic syllogistic had something to do with Theophrastus' views on the subject.

In Aristotle's problematic syllogistic, possible negations convert; that is to say—it is an unusual use of the word 'convert'—they are equivalent to possible affirmatives. Thus according to Aristotle, A holds possibly of no B if and only if A holds possibly of every B. A late commentary on the *Prior Analytics* informs us that

Theophrastus and Eudemus—and also the Platonists—do not want the possible negation to convert to the possible affirmation since in that case we shall have abandoned the sort of possible which holds for the most part, which is what the argument is about. For the syllogisms are advanced by those arts which are concerned with the possible which holds for the most part—if it is possible that no man has six fingers for the most part, then it is possible that every man (and that some man) has six fingers for the lesser part.

([Ammonius], *in APr* 45.42–46.2)[47]

That is far from pellucid—whatever does it mean to say that no man has six fingers for the most part? The other late texts which report the views of

---

[47] οἱ δ' ἑταῖροι αὐτοῦ Θεόφραστος καὶ Εὔδημος καὶ ἔτι οἱ Πλατωνικοὶ οὐ βούλονται ἐνδεχομένην ἀπόφασιν ἀντιστρέφειν πρὸς ἐνδεχομένην κατάφασιν, ἐπειδὴ οὐ μένει τὸ ὡς ἐπὶ τὸ πολὺ ἐνδεχόμενον, περὶ οὗ ὁ λόγος. οἱ γὰρ συλλογισμοὶ ὑπὸ τεχνῶν προβάλλονται αἳ περὶ τὸ ὡς ἐπὶ τὸ πολὺ ἐνδεχόμενον ἔχουσιν· εἰ γὰρ ἐνδέχεται μηδένα ἄνθρωπον ἑξαδάκτυλον εἶναι ὡς ἐπὶ τὸ πολύ, ἐνδέχεται πάντα ἄνθρωπον καὶ τινὰ ἄνθρωπον ἑξαδάκτυλον εἶναι ἐπ' ἔλαττον.

Theophrastus and Eudemus shed no light; and Alexander says nothing on the subject.

Nonetheless, one point is reasonably plain—and it is the point which matters here. It is this. Aristotle thought that there were two senses of 'possible' and hence, in principle, two sorts of problematical syllogism. The sciences which are concerned with contingent matters (medicine, for example, or navigation) employ 'possible' in only one of the two senses—and so problematical syllogistic may reasonably limit itself to that sense of 'possible'. Now in that sense,

A holds possibly of every B

will be true provided that A holds naturally of every B, or A holds for the most part of every B. But once possibility is so understood, the conversion rules which Aristotle proposes for problematic propositions will not work. In particular, the conversion from

A holds possibly of no B

to

A holds possibly of every B

must be dropped; for it is perfectly plain that

A holds naturally of no B

does not entail

A holds naturally of every B.

Now Aristotle's problematic syllogistic depends on his conversion rules. Hence it cannot be invoked by those sciences which deal with what holds for the most part.

Galen knew Theophrastus' logical works, on some of which he had written commentaries. Presumably he had read and digested Theophrastus' criticisms of Aristotle's problematic syllogistic; no doubt he saw that they made problematic syllogistic useless; and perhaps—utilitarian as he was—it was for that reason that he rejected the study of problematic arguments.

That is a plausible story; but I suppose that it is false. First, the Theophrastan criticism does not for a moment imply that problematic syllogistic is useless for the sciences. Rather, it suggests that Aristotle's problematic syllogistic is incapable of performing the scientific services for which it was allegedly designed. The moral to be drawn is not: Abandon problematic syllogistic. It is: Develop a better problematic syllogistic. After all, that is what Theophrastus set himself to do.

Secondly, al-Farabi indicates that Galen rejected apodictic as well as problematic syllogistic. True, Theophrastus had criticized certain aspects of

Aristotle's apodictic syllogistic, just as he had criticized certain fundamental aspects of his problematic syllogistic. But if it is just about conceivable that someone might have taken the Theophrastan criticisms of problematic syllogistic to indicate that the subject had better be abandoned *in toto*, it is quite unimaginable that anyone—let alone Galen—would have thought to abandon apodictic syllogistic on account of Theophrastus' criticisms of Aristotle.

So the question remains: Why did Galen reject modal syllogistic?

MOODS AND MATTER

Near the beginning of his commentary on the *Analytics*, Alexander makes a few preliminary remarks about modal operators and modal propositions; and he raises the question of why the things come into the *Prior Analytics* at all:

It seemed to me worth asking why, when in this book he is discussing syllogisms and figures, he also takes into consideration material differences among propositions—for the fact that something holds in this way or in that way is a material difference, and such differences among propositions will therefore seem pertinent not to something's being a syllogism *simpliciter* but rather to its being a syllogism of such-and-such a sort—a probative syllogism, say, or a dialectical syllogism.

(*in APr* 27.27–28.2)[48]

The propositions
Every triangle has an angle-sum of 180°
and
Every child ought to honour his parents
have a different modal status: the former is necessary, the latter merely reputable. But that—according to Alexander—is a material difference between the propositions: it may help to determine whether a certain syllogism is probative or not, but it has no bearing on the question whether a certain argument is a syllogism or not. From the point of view of predicative syllogistic, there is no difference between the two propositions. So why does Aristotle interest himself in modalities at all?

---

[48] ἄξιον δὲ ἔδοξεν ἐπισκέψεως εἶναί μοι τί δήποτε περὶ συλλογισμῶν καὶ σχημάτων τὸν λόγον ἐν τούτοις τοῖς βιβλίοις ποιούμενος παραλαμβάνει καὶ τὰς τῶν προτάσεων κατὰ τὴν ὕλην διαφοράς· ὑλικαὶ γὰρ διαφοραὶ τὸ οὕτως ἢ οὕτως ὑπάρχειν· ἤδη γὰρ δόξουσιν αἱ τοιαῦται διαφοραὶ τῶν προτάσεων οὐχ ἁπλῶς πρὸς συλλογισμὸν συντελεῖν, ἀλλὰ πρὸς τὸ τοιοῦτον ἢ τοιοῦτον αὐτὸν εἶναι, ἀποδεικτικόν, ἂν οὕτως τύχῃ, ἢ διαλεκτικόν.

Alexander offers what appears to be rather a confused answer to his question. He begins like this:

Or perhaps such differences among propositions are in general necessary to the method and study of syllogistic? After all, the conversions do not come about in the same ways when propositions differ in respect of the moods we have described ...

(*in APr* 28.2–5)[49]

But the conversions do 'come about in the same ways'; for, so far as conversions go, the propositions
    Every triangle has an angle-sum of 180°
and
    Every child ought to honour his parents
behave in exactly the same ways.

There are indeed differences in conversion, according to Aristotle, 'in respect of the moods'; but the differences are not between the two propositions which I have just illustratively cited but rather between the two related modalized propositions:
    Necessarily every triangle has an angle-sum of 180°,
and:
    Possibly every child ought to honour his parents.
For example, the latter proposition—according to Aristotle—entails that
    Possibly no child ought to honour his parents,
whereas the former does not entail
    Necessarily no triangle has an angle-sum of 180°.
Such differences are not, as Alexander would have put it, merely material: they hold in general between propositions of the form
    Necessarily every B is A
and
    Possibly every B is A.

It is one thing to ask what is the modal status of a proposition—does what it states hold necessarily or in point of fact or as a possibility? (Or, of course, not at all.) It is another thing to ask what modal operator the proposition carries—does it have the form 'Necessarily so-and-so' or 'Possibly so-and-so' or neither? In Alexander's terms, the former question asks after a material aspect of the proposition, the latter after a formal aspect. A

---

[49] ἢ αἱ διαφοραὶ αἱ τοιαῦται τῶν προτάσεων πρὸς τὴν συλλογιστικὴν μέθοδόν τε καὶ πραγματείαν ἀναγκαῖαι καθόλου· τῷ τε γὰρ μὴ ὁμοίως γίνεσθαι τὰς ἀντιστροφὰς τῶν κατὰ τοὺς προειρημένους τρόπους διαφερουσῶν προτάσεων ...

little earlier in his commentary Alexander had in fact made the pertinent distinction:

He claims that propositions take necessity and non-modality and possibility not from what underlies them and is meant by them but rather from the adjunct which is added and co-predicated and which says that this holds of that from necessity, or that it holds, or that it can hold.

(*in APr* 27.1–5)[50]

Modal logic—Aristotle's modal syllogistic—concerns propositions which predicate something necessarily or possibly of something; it concerns propositions which say that A holds M-ly of B. Modal syllogistic works with modalized propositions, and it is not concerned with the modal status of the propositions which are or may be modalized.

Since he has set down that point fairly clearly, it is strange that, a page or so later, Alexander should wonder why Aristotle deals with material aspects of propositions; for Aristotle does not do so. Nonetheless, what Alexander says—in passing—on the modal status of propositions is pertinent to the question of the applicability of modal syllogistic—and hence to the question: Why did Galen reject modal logic?

The modal status of a proposition, Alexander says, may help to determine whether a syllogism in which it appears is probative or dialectical or of some other character. Now proofs or probative syllogisms must, on a strict interpretation of a strict Aristotelian view, have premisses which are true and necessary. What matters, in other words, is their modal status. Modalization is not the issue. The apodictic proposition

Necessarily every triangle has an angle-sum of $190°$

could not, despite its modal operator, feature in a proof—after all, it is false. The non-apodictic proposition

Every triangle has an angle-sum of $180°$

can—and does—figure in proofs; for it is true, and it is necessary.

In general, if the proposition that such-and-such is to feature in a strict Aristotelian proof, then it must be the case that necessarily such-and-such. It does not follow, and it is not true, that if the proposition that such-and-such is to feature in a strict Aristotelian proof, then it must have the form 'Necessarily so-and-so' or say that necessarily so-and-so.

---

[50] οὐ γὰρ ἀξιοῖ τὰς προτάσεις ἀπὸ τῶν ὑποκειμένων αὐταῖς καὶ δηλουμένων ὑπ' αὐτῶν λαμβάνειν τὸ ἀναγκαῖον καὶ τὸ ὑπάρχον καὶ τὸ ἐνδεχόμενον, ἀλλὰ ἀπὸ τῆς προσθήκης τῆς προστιθεμένης καὶ προσκατηγορουμένης τῆς λεγούσης ὅτι τόδε τῷδε ἐξ ἀνάγκης ὑπάρχει ἢ ὑπάρχει ἢ ἐνδέχεται ὑπάρχειν.

Surely that cannot be right? After all, Aristotle invented apodictic syllogistic in order to satisfy the probative demands of those sciences whose propositions hold true by necessity; and apodictic syllogisms are constructed from modalized propositions, from propositions of the form 'Necessarily so-and-so'. So surely the apodictic proposition

Necessarily every triangle has an angle-sum of 180°

is more appropriate to scientific proofs than the non-modal proposition

Every triangle has an angle-sum of 180°?

No, it isn't. First, consider actual scientific practice. Pythagoras' theorem states that the square on the hypotenuse is equal to the sum of the squares on the other two sides: it does not state that necessarily the square on the hypotenuse etc. Euclid's *Elements* contains no modalized propositions: all its theorems are, if true, then necessary; but none has the form 'Necessarily so-and-so'. Secondly, the propositions which constitute a strict Aristotelian proof must hold of necessity. Hence the modalized proposition

Necessarily every triangle has an angle-sum of 180°

can feature in such a proof only if its own modal status is one of necessity; in other words, only if

Necessarily necessarily every triangle has an angle-sum of 180°.

Aristotle never considers such doubled modalities—nor has he any scientific reason to do so.

In other words, the sciences—even where they deal in necessities—do not use apodictic propositions. They therefore have no use for apodictic syllogisms. In just the same way, the sciences do not use problematic propositions. There are, to be sure, sciences of the contingent; and despite the official definition in the *Posterior Analytics* which requires necessity of every component proposition in a proof, Aristotle does in fact recognize—and in the *Posterior Analytics*—that some scientific proofs start from contingent premises and arrive at contingent conclusions. Such proofs, he thinks, deal with what happens 'for the most part'.

Thus, for example, it is a truth, and a contingent truth, that vines shed their leaves in autumn: they do not do so necessarily, but they do so by nature and for the most part. Let us follow Aristotle in imagining that that contingent truth is a theorem of the science of botany. Now the theorem is not:

Contingently, vines are lose their leaves in autumn.

It is:

Vines lose their leaves in autumn.

What goes for botany goes for medicine, and for navigation; and no doubt for gymnastics too.

When Alexander and al-Farabi urge the contrary thesis, stating that the theorems of such sciences are problematic propositions, they take themselves to be bowing both to Aristotle and to the truth. They are certainly not bowing to the truth; and although their reading of Aristotle is not whimsical—indeed, it is based firmly on some passages in the *Analytics*—it is not in the end the best overall interpretation of Aristotle's view of the nature of scientific proof.

The conclusion which Galen and Alexander should have drawn from such considerations is plain: modal arguments, *pace* Aristotle, have no probative utility; so they are not syllogisms; and they ought to be excluded from the purlieus of logic. Alexander did not draw that conclusion, which would doubtless have been embarrassing for an Aristotelian commentator who held an imperial chair in Peripatetic philosophy. Indeed, so far as I have noticed, Alexander nowhere hints that there may be something fundamentally odd about Aristotle's modal syllogistic. Galen, I suppose, drew the conclusion. That is to say, Galen recognized that the sciences do not use modal propositions, and he therefore concluded that modal syllogistic is superfluous. That is why he does not mention modality in his *Introduction to Logic*; and that is why no modal syllogism every appears in any of his voluminous writings—perhaps not even in *Simple Drugs*.

REPETITIVE ARGUMENTS

A utilitarian logician should have no time for modal syllogistic. But if modal syllogisms cannot be used to prove anything, that is not because of any formal deficiencies on their part but rather because of the nature of scientific theorems. Other would-be syllogisms were rejected by the utilitarians on purely formal grounds.

Aristotle's definition of the syllogism is found in three slightly different versions. In the *Analytics* it looks like this:

A syllogism is a saying in which, certain items being laid down, something other than the items laid down comes about by necessity from the fact that they are the case.

(*APr* 24b18–20)[51]

---

[51] συλλογισμὸς δέ ἐστι λόγος ἐν ᾧ τεθέντων τινῶν ἕτερόν τι τῶν κειμένων ἐξ ἀνάγκης συμβαίνει τῷ ταῦτα εἶναι.

In a syllogism, certain items—the premisses—are laid down, and something other—the conclusion—results. The ancient commentators read the definition minutely, and they gave each word a weight. Thus Alexander has a long discussion of the phrase 'something other'—or rather, he has two long discussions of it, one in his commentary on the *Analytics* and the other in his commentary on the *Topics*.

The passage in the commentary on the *Analytics*—in the state in which we have it—is not a smooth piece of writing. Commentaries in general are rough beasts which shamble from one lemma to the next. Moreover, they are functional items, not literary compositions; and their value is instrumental: the inventor of the instrument may himself produce later models; and an owner of the instrument may adapt it to his own uses. Certainly, many surviving ancient commentaries show signs of such a history. The best known case of the phenomenon is provided by Alexander himself: we have two versions of the earlier parts of his commentary on the *Metaphysics*, one of them (at least by and large) from his own hand and the other from the pen of some later professor. I suspect that parts of the commentary on the *Analytics*—among them the discussion of 'something other'—have been similarly written and rewritten. The comparable passage in the commentary on the *Topics* contains essentially the same material, here abbreviated and there expanded; and it runs more smoothly.

The passage in the commentary on the *Analytics* begins in the following way:

He was absolutely correct to add that the conclusion must be other than the items laid down. For it is useless—it destroys all syllogistic utility—to infer what is agreed and laid down. No syllogistic utility comes from

  If it is day, it is light
  But it is day
  Therefore it is day

—nor in general from what the more recent philosophers call non-differently concluding arguments. ... For a syllogism is a tool, and it is taken up for some useful purpose—for showing something. So what is not useful is not a syllogism at all.

                                                      (*in APr* 18.12–22)[52]

---

[52] πάνυ δὲ καλῶς τὸ δεῖν ἕτερον τῶν τεθέντων εἶναι τὸ συμπέρασμα προσέθηκεν· ἄχρηστον γὰρ καὶ συλλογιστικῆς χρείας φθαρτικὸν τὸ τὸ ὁμολογούμενον καὶ κείμενον ἐπιφέρειν. τὸ γὰρ χρειῶδες τοῦ συλλογισμοῦ οὐ παρέχεται τὸ εἰ ἡμέρα ἐστίν, φῶς ἐστιν· ἀλλὰ μὴν ἡμέρα ἐστίν· ἡμέρα ἄρα ἐστί, καὶ ὅλως οἱ λεγόμενοι ὑπὸ τῶν νεωτέρων ἀδιαφόρως περαίνοντες.

The 'more recent philosophers'—Alexander is referring to the Stoic logicians—studied certain sorts of argument which Aristotle excluded from the domain of syllogistic. Perhaps their exclusion was an unforeseen consequence of Aristotle's definition? Alexander does not think so: he notices—in a passage which I have already cited—that Aristotle explicitly repudiates any discussion of the indeterminate sort of possibility inasmuch as such possibility is not subject to scientific study; and then he adds:

> Hence it is clear that, in the case of those items which are useless for proofs and on which he said nothing and the more recent philosophers said their say, he omitted them too because of their uselessness and not because of his own ignorance. I mean, for example, the duplicated arguments ...
>
> (*in APr* 164.27–30)[53]

Aristotle's explicit attitude to certain useless modal arguments shows that he excluded the useless Stoic arguments not from ignorance but from policy: he excluded them because they are not syllogisms, because they do not satisfy one of the conditions which, according to his definition, every syllogism must satisfy.

A modern reader may wonder not merely whether Aristotle presciently rejected a number of arguments which the Stoics were later to promote but also whether the phrase 'something other' will bear the weight which Alexander puts upon it—and he may well be inclined to hope that it will not bear the weight and that Aristotle had no particular qualms about acknowledging arguments which conclude to one of their own premises. (After all, a modern logician has no such qualms.) In the *dictum de omni et nullo* Aristotle offers to explain what it is for one item to be in another as in a whole. But—or so I have urged—the phrase 'in another' is not to be pressed: he means to say what it is for something to be in something as in a whole. In the same way, when he says that the conclusion of a syllogism must be 'something other', perhaps the word 'other' is not to be pressed? Perhaps Aristotle doesn't really mean to exclude arguments which conclude to one of their own premises?

But he does, and Alexander's interpretation is correct. Had Aristotle simply said that the conclusion must be 'something other'—had he written 'from

---

... ὄργανον γὰρ ὁ συλλογισμὸς καὶ χρείας τινὸς χάριν καὶ δείξεως παραλαμβανόμενον, ὥστε τὸ μὴ χρήσιμον οὐδὲ συλλογισμός.

[53] ὅθεν δῆλον ὅτι καὶ ταῦτα περὶ ὧν αὐτὸς μὲν οὐκ εἴρηκε, λέγουσι δὲ οἱ νεώτεροι ἀχρήστων ὄντων πρὸς ἀπόδειξιν, δι' ἀχρηστίαν οὐ δι' ἄγνοιαν παρέλιπεν, οἷοί εἰσιν οἱ διφορούμενοι λόγοι ...

certain items laid down something other results'—then we might reasonably have set aside the strict implications of the word 'other'. But what he actually says is that the conclusion is 'something other than the items laid down'. And the expression 'than the items laid down' show that the word 'other' was conscientiously chosen and that Aristotle intended thereby to exclude certain arguments.

So a syllogism may not conclude to one of its own premises—it may not be repetitive, as I shall say. According to Alexander, repetitive arguments are not syllogisms inasmuch as they have no syllogistic utility. Why not? We might expect a speedy answer. Repetitive arguments cannot be used to prove anything, and for that reason they are not syllogisms. They cannot be used to prove anything because no argument can prove one of its own premises. The premises of a proof, as Aristotle put it, must be prior to the conclusion. Nothing can be prior to itself. So the conclusion of a proof cannot be identical with one of its premises. And quite apart from any Aristotelian reflections on priority, it must seem blindingly evident that a repetitive argument is no way to prove anything. The repetitive argument quoted by Alexander—

> If it is day, it is light.
> But it is day.
> Therefore it is day.

—is not and cannot be a proof that it is day. The useless sort of argument which that example illustrates is characterized by the following schema:

If P, then Q; P: therefore P

Circumscriptively:

> From a conditional and its antecedent, there is a valid inference to its antecedent.

No argument of that form could serve as a proof.

That would be enough for Galen. In principle, it is enough for Alexander. But in fact Alexander says rather more:

We shall see that this species of argument is not useful if we run through the species of arguments and ask in which of them it might be appropriate to infer one of the items laid down. In probative arguments?—But such arguments try to reveal what is unclear by way of what is evident and familiar, and what is posterior by way of what is prior. In dialectical arguments?—But such arguments try to show something which the interlocutor is unwilling to concede, and to do so by way of reputable items and items which he concedes, thus bringing him to a contradiction. In eristic arguments?—But they too are supposed to bring the answerer either to a contradiction or to an apparent contradiction by way of what he grants. They do not conclude to what he grants: they conclude by way of what he grants to what he is unwilling to grant, so that it is clear that they will conclude to something other that what is granted. Now if a genus exists in its own species, and if the syllogism is a genus of its species, and if in none of the species is the conclusion the same as a premiss, then it will not be so either in syllogism in general.

(in APr 18.22–19.3)[54]

All species of syllogism require a certain asymmetry between premisses and conclusion; and those asymmetries make it impossible for a syllogism to conclude to one of its premisses.

Alexander's argument is strange in one respect: surely a repetitive argument—suitably disguised by a glib sophist—might be just the ticket for a neat eristic refutation? In eristic argument, anything goes. You would expect Alexander to have urged that eristic syllogisms are syllogisms only homonymously, or else that the phrase 'eristic syllogism', like 'rhetorical syllogism', must be construed as a whole and does not designate a species of syllogism.

SOME PREDICATIVE PROBLEMS

Galen thinks that the Stoic logicians are peculiarly given to the study of useless forms of argument.

---

[54] ὅτι δὲ οὐ χρήσιμον τὸ τοιοῦτον εἶδος μάθοιμεν ἄν εἰ ἐπέλθοιμεν τὰ εἴδη τοῦ συλλογισμοῦ καὶ ἐξετάσαιμεν τίνι αὐτῶν οἰκεῖον τὸ τῶν κειμένων τι ἐπιφέρειν. πότερον γὰρ τῷ ἀποδεικτικῷ; ἀλλ' οὗτός γε τὸ ἄδηλον πειρᾶται διὰ τῶν φανερῶν καὶ γνωρίμων ἐκκαλύπτειν καὶ τὸ ὕστερον διὰ τῶν πρώτῳ. ἀλλὰ τῷ διαλεκτικῷ; ἀλλὰ καὶ οὗτος ὃ μὴ βούλεται συγχωρεῖν ὁ προσδιαλεγόμενος, τοῦτο πειρᾶται διὰ τῶν ἐνδόξων καὶ ὧν συγχωρεῖ δεικνύναι, εἰς ἀντίφασιν περιάγων. ἀλλὰ τῷ ἐριστικῷ; ἀλλὰ καὶ τούτῳ πρόκειται καὶ αὐτῷ ἢ εἰς ἀντίφασιν ἢ εἰς φαινομένην ἀντίφασιν περιαγαγεῖν τὸν ἀποκρινόμενον ἐξ ὧν δίδωσιν· οὐχ ὃ δίδωσι γοῦν συμπεραίνεται, ἀλλ' ἐξ ὧν δίδωσιν ὃ οὐ βούλεται δοῦναι· δῆλον οὖν ὡς ἄλλο τι τοῦ δεδομένου ἐποίσει. εἰ δ' ἐστὶ τὸ γένος ἐν τοῖς εἴδεσι τοῖς αὐτοῦ, καὶ ἔστιν ὁ συλλογισμὸς γένος τῶν αὐτοῦ εἰδῶν, ἐν οὐδενὶ δὲ αὐτῶν ταὐτὸν τῷ εἰλημμένῳ τὸ ἐπιφερόμενον, οὐδ' ἂν ἐν συλλογισμῷ εἴη ὅλως.

Against the Stoics, it is necessary to develop a long argument. They are men who are very well trained in the useless parts of logical theory whereas in the useful parts they are both entirely untrained and also brought up on bad methods of argument; so that it is necessary not only to teach them what is useful but also, and first, to wean them off the bad.

(PHP v 225–226)[55]

Galen exaggerates—Galen always exaggerates. But one of the items on which he has his mind is the repetitive argument, and he may well have supposed that such arguments were a Stoic property. Certainly, all the examples of repetitive arguments which Alexander considers are taken from Stoic logic; and Alexander does not stop to ask whether they may not have their counterparts in Aristotle's predicative syllogistic.

In fact, it is perfectly easy to construct such counterparts. Here is one:

Horses are animals, and animals are animals—so horses are animals.

The argument is repetitive inasmuch as its conclusion is identical with its first premiss. So the argument is not a syllogism: it cannot show any syllogistic utility; and in particular it cannot be used to prove that horses are animals. More generally, no argument of the form:

A holds of every B
B holds of every B
Therefore A holds of every B

can be probative. Such items are exactly on a level with the repetitive Stoic items to which Alexander refuses the title of syllogism and which he takes Aristotle's definition to exclude.

In arguments of that sort there are only two distinct terms, A and B. Consider, then, another argument which has only two distinct terms in it:

Men can laugh and anything which can laugh is a man—so men are men.

That is not a repetitive argument insofar as its conclusion is not identical with either of its premisses; but it is an argument which could not constitute an Aristotelian proof, if only because its premisses are not prior to its conclusion.

---

[55] πρὸς μέντοι τοὺς Στωϊκοὺς ἀναγκαῖόν ἐστι μακρὸν ἀνύεσθαι λόγον, ἀνθρώπους ἐν μὲν τοῖς ἀχρήστοις τῆς λογικῆς θεωρίας ἱκανῶς γεγυμνασμένους, ἐν δὲ τοῖς χρησίμοις ἀγυμναστοτάτους τε ἅμα καὶ μοχθηραῖς ὁδοῖς ἐπιχειρημάτων ἐντεθραμμένους· ὥστε ἀναγκαῖον εἶναι μὴ μόνον διδάσκειν αὐτοὺς ὅσον χρηστὸν ἀλλὰ πολὺ πρότερον ἀποστῆσαι τοῦ μοχθηροῦ.

In general, the Aristotelian conditions on proof will not tolerate any argument of the form:

A holds of every B.
B holds of every A.
Therefore A holds of every A.

Hence—on Alexander's and Galen's principles—such an argument form is not syllogistic.

Unlike the repetitive form, that form is not excluded by the clause in Aristotle's definition which demands that the conclusion be 'something other' than the premisses; nor is it excluded by any other clause in the definition. How then is it to be shut out? Aristotle begins his discussion of predicative syllogisms by saying that 'when three terms are so related to one another...' (*APr* 25b32);[56] and he thinks he can show that 'every proof will be through three terms' (41b36).[57] He does not say 'three different terms'; and his definition of the syllogism does not specify that the terms of a syllogism be different—indeed, it does not mention terms at all. But all of Aristotle's illustrative syllogisms invoke three different concrete terms; and a reader of the *Analytics* is likely to suppose, without reflecting on the matter, that the three terms of any syllogism must be different from one another—and perhaps he will also surmise that the different Greek letters which Aristotle uses picture that fact.

Alexander pretty clearly thought that a syllogism must contain three distinct terms, although so far as I have noticed he nowhere says so explicitly. For example, he once or twice refers to the middle term of a syllogism as 'the term which is taken twice over' (e.g. *in APr* 46.21):[58] that description picks out a particular term only on the assumption that every syllogism contains three distinct terms.

Just as a modern logician might hope that Aristotle did not really mean to require that the conclusion of a syllogism be different from its premisses, so he might hope that Aristotle did not really mean to insist that the terms of a syllogism be distinct from one another. The second hope is less forlorn than the first. After all, Aristotle never speaks explicitly of three different terms. Moreover, there is a passage in the *Analytics* in which—or so it is generally said—he expressly allows for the repetition of a term:

---

[56] ὅταν οὖν ὅροι τρεῖς οὕτως ἔχωσι πρὸς ἀλλήλους ὥστε ...
[57] πᾶσα ἀπόδειξις ἔσται διὰ τριῶν ὅρων ...
[58] ὁ δὶς λαμβανόμενος.

When A holds of the whole B and of C and is predicated of nothing else, and B holds of every C, then it is necessary for A and B to convert. For since A is said only of B and of C, and B is predicated both of itself and of C, it is evident that B will be said of everything of which A is said except of A itself.

(APr 68a16–21)⁵⁹

The argument runs thus: Suppose that A holds of every B and of every C, and of no other term. Suppose, secondly, that B holds of every B and of every C. Then B holds of every term of which A holds.

The argument explicitly supposes that B holds of every B; it implicitly supposes—in its last clause—that A holds of every A. And surely Aristotle must think, quite generally, that any term holds of all of itself? After all, to think that is to think that every so-and-so is a so-and-so—and who would be bold enough to deny that every gander is a gander and every goose a goose?

Nonetheless, it is only in this passage that Aristotle plainly admits that all ganders are ganders; and the passage is a curious one. It is curious in part because it invokes conversion in an odd sort of way. Normally, to say of two terms, A and B, that they convert is to say that A holds of every B and B of every A. Here, Aristotle says that A and B convert inasmuch as A holds of every B and B holds of all of everything of all of which A holds: that is to say, A holds of every B and for any X, if A holds of every X, then B holds of every X. What Aristotle says is true; for—as I have already noted in another context—B holds of every A if and only if B holds of all of everything of all of which A holds. Nonetheless, Aristotle's formulation is unusual—and it has misled more readers than one.

And there is more. For what Aristotle actually says is that A holds of every B and B holds of everything of which A holds except of A. And that is worse than odd—it is incoherent. At any rate, Aristotle appears to be denying that B holds of every A—and yet the suppositions of the argument ensure that there is no A of which B fails to hold.

Perhaps a closer analysis will find a more charitable interpretation. But whatever it means, the passage does not suggest, let alone establish, that syllogisms may contain fewer than three distinct terms. After all, it does not produce or discuss any syllogism. It is one thing to allow that every term holds of all of itself, another to admit such self-predications as components

---

⁵⁹ ὅταν δὲ τὸ Α ὅλῳ τῷ Β καὶ τῷ Γ ὑπάρχῃ καὶ μηδενὸς ἄλλου κατηγορῆται, ὑπάρχῃ δὲ καὶ τὸ Β παντὶ τῷ Γ, ἀνάγκη τὸ Α καὶ Β ἀντιστρέφειν· ἐπεὶ γὰρ κατὰ μόνων τῶν Β Γ λέγεται τὸ Α, κατηγορεῖται δὲ τὸ Β καὶ αὐτὸ αὑτοῦ καὶ τοῦ Γ, φανερὸν ὅτι καθ' ὧν τὸ Α, καὶ τὸ Β λεχθήσεται πάντων πλὴν αὐτοῦ τοῦ Α.

of syllogisms. No doubt all geese are geese—but perhaps such empty propositions have no place in real syllogisms?

There are a few other passages in the *Organon*, and in the commentaries upon it, which bear upon—or might be taken to bear upon—the question. But they do not overthrow the strong and general impression that syllogisms must contain three distinct terms. And I suppose that that impression is a fair representation, not of Aristotle's considered view of the matter, but of his implicit preconceptions about it.

If a syllogism must contain three distinct terms, then the argument

A holds of every B
B holds of every A
Therefore A holds of every A

is not a syllogism. Moreover, if syllogisms must contain three distinct terms, and if in addition each term in the conclusion must appear in exactly one of the premisses, then the conclusion of a syllogism must be different from each of its premisses, so that no repetitive argument is a syllogism. And that suggests that a utilitarian logician might have done well to rewrite Aristotle's definition: replace the clause which forbids repetitiveness in the conclusion by a clause which forbids repetition among the terms. The latter clause is necessary to exclude certain non-syllogisms; and if the latter clause is in place, the former clause is superfluous.

But how, it will be asked, can an Aristotelian consistently reject the two forms

A holds of every B
B holds of every B
Therefore A holds of every B

and

A holds of every B
B holds of every A
Therefore A holds of every A?

Surely those forms are special cases of Barbara—special cases of the general form:

A holds of every B
B holds of every C
Therefore A holds of every C?

Rejecting the two special cases involves the rejection of Barbara.

Not so. If Aristotle's definition is understood aright—or if it is appropriately rewritten—then the two unwanted forms are not special cases of Barbara; for Barbara is a syllogistic form, and the two special cases are not syllogistic forms. True, any syllogism of the form:

A holds of every B
B holds of every C
Therefore A holds of every C

is in Barbara; but it does not follow, and it is not true, that any argument of the form

A holds of every B
B holds of every C
Therefore A holds of every C

is in Barbara. For not every argument of that form is a syllogism.

It might be objected that the revised definition of the syllogism is unsatisfactory until some account of the identity of terms is supplied: if we can't count terms—if we don't know the criteria for their identity and diversity—then we shan't be able to tell a syllogism from a non-syllogism. The objection is a good one; but the same sort of remark can be made in connection with the unrevised definition: in order to understand that definition, we must be competent at counting propositions; for otherwise how can we tell if the conclusion is or is not other than the premisses? And counting Aristotelian propositions, it may be suspected, involves counting terms.

Such questions of identity have a modern ring to them; and there is no general discussion of them in any ancient text which I know of. But they are addressed in a particular context by Alexander. The context will occupy me a little later. Here is an anticipatory snippet:

It is not because 'It is not night' is other in expression than 'It is day' that they are not the same as one another. For where items which differ in expression signify the same item in the same way and primarily, then they make the same proposition, even if they are different utterances. For 'He has a dagger' and 'He has a poniard', if they are said of the same person, are the same proposition, because the same item is signified primarily by 'dagger' and by 'poniard'. So if 'It is not night' meant that it is day in the same way as 'It is day' does, in that case the propositions—the one saying it is day and the one saying it is not night—would not be different just because the expressions are different. Rather, it is because the two—'It is day' and 'It is not night'—do not mean the same thing primarily that they are other than and not the same as one another. For 'It is day' primarily posits that it is day and incidentally rejects that it is night, whereas its not being night primarily rejects night and incidentally posits day inasmuch as if it is not night then necessarily it is day.

(*in Top* 12.10–24)[60]

There are minor infelicities there of a sort which makes modern logicians turn pale and grind their teeth. But the central message is clear. The condition of identity for propositions is this: Two sentences express the same proposition if and only if they have the same primary meaning. No doubt we may say something similar for terms: Two term-expressions express the same term if and only if they have the same primary meaning.

Alexander's criterion is clear to the extent that the adverb 'primarily' is clear. In other words, not to a very great extent. Consider the following case. Definitions are among the principles of any science; and the principles function as premisses of the probative syllogisms which establish the theorems of the science. So a sentence such as

Every man is a two-legged rational animal

ought to be able to feature in syllogisms—in probative syllogisms. Hence it ought to have a different primary meaning from the sentence

Every man is a man,

a sentence which cannot feature in the expression of a syllogism. That is to say,

Every man is a two-legged rational animal

ought to contain two distinct terms. In that case, 'man' and 'two-legged rational animal' are distinct terms, and so ought to have different primary meanings. But a *definiens* and its *definiendum* must surely have the same meaning—how, otherwise, could the former define the latter? Well, of course they have the same meaning. But perhaps—or so Alexander must and presumably would claim—they do not have the same primary meaning. Perhaps that presumed claim is actually a true claim; but in order to assess it, we shall need

---

[60] οὐ γὰρ διότι ἕτερον τῇ λέξει τὸ οὐκ ἔστι νύξ τοῦ ἡμέρα ἐστί, διὰ τοῦτο οὐκ ἔστιν αὐτῷ ταὐτόν· ἐν οἷς γὰρ διαφέροντά τινα κατὰ τὴν λέξιν τοῦ αὐτοῦ τινος ὁμοίως καὶ προηγουμένως ἐστὶ δηλωτικά, ταῦτα τὴν αὐτὴν πρότασιν ποιεῖ, εἰ καὶ φωνὴν ἔχει διάφορον· τὸ γὰρ οὗτος ξίφος ἔχει τῷ οὗτος μάχαιραν ἔχει, εἰ ἐπὶ τοῦ αὐτοῦ λέγοιτο, ἡ αὐτὴ πρότασις, ὅτι ὑπὸ τοῦ ξίφους καὶ τῆς μαχαίρας τὸ αὐτὸ προηγουμένως δηλοῦται. οὕτως οὖν, εἰ καὶ τὸ οὐκ ἔστι νύξ τὸ ἡμέραν εἶναι ὁμοίως ἐσήμαινεν τῷ ἡμέρα ἐστίν, οὐ διὰ τὸ ἑτέραν εἶναι τὴν λέξιν ἕτεραι ἂν αἱ προτάσεις ἐγένοντο, ἥ τε λέγουσα ἡμέρα ἐστί καὶ ἡ λέγουσα οὐκ ἔστι νύξ, ἀλλ' ἐπεὶ ταὐτὸν προηγουμένως ἑκάτερον οὐ σημαίνει, τό τε ἡμέρα ἐστί καὶ οὐκ ἔστι νύξ, διὰ τοῦτο ἕτερα καὶ οὐ ταὐτὰ ἀλλήλοις. τὸ μὲν γὰρ ἡμέρα ἐστί προηγουμένως μὲν τίθησι τὸ ἡμέραν εἶναι, κατὰ συμβεβηκὸς δὲ ἀναιρεῖ τὸ εἶναι νύκτα· τὸ δὲ μὴ εἶναι νύκτα προηγουμένως μὲν ἀναιρεῖ τὴν νύκτα, κατὰ συμβεβηκὸς δὲ τίθησι τὴν ἡμέραν τῷ μὴ οὔσης νυκτὸς ἐξ ἀνάγκης ἡμέραν εἶναι.

to be told how to distinguish between the primary meaning of a term and the meaning of a term. Alexander does not help us towards such a distinction.

Nevertheless, let us suppose that such questions have been answered, and let us accept the revision of Aristotle's definition which stipulates that all the terms in any syllogism be distinct. Does not everything then swim along as before? Well, stipulations sometimes have unforeseen consequences. Here is a simple example.

In his commentary on the *Analytics* Alexander states—and ascribes to Aristotle—a general principle which he calls the synthetic theorem:

Here he delineates for us, rather clearly, the so-called synthetic theorem, which he himself discovered. Its circumscription is this: When an item is concluded from certain items, and the item concluded together with an item or items concludes to an item, then the items which were concludent of it, together with the item or items with which the last item is concluded, will themselves conclude to that same item. For, he says, the items which concluded to A and B through which C (say) was shown themselves conclude to what is concluded by A and B, namely C.

(*in APr* 274.20–25)[61]

Alexander's circumscription is marginally less opaque and convoluted in his Greek than it is in my English. This is what he means: 'When an item is concluded from certain items'—that is to say, given that

$P_1, P_2, \ldots, P_n$: therefore Q

is a syllogism; 'and the item concluded [i.e. Q] together with an item or items concludes to an item'—that is to say, given also that

$Q, R_1, R_2, \ldots, R_m$: therefore S

is a syllogism; 'then the items which were concludent of it [i.e. $P_1, P_2, \ldots, P_n$, which concluded to Q], together with the item or items with which the last item is concluded [i.e. $R_1, R_2, \ldots, R_m$, which conclude to S], will themselves conclude to that same item'—that is, to S.

In other words:

If '$P_1, P_2, \ldots, P_n$: therefore Q' is a syllogism, and '$Q, R_1, R_2, \ldots, R_m$: therefore S' is a syllogism, then '$P_1, P_2, \ldots, P_n, R_1, R_2, \ldots, R_m$: therefore S' is a syllogism.

---

[61] ὑπογράφει ἡμῖν φανερώτερον τὸ λεγόμενον συνθετικὸν θεώρημα, οὗ αὐτός ἐστιν εὑρετής. ἔστι δὲ ἡ περιοχὴ αὐτοῦ τοιαύτη· ὅταν ἔκ τινων συνάγηταί τι, τὸ δὲ συναγόμενον μετὰ τινὸς ἢ τινῶν συνάγῃ τι, καὶ τὰ συνακτικὰ αὐτοῦ, μεθ' οὗ ἢ μεθ' ὧν συνάγεται ἐκεῖνο, καὶ αὐτὰ τὸ αὐτὸ συνάξει. τὰ γὰρ τῶν Α Β συνακτικά, δι' ὧν δείκνυται τὸ Γ φέρε εἰπεῖν, ταῦτα συνάγειν φησὶ καὶ τὸ ὑπὸ τῶν Α Β συναγόμενον, ὃ ἦν τὸ Γ.

Alexander states that the theorem is to be found in the *Analytics*, and he also states that the Stoics took it and divided it up in order to form certain theorems of their own. Neither of those statements is particularly plausible, so far as the history of logic is concerned; and from a logical point of view it is not clear how—or that—you can cut the theorem up and produce the Stoic theorems. But I shall not chase those nifty hares. For in any event, the synthetic theorem seems to be a true theorem, and it is surely a powerful theorem.

Consider, for example, the three-premissed syllogism which I discussed briefly in another context:

A holds of every B; B holds of every C; C holds of every D: therefore A holds of every D.

The validity of that syllogism can be proved, as we saw, on the basis of Barbara. It can equally well be proved by an application of the synthetic theorem. An instance of the theorem is this:

If 'A holds of every B, B holds of every C: therefore A holds of every C' is a syllogism, and 'A holds of every C, C holds of every D: therefore A holds of every D' is a syllogism, then 'A holds of every B, B holds of every C, C holds of every D: therefore A holds of every D' is a syllogism.

The antecedent of that conditional proposition is true, for it says of a couple of syllogisms in Barbara that each is a syllogism. Hence the consequent is true—and the consequent states that the argument in question is a syllogism.

But now consider the following argument, which is a special case of the three-premissed syllogism which has just been proved valid:

A holds of every B, B holds of every C, C holds of every B: therefore A holds of every B.

That argument is not a syllogism; for its conclusion is identical with one of its premises. And yet it can be proved by an application of the synthetic theorem. For

A holds of every B, B holds of every C: therefore A holds of every C

and

A holds of every C, C holds of every B: therefore A holds of every B

are two impeccable syllogisms in Barbara.

So either there are syllogisms in which the conclusion repeats a premiss or else the synthetic theorem must be abandoned or modified. An apparently innocuous stipulation has unanticipated effects. Tinker with a system here, and it is likely to go out of kilter there. To be sure, the unanticipated effect in the case before us is not a catastrophe; for it is easy enough to modify the synthetic theorem. But modification is one of those activities which goes on and on—you can never be sure that there isn't another unexpected difficulty which requires another modification. Is it worth the fuss? Why not allow that some syllogistic forms are useless? The stipulation that a syllogism be useful, and that it be capable of delivering the probative goods, is merely that—a stipulation. Nothing is lost by dropping it: you will not find yourself suddenly producing non-probative arguments as if they were proofs.

DUPLICATED ARGUMENTS

Alexander does not discuss repetitive arguments which are predicative in structure. He thinks that the phrase 'something other' in Aristotle's definition was designed to outlaw certain argument-forms which the Stoic logicians would later patronize. If we take Alexander's words woodenly, then what he says is scarcely credible; for there is no reason to believe that Aristotle—or any of his contemporaries—had dreamed up duplicated arguments, and his definition of the syllogism cannot have been intended to outlaw a set of arguments of which he had never heard. But Alexander is right if we construe his words more generously; for presumably Aristotle deliberately excluded any arguments, of whatever form they might be and whencesoever they might emanate, in which the conclusion repeated one of the premisses.

Aristotle's definition of the syllogism excludes repetition. We have no rival definition from the Stoics—or from anyone else. Sextus says that, according to the logicians, an argument is a system of premisses and conclusions; and he further explains—in a passage I have already quoted—that

of arguments, some are concludent and others non-concludent. An argument is concludent when the conditional which starts from the conjunction of its premisses and ends in its conclusion is sound.

(*PH* ii 137)

But not all concludent arguments are syllogisms, and Sextus offers no account of how to differentiate syllogistic from non-syllogistic arguments—indeed, he does not notice a distinction between syllogistic and non-syllogistic arguments. Diogenes Laertius tells us that, according to the Stoics,

an argument is a system constituted from assumptions and conclusion, and a syllogism is a syllogistic argument so constituted.

(vii 45)[62]

But that is perfectly unilluminating.

True, a later passage in Diogenes' account of Stoic logic seems more promising.[63]

Of valid arguments, some share their name with the genus and are called valid, whereas others are called syllogistic. Syllogistic are those arguments which either are unproved or else reduce to the unproveds by virtue of one or more of the themata.

(vii 78)[64]

Syllogistic arguments are presumably the same things as syllogisms; so we may infer that an argument, according to the Stoics, is a syllogism if and only if either it is one of the unproveds or else it can be proved valid on the basis of the unproveds and by the aid of the 'themata' or rules of reduction.

No doubt that is true—but it is not an explanation of what the word 'syllogism' means. It says which arguments are in fact syllogisms: it does not say what it is about them which makes them syllogistic. It is as though you were to say that a man is a mafioso if and only if he is either a head of one of the Five Families or a henchman of one of the heads.

In the light of that meagre evidence, it is difficult to determine how the Stoic conception of a syllogism differed from the Aristotelian conception (if indeed it differed at all). Nevertheless, scholars generally suppose that the Stoic notion differed from the Aristotelian in at least one significant particular; for whereas Aristotle required that the conclusion of a syllogism be other than its premisses, surely the Stoics did not—on the contrary, they welcomed repetitive syllogisms. Perhaps they did; but it should be said that even that orthodox and unexciting claim goes beyond the texts at our disposal. For although Alexander says that the Stoic logicians studied certain arguments which are not syllogisms and which therefore—in his view—should not fall

---

[62] εἶναι δὲ τὸν λόγον αὐτὸν σύστημα ἐκ λημμάτων καὶ ἐπιφορᾶς· τὸν δὲ συλλογισμὸν λόγον συλλογιστικὸν ἐκ τούτων.

[63] Susanne Bobzien reminded me of the passage.

[64] τῶν δὲ περαντικῶν λόγων οἱ μὲν ὁμωνύμως τῷ γένει λέγονται περαντικοί· οἱ δὲ συλλογιστικοί. συλλογιστικοὶ μὲν οὖν εἰσιν οἱ ἤτοι ἀναπόδεικτοι ὄντες ἢ ἀναγόμενοι ἐπὶ τοὺς ἀναποδείκτους κατά τι τῶν θεμάτων ἢ τινα.

under the eye of the serious logician, he does not explicitly say that the Stoics treated those arguments as syllogisms.

However that may be, among the Stoic arguments which sinned by repetition were the so-called duplicated arguments, of which the stock example is this:

> If it is day, it is day.
> But it is day.
> Therefore it is day.

No doubt it is perfectly evident that no argument of that form can prove its conclusion, and hence—on the Alexandrian view—that the form is not a syllogistic form.

Nonetheless, in the commentary on the *Analytics* Alexander offers a suite of seven reasons for thinking that no such argument is a syllogism. The most interesting of them runs like this:

> Again, if it is non-syllogistic to co-assume the consequent of a conditional, and if in conditionals of this sort the antecedent is the same as the consequent, then the co-assumption is no more of the antecedent than of the consequent.
>
> (*in APr* 20.13–16)[65]

I argue thus:

> If it is day, then it is day
> It is day
> Therefore: it is day

What is my second premiss? Why, it is the consequent of my first premiss; so that my argument is a case of affirming the consequent—it has the general form:

> If P, then Q
> Q
> Therefore P

Circumscriptively:

> From a conditional and its consequent, there is a valid inference to its antecedent.

And that form is certainly non-syllogistic—after all, it is invalid.

---

[65] ἔτι τε εἰ ἡ τοῦ ἑπομένου πρόσληψις ἐν τοῖς συνεχέσιν ἀσυλλόγιστος, ἐν δὲ τοῖς τοιούτοις συνεχέσι ταὐτὸν τὸ ἡγούμενον τῷ ἑπομένῳ, ἡ πρόσληψις οὐ μᾶλλον τοῦ ἡγουμένου ἢ τοῦ ἑπομένου γίνεται.

Alexander is right to this extent: the duplicated argument which he cites does have the invalid form which we associate with the vice of affirming the consequent. But so what? Alexander invites us to infer that the duplicated argument is non-syllogistic on the grounds that it has an invalid form. But—as I have already recalled—every valid argument has numerous forms, among them invalid forms. Every predicative syllogism has invalid forms—after all, every predicative syllogism has the form

P, Q : therefore R.

That does not show that no predicative argument is not a syllogism, still less that none is valid. An argument is valid provided that at least one of the several forms which it has is a valid form, and it is syllogistic provided that at least one of its several forms is a syllogistic form.

In that case, Alexander's duplicated argument is a valid argument. For it has the following form, among others:

If P, then Q
P
Therefore Q

That is to say, the argument is a special case of the Stoic first unproved. So if Alexander rejects the argument as non-syllogistic, then presumably he must reject the Stoic first unproved as non-syllogistic.

Well, in fact Alexander does not think that first unproved arguments are syllogisms. Indeed, he does not think that any hypothetical arguments are syllogisms. When he comments upon Aristotle's 'syllogisms based on a hypothesis', which he identifies with hypothetical arguments, he has this to say:

As to Aristotle's expression, it is worth noting that he does not say that the hypotheticals are syllogisms without qualification but he does say that they conclude ... and that they are syllogisms based on a hypothesis (the phrase being taken as a whole). ... They will be simply concludent when the co-assumption is not posited by way of a syllogism, and hypothetical syllogisms when they have a co-assumption taken by way of a syllogism. Thus for Aristotle things are the opposite of what the more recent thinkers claim: hypothetical arguments are concludent but not syllogisms, as we have already said, whereas predicative arguments are syllogisms.

(*in APr* 390.9–18)[66]

---

[66] ἐκεῖνο δὲ ἄξιον ἐκ τῆς λέξεως ἐπισημήνασθαι ὅτι συλλογισμοὺς μὲν ἁπλῶς οὐ λέγει τοὺς ὑποθετικοὺς εἶναι, περαίνειν μέντοι αὐτοὺς λέγει, ... καὶ τὸ ὅλον ἐξ ὑποθέσεως συλλογισμούς· ... εἶεν δ᾽ ἂν περαίνοντες μὲν μόνον ὧν ἡ πρόσληψις οὐ διὰ συλλογισμοῦ τίθεται, ἐξ ὑποθέσεως

'As we have already said': earlier Alexander has explained that predicative arguments

> are syllogisms without qualification: the hypotheticals are not syllogisms without qualification but hypothetical syllogisms (the phrase being taken as a whole). For predicative arguments have no need of hypotheses in order to show the point at issue (that is why they are syllogisms without qualification, being sufficient in themselves), whereas hypothetical arguments show nothing without predicatives.
>
> (*in APr* 265.19–23)[67]

The phrase 'hypothetical syllogism', like the phrase 'rhetorical syllogism', does not designate a kind or species of syllogism: hypothetical syllogisms are not syllogisms at all. For a hypothetical syllogism cannot prove anything—or at least, it cannot prove anything unless it is aided by a predicative syllogism.

No first unproved is a syllogism. Every first unproved is a concludent or valid argument. A first unproved is a hypothetical syllogism if it is embedded in a longer argument—if its second premiss is the conclusion of a genuine syllogism. But hypothetical syllogisms are not syllogisms. They are false noses. Some Stoics—or at any rate, some of the younger logicians—had claimed that predicative arguments are not syllogisms and that hypothetical arguments are syllogisms. The truth—Alexander maintains—is the other way about: predicative arguments are syllogisms and hypothetical arguments are not syllogisms.

Alexander's reason for denying that hypothetical syllogisms are syllogisms will not stand examination; and as for the young Turks who denied that predicative syllogisms are syllogisms, we do not know how they urged their case, nor is it easy to imagine any persuasive advocacy on their behalf.

However that may be, insofar as Alexander holds that hypothetical arguments in general are not syllogisms, he has no need to argue that his duplicated argument in particular is not a syllogism. Nevertheless, he does so. Does that signify that, despite his official line, he is sometimes prepared to accept that certain

---

δὲ συλλογισμοὶ οἱ τὴν πρόσληψιν ἔχοντες εἰλημμένην διὰ συλλογισμοῦ· ὥστε ἀνάπαλιν κατ' αὐτόν ἢ ὡς οἱ νεώτεροι ἀξιοῦσιν, οἱ ὑποθετικοὶ λόγοι περαντικοὶ μὲν οὐ συλλογισμοὶ δέ, ὥσπερ φθάνομεν εἰρηκότες, συλλογισμοὶ δ' οἱ κατηγορικοί.

[67] διὸ καὶ ἁπλῶς ἐκεῖνοι συλλογισμοί, οἱ δ' ἐξ ὑποθέσεως οὐχ ἁπλῶς, ἀλλὰ τὸ ὅλον τοῦτο ἐξ ὑποθέσεως συλλογισμοί· οἱ μὲν γὰρ κατηγορικοὶ οὐδέν προσδέονται πρὸς τὸ δεῖξαι τὸ προκείμενον τῶν ὑποθέσεων (διὸ καὶ ἁπλῶς συλλογισμοὶ ἀρκοῦντες αὐτοῖς), οἱ δὲ ὑποθετικοὶ χωρὶς τούτων οὐδὲν δεικνύουσιν.

hypothetical arguments—for example, non-duplicated first unproveds—are genuine syllogisms? Or should we rather infer that when he argues against his duplicated argument he intends to show not merely that it is not a syllogism but that it is not even a hypothetical syllogism—better, that it cannot even function as a hypothetical syllogism?

The latter option is seductive; and although it must be admitted that there is no whiff of it in Alexander's text, it is certainly an option which he might have taken. For consider the following form of argument:

A holds of every B; B holds of every C; if A holds of every C, then P: therefore P.

That form can be shown to be valid, thus:

(1) A holds of every B   premiss
(2) B holds of every C   premiss
(3) If A holds of every C, then P premiss
(4) A holds of every C   1, 2, Barbara
(5) P   3, 4, first unproved

An argument of that sort might, according to Alexander, be a proof that P (or perhaps rather a hypothetical proof that P). And the hypothetical argument which forms part of it—steps (3) to (5)—may therefore function as a hypothetical syllogism.

But not every argument of that sort could be a proof that P, or even a hypothetical proof that P. In particular, an argument in which the first unproved is duplicated cannot be a proof. For example, you couldn't prove that A holds of every C by this argument:

(1) A holds of every B   premiss
(2) B holds of every C   premiss
(3) If A holds of every C, then A holds of every C   premiss
(4) A holds of every C   1, 2, Barbara
(5) A holds of every C   3, 4, first unproved

More generally, nothing of the form
   X; Y; if Z then Z: therefore Z
could ever be a proof that Z, nor even a hypothetical proof that Z.

Why not?—Because one of the premisses of any such argument must be redundant, and syllogisms may not have redundant premisses. I cite again Aristotle's definition:

A syllogism is a saying in which, certain items being laid down, something other than the items laid down comes about by necessity from the fact that they are the case.

(APr 24b18–20)

The conclusion must come about 'from the fact that they are the case': Alexander comments that

by this addition he will exclude arguments which contain any redundant element.

(in APr 22.30–23.1)[68]

And in his commentary on the *Topics* he explains that

in arguments in which a redundant proposition has been assumed, the conclusion is not inferred by way of the items laid down inasmuch as even if that proposition is removed it is still possible to make the same inference.

(in Top 13.29–31)[69]

In other words, if

$P_1, P_2, \ldots, P_n$: therefore Q

is a syllogism, then

$P_1, P_2, \ldots, P_n, P_{n+1}$: therefore Q

is not a syllogism. The notion of redundancy requires some refinement; and it may be wondered if Alexander's interpretation of the pertinent clause in the Aristotelian definition is not too elaborate; but it will be allowed that, at bottom, Alexander must be right. Of course, redundancy does not make an argument invalid. But surely it makes it non-probative.

However that may be, Alexander certainly rejects duplicated arguments as non-syllogistic: not every argument which, from a conditional assertible and its antecedent, infers the consequent of the conditional is thereby a syllogism—not even a hypothetical syllogism, or an argument capable of functioning as a hypothetical syllogism. But of course, just as it was possible to keep Barbara while rejecting as non-syllogistic some of its apparent instances, so too it is with the first unproved. The apparent instances of Barbara were not genuine instances inasmuch as Barbara is a syllogistic form and predicative syllogisms—according to the revised definition—have three distinct terms.

---

[68] παραιτοῖντο δ' ἂν διὰ τῆς προσθήκης ταύτης καὶ οἱ παρέλκον τι προσκείμενον ἔχοντες.
[69] ἐν οἷς γὰρ λόγοις πρότασίς τις εἴληπται παρέλκουσα, οὗτοι οὐ διὰ τῶν κειμένων συνάγουσι τὸ συμπέρασμα, εἴ γε καὶ ἀφαιρεθείσης ἐκείνης ἔτι οἷόν τε τὸ αὐτὸ συνάγεσθαι.

In the same way, it might be urged that the apparent instances of the first unproved are not genuine instances inasmuch as a first unproved is a syllogistic form—a hypothetical syllogistic form; and such forms—or so we shall expect a refined definition to require—must have two distinct assertibles.

As a first shot, you might simply stipulate that in a first unproved the antecedent of the conditional premiss be different from its consequent, thus:

Fom a conditional in which the antecedent differs from the consequent, together with its antecedent, there is an inference to its consequent.

But that is not quite good enough to meet Alexander's requirements. For a first unproved can only function as a hypothetical syllogism if the antecedent of its constitutive conditional proposition can be the conclusion of a syllogism—that is to say, of a predicative syllogism. So we must think of something along these lines:

From a conditional in which the antecedent both differs from the consequent and has a predicative form, together with the antecedent, there is an inference to the consequent.

Such a stipulative redefinition will have consequences; and some of them are likely to be tiresome. No Stoic logician had any particular reason for teasing out those consequences and avoiding the unwanted implications; and no Peripatetic logician was likely to bother his head over such matters.

DISJUNCTIVE ARGUMENTS

Alexander's attitude to duplicated instances—or apparent instances—of the first Stoic unproved is scarcely surprising; and we shall expect him to take a similar attitude in the case of the other Stoic unproveds, each of which has a duplicated cousin. To the second unproved there answers
    If P, P; not P: therefore not P.
For the third unproved we may set down:
    Not both P and not P; P: therefore P.
The fourth and the fifth unproveds suggest:
    Either P or not P; P: therefore P.
and
    Either P or not P; not P: therefore not P.
Those four schemata are instances of the last four unproveds in just the way in which the schema of Alexander's duplicated argument is an instance of a

first unproved. (And they can be turned into merely specious instances in the same way as the duplicated form could be turned into a specious instance of the first unproved.)

Alexander says nothing about the first two of those four schemata. But he discusses the last two. Each, he says, is a 'disjunctive syllogism based on a contradiction'. The word 'syllogism' is not a slip. For, contrary to every expectation, Alexander holds that disjunctive arguments based on a contradiction are syllogistical—that is to say, they are, or they may function as, hypothetical syllogisms. This is what he says in the commentary on the *Analytics*:

A disjunctive syllogism based on a contradiction does not infer its conclusion insofar as it is the same as the re-assumption (or the co-assumption, as the more recent thinkers say). For if you say

Either it is day or it is not day,

and then co-assume one of the items in the disjunction—either the negative, 'But it is not day', or the affirmative, 'It is day'—you have as conclusion either 'Therefore it is not day' or 'Therefore it is day', which seem to be the same as the co-assumptions, which were either 'But it is not day' or 'But it is day'. But the conclusion is inferred not insofar as it is the same as the co-assumption but rather insofar as it is opposite to the other item in the disjunction. It happens that, in such syllogisms, the opposite of that item is the same as the co-assumption. But there is a vast difference between taking the conclusion as being primarily the same as one of the premises and taking it as something different which then happens to be the same as it.

                                                      (*in APr* 19.3–15)[70]

Alexander's illustrative arguments are these:

Either it is day or it is not day.	Either it is day or it is not day.
It is day.	It is not day.
Therefore it is day.	Therefore it is not day.

---

[70] ὁ γὰρ ἐξ ἀντιφάσεως διαιρετικὸς συλλογισμὸς οὐχ ὡς ταὐτὸν τῷ μεταλαμβανομένῳ ἤ, ὡς οἱ νεώτεροί φασι, προσλαμβανομένῳ τὸ συμπέρασμα ἐπιφέρει· ὁ γὰρ λέγων ἤτοι ἡμέρα ἐστὶν ἢ οὐκ ἔστιν ἡμέρα, εἶτα προσλαμβάνων τὸ ἕτερον τῶν ἐν τῷ διαιρετικῷ, ἢ τὸ ἀποφατικὸν τὸ ἀλλὰ μὴν οὐκ ἔστιν ἡμέρα ἢ τὸ καταφατικὸν τὸ ἡμέρα ἐστίν, ἔχει μὲν συναγόμενον ἢ τὸ οὐκ ἄρα ἡμέρα ἐστίν ἢ τὸ ἡμέρα ἄρα ἐστίν, ὃ δοκεῖ ταὐτὸν εἶναι τῷ προσειλημμένῳ, ἤτοι τῷ ἀλλὰ μὴν οὐκ ἔστιν ἡμέρα ἢ τῷ ἀλλὰ μὴν ἡμέρα ἐστίν· οὐ μὴν ὡς ταὐτὸν ὂν αὐτῷ ἐπιφέρεται, ἀλλ' ὡς ἀντικείμενον τῷ ἑτέρῳ τῶν ἐν τῷ διαιρετικῷ· συμβαίνει δὲ τὸ ἐκείνῳ ἀντικείμενον ἐν τοῖς τοιούτοις συλλογισμοῖς ταὐτὸν γίνεσθαι τῇ προσλήψει. πάμπολυ δὲ διαφέρει τὸ προηγουμένως ταὐτὸν τῶν κειμένων τινὶ λαβεῖν τὸ συμπέρασμα ἢ λαβεῖν μὲν αὐτὸ ὡς ἄλλο συμπεσεῖν δὲ αὐτῷ τὸ ταὐτὸν αὐτῷ γενέσθαι.

Surely those arguments could not be used to prove that it is day or that it is not day? Surely, no argument of the forms

Either P or not-P	Either P or not-P
P	Not-P
Therefore P	Therefore not-P

could ever be used to prove anything? And for precisely the reason that in each case the conclusion is the same as one of the premises.

Why in heaven does Alexander want to defend such arguments? And how on earth can he do so? I shall address those questions as they apply to the repetitive version of the fourth unproved: the case of the fifth unproved is entirely parallel and needs no separate discussion.

Alexander does not explain why he defends the repetitive fourth unproved; but I suppose that he has his mind on a remark in the *Posterior Analytics*:

That everything is said or denied is assumed by proofs by way of the impossible—and that not always universally but rather so far as is sufficient, and it is sufficient if it is limited to the genus. (By to the genus I mean the genus about which the proofs are being produced.)

(*APst* 77a22–25)[71]

The phrase 'Everything is said or denied' is Aristotle's way of introducing the Law of Excluded Middle; and he means to claim that propositions of the form 'Either P or not P' will sometimes appear in proofs—in proofs by reduction to the impossible. In order to prove that P, you hypothesize that not-P. From the hypothesis you derive an impossibility, thereby establishing that you cannot accept that not-P. But either P or not-P. Hence P.

I have said earlier that ancient accounts of the workings of reduction to the impossible are surprisingly unsatisfactory; and the account implicit in the *Posterior Analytics* is curious enough. But it is Aristotelian—and presumably it explains why Alexander feels himself obliged to approve of certain arguments which, on general grounds, you would expect him to reject. Not that he need feel obliged to accept the arguments as syllogisms. Indeed, he should not do so, for they cannot be used on their own to formulate proofs. But he must accept them as hypothetical syllogisms.

---

[71] τὸ δ' ἅπαν φάναι ἢ ἀποφάναι ἢ εἰς τὸ ἀδύνατον ἀπόδειξις λαμβάνει, καὶ ταῦτα οὐδ' ἀεὶ καθόλου, ἀλλ' ὅσον ἱκανόν, ἱκανὸν δ' ἐπὶ τοῦ γένους. λέγω δ' ἐπὶ τοῦ γένους οἷον περὶ ὃ γένος τὰς ἀποδείξεις φέρει.

But how exactly does the disjunctive argument feature in proofs by reduction to the impossible? Consider Aristotle's proof of the validity of the second figure syllogism Baroco:

> Again, if M holds of every N and not of some X, it is necessary that N does not hold of some X. For if it holds of every X and M is predicated of every N, it is necessary that M holds of every X. But it was supposed that it does not hold of some.
>
> (*APr* 27a36-b1)[72]

There is no sniff of a disjunctive argument in that little proof. True, Aristotle's presentation is clipped; but when Alexander enlarges upon it he does not introduce any disjunction into the argument. Nonetheless, it is easy to formulate a reduction to the impossible which does use the disjunctive syllogism; and I suppose that Aristotle and Alexander must have had something like the following proof in mind:

(1) B holds of every A	premiss
(2) B does not hold of some C	premiss
(3) Either A does not hold of some C or it is not the case that A does not hold of some C	law of excluded middle
(4) It is not the case that A does not hold of some C	hypothesis
(5) A holds of every C	4, contradictories
(6) B holds of every C	1, 5, Barbara
(7) B holds of every C and B does not hold of some C	2, 6
(8) A does not hold of some C	4, 7, impossibility
(9) A does not hold of some C	3, 8, disjunctive syllogism

That is the proof. At the end of it—in the inference from (3) and (8) to (9)—there is a disjunctive argument from a contradiction. That is part of the proof, although it is not in itself a proof of anything. From a two-membered disjunction and one of the disjuncts it infers the opposite of the other disjunct. The second premiss—the disjunct—is introduced as the conclusion of a syllogism in Barbara. So the disjunctive argument may be called a hypothetical syllogism (as Alexander has explained the phrase).

---

[72] πάλιν εἰ τῷ μὲν Ν παντὶ τὸ Μ, τῷ δὲ Ξ τινὶ μὴ ὑπάρχει, ἀνάγκη τὸ Ν τινὶ τῷ Ξ μὴ ὑπάρχειν· εἰ γὰρ παντὶ ὑπάρχει, κατηγορεῖται δὲ καὶ τὸ Μ παντὸς τοῦ Ν, ἀνάγκη τὸ Μ παντὶ τῷ Ξ ὑπάρχειν· ὑπέκειτο δὲ τινὶ μὴ ὑπάρχειν.

A hypothetical syllogism is not thereby a syllogism; and reduction to the impossible does not show that repetitive disjunctive arguments are syllogisms. Alexander ought to have said that he takes such arguments to be hypothetical syllogisms, not syllogisms *tout court*. Perhaps it is not unreasonably generous to think that that is what he intended to say.

If that shows why Alexander wants to defend disjunctive arguments from a contradiction, it does not show how he can do so. But on that point he does attempt to explain himself. He suggests that the disjunctive arguments can be taken in either of two ways: on one reading they are syllogistic, or can function as hypothetical syllogisms, and on the other reading they are non-syllogistic, or cannot function as hypothetical syllogisms. For when you set down the conclusion you may do so either insofar as it is one of the premisses of the argument or else insofar as it is the contradictory of one of the disjuncts in the other premiss. The two readings of the argument might be represented as follows—where bold type indicates how the conclusion is to be attached to the premisses:

(A) Either P or not-P
P
Therefore **P**
(B) Either P or **not-P**
P
Therefore **P**

On reading (A), the argument cannot function as a hypothetical syllogism (let alone as a syllogism); for on reading (A) the conclusion of the argument repeats the second of its premisses. On reading (B), however, there may be a respectable hypothetical syllogism; for in argument (B) the conclusion is distinct from each of the premisses.

Alexander assures us that there is a vast difference between those two ways of taking the arguments; and he explains that

in the latter case <the conclusion> is indeed taken as something other <than the premisses>, since being this particular proposition is different from being opposite to the other item in the disjunction. So they are the same in expression but not in force.

(*in APr* 19.17–19)[73]

---

[73] καὶ τότε οὖν ὡς ἕτερον λαμβάνεται, εἴγε ἕτερόν ἐστι τὸ εἶναι τῷδέ τινι καὶ τὸ εἶναι ἀντικειμένῳ τοῦ ἑτέρου τῶν ἐν τῇ διαιρέσει· τῇ λέξει οὖν ταὐτὸν οὐ τῇ δυνάμει.

On reading (B), the conclusion, although the same in expression as one of the premisses, differs from it 'in force'—or in other words in meaning.

The point, which at first glance looks wholly sophistical, is elaborated in the commentary on the *Topics*:

> That the two are not taken as indicating the same item is clear from the fact that 'It is day' as it is taken in the co-assumption as primarily indicating that it is day, whereas in the inference it is inferred as rejecting 'It is not day', inasmuch as it is equal to 'Therefore it is not not day'. So, just as this does not primarily posit that it is day but rather rejects 'It is not day', so too with 'But it is day', when that is taken in its place—for it is taken in the conclusion as rejecting that proposition, and it is not the same to use it as rejecting that it is not day and as positing that it is day. For if someone uses it in order to reject that it is not day, then if there were something else, other than that it is day, which rejected it, he would make use of that in preference to this. Whereas someone wishing to signify that it is day would not use anything else except that which indicates it.
>
> (*in Top* 12.31–13.10)[74]

The sentence 'It is day' may be used to assert that it is day, and it may be used to deny that it is not day. Provided that it is used in one way in the co-assumption and in another in the conclusion, then there is no problem with the status of the argument.

The good construal of the argument, that is to say, is equivalent to this:

Either P or not P
P
Therefore not not P

There, it is plain that there is no repetitiveness: the conclusion is 'not not P', and that proposition does not figure among the premisses. In the same vein, the proof of Baroco might be emended near the end to read thus:

---

[74] ὅτι δὲ μὴ ὡς τοῦ αὐτοῦ δηλωτικὰ ἀμφότερα λαμβάνεται, δῆλον ἐκ τοῦ τὸ μὲν ἐν τῇ προσλήψει λαμβανόμενον ἡμέρα ἐστίν ὡς προηγουμένως τοῦ εἶναι ἡμέραν δηλωτικὸν προσλαμβάνεσθαι, τὸ δὲ ἐπιφερόμενον ὡς τοῦ οὐκ ἔστιν ἡμέρα ἀναιρετικὸν ἐπιφέρεσθαι, ὡς ἴσον ὂν τῷ οὐκ ἄρα οὐκ ἔστιν ἡμέρα. ὡς οὖν τοῦτο οὐ προηγουμένως τὸ ἡμέραν εἶναι τίθησιν ἀλλ' ἀναιρεῖ τὸ οὐκ ἔστιν ἡμέρα, οὕτως καὶ τὸ ἀλλὰ μὴν ἡμέρα ἐστί τὸ ἀντ' αὐτοῦ λαμβανόμενον· λαμβάνεται γὰρ ἐν τῇ ἐπιφορᾷ ὡς ἀναιροῦν ἐκεῖνο, οὐ ταὐτὸν δὲ τὸ ἢ ὡς ἀναιρετικῷ τοῦ μὴ εἶναι ἡμέραν χρῆσθαι αὐτῷ ἢ ὡς ἡμέραν εἶναι τιθέντι. ὁ μὲν γὰρ ὑπὲρ τοῦ ἀνελεῖν τὸ ἡμέραν μὴ εἶναι χρώμενος αὐτῷ, εἰ ἄλλο τι ἦν τὸ ἀναιροῦν αὐτὸ καὶ μὴ τὸ ἡμέραν εἶναι, ἐκείνῳ ἂν καὶ οὐ τούτῳ ἐχρήσατο· ὁ δὲ βουλόμενος τὸ ἡμέραν εἶναι σημῆναι οὐκ ἂν ἄλλῳ τινὶ ἢ τῷ τούτου δηλωτικῷ χρήσαιτ' ἄν.

(8) A does not hold of some C   4, 7, impossibility

(9) It is not the case that it is not the case
      that A does not hold of some C   3, 8, disjunctive syllogism

(10) A does not hold of some C   9, double negation

If that is the way of construing reductions to the impossible, then they do indeed involve disjunctive arguments from a contradiction; but the disjunctive arguments which they involve are not repetitive arguments, and they do not offend against the 'something other' clause in the Aristotelian definition of the syllogism.

But that cannot be how Alexander himself saw the matter; for had he seen it in that way, then he would have had no reason to discuss disjunctive arguments from a contradiction in his commentary on Aristotle's definition. He discusses such arguments only because they seem to offend against the definition.

What Alexander actually says about the arguments is perplexing. Of course, he is right when he remarks that 'It is day' can be used both to affirm that it is day and also to deny that it is not day. 'It's day', I cry: 'Yes, it's day', you murmur. 'It's not day', I groan. 'It's day', you retort. But his argument for thinking that there is a distinction between these two uses is odd: if I want to affirm that it is day, he says, then there is no sentence I would prefer to the trusty 'It's day'; but if I want to deny that it's not day, then I would choose some other sentence if only there were one—I would choose a sentence whose primary meaning was to deny that it's not day. But there is such a sentence, namely 'It's not not day'.

Again, insofar as Alexander imagines that there is an ambiguity in 'It's day' (and therefore in every sentence whatsoever), he is surely mistaken. In 'No, it's day', the sentence 'It's day' means just what it means in 'Yes, it's day'. Moreover, if there were a difference in meaning, then there would be a difference in meaning between 'It's day' and 'It's not not day'; and in that case—as I have already said—the argument which Alexander defends, and which he needs to defend, is not after all a repetitive argument. In any event, elsewhere, Alexander states that

'It is not not day' differs from 'It is day' only in expression.

(in APr 18.7–8)[75]

But in that case, how can there be any difference in force or meaning between the two uses of 'It's day'?

---

[75] τὸ γὰρ οὐχὶ οὐχ ἡμέρα ἐστί τοῦ ἡμέρα ἐστί μόνῃ τῇ λέξει διαφέρει.

In short, Alexander's attempt to distinguish the syllogistic from the non-syllogistic cases of disjunctive arguments is a failure.

Is it not worse than a failure? After all, if Alexander can find two different ways of taking a disjunctive argument from contradictories, he can surely do the same for duplicated arguments. He can distinguish between

(A)
　If P, P
　P
　Therefore **P**

and

(B)
　If P, **P**
　P
　Therefore **P**

On reading (A), the conclusion repeats the second premiss, and the argument is not syllogistic. On reading (B), the conclusion does not repeat the second premiss; for is there not a vast difference between affirming that so-and-so and setting it down as the consequent of a conditional?

There is a reply to that objection: 'The cases are not parallel; for the duplicated argument, unlike the disjunctive argument, cannot be used as part of a proof—it is not even a hypothetical syllogism.' But the duplicated argument can be used in a proof. Here, for example, is a proof of Cesare:

(1) B holds of no A	premiss
(2) B holds of every C	premiss
(3) If A holds of no C, then A holds of no C	identity
(4) A holds of no B	1, conversion
(5) A holds of no C	2, 4, Celarent
(6) A holds of no C	3, 5, duplicated syllogism

It will be retorted that the presence of the duplicated argument there is redundant; and that therefore—by Alexander's lights—the argument is not a proof. Well, the duplicated argument is indeed redundant. But then so too is the presence of the disjunctive argument in reductions to the impossible: therefore—by Alexander's lights—the reduction to the impossible which was designed to show the validity of Baroco and which contains a redundant disjunctive argument is not a proof.

Nonetheless, if what Alexander actually says about these disjunctive arguments will not wash, there is something washable underlying his words. To be sure, the argument

Either it is day or it is not day.
It is day.
Therefore it is day.

is not ambiguous in the way Alexander intimates. But it does have two distinct logical forms which correspond to the two parts of the alleged ambiguity. It fits the circumscription of the fourth unproved:

From a disjunction and one of its disjuncts, there is a valid inference to an opposite of the other disjunct.

Schematically, and with negation for opposition:

Either P or Q
P
Therefore not Q

Taking the argument in that way corresponds, more or less, to reading it in the virtuous manner. The argument also fits the following circumscription:

From a disjunction composed of an assertible and one of its opposites, together with one of the disjuncts, there is a valid inference to the opposite of the other disjunct.

Schematically, and with negation for opposition:

Either P or not P
P
Therefore P

Taking the argument in that way corresponds, less or more, to the vicious reading. We might therefore say, as it were on Alexander's behalf, that the argument is a syllogism inasmuch as it has the first of those two forms. It is not a syllogism insofar as it has the second form.

The same, of course, goes for duplicated arguments. They have the form of the first Stoic unproved, and insofar as they have that form they are syllogisms. They also have the form

If P, then P
P
Therefore P

—and in virtue of that form they are not syllogisms.

Alexander himself comes perilously close to saying just that. For there is a sentence in his account of duplicated arguments which I have thus far passed over in silence. It is this:

Such a thing can indeed be a syllogistic figure and a syllogistic conjugation, but it cannot be a syllogism.

(*in APr* 18.18–20).[76]

Alexander here applies the Peripatetic terminology of conjugations and figures to hypothetical syllogistic; but it is plain that by 'conjugation' he means the pair of premisses, and by 'figure' the general form or pattern of the argument. In any case, he means to say that a duplicated argument may have a decent syllogistic pedigree. He cannot mean that the duplicated form is itself syllogistic; and he must be referring to the form of the first unproved. Hence he allows that a duplicated argument may be a hypothetical syllogism: it is syllogistic in virtue of having the form of a first unproved.

He immediately adds: 'but it cannot be a syllogism'. If that is not to be incoherent, it must be taken to signify that a duplicated argument is not a hypothetical syllogism in its own right—it is not syllogistic in virtue of being a duplicated argument nor in virtue of the form which it shares with all and only duplicated arguments. It is syllogistic only insofar as it can feature in certain larger arguments. That is a lot to read into the text. But so far as I can see we must either read that (or something very like it) into the text or else leave Alexander to wallow in the mire of incoherence.

It is perhaps worth mentioning that not all repetitive arguments turn out, on this way of looking at things, to be syllogistic. For example the indifferently concluding argument

> If it is day, it is light
> It is day
> Therefore it is day

is not a syllogism, not even a hypothetical syllogism. For it has no syllogistic form. On the other hand, Alexander's duplicated argument is syllogistic (for it has the form of the first unproved); and his disjunctive arguments from a

---

[76] σχῆμα μὲν γὰρ συλλογιστικὸν δύναται καὶ τὸ τοιοῦτον εἶναι καὶ συζυγία συλλογιστική, συλλογισμὸς δὲ οὐδαμῶς.

contradiction are syllogistic (for they have the form of the fourth or the fifth unproved).

That is not, of course, what Alexander says. First, it places duplicated arguments and disjunctive arguments from a contradiction on the same level, whereas Alexander places the latter high and the former low. Secondly, it allows that some repetitive arguments are syllogistic, so that it offends against the Aristotelian definition of the syllogism. But it is a modified version of Alexander's view; and the modification makes for coherence. No repetitive argument is syllogistic in virtue of being repetitive: it is syllogistic in virtue of having a form which is non-repetitive. There are hypothetical syllogisms in which the conclusion repeats a premiss: there are no syllogistic forms in which the conclusion repeats a premiss.

Something similar can be said for predicative syllogistic. The argument

Horses are animals, and animals are animals—so horses are animals

is a predicative syllogism. For it has the form

A holds of every B
B holds of every C
Therefore A holds of every C

and that is the form of Barbara. The argument also has the form

A holds of every B
B holds of every B
Therefore A holds of every B

No argument of that form is a syllogism in virtue of having that form. Every argument of that form is a syllogism in virtue of being an argument in Barbara. If we choose to take that line, then we need not think to add any further clauses to Aristotle's definition of the syllogism—on the contrary, we may safely eliminate Aristotle's own clause which demands that the conclusion be 'something other' than the premisses.

In short: an argument is a syllogism if and only if it has a syllogistic form, and a form is syllogistic if and only if an argument might be a proof of its conclusion in virtue of the fact that it has that form. The utility of syllogisms and the link between syllogism and proof are preserved; but the unwelcome consequences which follow upon Alexander's way of forging the link are avoided—or at least, some of them are.

NEGATED CONJUNCTIONS

Historians of ancient logic often speak as though its two parts were one of them Peripatetic and the other Stoic: predicative syllogistic is Peripatetic, hypothetical syllogistic is Stoic. And of course, that is roughly true—but it is only roughly true. Some account of some hypothetical syllogisms had been developed by Theophrastus and Eudemus, who were only following up a memorandum of Aristotle's; and it should not be supposed that Peripatetic hypotheticals were in all ways the same as their Stoic cousins. Again, Galen presents an elementary hypothetical syllogistic in his *Introduction*; and it would be an egregious error—enough to make Galen turn in his urn—to think that he simply took over a part of Stoic logic.

One way in which Stoic hypothetical syllogistic differed from the logic of Galen, and also (it is reasonable to suppose) from Peripatetic hypothetical logic concerned the third of Chrysippus' unproveds. In his account of the five Stoic unproveds, Sextus states that

> third is the one which, from a negation of a conjunction and one of the items in the conjunction, infers the opposite of the other—for example:
> It is not the case that it is day and it is night
> But it is day
> Therefore it is not night.
>
> (*PH* ii 158)[77]

Galen offers the same circumscription; and he adds that

> the mode is this:
> Not at the same time the 1st and the 2nd
> But the 1st
> Therefore not the 2nd.
>
> (*inst log* vi 6)[78]

Just as the fourth and the fifth unproveds may be circumscribed for disjunctions with indefinitely many disjuncts, so too with the third unproved, the general circumscription of which is this:

---

[77] τρίτον τὸν ἐξ ἀποφατικοῦ συμπλοκῆς καὶ ἑνὸς τῶν ἐκ τῆς συμπλοκῆς τὸ ἀντικείμενον τοῦ λοιποῦ συνάγοντα, οἷον οὐχὶ ἡμέρα ἔστι καὶ νὺξ ἔστιν· ἡμέρα δὲ ἔστιν· οὐκ ἄρα νὺξ ἔστιν.

[78] ... τοιοῦτος ὁ τρόπος ἐστίν· οὐχ ἅμα τὸ πρῶτον καὶ τὸ δεύτερον· τὸ δὲ πρῶτον· οὐκ ἄρα τὸ δεύτερον.

From a negated conjunction and one of its conjuncts, there is an inference to the negation of the conjunction of its other conjuncts (or to the negation of its other conjunct if there is only one).

The general formulation happens not to be found in the surviving texts.

However that may be, the argument form is valid, and you can see why the Stoics might have presented it as an unproved item or as a form the validity of which needs no proof. Moreover, not only is the form syllogistic by Stoic lights: it seems also to satisfy the clauses in the Aristotelian definition of the syllogism. Alexander would, of course, have been revolted by any repetitive samples of the third unproved; but surely he need have found nothing nauseating in the third unproved itself? Perhaps no third unproveds are syllogisms; but surely they—like the four other unproveds—may function as hypothetical syllogisms?

In the *Analytics* Aristotle discussed, rather cursorily, a couple of types of 'arguments based on a hypothesis'; and he remarked that

many other arguments reach their conclusions based on a hypothesis, and they too should be considered and carefully distinguished. What these kinds of argument are, and in how many ways arguments based on a hypothesis come about, we shall say later.

(*APr* 50a39–b2)[79]

He never did say later; and in his commentary on the passage Alexander asked himself what kinds of hypothetical arguments Aristotle would have considered had he got around to it. His answer to that highly speculative question presumably draws on what Theophrastus and Eudemus had said on the subject. In any case, it runs in part like this:

He means arguments by way of a continuous proposition (which is also called a conditional) and the co-assumption, and those by way of a divisive or disjunctive proposition—and perhaps also those by way of a negated conjunction, if they are indeed different from those already mentioned.

(*in APr* 390.3–7)[80]

---

[79] πολλοὶ δὲ καὶ ἕτεροι περαίνονται ἐξ ὑποθέσεως, οὓς ἐπισκέψασθαι δεῖ καὶ διασημῆναι καθαρῶς. τίνες μὲν οὖν αἱ διαφοραὶ τούτων, καὶ ποσαχῶς γίνεται τὸ ἐξ ὑποθέσεως, ὕστερον ἐροῦμεν.

[80] λέγοι δ᾽ ἂν τούς τε διὰ συνεχοῦς, ὃ καὶ συνημμένον λέγεται, καὶ τῆς προσλήψεως ὑποθετικούς, καὶ τοὺς διὰ τοῦ διαιρετικοῦ τε καὶ διεζευγμένου· ἢ καὶ τοὺς διὰ ἀποφατικῆς συμπλοκῆς εἰ ἄρα οὗτοι ἕτεροι τῶν προειρημένων.—The punctuation, and hence the sense, of the last sentence are disputed.

Alexander's three classes of argument correspond, at least roughly, to the first two Stoic unproveds (which depend on conditional propositions), the last two unproveds (which depend on disjunctions), and the third unproved. But Alexander suggests—implicitly but unmistakably—that the third unproved may not be a genuine syllogism at all, or at any rate that it may not be a genuine syllogism distinct from the hypothetical syllogisms which he has already mentioned.

How might anyone think that a third unproved was either not a syllogism at all or else somehow the same syllogism as one of the other four unproveds? A text from Galen's *Introduction to Logic* suggests an answer:

> That not one syllogism by way of a negated conjunction is useful for proof ... has been proved elsewhere. ... The Chrysippeans think that a third unproved concludes from a negated conjunction and one of its members to the opposite of the other, as in
>
> Dio is not both in Athens and at the Isthmus;
> and we have shown that this too is useful for many proofs in ordinary life and in the law-courts.
>
> (*inst log* xiv 3–4)[81]

In the first sentence, Galen appears to say that arguments by way of negated conjunctions are not probative; in the second, that Chrysippus' third unproved is such an argument; and in the third, that the third unproved argument is useful for proofs. And that is self-contradictory.

The resolution of that little puzzle is found a few sentences later in the text. There Galen reminds us that he has earlier distinguished between complete conflict and partial conflict. (A set of propositions is in complete conflict if and only if at most one of its members can be the case at any given time and at least one of its members must be the case at any given time. A set is in partial conflict if and only if at most one of its members can be the case at any given time.) And he comments:

---

[81] ὅτι δὲ δι' ἀποφατικοῦ συμπεπλεγμένου συλλογισμὸς εἰς ἀπόδειξιν χρήσιμος οὐδὲ εἷς ἐστι, ... ἀποδέδεικται δι' ἑτέρων· ... τρίτον οὖν ἀναπόδεικτον τῶν περὶ τὸν Χρύσιππον ἡγουμένων ἐξ ἀποφατικοῦ συμπεπλεγμένου καὶ θατέρου τῶν ἐν αὐτῷ τὸ ἀντικείμενον τοῦ λοιποῦ περαίνοντα, ὡς ἐπὶ τῶν τοιούτων οὐχὶ καὶ Ἀθήνησίν ἐστι καὶ Ἰσθμοῖ Δίων, καὶ τόνδ' ἐπεδείξαμεν εἰς πολλὰς τῶν κατὰ τὸν βίον ἀποδείξεις εἶναι χρήσιμον ἄχρι καὶ τῶν δικαστηρίων.—The text is desperate in places; but although what I print is highly conjectural, it is scarcely to be disputed that it conveys the right sense.

It is in this latter sort of case that the syllogism we have described is useful: it has the same expression as Chrysippus, but it is constituted not on a conjunction but on conflicting items.

(inst log xiv 6)[82]

In other words, the arguments which Galen has shown to be useful for proofs may look just like third unproveds; but they are not third unproveds—for in fact they are not built around negated conjunctions. No argument constituted on a negated conjunction can be probative, and Chrysippus' third unproved is such an argument. So the third unproved is not a syllogism.

Take, for example, the argument:

Dio is not both in Athens and at the Isthmus.
Dio is in Athens.
Therefore Dio is not at the Isthmus.

Chrysippus takes that to be a third unproved, its first premiss being a negated conjunction. Galen observes that such an argument might well be used to prove something—say, in a court of law. We are perhaps likely to agree both with Chrysippus and with Galen, and to draw the conclusion that the third unproved is useful for proof. Galen, convinced that the third unproved is probatively valueless, concludes that the argument is not a third unproved inasmuch as it does not invoke a negated conjunction.

If the first premiss of the argument is not a negated conjunction, then what is it? Well, it is a proposition of partial conflict. Earlier, Galen has observed that

in the case of partial conflict, the Greeks customarily speak like this:

Dio is not both in Athens and at the Isthmus.

(inst log iv 3)[83]

And he has just explained that

when objects have a nature of the sort we have just described, it indicates a complete conflict, whereas the other nature indicates a partial conflict, in respect of which we say:

If Dio is in Athens, Dio isn't at the Isthmus.

(inst log iv 1)[84]

---

[82] ἐν τούτοις οὖν τοῖς πράγμασιν ὁ εἰρημένος συλλογισμὸς χρήσιμός ἐστι, τῇ μὲν αὐτῇ λέξει χρώμενος ᾗ Χρύσιππος, οὐ μὴν ἐπὶ συμπεπλεγμένῳ συνιστάμενος ἀλλ᾿ ἐπὶ τοῖς μαχομένοις.

[83] ἐπὶ μὲν οὖν τῆς ἐλλειπούσης μάχης ἐν ἔθει τοῖς Ἕλλησίν ἐστιν οὕτω λέγειν· οὐκ ἔστιν Ἀθήνησί τε καὶ Ἰσθμοῖ Δίων.

[84] ἡ μὲν οὖν τοιαύτη φύσις τῶν πραγμάτων τελείαν ἐνδείκνυται τὴν μάχην, ἡ δὲ ἑτέρα τὴν ἐλλιπῆ, καθ᾿ ἣν ὡδέ πως λέγομεν· εἰ Ἀθήνησίν ἐστιν Δίων, οὐκ ἔστιν Ἰσθμοῖ Δίων.

The argument which Chrysippus wrongly takes to be a third unproved may be expressed equally well as follows:

> If Dio is in Athens, then he is not at the Isthmus.
> Dio is in Athens.
> Therefore Dio is not at the Isthmus.

And that argument is evidently a first unproved. The sentence

> Dio is not both in Athens and at the Isthmus,

which Chrysippus takes to express a negated conjunction, in fact expresses a conditional assertible.

So where Alexander insinuates that the third unproved may not be a new sort of syllogism, Galen implies that those genuine syllogisms which appear to be third unproveds are in fact first unproveds. Two minds with but one thought.

The thought seems peculiar—or worse. After all, what is a negated conjunction but a proposition of the form

> Not (P_1 and P_2 and ... and P_n)?

So how can

> Dio is not in Athens and at the Isthmus

fail to be a negated conjunction? Surely, it negates

> Dio is in Athens and at the Isthmus,

and surely that is a conjunction?

But Galen's position, eccentric though it seems, is not insane. Galen agrees—of course—that the sentence 'Dio is in Athens and at the Isthmus' is conjunctive; and he agrees—of course—that the sentence 'Dio is not in Athens and at the Isthmus' is a negated conjunction so far as its expression is concerned. But he claims that, quite generally, it is not the mode of expression but the meaning of a sentence which determines whether it formulates a negated conjunction or a conditional or a disjunction or whatever.

That last and general claim is true—and uncontroversial. Evidently, it is the sense of a sentence which determines what it says or what you can say in uttering it. For example, it is not the presence of the sound 'eh' in an appropriate position between a couple of Greek sentences which makes the complex sentence express a disjunctive proposition. Sounds may express different senses. A Greek sentence which mouths 'eh' between two sentences expresses a disjunction only if the sound 'eh' represents the word 'ἤ' and the word '*ἤ*' functions as a disjunctive connector. What holds for 'eh' in Greek holds also for—say—'and' in English. The sentence

You invite her again and I go to Bath

may have a conjunctive sound to it—it may be, as Galen puts it, conjunctive so far as its expression goes; but it is most likely to express not a conjunctive but a conditional proposition. Such facts are familiar, and they underlie Galen's apparently eccentric view of negated conjunctions.

But if the foundations are solid, what about the structure which Galen here builds upon it? Galen's underlying principle may be true; but is not his particular view on negated conjunctions mistaken? He says that when the Greeks want to express a partial conflict, then they often produce a sentence of the form 'Not both P and Q'; and in that case they have expressed a conditional proposition. Allow—for the sake of argument—that he is right. It does not follow that whenever a Greek utters something of the form 'Not both P and Q' he has thereby expressed a conditional proposition. Nor, of course, does Galen assert anything so wild: he does not deny the existence of negated conjunctions, and he does not deny that a sentence of the form 'Not both P and Q' may express—indeed, is admirably adapted to express—a negated conjunction. What he denies is that negated conjunctions are of any interest to a logician or of any use in logic. But whyever does he deny that? And why, in particular, does he deny that the Stoic third unproved is a syllogistic form?

The background to his strange denial is sketched earlier in the *Introduction*. After he has discussed predicative propositions, Galen goes on to remark that

there is another kind of proposition with which we make assertions not about the holding of things but about what is the case something being the case, and what is the case something not being the case. Let such propositions be called hypothetical ...

(*inst log* iii 1)[85]

In Galen's view, there are just two sorts of hypothetical proposition—or at any rate, just two sorts in which hypothetical syllogistic has an interest. And in the next sentence he explains that such propositions are either conditionals or disjunctives. The two types are characterized in somewhat different ways in different parts of Galen's *œuvre*; but the commonest—and perhaps also

---

[85] γένος ἄλλο προτάσεών ἐστιν ἐν αἷς τὴν ἀπόφανσιν οὐ περὶ τῆς ὑπάρξεως ποιούμεθα τῶν πραγμάτων, ἀλλὰ περὶ τοῦ τίνος ὄντος τί ἐστι καὶ τίνος οὐκ ὄντος τί ἐστιν· ὑποθετικαὶ δὲ ὀνομαζέσθωσαν αἱ τοιαῦται προτάσεις ...

the clearest—characterization speaks in terms of implication and conflict, of entailment and exclusion, of ἀκολουθία and μάχη. Thus Galen will speak approvingly of

the men of old, logicians, scientists, practised in distinguishing the true and the false, knowing how to determine what is implied and what is in conflict, trained from youth upward in demonstrative method.

(MM x 10)[86]

Those GOM knew all there was to know about logic; and that *summa* can be summed up in the phrase 'what is implied and what is in conflict'.

If we say 'what is the case, something being the case', then we state an implication. (And to do so we might well use the conditional connector 'If … , then … '.) If we say 'what is the case, something not being the case', then we state a conflict. (And to do so we might well use the disjunctive connector 'Either … or … '.) The questions which concern hypothetical logic are two: Does X imply Y? Does X exclude Y? The logical relations with which hypothetical syllogistic is concerned are two: implication and exclusion. So insofar as Stoic logic appeals to conjunctions, it appeals to relations which are not logical—or to connexions which are not relations at all.

Galen's view here is not idiosyncratic. On the contrary, it was more or less commonplace outside the Stoa. True, it is not discussed elsewhere in the way in which Galen discusses it. But it is taken for granted by Alexander, and also by later commentators on Aristotle; and it also shows up in the rhetorical tradition in which there are two bases for argument—implication and conflict, ἀκολουθία and μάχη, *consequentia* and *repugnantia*.

The foundation of the view, at any rate in Galen's mind, was the familiar thesis that an argument-form which is not useful for proofs is not a syllogistic form. Galen claims that he has 'shown elsewhere' that the third unproved—and, more generally, any argument based upon a negated conjunction—is useless for proof. That is why Chrysippus' third unproved, and any congeners which it may have, are not syllogisms.

The elsewhere was no doubt somewhere in the lost work *On Proof*; but no other text, so far as I know, sheds any further light on the matter, and if we want to recover Galen's argument against third unproveds we must rely on pure speculation.

---

[86] … ἄνδρας παλαιοὺς, διαλεκτικοὺς, ἐπιστημονικοὺς, ἀληθὲς καὶ ψευδὲς διακρίνειν ἠσκηκότας, ἀκόλουθον καὶ μαχόμενον ὡς χρὴ διορίζειν ἐπισταμένους, ἀποδεικτικὴν μέθοδον ἐκ παίδων μεμελετηκότας, …

And not for the only time, pure speculation turns up trumps. The premisses of a proof, we know, must be prior to the conclusion, and prior in several ways. In particular, they must be prior in knowledge. That is to say, we must be able to come to know the premisses without already having come to know the conclusion—for how otherwise could the proof be a cognitive syllogism, a syllogism which breeds knowledge?

Consider, then, a genuine negated conjunction—say:

Unlike David Hume, John Locke wasn't both a philosopher and an historian.

How might we come to discover the truth on that particular matter? There is no logical relation of implication or exclusion between being a philosopher and being an historian, so that we cannot maintain, on entirely general or conceptual grounds, that history and philosophy won't marry and thence infer the negated conjunction about Locke. All we can do is consider the two elements in the negated conjunction one after another: industrious research will establish that Locke was a philosopher, and further research will prove that he wasn't a historian. Then we may affirm that he wasn't both a philosopher and an historian. Suppose that we then put forward the following argument, on the basis of the negated conjunction:

Locke wasn't both a philosopher and an historian.
Locke was a philosopher.
Therefore Locke wasn't an historian.

That argument may be logically impeccable in the sense that if its two premisses are true then its conclusion must be true. But it is not a proof, and it cannot be a proof. For in order to establish the truth of its complex premiss we had first to establish the truth of its conclusion.

Quite generally, it must seem, we can only come to know that not both P and Q (if that is a genuine negated conjunction and not a cryptic conditional) by first coming to know either that P and that not-Q or else that Q and that not-P. But the conclusion of a third unproved is either not-P or not-Q. Hence the negated conjunction, which is the premiss of such an argument, cannot be established without first establishing its conclusion; and for that reason the third unproved cannot be used to prove its conclusion. Given Galen's logical utilitarianism, it follows that the third unproved is not a syllogistic form—and that it should not be found in a text on logic.

The argument which I have just rehearsed has, I hope, a plausible air to it. Certainly, whenever I have put it forward, it has been well received. True, there is no hint of the argument—or of any other argument—in Galen's texts: to ascribe it to Galen is pure speculation. But it is an easy argument to dream up, and it is not at all easy to dream up any other argument.

Well, although the argument has often been smiled upon, in fact it is a rank bad argument. For it is quite untrue that the only way to establish a negated conjunction—a genuine negated conjunction—is to establish one of the conjuncts and disestablish the other. There are dozens of other ways in which you might come to learn the truth of a negated conjunction. A witness affirms that there was only one man in the dime-store at the time of the hold-up. The witness is a pretty reliable sort. Without knowing, or needing to know, anything whatever about the whereabouts of Smith and Wesson, I infer that it is not the case both that Smith was there and that Wesson was there. Or again, I know that the second letter in the answer to 1 across must be the same as the first letter in the answer to 2 down: I infer at once that it is not the case both that the answer to 1 across is 'aardvark' and that the answer to 2 down is 'zebu'. *Et caetera.*

In sum, the argument which pure speculation assigned to Galen is a rotten argument. Shall we conclude that pure speculation has failed, and that Galen's argument must have been something quite other? No—or at least, not without more ado. On the one hand, Galen was no slouch at logic—there is enough of his work still with us to vindicate that claim. And so, in looking to interpret his arguments, and to supply their missing pieces, we shall, in principle, be looking for a semi-respectable bit of reasoning. On the other hand, Galen was not infallible: there are errors and oversights in his extant texts, and it would be silly to suppose that the lost *On Proof* contained no mistakes. So in interpreting Galen, the respectable arguments which we look for need not always be true arguments.

I incline to think that, in the present case, it is on the whole plausible to ascribe to Galen a bad argument—a bad argument which nevertheless has appealed, at least temporarily, to many of my intelligent and informed colleagues.

ENVOI

A book wants a moral. That last story suggests one. We are all better at logic than Galen was—we are better at logic than Chrysippus was, and than

Aristotle was. Not, of course, that we are more inventive than the glorious dead—far, far from it. And I suppose that, in the whole history of logic, only two men have ever equalled Aristotle in logical creativity. Nonetheless, you and I are better logicians than Aristotle was inasmuch as we are often capable of spotting the mistakes which he made and are relatively unlikely to repeat them. That is not gasconade: it would be a scandal were things not so. But it is something which it is peculiarly easy to forget; and forgetting it, we think to squeeze delicious subtleties from dry texts and we let our imaginations picture a sophisticated interior where our eyes see only a very modest façade. We make Parmenides as profound as Dummett, and Plato as refined as Strawson. It is generous to do so, and it is clever. But it is not—it is not often—right to do so; and generosity and cleverness, no less than their unattractive opposites, have distorted many interpretations of ancient philosophical texts—among them, no doubt, several of the interpretations which you have just finished reading.

Onomasticon

The onomasticon catalogues pretty well all the ancient figures who are used or mentioned in the book. Dates are very often approximate.

ALEXANDER of Aphrodisias: *floruit* 210 AD, held the chair in Peripatetic philosophy at Athens; commentator on Aristotle.

AMMONIUS: *floruit* 500 AD, Alexandrian Platonist, commentator on Aristotle.

ANAXAGORAS of Clazomenae: *floruit* 425 BC, philosopher and rationalist.

ANDRONICUS of Rhodes: end of 1st century BC, Peripatetic philosopher, editor of and commentator upon Aristotle's works.

APOLLONIUS Dyscolus: 2nd century AD, Alexandrian scholar—the leading Greek grammarian.

APULEIUS of Madaurus: 2nd century AD, novelist, rhetorician and Platonist. The essay *On Interpretation* is probably not his work.

ARCHELAUS: *floruit* end of 5th century BC, philosopher, pupil of Anaxagoras.

ARISTOTLE: 384-322 BC, pupil of Plato and master of those who know.

Aemilius ASPER: 2nd century AD, Latin grammarian and critic. (The surviving *Art of Grammar* is not authentic.)

Anicius Manlius Severinus BOETHIUS: 480–524 AD, the last of the Romans— Platonist thinker who planned to translate Aristotle into Latin.

BOETHUS of Sidon: end of 1st century BC, Peripatetic philosopher and commentator on Aristotle.

CARNEADES of Cyrene: 214-129 BC, head of the sceptical Academy and its most celebrated controversialist.

CHAEREMON: 1st century AD, Egyptian priest and Stoic philosopher, tutor to the Emperor Nero.

Flavius Sosipater CHARISIUS: 4th century AD, Latin grammarian.

George CHOEROBOSCUS of Byzantium: 9th century AD, churchman and grammarian.

CHRYSIPPUS of Soli, in Cyprus; 280-207 BC, third head of the Stoic school.

CICERO: 106-43 BC, Roman statesman, orator, and philosopher.

CLEANTHES: 300-230 BC, second head of the Stoic school.

CLINOMACHUS of Thurii: *floruit* 350 BC, philosopher with logical interests.

COMINIANUS: Latin grammarian, *floruit* 300 AD.

DEMETRIUS: 2nd century BC (?) literary critic of Peripatetic persuasion.

DEMOSTHENES: 384-322 BC, Athenian statesman and orator.

DIODORUS Cronus: 3rd/2nd century BC, philosopher, logician, author of paradoxes.

DIOGENES LAERTIUS: 3rd century AD, author of *Lives of the Philosophers*.

DIOMEDES: *floruit* 500 AD, Latin grammarian.

DIONYSIUS of Halicarnassus: 1st century BC, historian and literary critic.

DIONYSIUS Thrax: 170-90 BC, Alexandrian grammarian. The surviving *Art of Grammar* is a later compilation.

Aelius DONATUS: *floruit* 350 AD, Latin grammarian, commentator on Terence and Vergil.

EPICTETUS: 55–130 AD, Stoic philosopher.

EPICURUS: 341-270 BC, Athenian, founder of the philosophical school based on atomism and hedonism.

EUCLID: *floruit* 300 BC, Alexandrian, mathematician.

EUDEMUS of Rhodes: *floruit* 320 BC, Peripatetic philosopher, pupil of Aristotle.

GALEN of Pergamum: 129-c.210 AD, the leading doctor and medical scientist of antiquity, who was also a philosopher.

Aulus GELLIUS: 130–180 AD, his *Attic Nights* is a collection of short essays on a variety of learned topics.

HEPHAESTION: *floruit* 150 AD, writer on poetical metres.

HERMINUS: 2nd century AD Peripatetic scholar; a teacher of Alexander of Aphrodisias.

Aelius HERODIAN: *floruit* end of 2nd century AD, son of Apollonius Dyscolus, and a grammarian like his father before him.

HIPPOCRATES of Chios: 5th century BC, mathematician and first author of *Elements*.

IAMBLICHUS of Chalcis: 250–325 AD, Platonist philosopher with a particular interest in Pythagoreanism.

ISIDORE of Seville: early 7th century AD, bishop and encyclopaedist.

JULIAN: 332-263, Emperor, anti-Christian, philosopher.

LUCIUS: 2nd century AD (?), Platonist (?), critic of Aristotle.

MARIUS VICTORINUS: 4th century AD, rhetorician, translator, philosopher, theologian; he converted to Christianity and became the bore of the century.

MARTIANUS CAPELLA: *floruit* 425 AD, his *Marriage of Mercury and Philology* is a mixture of elementary encyclopaedia and fey fantasy.

MAXIMUS: *floruit* 360 AD, Platonist philosopher in the mould of Iamblichus, attached to Julian.

NICOSTRATUS: 2nd century AD, Athenian, Platonist philosopher, critic of Aristotle.

Publius NIGIDIUS FIGULUS: 1st century BC, learned Roman, friend of Cicero, who wrote on grammar and theology and magic.

PHILO of Megara: 3rd/2nd century BC, philosopher and logician.

PHILODEMUS of Gadara: 1st century BC, Epicurean poet and philosopher, some of whose works were preserved by the lava of Vesuvius.

John PHILOPONUS: 6th Century AD, Christian Platonist, commentator on Aristotle.

PLATO: 429-347 BC, Athenian philosopher.

PLOTINUS: 205–270 AD, innovative and influential Platonist.

PLUTARCH of Chaeronea: 50–120 AD, historian and essayist, Platonist philosopher.

POMPEIUS: 5th/6th century AD, Latin grammarian, commentator on Donatus.

PORPHYRY of Tyre: 233–305 AD, polymath, pupil and editor of Plotinus.

POSIDONIUS of Apamea: 135-50 BC, Stoic philosopher, historian, teacher of Cicero and friend of Pompey.

PRAXIPHANES: 4th/3rd century BC, Peripatetic philosopher with an interest in grammar.

PRISCIAN: early 6th century AD, an African who taught Latin grammar in Greek Constantinople.

PROBUS: 4th century AD, Latin grammarian.

PROCLUS: 410–485, Platonist philosopher, who also wrote on astronomy, physics and geometry.

PROTAGORAS of Abdera: *floruit* 450 BC, sophist celebrated for his relativism.

Marcus Fabius Quintilianus: 30–100 AD, the most celebrated and influential of Latin rhetoricians.

Quintus Remmius Palaemon: 1st century AD, the first Latin grammarian—whose works are all lost.

scholiast to Dionysius Thrax: commentaries and notes on the *Art* of [Dionysius Thrax] from different hands and different centuries.

Servius: 4th/5th century AD, Latin grammarian and commentator on Vergil.

Sextus Empiricus: 2nd century AD, doctor and Pyrrhonist sceptic.

Simplicius: *floruit* 530 AD, Platonist philosopher and learned commentator on Aristotle.

Socrates: 469–399 BC, Athenian philosopher and gadfly, teacher of Plato.

Sphaerus: 3rd century BC, Stoic philosopher.

Stephanus: 7th century AD, Alexandrian who philosophized at Constantinople.

Stobaeus or John of Stobi: 5th century AD, anthologist.

Suda: tenth century Encyclopaedia.

Themistius: 320–390 AD, Platonist, paraphrast of Aristotle, favourite of Emperors, vicar of Bray.

Theodectes: 4th century BC; poet, orator, rhetorician.

Theophrastus of Eresus: 370-285 BC; pupil, friend, and successor to Aristotle.

Trypho: *floruit* 25 AD, Greek grammarian who worked at Rome.

Marcus Terentius Varro: 116–27 BC, the most learned Roman of his time.

Index of Passages

The index lists all the ancient works which are mentioned in the text, and all the passages in them which are cited or discussed. Mere mentions are not noticed.

Against each work there is an English version of its abbreviated Latin title, an indication of the edition used, and an explanation of the style of reference. The indications use these symbols:

BT   Bibliotheca Teubneriana
CIAG   Commentaria in Aristotelem Graeca
CMG   Corpus Medicorum Graecorum
GG   Grammatici Graeci
GL   Grammatici Latini
OCT   Oxford Classical Texts

The explanations use these abbreviations:

b   book
ch   chapter
l   line
p   page
s   section
sb   subsection
v   volume

Alexander		19.17–19	511–512
in APr: Commentary on Aristotle's Prior		20.13–16	502–503
Analytics; Wallies CIAG II i; p + l		20.24–27	458–459
1.3–9	454–455	22.30–23.1	506
3.10–13	457–458	24.4–5	367
6.8–12	458	24.30–25.2	389–390
6.15–21	278	25.18–21	390
6.23–25	372, 382, 385	27.1–5	487
14.28–29	107	27.27–28.2	483
18.7–8	513	28.2–5	484
18.12–22	488–489	32.8–21	418–419
18.18–20	516	46.21	493
18.22–19.3	490–491	53.28–54.2	339
19.1–3	266–267	54.9–12	403, 414
19.3–15	508–509	54.15–21	413

General Index

The Greek alphabet precedes the Roman.